PENGUIN CLASSICS

CAPITAL

VOLUME 2

KARL MARX was born at Trier in 1818 of a German-Jewish family converted to Christianity. As a student in Bonn and Berlin he was influenced by Hegel's dialectic, but he later reacted against idealist philosophy and began to develop his theory of historical materialism. He related the state of society to its economic foundations and mode of production, and recommended armed revolution on the part of the proletariat. In Paris in 1844 Marx met Friedrich Engels, with whom he formed a life-long partnership. Together they prepared the *Manifesto of the Communist Party* (1848) as a statement of the Communist League's policy. In 1848 Marx returned to Germany and took an active part in the unsuccessful democratic revolution. The following year he arrived in England as a refugee and lived in London until his death in 1883. Helped financially by Engels, Marx and his family nevertheless lived in great poverty. After years of research (mostly carried out in the British Museum), he published in 1867 the first volume of his great work, *Capital*. From 1864 to 1872 Marx played a leading role in the International Working Men's Association, and his last years saw the development of the first mass workers' parties founded on avowedly Marxist principles. Besides the two posthumous volumes of *Capital* compiled by Engels, Karl Marx's other writings include *The German Ideology*, *The Poverty of Philosophy*, *The 18th Brumaire of Louis Bonaparte*, *The Civil War in France*, *A Contribution to the Critique of Political Economy*, *Grundrisse: Foundations of the Critique of Political Economy* and *Theories of Surplus-Value*.

ERNEST MANDEL was born in 1923. He was educated at the Free University of Brussels, where he was later Professor for many years, and the École Pratique des Hautes Études in Paris. He gained his Ph.D. from the Free University of Berlin. He was a Member of the Economic Studies Commission of FGTB (Belgian TUC) from 1954 to 1963 and was chosen for the annual Alfred Marshall Lectures by Cambridge University in 1978. His many books include *The Formation of the Economic Thought of Karl Marx*, *Late Capitalism*, *The Long Waves of Capitalist Development*, *The Second Slump* and *The Marxist Theory of Bureaucracy*. His influential pamphlet, *An Introduction to Marxist Economics*, sold over half a million copies and was translated into thirty languages. Ernest Mandel died in July 1995. In its obituary the *Guardian* described him as 'one of the most creative and independent-minded revolutionary Marxist thinkers of the post-war world'.

KARL MARX **Capital**

A Critique of
Political Economy

Volume Two

Introduced by
Ernest Mandel

Translated by
David Fernbach

Penguin Books
in association with New Left Review

PENGUIN BOOKS

Published by the Penguin Group
Penguin Books Ltd, 27 Wrights Lane, London W8 5TZ, England
Penguin Books USA Inc., 375 Hudson Street, New York, New York 10014, USA
Penguin Books Australia Ltd, Ringwood, Victoria, Australia
Penguin Books Canada Ltd, 10 Alcorn Avenue, Toronto, Ontario, Canada M4V 3B2
Penguin Books (NZ) Ltd, 182–190 Wairau Road, Auckland 10, New Zealand

Penguin Books Ltd, Registered Offices: Harmondsworth, Middlesex, England

New Left Review, 7 Carlisle Street, London W1

This edition first published in Pelican Books 1978
Reprinted in Penguin Classics 1992
10 9 8 7 6 5 4

Printed in England by Clays Ltd, St Ives plc
Set in Monotype Times Roman

Contents

8 *Contents*

Introduction

I. THE PLACE OF VOLUME 2 IN MARX'S GENERAL ANALYSIS OF CAPITALISM

'The second volume is purely scientific, only dealing with questions *from one bourgeois to another*,' wrote Frederick Engels to the Russian populist, Lavrov, on 5 February 1884. Seventeen months later, he told Sorge: 'The second volume will provoke great disappointment, because it is purely scientific and does not contain much material for agitation.' Finally, on 13 November 1885, he wrote to Danielson: 'I had no doubt that the second volume would afford you the same pleasure as it has done to me. The developments it contains are indeed of such superior order that the vulgar reader will not take the trouble to fathom them and to follow them out. This is actually the case in Germany where all historical science, including political economy, has fallen so low that it can scarcely fall any lower. Our *Kathedersozialisten* have never been much more, theoretically, than slightly philanthropic *Vulgärökonomen*, and now they have sunk to the level of simple apologists of Bismarck's *Staatssozialismus*. To them, the second volume will always remain a sealed book . . . Official economic literature observes a cautious silence with regard to it.'[1]

These predictions were to be verified far beyond Engels's fears. In fact, ten years passed before two young Russian Marxists – Tugan-Baranowski followed by S. Bulgakov – made the first application of the main conceptual innovations of Volume 2. And it took nearly another decade for these concepts finally to penetrate Germany and the Western world, through an international debate in which Tugan-Baranowski – albeit

1. Engels to Lavrov: *Marx-Engels Werke*, vol. 36, p. 99; Engels to Sorge: ibid., pp. 296 and 324; Engels to Danielson: ibid., pp. 298 and 384 (see also Marx/Engels, *Selected Correspondence*, Moscow, 1975, pp. 365–6). For *Kathedersozialisten*, etc., see notes on pp. 88 and 101 below.

for the moment continuing to call himself a Marxist – began to revise some of Marx's key theories.[2] Volume 2 of *Capital* has indeed been not only a 'sealed book', but also a forgotten one. To a large extent, it remains so to this very day.

Grave misunderstandings arise, however, if the reader attempts to pass straight from Volume 1 to Volume 3, under-estimating the key place of Volume 2 in the monumental theoretical construction. Marx himself quite precisely clarified this place, in a letter sent to Engels on 30 April 1868: 'In Book I . . . we content ourselves with the assumption that if in the self-expansion process £100 becomes £110, the latter will *find already in existence* in the market the elements into which it will change once more. But now we investigate the conditions under which these elements are found at hand, namely the social intertwining of the different capitals, of the component parts of capital and of revenue ($= s$).'[3] This intertwining, conceived as *a movement of commodities and of money*, enabled Marx to work out at least the essential elements, if not the definitive form of a coherent theory of the trade cycle, based upon the inevitability of periodic disequilibrium between supply and demand under the capitalist mode of production. To forget this role of Volume 2 and jump to Volume 3 carries the danger of evacuating all problems *specific* to the inner contradictions of the commodity – problems of the market, of the realization of value and surplus-value, etc. – which, although touched upon in Volume 1, are only fully developed in Volume 2. We may even say that it was only by dealing with the reproduction of capital in its *totality* that Marx could bring out in their full complexity the inevitable contradictions of the basic cell of capitalist wealth – the individual commodity.

The 'intertwining of the different capitals, of the component parts of

2. Tugan-Baranowski's *Studies on the Theory and History of the Commercial Crises in England* originally appeared in Russian in 1894. According to Rosdolsky this version was radically different from the famous German edition of 1901 which sparked off the international debate (see Roman Rosdolsky, *The Making of Marx's Capital*, London, 1977, p. 470, note 66). Bulgakov's *On the Markets for Capitalist Production* was published in Russian in 1897. In autumn 1893, Lenin had made considerable use of Marx's reproduction schemas in a lengthy article, 'On the So-Called Market Question', which was based on a verbal report given to a St Petersburg social-democratic circle in answer to G. Krassin's lecture on the same subject. However, while the article seems to have circulated in manuscript form in Petersburg, it was not published at the time and was thought to have been lost until its publication in 1937. It now appears in Volume 1 of Lenin's *Collected Works*.

3. Marx/Engels, *Selected Correspondence*, op. cit., p. 191.

capital and of revenue' – that *dual movement* of both specific use-values and exchange-values, of supply and demand – also enabled Marx to develop an analysis of *the reproduction of capitalist economy and bourgeois society in its totality.* Of course, in this achievement, which is one of the greatest in the whole of social science, Marx did not have to start out from scratch; he was able to base himself above all on Quesnay's pioneering work, *Tableau économique.*[4] Nor should it be claimed that Marx solved 'all' problems of reproduction. In particular, he left only an unfinished sketch of the section on expanded reproduction and had no time to work on the vexed question of how it can attain occasional equilibrium while encompassing the famous 'laws of motion' of capital (especially those outlined in Volume 3: rising organic composition of capital; increasing rate of surplus-value; competition leading to concentration and centralization and to renewed competition, in spite of the tendency of equalization of the rate of profit; tendency of the average rate of profit to decline). Nevertheless, Volume 2 may be seen in a very real sense as the predecessor and initiator of modern aggregation techniques, which were sometimes even directly inspired by the book. On the road from Quesnay through Marx, Walras, Leontiev and Keynes, the leap forward made by Marx is immediately apparent. And the movement away from Marx in neo-classical and vulgar 'macro-economics' contains elements of enormous regression, of which contemporary economists are only now slowly beginning to take note.[5]

4. It should be stressed that from 1758 onwards Quesnay's writings demonstrate a clear understanding of a circuit of commodities and income, as well as a grasp that, in the last analysis, all incomes originate in production (see *Tableau économique, Extraits des économies réelles de Sully, Explication du tableau économique* and *Analyse de la forme économique du tableau*).

5. For an interesting comparison between Quesnay's *Tableau économique* and Marx's reproduction schemas, see Shigeto Tsuru, 'On Reproduction Schemes', in Paul M. Sweezy, *The Theory of Capitalist Development*, New York, 1942, pp. 365ff. Also worthy of note is Jacques Nagels, *Genèse, contenu et prolongements de la notion de reproduction du capital selon Karl Marx (Boisguillebert, Quesnay, Leontiev)*, Brussels, 1970.

While there seems to be a relation between Leontiev's input-output tables and the labour theory of value (see, for example, B. Cameron, 'The Labour Theory of Value in Leontiev's Models', in *Economic Journal*, March 1952), these tables reflect only the use-value inter-relationships ('exchanges') between different departments, and abstract from the question of the source of the purchasing power necessary to mediate these 'exchanges'. See also Koshimura's assessment: 'Leontiev, immersed in the minutiae of numerous small departments, fails to abstract or generalize and so ignores both the capital structure as a whole, and the component parts of commodities, i.e. c, v, and m ... For this reason his table, while useful for the statistical

Volume 2 of *Capital* carries the subtitle: *The Process of Circulation of Capital*, while Volume 1 was subtitled: *The Process of Production of Capital*. At first sight, the distinction is clear. Volume 1 is centred around the factory, the workplace. It explains the character of the production of commodities under capitalism as both a process of material production and one of valorization (i.e. production of surplus-value).[6] Volume 2, by contrast, is centred around the market-place. It explains not how value and surplus-value are produced, but how they are realized. Its *dramatis personae* are not so much the worker and the industrialist, but rather the money-owner (and money-lender), the wholesale merchant, the trader and the entrepreneur or 'functioning capitalist'. More broadly defined than simple industrialists, entrepreneurs are those capitalists who, having a certain amount of capital at their disposal (whether they own or borrow it is irrelevant here), try to increase that capital through the purchase of means of production and labour-power, the production and then the sale of commodities, the reinvestment of part of realized profit in additional machinery, raw materials and labour-power, and the production of an increased quantity of commodities.

The role of workers in Volume 2 will cause some surprise, both to non-Marxist readers heavily armed with current academic preconceptions of Marx as 'an outdated and typically nineteenth-century economist', and to dogmatic pseudo-Marxists whose understanding of Marx is based more on second-hand vulgarizations than on the genuine article. For if workers appear at all in Volume 2, it is essentially as *buyers of consumer goods* and, therefore, as *sellers* of the commodity labour-power, rather than as producers of value and surplus-value (although, of course, this latter quality, established in Volume 1, remains the solid foundation on which the whole of the unfolding analysis is based).

However, in order to grasp the deeper significance of the concept 'process of circulation of capital', as well as the exact place of Volume 2 in Marx's overall analysis of the capitalist mode of production attempted in his three-volume *magnum opus*, we have to understand the inner connection between the production of value and its realization. Commodity production is the expression of a specific form of social organization, which encompasses a basic contradiction. On the one hand, human

description of empirical phenomena, ignores the inner structure of capitalist production.' (Shinzaburo Koshimura, *Theory of Capital Reproduction and Accumulation*, Kitchener, Ont., 1975, p. 9.)

6. See my introduction to *Capital* Volume 1, London, 1976.

production has outgrown the primitive form of subsistence-farming and handicrafts, which prevailed in more or less isolated communities of producer-consumers. The progress of the division of labour and labour productivity, as well as the growth of transport and communications, have steadily increased the range and depth of human interdependence. More and more local, regional, even national and continental communities depend upon one another for the supply and combination of raw materials, instruments of labour and human producers themselves. The labour process has thereby become to an increasing extent *objectively socialized*. At the same time, however, private ownership of the means of production and circulation combines with the appearance and growth of (money) capital to make *private appropriation* both the starting-point and the goal of all productive endeavour. Thus, while labour is objectively more and more socialized, it remains to a greater degree than ever before organized on the basis of *private production*.

Commodity production, value production, the 'value form', as Marx calls it at the beginning of Volume 1, are rooted in this basic contradiction.[7] Production is impossible without *social* labour – without the co-operation of thousands (in some cases, hundreds of thousands) for the production of a given commodity, under optimum conditions of productivity of labour. But since production is based upon and tuned to private appropriation, social labour is not immediately organized as such – its input into the production process is not decided by society as a whole, and it is expended as *private labour*. Its social nature can only be recognized *a posteriori*, through the sale of the commodity, the realization of its value and, under capitalism, the appropriation in the form of profit by its capitalist owner of a given portion of the total surplus-value created by productive workers in their entirety. Value production or commodity production thus expresses the contradictory fact that goods are at one and the same time the product of social labour and private labour; that the social character of the private labour spent in their production cannot be immediately and directly established; and that *commodities must circulate*, their value must be *realized*, before we can know the proportion of private labour expended in their production that is recognized as social labour.

There is thus an indissoluble unity between the production of value and surplus-value on the one hand, and the circulation (sale) of commodities, the realization of value, on the other. Under commodity production, and even more so under its capitalist form, the one cannot

7. ibid., p. 131.

take place without the other. That is why the study of 'capital in general' – provisionally abstracted from competition and 'many capitals' – encompasses *both* the process of production and the process of circulation of commodities.[8]

However, once we begin to examine the circulation of commodities *under capitalism* (in the first place, their sale with the purpose of realizing their value) we are considering much more than simple *commodity* circulation. We are in fact dealing with the circulation of commodities *as capital*, that is to say, with the circulation of capital. In the course of his progressive analysis of the circulation process, Marx introduces a new and passionately interesting object of study: *the reproduction and circulation* ('turnover') *of the total social capital*. While formally this is the title of only the third Part of Volume 2, it could well be argued that it expresses the underlying subject-matter of the whole volume.

Marx himself explains[9] that the circulation and reproduction of each individual capital, analysis of which is begun in the first sections of Volume 2, must be seen as part of a more general movement of circulation and reproduction – that of the sum total of social capital. This is so not only because such a study must methodologically precede examination of the effects of competition on the division of surplus-value among various capitalist firms, but also because a broader question still has to be answered. How can an anarchic social system, based upon private determination of investment, 'factor-combination' and output, assure the presence of the objective, material elements necessary for further production and growth? What are the *absolute preconditions* of such growth? It was in order to answer these eminently 'modern' questions that Marx developed his famous reproduction schemas and showed that growth could be accommodated within his theory of capitalism.

Since capitalist production is production for profit (value production oriented towards an accretion of value), growth always has the meaning of *accumulation of capital*. While this is already made clear in Volume 1 of *Capital* (Chapters 22 and 23), the argument is only fully elaborated

8. Marxists have generally attached much less importance to problems of circulation than to those of production, often overlooking their essential unity. A rare example of bending the stick too far in the other direction is the book by the 'right-wing' Austro-Marxist and former president of the Austrian Republic, Dr Karl Renner – *Die Wirtschaft als Gesamtprozess und die Sozialisierung*, Berlin, 1924. Renner focuses his analysis entirely on the *circulation* of commodities and deliberately seeks to make of the sphere of circulation the springboard for the socialization of economic life.

9. See below, pp. 427–30.

in Volume 2. The key concepts are those of *capitalization of (part of)* *surplus-value* and *expanded reproduction*. For economic growth to occur, part of the surplus-value produced by the working class and appropriated by the capitalists must be *spent productively* and not wasted unproductively on consumer goods (and luxury goods) by the ruling class and its retainers and hangers-on. In other words, it must be transformed into additional constant capital (buildings, equipment, energy, raw materials, auxiliary products, etc.) and additional variable capital (money capital available to hire an increased labour force). The accumulation of capital is nothing other than this (partial) capitalization of surplus-value, i.e. the (partial) transformation of profit into additional capital.[10]

Expanded reproduction denotes a process whereby the turnover of capital (both individual capitals and total social capital, although not necessarily *all* individual capitals; given competition, we may even say: in the long run, *never* all capitals) leads, after a certain number of intermediary stages minutely studied in Volume 2, to *a larger and larger scale of productive operation*. More raw materials are transformed by more workers using more machinery into more finished products, with greater overall value than in the previous turnover cycle. This results in higher total sales and final profits, which in turn allow a higher absolute sum (if not in all cases a higher percentage) of profit to be added to capital. Thus does the spiral of growth continue . . .

The study of the circulation of commodities, the reproduction (and accumulation) of capital and the rotation of capital in its totality constantly encompasses the dialectical unity-and-contradiction of opposites contained in the commodity form of production, namely, the contradictory unity of use-value and exchange-value, doubled in that of commodities and money. One of the outstanding features of *Capital* Volume 2, to which insufficient attention has been paid by academic and Marxist commentators alike,[11] is precisely the masterly way in which Marx develops this initial theme of *Capital* Volume 1 throughout his analysis of the process of circulation. We shall have occasion to come back to this.

10. Most significantly, capital accumulation also requires that means of production producing *additional means of production* be added to means of production producing consumer goods or simply replacing means of production used up in current production.

11. An important exception is Rosdolsky, op. cit.

2. THE THREE FORMS OF CAPITAL

From the outset, Marx makes it clear that capital, in the capitalist mode of production,[12] appears in three forms: money capital, productive capital and commodity capital. Money capital is the original form and final purpose of the whole devilish undertaking. Productive capital is the basic precondition of the constantly enlarging spiral. Without the penetration of capital into the sphere of production, the social product and surplus product can only be re-apportioned and re-appropriated, not increased by capitalist enterprise. Under such conditions, capitalists would act essentially as parasites upon and plunderers of pre-capitalist (or post-capitalist) forms of production, rather than as masters of the production and appropriation of surplus-value (of the social surplus-product). As for commodity capital, it is the basic curse of capitalism that commodities *must* go through the phase in which they contain – in as yet unrealized form – the surplus-value produced by the working class. In other words, before money capital can return to its original form, swollen by surplus-value, it *has* to go through the intermediate stage of commodity-value – of value embodied in commodities which still have to pass the acid test by being sold.

Marx used the formula 'metamorphosis of capital' to indicate that, like a butterfly passing through the successive stages of larva, chrysalis and moth, capital takes on the forms of money capital, productive capital and commodity capital, before returning to the stage of money capital. While these three forms are to a large extent successive in the process of rotation of capital, they are also co-existent with one another. One of the most important and brilliant sections of Volume 2 is that which stresses again and again the *discontinuous* nature of reproduction of the three forms of capital, and the organic link of this discontinuity with the very essence of the capitalist mode of production.

Precisely because the capitalist mode of production is generalized production of commodities, money capital cannot and does not merely precede and succeed the widespread appearance of capital; it has to exist *side by side* with it. Similarly, money capital is not just the result of the sale of commodities; its social existence is a precondition of that sale. Finally, commodity capital is not simply the outcome of the function-

12. This specification is necessary. Although capital may appear and survive in pre-capitalist and post-capitalist societies (ones in transition from capitalism to socialism), it does so essentially outside the realm of production. In no case can it *dominate* the main sectors of production. This occurs only with the appearance of productive capital – the form proper to the capitalist mode of production.

ing of productive capital; it is also its necessary basis. Indeed, current production is only possible (and this applies especially to commodities with an above-average life span or production period) if all commodities produced during the previous turnover cycle have *not* already been sold to the final consumers – if, that is, *stocks and reserves* of raw materials, energy, auxiliary products, intermediary products and consumer goods needed to reproduce labour-power are available on a large scale. Continuity of the production process may be said to depend upon discontinuity or desynchronization of the turnover cycle of money capital, productive capital and commodity capital.

Furthermore, the very nature of capitalist relations of production requires the existence of money capital prior to the initiation of the production process. The separation of 'free' workers from their means of production and livelihood implies a *constraint* upon the owners of the means of production *to purchase* labour-power before the commencement of productive operations. And they must have at their disposal adequate money capital to effect the transaction: 'In the relation between capitalist and wage-labourer, the money relation, the relation of buyer and seller, becomes a relation inherent in production itself.'[13]

Thus, to a large extent, Volume 2 examines the *constant intertwining* of appearance and disappearance of money capital, productive capital and commodity capital – from the sphere of circulation into that of production, and back into the sphere of circulation, until the commodity is finally consumed. Each form passes over into the other, without expelling it entirely from the sphere of circulation, let alone from the overall social arena. Indeed, we can say that the dialectics of money (money capital) and commodities (commodity capital) is the basic contradiction examined in *Capital* Volume 2. Here again Marx's 'modernism' is particularly striking.

These considerations show the crucial importance of the 'time factor' in Marx's analysis of the capitalist mode of production. Its functioning cannot be understood if complete abstraction is made of time sequences and schedules, the duration of the production and turnover cycles of commodities, and the length of the turnover period of capital. Marx's important distinction between circulating capital and fixed capital is based exclusively on the amount of time required for each of these two parts of money capital to revert to its original form. Circulating capital (spent on raw materials and wages) is recovered by the capitalist firm after each production cycle and circulation cycle of commodities. Fixed

13. See below, p. 196.

capital, however, is recovered in its entirety only after n cycles of production and circulation, whose number depends on the longevity of machinery and buildings. As is well known, Marx worked on the hypothesis that the average longevity of machinery (not, of course, buildings) is equivalent to, and indeed *determines*, the average duration of the trade cycle. It would be a fruitful task for Marxist scholars to deepen our understanding of the role and function of this 'time dimension' in Marx's *Capital*. For time appears there as the measure of production, value and surplus-value (labour time); as the nexus connecting production, circulation and reproduction of commodities and capital (cycles of turnover and reproduction of capital); as the medium of the laws of motion of capital (trade cycles, cycles of class struggle, long-term historical cycles); and as the very essence of man (leisure time, life span, creative time, time of social intercourse).

The study of the process of circulation of commodities and capital is concerned essentially with metamorphosis – the change from one form to another which we have just mentioned. But this analysis, starting from a high level of abstraction and drawing nearer and nearer to the everyday 'phenomena' of capitalist life, itself represents this process of circulation in successive stages of concreteness. First there is the circulation of (money) capital in its most general form as we encountered it in Volume 1:

$$M-C-M' (M+AM)$$

Money buys commodities so that they may be sold with an accretion of money – a profit – part of which will be added to the initial money capital.

If we translate this formula into the real operations of the capitalist mode of production, we have to replace C, the commodities bought, with the specific operation of the industrialist, namely, the purchase of means of production and labour-power in order that the labour-power may produce additional value, surplus-value. This combination of means of production and labour-power gives rise, through the process of production, to new commodities embodying additional value which have to be sold to result in the formation of accumulated capital. Thus the initial formula becomes:

$$M-C<_L^{mp} \ldots \text{production} \ldots C'-M' \ (M+AM, \text{ where } AM =$$
$$\text{accumulated surplus-value})$$

3. THE DUAL ASPECT OF CAPITAL TURNOVER IN MARX'S ECONOMIC THEORY

Basing himself on the contradiction between use-value and exchange-value inherent in the commodity, Marx considered the problem of turnover of capital, of reproduction, as a *dual one*:

(a) In order that (at least simple, and normally expanded) reproduction may be achieved, the total value embodied in the produced commodities *must be realized*, that is to say, they must be sold *at their value*. Contrary to assumptions made by some of his most astute followers, principally Rudolf Hilferding, Otto Bauer and Nikolai Bukharin, Marx did not regard this process of realization as 'automatic'; nor did he derive it 'from his reproduction schemas', as some have naïvely suggested.[14] Indeed, a substantial section of the final Part of Volume 2, and most of the controversies which have been raging ever since Rosa Luxemburg raised the issue, have turned around a more or less detailed examination of *how* the value embodied in commodities as represented by the famous reproduction schemas *could* be realized by purchasing power generated in the production process.

(b) *At the same time*, at least simple – and normally expanded – reproduction require for their success that the *use-value of the commodities produced* should fulfil the *material* conditions for restarting production on either the existing or a broader scale. Reproduction could not take place in a situation where, on a technological base lower than total automation and in the absence of food reserves, the commodity package consisted entirely of raw materials and machinery; the workers and capitalists would starve and disappear before the available machinery could be used to restart agricultural production, or the existing stock of raw materials could be transformed into synthetic food. Similarly, reproduction would be impossible where the entire output of current commodity production, carried out with the large-scale use of sophisticated machinery, was composed of consumer goods and raw materials; if there were no stocks of machinery or spare parts, then machinery and

14. See especially Rudolf Hilferding, *Das Finanzkapital*, Vienna, 1923, p. 310; Nikolai Bukharin, *Imperialism and the Accumulation of Capital*, London, 1972, p. 226; and Otto Bauer, 'Die Akkumulation des Kapitals' in *Die Neue Zeit*, Vol. 31, 1913.

production would break down before the well-fed workers could build new machines out of simple raw materials.

We should add in passing that expanded reproduction, which is 'the norm' under capitalism, does not demand merely the existence (i.e. previous production) of use-values representing the necessary objective elements of reproduction (means of production to replace used-up equipment and raw materials; further means of production required to enlarge the scale of operation of material production; consumer goods to feed both already employed workers and additional recruits to the work force). Expanded reproduction also demands the presence of *a potential source of additional labour*. The *dual function* of the 'industrial reserve army of labour', both as regulator of wages (assuring that the rate of surplus-value remains above a certain level) and as material precondition of expanded reproduction, should not be overlooked. If 'traditional' means of increasing or maintaining that 'reserve army' are drying up (where, for example, independent peasants, handicrafts-men and shop-keepers have declined as a proportion of the total active population, or where substitution of machines for men in industry is slowing down), then new sources can always be tapped through sweeping transformation of housewives into wage-labourers; mass immigration of labour; extensive re-deployment of student youth onto the labour market, and so on.[15]

Marx's giant step forward in economic analysis may be gauged by the fact that, until this very day, most academic economists have still not fully grasped this basic innovation of his schemas of reproduction. They have broken up the totality of the process of reproduction of capital, based upon this 'unity of opposites', into a disconnected dichotomy. On the one hand, analysis centres on *physical coefficients* (especially at the level of inter-branch exchanges, as in Leontiev's input-output tables and all their derivations), i.e. it deals with use-values. On the other hand, as in the case of Keynesian and post-Keynesian treatises[16], the study focuses on money flows, income flows, that is to say on exchange-values largely disembodied from the commodities in the production of which

15. See Ernest Mandel, *Late Capitalism*, London, 1975, pp. 170–71.
16. Paul Samuelson's *Economics* (4th edition, New York, 1958, p. 41) attempts to correlate revenue flows and commodity flows by means of an inter-related system of 'supply-demand markets'. But it is the 'public' which buys 'consumer goods', while 'selling' land, labour and capital goods (i.e. factors of production) to 'business'! 'Business' in turn buys land, labour and capital from 'the public' and

they originated. Income theories are thereby more and more disconnected from production theories, and if the mediation of the 'production function' is employed at all, it remains largely inoperative, being considered at the micro-economic level rather than the macro-economic one.

Above all, *the constant combination and intertwining of the two* – the obvious fact that incomes are generated in the production of commodities with a given use-value, corresponding to the structure of socially recognized needs, and that disequilibrium is unavoidable without a structure of income congruent with that of value produced – this has not even been posed, still less tackled by traditional academic theory (with the marginal exception of certain students of the trade cycle and the theory of crisis). The technique of aggregation introduced by Keynes has, if anything, made matters even more confused by operating with undifferentiated money flows. For it evacuates the problem (not to mention its solution) of whether a given national income has a specific structure of demand (for consumer goods, for producer goods producing producer goods, for producer goods producing consumer goods, for luxury goods, for weapons and other commodities bought only by the state, etc.) which corresponds exactly to the specific structure of the total commodity-value created in the process of production.

In fact, most of the relevant academic theory (and not a little post-Marxian Marxist theory as well) for a long time assumed some kind of Say's law to be operative.[17] That is to say, it took for granted that a given value-structure of output is correlated with a congruent incomes structure (structure of purchasing power) through the normal operation of market forces. One of Marx's major purposes in Volume 2 of *Capital*

---

sells consumer goods to it. Samuelson does not seem to have noticed that, under capitalism, 'the public' (i.e. the mass of consumers) does not own 'capital goods' (i.e. raw materials and equipment) and that these are sold by certain 'businesses' to others. In his system, 'capital goods' are 'sold' without having been produced. It should be noted that Marx's reproduction schemas are not only of greater analytical and theoretical rigour; at the same time, they are more realistic, that is to say, they conform more closely to the real organization of capitalist economic life than the mystifying constructions of many species of academic economics.

17. For example, Oskar Lange, in his lengthy and interesting discussion of the reproduction schemas and derived equilibrium formulae, constantly abstracts from the *dual* flow of commodities and money, and assumes a relationship of pure barter between the two departments. (See Oskar Lange, *Theory of Reproduction and Accumulation*, Warsaw, 1969, pp. 24, 28, etc.)

is to show that this is not so: that such congruence depends upon certain exact proportions and structures, both of exchange-values and of use-values; that, for instance, wages *never* buy machines under capitalism; and that these exact proportions are extremely difficult to realize in the actual practice of capitalism.

It is thus all the more surprising that Joan Robinson reproaches Marx for having 'failed to realize how much the orthodox theory stands and falls with Say's Law and set himself the task of discovering a theory of crises which would apply to a world in which Say's Law was fulfilled, as well as the theory which arises when Say's Law is exploded'.[18] Would it not be more correct to state that Robinson herself, following Keynes's concept of 'effective demand', fails to realize how much Marx's theory of the commodity as a unity-and-contradiction of use-value and exchange-value not only underpins his concept of the necessary fluctuation of supply and demand at a macro-economic level, but actually intertwines it with his theory of income distribution (demand distribution) in capitalist society? Under capitalism, income distribution has a *class* structure determined by the very structure of the mode of production, and governed in the medium term by the class interests of the capitalists. Any increase in 'effective demand' which, instead of increasing the rate of profit, causes it to decline will never lead to a 'boom' under capitalism. *That* basic truth was well understood by Ricardo as well as Marx – though it is not by many latter-day Keynesians.

We said earlier that one of the basic functions of the reproduction schemas is to demonstrate that growth (i.e. the very existence of capitalism) is at least *possible* under the capitalist mode of production. Given the extremely anarchic nature of the organization of production (under *laissez-faire* capitalism on the home market, under monopoly capitalism on the world market), and given the very nature of competition, this is by no means as obvious as it sounds. The reproduction schemas locate the combination of value and use-value structures of the total commodity package within which growth *can* occur. But Marx never sought to prove that these proportions are automatically and constantly guaranteed by the 'invisible hand' of market forces. On the contrary, he insisted again and again[19] that these proportions are *difficult* to realize and impossible permanently to retain, and that they are

18. Joan Robinson, *An Essay on Marxian Economics*, New York, 1966, p. 51.

19. Cf. below: 'The fact that the production of commodities is the general form of capitalist production already implies that money plays a role, not just as means of circulation, but also as money capital within the circulation sphere, and gives

automatically upset by those same forces that bring them occasionally into being. In other words, the reproduction schemas show that equilibrium, not to speak of equilibrated growth, is the exception and not the rule under capitalism: that disproportions are far more frequent than proportionality, and that growth, being essentially uneven, inevitably produces the breakdown of growth – contracted reproduction or crisis.

When we say that Marx's reproduction schemas summarize the turnover of capital and commodities as *a dual movement*, we mean that they are based upon *a combined dual flow* – a flow of value produced in the process of production, and a flow of money (money revenue and money capital) unleashed in the process of circulation in order to realize the value of the commodities produced. The schemas are evidently not based upon barter: department I does not 'exchange' goods with department II simply according to 'mutual need'. *Before* the capitalists or employed workers of department I can obtain the goods they need, they must prove themselves to have sufficient purchasing power to *buy* them from department II *at their value*.[20] Furthermore, the difficulty cannot be solved by some legerdemain such as the sudden introduction *ex nihilo* of additional sources of purchasing power. If new sources of money do appear – and we shall see that they play a key role in Marx's schemas – they must be organically connected with the problem under examination. In other words, it has to be demonstrated that they are *necessarily coexistent* with the process of production and circulation of commodities under the capitalist mode of production.

The dual nature of the reproduction schemas, reflecting the dual nature of the commodity and commodity production in general, in no way circumvents or contradicts the operation of the law of value – a law which establishes, among other things, that the quantity and quality of value produced, both that of each individual commodity and that of the total sum of commodities, is independent of their use-value. Use-value

rise to certain conditions for normal exchange that are peculiar to this mode of production, i.e. conditions for the normal course of reproduction, whether simple or on an expanded scale, which turn into an equal number of conditions for an abnormal course, possibilities of crisis, since, on the basis of the spontaneous pattern of this production, this balance is itself an accident' (pp. 570–71). Cf. also Karl Marx, *Grundrisse*, London, 1973, pp. 413–14.

20. In Volume 2 of *Capital*, which, like Volume 1, features in Marx's general plan under the heading 'Capital in General' ('Das Kapital im Allgemeinen'), the author consciously abstracts from competition. Therefore, prices of production play no part, and calculations are strictly value calculations.

is a necessary *precondition* of commodity-value. A good which nobody wants to buy because it fulfils no need cannot be sold, and therefore has no exchange-value. Labour expended in its production is socially wasted, not socially necessary labour. Similarly, a certain use-value structure of total output – a given quantity of x raw materials, y pieces of equipment and z types of consumer goods – is a material and *social* precondition of the successful accomplishment of (simple or expanded) reproduction. But the use-value of these commodities will only be realized if their market prices can be matched, that is, if they can be bought. (Millions can – and do! – starve under capitalism, even though all the food they need is there, because they lack the purchasing power to buy it. Of course they would also starve if the food were really lacking, but, although this does happen occasionally, it is a much rarer occurrence.) Moreover, the system will be in equilibrium (i.e. expanded reproduction will be possible in value terms) only if these commodities are broadly speaking *sold at their value*, that is to say, if the surplus-value produced by the working class is realized in the form of profit. And this is by no means assured under capitalism.

A further preliminary condition of equilibrium has to be fulfilled before the dual flow of commodities and purchasing power between the departments can even be examined. The *sum total* of output of both departments must be equal to, not smaller or larger than, the total demand generated by expanded reproduction. Under simple reproduction this may be expressed as follows:

$$I = I_c + II_c$$
$$II = I_v + I_s + II_v + II_s$$

Under expanded reproduction this becomes:

$$I = I_c + AI_c + II_c + AII_c$$
$$II = I_v + AI_v + (I_s - AI_c - AI_v) + II_v + AII_v + (II_s - AII_c - AII_v)$$

The value and mass of the means of production produced must be equal to the value and mass of the means of production used up in both departments during the current production period (plus, under conditions of expanded reproduction, the value of the additional means of production needed in both departments). The value and mass of the consumer goods produced must be equal to the demand for consumer goods (wages+profits spent on unproductive consumption) in both departments.

4. THE SIGNIFICANCE OF MARX'S REPRODUCTION SCHEMAS

The so-called 'conditions of proportionality' in a two-department system (where the total mass of commodities is classified into a department I of means of production and a department II of consumer goods) were formulated by Marx himself. In the case of simple reproduction they are:

$$I_v + I_s = II_c$$

Otto Bauer and Bukharin derived from this a similar formula for expanded reproduction, which, although present in Volume 2, was not explicitly formulated by Marx:[21]

$$I_v + I_{s_\alpha} + I_{s_\gamma} = II_c + II_{s_\beta}{}^{22}$$

In conformity with the dual nature of the reproduction schemas, these conditions of proportionality simultaneously have two meanings:

(a) The *exchange-value* of the goods sold by department I to department II must be equal to the value of the goods sold by department II to department I (otherwise, there would emerge an unsaleable surplus in at least one of the two departments).

(b) The specific *use-value* of the commodities produced in both departments must correspond to their mutual needs. For instance, the purchasing power in the hands of the workers producing producer goods must encounter on the market not only 'commodities', but *actual consumer goods* equivalent to that sum of wages. (Under capitalism, workers are not supposed to spend their money on any commodities other than consumer goods.)

The commodity, non-barter nature of the reproduction schemas further implies a *dual flow* between the two departments. When department I *sells* raw materials and equipment to department II (to replace the value of II_c used up in the previous production cycle), commodities flow from department I to department II, while money flows from

21. See below, p. 593
22. Total surplus-value (s) in both departments is divided into three parts:
    α: unproductively consumed by the capitalists;
    β: accumulated in the form of constant capital;
    γ: accumulated in the form of variable capital.

department II to department I. It has to be determined where that money initially came from. Conversely, when department II sells consumer goods to the workers of department I, to enable them to reproduce their labour-power, commodities flow from II to I, while money flows from I to II.

From a purely technical point of view, there is nothing extraordinary or magical in this two-department schema. It is just the most elementary conceptual tool – an extreme simplification intended to bring out *the underlying assumptions of equilibrium* (or equilibrated, proportionate growth) *under conditions of commodity production.* For exchange to occur, there must exist at least two private capitals independent of each other. With these conceptual tools, it would be easy to draw up a three-department model (e.g. with gold as department III), or a four-department one (with both gold and luxury goods as additional departments – the difference between the two being that, while luxury goods are, like weapons, useless from the point of view of reproduction, gold does not enter into the reproduction process but mediates it, assisting the circulation of commodities for expanded reproduction). We could then move on to a five-department model (dividing department I into means of production producing means of production and means of production producing consumer goods) or a seven-department one (further dividing both sub-departments of department I into raw materials and machinery). Step by step, we would approach an inter-branch model reflecting the actual structure of a modern capitalist industrialized economy.[23]

A certain number of conditions of physical interdependence would have to be established among all these branches (they are clarified by Leontiev's input–output tables, based on either stable or changing technology). These would then have to be supplemented by a table of value equivalence (value equilibrium), since the only condition for equilibrium is *overall* realization of value. At this point, there appears an important difference between a two-department schema and a multi-department one. The former necessitates equivalence of exchange-values between the two departments, whereas this is not true of the latter.

23. Department III was first used by Tugan-Baranowski (*Studien zur Theorie und Geschichte der Handelskrisen in England*, Jena, 1901) and von Bortkiewicz as a means of representing the production of luxury goods or gold. Unknown to Tugan-Baranowski and other participants in that discussion, Marx had himself used a four-department schema in the *Grundrisse* (op. cit., p. 441), introducing separate departments for raw materials and machinery and, like Tugan-Baranowski, dividing the means of consumption between a department of workers' consumer goods and one of luxury goods ('surplus products') destined for the capitalists.

Department *C*, for instance (say, raw materials necessary for the production of consumer goods) could have a 'surplus' in its interchange with department *E* (finished mass consumer goods in a nine-department schema, where *F* is the luxury goods department and *G* the gold production one), while it had a 'deficit' in its interchange with department *B* (equipment for the production of producer goods, including raw materials).[24] In such a case, the system would still attain equilibrium provided that all the 'surpluses' and 'deficits' cancelled one another out *for each department* (i.e. were inter-related in a definitely proportionate and not arbitrary manner), and provided that each department realized the total value of the commodities produced within it and disposed of sufficient purchasing power to acquire the necessary objective elements of expanded reproduction (which would have to be supplied with their specific use-values by the current production of departments *A* to *E*).

However, the picture changes once we consider the two-department schema not as a simple conceptual or analytical tool, but as a model corresponding to a social *structure*. It then becomes clear that the choice of *these* two departments as basic sub-divisions of the mass of commodities produced is not at all an arbitrary one, but corresponds to the essential character of human production in general – not merely its specific expression under capitalist relations of production. Man cannot survive without establishing a material metabolism with nature. And he cannot realize that metabolism without using tools. His material production will, therefore, always consist of at least tools and means of subsistence. The two departments of Marx's reproduction schemas are nothing other than the specific *capitalist* form of this general division of human production, in so far as they (1) take the generalized form of commodities, and (2) assume that the workers (direct producers) do not

24. In order to avoid confusion, we shall use for a nine-department schema the letters *A*, *B* . . . *I*, rather than the Roman capitals I, II, etc. Thus, *A* denotes the department of raw materials used in the production of means of production; *B*: equipment employed in the production of means of production; *C*: raw materials used for the production of mass consumer goods; *D*: equipment employed in the production of mass consumer goods; *E*: raw materials used for the production of luxury goods; *F*: equipment employed in the production of luxury goods; *G*: mass consumer goods; *H*: luxury goods (and other goods not entering into the reproduction process – e.g. weapons); *I*: gold. The Soviet economist V. S. Dadajan has constructed a sophisticated 'feed-back' system for expanded reproduction which is based on a four-department system (*A*: means of production; *B*: raw materials; *C*: mass consumer goods; *D*: 'elements of non-productive funds and the rest of social production') See V. S. Dadajan, *Ökonomische Berechnungen nach dem Modell der erweiterten Reproduktion*, Berlin, 1969.

and cannot purchase that part of the commodity mountain which consists of tools and raw materials.[25]

Reverting to the two-department schema presented in *Capital* Volume 2, we can now outline the dual flow of commodities and money between the two departments, both in the case of simple reproduction and in that of expanded reproduction.

1. *Simple reproduction.* In department I, the workers buy commodities from department II to the equivalent of their wages, and the capitalists to the equivalent of their profits. *Both these flows are continuous* (workers and capitalists alike have to eat every day) *regardless* of whether department I commodities have already been sold. Therefore, even simple reproduction requires the *prior existence of money capital and money reserves* (for revenue expenditure) *in the hands of the capitalist class over and above the value of productive capital.*[26] With the money received from the sale of their commodities, the capitalists of department II buy from department I the means of production needed to reconstitute their own constant capital used up during the production process. This money returning to department I, after mediating the purchase-and-sale of means of production within that department, reconstitutes the initial money capital and money-revenue reserve with which the whole turnover process can recommence. Similarly, within department II the capitalists sell consumer goods to their own workers and thereby immediately reconstitute their own variable capital. They sell consumer and luxury goods to all industrialists active within that department, thus realizing the surplus-value contained in the sum total of consumer goods produced.

2. *Expanded reproduction.* Workers and capitalists of department I buy consumer goods from department II to a total value of $I_v + I_{s_\alpha}$. With this money, capitalists of department II buy means of production from department I in order to reconstitute their own constant capital used up

25. Rudolf Hickel (*Zur Interpretation der Marxschen Reproduktionsschemata*, p. 116 and p. 7 of footnotes) criticizes our use of a department III, thinking that we justify it by the fact that the state buys weapons or by the notion that weapons are 'waste'. This critique is altogether unfounded. The objective basis of department III lies in the fact that it includes *all* commodities not entering into the reproduction process (with the possible exception of monetary gold, in a four-department schema).

26. See below, pp. 548–9.

during the production process.[27] Now, capitalists of department I have the necessary means (if required, by drawing further on a reserve of money capital) to mediate the circulation of c within their own department and to hire additional workers, who will buy additional consumer goods (to the equivalent of I_{s_y}) from department II. The capitalists of department II thereby acquire the purchasing power to buy from department I the additional means of production necessary for their own expanded reproduction ($II_{s_\beta} = AII_c$), while the sale of consumer goods to workers and capitalists within department II operates as described above. Finally, with the further means obtained by the sale of AII_c to department II, the capitalists of department I can complete their own expanded reproduction, mediating the sale of AI_c within their department (as well as the purchase of the equivalent of AI_v from department II, if this has not been fully covered in the first stage of circulation).

5. USE AND MISUSE OF THE REPRODUCTION SCHEMAS

Marx's reproduction schemas have been used and abused in a number of ways during the past seventy years, ever since their analytical usefulness began to strike the imagination of followers and opponents alike. We have already indicated one of the most paradoxical forms of abuse of the schemas, namely, utilization of them as 'proof' that capitalism could grow harmoniously and unrestrictedly 'if only' the correct 'proportions' between the departments (the 'conditions of equilibrium') were maintained. The authors responsible for this aberration overlooked the basic assumption made by Marx: that the very structure of the capitalist mode of production, as well as its laws of motion, imply that the 'conditions of equilibrium' are *inevitably* destroyed; that 'equilibrium' and 'harmonious growth' are marginal exceptions to (or long-term averages of) normal conditions of disequilibrium ('overshooting' between the two departments) and uneven growth. We have dwelt on this problem elsewhere and shall not repeat the argumentation here. Suffice it to say that, under capitalism, both the *dynamics of value determination* and the *non-determination of consumer expenditure* make it impossible to maintain exact proportions between the two departments in such a way as to allow harmonious growth.

The very nature of expanded reproduction – capitalist reproduction –

27. Following the equilibrium formula: $II_c + II_{s_\beta} = I_v + I_{s_\alpha} + I_{s_y}$, it is clear that II_c may be equal to, or smaller than or greater than $I_v + I_{s_\alpha}$, depending on the relation of II_{s_β} to I_{s_y}.

under capitalism implies that production takes place not only on a broader scale, but also under changed technological conditions. Constant revolutions in the technique and cost of production are a basic character- istic of the system which Marx underlined much more sharply than any of his contemporaries (including the admirers and sycophants of capitalism). But these constant revolutions entail that the value of commodities as a *social* datum is subject to periodic change. It follows that values at input level do not automatically determine values at out- put level. Only after a certain interval will it be shown whether a fraction of the 'inputs' have been socially wasted. Neither the subjective will of 'monopolies' or 'the state', nor the cleverness of neo-Keynesian planners, can prevent the assertion of the law of value where private property and competition hold sway. Nothing can stop these long-term shifts in commodity values from leading to a *redistribution* of living labour inputs among different branches of production (and, ultimately, a redistribution of means of production as well).

Similarly, the avoidance of crises of over-production requires pro- portionality not only between departments, but also between output and 'final consumption' (i.e. consumption by the mass of wage and salary earners, above all in modern industrialized societies, where they generally form with their families more than 80 per cent of the total number of consumers). But this is impossible for two reasons. In the first place, the one freedom which cannot normally be taken away from the workers is the freedom to spend their wages as they wish – and there is no way in which it can be forecast with complete accuracy how they will do this (even if a prediction is 95 per cent correct, that could still leave a 5 per cent surplus of unsaleable consumer goods, which is enough to start an avalanche). Secondly, the laws of motion of capitalism have the inherent tendency to develop the capacity of production (including the production of consumer goods) beyond the limits within which the mode of production confines the purchasing power of those condemned to sell their labour-power. Thus, disproportion is intrinsic to the system itself.[28] However, it is not enough for a Marxist theory of the trade cycle and of crisis to demonstrate the reality of that inherent dispropor- tion (which is, after all, almost a truism, given the regular recurrence of crises of over-production for more than 150 years!); it must also discover

28. See *Grundrisse*, op. cit., p. 414. Cf. also *Capital* Volume 3, Chapter 15, 3, where Marx states that under capitalism 'the proportionality of the particular branches of production presents itself as a constant process through disproportion- ality'.

the *precise mechanisms* which relate that periodic disequilibrium to the basic laws of motion of capitalism.

In the Soviet Union and other countries where capitalism has been overthrown, Marx's reproduction schemas have been widely used as instruments of 'socialist planning'. We do not deny that, *by analogy*, these schemas may be useful tools for studying specific problems of inter-department structure and dynamics in all kinds of society. But it has first to be clearly understood what is being done in such a case. For, we repeat, the schemas refer to *commodity production* and to *dual flows* of commodities and money incomes. To extend their use to societies which have transcended generalized commodity production, where the means of production are, in their essential mass,[29] use-values distributed by the state (the planning authorities) according to a plan, rather than commodities sold on the basis of their 'value' – this leads to an accumulation of paradoxes, of which the authors are generally not even conscious.

A good example is provided by the late Maurice Dobb. In the fifties, he participated in a 'great debate' among Soviet and East European economists revolving around Stalin's so-called 'law of the priority development of the means of production under socialism' and the establishment of an optimum rate of growth for both departments.[30] Forgetting that what was involved in Marx's reproduction schemas was *value calculation of commodities*, Dobb 'proved' that an increased rate of growth of consumer goods in the future was 'impossible' unless the *present* rate of growth of department I was higher than that of department II. Now, a policy which sacrifices the consumption of four generations of workers and their families merely to increase the rate of growth of that consumption starting with the fifth generation has nothing in common with an 'ideal socialist norm', and cannot be rationally motivated except in terms of purely political contingencies. For Dobb's argumentation is, of course, completely spurious; all that his calculations show is that the *value* of consumer goods produced cannot grow at an increasing rate after x years unless the *value* of department I immediately rises at a faster rate than that of department II.

However, neither an individual worker nor the working class itself in

29. The exceptions are those means of production which are sold to agricultural cooperatives and small handicraftsmen or illegally channelled into the black (parallel) market.

30. Maurice Dobb, *On Economic Theory and Socialism*, London, 1955, pp. 330–31, 150–51, and elsewhere.

a post-capitalist society (not to speak of a *socialist commonwealth*) is interested in a constantly rising rate of growth of the *value* of consumer goods. On the contrary, they are concerned with *reducing* that 'value' as much as possible by raising the productivity of labour, and with the withering away of commodity production and market economy. Their basic interests lie in the most rapid optimum *satisfaction of rational consumer needs*, i.e. the production at lowest possible cost of an optimum basket of consumer goods (thereby combining maximum economy of the labour of the producers with maximum satisfaction of consumer needs). To believe that this is the same as maximization of capitalist commodity-value (or profit) is to commit not only a grave theoretical error, but also a disastrous political and social miscalculation.

Even worse were the attempts made in the sixties to revive a so-called 'structural law' of 'socialism', according to which department I must expand at a faster rate than department II.[31] All such endeavours abstract from the *value nature* of the reproduction schemas, and assume that optimum satisfaction of social needs implies both continuous, unlimited expansion of the output of means of production, and the allocation of an even higher fraction of the total labour potential of society to the creation of *material producer goods* (as against social services dealing with health, education, artistic creation, 'pure' scientific research, child-care, etc., etc.). None of these assumptions can be scientifically proven or justified. Indeed, their apologetic function – as a straightforward rationalization of existing practice in the USSR and the 'Peoples' Democracies' – is obvious to any critical observer.

It should be added that both Oskar Lange and Bronislaw Minc, while not clarifying the difference between capitalist and socialist reproduction schemas, correctly demonstrated that increased productivity of labour and technical progress do not necessarily require department I to grow more quickly than department II; nor do they imply increased current outlay on means of production per unit currently (annually) produced.[32]

Rosa Luxemburg well understood that the *form* of the reproduction

31. See, *inter alia*, P. Mstislawski, 'On the Methodology to Justify Optimal Proportions of Social Reproduction', in *Voprosy Ekonomiki*, No. 5, 1964; Helmut Koziolek, *Aktuelle Probleme der politischen Ökonomie*, Berlin, 1966; Rudolf Reichenberg, *Struktur und Wachstum der Abteilungen I und II im Sozialismus*, Berlin, 1968.

32. See Lange, op cit., pp. 32–3, and Bronislaw Minc, *Aktualne zagadnienia ekonomii politicznej socialismu* (Current Problems in the Political Economy of Socialism), Warsaw, 1956.

schemas applies only to capitalist commodity and value production, and that the laws of motion corresponding to that form can have no validity in non-capitalist societies. But even she erred by attaching to the 'equilibrium proportions' derived from the schemas an a-historical, eternal validity which they do not and cannot possess.[33]

If a socially appropriated surplus product is substituted for surplus-value, then the equilibrium formula takes on a new form which expresses the *different social goal* of reproduction, corresponding to the changed social structure. Surplus-value is not simply a part of the total value of commodities produced under capitalism, nor is it just a fraction of the newly produced value product (the national income). *It is also the goal of the capitalist production process.* As such, it is much more than a mere symbol in a reproduction schema which is intended to represent reality at a high level of abstraction. For Marx, the schemas refer to the reproduction of quantified use-value and exchange-value in a given proportion. But they also express the reproduction of capitalist relations of production themselves.[34] All that is implied in the formula $I_v + I_s =$ II_c. And all that changes under socialism, once s disappears.

Furthermore, in a society where commodity production has withered away, and where the concept of surplus labour is essentially reducible to that of *social service and economic growth*, the meaning of the notion of 'equilibrium' derived from the 'proportionality formula' is subject to a fundamental transformation. When proportionality is upset in a commodity-producing society, production of *both use-values and exchange-values* declines, because both are inextricably linked to each other. Under socialism, however, no such inexorable nexus survives – not even as a necessary proportion (in the form of an 'eternal law') between labour inputs and use-value inputs. Indeed, in *Capital* Volume 2, Marx goes so far as to state categorically that, after the abolition of capitalism, there will be 'constant relative over-production' of equip-

33. Rosa Luxemburg, *The Accumulation of Capital*, London, 1963, pp. 84–5. Earlier, however, she had specifically stated: 'In every planned system of production it is, above all, the relation between all labour, past and present, and the means of production (between $v+s$ and c, according to our formula), or the relation between the aggregate of necessary consumer goods (again, in the terms of our formula, $v+s$) and c which are subjected to regulation. Under capitalist conditions, on the other hand, all social labour necessary for the maintenance of the inanimate means of production and also of living labour power is treated as one entity, as capital, in contrast with the surplus labour that has been performed, i.e. with the surplus value s. The relation between these two quantities c and $(v+s)$ is a palpably real, objective relationship of capitalist society: it is the average rate of profit' (ibid., p. 79).

34. See *Capital* Volume 3, Chapter 51.

ment, raw materials and foodstuffs. 'Over-production of this kind', he says, 'is equivalent to control by the society over the objective means of its own reproduction.'[35]

It is easy to imagine a society which, having reached a certain level of consumption, consciously decides to give absolute priority to a single goal: reduction of the work load. Its efforts would then be concentrated on assuring the production and distribution of an 'ideal' *package of use-values* with fewer and fewer labour inputs. There would still be 'simple reproduction' at the level of use-values, but it would be achieved with, let us say, a reduction in man-days of 4 per cent per annum (if population increased by 1 per cent and labour productivity by 5 per cent). To call this a situation of 'contracted reproduction' would be wrong, both because a socialist society *would calculate essentially with use-values*, and because in Marx's reproduction schèma the concept of 'contracted reproduction' is logically connected with the notions of crisis, interrupted economic equilibrium and declining living standards, whereas the conditions just described involve smooth continuity of material production and reproduction, stable living standards and absence of any kind of crisis.

This does not mean that planned socialist production could do without specific proportions in the flow of labour, means of production and consumer goods between the two departments. Such proportional allocation of resources is indeed the very essence of socialist planning. It means only that there is a qualitative as well as a quantitative difference between value calculations and calculations in labour time – between the dynamics of, on the one hand, appropriation and accumulation of surplus-value, and, on the other hand, rising efficiency (labour productivity) achieved in successive phases of production and measured in quantities of use-values produced during a fixed length of time.[36]

35. See below, pp. 544–5.
36. Cf. the following passage from Engels's *Anti-Dühring*: 'From the moment when society enters into possession of the means of production and uses them in direct association for production, the labour of each individual, however varied its specifically useful character may be, becomes at the start and directly social labour. The quantity of social labour contained in a product need not then be established in a roundabout way; daily experience shows in a direct way how much of it is required on the average. Society can simply calculate how many hours of labour are contained in a steam-engine, a bushel of wheat of the last harvest, or a hundred square yards of cloth of a certain quality. It could therefore never occur to it still to express the quantities of labour put into the products, quantities which it will then know directly and in their absolute amounts, in a third product, in a measure which, besides, is only relative, fluctuating, inadequate, though formerly unavoidable for

Minc goes much farther than Luxemburg when, summing up the opinion of two generations of Stalinist and post-Stalinist East European and Soviet economists, he clearly asserts: 'The basic theses of Marx's theory of expanded reproduction, as expressed in the schemas, are entirely valid under socialism.'[37] Contrary to the explicit theory of

---

lack of a better, rather than express them in their natural, adequate and absolute measure, *time*. Just as little as it would occur to chemical science still to express atomic weights in a roundabout way, relatively, by means of the hydrogen atom, if it were able to express them absolutely, in their adequate measure, namely in actual weights, in billionths or quadrillionths of a gramme. Hence, on the assumptions we made above, society will not assign values to products. It will not express the simple fact that the hundred square yards of cloth have required for their production, say, a thousand hours of labour in the oblique and meaningless way, stating that they have the *value* of a thousand hours of labour. It is true that even then it will still be necessary for society to know how much labour each article of consumption requires for its production. It will have to arrange its plan of production in accordance with its means of production, which include, in particular, its labour-power. The useful effects of the various articles of consumption, compared with one another and with the quantities of labour required for their production, will in the end determine the plan.' Frederick Engels, *Anti-Dühring*, Moscow, 1969, pp. 366–7. Cf. also Marx's observation: 'Let us finally imagine, for a change, an association of free men, working with the means of production held in common, and expending their many different forms of labour-power in full self-awareness as one single social labour force . . . Labour-time would in that case play a double part. Its apportionment in accordance with a definite social plan maintains the correct proportion between the different functions of labour and the various needs of the associations. On the other hand, labour-time also serves as a measure of the part taken by each individual in the common labour, and of his share in the part of the total product destined for individual consumption' (*Capital* Volume 1, op. cit., pp. 171–2).

To what theoretical contortions the confusion of capitalist and socialist reproduction schemas necessarily leads is strikingly demonstrated by Reichenberg (op. cit.). First, he calmly includes the material *tools* of the service sector in a department II of consumer goods (p. 16). Next he speaks of an 'intensification of expanded reproduction' as a result of the 'scientific-technical revolution' – an intensification which expresses itself in the fact that 'if the difference between $(I_v + I_s)$ and II_c remains the same, a process of increased accumulation is possible' (p. 21). But he fails to specify the object of this accumulation. Is it the *value* of II_c? Obviously that would be nonsense. The difference between two value quantities cannot change if the quantities themselves do not change. Perhaps it is accumulation of *use-values*? No doubt. But surely an increase in the mass of raw materials and tools (for the output of consumer goods) produced by a given quantity of socially necessary labour is the very definition of an increase in labour productivity. And, at the same time, Reichenberg implies that the value of these goods (and therefore the dynamics of expanded reproduction in *value* terms) has not changed!

37. Bronislaw Minc, *L'Économie politique du socialisme*, Paris, 1974, p. 167.

Marx and Engels, such 'socialist production' would thus remain generalized commodity production, i.e. generalized production of value. We may well ask what kind of intrinsic 'law' of raising surplus labour would then be incorporated into these 'socialist production relations'. For Marx distinctly states that such a law underlies the schemas of expanded reproduction referring to the production of surplus-value.[38]

6. PRODUCTIVE AND UNPRODUCTIVE LABOUR

Marx's theory of reproduction is firmly rooted in his perfected labour theory of value, not only in the sense that his reproduction schemas are based upon a common *numéraire*, labour-time, but also in the sense that what they measure and express is the distribution (and movement) of the labour force available to society among different departments and branches of material production. Value, in Marx's theory, *is* abstract social labour.

Michio Morishima, who has devoted much effort and ingenuity to rehabilitating Marx in the eyes of academic economists as one of the principal forerunners of aggregation techniques, nevertheless continues to detect a contradiction between a macro-economic theory of value, based upon aggregation, and a micro-economic labour theory of value. While dismissing the trite 'contradiction' between Volume 1 and Volume

38. 'In this way a situation comes about in which the individual capitalists have command of increasingly large armies of workers (no matter how much the variable capital may fall in relation to the constant capital), so that *the mass of surplus-value, and hence profit which they appropriate grows*, along with and despite the fall in the rate of profit'(*Capital* Volume 3, Chapter 13, our emphasis). It should be noted that, in the previous sentence, Marx has explicitly referred to accumulation of capital, and thus expanded reproduction. This passage should be contrasted with the no less explicit one concerning economic growth under socialism: 'If however wages are reduced to their general basis, i.e. that portion of the product of his labour that goes into the worker's own individual consumption; if this share is freed from its capitalist limit and *expanded* to the scale of consumption that is both permitted by the existing social productivity (i.e. the social productivity of his own labour as genuinely social labour) and required for the full development of individuality; if surplus labour and surplus product are also *reduced*, to the degree needed under the given conditions of production, on the one hand to form an insurance and reserve fund, on the other hand for the steady expansion of reproduction *in the degree determined by social need* . . . i.e. if both wages and surplus-value are stripped of their specifically capitalist character, then nothing of these forms remains, but simply those foundations of the forms that are common to all social modes of production' (Volume 3, Chapter 50, our emphases). It is clear from these quotations that, for Marx, the difference *in form* implies a difference in quantities, especially in those dynamic quantities which are growth trends.

3, around which so much academic criticism of Marx has revolved for almost a century, he constructs quite an imposing straw man out of this 'new' contradiction.[39] In our opinion, however, his subtle distinction between Marx's 'two' labour theories of value is based upon a simple conceptual confusion. For Marx, value and value production are eminently *social* qualities, referring to relations between men, and not 'physical' attributes adhering to things once and for all. Thus, when Marx writes that the value of a commodity is the embodiment of human labour expended in its production, and when he goes on to say that its value is equal to the socially necessary labour contained within it, he is not making two different statements, but simply repeating the same thesis. For the value of a given commodity is determined only by that portion of labour spent in its production which corresponds to the social average (both the average productivity of labour and the average socially recognized need), that is to say, which is *recognized by society as socially necessary labour*. Labour expended in the production of a given commodity, but not recognized by society, is not productive of value *for the owner of that commodity*.

However, precisely because value and the production of value refer ultimately to the distribution and redistribution of the *total available labour-power of society engaged in production*, that macro-economic aggregate is a basic economic reality, a basic 'fact of life'. If five million workers work 2,000 hours a year in material production, the total value product *is* ten billion hours, independently of whether the socially recognized value of each individual commodity is equal to, or larger or smaller than, the actual number of labour hours expended in its production. It follows that if the value of a *given* commodity is less than the labour actually spent on its production, then there must be at least one other commodity whose value is greater than the quantity of labour actually embodied in it.[40] *Social recognition* of labour expenditure and

39. Michio Morishima, *Marx's Economics*, Cambridge, 1973, pp. 11–12. Cf. *Grundrisse* (op. cit., p. 135): 'What determines value is not the amount of labour time incorporated in products, but rather the amount of labour time necessary at a given moment.'

40. Cf. *Capital* Volume 3, Chapter 10, especially the following passage: 'Strictly speaking, in fact . . . the market value of the entire mass, as governed by the average values, is equal to the sum of its individual values . . . Those producing at the worst extreme then have to sell their commodities below their individual value, while those at the best extreme sell theirs above it.' See also below (p. 207): 'If the commodities are not sold at their values, then the sum of converted values remains unaffected; what is a plus for one side is a minus for the other.'

actual labour expenditure can differ only for individual commodities, not for the total mass.[41] In that sense, Morishima is right when he stresses that, in the last analysis, and for the capitalist mode of production (as distinct from petty commodity production), Marx's law of value is *fundamentally* an aggregate, macro-economic concept.[42]

The nexus between the reproduction schemas (and the problem of the circulation of capital in general) and the theory of value leads us back to one of the most hotly disputed issues of Marxist economic theory: the exact delimitation between productive and unproductive labour. As the schemas are *value* schemas, they express only *value production*, and automatically exclude economic activities which are not productive of value. What precisely are these activities?

It has to be admitted that the solution of this problem was made more difficult by Marx himself. There are undeniable differences – if only of nuance – between, on the one hand, the long section of *Theories of Surplus-Value* dealing with the problem of productive and unproductive labour and, on the other, those key passages of *Capital* (especially Volume 2) which treat the same subject. One striking illustration of this is the analysis of commerical agents and travellers. They are classified as productive workers in the *Theories*, and as unproductive workers in *Capital* Volumes 2 and 3.[43] In recent years, a long and often confused debate among Marxists has further complicated the matter.[44] It is also

41. I shall come back to this thesis when I deal with the so-called transformation problem in the introduction to Volume 3.

42. Morishima, op. cit., pp. 2–3.

43. *Theories of Surplus-Value*, Part I, Moscow 1969, p. 218; *Capital* Volume 3, Chapter 17; and see below, pp. 209–11. Even within Part 1 of *Theories of Surplus-Value*, there are striking contradictions on this question. Thus on page 157 Marx writes: 'An actor, for example, or even a clown, according to this definition, is a productive labourer if he works in the service of a capitalist.' And on page 172 he states: 'As for labours which are productive for their purchaser or employer himself – as for example the actor's labour for the theatrical entrepreneur – the fact that their purchaser cannot sell them to the public in the form of commodities but only in the form of the action itself would show that they are unproductive labours.'

44. See, *inter alia*, Jacques Nagels, *Travail collectif et travail productif dans l'évolution de la pensée marxiste*, Brussels, 1974; S. H. Coontz, *Productive Labour and Effective Demand*, London, 1965; Arnaud Berthoud, *Travail productif et productivité du travail chez Marx*, Paris, 1974; Ian Gough, 'Marx and Productive Labour', in *New Left Review*, No. 76, November–December 1972; Peter Howell, 'Once Again on Productive and Unproductive Labour', in *Revolutionary Communist*, No. 3/4, November 1975; Mario Cogoy, 'Werttheorie und Staatsausgaben', in *Probleme einer materialistischen Staatstheorie*, Frankfurt, 1973, pp. 164–71; P. Bischoff et al., 'Produktive und unproduktive Arbeit als Kategorien der Klassen-

intertwined with differences in judging the so-called service industries – which, to take one example, are not included in Soviet and East European accounting as contributing to national income, on the basis of a particular interpretation of Marx's theory of productive labour.[45] How then shall we unravel the problem?

A preliminary distinction which we need to draw goes to the heart of the matter. When Marx classifies certain forms of labour as productive and others as unproductive, he is not passing moral judgement or employing criteria of social (or human) usefulness. Nor does he even present this classification as an objective or a-historical one. The object of his analysis is the *capitalist mode of production*, and he simply determines what is productive and what is unproductive for the functioning, the *rationale* of that system, and that system alone. In terms of social usefulness or need, a doctor provides labour which is indispensable for the survival of any human society. His labour is thus eminently useful. Nevertheless, it is unproductive labour from the point of view of the production or expansion of *capital*. By contrast, the production of dum-dum bullets, hard drugs or pornographic magazines is useless and harmful to the overall interests of human society. But as such commodities find ready customers, the surplus-value embodied in them is realized, and capital is reproduced and expanded. The labour expended on them is thus productive labour.

In the framework of this socially determined and historically relativized concept, productive labour may then be defined as *all labour which*

analyse', in *Sozialistische Politik*, June 1970; Altvater and Huisken, 'Produktive und unproduktive Arbeit als Kampfbegriffe', in ibid., September 1970; Rudi Schmiede, *Zentrale Probleme der Marxschen Akkumulations- und Krisentheorie*, Diploma thesis, Frankfurt, 1972; I. Hashimoto, 'The Productive Nature of Service Labour', in *The Kyoto University Economic Review*, October 1966; K. Nishikawa, 'Productive and Unproductive Labour from the Point of View of National Income', in *Osaka City University Economic Review*, No. 1, 1965; K. Nishikawa, 'A Polemic on the Economic Character of Transport Labour', in ibid., No. 2, 1966. See also the article by Elisaburo Koga, Catherine Colliot-Thélème, Pierre Salama and Hugues Lagrange in *Critiques de l'économie politique*, Nos. 10 and 11/12 (January–March and April–September 1973); those by J. Morris and J. Blake in *Science and Society*, Nos. 22 (1958) and 24 (1960); and those by Fine, Harrison, Gough, Howell and others in the *Bulletin of the Conference of Socialist Economists*, 1973–5. There are numerous books on Marxist economic theory which deal with the same subject in passing.

45. See, for example, Jean Marchal and Jacques Lecaillon, *La Répartition du revenu national: Les modèles*, Vol. III, *Le modèle classique. Le modèle marxiste*, Paris, 1958, pp. 82–5; Bronislaw Minc, op. cit., pp. 159–65, and many others.

is exchanged against capital and not against revenue, i.e. all labour which enriches one or several capitalists, enabling them to appropriate a portion of the total mass of surplus-value produced by the total mass of value-producing wage-labour.[46] We could call it 'labour productive from the point of view of the individual capitalist(s)'. All wage-labour engaged by capitalist enterprise – as opposed to labour functioning for private households, for consumption needs – falls into that category. This is the level at which *Theories of Surplus-Value* stops.

But when he returns to the same problem in *Capital* Volume 2, from the point of view of the capitalist mode of production in its totality, and especially from that of the growth or accumulation of capital, Marx now distinguishes *labour productive for capital as a whole* from labour productive for the individual capitalist. For capital as a whole, only that labour is productive which *increases* the *total mass* of surplus-value. All wage-labour which enables an individual capitalist to appropriate a fraction of the total mass of surplus-value, without adding to that mass, may be 'productive' for the commercial, financial or service-sector capitalist whom it allows to participate in the general sharing of the cake. But from the point of view of capital as a whole it is unproductive, because it does not augment the total size of the cake.

Only commodity production makes possible the creation of value and surplus-value. Only within the realm of commodity production, then, is productive labour performed. No new surplus-value can be added in the sphere of circulation and exchange, not to speak of the stock exchange or the bank counter; all that happens there is the redistribution or reapportionment of previously created surplus-value. This point is made clear in *Capital* Volumes 2 and 3.[47] Most of the relevant passages from Volume 2 were drawn by Engels from Manuscripts II and IV. In other words, they were written in 1870 or between 1867 and 1870, some time after the *Theories of Surplus-Value* of 1861–3 (and even after the rough manuscript of Volume 3), and may therefore be considered to express Marx's definitive views on the question. Contrary to what is said in the *Theories*, they imply that wage-earning commercial clerks or travellers do not perform productive labour, at least not from the standpoint of capital as a whole. However, even when this basic principle is established, four additional problems remain to be solved.

First, there is the question of so-called 'immaterial goods': concerts, circus acts, prostitution, teaching, etc. In *Theories of Surplus-Value*,

46. See *Theories of Surplus-Value*, Part 1, op. cit., Chapter IV, 3.
47. See below, pp. 209–11; and *Capital* Volume 3, Chapters 16 and 17.

Marx tends to classify these as commodities, in so far as they are produced by wage-earners for capitalist entrepreneurs. Although in Volume 2 he does not explicitly contradict this, he insists strongly and repeatedly on the correlation between use-values embodied in commodities through a labour process which acts upon and transforms nature, and the production of value and surplus-value.[48] Moreover, he provides a general formula which implies the exclusion of wage-labour engaged in 'personal service industries' from the realm of productive labour: 'If we have a function which, although in and for itself unproductive, is nevertheless a necessary moment of reproduction, then when this is transformed, through the division of labour, from the secondary activity of many into the exclusive activity of a few, into their special business, this does not change the character of the function itself.'[49] If this is true of commercial travellers or book-keepers, it obviously applies all the more to teachers or cleaning services.

The definition of productive labour as *commodity-producing labour, combining concrete and abstract labour* (i.e. combining creation of use-values and production of exchange-values) logically excludes 'non-material goods' from the sphere of value production. Furthermore, this conclusion is intimately bound up with a basic thesis of *Capital*: production is, for humanity, the necessary mediation between nature and society; there can be no production without (concrete) labour, no concrete labour without appropriation and transformation of material objects.[50]

48. See below, Chapter 6. Of the more systematic analyses of this problem, those of Nagels and Bischoff (see note 44 above) adopt a similar position to our own. Gough supports the opposite view, basing himself especially on a passage of *Capital* Volume 1 (op. cit., p. 644), in which Marx explicitly includes wage-earners working for private capital (such as teachers) in the realm of productive labour. In our opinion, this passage, like several in *Theories of Surplus-Value*, only indicates that Marx had not yet completed his articulation of the contradictory determinants of 'productive labour' – on the one hand, exchange against capital rather than revenue, and on the other, participation in the process of commodity production (which involves the unity-and-contradiction of the labour process and the valorization process, use-value and exchange-value, concrete and abstract labour). What is the 'immaterial good' produced by a wage-earning teacher which could be conceptually contrasted with the 'immaterial service' produced by a wage-earning cleaner (working for a capitalist cleaning firm) or by a wage-earning clerk of a department store?

49. See below, p. 209.

50. See *Capital* Volume 1, op. cit., pp. 283ff. Jacques Gouverneur attempts, mistakenly in our opinion, to transcend this limitation. In order to be able to include the production of 'immaterial goods' by wage-labour in the category of

This becomes evident when Marx sets forth in *Capital* Volume 2 his reasons for classifying the transport industry in the realm of the production of value and surplus-value, rather than in that of circulation. The argument is clearly summarized in the following passage: 'The quantity of products is not increased by their transport. The change in their natural properties that may be effected by transport is also, certain exceptions apart, not an intended useful effect, but rather an unavoidable evil. But the use-value of things is only realized in their consumption, and their consumption may make a change of location necessary, and thus, in addition, the additional production process of the transport industry. The productive capital invested in this industry thus adds value to the products transported.'[51]

Now it is obvious that none of these arguments is applicable to the carrying of persons. Passenger transport is not an indispensable condition of the realization of use-values and adds no new value to any commodity. It is rather a personal service on which individuals (whether capitalists or workers) spend their own revenue. Thus, whether it is organized on the basis of wage-labour or not, the passenger transport industry can no more be considered as increasing the total mass of social value and surplus-value than can wage-labour employed in the fields of commerce, banking or insurance.

In striking contrast to the above passage is Marx's argument in Chapter 6, 3, of Volume 2. While explicitly stating that transportation of persons by capitalist enterprise does *not* create commodities or use-values of any kind, he notes that it is nevertheless a 'productive branch', even though the 'useful effect' (*Nutzeffekt*) is only consumable during the production process itself.[52]

Ranging this question under the broader heading of so-called service industries, we may say that, as a general rule, all forms of wage-labour which exteriorize themselves in and thus add value to a product (materials) are creative of surplus-value and hence productive for capitalism as a whole. This applies not only to manufacturing and mining industries, but also to transportation of goods,[53] 'public service' industries such as the production and transport of water or any form of

---

'productive labour', he extends Marx's formulation referred to above into 'transformation of nature *or the world*', where 'or the world' means 'or society'. Since wage-earning teachers 'transform society' without 'transforming nature', the implications are obvious. (Jacques Gouverneur, *Le Travail 'productif' en régime capitaliste*, Louvain, 1975, pp. 41ff.)

51. See below, pp. 226–7.   52. See below, pp. 134–5.   53. See below, Chapter 6.

energy (e.g. gas and electricity), the selling of meals in restaurants, the building and sale of houses and offices as well as provision of the material for constructing them, and of course agriculture. Many sectors which are often included under the heading 'service industries' are, therefore, parts of material production and employ productive labour. By contrast, the *letting* of apartment or hotel rooms, the service of transporting persons in buses, underground systems or trains, the performance of medical, educational or recreational wage-labour which is not objectivized outside the worker (the sale of specific forms of labour rather than of commodities), the work of commercial or banking clerks and of the employees of insurance companies or market research firms – these do not add to the sum total of social value and surplus-value produced, and cannot therefore be categorized as forms of productive labour.

An interesting illustration is provided by television. The production of television sets or *films* (including copies of such films) is obviously a form of commodity production, and wage-labour engaged in it is productive labour. But the hiring-out of completed films or the renting of a single television set to successive customers does not have the characteristics of productive labour. Similarly, wage-labour employed in making advertising films is productive, whereas the cajoling of potential clients to purchase or order such films is as unproductive as the labour of commercial representatives in general.

The second problem is to draw a precise demarcation between the spheres of production and circulation in capitalist society as a whole. Volume 2 of *Capital* leaves no room for doubt about Marx's view: only that labour which either adds to or is indispensable for the realization and conservation of a commodity's *use-value* adds to the total amount of abstract social labour embodied in that commodity (is productive of value).[54] Like the rest of Volume 2, the passages dealing with this question are but successive unfoldings of the basic analysis of the commodity – of its irreducible duality and the contradictions flowing therefrom.

Thirdly, we have to consider the different kinds of labour performed within the production process itself. Here Marx takes a much less simplistic attitude than some of his latter-day disciples. His fundamental doctrine is that of the 'collective labourer', as developed in 'Results of the Immediate Process of Production'.[55] Productive labour,

54. See below, pp. 225–6.
55. This text is included as an appendix in *Capital* Volume 1, op. cit. See our introduction to this appendix, as well as Chapter 14 of *Capital* Volume 1 itself.

as labour expended in the realm of production of commodities, is *all* wage-labour indispensable for that production process; that is to say, not only manual labour, but also that of engineers, people working in laboratories, overseers, and even managers and stock clerks, in so far as the physical production of a commodity would be impossible without that labour. But wage-labour which is indifferent to the specific use-value of a commodity and which is performed only to extort the maximum surplus-value from the work-force (e.g. the wage-labour of timekeepers) or to assure the defence of private property (security guards in and around a factory); labour linked to the particular *social and juridical forms* of capitalist production (lawyers employed as salaried staff by manufacturing firms); financial book-keepers; *additional* stock-checkers made necessary by the tendency to overproduction – none of these is productive labour for capital. It does not add value to the commodities produced (although it may be essential to the overall functioning of the capitalist system, or of bourgeois society as a whole).

The final case to be examined is that of petty commodity producers, independent peasants and handicraftsmen. While producing commodities and thus both use-values and exchange-values, these strata do not directly create surplus-value (except in marginal cases), although they may contribute indirectly to the mass of social surplus-value – for example, by depressing the value of food through their cheap labour. We believe that on this point Marx maintained the position put forward in *Theories of Surplus-Value*: such strata perform labour which is neither productive nor unproductive from the point of view of the capitalist mode of production, because they operate outside its framework.[56]

7. ARE UNPRODUCTIVE LABOURERS PART OF THE PROLETARIAT?

A precise definition of productive labour under capitalism is not only of theoretical importance. It also has major implications for social book-keeping (calculation *in value terms* of the national income)[57] and significantly affects our analysis of social classes and the political conclusions we draw from it.

56. *Theories of Surplus-Value*, Part 1, op cit., pp. 407–8.

57. It should be added that, for both analytical and practical reasons, it is quite legitimate for Marxists to introduce into calculations of national income a category such as 'total money incomes of all households and enterprises taken together', provided that it is clearly differentiated from the value of the annual product and incomes generated by annual production.

The narrowest position, which seeks to reduce the proletariat to the group of manual industrial workers, is in complete contradiction with Marx's explicit definition of productive labour, and we need not dwell on it here. At the other extreme, it is obviously absurd to extend the concept of the proletariat to all wage and salary earners without limitation (including army generals and managers earning 100,000 dollars a year). The defining structural characteristic of the proletariat in Marx's analysis of capitalism is the *socio-economic compulsion to sell one's labour-power*. Included in the proletariat, then, are not only manual industrial workers, but all unproductive wage-labourers who are subject to the same fundamental constraints: non-ownership of means of production; lack of direct access to the means of livelihood (the land is by no means freely accessible!); insufficient money to purchase the means of livelihood without more or less continuous sale of labour-power. Thus, all those strata whose salary levels *permit* accumulation of capital in addition to a 'normal' standard of living are excluded from the proletariat. Whether such accumulation actually takes place is in itself irrelevant (although monographs and statistics tend to confirm that, to a modest or sizeable degree, this social group does engage in it; this is the case especially of the so-called managers, who – notwithstanding a platitude which continues to circulate in spite of all evidence to the contrary – are part and parcel of the capitalist class, if not necessarily of its top layer of billionaires).

This definition of the proletariat, which includes the mass of unproductive wage-earners (not only commercial clerks and lower government employees, but domestic servants as well), and which considers productive workers in industry as the proletarian vanguard only in the broadest sense of the word, has been challenged recently by several authors.[58] It was, however, undoubtedly the one advanced by Marx and Engels and their most 'orthodox' followers: the mature (not the

58. Gillman groups 'the advertising managers, the directors of public relations, the legal counsel, the tax experts, the "sales engineers", the legislative lobbyists, their clerical assistants' together with 'the rest (!) of the growing host of white-collar workers' in the general category of 'third party consumers'. Although he does not explicitly say so, he thereby tends to exclude them from the proletariat (*The Falling Rate of Profit*, London, 1957, pp. 93 and 131). This view clearly influenced Paul Baran's analyses in *The Political Economy of Growth* (New York, 1957) and those of Baran and Paul Sweezy in *Monopoly Capital* (New York, 1966). Boccara et al. (*Le Capitalisme monopoliste d'état*, Paris, 1971) explicitly exclude the 'intermediate salaried layers' from the proletariat, reducing the latter to the sole group of productive workers (workers producing surplus-value). (See pp. 213 and 236ff.)

senile) Kautsky, Plekhanov, Lenin, Trotsky, Luxemburg et al.[59] But it raises a weighty objection. If only productive labour produces value and thereby reproduces the equivalent of its own wages (besides creating surplus-value),[60] does this not imply that the wages of unproductive labour are paid out of surplus-value produced by productive labour? And in that case, does there not arise a major conflict of interests between productive and unproductive labour, the first seeking to reduce surplus-value to a minimum, the second wishing it to be increased? How can such a basic conflict of interest be reconciled with the inclusion of both sectors in the same social class? Furthermore, should the industrial workers not be opposed to any expansion of state expenditure, even in

59. The sources are too numerous to be listed exhaustively. The following are particularly worthy of note: *Capital* Volume 1, op. cit., p. 798, where the unemployed sick, disabled, mutilated, widowed, elderly, etc., are designated as the 'pauperized sections [*Lazarusschichte*] of the working class'; *Capital* Volume 2 (see below, p. 516), where Marx defines the class of wage-labourers as those who are under constant (continuous) compulsion to sell their labour-power (on p. 561 servants – *die Bedientenklasse* – are also characterized as wage-labourers). Rosa Luxemburg (*Einführung in die Nazionalökonomie*, Berlin, 1925, pp. 263–4 and 277–8) similarly includes casually and occasionally employed workers, as well as paupers, the sick and unemployed and so on as members of the working class. Trotsky (*1905*, London, 1972, p. 43) groups domestic servants under the same heading, and Kautsky (*The Class Struggle: Erfurt Program*, New York, 1971, pp. 35–43) explicitly includes in the ranks of the proletariat commercial and industrial wage-earners. In his draft programme of the Russian Social Democratic Labour Party, Plekhanov defines the proletariat as those who are forced to sell their labour-power (see Lenin, *Collected Works*, Vol. 6, p. 19), later extending it to 'persons who possess no means of production and of circulation . . . All these persons are forced by their economic position to sell their labour-power constantly or periodically' (pp. 61–3). While Lenin contested the introduction of the words 'and of circulation', he raised no essential objection to the formulation.

60. An interesting borderline case is that of the so-called semi-proletariat – i.e. the layer which retains partial ownership of its own means of production. Its income, which is derived from agricultural and handicraft commodities privately produced at a productivity of labour far below the social average, barely exceeds its costs of production, and is therefore insufficient to secure the barest livelihood. The semi-proletariat is thus forced to work part of the time as wage-labour. But precisely because it sells its labour-power *only temporarily*, its wages can be driven far below the prevailing social minimum. Its social existence is characterized by a striking contradiction: while it is in no way involved in the extraction or consumption of surplus-value, both its immediate and its historic interests stand in a certain limited opposition to those of the proletariat proper. That is why the semi-proletariat, unlike unproductive workers and other straightforward wage-earners, cannot be regarded as a fraction of the proletariat; it represents rather a transitional phenomenon, with one foot in the petty bourgeoisie and another in the proletariat.

the realm of 'social services', since this is financed in the last analysis through an increase in surplus-value extracted from them?

This objection can be countered at two levels. To begin with, it is not true that all unproductive labour is paid out of currently produced surplus-value. An important part of that labour (e.g. commercial employees, workers in the financial sector and those in unproductive service industries) is paid not out of currently produced surplus-value, but out of that portion of *social capital* which is invested in these sectors. Only the *profits* of these capitals form part of currently produced surplus-value. It is true that social capital is the result of *past* extortion of surplus-value. But this applies also to variable capital, i.e. to wages currently paid out to productive workers. The important point here is that, since wages and salaries in all these sectors are not drawn from *currently produced* surplus-value, *their payment in no way reduces the currently paid wages* of productive workers.[61]

Part of the wages bill of unproductive labour, however, is financed out of currently produced surplus-value. This concerns essentially the wages and salaries of state employees in public services and administration (not, of course, the state industries, where autonomous commodity production and therefore value production occur). But in order to conclude from this that a reduction of state expenditure entails a reduction of surplus-value and an increase in real wages (or, which amounts to the same thing, that the rise in state expenditure has occurred through an increase in surplus-value and a reduction in real wages), it would be necessary to undertake a very detailed analysis of the trend of the rate of exploitation and of workers' living standards and needs since the 'explosion' of state expenditure. Such an examination is clearly beyond the scope of this introduction, but two crucial points should be made.

First, the concept of 'gross wages' (i.e. wages before tax) has no meaning in Marxist economic theory. Wages are means of reconstituting the

61. These wages increase the total mass of social capital among which the *given* quantity of surplus-value has had to be divided (in other words, they lower the average rate of profit). But as far as the industrialists are concerned, this is a lesser evil. If there were no autonomous commercial capital and commercial wage-earners, their own capital outlays to cover the costs of circulation would be significantly higher, and the rate of profit still lower (see *Capital* Volume 3, Chapter 17). Since this only concerns the distribution of a given mass of surplus-value between different forms of capital, with no *direct* bearing on the division of newly created value between wages and surplus-value (i.e. on the rate of exploitation of productive labour), there arises no conflict of interest between productive and commercial wage-earners.

worker's labour-power through the purchase of commodities and services. Thus money deducted from the worker's 'gross wage' to help the state buy aeroplanes has nothing at all to do with wages. It is from the outset part of social surplus-value. (Of course, if fresh taxes actually lower previously attained levels of real wages, they may indeed be said to have increased the rate of surplus-value. But again this will be measured by comparing successive amounts of net – real – wages, and not 'gross wages'.)

Similarly, it would be absurd to construe state medical, educational or transport services which help reconstitute the worker's labour-power (or maintain his family under normal living conditions) as derived from surplus-value; they represent rather *a socialized portion of the wage*, regardless of whether it passes through the form of 'state revenue', and regardless of whether it 'originated' in 'gross wages' (taxes paid by the worker), 'gross profits' (taxes paid by the capitalist), or the 'gross income' of independent middle classes.[62]

It thus proves meaningful after all to examine the impact of a rise or fall in state expenditure on *average working-class living standards*, independently of its servicing (mediation) by unproductive state employees. Where these living standards decline, the conclusion is obvious: the total price of labour-power (individual plus 'socialized' wages) has been reduced. Where they rise, however, no sophism can prove that this entails an increase in social surplus-value. (To be sure, it could be *accompanied* by such an increase, but then so could a rise in real direct wages. 'Accompanied by' is not synonymous with 'caused by', except for people with faulty logic.)

As Marxist economic theory rejects the notion of a rigid 'wages fund',

62. It has been objected that unemployment compensation can by no means be considered as the equivalent of the 'price' or 'value' of a commodity called 'labour-power', for by definition the unemployed do not sell their labour-power. However, this argument is based on a somewhat mechanistic reduction of the category 'socialized wages'. Nobody could assert that, if a worker places 10 per cent of his current wages in a chocolate box or a bank account in order to provide for the portion of his 'active adult life' during which he expects to be unemployed, that amount of money thereby ceases to be part of his wages. There is no fundamental difference between this and the situation where all workers use a collective chocolate box or bank account called the National Institute of Unemployment Insurance or National Institute of Social Security, and where the sums of money do not pass through the workers' pay packets but are transferred directly from the capitalists' accounts to these institutes. Only if this analysis is accepted, by the way, is it legitimate to demand that such funds be exclusively administered by the unions (for neither the employers nor the state should have any say in how the workers spend their own money!).

any analysis of the effects of varying levels of state expenditure upon the rate of exploitation would have to be aggregate and dynamic. Nothing flows automatically from either the expansion or contraction of state expenditure. Thus, for it to be shown that it was rising at the expense of the working class, it would have to be proved that, under the given economic, social and political conditions, a reduction in expenditure would lead to higher real wages rather than higher profits for the capitalist class. Without such detailed proof, the thesis would remain doubtful, to say the least. The analysis would have to take into account the probable dynamic of the political and social class struggle (a function of, among other things, the great historical shifts in the economic correlation of class forces within a given bourgeois society) and its precise impact upon the structure of both state revenue and state expenditure.

We seem to have strayed considerably from the problem of productive and unproductive labour, and its relation to the definition of the proletariat. But in reality, we have only now arrived at the heart of the problem. For the correct Marxist classification of the proletariat – the class which is forced by socio-economic compulsion to sell its labour-power to the capitalist owners of the means of production – implies that both variations in the level of the reserve army of labour, and the variegated relations between the 'purely physiological' and 'moral-historical' components of the value of labour-power,[63] are of decisive importance for the proletarian's immediate destiny.

Once we understand this, we can see the significance of the growth of unproductive wage-labour, which accompanies the absolute and relative increase in the size of the proletariat in contemporary capitalist countries.[64] Far from reflecting increased exploitation of productive labour or a

63. See my introduction to *Capital* Volume 1, op. cit., pp. 66–72, and *Late Capitalism*, op. cit., pp. 149–58.

64. *Wage earners (incl. unemployed) as % of total active population*

	1930s	1974
Belgium	65·2% (1930)	83·7%
Canada	66·7% (1941)	89·2%
France	57·2% (1936)	81·3%
Germany	69·7% (1939)	84·5% (West Germany)
Italy	51·6% (1936)	72·6%
Japan	41·0% (1936)	69·1%
Sweden	70·1% (1940)	91·0%
U.K.	88·1% (1931)	92·3%
U.S.A.	78·2% (1939)	91·5%

Sources: For the 1930s, *Annuaire des statistiques du travail*, 1945–6, Bureau International du Travail, Montreal, 1947; for 1974, *Office statistique des communautés européennes: statistiques de base, 1976*.

sharp rise in the rate of exploitation, it has rather established a ceiling above which the rate of exploitation can hardly climb under 'normal' political circumstances (excluding, that is, fascist or fascist-type régimes). For, despite the rapid replacement of living labour by dead labour (semi-automated machinery), it is this growth of unproductive wage-labour which, in many capitalist countries, has reduced the reserve army of labour for a whole historical period. Moreover, the services provided by a significant sector of unproductive wage-labour have been a major factor in developing the needs and living conditions of the proletariat far beyond the purely physiological bedrock. The new minimum standard which has arisen is, at least in the imperialist countries (and in some of the most developed semi-colonial countries with a powerful labour movement, like Argentina), much higher than the one existing in Marx's time.

This acquisition should obviously not be taken for granted or regarded as unassailable. It is nothing but a conquest made by the working class under favourable conditions on the labour market (long-term decline of structural unemployment) and rendered objectively possible by the long post-war period of accelerated economic growth. Since the early seventies, as was foreseeable, this basic economic situation has been reversed.[65] Massive structural unemployment has reappeared, together with savage attacks in many 'rich' countries on the real wages of the working class, be they aimed at 'direct' or 'socialized' wages or at both. Correctly, the workers have reacted strongly against massive cuts in social state expenditure, thereby showing that their class instinct is clearer than the 'science' of those theoreticians who persist in calling all state expenditure 'surplus-value' (the logical consequence of which would be indifference to, or even approval of the cut-backs).

8. LUXURY PRODUCTION, SURPLUS-VALUE AND ACCUMULATION OF CAPITAL

Also related to the integration of Marx's labour theory of value with his theory of reproduction is the question of the exact nature of the labour which produces luxury goods, as well as its function in repro-duction. This problem is important not so much because of the role of luxury consumption as such, but because of the obvious analogy between luxury products and another sector which has played an ominously

65. See Chapter 4 of *Late Capitalism*, op. cit.

growing role in capitalist economy ever since Marx wrote *Capital*. We are referring, of course, to *arms production*.

Controversy over the exact function of the arms sector under capitalism has been raging since the end of the nineteenth century, when the Russian populist V. Vorontsov raised for the first time the possibility of avoiding crises of over-production through 'absorption' of part of surplus-value by increased arms production.[66] In the thirties and forties, a long debate among Marxists took up the role of rearmament in overcoming the long-term stagnation of the international capitalist economy during the inter-war period. Since the war, the Vance–Cliff–Kidron school has assigned a crucial position to the 'permanent arms economy' in the explanation of the long economic 'boom'; and arms production occupies a central place in the process of 'surplus absorption' presented in Baran and Sweezy's *Monopoly Capital*.[67] More recently still, a new controversy has arisen between the author of this introduction and various other Marxist economists, centring on the specific relation of arms production to the evolution of the mass and rate of profit under late capitalism.[68]

Marx's theory sees the essence of value in abstract social labour, irrespective of the specific use-value of the commodity it produces. The existence of some kind of use-value is a precondition of the realization of exchange-value only in the immediate and obvious sense that nobody buys a good which has absolutely no use for him. But the social fact of purchase is sufficient proof of the use-value of a commodity, that is, of its usefulness to its buyer. Hence only *unsold* commodities do not embody socially necessary labour and thus have no value; those which are sold are by definition the product of socially necessary labour and increase through their production the mass of socially produced value. Under capitalism, also by definition, the production of all sold commodities created by wage-labour increases the total mass of surplus-

66. Quoted in Luxemburg, *The Accumulation of Capital*, op. cit., p. 282.

67. Here again, the list of books is too long to be reproduced in full. Leaving aside older works, the following deserve mention: Nathalia Moszkowska, *Zur Dynamik des Spätkapitalismus*, Zurich/New York, 1943; T. N. Vance, *The Permanent War Economy*, Berkeley, 1970; Adolf Kozlik, *Der Vergeudungskapitalismus*, Vienna, 1966; Baran and Sweezy, *Monopoly Capital*, op. cit.; Fritz Vilmar, *Rüstung und Abrüstung im Spätkapitalismus*, Frankfurt, 1965; Michael Kidron, *Western Capitalism since the War*, London, 1968. Of less direct relevance is Gillman, *The Falling Rate of Profit*, op. cit.

68. See my arguments in *Late Capitalism*, op. cit., Chapter 9, and those of Cogoy, *Werttheorie und Staatsausgaben*, op. cit., pp. 165–6. See also Paul Mattick, *Kritik der Neomarxisten*, Frankfurt, 1974.

value produced and realized (unless they are sold at a price so far below their cost of production that society does not recognize any part of the surplus labour contained in them).

In Volume 2, Marx clearly distinguishes production and realization of surplus-value (and, by implication, profit) from expanded reproduction of capital, i.e. capital accumulation. Not all commodities produced contribute to the process of expanded reproduction. But Marx states quite explicitly that all commodities produced and sold contribute to the increase of total surplus-value appropriated by the capitalists and their retainers.[69] By contrast, under conditions of simple reproduction, there would be no surplus-value and no profit whatsoever, since *all* surplus-value would be unproductively consumed without entering into the reproduction process.

The production of luxury consumer goods, purchased out of the portion of surplus-value which is not accumulated, remains within the sphere of the production of value and surplus-value, that is to say, it enlarges the mass of profit accruing to the capitalist class. By the same token, the production of arms or space equipment is a form of commodity production; the fact that the sole purchaser is here the state, whereas luxury products are exchanged for revenue of the bourgeoisie, makes no essential difference. In order to determine whether arms production depresses or raises the average rate of profit, the same questions have to be answered as for any other 'sub-department' of capitalist production. Is the organic composition of capital in that particular department equal, superior or inferior to the average organic composition in other departments? And does its rise (or fall) influence the average social rate of surplus-value?[70]

It is not as easy to define the contribution of armaments production to the accumulation of capital as it is to decide whether it constitutes a form of production of value and surplus-value which influences the oscillations of the rate of profit. Two basic situations have to be distinguished.

69. See below, pp. 146–9, 178, 508–9 etc.

70. This follows automatically from the commodity nature of the arms produced, that is to say, from the fact that capital invested in that sector is engaged in the production of commodities and the corresponding labour employed in the production of surplus-value. Thus, as in the case of the production of luxury goods, differences between the rate of profit within that branch and the rate outside it (due, for instance, to variations in the organic composition of capital) will lower or increase accordingly the social average rate of profit. In *Theories of Surplus-Value*, Marx explicitly defends this position against Ricardo.

In a situation of 'full employment of capital' (which can be, and often has been, accompanied by structural unemployment of wage-labour), the production of weapons, like the production of luxury goods not entering into the reproduction of labour-power, evidently does not contribute to the accumulation of capital. This is true in a double sense. Weapons, like luxury products, do not provide the objective material elements of expanded (re-)production. They furnish neither additional raw materials, machines or sources of energy, nor consumer goods capable of feeding an expanded work force. Nevertheless, that part of the national income which buys weapons could not have been spent on additional means of production or wages for additional productive workers. Thus, both because of their specific use-value, and because they are exchanged against the non-accumulated part of surplus-value, weapons do not contribute to expanded reproduction, to capital accumulation, under conditions of 'full employment' of social capital.

This does not necessarily imply that weapons production *reduces* capital accumulation, except in the most general sense that *all* forms of unproductive expenditure of surplus-value do so. For it to be shown that the appearance or expansion of an arms sector *has actually reduced* expanded reproduction, it would have to be demonstrated that it has appeared (or expanded) *at the expense* of the sector of means of production. If it has simply replaced luxury production, then, all other things being equal, neither the scope nor the potential rhythm of capital accumulation will have been changed.

But what if the weapons sector has appeared (or expanded) at the expense of the sector producing consumer goods for the workers, still assuming 'full employment' of capital? There are again two distinct possibilities to be considered. Where this substitution leads to a decline in the physical or moral working capacity of the labour force, the rate of capital accumulation will fall in consequence, perhaps even, after a certain time, to the extent of contracted reproduction.[71] But where this substitution leaves unchanged the capacity or willingness of the workers to accept the current 'norm' of social labour in the process of production, such a shift of resources from department II to department III would imply a rise in the average social rate of surplus-value. The same value product would then be produced with the same labour-power, but at the cost of less variable capital. The working class would simply receive a smaller share of the existing national income. Whether this would leave

71. See Ernest Mandel, *Marxist Economic Theory*, London, 1968, pp. 332–5, on the war economy.

the rate of accumulation unaltered, or whether it would actually lead to a higher level of capital accumulation or expanded reproduction, would then depend on the way in which this rise in the rate and mass of surplus-value influenced the division of surplus-value between the unproductively consumed portion (in which is included the weapons sector) and the accumulated part.[72]

At this point, we must abandon the initial supposition of 'full employment of capital' and examine the actual function of expanding arms production under conditions of long-term *plethora* of capital. The situation is by no means artificial or introduced purely for the sake of argument. On the contrary, it was already prevalent during the first massive arms drive in the history of capitalism, which took place during the two decades preceding the First World War.[73] It was even more marked in the thirties, during the second period of massive rearmament, starting with Japan's 'Manchurian Incident' and German policy after Hitler came to power, and becoming generalized after 1936. Such *plethora* of capital remained more than ever the rule in the phase of permanent arming which has lasted now for more than thirty years and shows no signs of coming to an end – quite the contrary.[74] It is thus entirely appropriate to investigate the effect upon capital accumulation of an armaments sector developing under conditions of large-scale *plethora* of capital.

Over-production of capital signifies, on the value side, the emergence of large sums of capital which have to be hoarded in savings accounts,

72. In *The Accumulation of Capital* (op. cit., pp. 455–7 and 461ff.), Luxemburg correctly stresses the circumstances under which increased military expenditure financed at the expense of the working class (for example, through indirect taxation of consumer goods) may lead to an increase both in the rate of surplus-value and in capital accumulation.

73. It is sufficient to refer here to Chapter 8 of Lenin's *Imperialism*.

74. On the controversy between those who see a current 'scarcity' of capital and those who argue that, on the contrary, there exists a plethora of capital, see 'Capital Shortage: Fact and Fancy' by the editors of *Monthly Review*, in Volume 27, No. 11, April 1976. In my own article, 'Waiting for the Upturn' (*Inprecor*, Nos. 40/41, December 1975), I put forward the same position as that of *Monthly Review*. It should be stressed that there is no contradiction between the appearance of a plethora of capital and an actual decline in the rate of profit (i.e. relative scarcity of the mass of surplus-value). Indeed, the latter *determines* the former. This appears paradoxical only to those who, ignoring one of the main lessons of Volume 2, evacuate the 'time' factor from the analysis of 'capital in general' and mistakenly identify capital with *currently produced* surplus-value. The problem disappears once capital is understood as the accumulation of quantities of surplus-value produced in a series of *past* operations.

or used for purchasing bonds and government securities, where they beget only the average rate of interest rather than the average rate of profit. On the use-value side, it is expressed in sizeable stocks of unused raw materials and productive capacity in plant, as well as in large reserves of unemployed workers. If, as a result of the appearance and expansion of a significant arms sector in the economy, money (or quasi-money) capital is productively reinvested, then the production of value and surplus-value increases. We know already that the manufacture of arms is productive of value and surplus-value. Hence, in the immediate sense, capital grows richer because more workers are exploited in the production of greater surplus-value.

Since department I I does not contribute to the creation of the material elements of expanded reproduction, its expansion cannot *directly* ensure a higher level of capital accumulation, But it can do so indirectly. For as additional workers are employed, the wages bill increases, leading to rising output and sale of consumer goods. Similarly, the consumption of additional raw materials in the weapons industry stimulates the production of mines and other centres of department I which had previously contracted their output. Material production will rise in all sectors of the economy, thereby augmenting the material elements of expanded reproduction, *provided that reserves of 'productive factors' are available* (which follows from the initial hypothesis of 'under-employment of capital') and/or provided that at least *part* of the additional surplus-value is not absorbed by the armaments sector or other unproductive departments, but remains available for capital accumulation.

These conditions apply with even greater force if the processes described are accompanied by a changed distribution of the national income between wages and surplus-value, that is to say, if rearmament is financed to some extent at the expense of the working class through a rise in the rate of surplus-value. The resultant combination would then be 'ideal' for the accumulation of capital: at one and the same time, there would occur an expansion of the mass of workers employed and exploited (i.e. an expansion of the value product, the mass of surplus-value, *and* market demand); an increase in the rate of surplus-value and (probably) the rate of profit; and a rise in the rate of accumulation (i.e. an increase of investment in the productive sector, over and above the growth in arms spending).[75]

75. This explains the important difference between Hitler's war economy and the post-war 'boom'. In the former case, as opposed to the latter, increased investment was by and large confined to the armaments sector; there occurred no real cumulative growth, involving expansion of the 'final consumers' market'.

Needless to say, this provides no 'long-term solution' to the problems of capitalist equilibrium, since the very 'success' of the operation inevitably reproduces the initial contradictions. Increased capital accumulation leads to a rise in the organic composition of capital, which in turn begins to depress the rate of profit. The higher level of employment (made possible by the absorption of part of the unemployed in the army or the state apparatus – a normal feature of a substantial rise in military spending) reduces the industrial reserve army of labour and thereby, except under a fascist-type dictatorship, tends to make it more difficult to neutralize the effects of the rising organic composition of capital by driving up further the rate of surplus-value. A decline in the rate of profit depresses productive investment and leads to both a crisis of over-production and a fall in the rate of capital accumulation; when that rate actually becomes 'negative', a process of devalorization of capital begins, which is the normal function of a crisis of over-production.

To counter this new crisis of capital accumulation through an intensification of armaments production, where a sizeable sector already exists in the economy, would modify the basic proportions both of the division of surplus-value between its accumulated and consumed portions, and of the allocation of productive resources between departments I and II, on the one hand, and department III, on the other. Whatever effect upon the process of expanded reproduction was initially obtained would be increasingly neutralized. Moreover, such a high rate of taxation of profits and wages would be necessary that, except under very special political conditions, the basic social classes (although not that sector of capitalists directly engaged in weapons production and procurement) would revolt against further development of the arms industry. Such an expansion is thus no cure-all for the ills of capitalist over-accumulation and over-production. But it can trigger off shorter or longer periods of economic upturn as long as those preconditions indicated above are satisfied.

9. HOW CAN COMMERCIAL AND FINANCIAL CAPITAL PARTICIPATE IN THE DISTRIBUTION OF SOCIAL SURPLUS-VALUE?

The distinction between productive and unproductive labour partially dovetails with the distinction between two general sectors of capital: capital invested in commodity *production* (be it in industry, agriculture, transport or productive branches of the so-called service industries) and capital invested elsewhere (i.e. between 'productive capital' and 'unproductive capital'). The latter category involves essentially commercial capital, banking and insurance capital, and capital invested in the 'unproductive' branches of service industries. We have seen before that, while wage-labour hired by these capitalists enables them to appropriate a fraction of the sum total of surplus-value accruing to the entire capitalist class, it does not itself add to that total. The question may, therefore, be posed: why do the industrial capitalists, or more precisely all those who invest in the 'productive' sectors, accept that a portion of the surplus-value produced by 'their' workers should be appropriated by capitalists whose capital does not contribute to the production of surplus-value?

This problem is dealt with at length in *Capital* Volume 3; but since a section of Volume 2 is devoted to it, we should briefly touch on it here. The answer becomes clear once we realize that, although capital invested outside the sphere of material production does not directly augment the mass of surplus-value, *it does contribute indirectly to its increase*. In other words, industrial and farming capitalists abandon a share of 'their' surplus-value to traders and bankers not out of the goodness of their hearts, but because these gentlemen help them to raise the mass of that surplus-value.

In order to demonstrate that this is so, Marx again introduces into his analysis that 'time dimension' which plays such a key role throughout Volume 2, and which in a certain sense structures the whole process of circulation and turnover of capital. Whereas the total turnover time of fixed capital stretches over many years, and is not basically affected by small shifts in the length of the period during which capital takes the form of commodity capital (i.e. during which commodities remain unsold in the sphere of circulation), the situation is entirely different in the case of circulating capital. If it takes three months to produce a given mass of commodities, and three months to sell them, circulating productive capital will turn over only twice a year unless it receives assistance. That part of it which is exchanged for labour-power, and thus makes possible the creation of surplus-value, would then remain sterile for six months of the year. If, however, commercial capital buys up a large proportion of the commodities as soon as they leave the factory, or if banking capital advances the money to pay the raw materials bill immediately after the commodities are produced and before they are sold, then, owing to the assistance of these sectors of the capitalist class, productive circulating capital can be reinvested as soon as a production cycle is completed. Consequently, variable capital will never remain idle. It will set workers to produce surplus-value twelve months, and not six months a year – as a result of which, all other things being equal, the total annual mass of surplus-value will be twice as great as it would otherwise have been. It naturally pays industrial capital to give a discount to wholesale traders, or to pay interest to bankers, if these rescue operations allow an overall increase in the production of surplus-value.

What this implies, however, is that only a fraction of total social capital is continuously engaged in production. An important segment remains constantly outside the realm of production. We have already noted why part of social capital necessarily takes the form of money capital. We now see that another portion has to take the form of transportation and banking capital, in order to shorten the circulation time of commodities. From the point of view of the capitalist class as a whole (and this is the one adopted by Marx in Volume 2; only in Volume 3 does he consider these different sectors as competing with one another for fractions of social surplus-value), this may be regarded as a *functional division of labour within that class*. Instead of each industrialist and capitalist farmer acting as his own treasurer, his own money changer, his own transporter, his own seller of commodities on the home and world markets, and his own advancer of additional money capital, all these various functions are socially centralized by sectors of the bourgeoisie specializing in different fields. This division of labour carries with it a considerable rationalization: the costs of overall social circulation, transportation and banking are lower than they would have been if each capitalist firm had had to accomplish these tasks itself. The overhead costs of production are thereby reduced, and the total mass of surplus-value is increased through continuous production. It is thus profitable for the bourgeoisie as a whole to maintain (and even expand, as the record of the 'service industries' demonstrates!) this functional division of labour.

What is the source of capital invested outside the realm of material production? Since all capital derives in the last analysis from surplus-value, and since, under the capitalist mode of production, all surplus-value is created by 'productive capital' (that is, by wage-labour engaged in material production), it may appear that all commercial and banking capital ultimately derives from industrial and agricultural 'productive' capital. This is partially true. In *Capital* Volume 2, Marx points out how money capital is periodically 'expelled' from the process of value production, thereby becoming temporarily available for other purposes. The best example of this is the depreciation fund of fixed capital. Reinvested only at certain intervals, rather than piecemeal after each production cycle, it serves for a time as an important source of money capital employed in credit and other operations.

However, such a view should not be generalized. Capital, after all, is older than the capitalist mode of production. Before surplus-value was produced in the process of production, vast wealth was accumulated through the plunder of peasants, the fleecing of feudal lords (for example, by over-pricing exotic merchandise), robbery of merchants (through piracy) and tribal communities (through the capture of slaves). Merchant, commercial and banking capital existed long before 'productive' capital was born in manufactures, not to speak of the industrial revolution. Thus, industrial capital not only reproduces commercial and banking capital by paying over fragments of the surplus-value created by 'its own' workers; it also finds these other forms of capital present at the moment of its own birth, and indeed as a condition of this. Commercial and banking capital, then, reproduce themselves both by continuing their former practices (i.e. appropriation of part of the social product originating *outside* the realm of *capitalist* relations of production, and transformation of it into surplus-value and money capital) and by appropriating part of the surplus-value created *within* the capitalist process of production proper. The interpenetration of pre-capitalist, semi-capitalist and capitalist relations of production, imposed upon colonies and semi-colonies by the power of capital on the world market and the violence of foreign political and military domination, has been an extremely important factor in the historical development of these twin sources of money capital accumulation. Through the operations of merchant, commercial, usury and banking capital, they have continued till this very day to play a key role in world-wide capitalist expansion, especially within the so-called third-world countries. Thus primitive accumulation of capital and 'productive' accumulation of capital (through the creation of surplus-value in commodity *production*) are not only successive historical stages, but also simultaneous and combined phenomena. Nor does primitive accumulation automatically lead to a commensurate spread of 'productive' capital and industrialization; it may instead simply condense into a 'one-sided' expansion of the above-mentioned forms of 'unproductive' capital. This circumstance, together with the impact of foreign imperialist domination, clarifies one of the mysteries of underdevelopment under capitalism.

10. LUXEMBURG'S CRITIQUE OF MARX'S REPRODUCTION SCHEMAS

In the history of Marxist thought and the international labour movement, the most important controversy to have arisen in connection with Volume 2 was sparked off by Luxemburg's critique of Marx's reproduction schemas in her *The Accumulation of Capital*. Involved in the debate have been truly formidable questions: Marx's theory of crisis; the historical limits of the capitalist mode of production (the so-called 'breakdown theory' or *Zusammenbruchstheorie*); and the origins and functions of imperialism, colonialism, militarism and wars in the imperialist epoch.[76] We shall confine ourselves, in this introduction, to that part of Luxemburg's contribution which is directly related to the subject-matter of *Capital* Volume 2 – the circulation, turnover and reproduction of the total social capital.

Luxemburg's critique is essentially centred on a single theme: how can that part of the value of commodities which corresponds to the accumulated portion of surplus-value be realized? What purchasing power is available for its realization? Why do capitalists expand production, if not because they are assured of, or expect to have, additional customers? Who are these new customers? She first rejects the idea that they could be workers, since the purchasing power of the latter originates with capital, and expansion of production merely to satisfy the new needs of an enlarged work-force would be inconceivable for the capitalist class *in its totality*. (Of course, this is not true of capitalists taken individually, for whom all workers *except their own* are potential customers; but, as Luxemburg flatly states, for the capitalist class as a whole, *all* workers are 'their own workers', and it makes no sense to treat them as a source of increased sales.[77]) She also dismisses the notion that these additional customers could be other capitalists. For how could the capitalist class *in its totality* enrich itself if the money to buy the

76. The main contributions to the discussion on Luxemburg's *The Accumulation of Capital* were the reviews by Otto Bauer (in *Die Neue Zeit*, No. 24, 1913), Anton Pannekoek (in *Bremer Bürgerzeitung*, 29 January 1913) and G. Eckstein (in *Vorwärts*, 16 February 1913), and the book by Bukharin, *Imperialism and the Accumulation of Capital*, op. cit. Henryk Grossmann (*Das Akkumulations- und Zusammenbruchsgesetz des kapitalistischen Systems*, Leipzig, 1929) deals in a number of places with Luxemburg's theory. See also the recent discussion in Arghiri Emmanuel, *Le Profit et les crises*, Paris, 1975, and Joan Robinson's introduction to the English translation of *The Accumulation of Capital* (ed. cit.).

77. Luxemburg, *The Accumulation of Capital*, op. cit., pp. 289–90.

surplus product came out of its own pocket?[78] Nor could they be so-called third persons, who are essentially the cronies, hangers-on and servants of the capitalist class (or of landowners appropriating ground-rent). For, in the last analysis, the revenue of all these social layers is derived from surplus-value. If surplus-value were the only source of purchasing power available for buying up the increased mass and value of commodities, it would mean that capitalists become richer by spending their own money.

For Luxemburg, then, the conclusion is inescapable. The additional purchasing power which has to be sucked into the process of capitalist circulation can only come from *outside* capitalist relations of production properly called, through forcing non-capitalist social classes (essentially peasants and pre-capitalist landowners) ruinously to spend their revenue on capitalist commodities. Only in this way can expanded production and reproduction, capital accumulation and capitalist economic growth in general take place. The end result of the argument is equally obvious. By destroying the non-capitalist milieu on which its expansion is based, capitalism undermines the conditions of its own growth. The disappearance of this non-capitalist (pre-capitalist) environment thus marks the absolute limit of capitalist development.[79]

While the main thrust of Luxemburg's argument is clear and simple, much of the controversy surrounding *The Accumulation of Capital* has been diverted away from her central thesis, largely because she herself combined it with a series of further criticisms of Marx's reproduction schemas which are much easier to answer. Thus, when she asserts that Marx confuses the function of money as means of circulation with the role of income (purchasing power) as necessary prerequisite of the realization of commodity-value, she is quite evidently mistaken.[80] And when she implies that the reproduction schemas do not correspond to the reality of the capitalist mode of production, she mixes up levels of abstraction which are clearly differentiated in Marx's method. She is no less misguided when she surmises that, because Marx's figures do not incorporate the 'laws of motion' of capital (they allow for no increase in the organic composition of capital), they *could not* incorporate these

78. ibid., pp. 127–33.

79. The notion that a non-capitalist milieu is necessary for expanded reproduction and accumulation was first advanced by Heinrich Cunow ('Die Zusammenbruchs-theorie', in *Die Neue Zeit*, No. 1, 1898) and later defended by Karl Kautsky ('Krisentheorien', in *Die Neue Zeit*, No. 2, 1902) and Louis B. Boudin (*The Theoretical System of Karl Marx*, Chicago, 1907, especially pp. 163–9 and 241–53).

80. Luxemburg, op. cit., pp. 143–5. Cf. below, pp. 442–4.

laws. Similarly, it does not follow at all from the evident truth that department I is the *primum movens* of the accumulation process, that department II is somehow 'sacrificed to' or 'dependent upon' department I, in contradiction to the laws of private property and competition.[81] And so on and so forth. On all these secondary issues, controversy has been raging fiercely, generally at Luxemburg's expense. But although it still erupts from time to time, it has little relevance to the principal question that she raised.

Luxemburg's main argument has to be answered at three successive levels of abstraction. First, and most abstractly, she committed a methodological error by situating within the framework of 'capital in its totality' a problem that can only be considered in relation to the 'competition of many capitals'.[82] It is impossible to conduct an analysis simultaneously at these two distinct levels, since capital in its totality *abstracts by definition* from many capitals, from competition. Thus the argument that the capitalist class cannot enrich itself by purchasing its own surplus product overlooks the fact that, under a system of private property, the surplus product can *never* be owned by 'a single total capital'. Capitalist competition implies that capitalists can indeed grow richer by buying one another's 'surplus product'. Marx himself explicitly states that 'the *surplus-value* created at one point requires the creation of surplus-value at another point, for which it may be exchanged'.[83] He also indicates that, in the absence of competition, growth would actually disappear.[84]

In short, for Marx, growth is possible in a 'purely' capitalist milieu (i.e. where no part of the social surplus product can find 'non-capitalist' customers) provided that the interests and growth rates of all capitalists are assumed to be not identical, but on the contrary *rooted in competition*. The realization question *does not*, and *cannot*, arise within the realm of 'capital in general'; it appears, together with the theory of crises and the trade cycle, only within the sphere of 'many capitals'. This Marx repeatedly stated himself.[85]

It follows that reproduction schemas which imply competition should

81. Schemas incorporating these laws of motion have been worked out by Bauer, Grossmann, Léon Sartre, Glombowski, Hosea Jaffe and many others. Whether they assure long-term equilibrium conditions is, of course, quite a different question.

82. This point was first made by Rosdolsky (op. cit., pp. 63–72).

83. *Grundrisse*, op. cit., p. 407.

84. *Capital* Volume 3, Chapter 15, 3.

85. *Theories of Surplus-Value*, op. cit., Part II, pp. 532–4.

assume *as a rule* the existence of *different, rather than equal* rates of accumulation in the two departments, only occasionally leading to equalization of the rate of profit. This corresponds to the real *modus operandi* of the capitalist system. It also points the way to a solution of the technical problem seen by Luxemburg in the fact that the 'unsaleable' portion of commodities of department II embodies part of the surplus-value created in that department. As a matter of fact, Luxemburg dismissed out of hand Marx's convincing solution, which was later developed at length by Otto Bauer.[86] Part of the surplus-value produced in department II *is* periodically transferred to department I, precisely when (and because) department I exhibits, over a considerable length of time, a higher organic composition of capital than that of department II.

At this most abstract level of reasoning, the problem has been posed as one of quasi-static equilibrium. But at a second level which, while still abstract, is a step nearer to the historical reality of the capitalist mode of production, accumulation of capital must be examined as *a discontinuous process* with a view to understanding its actual dynamics. The first question I posed was the following: can customers be found for those commodities which embody the accumulated part of surplus-value, if we assume that all purchasing power originates as either wages or surplus-value within the capitalist process of production itself? Marx's simple answer is: yes, so long as we do not take surplus-value to be a single mass, owned by a solitary capitalist (who would then obviously be condemned to 'buy' his own goods). The second question may now be re-posed as follows: what is the effect upon the realization of the value of commodities embodying the accumulated part of surplus-value, if and when (1) the organic composition of capital rises in both departments; (2) department I grows at a faster rate than II (which is the unavoidable result of the rising organic composition of capital); and (3) the rate of profit declines (i.e. the growth in the rate of surplus-value is insufficient to compensate for the rising organic composition of capital)? In other words, is full realization of surplus-value possible when the laws of motion of the capitalist mode of production assert themselves?

This second question requires a more complex answer than the previous one. Theoretically, full realization of surplus-value *is* possible, and several ingenious mathematical models have been constructed – by, among others, O. Benedikt, Shinzaburo Koshimura, Oskar Lange, J.

86. Luxemburg, op. cit., pp. 294–5.

Caridad Mateo and Hosea Jaffe[87] – in order to show that it is. By contesting this. Luxemburg denied that 'pure' capitalism was possible, thus taking a position exactly opposite to the one which Marx tried to demonstrate with his reproduction schemas. It should be immediately added, however, that the real *socio-economic conditions* expressed by these algebraic formulas have to be precisely defined.[88] Furthermore, those of her critics who replied that the schemas 'prove' by themselves the possibility of unlimited, smooth progress of reproduction [89] forgot one small point: capitalism has been generating periodic crises of over-production for more than 150 years, and continues to do so with the regularity of a 'natural law'. We can reject out of hand the hypothesis that each successive crisis has been due entirely to 'specific' causes, unrelated to the inner logic of the capitalist mode of production, and extraneous to the inter-relation of the growth rates of c, v, s/v, accumulated s/total s, both within and between the two departments. The very periodicity of these crises is enough to refute the 'harmony theorists' and the view that capital accumulation can go on for ever 'on the basis of the schemas'. In this respect, the superiority of Luxemburg over certain of her critics is obvious.[90]

Nevertheless, did she succeed in proving her case in a technically satisfactory manner? We do not believe so; for she narrowed down the problem to an excessively monocausal one. In order to prove that, under capitalism, equilibrium *must* beget disequilibrium, that expanded

87. O. Benedikt, 'Die Akkumulation des Kapitals bei wachsender organischer Zusammensetzung', in *Unter dem Banner des Marxismus*, No. 3, 1929; Koshimura, op. cit.; J. Caridad Mateo, *Reproducción del capital social*, Mexico, 1974; Hosea Jaffe, *Processo capitalista e teoria dell'accumulazione*, Milan, 1973, and in a personal communication to myself.

88. Let us take a single example. In order to reconcile equilibrium with a rising organic composition of capital and a falling rate of profit, Koshimura has to modify the initial relations between the three departments and to increase considerably the organic composition of department III (which makes little sense from a historical point of view). Next, he has to lower the total price of production of department II (workers' wages) to the extent of an absolute decline. 'Offsetting' the falling rate of profit by a rising *rate* of surplus-value (which is plausible), Koshimura arrives at an absolute decrease in workers', and even capitalists' consumption (which is not only implausible but contrary to both Marx's basic assumption in *Capital* Volume 2, and to the existing empirical data). (See Koshimura, op. cit., pp. 122–4 and 124–6.)

89. See the above-mentioned critique by Eckstein and the article by Helene Deutsch (in *Der Kampf*, 1913, the theoretical journal of Austrian Social Democracy). This is also partially true of the critiques by Bauer and Emmanuel.

90. See especially her 'Anti-Critique', in Luxemburg and Bukharin, *Imperialism and the Accumulation of Capital*, op. cit.

reproduction *must* generate over-production, and that accumulation of capital *must* lead to devalorization of capital it is necessary to bring all the inter-related variables of the reproduction schemas into play. And this she docs not do. Thus, while *The Accumulation of Capital* raises the correct problems, it does not provide acceptable solutions to them.[91]

Synthetically, we may say that the equilibrium formula of expanded reproduction: $I_v + I_{s_\alpha} + I_{s_\gamma} = II_c + II_{s_\beta}$, implies an identity of the rate of growth of demand for consumer goods generated by department I, and the rate of growth of constant capital in department II. Now, the rise in the organic composition of capital entails that the demand for consumer goods generated in department I will normally grow more slowly than constant capital in that sector (unless the slower rate of growth of variable capital is compensated by a rate of growth of unproductively consumed surplus-value higher than that of constant capital, which is extremely unlikely in the long run). The precondition of equilibrium is consequently a rate of growth of constant capital in department II lower than the one in department I. If the rates in the two departments are equal, the conditions of equilibrium will be upset.

However, a rate of growth of constant capital in department II which is *permanently* lower than that in department I is incompatible with private property and competition. There is no reason why capitalists engaged in the production of consumer goods should forever abstain from trying to incorporate all existing technology, all means of reducing costs of production, all potentially useable machinery. Therefore, $II_c + II_{s_\beta}$ will from time to time be greater than $I_v + I_{s_\alpha} + I_{s_\gamma}$, just as, *periodically*, under conditions of rising organic composition of capital (biased development of labour-saving technology), $A[II_c + II_{s_\beta}]$ will be equal to $A[I_c + I_{s_\beta}]$, and $A[I_c + I_{s_\beta}]$ will be greater than $A[I_v + I_{s_\alpha} + I_{s_\gamma}]$. It

91. Nor can it be accepted that Grossmann (op. cit.) provides these solutions. His own standpoint – a denial that at the bottom of the crisis are problems of realization of surplus-value and of disproportionality between production and consumption – is fundamentally unsound. By converting the decline of the rate of profit into the sole cause of the final breakdown of capitalism, he overlooks the fact that this *tendency* is offset by periodical devalorization of capital. Whereas he seeks to establish a mechanical unity between the theory of crises of over-production and that of the breakdown of capitalism, the real, dialectical link between the two embodies the following contradiction: crises of over-production are the precise mechanism which allows the decline in the rate of profit to be periodically *overcome* – both through devalorization of the total mass of social capital and through a rise in the rate of surplus-value.

therefore seems impossible to avoid periodic over-production of consumer goods, as well as a decline in the rate of profit and of the ratio *acc. sv/sv*, entailing an abrupt halt to the accumulation of capital.

Donald Harris has concluded from Marx's 'assumptions' that equilibrium obtains only if (in a value system) there is proportional hiring of labour in the two departments, or if (in a prices of production system) there is an equal ratio of investment – accumulation – of surplus-value.[92] However, all these calculations are based upon a misunderstanding of Marx's method. While Marx does assume an equal rate of exploitation in both departments (an assumption based on the concept of an average national *value of labour-power*, for which quite strong empirical evidence exists under developed capitalism), he does not 'assume' either that the organic composition of capital will remain equal or that the rate of surplus-value will stay the same. His method of successive approximation to the 'appearances' of day-to-day capitalist economy led him to *abstract*, at a given stage of the inquiry, from a number of additional *variables*, in order to clarify certain preliminary problems. This has nothing to with 'assuming' historical trends.

Finally, on the third level, that of the *actual historical process* of capital accumulation, Luxemburg seems fundamentally correct. Capitalism was born essentially in a non-capitalist milieu; it has immensely enriched itself by plundering that milieu; and the same value-transferring metabolism has continued to this very day. 'Pure' capitalism has never existed in real life and, as Engels rightly predicted, it never will exist, because 'we shall not let it come to that'. The Russian October Revolution, and the subsequent expansion of a post-capitalist sector of world economy, indicates that Engels's instinct was a sure one in that respect. Luxemburg's analysis of the ways and means whereby capitalism sucks wealth and value from pre-capitalist communities and classes was an impressive first contribution to three-quarters of a century of anti-colonialist and anti-imperialist world literature. It has still to be equalled in either theoretical insight or economic lucidity.[93]

The final balance-sheet of Luxemburg's critique, then, must be a nuanced one. We cannot say baldly that she is right or that she is wrong. While many of her partial theses, as well as her final answer, are inadequate, she certainly poses relevant questions and puts her finger on real problems which Volume 2 does not and cannot answer. In particular,

92. Donald J. Harris, 'On Marx's Scheme of Reproduction and Accumulation', in *Journal of Political Economy*, Vol. 80, 1972, pp. 505ff.

93. See especially *The Accumulation of Capital*, Chapters 27–30.

the contradictory character of capitalist growth, discussion of which was stimulated by her seminal *The Accumulation of Capital*, cannot be simply subsumed under the formulas 'anarchy of production' and 'disproportionality'.[94] The specific place which unavoidable disproportions between production and mass consumption occupy in the dynamics of capitalism has to be integrated into any overall explanation of capitalist disequilibrium and crisis.

II. VOLUME 2 OF CAPITAL AND MARX'S EXPLANATION OF CAPITALIST CRISES OF OVER-PRODUCTION

Our discussion of Luxemburg's critique of Marx's reproduction schemas leads logically on to an examination of his theory of crises, as it appears in Volume 2 of *Capital*. It is well known that the four volumes of *Capital* which Marx left behind contain no systematic analysis of that key aspect of the capitalist mode of production: the inevitable periodic occurrence of such crises. In his original plan, Marx had reserved a full treatment of the question for a sixth volume dealing with the world market and crises.[95] But partial considerations are interspersed through the text, especially in Volume 4 (*Theories of Surplus-Value*) and Volumes 2 and 3. It is on these that we wish to touch briefly here.

In Volume 2, Marx makes a number of crucial points about capitalist crises of over-production. First, he insists upon the fact that the role of commercial capital as intermediary between industrial capitalist and

94. The 'neo-harmonicist' versions of the Austro-Marxists Hilferding and Bauer were clearly inspired by Tugan-Baranowski's book *Studien zur Theorie* (op. cit.). Although both polemicized against Tugan-Baranowski, they fell under the spell of his mathematical 'juggling' with the reproduction schemas. Hilferding's statement in his *magnum opus* of 1909, *Finanzkapital*, is especially striking: 'A general cartel regulating total social production and thereby overcoming crises is, in principle, economically imaginable, even if such a social and political state of affairs is an impossibility' (op. cit., p. 372). Bukharin was influenced by the same trend of thought, as clearly emerges from the assertion in *Imperialism and the Accumulation of Capital* (op. cit., p. 226) that under state capitalism, where anarchy of production has been overcome, there could be no crises of over-production. Drawing on these arguments, Tony Cliff and his disciples have attempted to justify their use of the term 'state capitalism' to define the Soviet economy – an economy which has witnessed no crisis of over-production for more than half a century. (See Cliff, *Russia: A Marxist Analysis*, London, 1964, pp. 167–75). For a thorough critique of the neo-harmonicist interpretation of *Capital* Volume 2, see Rosdolsky, op. cit., pp. 569–80 and pp. 586–94.

95. See my introduction to *Capital* Volume 1, op. cit., pp. 28–31.

'final consumer', while helping to shorten the circulation time of commodities and hasten the turnover of productive circulating capital, at the same time *masks* the growing disproportion between expanding production and lagging final demand.[96] More precisely, Marx adds: 'The periods in which capitalist production exerts all its forces regularly show themselves to be periods of over-production; because the limit to the application of the productive powers is not simply the production of value, but also its realization. However, the sale of commodities, *the realization of commodity capital, and thus of surplus-value, is restricted not by the consumer needs of society in general, but by the consumer needs of a particular society in which the great majority are always poor and must always remain poor. This however belongs rather to the next part.*'[97] This is but an echo of the famous passage in Volume 3, in which Marx summarizes his theory of crises, ending with the following words: 'The ultimate reason for all real crises always remains the poverty and restricted consumption of the masses, in the face of the drive of capitalist production to develop the productive forces as if only the absolute consumption power of society set a limit to them.[98]

However, Marx states no less categorically in Volume 2: 'It is a pure tautology to say that crises are provoked by a lack of effective demand or effective consumption. The capitalist system does not recognize any forms of consumer other than those who can pay, if we exclude the consumption of paupers and swindlers. The fact that commodities are unsaleable means no more than that no effective buyers have been found for them, i.e. no consumers (no matter whether the commodities are ultimately sold to meet the needs of productive or individual consumption). If the attempt is made to give this tautology the semblance of greater profundity, by the statement that the working class receives too small a portion of its own product, and that the evil would be remedied if it received a bigger share, i.e. if its wages rose, we need only note that crises are always prepared by a period in which wages generally rise, and the working class actually does receive a greater share in the part of the annual product destined for consumption. From the standpoint of these advocates of sound and 'simple' (!) common sense, such periods should rather avert the crisis. It thus appears that capitalist production involves certain conditions, independent of people's good or bad intentions, which permit the relative prosperity of the working class only temporarily, and moreover always as a harbinger of crisis.'[99] Is there a

96. See below, pp. 155–6.   97. See below, p. 391, note. Our emphasis.
98. *Capital* Volume 3, Chapter 30.   99. See below, pp. 486–7.

contradiction between these two explanations? What lies behind the frenetic accusations of 'under-consumptionism', referred to as some grave 'deviation' or shameful disease, and levelled by some of Marx's followers against others?

In our opinion, there is no contradiction whatsoever between the above two sets of comments made by Marx on capitalist crises of over-production. What he rejects is the common-or-garden reformist or 'liberal' platitude, according to which crises could be avoided if, in the period immediately preceding or coinciding with the onset of over-production, the purchasing power in the hands of the masses were to be significantly increased. This simplistic view overlooks two facts. Under capitalism, not all commodities are consumer goods; an important fraction of the total 'commodity mountain', namely, all means of production, cannot be, and are not intended to be, bought by workers. Therefore, an increase in sales of consumer goods, in and of itself, tells us nothing of the course of sales of equipment and raw materials. It does not lead automatically to greater productive investment. Indeed, a redistribution of the national income at the expense of profits (which would be the outcome of a sudden large rise in wages) would result in a collapse of investment, i.e. of sales of means of production. If this succeeded a period of actual decline in the rate of profit, then capital accumulation would contract very violently indeed and the crisis would remain unavoidable. Inasmuch as they forget this basic correlation of the trade cycle with medium-term fluctuations of the rate of profit, all economists (whether Marxist or non-Marxist) who explain the crisis exclusively or mainly in terms of the relation between the purchasing power of consumers and the national income are truly guilty of 'under-consumptionism', that is to say, of a one-sided and therefore erroneous theory of over-production and the trade cycle.[100]

But the same is true of the opposite theory, which concentrates exclusively or mainly on the 'disproportion' between the two departments, explaining crises by the anarchy of production and the difficulty (impossibility) of establishing the 'right proportions' spontaneously (as if 'organized capitalism' or a 'general cartel' *could* avoid crisis!).[101]

100. The most noteworthy Marxist author of this type is Nathalia Moszkowska (*Zur Kritik moderner Krisentheorien*, Prague, 1935), but Fritz Sternburg and Paul Sweezy should also be mentioned in this context. The list of non-Marxist economists is very long indeed, running from Simonde de Sismondi and Malthus to Lederer and Keynes.

101. See note 94 above.

Overlooked in such a thesis is the fact, which Marx himself pointed out,[102] that the 'disproportion' between the tendency of unlimited development of the productive forces and the narrow constraints placed upon consumption by the bourgeois mode of distribution, is itself a specific source of disequilibrium, autonomous from the disturbance of 'equilibrium relations' between the two departments. Supporters of this view also forget, like Tugan-Baranowski, the father of pure 'disproportionism', that unlimited growth of department I leads to ever faster growth of the *productive capaity* of department II (although not necessarily in the same proportion); in other words, that under capitalist *commodity relations* production can never fully emancipate itself from sales to the final consumer.[103] Thus theories of 'pure disproportionism' are as wrong as ones of 'pure under-consumptionism'. The basic causes of periodic crises of over-production are, at one and the same time, the inevitable periodic decline of the rate of profit, the capitalist anarchy of production, and the impossibility under capitalism of developing mass consumption in correlation with the growth of the productive forces.

As we have explained elsewhere,[104] the basic curse of capitalism – the fact that surplus-value embodied in commodities can only be realized if they are *sold at their value* – implies the presence of an insoluble contradiction at a given point of expanded reproduction. Any measure which tries suddenly to reverse the decline of the rate of profit provokes a shrinking of the market of 'final consumers'. And any attempt suddenly to reverse that shrinking accentuates the decline of the rate of profit. Capitalist growth and prosperity require *both* a rising rate of profit (of currently realized as well as anticipated profits) *and* an expanding market (as present reality and future trend). But the coincidence of these conditions can never be permanent, for the very forces which bring it into being at a given point in the trade cycle work towards its undoing at a subsequent stage.[105] In that sense, crises of over-production are

102. *Grundrisse*, op. cit., pp. 420–42; *Theories of Surplus-Value*, op. cit., Part III, pp. 120–21. See also *Grundrisse*, p. 155.

103. 'It is quite the same with the demand created by production itself for raw material, semi-finished goods, machinery, means of communication, and for the auxiliary materials consumed in production, such as dyes, coal, grease, soap, etc. This effective, exchange-value-positing demand is adequate and sufficient as long as the producers exchange among themselves. Its inadequacy shows itself as soon as the final product encounters its limit in direct and final consumption' (*Grundrisse*, p. 421).

104. Mandel, *Marxist Economic Theory*, op. cit., p. 370.

105. Among these should be included not only 'purely' economic factors, but also the interwining of the trade cycle with the partially autonomous cycle of the class struggle.

unavoidable under capitalism. According to even the most optimistic hypothesis, 'anti-cyclical policies' can only reduce their scope temporarily; they cannot prevent the very 'moderation' obtained during one period from leading, in the long run, to more explosive side-effects (such as the cumulative movement of inflation, or the precipitate growth of the burden of company debt).[106]

The objective logic of crises of over-production, connected with the operation of the law of value, is clarified by an important remark made by Marx in *Capital* Volume 2.[107] Equlibrium of the process of expanded reproduction presupposes that commodities are sold at their value, or more precisely, *at the value they had at the moment of their production*. However, the very dynamic of expanded reproduction involves regular revolutions in technology, unceasing attempts by industrialists to win the competitive struggle by reducing their costs of production and growing substitution of machines for manual labour. All these phenomena, which are translated into regular increases in the average labour productivity of most branches of production, imply *a tendency for the value of each commodity to decline*. Seen in this light, crises of over-production are nothing other than objective mechanisms through which the adjustment of market prices to declining commodity-values is achieved.[108] Capital thereby incurs important losses (i.e. devalorizations of capital), whether directly, through the reduction in value of commodity capital, or indirectly, through the bankruptcy and closure of the least efficient firms.

Marx further stresses in *Capital* Volume 2 that there exists a nexus between the trade cycle and the turnover cycle of fixed capital which is distinct from the usually mentioned one of determination *grosso modo* of the length of the former by that of the latter. Fixed capital expenditure is discontinuous in a double sense. Machines are replaced not piecemeal (except, of course, so far as current repairs are concerned) but *in toto*, say once every seven or ten years. Their replacement tends to occur at the same time in numerous, inter-connected key branches of industry, precisely because the process is not only, or even essentially, a function of physical wear and tear,[109] but rather a response to financial incentives

106. On the roots, functions and consequences of permanent inflation in contemporary capitalism, see Chapter 13 of my *Late Capitalism*, op. cit.

107. See below, p. 153.

108. Declining value expressed in gold prices and not, of course, in inflated paper currency.

109. 'Moral' wearing-out of equipment (obsolescence) generally predates 'physical' breakdown under capitalism, given the pressure of competition and accelerated technical progress.

to introduce more advanced technology. (The principal criteria of profit calculation are here: availability of sufficient money capital reserves; rising rate of profit and profit expectations; and the existence and/or anticipation of a sudden market expansion.) These incentives coincide only at a certain point in the trade cycle; but when this occurs, there follows a massive investment in the renewal of fixed capital. This in turn sets up a dynamic of accelerated capital accumulation and economic growth, together with rapid expansion of markets, which leads finally to an increase in the organic composition of capital, a declining trend of the rate of profit and a tendency to slow down investment and renewal of fixed capital.

Discontinuous renewal of fixed capital is, therefore, one of the key determinants of the trade cycle. The difficulty is compounded by the fact that the productive capacity of the sub-branch of department I which produces means of production for the production of means of production, must normally be geared to the *general demand for the renewal* of fixed capital (at least in its social average). Thus while this sub-branch may be overtaken by peak demand at the moment of 'overheating', it will suffer from unused capacity during a considerable part of the trade cycle.[110]

12. MONEY CIRCULATION, MONEY CAPITAL AND MONEY HOARDING

One of the most 'modern' aspects of Marx's analysis is the treatment in Volume 2 of the 'commodity–money' dialectic, and its correlation with problems relating to the reproduction of social capital and the trade cycle. Here, Marx fundamentally anticipates the Keynesian problematic of money hoarding, that is, withdrawal of money from the process of productive circulation (i.e. circulation geared to the realization and reproduction of surplus-value). Marx starts from the assumption that, in order for the process of reproduction to flow smoothly, all income generated in the production process must be spent on the commodities produced. Any additional purchasing power injected into the repro-duction process at a given point must be expelled at another point, if the process is to continue in a balanced way.

Now, it so happens that the very functioning of the capitalist mode of production leads to periodic hoarding of money capital. We have already

110. See below, pp. 542–5. Of course, academic economic theory later took over this essentially Marxist contribution to the theory of the trade cycle.

encountered this problem with regard to discontinous renewal of fixed capital. Marx points out that successive expansions and contractions of the circulation time of commodities – related to phases of the trade cycle – result in periodic expansions and contractions of money capital as compared with productive capital. In the same way, the shortening or lengthening of the production process itself (for instance, increase or reduction of the weight within the total product-mix of commodities requiring a lengthy production time) gives rise to contraction or expansion of the volume of money capital in circulation. The shorter the production time, the quicker will be the turnover of productive capital itself, and the smaller will be the money reserves which the capitalists have to throw into circulation, in order to cover the wages bill and their own consumption needs until the commodities worked upon in their factories are finished and sold. Conversely, a lengthening of the production time will result in a lengthening of the turnover time of capital, and an increase in the reserves of money capital and money revenue that have to be injected into the circulation process to maintain consumption until the production and sale of the commodities is completed.[111]

More generally, the harmonious flow of expanded reproduction is constantly threatened (not permanently upset, of course), because there are always capitalists who buy without selling, and others who sell without buying. Money is continually being withdrawn from circulation, and additional money is forever being injected. Only if these movements roughly cancel each other out will the partially *autonomous* character of the money flow not conflict with the need to realize the total value of commodities produced. While the banking system objectively strives to achieve that balance (and thus represents a force of social accounting and centralization far superior to anything private ownership could accomplish in the realm of production), it does not have the means to ensure automatic and continual balancing. Here there appears a further cause of discontinuity or interruption of expanded production – a cause which, though derived from monetary phenomena, is of course essentially rooted in the contradictory nature of the commodity and of the production of value and surplus-value.

It follows that a series of proportions, additional to those which emerge *prima facie* from the reproduction schemas, play an important role in *amplifying*, if not triggering off, the trade cycle. The way in which the total money stock is divided between circulating money and hoarded

111. See below, pp. 358–9, 364–6.

money[112]; the way in which circulating money is divided between circulating money capital and circulating revenue; the way in which hoarded money is divided between *latent* (*potential*) *productive capital* (i.e. money capital which will tend to contribute to increased production of surplus-value) and capital which is more or less permanently hoarded (i.e. withdrawn from both the sphere of production and the sphere of circulation *of commodities*) – all these proportions significantly influence the volume and rhythm of capital accumulation.[113]

Keynes was correct when he discarded the assumption of more or less permanent full employment of manpower and capital (or at least, the hypothesis that it could be achieved automatically through the operation of market forces). He was also right to point out that capital or revenue *not spent* (i.e. hoarded) is an important source of disequilibrium and under-employment of productive resources in an economy based upon generalized commodity production. In fact, Marx had argued as much sixty-five years earlier, in *Capital* Volume 2. But the latter's understanding of the fundamental mechanisms of the capitalist mode of production proved more profound than that of Keynes. For Marx went a step further by distinguishing between *productive* investment (i.e. investment leading to increased production of surplus-value) and unproductive 'investment' (which cannot directly augment the total social wealth and real income, but only contribute indirectly to re-allocation and re-deployment of existing resources). After all, building pyramids and digging canals in order to fill them up again does not have the same effect upon economic growth, capital accumulation and expanded reproduction as building new factories and opening up new oil fields. Buying government bonds in order to finance the building of pyramids is evidently not the same kind of activity as the investment of productive capital.[114]

112. See below, pp. 260–61.

113. In his latest book, Emmanuel correctly stresses the role of hoarding in Marx's theory of crises. He uses the expression *vouloir d'achat* (purchasing desire) as opposed to *pouvoir d'achat* (purchasing power) (op. cit., pp. 61ff.).

114. Paul Mattick (*Marx and Keynes*, London, 1969) does not make the matter any clearer by a confused use of the concept 'waste production'. 'Waste', in the sense of products not entering into the reproduction process, and 'waste' in the sense of unsellable products, are not at all identical concepts. Luxury products are – like arms – commodities, and they find buyers. Public works and other infrastructural outlays are not carried out for the purpose of sale, but in order to accelerate the turnover of capital and thereby indirectly to increase the production of surplus-value. However, pyramids or canals which are dug and then filled up again are pure waste – they are neither commodities to be sold nor means of hastening the turnover of capital.

From the elements of monetary analysis dispersed throughout Volume 2, it is possible to identify, within the framework of Marxist economic theory, four distinct *causes of rising commodity prices*. These causes are the following.

(a) *A fall in the average productivity of labour in a given branch of output* (for example, in certain agricultural or mining branches, where a decline in natural fertility is not completely offset by technological progress); prices would then rise as the result of an increase in value of particular commodities (i.e. in the quantity of social labour necessary for their production).

(b) *A sudden increase of labour productivity in the gold-mining industry* (and thus a decline in the value of gold); all other things remaining equal, the same mass of commodities would then be exchanged for a greater amount of gold (produced by the same quantity of labour as before). In other words, the gold price of commodities would rise.

(c) *An upward trend of market price-fluctuations* around an *unchanged* axis of values. This may occur, even when the gold currency remains stable and when there is no paper money inflation, at that precise stage of the trade cycle marked by the periodic contraction of the hoarded part of money as compared to the circulating part.

(d) *An inflationary movement of money signs*. In this case, a constant amount of gold, which exchanges against the same amount of commodities as before on the basis of an unaltered quantity of socially necessary labour, becomes represented by a greater sum of paper money signs (or of bank money, credit money).[115]

13. GROWTH AND CRISIS

The central 'message' of Volume 2, like that of Volume 1, refers to a terrifyingly dynamic process. Volume 1 indicates why capital, by its very essence, is value in perpetual search of additional value, produced by the workers in the process of production. The unquenchable thirst for surplus-value is the fundamental motor of economic growth, technological revolution, 'research and development' spending, improvement of communications, 'third-world aid', the sales drive and market research. A corresponding quest for individual enrichment appears at the core of every level of bourgeois society, together with increasing

115. Karl Marx, *A Contribution to the Critique of Political Economy*, Moscow, 1971, pp. 118–20. See also *Grundrisse*, op. cit., pp. 121–2 and 212–13.

alienation of workers and all human beings, and a growing threat that the forces of production will be transformed into forces of destruction. Paradoxically, mankind increasingly loses control over its own products and productive endeavour at the very moment when its mastery of nature and natural forces seems to be developing by leaps and bounds.[116]

In Volume 2 of *Capital*, we follow the commodities, containing the surplus-value produced by the workers, on their travels outside the factory. A 'spiralling movement' of growth is unleashed – a veritable avalanche.[117] The sale of commodities at their value enables profit to be realized and additional capital to be accumulated. More capital begets more surplus-value, which in turn begets more capital. Obstacles on the road of self-expansion – such as the enforced lingering of commodities in the sphere of circulation, or the protracted character of the production process itself – are swept away by the avalanche, thanks to social division of labour within the capitalist class; the appearance of commercial and banking capital; and the constant striving to accelerate the transport of commodities, build up a world-wide system of communications and reduce the length of the circulation process to a minimum. An immense mountain of commodities is distributed with lightning speed around the globe, so that a steadily growing stream of value (money capital) may be concentrated in the hands of an ever smaller percentage (if not necessarily a shrinking absolute number) of the world's active population. Today's real masters are to be found in probably no more than 1,000 or 2,000 firms the world over.[118]

116. This domination of nature increasingly takes the form of the destruction (*Raubbau*) of nature, as is shown by the threats to ecological equilibrium.

117. Marx and Luxemburg borrowed the image of the spiral as an expression of the form of capitalist development from Simonde de Sismondi.

118. This does not mean, of course, that the hundreds of thousands of smaller capitalist entrepreneurs, and the several million capitalist *rentier* families, are not part of the world bourgeoisie, but simply that they no longer command the decisive means of production or take the key investment decisions. Bourgeois society has the form of a pyramid in which the summit of monopolists could not survive without the support of different strata of large and medium bourgeois and their retainers (as well as the, at least partial, support of sections of the petty bourgeoisie). The notion that capitalism could be abolished by eliminating the monopolists alone does not take account of the fact that capitalism inevitably grows out of even petty commodity production where conditions of money circulation and widespread private ownership of the means of production prevail. If a significant sector of medium-sized capitalist firms is retained (and some of the 'non-monopolist' capitalists are rather large-scale ones!) then capitalism would not only survive, but flourish and open up the road leading to the formation of new monopolies.

This frenetic search for additional wealth in order to create even more wealth becomes increasingly divorced from basic human needs and interests, increasingly opposed to the 'production of a rich individuality' and the 'rich development of social relations' encompassing all human beings. But the process cannot continue smoothly and uninterruptedly: capital is powerless to overcome the basic contradictions of the commodity and private property. From both sides, the contradictions of production for its own sake (i.e. production in order to augment the profits of those who own the major means of production) must lead to periodic discharge in huge social and economic convulsions.

Following the social explosion initiated in the Western world by May '68 in France, the severe generalized recession of 1974–5[119] has confirmed Marx's basic analysis. Capitalist growth cannot but be uneven, disproportionate and unharmonious. Expanded reproduction necessarily gives rise to contracted reproduction. Prosperity inexorably leads to over-production. The search for the philosopher's stone which would enable market economy (i.e. private property, i.e. competition) to coincide with balanced growth, and mass consumption to develop apace with productive capacity (despite the capitalists' drive to force up the rate of exploitation) – this search will go on as long as the system survives. But it will be no more crowned with success than that which has already been conducted for more than 150 years. The only possible remedy for economic crises of over-production and social crises of class struggle is the elimination of capitalism and class society. No other solution will be found, either in theory or in practice. This awe-inspiring prediction made by Marx has been borne out by empirical evidence ever since *Capital* was written. There is no sign that it will be contradicted by current or future developments.

ERNEST MANDEL

119. See the last chapter of *Late Capitalism* (op. cit.), and my articles on the generalized recession of the international capitalist economy in *Inprecor* (16 January 1975, 5 June 1975, 18 December 1975 and 15 September 1976).

Translator's Preface

The three volumes of *Capital* form a single integral work. As Ernest Mandel explains in his introduction, the later volumes extend, if they do not wholly complete, the theoretical depiction of the capitalist mode of production which Marx embarked upon with Volume 1.

The Pelican Marx Library *Capital* has therefore been planned and executed as a coherent new edition. Though Volumes 2 and 3 have a different translator from Volume 1, Ben Fowkes and myself have each been able to read the other's work and give advice. On virtually all technical points and matters of terminology, Volumes 2 and 3 follow the lead given in Volume 1.

As far as the style of writing is concerned, the differences to be found between the later volumes and Volume 1, while in some part inevitably reflecting the preferences of the translators, are due to a far greater extent to differences in the original texts. Volume 1 of *Capital*, which Marx himself prepared for the press – and revised after its first publication – is palpably presented to the public as a work of science that is also a work of world literature. Hence not only the splendid rhetoric of many well-known passages, but also the copious references to the works of classical antiquity and Renaissance Europe.

Volumes 2 and 3 follow much more in the wake of the less purple passages of Volume 1. Their content is to a far greater extent technical, even dry; and Volume 2, above all, is renowned for the arid deserts between its oases. From the scientific point of view, this is all quite contingent; but it has caused many a non-specialist reader to turn back in defeat. As translator, I have tried to ease the passage as best I could by rendering Marx's prose into as straightforward and contemporary an English as possible. Translator's footnotes and cross-references are designed with the same end in view. But though it is not hard for a new translator to improve on previous editions, I certainly could not claim to have made the later volumes of *Capital* easy reading. Happily, the reader of the present edition also has Ernest Mandel's introduction as a guide, and this will come to the rescue, I am sure, at many a tricky point.

DAVID FERNBACH

NOTE

In compiling the editorial footnotes, indicated by asterisks etc., the translator has derived much assistance from the *Marx-Engels-Werke* (*MEW*) edition of *Capital*.

Note

In this edition numbered footnotes
are those of the original text.
Those marked by asterisks, etc., are
the translator's.

Preface

It was not an easy job to prepare the second volume of *Capital* for publication, and particularly in such a way that it appeared not only as an integrated work, as complete as possible, but also as the exclusive work of its author, and not its editor. The task was made more difficult by the large number of versions, most of them incomplete. Only one of these, Manuscript IV, had been completely prepared for publication, though even here the greater part had been made obsolete by drafts of a later date. The main body of the material, if it was fully worked out in content, in the main, was not so in its language. It was composed in the idiom that Marx customarily used in preparing his summaries: a negligent style, colloquial and often coarsely humorous expressions and usages, English and French technical terms, frequently whole sentences and even pages in English. This is the expression of ideas in the immediate form in which they developed in the author's head. Alongside particular sections that were worked out in detail, there were others, equally important, that were only sketched in outline. The material for factual illustration had been assembled, but hardly arranged, let alone worked up. At the end of a chapter, in his haste to go on to the next, Marx often left a few disconnected sentences to serve as the guidelines for an as yet unfinished analysis. Finally, there was the notorious handwriting, which even the author himself was sometimes unable to read.

I have confined myself to reproducing the manuscripts as literally as possible, altering in the style only what Marx himself would have altered, and only putting in explanatory parentheses and bridging passages where this was absolutely necessary, and the sense quite unambiguous. Whenever there was even the faintest doubt as to the meaning of a sentence, I preferred to print it word for word. The reworkings and interpolations that originate from me amount altogether to less than ten printed pages, and are of a purely formal character.

It is sufficient to enumerate the manuscript material that Marx left for Volume 2 to show the incomparable conscientiousness and severe self-criticism with which he strove to bring his great economic discoveries to the utmost degree of perfection before publishing them. This self-criticism seldom allowed him to adapt his presentation, either in content or in form, to his mental horizon, which was constantly expanding as the result of new studies. The material, then, consists of the following manuscripts.

Firstly a manuscript entitled 'Zur Kritik der politischen Ökonomie', 1,472 pages in twenty-three notebooks, written between August 1861 and June 1863. This is the continuation of the volume of the same title published in Berlin in 1859.* The themes investigated in Volume 1 of *Capital* are dealt with in pp. 1–220 (notebooks I–V) and again in pp. 1159–1472 (notebooks XIX–XXIII), from the transformation of money into capital through to the conclusion. This is the first existing draft for Volume 1. Pages 973–1158 (notebooks XVI–XVIII) deal with capital and profit, rate of profit, merchant's capital and money capital, i.e. themes that were later developed in the manuscript for Volume 3. The themes treated in Volume 2, however, as well as many treated later in Volume 3, are not yet grouped together. They are dealt with in passing in the section that forms the main body of the manuscript, pp. 220–972 (notebooks VI–XV): *Theorien über den Mehrwert*. This section contains a detailed critical history of the crucial question in political economy, the theory of surplus-value, while at the same time most of the points that were specifically investigated later in the manuscript for Volumes 2 and 3, in their logical context, are developed here in polemical opposition to Marx's predecessors. My intention is to publish the critical portion of this manuscript, leaving aside the passages already covered in Volumes 2 and 3, as Volume 4 of *Capital*.† But valuable though this manuscript is, it was of little use for the present edition of Volume 2.

The next manuscript in chronological order is that of Volume 3. The

---

* *Zur Kritik der politischen Ökonomie*, Berlin, 1859. English translation: *A Contribution to the Critique of Political Economy*, tr. S. W. Ryazanskaya, London, 1971.

† *Theorien über den Mehrwert* was first published in 1905–10, edited by Karl Kautsky, who took on the work after Engels's death. This edition, however, was far from accurate, and is now generally neglected in favour of that published by the Institute for Marxism-Leninism, Berlin, 1956-62. The remaining part of Marx's gigantic 'Zur Kritik...' of 1861-3, approximately half its total 1½ million words, has yet to be published

bulk of this, at least, was written in 1864 and 1865. Only after this was essentially complete did Marx proceed to finish off Volume 1, which appeared in 1867. This manuscript of Volume 3 I am now preparing for publication.

From the next period – after the appearance of Volume 1 – we have a collection of four folio manuscripts for Volume 2, numbered I–IV by Marx himself. Manuscript I (150 pages), which appears to date from 1865 or 1867, is the first independent version of Volume 2 in its present arrangement, but a more or less incomplete one. Here, too, nothing could be used. Manuscript III consists partly of a compilation of quotations and references to Marx's extract-books (mostly related to the first part of Volume 2), partly of elaborations of individual points, in particular criticisms of Adam Smith's* ideas on fixed and circulating capital, and on the source of profit; there is also a presentation of the relation between rate of surplus-value and rate of profit, which belongs to Volume 3. The references provided little that was new, while the elaborations were superseded by later versions, both for Volume 2 and Volume 3, and so also had to be mostly set aside. Manuscript IV is a version of Part One of Volume 2, and the first chapter of Part Two, which Marx left ready for publication, and it has been used in its due place. Even though it was evidently composed earlier than No. II, it is more complete in form, and could thus be used to advantage for the appropriate portion of the book. It only needed some additions from Manuscript II. This last manuscript is the only version of Volume 2 we possess which has been even approximately finished, and it dates from 1870. The notes for the final draft, which I shall discuss in a moment, say expressly that 'the second version must be used as a basis'.

After 1870 there is a further pause, principally occasioned by illness. As usual, Marx filled this time with study: agronomy, American and particularly Russian rural conditions, the money market and banking, as well as natural science – geology and physiology, and in particular independent mathematical work – form the content of numerous extract-books of this period. Early in 1877 Marx felt sufficiently restored

---

*Adam Smith, author of *The Wealth of Nations* (1776), gave bourgeois political economy its classical form, in a work that was both scientifically important and a major ideological weapon for the developing industrial capitalist class. For both these reasons, Smith's work forms a constant reference point for Marx throughout *Capital*. In *Theories of Surplus-Value*, in particular (Part 1, Chapter III), Marx develops his fullest critique of Smith's fundamental theoretical conceptions. See also Chapters 10 and 19 in the present volume.

to health to be able to proceed again with his own proper work. References and notes dating from the end of March 1877, taken from the above four manuscripts, form the basis for a new version of Volume 2, begun in Manuscript V (fifty-six folio pages). This covers the first four chapters, but is not very thoroughly elaborated. Essential points are treated in notes below the text; the material is collected rather than sifted, but this is the last complete presentation of the most important portion of Part One. A first attempt to derive a publishable manuscript from this was made in Manuscript VII (between October 1877 and July 1878): only seventeen quarto pages, covering the bulk of the first chapter. A second, final attempt, Manuscript VII, dated '2 July 1878', is only seven folio pages.

By this time Marx seems to have realized that, save for a complete transformation in the state of his health, he would never manage to complete a version of the second and third volumes that he would himself be satisfied with. Indeed, Manuscripts V–VIII bear only too frequently the traces of violent struggle against the oppression of illness. The most difficult bit of the first part was worked over afresh in Manuscript V; the remainder of the first part and the whole of the second part presented no significant theoretical difficulties (with the exception of Chapter 17), but the third part, on the reproduction and circulation of the social capital, seemed to him strongly in need of revision. In Manuscript II, for example, reproduction was treated firstly without regard to the money circulation that mediates it, and then once again taking this into account. This was to be jettisoned, and the whole part completely revised so as to correspond to the author's expanded horizon. This is how Manuscript VIII came into being, a notebook of only seventy quarto pages; but what Marx managed to compress into this space can be seen from Part Three in its published form, subtracting the pieces interposed from Manuscript II.

This manuscript too is only a provisional treatment of the subject, the main point being to set down and develop the new perspectives arrived at since Manuscript II, ignoring those points on which there was nothing new to say. An important section of Chapter 17 in Part Two, which overlaps somewhat into the third part, was also considered again and expanded. The logical sequence is frequently interrupted, and the treatment in places punctuated and especially at the end quite incomplete. And yet what Marx intended to say is said there, in one way or another.

That is the material for Volume 2, from which I was to 'make something', as Marx put it to his daughter Eleanor shortly before his death. I interpreted this commission in the narrowest sense. Wherever possible, I have confined my activity to mere selection between the various drafts, and indeed always used the last existing draft as the basis, comparison being made with the earlier ones. Real difficulties, i.e. those other than merely technical, arose only in the first and third parts, although they were in no way slight. I have sought to resolve them exclusively in the spirit of the author.

I have mostly translated [into German] the quotations in the text, where evidence of a factual nature was involved or where, as with passages from Adam Smith, the original is available to anyone who wants to go more deeply into the matter. Only in Chapter 10 was this not possible, as here the English text is criticized directly. The quotations from Volume 1 carry page references to the second edition, the last to appear in Marx's lifetime.*

For Volume 3, besides the first version contained in the manuscript 'Zur Kritik', the pieces in Manuscript III already mentioned, and short notes occasionally interspersed in extract-books, we have just the folio manuscript of 1864–5 as mentioned, elaborated to approximately the same degree of completeness as Manuscript II for Volume 2, and finally a notebook of 1875, entitled 'The Relation of the Rate of Surplus-Value to the Rate of Profit', which is a mathematical treatment (in equations). Rapid progress is being made in preparing this volume for publication. As far as I can judge at this moment, it will chiefly involve only technical difficulties, with the exception of a few, though very important sections.†

*

It is a suitable place here to rebut a certain accusation made against Marx, first only cautiously and sporadically, but now, after his death, proclaimed by German academic and state socialists and their hangers-on as an established fact – the accusation that Marx plagiarized the

---

*In the present volume, these references have been replaced throughout by corresponding references to the Pelican Marx Library edition. The reader is also reminded that the division there into chapters and parts follows that made by Engels for the original English edition of 1886, and is different from that of the various German editions. The table on p. 110 of Volume 1 shows the relationship between English and German divisions.

† In fact, nine years were to elapse before the publication of Volume 3. See Engels's Preface to that volume.

work of Rodbertus.* I have already said elsewhere what it was most urgent to say on this matter,[1] but only here can I introduce for the first time the decisive evidence.

As far as I know, the accusation was first made by R. Meyer in his *Emancipationskampf des vierten Standes*, p. 43: 'It can be demonstrated that Marx borrowed the greater part of his critique from these publications' (i.e. the works of Rodbertus dating back to the latter half of the 1830s).

I might well take it, until evidence to the contrary is forthcoming, that the entire 'demonstration' of this statement consists in the fact that Rodbertus assured this Herr Meyer of it. In 1879, Rodbertus himself appeared on the scene,† and wrote to J. Zeller (*Zeitschrift für die gesammte Staatswissenschaft*, Tübingen, 1879, p. 219) with reference to his text, *Zur Erkenntnis unsrer staatswirthschaftlichen Zustände* (1842), 'You will find that thé same thing' (the line of thought there developed) 'has already been nicely used by Marx, of course without acknowledgement to me.'

This was then echoed in so many words by his posthumous editor T. Kozak ('*Das Kapital' von Rodbertus*, Berlin, 1884, Introduction, p. xv). Finally, in the *Briefe und socialpolitische Aufsätze von Dr Rodbertus-Jagetzow* published by R. Meyer in 1881, Rodbertus says straight out, 'Today I find myself robbed by Schäffle‡ and Marx, without my name

1. In the Preface to Marx's *The Poverty of Philosophy*, translated [into German] by E. Bernstein and K. Kautsky, Stuttgart, 1885. [This work of Marx's, first published in 1847 as a reply to Proudhon's book *The Philosophy of Poverty*, was written in French.]

---

*The academic socialists (*Kathedersozialisten*) mentioned here, who flirted with socialism from the safety of their university chairs, first made their appearance in the 1870s. Prominent among them were Gustav Schmoller, Lujo Brentano, Adolph Wagner, Karl Bücher and Werner Sombart. They were outside and generally opposed to the Social-Democratic Party. 'State socialism', the ideology that presents state intervention in the capitalist economy as *ipso facto* 'socialist', was a constant object of attack by Marx and Engels (as in the *Communist Manifesto*, ch. III, 2, and the *Critique of the Gotha Programme*). In Germany in the 1880s it was Bismarck's nationalization of the railways, in particular, that was dressed up as 'socialist' in this way, mainly by the 'academic socialists'. Johann Karl Rodbertus-Jagetzow, a Prussian landowner, was the doyen of state socialism in Germany, in practice seeking state support for the development of large-scale capitalist agriculture.

†Rodbertus had in fact died in 1875. The letter published in the Tübingen *Zeitschrift* was written on 14 March 1875.

‡Albert Eberhard Schäffle, a vulgar economist (see p. 101, note) and bourgeois sociologist. Marx refers to him in his 'Notes on Wagner'.

being mentioned' (Letter no. 60, p. 134). In a further passage Rodbertus's claim assumes more specific form: 'I showed in the third of my
Social Letters* how the capitalist's surplus-value is derived, essentially
the same way as Marx, only clearer and more briefly' (Letter no. 48,
p. 111).

Marx never came across these accusations of plagiarism. In his copy
of the *Emancipationskampf* the only pages cut were those of the part
relating to the International, until I myself cut the remainder after his
death. He never saw the Tübingen *Zeitschrift*. The *Briefe, etc.* to R.
Meyer remained equally unknown to him, and I came to know of the
passage about the 'robbery' only in 1884, through the good offices of
Herr Dr Meyer himself. But Marx was familiar with letter no. 48; Herr
Meyer had been kind enough to send the original to Marx's youngest
daughter. After some furtive gossip that the secret sources of his critique
were to be found in Rodbertus had reached his ears, Marx showed me
the note in question. Here he finally had authentic information as to
what Rodbertus himself claimed. If this was all Rodbertus was saying,
then Marx was not worried; and if Rodbertus held his own presentation
to be briefer and clearer, Marx could also allow him this indulgence.
Indeed, Marx believed that the whole matter started and finished with
this letter of Rodbertus.

Marx was particularly inclined to let the matter lie because, as I know
for a fact, he had been quite unaware of Rodbertus's literary activity up
till around 1859, by which time his own Critique of Political Economy
was finished not only in outline, but even in the most important details.
Marx began his economic studies in Paris in 1843 with the great English
and French writers; of the Germans, he was familiar only with Rau and
List,† and that was enough. Neither Marx nor I had any word of Rodbertus's existence until 1848, when we had to criticize his speeches as a
Berlin deputy, and his actions as a minister, in the *Neue Rheinische
Zeitung*. We were so ignorant that we had to ask the Rhineland deputies
who this Rodbertus was, who had suddenly become a minister. But that
Marx already knew very well, even without Rodbertus's help, 'how the

*The third of Rodbertus's *Soziale Briefe an von Kirchmann*, in which he put
forward his theory of rent against Ricardo's, was published in Berlin in 1851.

†Karl Heinrich Rau was a German economist who vulgarized the theories of
Smith and Ricardo, and supported the doctrine of the factors of production put
forward by Say (see p. 227, note). Friedrich List, the most important German
economist of the first half of the nineteenth century, accurately expressed the
demands of the embryonic industrial bourgeoisie in Germany, and is particularly
remembered for his forceful arguments for protective tariffs.

capitalist's surplus-value is derived', is shown by *The Poverty of Philosophy*, 1847, and by his lectures on *Wage-Labour and Capital*, delivered in Brussels in 1847 and published in 1849 in the *Neue Rheinische Zeitung*, nos. 264–269. It was only around 1859, via Lassalle,* that Marx discovered there was also an economist Rodbertus, and he then found the latter's *Third Social Letter* in the British Museum.

These are the facts of the case. What then about the material of which Marx is supposed to have 'robbed' Rodbertus?

'I showed in the third of my *Social Letters* how the capitalist's surplus-value is derived, essentially the same way as Marx, only clearer and more briefly.'

This then is the decisive point, the theory of surplus-value, and it is hard to say what else there is in Marx that Rodbertus could have claimed as his property. Rodbertus here declares that he was the true founder of the theory of surplus-value, and that Marx 'robbed' him of it.

Now what does the *Third Social Letter* tell us as to the origin of surplus-value? Simply that 'rent' (which is how he lumps together ground-rent and profit) does not arise as an 'addition' to the value of a commodity, but rather 'as a result of a deduction of value suffered by wages, in other words because wages only amount to a part of the value of the product', and if labour is sufficiently productive, 'they do not need to be equal to the natural exchange-value of the product, so that some of this still remains over for capital replacement (!) and rent'. We are not told what 'natural exchange-value of the product' it is which does not leave anything over for 'capital replacement', i.e. for the replacement of raw material and the wear and tear of tools.

Fortunately we are able to confirm the impression Rodbertus's epoch-making discovery made on Marx. In the manuscript 'Zur Kritik', we find in notebook X, pp. 445 ff., 'Herr Rodbertus. New Theory of Rent. (Digression)'. It is only from this point of view that the *Third Social Letter* is considered here. Rodbertus's theory of surplus-value in general is dismissed here with the ironic remark, 'Herr Rodbertus first investigates the situation in a country where there is *no separation* between land ownership and ownership of capital. And here

* Ferdinand Lassalle, who at this time professed to be a disciple of Marx, one of only a small handful who had been able to remain in Germany after the failure of the 1848 revolution, became in the early 1860s the inspirer and chief organizer of the first mass movement of the modern German working class. Politically, however, he played an ambiguous role in relation to the Bismarck regime; see *The First International and After*, Pelican Marx Library, pp. 20 ff.

he comes to the important conclusion that rent (by which he means the entire *surplus-value*) is simply equal to the unpaid labour or the quantity of products which it represents.'*

The capitalist world has been producing surplus-value for several centuries, and has gradually come to develop ideas about its origin. The first view was that arising directly from commercial practice, that surplus-value is derived from an addition to the value of the product. This was the prevailing view among the mercantilists, but James Steuart† already saw that if this were the case, what one man gained, the other would necessarily lose. All the same, this view continued to haunt men's minds for a long time, particularly the minds of socialists, though it was expelled from classical [economic] science by Adam Smith.

Smith wrote in *The Wealth of Nations*, Book One, Chapter VI:

'As soon as stock has accumulated in the hands of particular persons, some of them will naturally employ it in setting to work industrious people, whom they will supply with materials and subsistence, in order to make a *profit* by the sale of their work, or by *what their labour adds to the value of the materials* . . . The *value* which the workmen *add to the materials*, therefore, resolves itself into *two parts*, of which the one pays *their wages*, the other the *profits of their employer* upon the whole stock of materials and wages which he advanced' [Pelican edn, p. 151].‡

And a little further on,

'As soon as the land of any country has all become private property, the landlords, like all other men, love to reap where they never sowed, and demand a rent even for its natural produce . . . the labourer . . . must *give up* to the landlord *a portion* of what his *labour* either collects or produces. This portion, or, what comes to the same thing, the price of this portion, constitutes the *rent of land*.'

In the above-mentioned manuscript 'Zur Kritik', p. 253, Marx remarks on this passage:

* *Theories of Surplus-Value*, London, 1969–72, Part II, pp. 15–16.

† Sir James Steuart's *Inquiry into the Principles of Political Economy* was first published in 1767. Steuart was the last representative of the Mercantilist school (see below, p. 139, note), and his work already represehts a transition towards the classical bourgeois analysis of capitalist production by Adam Smith. It is with a short chapter on Steuart, therefore, that Marx opens his *Theories of Surplus-Value*.

‡ This passage and those following are quoted by Marx in the manuscript of *Theories of Surplus-Value* (Part I, Chapter III, 2; pp. 78–85 of the English translation), interspersed with Marx's comments, as cited below by Engels. Marx's emphases in his quotations from Smith, however, differ somewhat in the published version – and thus presumably in the manuscript as well – from those made by Engels here.

'Thus Adam Smith conceives *surplus-value* – that is, surplus labour, the excess of labour performed and objectified in the commodity *over and above* the paid labour, the labour which has received its equivalent in wages – as the *general category*, of which profit in the strict sense and rent of land are merely branches.'*

Adam Smith says further (Book One, Chapter VIII):

'As soon as land becomes private property, the landlord demands a share of almost all the produce which the labourer can either raise, or collect from it. His rent makes the *first deduction* from the *produce of the labour which is employed upon land.* It seldom happens that the person who tills the ground has wherewithal to maintain himself till he reaps the harvest. His maintenance is generally advanced to him from the stock of a master, the farmer who employs him, and who would have no interest to employ him, unless he was to *share in the produce of his labour*, or unless his stock was to be replaced to him with a profit. This profit makes a *second deduction* from the [produce of the] labour which is employed upon land.

'The produce of almost all other labour is liable to the like deduction of profit. In all arts and manufactures the greater part of the workmen stand in need of a master to advance them the materials of their work, and their wages and maintenance till it be completed. He *shares* in the *produce of their labour*, or in the value which it adds to the materials upon which it is bestowed; and in this share consists his profit' [Pelican edn, p. 168].

Marx comments (p. 256 of the manuscript):

'Here therefore Adam Smith in plain terms describes rent and profit on capital as mere *deductions* from the workman's product or the value of his product, which is equal to the quantity of labour added by him to the material. This deduction, however, as Adam Smith has himself previously explained, can only consist of that part of the labour which the workman adds to the materials, over and above the quantity of labour which only pays his wages, or which only provides an equivalent for his wages; that is, the surplus labour, the unpaid part of his labour.'†

Adam Smith was thus already aware 'how the capitalist's surplus-value is derived', and that of the landlord into the bargain. Marx recognized this quite frankly back in 1861, while Rodbertus and his crowd of admirers, springing up like mushrooms under the warm summer rain of state socialism, seem to have totally forgotten it.

*op. cit., p. 82.   †ibid., p. 85.

'Nevertheless,' Marx continues, 'he does not distinguish surplus-value as such as a category on its own, distinct from the specific forms it assumes in profit and rent. This is the source of much error and inadequacy in his inquiry, and of even more in the work of Ricardo.'*

This statement applies word for word to Rodbertus. His 'rent' is simply the sum of ground-rent and profit; he makes up a totally false theory of ground-rent, and takes over profit just as he finds it in his predecessors. Marx's surplus-value, however, is the *general form* of the sum of value appropriated without equivalent by the owners of the means of production, which is decomposed into the particular, *transformed* forms of profit and ground-rent according to quite specific laws that were first discovered by Marx. These laws are developed in Volume 3, where it will be seen how many intermediate terms are necessary in order to proceed from understanding surplus-value in general to understanding its transformation into profit and ground-rent, and thus to understanding the laws of distribution of surplus-value within the capitalist class.

Ricardo already went significantly further than Adam Smith. He founded his conception of surplus-value on a new theory of value, which although it was present in embryo in Smith, was time and again forgotten in the latter's exposition, a theory that became the starting-point of all subsequent economic science. In Ricardo's view, the value of a commodity is determined by the amount of labour realized in it. From this Ricardo derived the distribution between worker and capitalist of the quantum of value added by labour to the raw materials, its division into wages and profit (i.e. surplus-value). He showed that the value of commodities remains the same, however the ratio of these two parts may change, a law to which he admits only a few exceptions. He even established some basic laws on the changing ratio between wages and surplus-value (conceived in the form of profit), even if in too general a sense (Marx, *Capital* Volume 1, Chapter 17, 1), and showed ground-rent to be an excess over profit that in certain circumstances does not arise. In none of these points has Rodbertus gone beyond

*p. 81. David Ricardo's main work, *On the Principles of Political Economy, and Taxation*, first appeared in 1817. Ricardo marked the high point of classical political economy, as after 1830 the irrepressible fact of the class struggle of the industrial workers led bourgeois economics to retreat from its own previous scientific discoveries, and to the rise of vulgar economics (see p. 101, note). Like that of Adam Smith, Ricardo's work forms a constant reference point throughout *Capital*, and the bulk of Part II of *Theories of Surplus-Value*, in particular, is devoted to a critique of Ricardo's ideas.

Ricardo. Either he remained quite unaware of the internal contradictions of Ricardo's theory, which led to the collapse of the Ricardian school, or these led him to utopian demands instead of economic solutions (*Zur Erkenntnis . . .*, p. 130).

Ricardo's doctrine of value and surplus-value did not have to wait for Rodbertus's *Zur Erkenntnis . . .* to be turned to a socialist purpose. In Volume 1 of *Capital*, p. 734, Marx refers to a pamphlet entitled *The Source and Remedy of the National Difficulties. A Letter to Lord John Russell*, London, 1821, containing the phrase 'the possessors of surplus-produce or capital'. The significance of this pamphlet of forty pages, which Marx rescued from its oblivion, is already indicated by the expression 'surplus-produce or capital'. It goes on to say:

'Whatever may be due to the capitalist' (from the capitalist's standpoint), 'he can only receive the surplus-labour of the labourer; for the labourer must live' (p. 23).

But *the manner in which* the worker lives, and hence the magnitude of the surplus labour appropriated by the capitalist, are subject to considerable variation:

'If capital does not decrease in value as it increases in amount, the capitalists will exact from the labourers the produce of every hour's labour beyond what it is possible for the labourer to subsist on . . . the capitalist may . . . eventually say to the labourers, "You shan't eat bread, because . . . it is possible to subsist on beet root and potatoes." And to this point we have come!' (pp. 23–4). '. . . if the labourer can be brought to feed on potatoes instead of bread, it is indisputably true that more can be exacted from his labour; that is to say, if when he fed on bread he was obliged *to retain* for the maintenance of himself and family *the labour of Monday and Tuesday*, he will, on potatoes, require only the *half of Monday*; and the remaining half of Monday and the whole of Tuesday *are available* either for the service of the state or *the capitalist*' (p. 26). 'It is admitted that the interest paid to the capitalists, whether in the nature of rents, interests of money, or profits of trade, is paid out of the labour of others' (p. 23).

Here then we have precisely Rodbertus's 'rent', only instead of rent it is called 'interest'.

Marx notes on this ('Zur Kritik', p. 852),

'This scarcely known pamphlet (about forty pages) [which appeared] at a time when McCulloch, "this incredible cobbler",* began to make a

---

*John Ramsay McCulloch vulgarized Ricardo's doctrines; the description was applied to him by a critic, Mordecai Mullion (pseudonym of John Wilson), in *Some Illustrations of Mr McCulloch's Principles of Political Economy*, Edinburgh, 1826.

stir, contains an important advance on Ricardo. It bluntly describes surplus-value – or "profit", as Ricardo calls it (often also "surplus produce"), or "*interest*", as the author of the pamphlet terms it – as "*surplus labour*", the labour which the worker performs gratis, the labour he performs over and above the quantity of labour by which the value of his labour-power is replaced, i.e., by which he produces an equivalent for his wages. Important as it was to reduce *value* to labour, it was equally important [to present] *surplus-value*, which manifests itself in *surplus product*, as *surplus labour*. This was in fact *already stated by Adam Smith and constitutes one of the main elements in Ricardo's argumentation*. But nowhere did he clearly express it and record it in an absolute form'.*

Marx goes on to say:

'For the rest, the author remains a captive of the economic categories as he finds them. Just as in the case of Ricardo the confusion of surplus-value with profit leads to undesirable contradictions, so in his case the fact that he christens surplus-value the interest of capital.

'To be sure, he is in advance of Ricardo in that he first of all reduces all surplus-value to surplus labour, and when he calls surplus-value interest of capital, he at the same time emphasizes that by this he understands the general form of surplus labour in contrast to its special forms – rent, interest of money and industrial profit . . . But on the other hand, he applies the name of one of these particular forms – interest – to the general form. And this suffices to make him relapse into economic slang.'†

This last passage fits our Rodbertus like a glove. He too remains a captive of the economic categories as he finds them. He too christens surplus-value with the name of one of its particular subordinate forms, rent, which for him, moreover, is something quite indefinite. As a result of these two blunders, he again relapses into economic slang, fails to make any further critical development of his advance over Ricardo, and instead lets himself be diverted into making his unfinished theory, before it has even fully emerged from its shell, the basis of a utopia – which like everything else, he produces too late. The pamphlet quoted above appeared in 1821, and is already a complete anticipation of the Rodbertian 'rent' of 1842.

This pamphlet is only the most advanced outpost of a whole group of writings of the 1820s, which turned the Ricardian theory of value and

* *Theories of Surplus-Value*, Part III, pp. 238–9.
† ibid., p. 254.

surplus-value against capitalist production in the interest of the proletariat, and fought the bourgeoisie with its own weapons. The whole of Owen's communism,* in so far as it engaged in economic polemics, was based on Ricardo. But besides Owen there was a whole series of writers, of whom Marx mentioned just a few in 1847 in his book against Proudhon, *Misère de la Philosophie*, p. 49†: Edmonds, Thompson, Hodgskin, etc. 'and four pages more of *etc.*'.‡ From this plethora of writings, I take just one at random, *An Inquiry into the Principles of the Distribution of Wealth, most conducive to Human Happiness*, by William Thompson; a new edition, London, 1850. This text, written in 1822, first appeared in 1824. Here, too, the wealth appropriated by the non-producing classes is described throughout as a deduction from the product of labour, and this in fairly strong terms.

'The constant effort of what has been called society, has been to deceive and induce, to terrify and compel, the productive labourer to work for the smallest possible portion of the produce of his own labour' (p. 28). 'Why not give him the whole absolute produce of his own labour?' (p. 32). 'This amount of compensation, exacted by capitalists from the productive labourers, under the name of rent or profits, is claimed for the use of land or other articles ... For all the physical materials on which, or by means of which, his productive powers can be made available, and their consent being a necessary preliminary to any exertion on his part, is he not, and must he not always remain, at the mercy of these capitalists for whatever *portion of the fruits of his own labour* they may think proper to leave at his disposal in compensation for his toils?' (p. 125). '... in proportion to the amount of *products withheld*, whether called profits, or taxes, or theft' (p. 126), etc.

I admit that I am somewhat ashamed to have to write these lines. The fact that the English anti-capitalist literature of the 1820s and 1830s is so completely unknown in Germany, despite the fact that Marx directly referred to it in *The Poverty of Philosophy*, and quoted a good deal of it,

* Robert Owen was the great English representative of utopian communism in the early nineteenth century, See in particular Engels's *Anti-Dühring*, Part III 'Socialism', Chapter I 'Historical'.

† *The Poverty of Philosophy*, London, 1966, p. 60.

‡ Besides Marx's brief reference in *The Poverty of Philosophy*, a chapter of *Theories of Surplus-Value* is devoted to 'Opposition to the Economists (Based on the Ricardian Theory)' (Part III, Chapter XXI). This deals principally with the works of William Thompson, Piercy Ravenstone and Thomas Hodgskin. Thomas Edmonds, however, the author of *Practical Moral and Political Economy* (1828), does not reappear in *Theories of Surplus-Value*.

in several places, in Volume 1 of *Capital* – this in itself may pass muster. But that not only the *literatus vulgaris*,* desperately clinging on to Rodbertus's coat-tails, 'who really has learnt nothing', but also the professor in high office, who 'brags of his learning',† have forgotten their classical economics to such an extent as to seriously reproach Marx for purloining from Rodbertus things that can already be read in Smith and Ricardo – this indicates the depths to which official economics has sunk today.

But what then did Marx say about surplus-value that was new? How did it happen that Marx's theory of surplus-value burst like a bolt from the blue, in all civilized countries, while the theories of all his socialist precursors, Rodbertus included, petered out ineffectually?

The history of chemistry offers us a parallel.

Towards the end of the last century, as is well known, the phlogiston theory still prevailed. According to this theory, the essence of all combustion consisted in a hypothetical substance detaching itself from the burning body, an absolute combustible that was given the name phlogiston. This theory was sufficient to explain the greater part of chemical phenomena known at that time, even if the explanation was rather strained in some cases. Now in 1774 Priestley prepared a kind of air 'which he found so free of phlogiston that even ordinary air seemed adulterated by comparison'. He named this 'de-phlogisticated air'. Shortly afterwards, Scheele prepared the same kind of air in Sweden, and demonstrated its presence in the atmosphere. He also found that it vanished if a body was burned in it or in ordinary air, and therefore called it 'fire-air'.

'From these results, he [Priestley] now drew the conclusion that the combination produced by the union of phlogiston with one of the components of air' (i.e. by combustion) 'was nothing more than fire or heat, which escaped through the glass.'[2]

2. Roscoe and Schorlemmer,* *Ausführliches Lehrbuch der Chemie*, Braunschweig, 1877, I, pp. 13, 18.

*Karl Schorlemmer, a German exile and Professor of Organic Chemistry at Manchester University from 1874, was a personal friend of Marx and Engels, and accompanied Engels on his visit to the United States in 1888. He was one of the first natural scientists to adhere to the philosophy of dialectical materialism, as well as a member of the German Social-Democratic Party.

---

*Common *littérateur*. Here an allusion to R. Meyer.

†This is an allusion to Adolph Wagner (see above, p. 88, note). Wagner specifically attacked Marx's economic theory in his book *The General or Theoretical Doctrine of Political Economy* (1879). Marx's manuscript 'Marginal Notes' dealing with Wagner's critique, written in 1881–2, form his final economic writing.

Both Priestley and Scheele had produced oxygen, but they were unaware of what they had laid their hands on. They remained captives of the phlogistic categories they had inherited. The element that was to overthrow the whole phlogistic conception and revolutionize chemistry was stricken with barrenness in their hands. However, Priestley had immediately informed Lavoisier in Paris of his discovery, and Lavoisier now investigated the whole of phlogistic chemistry with the aid of this new fact. He was the first to discover that the new type of air was a new chemical element, that what happened in combustion was not that a mysterious phlogiston *escaped* from the burning body, but that this new element *combined* with the body, and he thus put the whole of chemistry, which in its phlogistic form was standing on its head, onto its feet for the first time. Even if Lavoisier did not himself produce oxygen at the same time as the others, as he later claimed, he remains none the less the real *discoverer* of oxygen, as opposed to Priestley and Scheele, who merely *produced* it, without having the slightest inkling of *what* they had produced.

Marx is related to his predecessors in the theory of surplus-value as Lavoisier is to Priestley and Scheele. The *existence* of the part of the value produced that we now call surplus-value was established long before Marx; what it consists of, i.e. the product of labour, for which the appropriator has paid no equivalent, was also formulated with a greater or lesser degree of clarity. But this was as far as it went. Some people – the classical bourgeois economists – investigated primarily the ratio in which the product of labour was distributed between the worker and the proprietor of the means of production. Others – the socialists – found this distribution unjust and sought to remove the injustice by utopian means. Both remained captive of the economic categories as they had found them.

Then Marx appeared. And he stood in direct opposition to all his predecessors. Where they had seen a *solution*, he saw only a *problem*. He saw that what was involved here was neither dephlogisticated air nor fire-air, but rather oxygen; that it was neither a matter of simply recording an economic fact, nor of a conflict between this fact and eternal justice or true morality, but rather of a fact which was destined to revolutionize economics, and which provided the key to the understanding of the whole of capitalist production – for the person who knew how to use it, that is. With the aid of this fact Marx investigated all the existing categories of economics, as Lavoisier had investigated the existing categories of phlogistic chemistry with the aid of oxygen. In order to know what surplus-value was, he had to know what value was. First and foremost, Ricardo's theory of value itself had to be subjected to criticism. Marx therefore investigated labour from the point of view of its value-forming quality, and established for the first time *what* labour, why, how it formed value, and that value in general is nothing more than congealed labour of *this* kind – a point Rodbertus never grasped to the end of his days. Marx then investigated the relation between commodities and money, and demonstrated how and why, by virtue of their inherent value property, commodities and commodity exchange must give rise to the antithesis of commodities and money; the theory of money which Marx founded on this basis is the first comprehensive theory of money, and it is now everywhere tacitly accepted. He investigated the transformation of money into capital, and proved that this rested on the sale and purchase of labour-power for labour as the value-creating property, Marx solved at a single stroke one of the difficulties which had caused the Ricardian school to founder: the impossibility of bringing the mutual exchange of capital and labour into accordance with the Ricardian law of the determination of value by labour. By distinguishing between constant and variable capital, Marx was able for the first time to depict the process of surplus-value formation in its true course, even in the minutest details, and thus to explain it – which none of his predecessors were able to do. He thereby established a distinction within capital itself, which neither Rodbertus nor the bourgeois economists was in a position even to approach, but which provides the key for solving the most intricate economic problems; the present Volume 2, and still more so, as we shall see, Volume 3, offer the most striking proof of this. In the further investigation of surplus-value itself, Marx discovered its two forms, absolute and relative surplus-value, and demonstrated the different, but in both cases decisive, roles that these have played in the historical development of capitalist production. On the basis of surplus-value Marx developed the first rational theory of wages that we have, and presented for the first time the basic elements of the history of capitalist accumulation, as well as depicting its historical tendency.

And Rodbertus? After he had read all this, he found in it, true to the partisan economist he invariably was, an 'assault on society',* took the view that he himself had already described the origin of surplus-value more clearly and briefly and, finally, asserted that, while all this does apply to 'the present form of capital', as it historically exists, it

* *Briefe und socialpolitische Aufsätze*, op. cit., p. 111.

does not apply to 'the concept of capital', i.e. the utopian idea that Herr Rodbertus has of capital. Just like old Priestley, who swore by phlogiston to the end, and would hear nothing of oxygen. Only Priestley really was the first to produce oxygen, whereas Rodbertus with his surplus-value, or rather 'rent', simply rediscovered a commonplace, while Marx, in contrast to Lavoisier, disdained to claim that he was the first to have discovered the *fact* of the existence of surplus-value.

Everything else that Rodbertus accomplished as an economist is on the same level. His elaboration of surplus-value into a utopia was already criticized by Marx, unknowingly, in *The Poverty of Philosophy*; everything else that there is to say, I have already said in the Preface to the German translation of that work.* His explanation of trade crises as a result of under-consumption on the part of the working class is to be found already in Sismondi's *Nouveaux Principes de l'économie politique*, Book iv, Chapter iv.³ The only difference is that Sismondi constantly had in mind here the world market, while Rodbertus's horizon stretches no further than the Prussian frontier. His speculations as to whether wages stem from capital or revenue pertain to scholasticism and are finally laid to rest in the third part of this second volume of *Capital*. His theory of rent remains his very own property, and can sleep on until Marx's manuscript criticizing it is published.† Finally, his proposals to emancipate landed property in the old Prussian provinces from the pressure of capital are again thoroughly utopian; they avoid the only practical question which is involved, i.e. how can the Prussian Junker receive, say, 20,000 marks and spend 30,000 marks, year after year, without running into debt?

Around 1830, the Ricardian school foundered on surplus-value. What

---

3. 'Thus the home market becomes ever more constricted by the concentration of riches in the hands of a small number of proprietors, and industry is forced more and more to seek its outlets in foreign markets, where still greater revolutions await it' (i.e. the crisis of 1817, which Sismondi goes on to describe). 1819 edition, I, p. 336.*

* Jean-Charles Simonde de Sismondi was a Swiss economist and historian. Contemporary with the utopian socialists, he also criticized certain of the contradictions of the developing capitalist society, but this was from the restricted standpoint of the petty bourgeoisie; Sismondi idealized petty commodity production.

---

* English translation, pp. 5–19.
† 'Herr Rodbertus. New Theory of Rent', pp. 15–113 of *Theories of Surplus-Value*, Part II, London, 1969.

it was unable to solve remained still more insoluble for its successors, the vulgar economists.*

The two points on which it came to grief were as follows.

(1) Labour is the measure of value. Now living labour, in exchange with capital, has a lesser value than the objectified labour for which it is exchanged. Wages, the value of a definite quantity of living labour, are always smaller than the value of the product that is produced by this quantity of living labour, or in which this is expressed. The question is in fact insoluble in this form. Marx posed it correctly, and thereby answered it. It is not the labour that has a value. Labour, as value-creating activity, can just as little have a particular value as heaviness can have a particular weight, heat a particular temperature, or electricity a particular intensity of current. It is not labour that is bought and sold as a commodity, but rather labour-*power*. Once this becomes a commodity, its value is governed by the labour embodied in it as a social product; it is equal to the labour necessary for its production and reproduction. Thus the sale and purchase of labour-power on the basis of its value in no way contradicts the economic law of value.

(2) According to the Ricardian law of value, two capitals which employ the same amount of living labour at the same rate of pay, assuming all other circumstances to be also the same, produce in the same period of time products of the same value, and similarly the same amount of surplus-value or profit. If they employ unequal amounts of living labour, then they cannot produce the same surplus-value, or profit as the Ricardians say. However, the contrary is the case. In point of fact, equal capitals produce, on average, equal profits in the same time, irrespective of how much or how little living labour they employ. This contradiction to the law of value was already known to Ricardo, but neither he nor his followers were able to resolve it. Even Rodbertus could not ignore the contradiction, but instead of resolving it, he makes it one of the starting-points for his utopia (*Zur Erkenntnis . . .*, p. 131). Marx had already resolved this contradiction in his manuscript 'Zur Kritik';† in the plan of *Capital*, the solution is to be included in Volume 3.‡ Some months will still pass until its publication.§ And so the economists who would like to discover Marx's secret source in Rod-

* For Marx's explanation of the rise of 'vulgar economics', see the Postface to the second German edition of *Capital* Volume 1, Penguin Marx Library edition, pp. 97–8; also Chapter 1, note 34, pp. 174–5.

† See *Theories of Surplus-Value*, Part II, Chapter VIII, 3a and 6, and Chapter X.

‡ Parts One and Two.

§ See above, p. 87, and Engels's Preface to Volume 3.

bertus, as well as his superior predecessor, have here an opportunity to show what Rodbertus's economics can accomplish. If they show how an average rate of profit can and must come about, not only without violating the law of value, but precisely on the basis of this law, then we shall have to continue our discussion. In the meantime, they had better hurry. The brilliant investigations of this Volume 2, and its entirely new results in areas that up to now have been almost untrodden, are simply premises for the material of Volume 3, in which the final results of Marx's presentation of the process of social reproduction on the capitalist basis are developed. When this Volume 3 appears, little more will be heard of an economist named Rodbertus.

The second and third volumes of *Capital* were to be dedicated, as Marx frequently told me, to his wife.

Frederick Engels

London, on Marx's birthday, 5 May 1884

Preface to the Second Edition

The present second edition is in essentials a word-for-word reprint of the first. Printers' errors have been corrected, a few stylistic faults eliminated, and a few short paragraphs that contain only repetitions have been taken out.

Volume 3, which has presented quite unexpected difficulties, is now also nearly ready in manuscript. If I remain in good health, it will be able to go to press this autumn.

F. Engels

London, 15 July 1893

*

For the sake of convenience, a brief summary is given here of the various manuscripts (II–VIII) from which this volume is compiled:

	Pages	Manuscript	Date
Part One			
	109	II	1870
	110–20	VII	1878
	120–23	VI	1877–8
	123–96	V	1877
	196–9	note found among extracts from books	1877–8
	200–206	IV	before 1870
	207–8	VIII	after 1878
	208–29	IV	before 1870

(pp. 211–12 and 218, notes from MS. II, 1870)

	Pages	Manuscript	Date
Part Two			
	233–42	IV	before 1870
	242–424	II	1870
Part Three			
	427–34	II	1870
	435–65	VIII	1878
	465–70	II	1870
	470–71	VIII	1878
	471–4	II	1870
	474–97	VIII	1878
	498–513	II	1870
	513–56	VIII	1878
	556–64	II	1870
	565–99	VIII	1878

Capital

Volume Two

Part One

The Metamorphoses
of Capital and their
Circuit

Chapter 1: The Circuit of Money Capital

The circuit of capital comprises three stages. As we have depicted them in Volume 1, these form the following series:

First stage: The capitalist appears on the commodity and labour markets as a buyer; his money is transformed into commodities, it goes through the act of circulation $M-C$.

Second stage: Productive consumption by the capitalist of the commodities purchased. He functions as capitalist producer of commodities; his capital passes through the production process. The result: commodities of greater value than their elements of production.

Third stage: The capitalist returns to the market as a seller; his commodities are transformed into money, they pass through the act of circulation $C-M$.

Thus the formula for the circuit of money capital is

$$M-C\ldots P\ldots C'-M'.$$

The dots indicate that the circulation process is interrupted, while C' and M' denote an increase in C and M as the result of surplus-value.

In Volume 1, the first and third stages were discussed only in so far as this was necessary for the understanding of the second stage, the capitalist production process. Thus the different forms with which capital clothes itself in its different stages, alternately assuming them and casting them aside, remained uninvestigated. These will now be the immediate object of our inquiry.

In order to grasp these forms in their pure state, we must first of all abstract from all aspects that have nothing to do with the change and constitution of the forms as such. We shall therefore assume here, both that commodities are sold at their values, and that the circumstances in which this takes place do not change. We shall also ignore any changes of value that may occur in the course of the cyclical process.[1]

1. This introductory section is taken from Manuscript II.

I. FIRST STAGE. M–C[2]

M–C represents the conversion of a sum of money into a sum of commodities; the buyer transforms his money into commodities, the sellers their commodities into money. What makes this particular act of commodity circulation a part of the whole process with a well-defined function in the independent circuit of an individual capital is not primarily the form of the act, but rather its material content, the specific use character of the commodities that change place with money. These are on the one hand means of production, on the other, labour-power, the material and the personal factors of commodity production; their precise nature must of course depend on the type of article to be produced. If we call labour-power L, means of production mp and the sum of commodities to be purchased C, then we have $C = L + mp$. To abbreviate, $C{<}{L \atop mp}$. The act M–C, considered in respect of its content, is thus represented by M–$C{<}{L \atop mp}$; M–C breaks up into M–L and M–mp. The money M divides into two portions, one for the purchase of labour-power, the other for means of production. The two sets of purchases pertain to completely different markets: one to the commodity market proper, the other to the labour market.

But apart from this qualitative division of the commodities into which M is transformed, M–$C{<}{L \atop mp}$ also exhibits a most characteristic quantitative relationship.

We know that the value or price of labour-power is paid to its proprietor, who offers it for sale as a commodity, in the form of wages, i.e. as the price of a sum of labour that contains surplus labour. Thus, if the value of a day's labour-power is 3 shillings, the product of five hours' labour, this sum may figure in the contract between buyer and seller as the price or wage for perhaps ten hours' labour. If a contract of this kind is made with fifty workers, they have to provide the buyer with a total of 500 hours' labour each day, half of this – 250 hours, or twenty-five ten-hour working-days – consisting simply of surplus labour. The means of production to be purchased must be sufficient in quantity and volume to employ this amount of labour.

Thus M–$C{<}{L \atop mp}$ does not simply express the qualitative relationship

2. From here Manuscript VII, begun 2 July 1878.

in which a certain sum of money, e.g. £422, is transformed into means of production and labour-power of a corresponding sum, but also a quantitative ratio between the portions of the money spent on labour-power L and on means of production mp, this ratio being conditioned from the start by the excess or surplus labour that the number of workers involved have to expend.

If the weekly wages of fifty workers in a spinning mill come to £50, for example, then it will be necessary to spend £372 on means of production, if this is the value of the means of production that a working week of 3,000 man-hours, 1,500 of these being surplus labour, transforms into yarn.

The degree to which the expenditure of excess labour requires an excess value in the form of means of production is quite unimportant here. The point is simply that under all circumstances the part of the money that is spent on means of production – the means of production bought in M–mp – must be sufficient, i.e. must be reckoned up from the start and be provided in appropriate proportions. To put it another way, the means of production must be sufficient in mass to absorb the mass of labour which is to be turned into products through them. If sufficient means of production are not present, then the surplus labour which the purchaser has at his disposal cannot be made use of; his right to dispose of it will lead to nothing. If more means of production are available than disposable labour, then these remain unsaturated with labour, and are not transformed into products.

Once the movement M–$C{<}{\begin{smallmatrix}L\\mp\end{smallmatrix}}$ is completed, the purchaser does not merely have at his disposal the means of production and labour-power needed to produce a useful article. He has also a greater capacity to set labour-power in motion, or a greater quantity of labour, than is needed to replace the value of the labour-power, as well as the means of production that are required to realize or objectify this amount of labour. He thus controls the factors of production for articles of a greater value than their elements of production, for a mass of commodities containing surplus-value. The value that he has advanced in the form of money thus now exists in a natural form in which it can be realized as value which breeds surplus-value (in the shape of commodities). In other words, it exists in the state or form of *productive capital*, with the ability to function as creator of value and surplus-value. We call capital in this form P.

The value of P, however, equals the value of $L+mp$, that of the money M transformed into $L+mp$. M is the same capital value as P, only in a different mode of existence, i.e. capital value in the state or form of money – *money capital*.

$M-C{<}^{L}_{mp}$, or $M-C$ in its general form, a sum of commodity purchases – this act of general commodity circulation is thus at the same time, as a stage in the independent circuit of capital, the transformation of capital value from its money form into its productive form, or more briefly the transformation of money capital into productive capital. In the first figure of the circuit to be considered here, money appears as the original bearer of the capital value, and hence money capital appears as the form in which capital is advanced.

As money capital, it exists in a state in which it can perform monetary functions, in the present case the functions of general means of purchase and payment. (The latter, in that although labour-power is bought beforehand, it is paid for only after it has done its work. In so far as the means of production are not readily available on the market, but have to be ordered, money also functions as means of payment in $M-mp$.) Money capital does not possess this capacity because it is capital, but because it is money.

On the other hand, the capital value in its monetary state can perform only monetary functions, and no others. What makes these into functions of capital is their specific role in the movement of capital, hence also the relationship between the stage in which they appear and the other stages of the capital circuit. In the present case, for instance, money is converted into commodities which in their combination constitute the natural form of productive capital; this form therefore already bears latently within it, as its possibility, the result of the capitalist production process.

A part of the money that performs the function of money capital in $M-C{<}^{L}_{mp}$ passes over, by accomplishing this very circulation, into a function in which its capital character vanishes though its money character remains. The circulation of money capital M breaks up into $M-mp$ and $M-L$, purchase of means of production and purchase of labour-power. Let us consider the latter process by itself. $M-L$, on the capitalist's part, is the purchase of labour-power; it is the sale of labour-power on the part of the worker, the owner of labour-power (we can say 'labour' here, as the wage form is presupposed). What is $M-C(M-L)$ for the purchaser, is here, as in every sale, $L-M(C-M)$ for the seller (the worker), in this case the sale of his labour-power. The latter is for the seller of labour the first stage of circulation, or the first metamorphosis of the commodity (Volume 1, Chapter 3, 2, a); it is the transformation of his commodity into its money form. The worker spends the money thus received bit by bit on a sum of commodities that satisfy his needs, on articles of consumption. The overall circulation of his commodity thus presents itself as $L-M-C$, i.e. firstly $L-M(C-M)$ and secondly $M-C$, i.e. in the general form of simple commodity circulation $C-M-C$, where money figures simply as an evanescent means of circulation, as merely mediating the conversion of one commodity into another.

$M-L$ is the characteristic moment of the transformation of money capital into productive capital, for it is the essential condition without which the value advanced in the money form cannot really be transformed into capital, into value-producing surplus-value. $M-mp$ is necessary only in order to realize the mass of labour bought by way of $M-L$. This is why $M-L$ was presented from this point of view in Volume 1, Part Two, 'The Transformation of Money into Capital'. Here we have to consider the matter from a further aspect, with special reference to money capital as a form of appearance of capital.

$M-L$ is generally regarded as characteristic of the capitalist mode of production. But this is in no way for the reason just given, i.e. because the purchase of labour-power is a contract of sale which determines that a greater quantity of labour is provided than is necessary to replace the price of the labour-power, the wage; i.e. because surplus labour is provided, which is the basic condition for the capitalization of the value advanced, or, what comes to the same thing, for the production of surplus-value. It is rather on account of its form, because in the form of wages labour is bought *with money*, and this is taken as the characteristic feature of a 'money economy'.

Here again, it is not the irrationality of the form that is taken as characteristic. This irrationality is rather overlooked. The irrationality consists in the fact that labour as the value-forming element cannot itself possess any value, and so a certain quantity of labour cannot have a value that is expressed in its price, in its equivalence with a certain definite quantity of money. We know, however, that wages are simply a disguised form, a form in which the price of a day's labour-power, for example, presents itself as the price of the labour set in motion in the course of a day by this labour-power, so that the value produced by this labour-power in six hours' labour, say, is expressed as the value of its twelve-hour functioning or labour.

$M-L$ is taken as the characteristic feature or hallmark of the so-called money economy because labour appears here as the commodity of its possessor, and hence money as its buyer – in other words because of the money relation (sale and purchase of human activity). But money appears very early on as a buyer of so-called services, without its being transformed into money capital, and without any revolution in the general character of the economy.

It is quite immaterial, as far as the money is concerned, what sort of commodities it is transformed into. Money is the universal equivalent form of all commodities, which already show in their prices that they ideally represent a specific sum of money, expect to be transformed into money, and only receive the form in which they can be converted into use-values for their possessor by changing places with money. Thus once labour-power is found on the market as a commodity, its sale taking place in the form of a payment for labour, in the wage form, then its sale and purchase is no more striking than the sale and purchase of any other commodity. What is characteristic is not that the commodity labour-power can be bought, but the fact that labour-power appears as a commodity.

By way of $M\text{–}C{<}{L \atop mp}$, the transformation of money capital into productive capital, the capitalist effects a connection between the objective and the personal factors of production, in so far as these factors consist of commodities. If money is to be transformed for the first time into productive capital, or to function as money capital for the first time for its possessor, then he must first buy the means of production, i.e. buildings, machines, etc. before he buys labour-power; for when the labour-power passes into his control, the means of production must also be present before it can be applied as labour-power.

This is how the matter presents itself from the capitalist's side.

From the worker's side, the productive application of his labour-power is possible only when this has been associated with the means of production, as the result of its sale. Before the sale, this labour-power exists in a state of separation from the means of production, from the objective conditions of its application. In this state of separation, it can be directly used neither for the production of use-values for its possessor, nor for the production of commodities which he could live from selling. But as soon as it is associated with the means of production, by being sold it forms a component of the productive capital of its buyer just as much as the means of production do.

Hence, although in the act $M\text{–}L$ the possessor of money and the possessor of labour-power relate to each other only as buyer and seller, confront each other as possessor of money and possessor of a commodity, and are thus from this point of view simply in a money relationship with each other, the buyer appears right from the start as the possessor of the means of production which form the objective conditions for the productive expenditure of labour-power by its possessor. In other words, these means of production confront the possessor of labour-power as someone else's property. The buyer, conversely, is confronted by the seller of labour as another's labour-power which must pass into his control, and has to be incorporated into his capital in order for this really to function as productive capital. The class relation between capitalist and wage-labourer is thus already present, already presupposed, the moment that the two confront each other in the act $M-L$ ($L-M$ from the side of the worker). This is a sale and purchase, a money relation, but a sale and purchase in which it is presupposed that the buyer is a capitalist and the seller a wage-labourer; and this relation does in fact exist, because the conditions for the realization of labour-power, i.e. means of subsistence and means of production, are separated, as the property of another, from the possessor of labour-power.

We are not concerned here with how this separation arises. If $M-L$ takes place, it already exists. What is important here is that, if $M-L$ appears as a function of money capital, or money appears here as a form of existence of capital, then this is in no way simply because money is involved here as the means of payment for a human activity with a useful effect, for a service; thus in no way because of money's function as means of payment. Money can be spent in this form only because labour-power is found in a state of separation from its means of production (including the means of subsistence as means of production of labour-power itself); and because this separation is abolished only through the sale of labour-power to the owner of the means of production, a sale which signifies that the buyer is now in control of the continuous flow of labour-power, a flow which by no means has to stop when the amount of labour necessary to reproduce the price of labour-power has been performed. The capital relation arises only in the production process because it exists implicitly in the act of circulation, in the basically different economic conditions in which buyer and seller confront one another, in their class relation. It is not the nature of money that gives rise to this relation; it is rather the existence of the relation that can transform a mere function of money into a function of capital.

In the conception of money capital we customarily find two inter-connected errors (for the time being we only deal with money capital in connection with the specific function in which it confronts us here). Firstly, the functions that capital value performs as money capital, and which it is able to perform because it happens to be in the money form, are erroneously ascribed to its character as capital, whereas they are simply due to the money state of the capital value, its form of appearance as money. Secondly, and inversely, the specific content of the money function that makes it simultaneously a function of capital is deduced from the nature of money (money is here confused with capital), whereas this function presupposes social conditions, as here in the act $M-L$, that are in no way given simply by commodity circulation and the money circulation corresponding to it.

The purchase and sale of slaves is also in its form a purchase and sale of commodities. Without the existence of slaves, however, money cannot fulfil this function. If there is slavery, then money can be spent on the acquisition of slaves. But money in the hand of the buyer is in no way a sufficient condition for the existence of slavery.

If the sale of one's own labour-power (in the form of the sale of one's own labour, or the wage form) is not an isolated phenomenon, but the socially decisive precondition for the production of commodities, i.e. if money capital performs the function here considered, $M-C\mathord{<}^{L}_{mp}$, throughout society, this fact implies the occurrence of historic processes through which the original connection between means of production and labour-power was dissolved; processes as a result of which the mass of the people, the workers, come face to face with the non-workers, the former as non-owners, the latter as the owners, of these means of production. It is quite irrelevant whether the original connection, before it was destroyed, took the form that the worker belonged together with the other means of production as a means of production himself, or whether he was their owner.

Thus the situation that underlies the act $M-C\mathord{<}^{L}_{mp}$ is one of distribution; not distribution in the customary sense of distribution of the means of consumption, but rather the distribution of the elements of production themselves, with the objective factors concentrated on one side, and labour-power isolated from them on the other.

The means of production, the objective portion of productive capital, must thus already face the worker as such, as capital, before the act $M-L$ can become general throughout society.

We have already seen* how capitalist production, once it is established, not only reproduces this separation in the course of its development, but also expands on an ever greater scale until it has become the generally prevailing social condition. But this also has another side to it. For capital to be formed and to take hold of production, trade must have developed to a certain level, hence also commodity circulation and, with that, commodity production; for articles cannot go into circulation as commodities except in so far as they are produced for sale, i.e. as commodities. It is only on the basis of capitalist production that commodity production appears as the normal, prevailing character of production.

The Russian landowners, who in consequence of the so-called emancipation of the peasants now conduct their farming with wage-labourers instead of with the forced labour of serfs, have two complaints. Firstly, they complain of the lack of money capital. They say for example that before the harvest is sold, the wage-labourers have to be paid a considerable amount, and the basic condition for this, a supply of ready cash, is lacking. Capital in the form of money must constantly be available, precisely for the payment of wages, in order that production may be conducted on a capitalist basis. But the landlords need not worry. Everything comes to those who wait, and in time the industrial capitalist will have at his disposal not only his own money, but also *l'argent des autres*.†

The second complaint is more typical, namely that, even when they have money, the labour-power to be bought is not available in sufficient quantity and at the right time. This is because the Russian agricultural worker, owing to the common ownership of the soil by the village community, is not yet fully separated from his means of production, and is thus still not a 'free wage-labourer' in the full sense of the term. But the presence of such 'free wage-labourers' throughout society is the indispensable condition without which $M-C$, the transformation of money into commodities, cannot take the form of the transformation of money capital into productive capital.

It goes without saying, therefore, that the formula for the circuit of money capital: $M-C\ldots P\ldots C'-M'$, is the self-evident form of the circuit of capital only on the basis of already developed capitalist production, because it presupposes the availability of the class of wage-

* See *Capital* Volume 1, Parts Seven and Eight, particularly Chapter 32.

† Other people's money. For Marx's definition of 'industrial capital' in this sense see below, p. 133.

labourers in sufficient numbers throughout society. As we have seen, capitalist production produces not only commodities and surplus-value; it reproduces, and on an ever extended scale, the class of wage-labourers, and transforms the immense majority of direct producers into wage-labourers. Since the first precondition of $M-C...P...C'-M'$ is the continuous availability of the class of wage-labourers, it already implies the existence of capital in the form of productive capital, and hence the form of the circuit of productive capital.

2. SECOND STAGE. THE FUNCTION OF PRODUCTIVE CAPITAL

The circuit of capital being considered here begins with the act of circulation $M-C$, the transformation of money into commodities, i.e. purchase. This circulation must therefore be supplemented by the opposite metamorphosis $C-M$, the transformation of commodities into money, i.e. sale. But the direct result of $M-C\begin{smallmatrix}L\\mp\end{smallmatrix}$ is an interruption in the circulation of the capital value advanced in the money form. By the transformation of money capital into productive capital, the capital value has received a natural form in which it cannot circulate any further, but has to go into consumption, that is into productive consumption. The use of labour-power, labour, can be realized only in the labour process. The capitalist cannot sell the worker again as a commodity, for he is not his slave, and the capitalist has bought nothing more than the utilization of his labour-power for a certain time. He can make use of this labour-power only in so far as it enables him to make use of the means of production to fashion commodities. The result of the first stage is thus capital's entry into the second stage, its productive stage.

The movement presents itself as $M-C\begin{smallmatrix}L\\mp\end{smallmatrix}...P$, the dots indicating that the circulation of capital is interrupted; but its circuit continues, with its passage from the sphere of commodity circulation into that of production. The first stage, the transformation of money capital into productive capital, thus appears as no more than the prelude and introduction to the second stage, the function of productive capital.

$M-C\begin{smallmatrix}L\\mp\end{smallmatrix}$ presupposes that the individual who performs this act does not just have at his disposal values in some useful form or other, but that he possesses these values in money form, that he is the possessor of money. The act, however, consists precisely in letting go of money, and the possessor of money can only remain so in so far as the money will implicitly flow back to him as a result of the very act of letting go of it. This act thus presupposes that he is a commodity producer.

$M-L$. The wage-labourer lives only from the sale of his labour-power. Its maintenance – his own maintenance – requires daily consumption. His payment must therefore be constantly repeated at short intervals, to enable him to repeat the purchases – the act $L-M-C$ or $C-M-C$ – that are needed for this self-maintenance. Hence the capitalist must constantly confront him as money capitalist, and his capital as money capital. On the other hand, however, in order that the mass of direct producers, the wage-labourers, may perform the act $L-M-C$, they must constantly encounter the necessary means of subsistence in purchasable form, i.e. in the form of commodities. Thus this situation in itself demands a high degree of circulation of products as commodities, i.e. commodity production on a large scale. As soon as production by way of wage-labour becomes general, commodity production must be the general form of production. Assuming this to be the case, commodity production in turn brings about an ever growing division of social labour, i.e. an ever greater specialization of the products produced as commodities by particular capitalists, an ever greater division of complementary production processes into independent ones. $M-mp$ therefore develops to the same degree as $M-L$, i.e. the production of means of production is separated to the same extent from the production of the commodities whose means of production they are; these too confront each commodity producer as commodities which he does not himself produce, but buys for the purpose of his particular production process. They come from branches of production that are pursued in complete separation and independence from his own, and enter his branch of production as commodities, which must therefore be bought. The material conditions of commodity production confront him to an ever greater extent as the products of other commodity producers, as commodities. The capitalist must appear to the same extent as a money capitalist, i.e. his capital must function in a greater measure as money capital.

On the other hand, the same circumstance that produces the basic condition for capitalist production, the existence of a class of wage-labourers, encourages the transition of all commodity production to capitalist commodity production. To the extent that the latter develops, it has a destroying and dissolving effect on all earlier forms of production, which, being pre-eminently aimed at satisfying the direct needs of the producers, only transform their excess products into commodities. It makes the sale of the product the main interest, at first without apparently attacking the mode of production itself; this was for example the first effect of capitalist world trade on such peoples as the Chinese, Indians, Arabs, etc. Once it has taken root, however, it destroys all forms of commodity production that are based either on the producers' own labour, or simply on the sale of the excess product as a commodity. It firstly makes commodity production universal, and then gradually transforms all commodity production into capitalist production.[3]

Whatever the social form of production, workers and means of production always remain its factors. But if they are in a state of mutual separation, they are only potentially factors of production. For any production to take place, they must be connected. The particular form and mode in which this connection is effected is what distinguishes the various economic epochs of the social structure. In the present case, the separation of the free worker from his means of production is the given starting point, and we have seen how and under what conditions the two come to be united in the hands of the capitalist – i.e. as his capital in its productive mode of existence. The actual process which the personal and material elements of commodity formation, brought together in this way, enter into with each other, the process of production, therefore itself becomes a function of capital – the capitalist production process, whose nature we have gone into in detail in the first volume of this work. All pursuit of commodity production becomes at the same time pursuit of the exploitation of labour-power; but only capitalist commodity production is an epoch-making mode of exploitation, which in the course of its historical development revolutionizes the entire economic structure of society by its organization of the labour process and its gigantic extension of technique, and towers incomparably above all earlier epochs.

By the different roles that they play during the production process in connection with the formation of value, and thus in the creation of surplus-value, means of production and labour-power, in so far as they are forms of existence of the capital value advanced, are distinguished as constant and variable capital. They are further distinguished, as

3. Up to here Manuscript VII. From here Manuscript VI.

different components of productive capital, by the fact that the means of production, once in the possession of the capitalist, remain his capital even outside the production process, whereas labour-power becomes the form of existence of an individual capital only within this process. If labour-power is only a commodity in the hands of its seller, the wage-labourer, it only becomes capital in the hands of its buyer, the capitalist, to whom falls its temporary use. The means of production, for their part, become objective forms of productive capital, or productive capital proper, only from the moment that labour-power, as the personal form of existence of productive capital, can be incorporated into them. The means of production are no more capital by nature than is human labour-power. They receive this specific social character only under certain particular conditions that have historically developed, just as it is only under such conditions that precious metals are stamped with the character of money, or money with that of money capital.

In the course of its functioning, productive capital consumes its own components, to convert them into a mass of products of a higher value. Since labour-power operates only as an organ of capital, the excess value with which surplus labour endows the product, over and above that of its constituent elements, is also the fruit of capital. Labour-power's surplus labour is labour performed gratis for capital, and hence forms surplus-value for the capitalist, a value that costs him no equivalent. The product is therefore not only a commodity, but a commodity impregnated with surplus-value. Its value is $P+s$, the value of the productive capital P consumed in its production plus that of the surplus-value s it engenders. Let us suppose that this commodity consists of 10,000 lb of yarn, with means of production to the value of £372 and labour-power to the value of £50 used up in its production. During the spinning process, the spinners transferred to the yarn the value of the means of production consumed in the process by means of their labour, £372, while they simultaneously produced a new value of, say, £128, corresponding to their expenditure of labour. The 10,000 lb. of yarn is therefore the bearer of a value of £500.

3. THIRD STAGE. C′–M′

Commodities become *commodity capital* as the functional form of existence of the already valorized capital value that has arisen directly from the production process itself. If commodity production were carried out on a capitalist basis throughout the whole society, then every commodity would be from the start the element of a commodity capital, whether it consisted of pig-iron or Brussels lace, sulphuric acid or cigars. The problem as to which varieties out of the host of commodities are destined by their properties for the rank of capital, and which others for common commodity service, is one of the charming vexations that scholastic economics inflicts on itself.

In commodity form, capital must perform commodity functions. The articles it consists of, which are produced from the start for the market, must be sold, transformed into money, and thus pass through the movement $C-M$. The capitalist's commodity consists of 10,000 lb. of cotton yarn. If means of production to a value of £372 were consumed in the spinning process, and a new value of £128 created, then the yarn has a value of £500, expressed in its corresponding price. This price is to be realized by the sale $C-M$. What is it that makes this simple act of all commodity circulation simultaneously a function of capital? It cannot be a change undergone in the act itself, neither with respect to its useful character, for it is as an object of use that the commodity passes to the buyer, nor with respect to its value, for this does not suffer a change of magnitude, but only one of form. It first existed in yarn, and now exists in money. There is thus an essential distinction between the first stage $M-C$ and the final stage $C-M$. Formerly the money advanced functioned as money capital because it was converted through circulation into commodities with a specific use-value. Now the commodity can function as capital only in so far as it actually brings this character with it from the production process, before its circulation begins. During the spinning process the spinners created yarn to the value of £128, of which £50, say, was simply an equivalent to the capitalist for his outlay on labour-power, and £78 formed surplus-value – a rate of exploitation of labour-power of 156 per cent. The value of the 10,000 lb. of yarn thus contains, firstly, the value of the consumed productive capital P, its constant part being £372, its variable part £50 and their sum £422 = 8,440 lb. of yarn. The value of the productive capital P is equal to C, the value of its formative elements, which in the stage $M-C$ confronted the capitalist as commodities in the hands of their sellers. Secondly, however, the value of the yarn contains a surplus-value of £78 = 1,560 lb. of yarn. Thus as the value expression of the 10,000 lb. of yarn, $C = C+\Delta C$, C plus an increment (£78) which we shall call c, as it exists in the same commodity form as the original value now does.*

* We have chosen to adhere here to the traditional English symbolism for Marx's categories, even at the risk of perpetuating a possible source of confusion. Since

The value of 10,000 lb. of yarn, £500, is thus $C+c = C'$. What makes C, as the value expression of the 10,000 lb. of yarn, into C' is not the absolute amount of its value (£500), for this is determined, like the value expression of any other sum of commodities, by the amount of labour objectified in it. It is rather the relative magnitude of its value, its value compared with the value of the capital P consumed in its production. The value contained in it is this value plus the surplus-value provided by the productive capital. Its value is greater, i.e. it exceeds the capital value P, by the surplus-value c. The 10,000 lb. of yarn is the bearer of a capital value which has been valorized, enriched with a surplus-value, and this is because it is the product of the capitalist production process. C' expresses a value ratio, the ratio of the value of the commodity product to that of the capital consumed in its production, i.e. it expresses the composition of its value out of capital value and surplus-value. The 10,000 lb. of yarn are commodity capital, C', only as the transformed form of the productive capital P, thus in a relationship that exists at first only in the circuit of this individual capital, or for the capitalist who has produced yarn with his capital. It is so to speak only an internal relation, not an external one, that makes the 10,000 lb. of yarn, as bearer of value, into commodity capital. The yarn bears its capitalist birth-mark not in the absolute magnitude of its value, but in its relative magnitude, in the magnitude of its value compared with the value of the productive capital contained in it before it was transformed into commodities. If the 10,000 lb. of yarn is sold at its value of £500, this act of circulation, considered in itself, is $C-M$, the simple transformation of a value that remains the same from the commodity form into the money form. However, as a particular stage in the circuit of an individual capital, this same act is the realization of a capital value of £422 plus a surplus-value of £78, both borne by the commodity, i.e. $C'-M'$, the transformation of the capital value from its commodity form into the money form.[4]

The function of C' is now that of every commodity product, to be transformed into money and sold, to pass through the phase of circulation $C-M$. As long as the now valorized capital persists in the form of commodity capital, is tied up on the market, the production process

---

C, M and P are used for the three forms of industrial capital in its circuit, 'c' has to be used for the increment to C, i.e. the surplus-value in its commodity form. However, c, v and s are conventionally used in English for constant capital, variable capital and surplus-value, and this trio reappears later in Volume 2.

4. Up to here Manuscript VI. From here Manuscript V.

stands still. The capital operates neither to fashion products nor to form value. According to the varying speed with which the capital sheds its commodity form and assumes its money form, i.e. according to the briskness of the sale, the same capital value will serve to a very uneven degree in the formation of products and value, and the scale of the reproduction will expand or contract. It was shown in the first volume that the degree of effectiveness of a given capital is conditioned by forces in the production process that are to a certain extent independent of its own magnitude.* Now we see that the circulation process sets in motion new forces independent of the magnitude of value, which affect the degree of effectiveness of the capital, its expansion and its contraction.

The mass of commodities C', as bearer of the valorized capital, must fully undergo the metamorphosis $C'-M'$. The quantity sold is here the essential determinant. The individual commodity figures only as an integral part of the total quantity. The value of £500 exists in 10,000 lb. of yarn. If the capitalist succeeds in selling only 7,440 lb., at its value of £372, then he has only replaced the value of his constant capital, the value of the means of production consumed; if he sells 8,440 lb., then he still replaces only the value of the total capital advanced. He must sell more, if he is to realize surplus-value, and he must sell the entire 10,000 lb. of yarn if he is to realize the whole surplus-value of £78 (=1,560 lb. of yarn). He receives in the £500 only an equal value for the commodities sold; his transaction within the circulation sphere is simply $C-M$. If he had paid his workers £64 instead of £50, then his surplus-value would be only £64, instead of £78, and the rate of exploitation only 100 per cent instead of 156 per cent. But the value of his yarn would be unchanged; only the ratio of its various component portions would be different; the circulation act $M-C$ would still be the sale of 10,000 lb. of yarn for £500, its value.

$C' = C + c$ (=£422+£78). C is equal in value to P or the productive capital, and this is also equal in value to the M advanced in $M-C$, the purchase of the elements of production: in our example, £422. If the mass of commodities is sold at its value, then $C =$ £422, and $c =$ £78, the value of the surplus product of 1,560 lb. of yarn. If we call c, expressed in monetary terms, m, we have $C'-M'$, or $(C+c)-(M+m)$, and the circuit $M-C \ldots P \ldots C'-M'$ in its expanded form is thus

$$M-C{<}^{L}_{mp}\ldots P\ldots(C+c)-(M+m).$$

*See *Capital* Volume 1, Chapter 24, 4, pp. 747 ff.

In the first stage, the capitalist withdraws articles of use, both from the commodity market proper and from the labour market; in the third stage he puts commodities back, though only into one market, the commodity market proper. But if he withdraws more value from the market by way of his commodities than he originally put into it, this is only because he puts in a greater value of commodities than he originally withdrew. He puts in the value M and withdraws the same value C; he puts in $C+c$, and withdraws the same value $M+m$. In our example, M was equal in value to 8,440 lb. of yarn; the capitalist, however, puts 10,000 lb. of yarn into the market, i.e. gives back a greater value than he took from it. On the other hand, he has only put in this increased value because he produced surplus-value (as an aliquot part of the product, expressed in surplus product) in the production process, by the exploitation of labour-power. It is only as the product of this process that the mass of commodities is commodity capital, the bearer of the valorized capital value. By accomplishing $C'-M'$, the capital value advanced is realized together with the surplus-value. The two are realized together in the sale, either by stages or at one stroke, of the total mass of commodities, expressed as $C'-M'$. However, the same circulation process $C'-M'$ differs for the capital value and for the surplus-value in so far as it expresses in each case a different stage of their circulation, a different section in the series of metamorphoses that they have to pass through within the circulation sphere. The surplus-value, c, first came into the world within the production process. It is thus now entering the commodity market for the first time, and moreover in the commodity form; this is its first form of circulation, and hence the act $c-m$ is its first act of circulation or its first metamorphosis, which thus still has to be supplemented by the opposite circulation act, the converse metamorphosis $m-c$.[5]

It is a different matter with the circulation accomplished by the capital value C in the same circulation act $C'-M'$, which for it is the circulation act $C-M$, where $C = P$, equal to the originally advanced M. This started its first act of circulation as M, money capital, and it now returns to the same form via the act $C-M$; it has thus passed through the two opposing phases of circulation (1) $M-C$ and (2) $C-M$, and exists once again in the form in which it can begin the same cyclical process afresh. The transformation from the commodity form to the money

5. This holds irrespective of the manner in which we divide up capital value and surplus-value. 10,000 lb. of yarn contain 1,560 lb. = £78 surplus-value, but 1 lb. of yarn = 1 shilling also contains 2·496 oz. = 1·872 d. surplus-value.

form, which is for the surplus-value its first transformation, is for the capital value its return or transformation back into its original money form.

The money capital was converted into a sum of commodities of equal value, L and mp, by way of $M-C{<}^{L}_{mp}$. These commodities now no longer function as commodities, as articles for sale. Their value now exists in the hands of their buyer, the capitalist, as the value of his productive capital P. And in the function of P, productive consumption, they are transformed into a kind of commodity materially different from the means of production, into yarn, with the value not only being maintained, but increased, from £422 to £500. Through this real metamorphosis, the commodities withdrawn from the market in the first stage $M-C$ are replaced by materially different commodities of different value, which must now fur.ction as commodities, be transformed into money and sold. Hence the production process appears simply as an interruption in the circulation of capital value, which up till then has only passed through the first phase $M-C$. It passes through the second and final phase, $C-M$, with C altered both materially and in value. But as far as the capital value taken by itself is concerned, all it has undergone in the production process is a change in its use form [*Gebrauchsform*]. It existed as £422 of value in L and mp, and it now exists as £422, the value of 8,440 lb. of yarn. Thus if we simply consider the two phases of the circulation process of the capital value, separately from its surplus-value, it passes through (1) $M-C$ and (2) $C-M$, where the second C has a changed form, but the same value, as the first C; we thus have $M-C-M$, a form of circulation which, by way of a two-fold displacement in opposite directions, the transformation of money into commodities and commodities into money, necessarily determines the return of the value advanced as money to its money form: its transformation back into money.

The same act of circulation $C'-M'$, which is the second and concluding metamorphosis for the capital value advanced in money, its return to the money form, is, for the surplus-value that is simultaneously borne along by the commodity capital, and realized together with it when it is converted into the money form, its first metamorphosis, the transformation from the commodity form into the money form, $C-M$, the first phase of circulation.

Two things should be noted here. Firstly, the ultimate transformation of capital value back into its original money form is a function of commodity capital. Secondly, this function includes the first formal trans-formation of the surplus-value from its original commodity form into the money form. The money form plays a double role here; on the one hand it is the returning form of a value originally advanced in money, i.e. the money returns to the form of value that opened the process; on the other hand it is the first transformed form of a value that originally enters into circulation in the commodity form. If the commodities of which the commodity capital consists are sold at their value, as we assume here, then $C+c$ is transformed into $M+m$ with the same value; it is in this last form, $M+m$ (£422+£78 = £500), that the realized commodity capital now exists in the hands of the capitalist. Capital value and surplus-value now exist as money, i.e. in the form of the universal equivalent.

At the end of the process, the capital value is thus once again in the same form in which it entered it, and can therefore open the process afresh and pass through it as money capital. And indeed because the initial and concluding form of the process is that of money capital (M), we call this form of the circuit the circuit of money capital. It is not the form of the value advanced, but only its magnitude, that is changed at the end.

$M+m$ is nothing more than a sum of money of a certain magnitude, in our case £500. But as the result of the circuit of capital, as realized commodity capital, this sum of money contains the capital value and the surplus-value; moreover, these are no longer inextricably entwined, as in the yarn; they are now simply juxtaposed. Their realization has given each of the two an independent money form. 211/250 of the money is the capital value, £422, and 39/250 the surplus-value of £78. This separation effected by the realization of the commodity capital does not only have the formal content we shall speak of in a moment; it is important in the reproduction process of capital, according to whether m is added on to M in its entirety, in part, or not at all, thus according to whether or not it continues to function as a component of the capital value advanced. M and m can even pass through quite different circulations.

In M', the capital returns once more to its original form M, its money form, but in a form in which it has been realized as capital.

Firstly, there is a quantitative difference. It was M, £422; it is now M', £500, and this difference is expressed in $M \ldots M'$, the quantitatively different extremities of the circuit, the actual movement of which is indicated simply by the dots. M' is greater than M; M' minus $M = s$, the surplus-value. But all that exists as the result of the cycle $M \ldots M'$ is M'; the process of formation has been obliterated in the product. M' now exists independently in its own right, it is independent of the movement that produced it. The movement is past, and M' is there in its place.

But as $M+m$, £422 advanced capital plus an increment of £78 on the same, M' or £500 also exhibits a qualitative relation, although this qualitative relation itself exists only as a relation between the parts of a corresponding sum, i.e. as a quantitative ratio. M, the capital advanced, which is once again present in its original form (£422), exists now as realized capital. It has not only maintained itself, but it has also realized itself as capital, in so far as it has differentiated itself from m (£78), which is related to it as *its* increase, *its* fruit, an increment that it itself has bred. It is realized as capital, because it is value that has bred value. M' exists as a capital relation; M no longer appears as mere money, but is expressly postulated as money capital, expressed as value that has valorized itself, i.e. thus also possesses the property of valorizing itself, of breeding more value than it itself has. M is posited as capital by its relation to another part of M' as to something posited by itself, as to the effect of which it is the cause, as to the consequence of which it is the ground. M' thus appears as a sum of values which is internally differentiated, undergoes a functional (conceptual) self-differentiation, and expresses the capital-relation.

But this is expressed simply as a result, without the mediation of the process whose result it is.

Portions of value are not qualitatively distinguished from each other as such, save in so far as they appear as the values of different articles, concrete things, thus in various different useful forms, as values of different bodies of commodities – a distinction that does not arise from their existence as mere portions of value. In money, every difference between commodities is obliterated, because money is precisely the equivalent form common to all of them. A sum of money of £500 consists of nothing but isomorphous elements of £1. Since the mediating effect of its history is obliterated in the simple existence of this sum of money, and every trace of the specific difference which the various component parts of capital possess in the production process has vanished, the only remaining distinction is the crude, non-conceptual*

---

* The word *begrifflich*, which appears here in the original, is clearly inappropriate, in view of the general sense of the passage. We have therefore assumed that Marx intended to write *begriffslos*.

distinction between a 'principal', as it is called in English, i.e. the capital of £422 which was advanced, and an additional sum of value of £78. Let M' be £110, of which £100 is M, the principal, and £10 is s, surplus-value. There is absolute homogeneity, a complete absence of conceptual distinction, between the two constituent parts of the sum of £110. Any £10 is always one eleventh of the total sum of £110, whether it is a tenth of the principal advanced, or the additional £10 over and above this. Principal and increment, capital and surplus, can therefore both be expressed as fractions of the total sum; in our example ten elevenths is the principal or capital, and one eleventh the surplus. At the conclusion of its process the realized capital therefore appears as a sum of money, within which the distinction between principal and surplus expresses, in a naïve, non-conceptual manner, the capital-relation.

This is also true, moreover, for C' ($=C+c$). But with the difference that C', in which C and c are simply proportional value portions of the same homogeneous mass of commodities, indicates its origin in P, whose direct product it is, whereas in M', a form arising directly from the circulation sphere, the direct connection with P has vanished.

The superficial distinction between principal and increment that is contained in M', in so far as this expresses the result of the movement $M \ldots M'$, vanishes immediately, as soon as M' functions actively once more as money capital, rather than being fixed as the money expression of the valorized industrial capital. The circuit of money capital can never begin with M', but only with M (even though it is M' that now functions as M); i.e. never as an expression of the capital relation, but only as the form in which the capital value is advanced. As soon as the £500 is advanced afresh as capital, in order to be valorized once more, it is the starting-point rather than the point of return. Instead of a capital of £422, one of £500 has now been advanced; more money than before, more capital value, but the relation between the two components has gone. The sum of £500 now functions as capital, rather than £422, just as, originally, a sum of £500 might have functioned, rather than a sum of £422.

It is not the active function of money capital to present itself as M'; its own presentation as M' is rather a function of C'. Already in simple commodity circulation, (1) C_1-M, (2) $M-C_2$, M functions actively only in the second act $M-C_2$; its presentation as M is only the result of the first act, by virtue of which it first appears as the transformed form of C_1. The capital relation contained in M', the connection between one of its parts as a part of capital value and the other as the value increment to this, does receive a functional significance, however, in so far as M' divides into two circulations, the circulation of capital and the circulation of surplus-value, when the circuit $M...M'$ is constantly repeated. The two parts M and m then fulfil functions that differ not just quantitatively, but also qualitatively. Considered in itself, however, the form $M...M'$ does not include the consumption of the capitalist, but expressly only capital's self-valorization and accumulation, in so far as the latter is first expressed in the periodic growth of the money capital that is constantly advanced afresh.

Although it is a crude and conceptually undifferentiated form of capital, $M' = M+m$ is at the same time money capital in its first realized form, money that has bred money. This must be distinguished from the function of money capital in the first stage $M-C{<}^{L}_{mp}$. In this first stage, M circulates as money. It functions as money capital simply because it is only in its monetary state that it performs a monetary function, and can be converted into the elements of P that face it as commodities, L and mp. In this act of circulation, it functions only as money; but because this act is the first stage of capital value in process, it is simultaneously a function of money capital, by virtue of the specific useful form of the commodities L and mp that are bought. M' on the other hand, composed of M, the capital value, and m, the surplus-value created by it, expresses valorized capital value, the purpose and the result, the function of the total process of the circuit of capital. If it expresses this result in money form, as realized money capital, this is not because it is the money form of capital, *money* capital, but rather the reverse, because it is money *capital*, capital in the money form, and that it was in this form that capital opened the process, was advanced in its money form. The transformation back into the money form is a function of the commodity capital C', as we saw, not of money capital. And as far as the difference m between M' and M is concerned, this is only the money form of c, the increment to C; M' is only equal to $M+m$ because C' equals $C+c$. In C', therefore, this difference, and the relation between the capital value and the surplus-value bred by it, is present and is expressed before they are both transformed into M', into a sum of money in which the two portions of value confront each other from a position of independence and can therefore also be applied to independent and different functions.

M' is only the result of the realization of C'. Both of these, C' as well as M', are only different forms, the commodity form and the money form, of the valorized capital value; both have it in common that they are valorized capital value. Both are realized capital, because here capital value exists as such together with surplus-value as the fruit that is separate from it but produced by it, although this relation is expressed only in the naïve form of the ratio between two parts of a sum of money or a commodity value. As expressions of capital, however, both related to and distinct from the surplus-value created by it, i.e. as expressions of valorized value, M' and C' are the same, and express the same thing, only in different forms; they are not distinguished from each other as money capital and commodity capital, but rather as money and commodity. In so far as they represent valorized value, capital active as capital. they simply express the result of the function of productive capital, the only function in which capital value breeds value. What they have in common is that both of them, money capital and commodity capital, are modes of existence of capital. The one is capital in its money form, the other in its commodity form. The specific functions that distinguish them can thus be nothing other than distinctions between the money function and the commodity function. The commodity capital, as the direct product of the capitalist production process, recalls its origin and is therefore more rational in its form, less lacking in conceptual differentiation, than the money capital, in which every trace of this process has been effaced, just as all the particular useful forms of commodities are generally effaced in money. Hence it is only when M' itself functions as commodity capital, when it is the direct product of a production process and not the transformed form of this product, that its bizarre form disappears – i.e. in the production of the money material itself. The formula for the production of gold, for example, would be $M-C{<}^{L}_{mp}\ldots P\ldots M'\,(M+m)$, where M' figures as the commodity product in so far as P provides more gold than was advanced for the elements of production of gold in the first M, the money capital. The expression $M\ldots M'\,(M+m)$ is irrational, in that, within it, part of a sum of money appears as the mother of another part of the same sum of money. But here this irrationality disappears.

4. THE CIRCUIT AS A WHOLE

We have seen how the circulation process, after its first phase $M-C{<}^{L}_{mp}$ has elapsed, is interrupted by P, in which the commodities bought on the market, L and mp, are consumed as material and value components of the productive capital; the product of this consumption is a new commodity, M', altered both materially and in value. The interrupted circulation process, $M-C$, must be supplemented by $C-M$. But it is C' that appears as the bearer of this second and concluding phase, a commodity different materially and in value from the original C. The circulation series thus presents itself as (1) $M-C_1$; (2) C'_2-M', in which the first commodity C_1 has been replaced in the second phase by one of higher value and a different useful form, C'_2, during the interruption that is occasioned by the function of P, i.e. the production of C' from the elements of C, the forms of existence of the productive capital P. The first form of appearance in which we met with capital, on the other hand (Volume 1, Chapter 4), $M-C-M'$ (broken down: (1) $M-C_1$; (2) C_1-M'), exhibits the same commodity twice over. It is the same commodity into which money is transformed in the first phase and which is transformed back into more money in the second phase. Despite this essential difference, both circulations have in common that in their first phase money is transformed into commodities and in their second phase commodities into money, that the money that is spent in the first phase flows back again in the second. On the one hand they have in common this stream of money back to its starting-point, on the other hand the excess of the money that flows back over that advanced. In this respect, $M-C\ldots C'-M'$ too appears to be contained in the general formula $M-C-M'$.

It further results here that in both metamorphoses pertaining to the circulation sphere, $M-C$ and $C'-M'$, equally large and simultaneously present values always confront and replace each other. The change in value belongs solely to the metamorphosis P, the production process, which thus appears as the real metamorphosis of capital, as opposed to the merely formal metamorphoses of the circulation sphere.

Let us now consider the total movement $M-C\ldots P\ldots C'-M'$, or its expanded form $M-C\begin{smallmatrix}L\\<\\mp\end{smallmatrix}\ldots P\ldots C'(C+c)-M'(M+m)$. Here capital appears as a value that passes through a sequence of connected and mutually determined transformations, a series of metamorphoses that form so many phases or stages of a total process. Two of these phases belong to the circulation sphere, one to the sphere of production. In each of these phases the capital value is to be found in a different form, corresponding to a different and special function. Within this movement the value advanced not only maintains itself, but it grows, increases its magnitude. Finally, in the concluding stage, it returns to the same form in which it appeared at the outset of the total process. This total process is therefore a circuit.

The two forms that the capital value assumes within its circulation stages are those of *money capital* and *commodity capital*; the form pertaining to the production stage is that of *productive capital*. The capital that assumes these forms in the course of its total circuit, discards them again and fulfils in each of them its appropriate function, is *industrial capital* – industrial here in the sense that it encompasses every branch of production that is pursued on a capitalist basis.

Money capital, commodity capital and productive capital thus do not denote independent varieties of capital, whose functions constitute the content of branches of business that are independent and separate from one another. They are simply particular functional forms of industrial capital, which takes on all three forms in turn.

The circuit of capital proceeds normally only as long as its various phases pass into each other without delay. If capital comes to a standstill in the first phase, $M-C$, money capital forms into a hoard; if this happens in the production phase, the means of production cease to function, and labour-power remains unoccupied; if in the last phase, $C'-M'$, unsaleable stocks of commodities obstruct the flow of circulation.

It lies in the nature of the case, however, that the circuit itself determines that capital is tied up for certain intervals in the particular sections of the cycle. In each of its phases industrial capital is tied to a specific form, as money capital, productive capital or commodity capital. Only after it has fulfilled the function corresponding to the particular form it is in does it receive the form in which it can enter a new phase of transformation. In order to make this clear, we have assumed in our example that the capital value of the mass of commodities created in the production stage is equal to the total value originally advanced as money, in other words that the whole capital value advanced as money moves all at once from one stage into the subsequent one. We have already seen, however (Volume 1, Chapter 8), that a part of the constant capital, the actual instruments of labour (e.g. machines), serve continuously throughout a greater or smaller number of repetitions of the same production process, and for this reason give up their value to the product only bit by bit. We shall show later on how far this circumstance modifies the circuit of capital. The following will suffice for the time being. In our example, the value of the productive capital, £422, contained only the average calculated wear and tear of factory buildings, machinery, etc., thus only the portion of value that they carry over in the course of transforming 10,000 lb. of raw cotton into 10,000 lb. of yarn, the product of a weekly spinning process of sixty hours. The instruments of labour – buildings, machinery, etc. – therefore figured in the means of production into which the constant capital advanced was transformed, as if they were simply hired on the market in return for a weekly payment. This however alters absolutely nothing as far as the substance of the matter is concerned. We need only multiply the weekly output of yarn, 10,000 lb., by the number of weeks contained in a given series of years, and the entire value of the instruments of labour bought and used up in this period will have been carried over. It is clear then that the money capital advanced must first be transformed into these means of production, and must therefore have made its exit from the first phase $M-C$, before it can function as productive capital P. It is just as clear in our example that the capital value of £422, which is incorporated into the yarn during the production process, cannot enter into the circulation phase $C'-M'$ as a component of the 10,000 lb. of yarn before the process is finished. The yarn cannot be sold until it has been spun.

In the general formula, the product of P is considered as a material thing different from the elements of the productive capital, an object that has an existence of its own, apart from the production process, possessing a useful form different from that of the elements of production. In so far as the result of the production process does appear as a thing, this is always the case, even when a part of the product enters once more as an element into the renewed production process. Thus grain serves as seed-corn for its own production, but the product consists only of grain, and thus has a different physical shape from the elements applied together with it: labour-power, instruments of labour, fertilizer. There are however particular branches of industry in which the product of the production process is not a new objective product, a commodity. The only one of these that is economically important is the communication industry, both the transport industry proper, for moving commodities and people, and the transmission of mere information – letters, telegrams, etc.

A. Chuprov says on this point:

'The manufacturer can produce articles first and look for customers afterwards.' (His product, after it is ejected in finished form from the production process, passes into circulation as a commodity separate from this process.) 'Production and consumption thus appear as two acts separated in time and space. In the transport industry, however, which does not create new products, but only displaces people and things, these two acts coincide; the services' (the change of place) 'are necessarily consumed the moment they are produced. This is why the area within which railways can seek their customers is at most 50 versts' (53 km.) 'on either side.'[6]

The result in each case, whether it is people or commodities that are transported, is a change in their spatial location, e.g. that the yarn finds itself in India instead of in England, where it was produced.

But what the transport industry sells is the actual change of place itself. The useful effect produced is inseparably connected with the transport process, i.e. the production process specific to the transport industry. People and commodities travel together with the means of transport, and this journeying, the spatial movement of the means of transport, is precisely the production process accomplished by the transport industry. The useful effect can only be consumed during the production process; it does not exist as a thing of use distinct from this process, a thing which functions as an article of commerce and circulates as a commodity only after its production. However the exchange-value of this useful effect is still determined, like that of any other commodity, by the value of the elements of production used up in it (labour-power and means of production), plus the surplus-value created by the surplus labour of the workers occupied in the transport industry. In respect of its consumption, too, this useful effect behaves just like other commodities. If it is consumed individually, then its value vanishes with its consumption; if it is consumed productively, so that it is itself a stage of production of the commodity that finds itself transported, then its value is carried over to the commodity as an addition to it. The formula for the transport industry is thus $M-C<^{L}_{mp}\ldots P\ldots M'$, for it is the production process itself, and not a product separable from it, that is paid for and consumed. This therefore has almost exactly the same form as that for the production of precious metals, except that M' is here the transformed form of the useful effect produced in the course of the production process, and not the natural form of the gold and silver that is produced during this process and ejected from it.

Industrial capital is the only mode of existence of capital in which not

6. A. Chuprov, *Zhelyeznodorozhnoye Khozyaistvo* [*The Railway Industry*], Moscow, 1875, pp. 69, 70.

only the appropriation of surplus-value or surplus product, but also its creation, is a function of capital. It thus requires production to be capitalist in character; its existence includes that of the class antagonism between capitalists and wage-labourers. To the degree that it takes hold of production, the technique and social organization of the labour process are revolutionized, and the economic-historical type of society along with this. The other varieties of capital which appeared previously, within past or declining conditions of social production, are not only subordinated to it and correspondingly altered in the mechanism of their functioning, but they now move only on its basis, thus live and die, stand and fall together with this basis. Money capital and commodity capital, in so far as they appear and function as bearers of their own peculiar branches of business alongside industrial capital, are now only modes of existence of the various functional forms that industrial capital constantly assumes and discards within the circulation sphere, forms which have been rendered independent and one-sidedly extended through the social division of labour.

On the one hand, the circuit $M \ldots M'$ is inextricably linked with the general circulation of commodities, issues from it and flows back into it, forming a part of it. On the other hand, it forms for the individual capitalist an independent movement peculiar to his capital value, a movement which proceeds in part within the general circulation of commodities, in part outside it, but which always retains its independent character. It does so firstly because both of the phases that it goes through in the circulation sphere, $M–C$ and $C–M$, possess a functionally specific character as phases of the movement of capital; in $M–C$, C is determined in its material content as labour-power and means of production; in $C'–M'$ the capital value is realized together with the surplus-value. In the second place, P, the production process, includes productive consumption. Thirdly, the return of money to its starting-point makes the movement $M \ldots M'$ a cyclical movement complete in itself.

On the one hand, therefore, each individual capital, in the two halves of its circulation $M–C$ and $C'–M'$, is an agent of the general circulation of commodities, in which it functions and of which it forms a link, either as money or as commodity. Hence it is a member of the general series of metamorphoses of the commodity world. On the other hand, it describes its own independent circuit within the general circulation, one in which the sphere of production forms a transitional stage, and in which it returns to its starting-point in the same form in which it left it. Within its own circuit, which includes its real metamorphosis in the production process, the magnitude of its value also changes. It returns not only as money value, but as increased and expanded money value.

If we finally consider $M-C...P...C'-M'$ as a special form of the circuit of capital, alongside the other forms that will be investigated later on, it is marked by the following features.

1. It appears as the *circuit of money capital* because industrial capital in its money form, as money capital, forms the starting-point and the point of return of the whole process. The formula itself expresses that the money is not spent here as money, but is only advanced, and is thus simply the money form of capital, money capital. It further expresses the fact that it is the exchange-value, not the use-value, that is the decisive inherent purpose of the movement. It is precisely because the money form of value is its independent and palpable form of appearance that the circulation form $M...M'$, which starts and finishes with actual money, expresses money-making, the driving motive of capitalist production, most palpably. The production process appears simply as an unavoidable middle term, a necessary evil for the purpose of money-making. (This explains why all nations characterized by the capitalist mode of production are periodically seized by fits of giddiness in which they try to accomplish the money-making without the mediation of the production process.)*

2. In this circuit, the stage of production, the function of P, forms an interruption in the circulation process $M-C...C'-M'$, whose two phases are in turn only a mediation of simple circulation $M-C-M'$. The production process here appears formally and explicitly, in the actual form of the circuit itself, for what it actually is in the capitalist mode of production, a mere means for the valorization of the value advanced; i.e. enrichment as such appears as the inherent purpose of production.

3. Because the sequence of phases is opened by $M-C$, $C'-M'$ is the second term in the circulation; the starting-point is M, the money capital to be valorized, the conclusion M', the valorized money capital $M+m$, in which M figures alongside its offshoot m as realized capital. This distinguishes the circuit of money capital from the two other circuits P and C', and in two ways. On the one hand, through the money form of the two extremes; money is the independent and palpable form of existence of value, the value of the product in its independent value form, in which all trace of the commodities' use-value has been effaced. On the other hand, the form $P...P$ does not necessarily become $P...$

*The sentence in parentheses was introduced by Engels in the second (1893) edition.

$P'(P+p)$, while in the form $C' \ldots C'$, no value difference at all is visible between the two extremes. It is thus characteristic of the formula $M \ldots M'$, on the one hand, that the capital value forms the starting-point and the valorized capital the point of return, so that the advancing of the capital value appears as the means, the valorized capital value as the goal of the whole operation; on the other hand, that this relation is expressed in the money form, the independent value form, hence money capital as money breeding money. The creation by value of surplus-value is not only expressed as the alpha and omega of the process, but explicitly presented in the glittering money form.

4. Since M', the money capital realized as the result of $C'-M'$, the complementary and concluding phase of $M-C$, exists in absolutely the same form as that in which it opened its first circuit, it can, as it emerges from this, reopen the same circuit as augmented (accumulated) money capital, $M' = M+m$; at least it is in no way expressed in the form of $M \ldots M'$ that the circulation of m separates itself from that of M when the circuit is repeated. Considered by itself in isolation, from the formal standpoint, the circuit of money capital thus expresses only the process of valorization and accumulation. Consumption, therefore, is expressed in it only as productive consumption, $M-C<^{L}_{mp}$; this is all that is accounted for in this circuit of the individual capital. $M-L$ is $L-M$ or $C-M$ from the point of view of the worker, i.e. the first phase of the circulation that mediates his individual consumption: $L-M-C$ (means of subsistence). The second phase, $M-C$, no longer falls within the circuit of the individual capital; but it is introduced by it and presupposed by it, for the worker, in order to continue to exist on the market as exploitable material for the capitalist, must before all else keep alive, and therefore maintain himself by individual consumption. This consumption itself, however, is assumed here only as a precondition for the productive consumption of labour-power by capital, thus only in so far as the worker maintains and reproduces himself as labour-power by his individual consumption. The means of production (mp), however, the actual commodities that are involved in the circuit, are simply the means of nourishment for productive consumption. The act $L-M$ mediates the individual consumption of the worker, the transformation of means of subsistence into his flesh and blood. But the capitalist must also exist, thus also live and consume, in order to function as capitalist. In actual fact, he needs to consume only as a worker, and hence no more than this is assumed in this form of the circulation process. But

even this is not expressed formally, since the formula closes with M', i.e. a result that can function again immediately as increased money capital.

$C'-M'$ directly contains the sale of C'; but $C'-M'$, which is from one side a sale, is $M-C$, a purchase, from the other side, and in the last instance commodities are bought only for the sake of their use-value (we ignore intermediate transactions here), in order to enter the process of consumption, either individual or productive, according to the nature of the article bought. This consumption, however, does not enter the circuit of the individual capital of which C' is the product; the product C' is precisely ejected from the circuit as a commodity to be sold. It is expressly destined for the consumption of others. We therefore find among the exponents of the Mercantile System* (which is based on the formula $M-C...P...C'-M'$) long sermons to the effect that the individual capitalist should consume only in his capacity as a worker, and that a capitalist nation should leave the consumption of its commodies and the consumption process in general to other more stupid nations, while making productive consumption into its own life's work. These sermons are often reminiscent in both form and content of analogous ascetic exhortations by the Fathers of the Church.

*

The circuit of capital is thus a unified process of circulation and production, it includes both. In so far as the two phases $M-C$ and $C'-M'$ are processes of circulation, the circulation of capital forms part of the general circulation of commodities. But by taking part in functionally determined sections or stages in the circuit of capital, which do not just pertain to the sphere of circulation, but also to that of production, capital performs its own circuit within the general circulation of commodities. This general circulation enables it, in the first stage, to assume the form in which it can function as productive capital; in the second stage, to cast off the commodity function in which it cannot renew its circuit; it equally gives it the possibility of separating its own capital circuit from the circulation of the surplus-value that has adhered to it.

---

* Marx did not leave a systematic examination of the Mercantile System as he conceived it, although he devotes a few paragraphs to it in *A Contribution to the Critique of Political Economy*, London, 1971, pp. 157–9. The view he attributes to the Mercantilists is expressed clearly by D'Avenant in *An Essay on the East-India Trade*, London, 1697, quoted by Marx in *Theories of Surplus-Value*, Part I, p. 179: 'By what is consum'd at Home, one loseth only what another gets, and the Nation in General is not at all the Richer; but all Foreign Consumption is a clear and certain Profit.'

The circuit of money capital is thus the most one-sided, hence most striking and characteristic form of appearance of the circuit of industrial capital, in which its aim and driving motive – the valorization of value, money-making and accumulation – appears in a form that leaps to the eye (buying in order to sell dearer). The fact that the first phase is $M–C$ displays the provenance of the components of productive capital on the commodity market. It also shows that the capitalist production process is conditioned by circulation, trade. The circuit of money capital is not just commodity production; it only comes into being by way of circulation, and presupposes this. This is already shown by the fact that the form M pertaining to circulation appears as the first and pure form of the capital value advanced, which is not the case with the two other forms of the circuit.

The circuit of money capital remains the permanent general expression of industrial capital, in so far as it always includes the valorization of the value advanced. In $P\ldots P$, the money expression of the capital emerges only as the price of the elements of production, thus only as value expressed in money of account, the form in which it is found in book-keeping.

$M\ldots M'$ becomes a particular form of the circuit of industrial capital in so far as newly appearing capital is first advanced as money and is withdrawn in the same form, whether on its transfer from one branch of business to another, or when industrial capital is withdrawn from business altogether. This includes the capital function of the surplus-value first advanced in the money form, and emerges most strikingly when this functions in a business other than that from which it origininates. $M\ldots M'$ can be the first circuit of a capital, it can be its last; it can be taken as the form of the total social capital; it is the form of capital that is newly invested, whether as newly accumulated capital in the money form, or old capital that is completely transformed into money in order to be transferred from one branch of production to another.

As a form that is comprised in all circuits, money capital performs this circuit precisely for that part of the capital that creates surplus-value, the variable capital. The normal form of advance for wages is payment in money; this process must be steadily repeated at short intervals, as the worker lives from hand to mouth. Hence the worker must constantly come face to face with the capitalist as money capitalist, and with his capital as money capital. Here there can be no question, as in the purchase of means of production and the sale of productive commodities, of a direct or indirect balancing of accounts (so that the greater part of money capital actually figures only in the form of commodities, money only in the form of money of account, and finally cash only for the settlement of the balances). On the other hand, a part of the surplus-value arising from the variable capital is spent by the capitalist for his personal consumption; this pertains to the retail trade, and, after however roundabout a journey, is ultimately spent as cash, in the money form of the surplus-value. Whether this part of the surplus-value is great or small in no way affects the matter. The variable capital constantly appears anew as money capital invested in wages $(M-L)$, and m as surplus-value that is spent to defray the personal needs of the capitalist. Thus both M, as the variable capital value advanced, and m, as its increment, are necessarily retained in the money form, to be spent as such.

The formula $M-C...P...C'-M'$, with the result $M' = M+m$, contains in its form a certain deception; it bears an illusory character that derives from the existence of the advanced and valorized value in its equivalent form, in money. What is emphasized is not the valorization of the value, but the *money form* of this process, the fact that more value in the money form is finally withdrawn from the circulation sphere than was originally advanced to it, i.e. the increase in the mass of gold and silver belonging to the capitalist. The so-called Monetary System* is simply the expression of the superficial form $M-C-M'$, a movement that proceeds exclusively in the circulation sphere, and hence can only explain the two acts (1) $M-C$ and (2) $C-M'$ by saying that C in the second act is sold above its value, and therefore withdraws more money from the circulation sphere than was cast into it by its purchase. On the other hand, however, $M-C...P...C'-M'$, when regarded as the exclusive form, is the basis for the more developed Mercantile System, in which it is not simply the circulation of commodities but also their production that appears as a necessary element.

The illusory character of $M-C...P...C'-M'$, and the corresponding

---

*The Monetary System (sometimes called bullionism) preceded the Mercantile System or mercantilism. Marx describes the Mercantile System as a 'variant' of the Monetary System. He distinguishes the two most clearly in the *Grundrisse* (Pelican edition, p. 327): 'The Monetary System had understood the autonomy of value only in the form in which it arose from simple circulation – *money* ... Then came the Mercantile System, an epoch where industrial capital and hence wage labour arose in manufactures ... The Mercantilists already have faint notions of money as capital, but actually again only in the form of money, of the circulation of *mercantile* capital.'

illusory significance it is given, is there as soon as this form is regarded as the sole form, not as one that flows and is constantly repeated; i.e. as soon as it is taken not just as one of the forms of the circuit, but rather as its exclusive form. In itself, however, it refers to other forms.

Firstly, this whole circuit presupposes the capitalist character of the production process, and hence this production process itself as a basis, as well as the specific social relations determined by it. $M-C = M-C{<}{L \atop mp}$, but $M-L$ implies that the wage-labourer, and therefore the means of production too, are a part of the productive capital; hence the labour and valorization process, the production process is already a function of capital.

Secondly, if $M...M'$ is repeated, the return to the money form appears just as evanescent as the money form in the first stage. $M-C$ vanishes, in order to make way for P. The permanently repeated advance in money, as well as its permanent return in money, themselves appear simply as evanescent moments in the circuit.

Thirdly,

$$M-C...P...C'-M'.\,M-C...P...C'-M'.\,M-C...P...\ \text{etc.}$$

With the second repetition of the circuit, we already have the circuit $P...C'-M'.\,M-C...P$, before the second circuit of M is even complete, and thus all further circuits can be considered in the form $P...C'-M-C...P$; $M-C$, therefore, as the first phase of the first circuit, simply forms an evanescent prelude to the constantly repeated circuit of productive capital, as is in fact the case when industrial capital is invested for the first time, in the form of money capital.

Furthermore, before the second circuit is complete, the first circuit $C'-M'.\,M-C...P...C'$ (abbreviated $C'...C'$) has been described, the circuit of commodity capital. Thus the first form already contains the two others, and the money form vanishes, in so far as it is not just an expression of value, but an expression of value in the equivalent form, in money.

Finally, if we take a newly appearing individual capital, which describes the circuit $M-C...P...C'-M'$ for the first time, then $M-C$ is a preparatory phase, the precursor of the first production process performed by this individual capital. This phase $M-C$ is therefore not the presupposition, but is rather posited or conditioned by the production process. However, this holds only for this individual capital. The general form of the circuit of industrial capital is the circuit of money capital, in so far as the capitalist mode of production is presupposed, i.e. within a specific state of society determined by capitalist production. Hence the capitalist production process is the basic pre-condition, it is prior to all else, if not within the first circuit of the money capital of a newly invested industrial capital, then outside it; the continued existence of this production process assumes the constantly repeated circuit of $P \ldots P$. This assumption is already made within the first stage $M-C\genfrac{}{}{0pt}{}{L}{mp}$, in so far as this stage presupposes on the one hand the existence of the class of wage-labourers, and on the other hand what is the first stage $M-C$ for the purchaser of the means of production, and $C'-M'$ for their seller. It presupposes, therefore, that C' is commodity capital, and therefore that the commodity itself is the result of capitalist production; with this we must also presuppose the function of productive capital.

Chapter 2: The Circuit of Productive Capital

The circuit of productive capital has the general formula:

$$P \ldots C'-M'-C \ldots P.$$

It signifies the periodically repeated function of the productive capital, i.e. reproduction. In other words it signifies that its production process is a reproduction process in respect of valorization; not only does production occur, but also the periodic reproduction of surplus-value. It signifies that the function of the industrial capital that exists in its productive form does not take place once and for all, but is periodically repeated, so that the new beginning is given by the point of departure itself. A part of C' (in certain cases, in the investment branches of industrial capital) may directly re-enter, as means of production, the same labour process from which it emerged as a commodity; all this does is circumvent the need to transform its value into real money or money tokens; in other words the only independent expression it receives is as money of account. This part of the value does not enter the circulation process. The same holds for the part of C' that the capitalist consumes in kind, as part of the surplus product. This is however insignificant for capitalist production; at most it comes into consideration in agriculture.

Two things about this form immediately catch the eye.

Firstly, while in the first form, $M \ldots M'$, the production process, the function of P, interru᷉ the circulation of money capital and appears only as mediator between its two phases $M-C$ and $C'-M'$, here the entire circulation process of industrial capital, its whole movement within the circulation phase, merely forms an interruption, and hence a mediation, between the productive capital that opens the circuit as the first extreme and closes it in the same form as the last extreme, i.e. in the form of its new beginning. Circulation proper appears only as the mediator of the reproduction that is periodically repeated and made continuous through this repetition.

Secondly, the entire circulation presents itself in the opposite form from that which it possessed in the circuit of money capital. There it was $M–C–M$ ($M–C. C–M$), disregarding the value determination; here, again disregarding the value determination, it is $C–M–C$ ($C–M. M–C$), i.e. the form of simple commodity circulation.

I. SIMPLE REPRODUCTION

Let us consider first of all the process $C'–M'–C$ that runs its course between the extremes $P...P$ in the sphere of circulation.

The starting-point of this circulation is the commodity capital: $C' = C+c = P+c$. The function of the commodity capital $C'–M'$ (the realization of the capital value P contained in it, which now exists as a commodity component C, as well as of the surplus-value it contains, which exists as a component of the same commodity mass with the value c) was treated in the first form of the circuit. There, however, it formed the second phase of the interrupted circulation, and the concluding phase of the entire circuit. Here it forms the second phase of the circuit, but only the first phase of circulation. The first circuit ends with M', and since M', just as much as the original M, can reopen the second circuit as money capital, it was at first unnecessary to see whether the M and m (surplus-value) contained in M' continue their paths together, or whether they describe different paths. This would only have been necessary if we had pursued the first circuit further, in its repetition. But in the circuit of productive capital this point must be decided, since the very definition of the first circuit depends on it, and because $C'–M'$ appears in it as the first phase of circulation, which is to be supplemented by $M–C$. It depends on this decision whether the formula depicts simple reproduction or reproduction on an expanded scale. The character of the circuit is altered according to this decision.

Let us therefore start by taking the simple reproduction of the productive capital, in which connection we assume, as in the first chapter, that other circumstances remain the same and that commodities are bought and sold at their values. On this assumption, the entire surplus-value goes into the personal consumption of the capitalist. As soon as the commodity capital C' has been transformed into money, the part of the money that represents the capital value goes on circulating in the circuit of industrial capital; the other part, which is surplus-value turned into gold, goes into the general circulation of commodities; it is money circulation proceeding from the capitalist, but it takes place outside the circulation of his individual capital.

In our example, we had a commodity capital C' of 10,000 lb. of yarn to the value of £500. £422 of this was the value of the productive capital, and continues the capital circulation begun with C' as the money form of 8,440 lb. of yarn, while the surplus-value of £78, the money form of 1,560 lb. of yarn, the excess portion of the commodity product, makes its exit from this circulation and describes a separate path within the general circulation of commodities.

$$C'\begin{pmatrix} C \\ + \\ c \end{pmatrix} \begin{matrix} - \\ - \\ - \end{matrix} M'\begin{pmatrix} M \\ + \\ m \end{pmatrix} \begin{matrix} -C<^{\textstyle L}_{\textstyle mp} \\ \\ -c \end{matrix}$$

m–c is a series of purchases made with the money that the capitalist spends, whether on commodities as such or on services, for his esteemed self and family. These purchases are fragmented, and take place at different times. The money thus exists temporarily in the form of a money reserve or hoard destined for current consumption, since it is in the form of a hoard that any money whose circulation is interrupted exists. In its function as a means of circulation, which also includes its temporary form of a hoard it does not enter into the circulation of the capital in its money form M. The money is not advanced, but spent.

We have assumed that the total capital advanced is constantly passing from one of its phases into another, and that here, therefore, the commodity product of P carries the total value of the productive capital P, £422, plus the surplus-value created during the production process, £78. In our example, where we are concerned with a discrete commodity product, the surplus-value exists in the form of 1,560 lb. of yarn; just as it exists as 2·496 ounces in each lb. of yarn. If however the commodity product was a machine worth £500, for example, and with the same value composition, then there would certainly still be a portion of the machine's value that equalled the £78 surplus-value, but this £78 would exist only in the total machine; this could not be divided into capital value and surplus-value without being broken into pieces and thus destroying its value together with its use-value. The two value components could thus be depicted only ideally as components of the physical body of the commodity, not as independent elements of the commodity C', in the way that each lb. of yarn can be depicted as a separate, independent commodity element of the 10,000 lb. In the one case, the total commodity or commodity capital, the machine, must be sold in its entirety before *m* can embark on its own particular circulation. But if the capitalist sells 8,440 lb. of yarn, in the other case, then the sale of the remaining 1,560 lb. exhibits a completely separate circulation of the surplus-value in the form *c* (1,560 lb. of yarn)–*m* (£78)–*c* (articles of consumption). The value elements of each individual portion of the yarn product of 10,000 lb., moreover, can be depicted as parts of the product just as much as the total product can. Just as the 10,000 lb. of yarn can be partitioned into constant capital value (*c*), 7,440 lb. of yarn with a value of £372, variable capital value (*v*), 1,000 lb. of yarn with a value of £50, and surplus-value (*s*), 1,560 lb. of yarn with a value of £78, so each lb. of yarn can be partitioned into *c*, 11·904 ounces with a value of 8·298 d., *v*, 1·600 ounces with a value of 1·200 d., and *s*, 2·496 ounces of yarn with a value of 1·872 d.* The capitalist can therefore successively consume the elements of surplus-value contained in the 10,000 lb. of yarn by its successive sale in successive portions, and also successively realize the sum of *c*+*v* in this way. But this operation similarly presupposes that the entire 10,000 lb. is sold, and that the value of *c* and *v* is therefore replaced by the sale of 8,440 lb. (Volume 1, Chapter 9, 2).

However this might be, by way of *C′–M′* both the capital value and the surplus-value contained in *C′* acquire a separable existence, the existence of different sums of money; both *M* and *m* are in each case actually the transformed form of the value that originally possessed its own expression merely as the price of the commodity, i.e. a merely ideal expression.

c–m–c is simple commodity circulation, the first phase of which, *c–m*, is included in the circulation of the commodity capital *C′–M′*, and therefore in the circuit of capital; its complementary phase *m–c*, on the other hand, falls outside this circuit, as a separate process of general commodity circulation. The circulation of *C* and *c*, capital value and surplus-value, divides after the transformation of *C′* into *M′*. It follows from this:

Firstly, that when the commodity capital is realized by way of *C′–M′*, i.e. *C′–(M+m)*, the movement of capital value and surplus-value which, in *C′–M′*, was still common to both, and was borne by the same mass of commodities, becomes divisible, as the two now possess independent forms as sums of money.

Secondly, if this division takes place, with *m* being spent by the

---

* See above, p. 122, note.

capitalist as revenue, while M continues the path prescribed for it by the circuit as the functional form of capital value, the first act $C'-M'$, together with the subsequent acts $M-C$ and $m-c$, can be depicted as two different circulations: $C-M-C$ and $c-m-c$; both of these, in their general form, are series that belong to the ordinary commodity circulation.

Moreover, it happens in practice that where commodities are continuous in their physical composition, and hence indivisible, the value components are isolated ideally. In the London building trade, for example, which is conducted for the most part on credit, the contractor receives advances in various stages as the building of the house progresses. None of these stages is a house; each of them is rather a really existing component of a future house that is coming into being; despite its reality, it is thus only an ideal fraction of the whole house, but it is sufficiently real, all the same, to serve as security for an additional advance. (For more on this subject see Chapter 12 below.)

Thirdly, if the common movement of capital value and surplus-value in C and M only divides in part (so that a part of the surplus-value is not spent as revenue), or not at all, then a change in capital value takes place within the circuit of the capital value itself, before the circuit is completed. In our example, the value of the productive capital was £422. If $M-C$ continues as £480, for example, or £500, then it traverses the final stages of the circuit as a value £58 or £78 greater than it originally was. This can also occur in combination with a change in its value composition.

$C'-M'$, the second stage of circulation and the concluding stage of circuit I $(M...M')$, is the second stage of the present circuit and the first stage of commodity circulation in it. In so far as circulation comes into consideration, it must thus be supplemented by $M'-C'$. However $M'-C'$ does not just have the process of valorization already behind it (in this case the function of P, the first stage), but its result, the commodity product C', has already been realized. The valorization of capital, as well as the realization of the commodity product in which the valorized capital value is represented, thus ends with $C'-M'$.

We have assumed simple reproduction, i.e. that $m-c$ completely separates off from $M-C$. Since both circulations, $c-m-c$ and $C-M-C$, belong in their general form to commodity circulation (and thus do not exhibit any difference in value between their extremes), it is quite easy to conceive the capitalist production process, as the vulgar economists* do,

* See above, p. 101, note.

as the simple production of commodities, use-values destined for consumption of some kind or other, which the capitalist produced only in order to replace them with commodities of a different use-value, or to exchange them with these, as vulgar economics incorrectly puts it.

C' appears from the start as commodity capital, and the aim of the entire process, enrichment (valorization), by no means excludes a growth in the capitalist's consumption in line with the increase in the magnitude of surplus-value. In fact it absolutely includes it.

In the circulation of the capitalist's revenue, the commodity which has been produced, C (or the corresponding ideal fraction of the commodity product C'), serves in point of fact only to convert this revenue into money and from money into a series of other commodities for the purpose of private consumption. But in this connection one should not overlook the little fact that c is a commodity value which has not cost the capitalist anything; it is the embodiment of surplus labour, which originally stepped forth onto the stage as a component of the commodity capital C'. This c is thus itself already linked in its existence to the circuit of the capital value in process, and if this comes to a halt or is disturbed in some way, it is not only the consumption of c that is restricted, or completely ceases, but in addition the market for the set of commodities that form the replacement for c. This is similarly the case if $C'-M'$ goes awry or only a portion of C' can be sold.

We have seen that $c-m-c$, as the circulation of the capitalist's revenue, enters into the capital circulation only in so far as c is a value portion of C', capital in its functional form as commodity capital. But as soon as it becomes independent through $m-c$, thus in the form as a whole, $c-m-c$, it does not enter into the movement of the capital advanced by the capitalist, even though it proceeds from this. It is related to it in so far as the existence of capital presupposes the existence of the capitalist, and this latter is conditional on his consumption of surplus-value.

Within the general circulation, C' functions for example as yarn, simply as a commodity; but as a moment of the circulation of capital it functions as *commodity capital*, a form that the capital value alternately assumes and discards. When the yarn is sold to the merchant it is removed from the circuit of that capital whose product it is, but still continues as a commodity in the orbit of general circulation. The circulation of this mass of commodities continues, even though it has ceased to form a moment in the independent circuit of the capital of the spinner. The really definitive metamorphosis of the mass of commodities thrown into circulation by the capitalist, $C-M$, its final abandonment to consumption, can thus be completely separated in time and space from the metamorphosis in which this mass of commodities functions as his commodity capital. The same metamorphosis that has already been accomplished in the circulation of this capital remains still to be completed in the sphere of the general circulation.

Nothing is changed if the yarn now enters the circuit of another industrial capital. The general circulation includes the intertwining of the circuits of the various independent fractions of the social capital, i.e. the totality of individual capitals, as well as the circulation of those values that are not placed on the market as capital, in other words those going into individual consumption.

The relation between the circuit of capital as it forms part of general circulation, and as it provides the links in an independent circuit, is further displayed if we consider the circulation of $M' = M + m$. M, as money capital, continues the circuit of capital. m, spent as revenue ($m-c$), goes into the general circulation, but is cast out of the circuit of capital. Only that part of it enters the latter circuit that functions as additional money capital. In $c-m-c$, money functions simply as coin; the purpose of this circulation is the individual consumption of the capitalist. Vulgar economics shows its characteristic cretinism by the way that it depicts this circulation, which does not enter into the circuit of capital – the circulation of the portion of the value product that is consumed as revenue – as the characteristic circuit of capital.

In the second phase, $M-C$, the capital value $M = P$ (the value of the productive capital that opens this circuit of industrial capital) is again present, having rid itself of the surplus-value, i.e. with the same value magnitude as in the first stage of the circuit of money capital $M-C$. Despite the different position, the function of the money capital into which the commodity capital has now been changed remains the same: its transformation into mp and L, means of production and labour-power.

The capital value in the function of the commodity capital $C'-M'$ has thus passed through the phase $C-M$, at the same time as $C-M$, and it now moves into the complementary phase $M-C<^{L}_{mp}$; its overall circulation is thus $C-M-C<^{L}_{mp}$.

Firstly, the money capital M appeared in form I (circuit $M \ldots M'$) as the original form in which the capital value was advanced; now it appears from the start as a part of the sum of money into which the commodity capital has been transformed in the first phase of circulation $C'-M'$, thus from the start as a transformation, mediated by the sale of the commodity product, of P, the productive capital, into the money form. Here the money capital exists from the outset neither as the original nor as the concluding form of the capital value, since it is only through repeatedly stripping off the money form that the phase $M-C$ that complements the phase $C-M$ can be completed. Hence the portion of $M-C$ that is simultaneously $M-L$ also appears no longer as a mere advance of money for acquiring labour-power, but as an advance in which the same 1,000 lb. of yarn with a value of £50 is advanced for the labour-power in the money form, and this forms a portion of the commodity value produced by the labour-power. The money that is here advanced to the worker is only the transformed equivalent form of a portion of the commodity value that he himself produces. And for this reason alone, the act $M-C$, in so far as it is $M-L$, is in no way simply the substitution of commodities in use form for commodities in money form, but includes other elements that are independent of the general circulation of commodities as such.

M' appears as the transformed form of C', which is itself the product of the past function of P, the production process; the entire sum of M' thus appears as the monetary expression of past labour. In our example, 10,000 lb. of yarn = £500, the product of the spinning process; 7,440 lb. of this equals the constant capital advanced, c = £372; 1,000 lb. equals the variable capital advanced, v = £50; and 1,560 lb. of yarn equals the surplus-value, s = £78. If, out of M', it is only the original capital of £422 that is advanced afresh, other circumstances remaining the same, then the worker merely receives as the next week's advance in $M-L$ a portion of the 10,000 lb. of yarn produced in this week (the money value of 1,000 lb. of yarn). As the result of $C-M$, the money is throughout the expression of past labour. In so far as the complementary act $M-C$ is immediately performed on the commodity market, and M is thus converted into existing commodities found on the market, there is again a conversion of past labour from one form (money) into another (commodity). But $M-C$ is separate from $C-M$ in time. It can in exceptional cases be simultaneous, if for example the capitalist who performs $M-C$ and the capitalist for whom this act is $C-M$ transfer their respective commodities to each other at the same time, and M simply settles the balance. The difference in time between the execution of $C-M$ and that of $M-C$ may be more or less considerable. Although, as the result of the act $C-M$, M represents past labour, M can represent for the act $M–C$ the transformed form of commodities that are not yet present on the market at all, but will be there only in the future, since $M–C$ does not need to take place until C has been produced afresh. In the same way, M may represent commodities that are produced simultaneously with the C whose monetary expression it is. In the conversion $M–C$, for example (acquisition of means of production), coal may be purchased before it is extracted from the mine. In so far as m figures as accumulation of money, and is not spent as revenue, it can represent cotton that will only be produced next year. The same applies to the expenditure of the capitalist's revenue, $m–c$, and holds even for the wages of labour = £50; this money is not only the monetary form of the workers' past labour, but also a draft on simultaneous or future labour that will only be realized, or is supposed to be realized, in the future. The worker may use it to buy a coat that will only be made one week later. This is in particular the case with the very large number of necessary means of subsistence that must be consumed almost immediately, the moment they are produced, if they are not to spoil. In the money with which his wage is paid, therefore, the worker receives the transformed form of his own future labour or that of other workers. With one part of his past labour the capitalist gives him a draft on his own future labour. It is his own simultaneous or future labour which forms the as yet non-existent reserve stock with which his past labour is paid for. Here the idea that a stock has to be formed is completely demolished.

Secondly, in the circulation $C–M–C\mathopen{<}^{L}_{mp}$, the same money changes its position twice; the capitalist first receives it as a seller, and then gives it out again as buyer. The transformation of the commodity into the money form only serves to transform it from the money form into the commodity form again, and so the money form of capital, its existence as money capital, is thus only an evanescent moment in this movement. Alternatively, the money capital, in so far as the movement is fluid, appears as a means of circulation only when it serves as a means of purchase; it appears as an actual means of payment only when capitalists buy from each other, hence when there is simply a balance of payments to be settled.

Thirdly, the function of money capital, whether it serves as mere means of circulation or as means of payment, is simply to mediate the replacement of C by L and mp, i.e. to replace the yarn, the commodity product which is the result of the activity of the productive capital (after deduction of the surplus-value spent as revenue), with its own elements of production, i.e. to transform capital value back from its form as commodity into the elements of formation of this commodity; it thus mediates, in the last instance, only the transformation of commodity capital back into productive capital.

In order for the circuit to run its normal course, C' must be sold at its value and as a whole. Furthermore, C–M–C does not just include the replacement of one commodity by another, but its replacement in the same value relations. We have made the assumption that this is what happens here. In fact, however, the value of the means of production varies; capitalist production is precisely marked by a continuous change in value relations, if only because of the constant change in the productivity of labour that characterizes it. We shall deal with this change n the value of the factors of production later,* and for the moment we merely indicate it. The transformation of the elements of production into the commodity product, P into C', proceeds in the sphere of production, while the transformation of C' back into P takes place in the circulation sphere. It is mediated by the simple metamorphosis of commodities. Its content, however, is a moment of the reproduction process considered as a whole. C–M–C, as a form of circulation of capital, includes a functionally specific interchange of material. The conversion C–M–C further requires that C be equal to the elements of production of the commodity quantum C', and that these maintain their original value relations to each other; thus it is not only assumed that the commodities are bought at their values, but also that they do not suffer any change of value during the circuit; if this is not the case, then the process cannot run its normal course.

In $M \ldots M'$, M is the original form of the capital value, and is cast aside only in order to be re-assumed later. In $P \ldots C'$–M'–$C \ldots P$, M is only a form assumed in the process, and is already cast aside again within this. Here the money form appears simply as an evanescent form of value of the capital; the capital as C' is anxious to assume the money form but the capital as M' is equally anxious to get rid of it, as soon as it has pupated into it, in order to convert itself once more into the form of productive capital. As long as it persists in the shape of money, it does not function as capital, and thus is not valorized; the capital remains idle. M functions here as a means of circulation, even though a means of circulation of capital.† The appearance of inde-

* See below, Chapter 15, 5, pp. 360–68.

† Marx's manuscript here carries the note: 'Against Tooke'. Thomas Tooke was

pendence that the money form of the capital value possesses in the first form of the circuit (that of money capital), vanishes in this second form, which thus constitutes a critique of form I, and reduces this to a mere particular form. If the second metamorphosis $M-C$ comes up against obstacles (e.g. if the means of production are unobtainable on the market), then the circular flow of the reproduction process is interrupted, just as if the capital was tied up in the form of commodity capital. The difference, however, is that it can last out longer in the money form than in its previous commodity form. It does not cease to be money when it functions as capital; but it does cease to be a commodity, and in fact a use-value in general, if it is detained too long in its function as commodity capital. Secondly, in the money form it is able to assume a form other than its original one of productive capital, while as C' it can move no further.

In its form, $C'-M'-C$ includes for C' only acts of circulation which are moments of its reproduction; but the real reproduction of the C into which C' is converted is necessary to the performance of $C'-M'-C$; this is however conditional on reproduction processes outside the reproduction process of the individual capital depicted in C'.

In form I, $M-C{<}^{L}_{mp}$ simply prepared the first transformation of money capital into productive capital; in form II it prepares the transformation of commodity capital back into productive capital; thus, in so far as industrial capital remains invested in the same business, it prepares the transformation of commodity capital back into the same elements of production from which it emerged. It therefore appears here, as in form I, as a preparatory phase for the production process, but as a return to this process, a repetition of it, hence as a forerunner to the reproduction process, and so also to the repetition of the valorization process.

We again have to note here that $M-L$ is not simple commodity exchange, but the purchase of a commodity L that is to serve for the production of surplus-value, while $M-mp$ is only a procedure that is materially indispensable to the accomplishment of this end.

---

the author of the six-volume *A History of Prices* (1838–57), a work frequently praised by Marx, who called Tooke 'the last English economist of any value'. Marx's present point is explained in more detail in Volume 3 of *Capital*, Chapter 23. Here Marx attacks Tooke for failing to distinguish between money as means of circulation and money as capital: 'If the money-capitalist gets his money back, he must always loan it out again, so long as it is to function for him as capital.'

With the completion of $M-C\underset{mp}{\overset{L}{<}}$, M has been transformed back into productive capital, and begins the circuit afresh.

The form $P\ldots C'-M'-C\ldots P$ can therefore be expanded as follows:

$$P\ldots C'\begin{Bmatrix}C\\+\\c\end{Bmatrix}\begin{matrix}-\\-\end{matrix}\begin{Bmatrix}M\\+\\m\end{Bmatrix}\begin{matrix}-C\underset{mp}{\overset{L}{<}}\ldots P\\-c\end{matrix}$$

The transformation of money capital into productive capital is the purchase of commodities for the purpose of commodity production. It is only in so far as consumption is productive consumption of this kind that it falls within the actual circuit of capital; the condition for consumption to occur is that surplus-value is made by means of the commodities thus consumed. And this is something very different from production, even commodity production, whose purpose is the existence of the producers; such a replacement of commodity by commodity conditioned by surplus-value production is something quite other than an exchange of products that is simply mediated by money. But this is how the matter is presented by the economists, as proof that no overproduction is possible.

Besides the productive consumption of M, transformed into L and mp, the circuit contains the first link of $M-L$, which for the worker is $L-M = C-M$. Of the worker's circulation $L-M-C$, which includes his consumption, only the first link falls into the circuit of capital, as the result of $M-L$. The second act, i.e. $M-C$, does not fall into the circulation of the individual capital, although it proceeds from it. The constant existence of the working class, however, is necessary for the capitalist class, and so, therefore, is the consumption of the worker mediated by $M-C$.

The act $C'-M'$ merely assumes that C' is transformed into money, is sold, so that the circuit of the capital value can continue, and the surplus-value can be consumed by the capitalist. The commodity is of course bought only because it is a use-value, i.e. is suitable for some kind of consumption, productive or individual. But if C' circulates further, e.g. in the hands of the merchant who has bought the yarn, this in no way disturbs – initially at least – the continuation of the circuit of the individual capital that has produced the yarn and sold it to the merchant. The whole process follows its course, and with it also the individual consumption of the capitalist and the worker that is conditional on it. This point is an important one in considering crises.

As soon as C' is sold, is transformed into money, it can be transformed back into the real factors of the labour process, and hence of the reproduction process. Hence whether C' is bought by the final consumer or by the merchant who intends to sell it again does not directly alter the matter in any way. The volume of the mass of commodities brought into being by capitalist production is determined by the scale of this production and its needs for constant expansion, and not by a predestined ambit of supply and demand, of needs to be satisfied. Besides other industrial capitalists, mass production can have only wholesale merchants as its immediate purchasers. Within certain bounds, the reproduction process may proceed on the same or on an expanded scale, even though the commodities ejected from it do not actually enter either individual or productive consumption. The consumption of commodities is not included in the circuit of the capital from which they emerge. As soon as the yarn is sold, for example, the circuit of the capital value represented in the yarn can begin anew, at first irrespective of what becomes of the yarn when sold. As long as the product is sold, everything follows its regular course, as far as the capitalist producer is concerned. The circuit of the capital value that he represents is not interrupted. And if this process is expanded (which includes an expansion of the productive consumption of the means of production), then this reproduction of capital can be accompanied by a more expanded individual consumption (and thus demand) on the part of the workers, since this is introduced and mediated by productive consumption. The production of surplus-value and with it also the individual consumption of the capitalist can thus grow, and the whole reproduction process find itself in the most flourishing condition, while in fact a great part of the commodities have only apparently gone into consumption, and are actually lying unsold in the hands of retail traders, thus being still on the market. One stream of commodities now follows another, and it finally emerges that the earlier stream had only seemed to be swallowed up by consumption. Commodity capitals now vie with each other for space on the market. The late-comers sell below the price in order to sell at all. The earlier streams have not yet been converted into ready money, while payment for them is falling due. Their owners must declare themselves bankrupt, or sell at any price in order to pay. This sale, however, has absolutely nothing to do with the real state of demand. It has only to do with the *demand for payment*, with the absolute necessity of transforming commodities into money. At this point the crisis breaks out. It first becomes evident not in the direct reduction of consumer demand, the demand for individual consumption, but rather in a decline in the number of exchanges of capital for capital, in the reproduction process of capital.

In order to fulfil its function as money capital, as a capital value destined to be transformed back into productive capital, M is converted into the commodities mp and L. If these commodities are to be purchased or paid for at different dates, M–C then takes the form of a series of successive purchases and payments, so that a part of M performs the act M–C, while another part persists in the money state, and only serves for simultaneous or successive acts M–C at a time determined by the conditions of the process itself. It is withdrawn from circulation only temporarily, to step into action and fulfil its function at a definite point in time. This storing of money is then itself a function determined by its circulation and for circulation. Its existence as a fund for purchase and payment, the suspension of its movement, its state of interrupted circulation, is then a situation in which the money fulfils one of its functions as money capital. For, in this case, the money that is temporarily dormant is itself a part of the money capital M (of M' minus $m = M$), of the value portion of the commodity capital equal to P, the value of the productive capital, from which the money that is withdrawn originates. Furthermore, all the money that is withdrawn from circulation exists in the form of a hoard. The hoard form thus becomes here a function of the money capital, just as in M–C the function of money as a means of purchase or payment becomes a function of the money capital, and indeed, precisely because the capital value exists here in the form of money, the money state is here a state of industrial capital in one of its stages, prescribed by the circuit as a whole. But it also proves true once again here that, within the circuit of industrial capital, money capital performs no other functions than those of money, and these money functions have the significance of capital functions only through their connection with the other stages of the circuit.

The expression of M' as a relation between m and M, as a capital relation, is not a direct function of the money capital, but rather of the commodity capital C', which in turn expresses, as a relation between c and C, only the result of the production process, of the self-valorization of the capital value that takes place within it.

If the circulation process comes up against obstacles, so that M has to suspend its function M–C as a result of external circumstances – the state of the market, etc. – and on this account persists for a shorter or longer time in its money state, then this is again a form of hoarding, which can also arise in simple commodity circulation if the transition from *C–M* to *M–C* is interrupted by external circumstances. It is the involuntary formation of a hoard. In our case, the money thus has the form of latent money capital, money capital that lies idle. However, we shall not go into this any further for the moment.

In both cases, the persistence of money capital in its money state appears as the result of interrupted movement, whether this is expedient or inexpedient, voluntary or involuntary, functional or dysfunctional.

2. ACCUMULATION AND REPRODUCTION ON AN EXPANDED SCALE

Since the proportions in which the production process can be expanded are not arbitrary, but are prescribed by technical factors, the surplus-value realized, even if it is destined for capitalization, can often only grow to the volume at which it can actually function as additional capital, or enter the circuit of capital value in process, by repeating a number of circuits. (Until then, therefore, it must be stored up.) The surplus-value thus builds up into a hoard, and in this form it constitutes latent money capital. Latent, because as long as it persists in the money form, it cannot function as capital.[1] Thus the formation of a hoard appears here as a moment that is comprised within the process of capitalist accumulation, accompanies it but is at the same time essentially different from it. For the reproduction process is not itself expanded by the formation of latent money capital. On the contrary. Latent money capital is formed here because the capitalist producer cannot directly expand the scale of his production. If he sells his surplus-product to a gold or silver producer, who thereby throws new gold or silver into circulation – or, what comes to the same thing, if he sells it to a merchant who uses part of the national surplus product to import additional gold or silver from abroad – then his latent money capital forms an increment to the national gold or silver hoard. In all other cases, the £78, say, that was means of circulation in the hands of the purchaser, has assumed in the hands of the capitalist only the form

1. The expression 'latent' is borrowed from the physical concept of latent heat, which has now been more or less displaced by the theory of the transformation of energy. In Part Three, therefore, which is a later draft, Marx used the expressions 'potential capital', borrowed from the concept of potential energy, or by analogy with D'Alembert's virtual velocities, 'virtual capital'. – F. E.

of a hoard; thus all that has taken place is a new distribution of the national gold or silver hoard.

If money functions as means of payment in our capitalist's transactions (so that the commodity only has to be paid for by the purchaser at a later date), then the surplus product destined for capitalization is not transformed into money, but into claims for payment, titles to property equivalent to a sum that the purchaser either already has in his possession or expects to come into. It does not enter into the reproduction of the circuit, any more than the money that is invested in interest-bearing securities, etc., even though it can enter the circuits of other individual industrial capitals.

The whole character of capitalist production is determined by the valorization of the capital value advanced, thus in the first instance by the production of the greatest possible amount of surplus-value; secondly, however (see Volume 1, Chapter 24), by the production of capital, i.e. the transformation of surplus-value into capital. Accumulation, or production on an expanded scale, which first appears as a means towards the constantly extended production of surplus-value, hence the enrichment of the capitalist, as the personal end of the latter, and is part of the general tendency of capitalist production, becomes in the course of its development, as was shown in the first volume, a necessity for each individual capitalist. The constant enlargement of his capital becomes a condition for its preservation. However, it is not necessary here to come back to what was already developed earlier.

We first considered simple reproduction, in which connection it was assumed that the whole of the surplus-value is spent as revenue. In actual fact, a part of the surplus-value must always be spent as revenue in normal circumstances, and another part capitalized, and it is quite immaterial in this connection that at certain periods the surplus-value produced is completely consumed, and at others completely capitalized. If the movement takes its average course, and this is all that the general formula can express, there is a bit of both. In order not to complicate the formula, it is better to assume that the whole of the surplus-value is accumulated. The formula $P \ldots C'-M'-C'{<}\frac{L}{mp} \ldots P'$ then expresses:

productive capital which is to be reproduced on a larger scale and with greater value, and begins its second circuit – or what comes to the same thing, repeats its first circuit – as augmented productive capital. As soon as this second circuit begins, we once again have P as the point of departure; it is simply that P is now a larger productive capital than the first P was. Similarly, in the formula $M \ldots M'$, the second circuit begins with M', and M' functions as M, as money capital of a specific magnitude, which has been advanced; it is a larger money capital than that with which the first circuit commenced, but all reference to its augmentation through the capitalization of surplus-value has vanished, once it steps forth in the function of money capital advanced. This origin was obliterated in its form as money capital just beginning its circuit. It is just the same with P', as soon as it functions as the point of departure for a new circuit.

If we compare $P \ldots P'$ with $M \ldots M'$, the first circuit, we see that each has a quite different significance. $M \ldots M'$, taken by itself as an isolated circuit, simply expresses that M, the money capital (or industrial capital in its circuit as money capital), is money breeding money, value breeding value, and brings forth surplus-value. In the circuit of P, on the contrary, the process of valorization is already complete as soon as the first stage, the production process, has taken place, and once it has passed through the second stage $C'-M'$ (the first of the circulation stages), capital value and surplus-value already exist as realized money capital, as M', which in the first circuit appeared as the final extremity. The fact that surplus-value is produced was depicted in the first form of $P \ldots P$ that was considered (see the expanded formula on p. 79) by $c-m-c$, the second stage of which falls outside the circulation of capital and represents the circulation of surplus-value as revenue. In this form, in which the entire movement is represented by $P \ldots P$, and there is thus no difference in value between the two end points, the valorization of the value advanced, the creation of surplus-value, is depicted as much as it is in $M \ldots M'$; it is simply that the act $C'-M'$ appears as the final stage in $M \ldots M'$, but as the second stage in the circuit. and first of the circulation stages, in $P \ldots P'$.

In $P \ldots P'$, P' does not express the fact that surplus-value is produced, but rather that the produced surplus-value is capitalized, i.e. that capital has been accumulated, and hence P', as opposed to P, consists of the original capital value plus the value of the capital accumulated through its movement.

M', as the simple conclusion of $M \ldots M'$, as also C', as it appears within all these circuits, express, taken by themselves, not the movement, but rather its result; the valorization of the capital value realized in the commodity or money form, and hence the capital value as $M+m$ or as $C+c$, as the relation of the capital value to the surplus-value as its derivative. These express this result as different forms of circulation of the capital value that has been valorized. But neither in the form C' nor in the form M' is the valorization that has taken place a function of the money capital or the commodity capital. As a specific and distinct form or mode of existence that corresponds to the particular functions of industrial capital, money capital can perform only money functions, and commodity capital only commodity functions; the distinction between them is simply that between money and commodity. In the same way, industrial capital in its form as productive capital can consist only of the same elements as those of any other labour process that fashions products: on the one hand the objective conditions of labour (means of production), on the other hand productively (purposively) active labour-power. As industrial capital within the sphere of production can exist only in the combination corresponding to the production process in general, and thus also to the non-capitalist production process, so it can exist in the sphere of circulation only in the two forms of commodity and money that correspond to this. Just as the sum of the elements of production proclaims itself from the start to be productive capital, in so far as the labour-power is the labour-power of others which the capitalist has bought from its owners; just as he has bought his means of production from the owners of other commodities, hence just as the production process itself appears as a productive function of industrial capital – so money and commodities appear as forms of circulation of this industrial capital, and thus also their functions as its circulation functions, which either pave the way for the functions of productive capital, or derive from them. It is only through their connection as functional forms which industrial capital has to go through in the various stages of its circuit that the money function and the commodity function are here at the same time functions of money capital and commodity capital. It is wrong, therefore, to seek to ascribe the specific properties and functions that characterize money as money and commodities as commodities to their character as capital, and it is just as wrong, conversely, to derive the properties of productive capital from its mode of existence in the means of production.

When M' or C' are depicted as $M+m$, $C+c$, i.e. as a relation between the capital value and the surplus-value as its offshoot, this relation is expressed in one case in the money form, and the other case in the commodity form, but this does not alter the matter in any way. This relation thus does not arise from properties and functions that can be ascribed either to the money or the commodity as such. In both cases, the characteristic property of capital, that it is money which breeds money, is only expressed as the result. C' is always the product of the function of P, and M' is always simply the form into which C' has been transformed in the circuit of industrial capital. Hence, as soon as the realized money capital recommences its particular function as money capital, it ceases to express the capital-relation contained in $M' = M+m$. When the movement $M \ldots M'$ has been passed through, and M' begins the cycle anew, it does not figure as M', but rather as M, even if the entire surplus-value contained in M' has been capitalized. In our case, the second circuit begins with a money capital of £500, instead of with £422 as did the first circuit. The money capital that opens the circuit is £78 greater than previously and this difference exists when one circuit is compared with another, but such a comparison is not made within the individual circuit itself. The £500 now advanced as money capital, of which £78 existed earlier as surplus-value, does not play a different role from the £500 which another capitalist might use to open his first circuit. The same applies in the circuit of productive capital. The enlarged P' appears as P when the circuit is begun again, just like P in the simple reproduction $P \ldots P$.

At the stage $M'-C'{<}{\stackrel{L}{mp}}$, the augmented magnitude is indicated simply by C', and not by L' and mp'. Since C is the sum of L and mp, it is already indicated by C' that the sum of the L and mp contained in it is greater than the original P. Secondly, however, the designations L' and mp' would be false, as we know that the growth of capital involves a change in its value composition, in the course of which the value of mp constantly grows, while that of L always declines relatively, and often even absolutely.

3. ACCUMULATION OF MONEY

Whether m, surplus-value in its golden form, is immediately added on to the capital value in process, and can thus embark on the circuit together with the capital M, making a total magnitude of M', depends on circumstances that are independent of the mere presence of m. If m is to serve as money capital in a second independent business alongside the first, it is clear that it can be invested in this only if it possesses the minimal magnitude required for such a business. If it is invested in extending the original business, then the relationship between the material factors of P, as well as their value relationship, similarly determines a certain minimal magnitude for m. Between all means of production operating in this business there is not only a qualitative relation, but also a quantitative ratio, a proportionality. The above-mentioned material factors and the value relationships, borne by them, between the factors which enter into the productive capital, determine the minimum size that m must possess in order to be convertible either into additional means of production and labour-power, or into the former alone, as an increase of productive capital. Thus the mill-owner cannot increase the number of his spindles without simultaneously purchasing a corresponding number of carding machines and roving-frames, to say nothing of the increased outlay on cotton and wages that this extension of his business would demand. For him to extend his business in this way, therefore, the surplus-value must already amount to a fair sum (£1 per additional spindle is generally reckoned on). As long as m has not reached this minimum size, the capital circuit must be repeated several times, until the sum of the m's successively produced by it can function together with M in the form $M'-C'<^{L}_{mp}$. Even detailed changes in the spinning machinery, for example, that make it more productive, require greater outlay on raw material, extension of the roving machinery, etc. In the meantime, therefore, m is stored up, and its accumulation is not its own function, but the result of repeated $P\ldots P$. Its own function is its persistence in the money state until the repeated circuits of valorization, i.e. an external factor, have added to it sufficiently for it to have attained the minimum magnitude required for it to function actively, the magnitude at which it can really function for the first time as money capital, i.e. in the given case enter into the function of the money capital M as an accumulated portion of the latter. In the meantime it is stored up, and exists only in the form of a hoard in the process of formation and growth. Thus the accumulation of money, the formation of a hoard, appears here as a process that temporarily accompanies an extension of the scale on which industrial capital operates. Temporarily, because as long as the hoard persists in its state as a hoard, it does not function as capital, does not participate in the valorization process, but remains a sum of money that grows only because money available to it without any effort on its part is cast into the same coffer.

The form of the hoard is simply the form of money not in circulation, money that is interrupted in its circulation and is therefore preserved in its money form. As far as the process of hoard formation itself is concerned, this is common to all commodity production, and it is only in the undeveloped pre-capitalist forms of the latter that it plays a role as an end in itself. In our case, however, the hoard appears as a form of money capital, and hoard formation as a process that temporarily accompanies the accumulation of capital, because and in so far as money figures here as *latent money capital*; because the formation of a hoard, the hoarded state of the surplus-value present in money form, is a functionally determined preparatory stage that proceeds outside the circuit of capital, and paves the way for the transformation of surplus-value into really functioning capital. This characteristic is what makes it latent money capital, and is also why the scale that it must have attained in order to enter the process is determined by the value composition of the productive capital in each particular case. As long as it persists in the state of a hoard, it does not yet function as money capital, it is still money capital lying fallow; not interrupted in its function, as in the previous case, but rather as yet incapable of performing this function.

Here we take the accumulation of money in its original real form, as a real hoard of money. It can also exist merely in the form of favourable balances, of sums owed to the capitalist who has sold C'. As far as concerns the other forms, in which this latent money capital may in the interval exist in the actual shape of money which breeds money, e.g. as interest-bearing deposits in a bank, bills of exchange or securities of one kind or other, these do not belong here. In that case, the surplus-value realized in money performs particular capital functions outside the circuit of the industrial capital from which it arose; functions which have nothing to do with that circuit as such, and assume the existence of functions of capital distinct from the functions of industrial capital, which have not yet been developed here.

4. THE RESERVE FUND

In the form just considered, the hoard in which the surplus-value exists, the money accumulation fund, is the money form which capital accumulation temporarily possesses, and in this respect it is itself a condition for this accumulation. But the accumulation fund can also perform particular ancillary services, i.e. it can enter into the circulation process of capital, without the latter possessing the form $P \ldots P'$, i.e. without capitalist reproduction on an expanded scale.

If the process $C'-M'$ extends beyond its normal duration, then the commodity capital is abnormally delayed in its transformation into the money form; alternatively, if, when the transformation is completed, the price of the means of production into which the money capital must be converted has risen, for example, above the level that it had at the beginning of the circuit, then the hoard that functions as accumulation fund can be used to take the place of money capital, or a part of this. The money accumulation fund then serves as a reserve fund to cope with disturbances in the circuit.

As a reserve fund of this kind, it is different from the fund for purchase and payment considered in the circuit $P\ldots P$. The latter was a part of the functioning money capital (thus the form of existence of a part of the total capital value in process), the parts of which functioned successively at different points in time. It formed a constant reserve of money capital in the continuity of the production process, as one day money is received and no payments have to be made until later, while another day large quantities of commodities are sold, and only at a later date do large quantities of commodities have to be bought; within these intervals, therefore, a part of the circulating capital always exists in the money form. The reserve fund, on the other hand, is not a component part of the functioning capital, or, more precisely, the money capital, but rather capital going through a preliminary stage of its accumulation, surplus-value that has not yet been transformed into active capital. It goes without saying, of course, that when the capitalist is in need, he in no way ponders over the specific functions of the money that he has in his hands, but uses whatever he has in order to get the circulation process of his capital moving again. In our example, for instance, $M = £422$, $M' = £500$. If part of the capital of £422 exists as a fund for purchase and payment, as a monetary reserve, it is reckoned that, with circumstances remaining the same, it will enter as a whole into the circuit, and will also be sufficient for this purpose. The reserve fund, however, is a part of the £78 surplus-value; it can enter the circuit of the capital of £422 only in so far as this circuit is accomplished in altered circumstances; for it is a part of the accumulation fund, and it figures here without an expansion in the scale of reproduction.

In the money accumulation fund, money already exists as latent money capital, and is thus transformed into money capital.

The general formula for the circuit of productive capital, which comprises both simple reproduction and reproduction on an expanded scale, is:

$$P\ldots \overset{\overset{1}{\frown}}{C'-M'}.\overset{\overset{2}{\frown}}{M-C}\!\!<^{L}_{mp}\ldots P(P')$$

If $P = P$, then M in (2) = M' minus m; if $P = P'$, then M in (2) is greater than M' minus m; i.e. m has been wholly or partly transformed into money capital.

The circuit of productive capital is the form in which the classical economists have considered the circuit of industrial capital.

Chapter 3: The Circuit of Commodity Capital

The general formula for the circuit of commodity capital is:

$$C'-M'-C\ldots P\ldots C'.$$

Here C' does not just appear as the product of the two earlier circuits, but also as their premise, since what is $M-C$ for one capital already involves $C'-M'$ for another, at least in so far as a part of the means of production are themselves the commodity product of other individual capitals in their circuits. In our case, for example, coal, machinery, etc. are the commodity capital of the mine-owner, the capitalist engineer, etc. It has already been shown in Chapter 1, 4, moreover, that when $M\ldots M'$ is being repeated for the first time, even before this second circuit of the money capital is completed, not only is the circuit $P\ldots P$ presupposed, but also the circuit $C'\ldots C'$.

If there is reproduction on an expanded scale, then the concluding C' is greater than the starting C', and will therefore be designated here as C''.

The difference between the third form and the two previous ones is first apparent in that here the circuit commences with the entire circulation, in its two opposing phases, whereas in form I the circulation was interrupted by the production process, and in form II the entire circulation and its two complementary phases simply appeared as a mediation for the reproduction process, and hence formed the mediating movement between $P\ldots P$. With $M\ldots M'$, the form of circulation is $M-C\ldots C'-M'$, or $M-C-M$. With $P\ldots P$, it is conversely $C'-M'$, $M-C$, or $C-M-C$. In $C'\ldots C'$ it similarly has this latter form.

Secondly, when the circuits I and II are repeated, even if the final points M' and P' form the points of departure for a new circuit, the form in which they were produced vanishes. Both $M' = M+m$, and $P' = P+p$, begin the new process once more as M and P. In form III, however, the starting-point C must be designated as C', even when the circuit is renewed on the same scale. The reason for this is as follows. In form I, as soon as M', as such, opens a new circuit, it functions as money capital M, the advance in monetary form of the capital value which is to be valorized. The magnitude of the money capital advanced has increased, for it has grown by way of the accumulation accomplished in the first circuit. But whether the magnitude of the money capital advanced is £422 or £500 in no way alters the fact that it appears simply as capital value. M' no longer exists as valorized capital, as capital pregnant with surplus-value, as a capital-relation. It is only in the course of the process that it is to be valorized. The same holds for $P\ldots P'$; P' must always continue to function as P, as capital value which should produce surplus-value, and always repeat the circuit. The circuit of commodity capital, on the other hand, does not just open with capital value, but with expanded capital value in the commodity form, and thus it includes from the start not only the circuit of the capital value present in the commodity form, but also that of the surplus-value. Hence if simple reproduction takes place in this form, this involves at the close of the circuit a C' of equal magnitude to the one at its starting-point. If a part of the surplus-value goes into the capital circuit, then what appears at the end is in fact not C' but C'', a bigger C'; but the following circuit still opens with C', which is simply a greater C' than in the previous circuit and begins its new circuit with a greater accumulated capital value, hence also with relatively more newly produced surplus-value. In all cases, C' always opens the circuit as a commodity capital equal to capital value plus surplus-value.

In the circuit of an individual industrial capital, C' as C appears not as the form of this capital, but as the form of another industrial capital, in so far as the means of production are the product of this other capital. The act $M-C$ (i.e. $M-mp$) of the first capital is for this second capital $C'-M'$.

In the act of circulation $M-C{<}^{L}_{mp}$, L and mp behave identically in so far as they are commodities in the hands of their sellers, in the one case the workers who sell their labour-power, in the other the possessors of the means of production, who sell the latter. For the buyer, whose money functions here as money capital, both these things function merely as commodities, as long as he has not yet bought them, thus as long as they confront his capital, existing in the money form, as the commodities of others. mp and L are distinguished here only in so far as mp is C' in the hands of its seller, and can thus be capital if mp is the commodity form of his capital, whereas L is always just a commodity for the worker, and becomes capital only in the hands of the buyer, as a component part of P.

C' can therefore never open a circuit as mere C, as merely the commodity form of the capital value. As commodity capital, it always has a dual aspect. From the point of view of use-value, it is the product of the function of P, here yarn, whose elements L and mp, emerging from circulation as commodities, have only functioned to fashion this product. Secondly, from the point of view of value, it is the capital value P plus the surplus-value m produced in the function of P.

It is only in the circuit of C' itself that $C = P =$ the capital value can and must separate itself from the portion of C' in which surplus-value exists, from the surplus product in which the surplus-value is hidden, whether the two are actually separable, as in the case of yarn, or not, as in the case of the machine. They become separable in any case, as soon as C' has been transformed into M'.

If the total commodity product is divisible into independent and homogeneous partial products, as for example our 10,000 lb. of yarn, and if the act $C'-M'$ can thus be represented as a sum of successively performed sales, then the capital value can function as C in the commodity form and separate itself off from C' before the surplus-value is realized, therefore before C' is realized as a whole.

Of the 10,000 lb. of yarn with a value of £500, the value of 8,440 lb. $=$ £422 $=$ the capital value, separated from the surplus-value. If the capitalist first sells 8,440 lb. for £422, then this 8,440 lb. represents C, the capital value in commodity form; the additional surplus product contained in C', which consists of 1,560 lb. of yarn and $=$ a surplus-value of £78, only circulates later; the capitalist could complete

$C\text{–}M\text{–}C{<}_{mp}^{L}$ before the circulation of the surplus product $c\text{–}m\text{–}c$.

Alternatively, if he firstly sells 7,440 lb. of yarn at its value of £372, and then 1,000 lb. at its value of £50, he could replace the means of production (the constant capital c) with the first part of C, and the variable capital v, i.e. the labour-power, with the second part of C, and then proceed as before*.

But if there are successive sales of this kind, and the conditions of the circuit allow it, then the capitalist, instead of dividing C' into $c+v+s$, can undertake this division also for aliquot parts of C'.

For example, 7,440 lb. of yarn, $=$ £372, which as a portion of C'

* See above, p. 122, note.

(10,000 lb. of yarn = £500) represents the constant capital, can itself be further broken down into 5,535·360 lb. of yarn with a value of £276·768 which simply replaces the constant part, the value of the means of production used up in the 7,440 lb.; 744 lb. of yarn with a value of £37·200, which replaces the variable capital; and 1,160·640 lb. of yarn with a value of £58·032, which carries the surplus-value in the form of surplus product. Having thus sold 7,440 lb., he can replace the capital value contained in it from the sale of 6,279·360 lb. at a price of £313·968, and spend the value of the surplus product of 1,160·640 lb. = £58·032 as revenue.

He can in the same way break down 1,000 lb. of yarn = £50 = the variable capital, and accordingly sell: 744 lb. of yarn for £37·200, the value of the constant capital in 1,000 lb. of yarn; 100 lb. of yarn for £5, the variable capital value of the same – thus 844 lb. of yarn for £42·200 replace the capital value contained in the 1,000 lb. of yarn; finally, 156 lb. of yarn at its value of £7·800, which represents the surplus product contained in the 1,000 lb. and may be consumed as such.

Finally he can break down the remaining 1,560 lb. of yarn, with its value of £78, when he manages to sell it, in such a way that the sale of 1,160·640 lb. for £58·032 replaces the value of the means of production contained in this 1,560 lb., and 156 lb. at its value of £7·800 replaces the variable capital value – together this makes 1,316·640 lb. of yarn = £65·832, the replacement of the total capital value; so that finally the surplus product of 243·360 lb. = £12·168 remains to be spent as revenue.

As each of the elements *c*, *v* and *s* existing in the yarn is divisible into the same component parts, so is each individual lb. of yarn with a value of 1 shilling or 12d.

$$c = 0·744 \text{ lb.} \quad \text{yarn} = 8·928 \text{ d.}$$
$$v = 0·100 \text{ ,, } \quad \text{ ,, } = 1·200 \text{ d.}$$
$$s = 0·156 \text{ ,, } \quad \text{ ,, } = 1·872 \text{ d.}$$
$$\overline{c+v+s = 1 \text{ lb.} \qquad \text{yarn} = 12 \text{ d.}}$$

If we add together the results of the three partial sales as above, then we get the same result as if the entire 10,000 lb. of yarn was sold at one stroke.

In constant capital:

1st sale:	5,535·360 lb.	yarn =	£276·768
2nd sale:	744·000 ,,	,, =	£37·200
3rd sale:	1,160·640 ,,	,, =	£58·032
together	7,440 lb.	yarn =	£372

In variable capital:

1st sale:	744·000 lb.	yarn	=	£37·200
2nd sale:	100·000 „	„	=	£5·000
3rd sale:	156·000 „	„	=	£7·800
together	1,000 lb.	yarn	=	£50

In surplus-value:

1st sale:	1,160·640 lb.	yarn	=	£58·032
2nd sale:	156·000 „	„	=	£7·800
3rd sale:	243·360 „	„	=	£12·168
together	1,560 lb.	yarn	=	£78

Grand total:

constant capital:	7,440 lb.	yarn	=	£372
variable capital:	1,000 „	„	=	£50
surplus-value	1,560 „	„	=	£78
together	10,000 lb.	yarn	=	£500

Taken by itself, $C'-M'$ is nothing more than a sale of 10,000 lb. of yarn. The 10,000 lb. of yarn is a commodity like all other yarn. What interests the buyer is the price of 1 shilling per lb., or £500 for 10,000 lb. If he goes into the value composition in the course of his bargaining, he does so only with the crafty intention of showing that it could be sold below 1 shilling per lb. and the seller would still be doing good business. But the quantity that he buys will depend upon his needs; if he is the owner of a weaving-mill, for example, it will depend on the composition of his own capital functioning in this weaving-mill and not on that of the capital of the spinner from whom he buys it. The ratio in which C' has to serve, on the one hand to replace the capital utilized in it (or its various components), on the other hand as surplus product, whether the surplus-value is destined to be spent or for capital accumulation, exists only in the circuit of the capital whose commodity form is represented by the 10,000 lb. of yarn. It has nothing to do with the sale as such. It is assumed here, moreover, that C' is sold at its value, and so all that is involved is its transformation from the commodity form into the money form. It is of course decisive for C', as a functional form in the circuit of this individual capital, whether and to what extent price and value diverge from one another in the sale, but here, where we are merely considering distinctions of form, this is of no concern.

In form I, $M \ldots M'$, the production process appears in the middle, between the two complementary and mutually opposed phases of the circulation of capital; it is over with before the concluding phase $C'-M'$

begins. Money is advanced as capital, first transformed into the elements of production, then transformed from these into the commodity product, and this commodity product then again converted into money. This is a finished and complete cycle of business, the result being money which can be used by anyone for anything. Thus the recommencement of the cycle is indicated only as a possibility. $M \ldots P \ldots M'$ may just as well be the final circuit, concluding the functioning of the individual capital, which is then withdrawn from the business, or else the first circuit of a capital that newly enters into its function. Here the general movement is $M \ldots M'$, from money to more money.

In form II, $P \ldots C'-M'-C \ldots P(P')$, the entire circulation process follows the first P and precedes the second; but it follows in the opposite order to that of form I. The first P is productive capital, and its function is the production process, as precondition for the subsequent process of circulation. The concluding P, on the contrary, is not the production process; it is only the renewed existence of the industrial capital in its form of productive capital. Furthermore, this is the result of the transformation of the capital value into $L+mp$ that is accomplished in the final circulation phase, into the objective and subjective factors that constitute, in their union, the form of existence of productive capital. Whether the capital is P or P', it is present once more at the conclusion in a form in which it must function once more as productive capital, must again accomplish the production process. The general form of the movement $P \ldots P'$ is the form of reproduction, and does not indicate, as does $M \ldots M'$, that valorization is the purpose of the process. For this reason, classical economics found it all the more easy to ignore the specifically capitalist form of the production process, and to present production as such as the purpose of the process – to produce as much and as cheaply as possible, and to exchange the product for as many other products as possible, partly for the repetition of production $(M-C)$, partly for consumption $(m-c)$. In this connection, since M and m appear here only as evanescent means of circulation, the peculiarities of both money and money capital could be overlooked, the whole process then appearing simple and natural, i.e. possessing the naturalness of superficial rationality. In the case of commodity capital, similarly, profit was occasionally forgotten, and this capital figured, in so far as there was any mention of the production circuit as a whole, simply as a commodity; though as soon as the component parts of value were discussed, it figured as commodity capital. Accumulation, of course, appeared in the same light as production.

In form III, $C'-M'-C...P...C'$, it is the two phases of the circulation process that open the circuit, and in fact in the same order as in form II, $P...P$; P then follows, together with its function, the production process, as in form I; the circuit closes with the result of this process, C'. Just as in form II the circuit closed with P, the merely renewed existence of the productive capital, so here it closes with C', the renewed existence of the commodity capital; just as in form II the capital in its concluding form P had to begin the process again as a production process, so here it must reopen the circuit with the reappearance of the industrial capital in the form of commodity capital, with the circulation phase $C'-M'$. Both forms of the circuit are incomplete, because they do not conclude with M', with the valorized capital value transformed back into *money*. Both must thus be continued further, and hence include reproduction. The overall circuit in form III is $C'...C'$.

What differentiates the third form from the two earlier ones is that it is only in this circuit that the valorized capital value, and not the original capital value that has still to be valorized, appears as the starting-point of its own valorization. C', as capital-relation, is here the point of departure, and thus has a determining effect on the whole circuit, in so far as this includes, even in its first phase, both the circuit of the capital value and that of the surplus-value; and surplus-value must on average, even if not in every individual circuit, be partly spent as revenue and pass through the circulation $c-m-c$, and partly function as an element of capital accumulation.

In the form $C'...C'$, the consumption of the entire commodity product is presupposed as the condition for the normal course of the circuit of capital itself. The individual consumption of the worker and the individual consumption of the non-accumulated part of the surplus product comprise, taken together, the total individual consumption. Thus consumption in its entirety – both individual and productive consumption – enters into the circuit of C' as a precondition. Productive consumption (which in the nature of the case includes the individual consumption of the worker, for labour-power is the permanent product, within certain limits, of the worker's individual consumption) is carried on by every individual capital. Individual consumption – other than is necessary for the existence of the individual capitalist – is presupposed only as a social act, in no way as the act of the individual capitalist.

In forms I and II, the overall movement presents itself as a movement of the capital value advanced. In form III, the valorized capital, in the shape of the total commodity product, forms the starting-point, and possesses the form of capital in movement, commodity capital. It is only after its transformation into money that this movement splits up into movement of capital and movement of revenue. The division of the total social product, as well as the particular division of the product of every individual commodity capital, into an individual consumption fund on the one hand and a reproduction fund on the other, is included in this form of the circuit of capital.

$M \ldots M'$ allows for the possible expansion of the circuit, according to the scale on which m enters the new circuit.

In $P \ldots P$, P can begin the new circuit with the same value, perhaps even with a lesser value, and yet still represent reproduction on an expanded scale; if for example the commodity elements are cheapened as a result of the increased productivity of labour. Conversely, in the opposite case, a productive capital that has grown in value may represent reproduction on a materially more restricted scale, if for example the elements of production have become dearer. The same applies for $C' \ldots C'$.

In $C' \ldots C'$, capital in the commodity form is the premise of production; it reappears as a premise within this circuit in the second C. If this C is not yet produced or reproduced, then the circuit is inhibited; this C must be reproduced, for the most part as the C' of another industrial capital. In this circuit, C' exists as the point of departure, the point of transit and the conclusion of the movement; in other words it is always there. It is a permanent condition for the reproduction process.

$C' \ldots C'$ is distinguished from forms I and II by a further characteristic. All three circuits have in common that the form in which the capital opens its circuit is also the form in which it closes it, and it therefore finds itself back once more in the initial form, and in this form recommences the same circuit. The initial forms M, P and C' are always the forms in which the capital value is advanced (in form III together with the surplus-value that has adhered to it), i.e. their original forms as far as the circuit is concerned; the concluding forms M', P and C' are in each case the transformed form of a preceding functional form in the circuit which is not the original form.

Thus in form I, M' is the transformed form of C', while the closing P in form II is the transformed form of M (and in forms I and II this transformation is effected by way of a simple process of commodity circulation, by a formal change of position between commodity and money); in form III, C' is the transformed form of P, the productive capital. But in this form III, the transformation firstly does not just affect the functional form of the capital, but also the magnitude of its value; while secondly, the transformation is not the result of a merely formal change of position belonging to the circulation process, but rather the real transformation which the use form and the value of the commodity components of the productive capital have undergone in the production process.

The form of the first extreme M, P and C' is given for each circuit, I, II or III; the returning form at the closing extreme is produced and hence determined by the series of metamorphoses of the circuit itself. C', as the closing point of the circuit of an individual industrial capital, only presupposes the form P of the same industrial capital, which does not belong to the circulation sphere, and it is the product of the form P. M', as the closing point in I, the transformed form of $C'(C'-M')$, presupposes M in the hands of the buyer, as existing outside the circuit $M \ldots M'$, brought into it by the sale of C' and made into its own closing form. Thus, in form II, the closing P presupposes L and mp (C) as existing outside it and incorporated into it as the closing form by $M-C$. But apart from the final extreme, the circuit of the individual money capital does not presuppose the existence of money capital as such, and the circuit of the individual productive capital does not presuppose the existence of productive capital in the circuit itself. In form I, M may be the only money capital, and in form II P may be the only productive capital, that appears on the historical scene. In III, however, i.e.

$$C'\begin{cases} C- \\ -M' \\ c- \end{cases} \begin{cases} M-C{<}^{L}_{mp} \ldots P \ldots C', \\ \\ m-c \end{cases}$$

C is twice presupposed outside the circuit. Firstly in the circuit $C'-M'-C{<}^{L}_{mp}$. This C, in so far as it consists of means of production, is a commodity in the hands of its seller; it is itself commodity capital, in so far as it is the product of a capitalist production process; and even when this is not the case, it appears as commodity capital in the hands of the merchant. It is further presupposed in the second c of $c-m-c$, which must similarly be present as a commodity in order to be bought. In either case, whether commodity capital or not, L and mp are commodities as much as C' is, and act towards one another as commodities. The same holds for the second c in $c-m-c$. Thus, in so far as $C' = C$ $(L+mp)$, commodities are its own elements of formation, and must be replaced by equivalent commodities in the course of circulation, just as must the second c in $c-m-c$.

Moreover, on the basis of the capitalist mode of production, as the prevailing mode, all commodities must be commodity capital in the hands of their sellers. They continue to be so in the hands of the merchant, or they become so if they were not so previously. Alternatively, they can be commodities such as imported articles, which replace original commodity capital, hence simply give it another form of existence.

The commodity elements L and mp, of which the productive capital, P, consists, do not possess the same shape, as forms of existence of P, as they did on the various commodity markets from which they were brought together. They are now united, and in their combination they can function as productive capital.

If it is only in this form III, within the circuit itself, that C appears as a premise of C, this is because the starting-point is capital in the commodity form. The circuit is opened by the conversion of C' (in so far as it functions as capital value, whether or not increased by the addition of surplus-value) into the commodities that form its elements of production. But this conversion comprises the entire circulation process $C–M–C (=L+mp)$ and is its result. C thus stands here at both extremes, though the second extreme, which receives its form C from outside, from the commodity market, by way of $M–C$, is not the last extreme of the circuit, but only the latter of the first two stages that comprise its circulation process. Its result is P, and then P's function begins, the production process. It is only as the result of this, i.e. not as the result of the circulation process, that C' appears as the close of the circuit and in the same form as the original extreme C'. In $M\ldots M'$ and $P\ldots P$, on the other hand, the closing extremes M' and P are the direct results of the circulation process. This is why it is only at the close that M' in the first case, and P in the second case, are assumed to be in the hands of others. In so far as the circuit takes place between these extremes, neither M in the one case nor P in the other – the existence of M as someone else's money, and of P as another production process – appears as a precondition for these circuits. $C'\ldots C'$, on the other hand, presupposes $C (=L+mp)$ as other commodities in the hands of others, commodities which are drawn into the circuit and changed into productive capital by way of the opening process of circulation. Then, as the result of productive capital's function, C' once again becomes the closing form of the circuit.

But precisely because the circuit $C'\ldots C'$ presupposes in its description the existence of another industrial capital in the form $C (=L+mp)$

(and *mp* comprises other capitals of various kinds, e.g. in our case machines, coal, oil, etc.), it itself demands to be considered not only as the *general* form of the circuit, i.e. as a social form in which every individual industrial capital can be considered (except in the case of its first investment), hence not only as a form of motion common to all individual industrial capitals, but at the same time as the form of motion of the sum of individual capitals, i.e. of the total social capital of the capitalist class, a movement in which the movement of any individual industrial capital simply appears as a partial one, intertwined with the others and conditioned by them. If we consider, for example, the total annual commodity product of a country, and analyse the movement in which one part of this replaces the productive capital of all individual businesses, and another part goes into the individual consumption of the different classes, then we are considering $C' \ldots C'$ as a form of motion of both the social capital and of the surplus-value or surplus product produced by this. The fact that the social capital is equal to the sum of the individual capitals (including joint-stock capital and also state capital, in so far as governments employ productive wage-labour in mines, railways, etc., and function as industrial capitalists), and that the total movement of the social capital is equal to the algebraic sum of the movements of the individual capitals, in no way prevents this motion, as the motion of an isolated individual capital, from displaying phenomena different from those displayed by the same motion, when it is viewed as a part of the total motion of the social capital, i.e. in its connection with the motions of the other parts of this; in this latter aspect, problems can be resolved whose solution must be presupposed in considering the circuit of a single individual capital, instead of resulting from the study of this.

$C' \ldots C'$ is the only circuit in which the capital value originally advanced forms only a part of the extreme that opens the movement, and in which the movement in this way proclaims itself from the start as a total movement of industrial capital; a movement both of the part of the product that replaces the productive capital and of the part that forms surplus product and is on average partly spent as revenue, and partly has to serve as an element of accumulation. In so far as the expenditure of surplus-value as revenue is included in this circuit, individual consumption is also involved. This latter, however, is also included in so far as the starting-point *C*, the commodity, exists as some particular kind of useful article; every capitalistically produced article is commodity capital, irrespective of whether its use form destines it for productive or individual consumption, or for both. $M \ldots M'$ indicates only the value aspect, the valorization of the capital value advanced as the purpose of the whole process; $P \ldots P (P')$ points to the production process of capital as a reproduction process with the productive capital remaining the same or growing in magnitude (accumulation); $C' \ldots C'$, while it already proclaims itself in its initial extreme as a form of capitalist commodity production, comprises both productive and individual consumption from the start; productive consumption and the valorization included in it appear simply as a branch of its movement. Finally, since C' can exist in a use form incapable of entering any further production process, it is apparent from the start that the various value components of C', expressed in portions of the product, must assume a different position, according to whether $C' \ldots C'$ is taken as a form of motion of the total social capital or as the independent movement of an individual industrial capital. In all these peculiarities, this circuit points beyond its own existence as the isolated circuit of a merely individual capital.

In the figure $C' \ldots C'$, the movement of the commodity capital, i.e. of the capitalistically produced total product, appears both as premise of the independent circuit of the individual capital, and as conditioned by it in turn. Hence if this figure is conceived in its particularity, it is no longer sufficient to rest content with the fact that the metamorphoses $C'-M'$ and $M-C$ are on the one hand functionally determined sections of the metamorphosis of the capital, and on the other hand links in the general circulation of commodities. It is necessary to make clear how the metamorphoses of an individual capital are intertwined with those of other individual capitals, and with the part of the total product that is destined for individual consumption. This is why our analysis of the circuit of the individual industrial capital was primarily based on the first two forms.

In agriculture, for example, where they reckon from one harvest to the next, the circuit $C' \ldots C'$ does appear as the form of a single individual capital. Figure II proceeds from the sowing, and figure III from the harvest, or, as the Physiocrats put it, from *avances* and *reprises* respectively.* In figure III the movement of the capital value appears

---

*Advances and returns. The French Physiocratic writers of the 1750s and 60s, in particular Quesnay and Turgot, were the first economists to begin to analyse production rather than simply circulation. They believed however that only agricultural labour was truly productive. Marx explains the characteristic doctrines of the Physiocrats and their origins in *Theories of Surplus-Value*, Part I, Chapter II.

from the start simply as a part of the movement of the general mass of products, while in figures I and II the movement of C' simply forms a moment in the movement of a single capital.

In figure III the commodities on the market form the permanent premise of the process of production and reproduction. Hence if attention is fixed exclusively on this figure, all the elements of the production process seem to proceed from commodity circulation and to exist only as commodities. This one-sided conception overlooks the elements of the production process that are independent of the commodity elements.

Since in $C' \ldots C'$ the total product (the total value) is the point of departure, it is evident here that, leaving aside foreign trade, reproduction on an expanded scale, with productivity otherwise remaining the same, can take place only if the material elements of the additional productive capital are already contained in the part of the surplus product to be capitalized. That is to say, in so far as the production of one year serves as precondition for that of the next, or, in so far as production can occur together with the simple reproduction process within a year, surplus product is immediately produced in the form that enables it to function as additional capital. Increased productivity can increase only the material substance of capital, and cannot raise its value; but it still forms additional material for valorization.

$C' \ldots C'$ is the basis of Quesnay's *Tableau économique*, and it shows great discernment on his part that he selected this form in opposition to $M \ldots M'$ (the form fixed on and isolated by the Mercantile System), and not $P \ldots P$.

Chapter 4: The Three Figures of the Circuit

Taking Tc to stand for the total circulation process, we can depict the three figures as follows:

(I) $M-C\ldots P\ldots C'-M'$

(II) $P\ldots Tc\ldots P$

(III) $Tc\ldots P\,(C')$.

It we take all three forms together, then all the premises of the process appear as its result, as premises produced by the process itself. Each moment appears as a point of departure, of transit, and of return. The total process presents itself as the unity of the process of production and the process of circulation; the production process is the mediator of the circulation process, and vice versa.

Common to all three circuits is the valorization of value as the determining purpose, the driving motive. In figure I, this is actually expressed in the form. Form II begins with P, the valorization process itself. In form III, the circuit begins with the valorized value, and closes with the newly valorized value, even when the movement is repeated on the same scale.

In so far as $C-M$ is $M-C$ for the buyer and $M-C$ is $C-M$ for the seller, the circulation of capital simply displays the general metamorphosis of commodities, and the laws developed in connection with this (Volume 1, Chapter 3, 2), governing the amount of money in circulation, apply here too. However, if we do not just dwell on this formal aspect of the matter, but consider the real connection between the metamorphoses of the various individual capitals, in fact the connection between the circuits of individual capitals as partial movements of the reproduction process of the total social capital, then this process cannot be explained in terms of the simple change of form between money and commodity.

In a constantly rotating orbit, every point is simultaneously a starting-point and a point of return. If we interrupt the rotation, then not every starting-point is a point of return. Thus we have seen that not only does every particular circuit (implicitly) presuppose the others, but also that the repetition of the circuit in one form includes the motions which have to take place in the other forms of the circuit. Thus the entire distinction presents itself as merely one of form, a merely subjective distinction that exists only for the observer.

In so far as each of these circuits is considered as a particular form of the movement in which different individual industrial capitals are involved, this difference also exists throughout simply at the individual level. In reality, however, each individual industrial capital is involved in all three at the same time. The three circuits, the forms of reproduction of the three varieties of capital, are continuously executed alongside one another. One part of the capital value, for example, which for the moment functions as commodity capital, is transformed into money capital, while at the same time another part passes out of the production process into circulation as new commodity capital. Thus the circular form of $C' \ldots C'$ is constantly described, and the same is the case with the two other forms. The reproduction of the capital in each of its forms and at each of its stages is just as continuous as is the metamorphosis of these forms and their successive passage through the three stages. Here, therefore, the entire circuit is the real unity of its three forms.

We have assumed in our discussion that the capital value appears either as money capital, productive capital or commodity capital to the full extent of its magnitude. We thus had the £422, for example, first completely as money capital, then transformed fully into productive capital, finally as commodity capital: yarn to the value of £500 (including £78 surplus-value). The various stages here constitute an equal number of interruptions. For example, as long as the £422 persists in its money form, i.e. until the purchases $M-C\!\!<^{L}_{mp}$ are completed, the total capital exists and functions simply as money capital. Once it is transformed into productive capital, it functions neither as money capital nor as commodity capital. Its entire circulation process is interrupted, just as on the other hand its entire production process is interrupted as soon as it functions in one of the two stages of circulation, whether as M or as C'. Thus the circuit $P \ldots P$ would present itself not only as a periodic renewal of the productive capital, but equally as an interruption in its function, the production process, until the circulation process had been completed; instead of taking place continuously, production would be pursued only in spasms and be repeated only after periods of time of accidental duration, according to whether the two stages of the circulation process were accomplished quicker or more slowly. This would be the case, for example, with a Chinese handicraftsman, who works only for individual clients, and whose production process comes to a halt between one order and the next.

This is in fact true for each individual portion of capital in motion, and all portions of the capital go through this movement in succession. Assume that the 10,000 lb. of yarn is one week's output of a spinning-mill. This 10,000 lb. of yarn moves in its entirety from the sphere of production into that of circulation; the capital value contained in it must be entirely transformed into money capital, and, as long as it persists in the form of money capital, it cannot re-enter the production process; it must first enter circulation and be transformed back into the elements of the productive capital, L and mp. The circuit of capital is a constant process of interruption; one stage is left behind, the next stage embarked upon; one form is cast aside, and the capital exists in another; each of these stages not only conditions the other, but at the same time excludes it.

But continuity is the characteristic feature of capitalist production, and is required by its technical basis, even if it is not always completely attainable. Let us see how things proceed in reality. While our 10,000 lb. of yarn steps onto the market as commodity capital, and accomplishes its transformation into money (whether as means of payment, means of purchase or simply money of account), new cotton, coal, etc. comes into the production process in its place. All this has there-fore already been transformed back from both the money form and the commodity form into the form of productive capital, and begins its function as such; moreover, while the first 10,000 lb. of yarn is being converted into money, a previous 10,000 lb. is already describing the second stage of its circulation, and being transformed back from money into the elements of productive capital. All portions of the capital go through the circuit in succession, and, at any one time, they find themselves in various stages of it. Thus industrial capital in the continuity of its circuit is simultaneously in all of its stages, and in the various functional forms corresponding to them. While the circuit $C' \ldots C'$ has only just begun for that part which is transformed from commodity capital into money for the first time, for industrial capital, considered as a self-moving totality, the same circuit $C' \ldots C'$ has already been traversed. Money is given out with one hand and taken in with the other; what is at one point the commencement of the circuit $M \ldots M'$ is simultaneously at another point its conclusion. The same applies for the productive capital.

The real circuit of industrial capital in its continuity is therefore not only a unified process of circulation and production, but also a unity of all its three circuits. But it can only be such a unity in so far as each different part of the capital runs in succession through the successive phases of the circuit, can pass over from one phase and one functional form into the other; hence industrial capital, as the whole of these parts, exists simultaneously in its various phases and functions, and thus describes all three circuits at once. The succession [*Nacheinander*] of the various parts is here determined by their coexistence [*Nebeneinander*], i.e. by the way in which the capital is divided. In the developed factory system, the product is continuously at the various stages of its formation, and in transition from one phase of production to another. Since each individual industrial capital has a definite size, which is dependent on the means of the capitalist and has a definite minimum for each branch of industry, definite numerical ratios must obtain in its division into parts. The size of the capital involved determines the scale of the production process, and this determines the volume of commodity capital and money capital, in so far as these function alongside the production process. The coexistence which determines the continuity of production, however, exists only through the movement in which the portions of capital successively describe the various stages. The coexistence is itself only the result of the succession. If $C'–M'$ comes to a halt in the case of one portion, for example, if the commodity is unsaleable, then the circuit of this part is interrupted and its replacement by its means of production is not accomplished; the successive parts that emerge from the production process as C' find their change of function barred by their predecessors. If this continues for some time, production is restricted and the whole process brought to a standstill. Every delay in the succession brings the coexistence into disarray, every delay in one stage causes a greater or lesser delay in the entire circuit, not only that of the portion of the capital that is delayed, but also that of the entire individual capital.

The immediate form in which the process presents itself is that of a succession of phases, so that the transition of the capital into a new phase is determined by its abandonment of the previous one. Thus every particular circuit has one of the functional forms of the capital as its starting-point and point of return. On the other hand the total process is in fact the unity of the three circuits, which are the different forms in which the continuity of the process is expressed. The total circuit presents itself for each functional form of capital as its own specific circuit, and indeed each of these circuits conditions the continuity of the overall process; the circular course of one functional form determines that of the others. It is a necessary condition for the overall production process, in other words for the social capital, that this is at the same time a process of reproduction, and hence the circuit of each of its moments. Different fractions of the capital successively pass through the different stages and functional forms. Each functional form thus passes through its circuit simultaneously with the others, though it is always a different part of the capital that presents itself in it. A part of the capital exists as commodity capital that is being transformed into money, but this is an ever-changing part, and is constantly being reproduced; another part exists as money capital that is being transformed into productive capital; a third part as productive capital being transformed into commodity capital. The constant presence of all three forms is mediated by the circuit of the total capital through precisely these three phases.

As a whole, then, the capital is simultaneously present, and spatially coexistent, in its various phases. But each part is constantly passing from one phase or functional form into another, and thus functions in all of them in turn. The forms are therefore fluid forms, and their simultaneity is mediated by their succession. Each form both follows and precedes the others, so that the return of one part of the capital to one form is determined by the return of another part to another form. Each part continuously describes its own course, but it is always another part of capital that finds itself in this form, and these particular circuits simply constitute simultaneous and successive moments of the overall process.

It is only in the unity of the three circuits that the continuity of the overall process is realized, in place of the interruption we have just delineated. The total social capital always possesses this continuity, and its process always contains the unity of the three circuits.

For individual capitals, the continuity of reproduction is at certain points interrupted, to a greater or lesser degree. Firstly, the quantities of value are frequently distributed amongst the various stages and functional forms in unequal portions, at different times. Secondly, these portions may be differently divided, according to the character of the commodity which has to be produced, thus according to the particular sphere of production in which the capital has been invested. Thirdly, the continuity may be more or less interrupted in branches of production that depend on the season, either as a result of natural conditions (agriculture, fishing for herrings, etc.), or as a matter of convention as is the case with so-called seasonal work, for example. It is in the factory and in mining that the process occurs most regularly and uniformly. But this difference between branches of production does not give rise to any difference in the general forms of the circuit.

Capital, as self-valorizing value, does not just comprise class relations, a definite social character that depends on the existence of labour as wage-labour. It is a movement, a circulatory process through different stages, which itself in turn includes three different forms of the circulatory process. Hence it can only be grasped as a movement, and not as a static thing. Those who consider the autonomization [*Verselbstständigung*] of value as a mere abstraction forget that the movement of industrial capital is this abstraction in action. Here value passes through different forms, different movements in which it is both preserved and increases, is valorized. Since we are firstly dealing here simply with the forms of movement, we have not considered the revolutions that the capital value may suffer in its circulatory process; it is clear however that despite all revolutions in value, capitalist production can exist and continue to exist only so long as the capital value is valorized, i.e. describes its circuit as value that has become independent, and therefore so long as the revolutions in value are somehow or other mastered and balanced out. The movements of capital appear as actions of the individual industrial capitalist in so far as he functions as buyer of commodities and labour, seller of commodities and productive capitalist, and thus mediates the circuit by his own activity. If the social capital value suffers a revolution in value, it can come about that his individual capital succumbs to this and is destroyed, because it cannot meet the conditions of this movement of value. The more acute and frequent these revolutions in value become, the more the movement of the independent value, acting with the force of an elemental natural process, prevails over the foresight and calculation of the individual capitalist, the more the course of normal production is subject to abnormal speculation, and the greater becomes the danger to the existence of the individual capitals. These periodic revolutions in value thus confirm what they ostensibly refute: the independence which value acquires as capital, and which is maintained and intensified through its movement.

This sequence of metamorphoses of capital in process implies the continuous comparison of the change in value brought about in the circuit with the original value of the capital. The independence of value in relation to the value-forming power, labour-power, is introduced by the act *M–L* (purchase of labour-power), and is realized during the production process as exploitation of labour-power. But this independence does not reappear in the circuit in which money, commodity and elements of production are only alternating forms of the capital value in process, and in which the past magnitude of the value is compared with the present, changed value of the capital.

'Value,' says Bailey, opposing the autonomization of value which characterizes the capitalist mode of production, and which he treats as the illusion of certain economists, 'value is a relation between contemporary commodities, because such only admit of being exchanged with each other.'*

He says this in opposition to the comparison of commodity values at different points in time, a comparison which, if the value of money at each period is taken as fixed, is simply a comparison between the expenditure of labour required in different epochs for the production of the same kind of commodities. This derives from his general misunderstanding, according to which exchange-value equals value, the form of value is value itself; thus commodity values cease to be comparable once they no longer actively function as exchange-values, and cannot actually be exchanged for one another. He does not in the least suspect, therefore, that value functions as capital value or capital only in so far as it remains identical with itself and is compared with itself in the different phases of its circuit, which are in no way 'contemporary', but rather occur in succession.

In order to consider the formula of the circuit in its pure state, it is not sufficient to assume that commodities are sold at their values; this must also take place in circumstances that in other respects, too, remain the same. If we take the form *P* . . . *P*, for example, we must disregard all technical revolutions in the production process which may devalue the productive capital of a particular capitalist; we must also disregard any repercussions that a change in the value elements of the productive capital might have on the value of the existing commodity capital (which may rise or fall if there is a stock of this on hand). Let *C'*, the 10,000 lb. of yarn, be sold at its value of £500; 8,440 lb. = £422 replaces

---

*This quotation is from Samuel Bailey's *A Critical Dissertation on the Nature, Measures, and Causes of Value; Chiefly in Reference to the Writings of Mr Ricardo and His Followers*, London, 1825, p. 72. Although a vulgar economist who held value to be merely relative, Bailey did expose certain contradictions in the Ricardian theory. See *Theories of Surplus-Value*, Part III, Chapter XX, pp. 124 ff.

the capital value contained in it. But if the value of cotton, coal etc. rises (here we disregard mere price-fluctuations), then this £422 may not be sufficient to replace completely the elements of the productive capital; additional money capital is then necessary, i.e. money capital is tied up. Conversely, if these prices fall, money capital is set free. The process takes place quite normally only if value relations remain constant; in practice it runs its course as long as disturbances in the repetition of the circuit balance each other out; the greater the disturbances, the greater the money capital that the industrial capitalist must possess in order to ride out the period of readjustment; and since the scale of each individual production process grows with the progress of capitalist production, and with it the minimum size of the capital to be advanced, this circumstance is added to the other circumstances which increasingly turn the function of industrial capitalist into a monopoly of large-scale money capitalists, either individual or associated.

We may remark here, in passing, that when there is a change in the value of the elements of production, a distinction arises between the form $M \ldots M'$ on the one hand, and the forms $P \ldots P$ and $C' \ldots C'$ on the other.

In $M \ldots M'$, as the formula for newly invested capital, which first appears as money capital, a fall in the value of the means of production, e.g. raw materials, ancillaries, etc., means that a smaller outlay of money capital than previously is required in order to open a business of a particular size, since, given that the level of the productive forces remains the same, the scale of the production process depends only on the volume and scale of the means of production that a given quantity of labour-power can cope with, and not on the value of those means of production, or on that of the labour-power (the latter simply has an effect on the magnitude of the valorization). Conversely, if there is an increase in the value of the elements of production of the commodities which form the elements of productive capital, then more money capital is necessary in order to found a business of a given size. In both cases, it is only the amount of the money capital to be newly invested that is affected; in the first case, some money capital becomes superfluous, in the second case, more money capital is tied up, provided that the rate of increase of a new individual industrial capital proceeds as is usual in the given branch of production.

The circuits $P \ldots P$ and $C' \ldots C'$ behave in the same way as $M \ldots M'$ only in so far as the movement of P and C' is at the same time accumulation, i.e. in so far as excess m, money, is transformed into money capital.

Otherwise, they are affected differently from $M \ldots M'$ by a change in the value of the elements of productive capital; here we once again disregard the impact a change in value of this kind has on the components which are already involved in the production process. Here it is not the original outlay that is directly affected, but rather an industrial capital involved not in its first circuit but in its process of reproduction, i.e. $C' \ldots C {<}^{L}_{mp}$, the conversion of commodity capital back into its elements of production, in so far as these consist of commodities. With a fall in value (or price), three cases are possible: first, the reproduction process may be continued on the same scale, in which case a part of the former money capital is set free, and money capital is stored up, though neither real accumulation (production on an expanded scale) nor the preliminary and accompanying transformation of m (surplus-value) into an accumulation fund has taken place; second, the reproduction process may be expanded to a larger scale than would have otherwise been the case, if the technical proportions permit this; or third, a larger reserve of raw materials, etc., may be built up.

The opposite happens with a rise in the value of the replacement elements of commodity capital. Reproduction then no longer takes place on its normal scale (e.g. working hours may be cut); or, additional money capital has to be injected, in order to continue the former scale of reproduction (money capital is tied up); or, finally, the monetary accumulation fund, where there is one, has to serve in whole or in part for pursuing the reproduction process on its old scale, instead of expanding it. This also involves the tying up of money capital, although here the additional money capital does not come from an external source, from the money market, but rather from the resources of the industrial capitalist himself.

But there can be modifying circumstances to $P \ldots P$ and $C' \ldots C'$. If our cotton spinner has a large reserve of raw cotton, for example (i.e. a large part of his productive capital is in the form of a cotton stock), then a part of his productive capital will be devalued by a fall in cotton prices; if these rise, then this part of his productive capital conversely rises in value. On the other hand, if he has large quantities tied up in the form of commodity capital, e.g. in cotton yarn, then a fall in cotton prices will devalue a part of his commodity capital, and thus a part of his overall capital in the circuit; conversely with a rise in cotton prices.

In the process $C'{-}M{-}C {<}^{L}_{mp}$, finally: if $C'{-}M$, the realization of commodity capital, has taken place before the change in value of the elements of C, then the capital is affected only in the way considered in the first case, i.e. in the second act of circulation $M-C<^{L}_{mp}$; but if the change in value occurs before the completion of $C'-M$, then, with other circumstances remaining the same, the fall in the price of cotton leads to a corresponding fall in the price of yarn, and a rise in the price of cotton to a rise in the price of yarn. The effect on the various individual capitals invested in the same branch of production can be very different according to the different circumstances in which they are found. Money capital may also be set free or tied up as the result of differences in the duration of the circulation process, i.e. in the speed of circulation. This however belongs to the discussion of turnover. What interests us here is simply the real distinction which emerges between $M \ldots M'$ and the two other forms of the circuit with respect to changes in value of the elements of productive capital.

In the section of circulation $M-C<^{L}_{mp}$, in the epoch when the capitalist mode of production is already developed, and hence dominant, a large part of the commodities which the means of production (mp) consist of are themselves the functioning commodity capital of others. From the standpoint of the seller, therefore, what takes place is $C'-M'$, the transformation of commodity capital into money capital. But this does not hold good absolutely. On the contrary. Within its circulation process, in which industrial capital functions either as money or as commodity, the circuit of industrial capital, whether in the form of money capital or commodity capital, cuts across the commodity circulation of the most varied modes of social production, in so far as this commodity circulation simultaneously reflects commodity production. Whether the commodities are the product of production based on slavery, the product of peasants (Chinese, Indian ryots), of a community (Dutch East Indies), of state production (such as existed in earlier epochs of Russian history, based on serfdom) or of half-savage hunting peoples, etc. – as commodities and money they confront the money and commodities in which industrial capital presents itself, and enter both into the latter's own circuit and into that of the surplus-value borne by the commodity capital, in so far as the latter is spent as revenue; i.e. in both branches of the circulation of commodity capital. The character of the production process from which they derive is immaterial; they function on the market as commodities, and as commodities they enter both the circuit of industrial capital and the circulation of the surplus-value borne by it. Thus the circulation process of industrial capital is characterized by the many-sided character of its origins, and the existence of the market as a world market. What holds for foreign commodities holds also for foreign money; as commodity capital functions in relation to money simply as commodity, so this money functions towards commodity capital simply as money; the money functions here as world money.

Now, however, there are two further points to be made.

Firstly. As soon as the act $M-mp$ is completed, the commodities (mp) cease to be commodities and become one of the modes of existence of industrial capital in its functional form P, productive capital. Their provenance is therefore obliterated; they now exist simply as forms of existence of industrial capital, and are incorporated into it. Yet it remains the case that their replacement requires their reproduction, and to this extent the capitalist mode of production is conditioned by modes of production lying outside its own stage of development. Its tendency, however, is to transform all possible production into commodity production; the main means by which it does this is precisely by drawing this production into its circulation process; and developed commodity production is itself capitalist commodity production. The intervention of industrial capital everywhere promotes this transformation, and with it too the transformation of all immediate producers into wage-labourers.

Secondly. Whatever the origin of the commodities that go into the circulation process of industrial capital (and these include the necessary means of subsistence into which variable capital is transformed after being paid to the workers so that they can reproduce their labour-power), whatever therefore may be the social form of the production process from which these commodities derive – they confront industrial capital straight away in its form of commodity capital, they themselves having the form of commodity-dealing or merchant's capital; and this by its very nature embraces commodities from all modes of production.

As the capitalist mode of production presupposes production on a large scale, so it also necessarily presupposes large-scale sale; sale to the merchant, not to the individual consumer. In so far as this consumer is himself a productive consumer, i.e. an industrial capitalist, i.e. in so far as industrial capital in one branch of production supplies means of production to another branch, there is also direct sale by one industrial capitalist to several others (in the form of orders, etc.). Each industrial capitalist is a direct seller in so far as he is himself his own merchant, which he is moreover also when he sells to a merchant.

Commodity trade is presupposed, as a function of merchant's capital, and this develops ever further with the development of capitalist production. Thus we occasionally take its existence for granted in illustrating particular aspects of the capitalist circulation process; but in this general analysis we assume direct sale without the intervention of the merchant, since this intervention conceals various moments of the movement.

We may quote Sismondi, who presents the matter rather naïvely:

'Commerce employs a considerable capital, and this appears at first glance not to form part of that whose course we have charted. The value of the cloth accumulated in the stores of the draper seems at first to be completely different from the part of the year's production that the rich man gives to the poor man as a wage to have him work for him. But this capital has simply replaced that of which we have been speaking. In order to grasp clearly the progress of wealth, we started with its creation, and we have followed it through to its consumption. The capital employed in the manufacture of cloth, for example, we regarded as remaining constant. Exchanged against the revenue of the consumer, it divided into only two parts. One of these served as revenue for the manufacturer, in the form of profit, the other served as revenue for the workers in the form of wages, while they were manufacturing more cloth.

'But it was soon found to be to everyone's advantage for the various parts of this capital to replace one another, so that, if 100,000 crowns was sufficient for the whole circulation between the manufacturer and the consumer, this 100,000 crowns would be shared equally between the manufacturer, the wholesale merchant and the retailer. The first of these, who receives only a third of the total, does the same work as he did when he received the whole lot, because the moment its manufacture is completed, he finds the merchant to buy it much sooner than he would have found the consumer. The wholesaler's capital, for its part, is replaced by that of the retailer much sooner . . . The difference between the sums advanced in wages and the purchase price for the final consumer forms the profit on the capitals. It is divided between the manufacturer, the wholesaler and the retailer, after they have divided their functions between them, and the task accomplished is the same, even though it has employed three persons and three fractions of capital in place of one' (*Nouveaux Principes,* I, pp. 139, 140). 'All these' (the merchants) 'indirectly participated in production; for as the aim of production is consumption, it cannot be considered accomplished until it has placed the object produced at the disposal of the consumer' (ibid., p. 137).

In considering the general forms of the circuit, and throughout this second volume in general, we take money to be metal money, excluding symbolic money, mere tokens of value which are specific to particular countries, as well as credit money, which we have not yet developed. Firstly, this is the course taken by history: credit money played no role, or at least not a significant one, in the early period of capitalist production. Secondly, the necessity of this course can be proved theoretically, in so far as everything critical that has so far been said about the circulation of credit money by Tooke and others compelled them time and again to look back at how the matter would present itself on the basis of mere metallic circulation. It should not be forgotten, however, that metallic money can not only function as means of purchase, but also as means of payment. For the sake of simplification, we generally take it, in this second volume, only in the first functional form.

The circulation process of industrial capital, which forms only one part of its individual circuit, is determined, in so far as it represents only a series of acts within the general commodity circulation, by the general laws that have already been developed (Volume 1, Chapter 3). The same quantity of money, e.g. £500, puts correspondingly more industrial capitals into circulation (i.e. individual capitals in their form as commodity capitals), the greater the velocity of circulation of the money, thus the faster each individual capital passes through its series of metamorphoses into commodities and money. Capital of the same value accordingly requires less money for its circulation, the more the money functions as means of payment (e.g. the more that it is only balances that have to be settled when a commodity capital is replaced by its means of production), and the shorter the periods of payment (e.g. in the payment of wages). On the other hand, assuming that the velocity of circulation and all other circumstances remain the same, the amount of money needed to circulate as money capital, is determined by the sum of the prices of the commodities (price multiplied by the quantity of commodities), or alternatively, given the quantity and values of the commodities, by the value of the money itself.

But the laws of general commodity circulation apply only in so far as the circulation process of capital is a series of simple acts of circulation, and not in so far as the latter form functionally specific sections of the circuits of individual industrial capitals.

In order to make this clear, it is best to consider the circulation process in its uninterrupted interconnection, as it appears in the two forms:

(II)

$$P \ldots C' \begin{cases} C- \\ -M' \\ c- \end{cases} \begin{cases} M-C \underset{mp}{\overset{L}{\diagdown}} \ldots P \ (P') \\ m-c \end{cases}$$

(III)

$$C' \begin{cases} C- \\ -M' \\ c- \end{cases} \begin{cases} M-C \underset{mp}{\overset{L}{\diagdown}} \ldots P \ldots C' \\ m-c \end{cases}$$

As a series of acts of circulation in general, the circulation process (whether as $C-M-C$ or as $M-C-M$) simply presents two opposing series of commodity metamorphoses, each individual metamorphosis including the opposite metamorphosis on the part of the other person's commodity or money that confronts it.

$C-M$ on the part of the commodity possessor is $M-C$ on the part of the purchaser; the first metamorphosis of the commodity in $C-M$ is the second metamorphosis of the commodity which steps forth as M; conversely with $M-C$. What was previously demonstrated, concerning the intertwining of the metamorphoses of a commodity at one stage with those of another commodity at another stage, therefore holds good for the circulation of capital, in so far as the capitalist is buyer and seller of commodities, and his capital accordingly functions as money towards others' commodities, or as a commodity towards others' money. This intertwining, however, is not by this token alone an entwining of the metamorphoses of capitals.

Firstly, $M-C$ (mp), as we have seen, can depict an entwining of the metamorphoses of various individual capitals. The commodity capital of the cotton-spinner, yarn, for example, is in part replaced by coal. A part of his capital exists in the money form and is converted from this into the commodity form, while the capital of the mine-owner exists in the commodity form and is therefore converted into the money form; the same act of circulation here represents opposite metamorphoses on the part of two industrial capitals (which belong to different branches of production), i.e. an entwining of the series of metamorphoses of these capitals. As we have seen, however, the mp into which M is converted need not be commodity capital in the categorical sense, i.e. need not be a functional form of industrial capital, produced by a capitalist. It is always $M-C$ on the one hand, and $C-M$ on the other, but not always an entwining of metamorphoses of capital. Furthermore, $M-L$, the acquisition of labour-power, is never an entwining of capital metamorphoses, for, while labour-power is certainly a commodity for the worker, it becomes capital only when it is sold to the capitalist. In the process $C'-M'$, on the other hand, M' does not need to be converted commodity capital; it can be the expression in money of the commodity labour-power (i.e. wages), or of a product produced by an independent worker, a slave, a serf or a community.

Secondly, it is by no means always the case that the functionally determined role played by every metamorphosis that takes place within the circulation process of an individual capital represents the corresponding opposite metamorphosis in the circuit of the other capital, particularly if we assume that the whole of production for the world market is pursued on a capitalist basis. In the circuit $P \ldots P$, for example, the M' that turns C' into cash may be on the side of the buyer simply the monetary expression of his surplus-value (if the commodity is an article of consumption); alternatively. in $M'-C' <^{L}_{mp}$ (i.e. where accumulated capital is involved), it may be for the buyer of mp simply a replacement for his capital advance, or it may not re-enter his capital circulation at all, particularly if this branches off into expenditure of revenue.

The way in which the various components of the total social capital, of which the individual capitals are only independently functioning components, alternately replace one another in the circulation process – both with respect to capital and to surplus-value – is thus not the result of the simple intertwining of the metamorphoses that occurs in commodity circulation, and which the acts of capital circulation have in common with all other processes of commodity circulation, but rather requires a different mode of investigation. Up till now, mere phrases have been taken as sufficient in this respect, although, when these are analysed more closely, they contain nothing more than indefinite notions, simply borrowed from the intertwining of metamorphoses that is common to all commodity circulation.

*

One of the most obvious peculiarities of the circuit of industrial capital, and thus of capitalist production, is the situation that on the one hand the elements from which productive capital is formed stem from the commodity market, and must be continually renewed from it, bought as commodities; and on the other hand the product of the labour process emerges from it as a commodity, and must constantly be sold anew as a commodity. A modern farmer in the lowlands of Scotland might for example be contrasted with an old-fashioned small peasant on the Continent. The former sells his entire product and thus has to replace all its elements, even the seed-corn, on the market, while the latter consumes the greater part of his product directly, buys and sells as little as possible, and as far as possible produces his tools, clothing, etc. himself.

Natural economy, money economy and credit economy have for this reason been counterposed as the three characteristic economic forms of motion of social production.

Firstly, these three forms do not represent phases of development of the same status. The so-called credit economy is itself only a form of the money economy, in so far as both terms express functions or modes of commerce [*Verkehr*]* between the producers themselves. In developed capitalist production, the money economy simply appears as the basis of the credit economy. Thus money economy and credit economy merely correspond to different stages of development of capitalist production; they are in no way different independent forms of commerce as opposed to natural economy. It would be just as valid to counterpose the very varied forms of natural economy as equal in status to the other two.

Secondly, what is emphasized in the categories money economy and credit economy, and stressed as the distinctive feature, is actually not the economy proper, i.e. the production process itself, but rather the mode of commerce between the various agents of production or pro-

---

*The term *Verkehr* plays an important role in *The German Ideology*, where it is conventionally translated as 'intercourse'. The concept this denotes was later to be rejected by Marx and Engels in favour of that of relations of production, as Göran Therborn explains in *Science, Class and Society*, NLB, 1976, pp. 368ff. The present passage, written in 1877, seems to be the only time that '*Verkehr*' reappears in a conceptual sense in any of the volumes of *Capital*. Its meaning here, however, has clearly little to do with the early concept of *The German Ideology*. It rather covers what Marx and Engels more usually referred to as 'exchange' (*Austausch*), in the sense of 'mode of production and exchange'. The reason why Marx uses *Verkehr* here instead of the more usual *Austausch* would seem to be then that he needs to use the term *Tausch* (exchange or barter) to refer to a particular form of 'commerce' between producers – the non-monetary exchange corresponding to a 'natural economy' – and, since *Tausch* and *Austausch* are almost interchangeable in German usage, selects the looser term *Verkehr* to emphasize the general concept of which barter and monetary exchange (with the latter's sub-type credit) are the variants.

ducers that corresponds to the economy, and so this should also be done in the case of the first category. Instead of natural economy, we would then have barter economy. A completely enclosed natural economy, such as the Inca state of Peru, would fall into none of these categories.

Thirdly, money economy is common to all commodity production, and the product appears as a commodity in the most diverse organisms of social production. Thus it would simply be the scale on which the product was produced as an article of trade, as a commodity, and thus also the extent to which its own formative elements must again enter the economy from which it derives as articles of trade, as commodities, which would characterize capitalist production.

In point of fact, capitalist production is commodity production as the general form of production, but it is only so, and becomes ever more so in its development, because labour itself here appears as a commodity, because the worker sells labour, i.e. the function of his labour-power, and moreover, as we have assumed, at a value determined by the costs of its reproduction. The producer becomes an industrial capitalist to the same extent that labour becomes wage-labour; hence capitalist production (and thus also commodity production) appears in its full extent only when the direct agricultural producer is also a wage-labourer. In the relation between capitalist and wage-labourer, the money relation, the relation of buyer and seller, becomes a relation inherent in production itself. But this relation rests fundamentally on the social character of production, not on the mode of commerce; the latter rather derives from the former. It is typical of the bourgeois horizon, moreover, where business deals fill the whole of people's minds, to see the foundation of the mode of production in the mode of commerce corresponding to it, rather than the other way round.[1]

*

The capitalist casts less value into circulation in the form of money than he draws out of it, because he casts in more value in the form of commodities than he has extracted in the form of commodities. In so far as he functions merely as the personification of capital, as industrial capitalist, his supply of commodity-value is always greater than his demand for it. If his supply and demand matched one another in this respect, this would be equivalent to the non-valorization of his capital; it would

1. Up to here, Manuscript V. The remainder of this chapter consists of a note found among extracts from books in a notebook of 1877 or 1878.

not have functioned as productive capital; productive capital would have been transformed into commodity capital that had not been impregnated with surplus-value; it would not have extracted from labour-power during the production process any surplus-value in the commodity form, and thus not functioned as capital at all. The capitalist must indeed 'sell dearer than he has bought', but he manages to do this only because the capitalist production process enables him to transform the cheaper, because less valuable, commodities that he has bought into more valuable and hence dearer ones. He sells dearer, not because he sells above the value of his commodities, but because he sells commodities of a value greater than the sum of values of the ingredients required to produce them.

The greater the difference between the capitalist's supply and his demand, i.e. the greater the additional commodity value that he supplies over the commodity value that he demands, the greater the rate at which he valorizes his capital. His goal is not simply to cover his demand with his supply, but to have the greatest possible excess of supply over demand.

What is true for the individual capitalist, is true also for the capitalist class.

In so far as the capitalist simply personifies industrial capital, his own demand consists simply in the demand for means of production and labour-power. His demand for *mp* is smaller in value terms than the capital he has advanced; he buys means of production to a smaller value than the value of his capital, and hence to a still smaller value than that of the commodity capital that he supplies.

As far as his demand for labour-power is concerned, it is determined in its value by the ratio between his variable capital and his total capital, i.e. $v:C$. In capitalist production, therefore, this demand grows at a smaller rate than his demand for means of production. The capitalist buys more of *mp* than of L, and to a steadily increasing extent.

In so far as the worker converts his wages almost wholly into means of subsistence, and by far the greater part into necessities, the capitalist's demand for labour-power is indirectly also a demand for the means of consumption that enter into the consumption of the working class. But this demand equals v, and not an atom more (if the worker saves something out of his wages – we necessarily leave the matter of credit out of consideration here – this means that he transforms a part of his wage into a hoard and to this extent does not appear as a customer). The maximum limit of the capitalist's demand is $C = c+v$, but his supply is $c+v+s$; thus if the composition of his commodity capital is $80_c+20_v+20_s$, then his demand is 80_c+20_v, a value one fifth smaller than his supply. The greater the percentage of s produced (the rate of profit), the smaller his demand in relation to his supply. Although, as production advances, the capitalist's demand for labour-power, and hence indirectly for necessary means of subsistence, becomes progressively smaller than his demand for means of production, it should not be forgotten that his demand for *mp* is always smaller than his capital, considering this day by day. His demand for means of production must thus always be smaller in value than the commodity product of the capitalist who works with the same capital and under otherwise similar conditions, and supplies him with these means of production. That many capitalists are involved here, and not just one, in no way affects the matter. Assume that his capital is £1,000, the constant part of this being £800; then his demand on all these capitalists is £800. Together they supply for each £1,000 (no matter how much of this falls to each one of them and what portion this may constitute in his total capital), assuming the same rate of profit, means of production to a value of £1,200; thus his demand only covers two thirds of their supply, while his own total demand is only four fifths of his own supply, considered in value terms.

We still have to investigate the question of turnover, for the time being only in passing. Assume that his total capital is £5,000, of which £4,000 is fixed and £1,000 circulating; this $1,000 = 800_c+200_v$, according to the above assumption. His circulating capital must turn over five times in the year in order for his total capital to turn over once. His commodity product is then £6,000, i.e. £1,000 greater than the capital he advanced, which once again gives the same ratio of surplus-value as above: $5,000\ C{:}1,000_s = 100_{(c+v)}{:}20_s$. Thus this turnover in no way alters the ratio of his total demand to his total supply, the former remaining one fifth smaller than the latter.

Let us assume that his fixed capital has to be renewed in ten years. Each year, then, he amortizes $1/10 =$ £400. [After the first year] he has a value of £3,600 in fixed capital and £400 in money. In so far as repairs are necessary, and these do not exceed the average amount, they are simply capital that is invested at a later date. We can consider the matter as if he had allowed for all the repair costs when he assessed the value of his invested capital, in so far as this enters into the annual commodity product, so that these are included in the one tenth amortization. (If his repair needs are lower than average, this is simply a bonus for him, just as it is to his disadvantage if they are higher.) In any case, although (on the assumption that his total capital turns over once in the year) his annual demand remains £5,000, the same as the original capital value he advanced, it increases with respect to the circulating part of the capital, while it steadily declines with respect to the fixed part.

We now come to reproduction. Assume that the capitalist consumes the entire surplus-value *m* and reconverts only the original capital sum *C* into productive capital. The capitalist's demand is now equal in value to his supply. But this is not so in respect of the movement of his capital; as capitalist he exerts a demand only on the basis of four fifths of his supply (in value terms). The remaining fifth he consumes as non-capitalist, not in his function as capitalist, but for his private requirements or pleasures.

His account, reckoned in percentages, is then:

Demand as capitalist	100, supply 120
Demand as man of the world	20, „ –
Total demand	120, supply 120

This assumption is equivalent to assuming the non-existence of capitalist production and therefore the non-existence of the industrial capitalist himself. For capitalism is already essentially abolished once we assume that it is enjoyment that is the driving motive and not enrichment itself.

It is moreover also technically impossible. The capitalist must not only form a reserve capital to guard against price fluctuations, and in order to be able to await the most favourable conjunctures for buying and selling; he must accumulate capital, in order to extend production and incorporate technical advances into his productive organism.

In order to accumulate capital, he must first withdraw from circulation a part of the surplus-value that he obtained from it, and let it grow in the form of a hoard until it has assumed the requisite dimensions for an extension of his old business or the opening of a new line. As long as the hoarding continues, the capitalist's demand is not increased; the money is immobilized and does not withdraw from the commodity market an equivalent in commodities for the money equivalent that it has withdrawn for commodities supplied.

We have ignored credit here, and it pertains to credit if the capitalist deposits the money that he accumulates in a bank, for example, on current account bearing interest.

Chapter 5: Circulation Time[1]

As we have seen, the movements of capital through the production sphere and the two phases of the circulation sphere are accomplished successively in time. The duration of its stay in the production sphere forms its production time, that in the circulation sphere its circulation time. The total amount of time it takes to describe its circuit is therefore equal to the sum of its production time and its circulation time.

The production time includes, of course, the period of the labour process; but this is not all. We should first recall that a part of the constant capital exists in means of labour such as machines, buildings, etc. which serve for constant repetitions of the same labour process until they are worn out. The periodic interruption of the labour process, at night for example, may interrupt the function of these means of labour, but it does not affect their stay in the place of production. They belong to this not only when they function, but also when they do not function. What is more, the capitalist must hold in reserve a certain stock of raw and ancillary materials, so that the production process can keep going for shorter or longer intervals on the previously determined scale, without depending on the accidents of daily supply on the market. This reserve of raw materials etc. is only gradually consumed productively. There is therefore a difference between the capital's production time[2] and its functioning time. The production time of the means of production generally comprises (1) the time during which they function as means of production, and thus serve in the production process; (2) the pauses during which the production process, and thus also the functioning of the means of production incorporated in it, is interrupted; (3) the time during which they are held in reserve as conditions of the

1. From here onwards, Manuscript IV.
2. The expression 'production time' is to be taken here in the active sense: the production time of the means of production is not the time that it takes to produce them, but that for which they participate in the production process of a commodity product. – F.E.

process, and thus already represent productive capital, but are not yet engaged in the production process.

The difference so far considered is in each case a difference between the time that the productive capital remains in the production sphere and its time in the actual production process. But the production process may itself involve interruptions of the labour process and hence of working time, intervals in which the object of labour is exposed to the action of physical processes, without further addition of human labour. The production process, and hence the function of the means of production, continues in this case, even though the labour process, and hence the function of the means of production as means of labour, is interrupted. This is the case for example with corn that is sown, wine that ferments in the cellar, or material of labour that is exposed to chemical processes, as in many industries such as tanning. Here the production time is greater than the working time. The difference between the two consists in an excess of the production time over the working time. This excess is always based on the fact that the productive capital exists in a *latent* state in the production sphere, without functioning in the production process itself, or that it functions in the production process without being involved in the labour process.

The part of the latent productive capital that is simply held in readiness as a condition for the production process, such as cotton, coal, etc. in the spinning mill, acts neither to form products nor values. It is idle capital, although its idleness forms a condition for the uninterrupted flow of the production process. The buildings, apparatus, etc. that are necessary for storing the productive reserve (the latent capital) are conditions of the production process and hence form components of the productive capital advanced. They fulfil their function by maintaining the productive components in the preliminary stage; they make the raw material, etc. dearer, but since a part of this labour, in the same way as a part of all other wage-labour, is not paid for, it is productive labour and creates surplus-value. The normal interruptions of the overall production process, i.e. the intervals in which the productive capital does not function, produce neither value nor surplus-value. Hence the drive towards night work (Volume 1, Chapter 10, 4). The intervals in the working time that the object of labour has itself to undergo during the production process create neither value nor surplus-value; but they further the product, form a part of its life, a process that it must pass through. The value of the apparatus, etc. is carried over to the product in proportion to the entire period during which it functions; the product is placed in this stage by labour itself, and the use of this apparatus is just as much a condition of production as the reduction to dust of a part of the cotton that does not go into the product, but still carries its value over to it. The other part of the latent capital, such as the buildings, machines, etc., i.e. the means of labour whose function is interrupted only by the regular pauses in the production process – irregular interruptions as a result of a restriction of production, crises, etc. are pure loss – adds value, without entering into the formation of the product. The total value that the means of labour add to the product is determined by the average length of their life; they lose value because they lose use-value, not only in the time during which they are functioning, but also in the time during which they are not.

Finally, the value of that part of the constant capital that continues in the production process even when the labour process is interrupted appears once again in the result of the production process. The means of production are here placed by labour itself in conditions in which they undergo by themselves certain specific natural processes, the result of which is a specific useful effect or a changed form of their use-value. Labour always carries over the value of the means of production to the product, to the extent that it actually consumes these deliberately as means of production. Nothing is altered here by whether the labour must, through the means of labour, act continuously on the object of labour, in order to produce this effect, or whether it need only give the first impulse by placing the means of production in conditions in which they themselves undergo the intended alteration, without labour's further collaboration, as a result of natural processes.

Whatever may be the reason for the excess of production time over working time – whether it is because the means of production form only latent productive capital, i.e. still exist in a stage preliminary to the production process proper, or because their specific function is interrupted within the production process by the pauses in it, or because finally the production process itself requires interruptions in the labour process – in none of these cases do the means of production function to absorb labour. If they absorb no labour, then they absorb no surplus labour. Hence there is no valorization of the productive capital, as long as this finds itself in that part of its production time that is in excess of the working time, no matter how inseparable these pauses may be from the accomplishment of the valorization process. It is clear that the nearer production time and working time approach to equality, the greater the productivity and valorization of a given productive capital in a given space of time. The tendency of capitalist production is therefore to shorten as much as possible the excess of production time over working time. But although the production time of capital may diverge from its working time, it always includes the latter, and the excess itself is a condition of the production process. Thus the production time is always the time that the capital takes to produce use-values and valorize itself, hence to function as productive capital, although it includes time in which it is either latent or produces without being valorized.

Within the circulation sphere, capital exists as commodity capital and money capital. Its two circulation processes consist in transforming itself from the commodity form into the money form and from the money form into the commodity form. The circumstance that the transformation of the commodity into money is here at the same time the realization of the surplus-value embodied in the commodity, and that the transformation of money into commodity is at the same time the transformation of capital value into, or back into, the form of its elements of production, in no way changes the fact that these processes, as processes of circulation, are processes of simple commodity metamorphosis.

Circulation time and production time are mutually exclusive. During its circulation time, capital does not function as productive capital, and therefore produces neither commodities nor surplus-value. If we consider the circuit in its simplest form, so that the entire capital value always moves at one stroke from one phase to the other, then it is obvious that the production process is interrupted, and with it therefore the self-valorization of capital, so long as its circulation time lasts, and that according to the duration of the latter, the production process will be repeated sooner or later. If the various parts of the capital pass through the circuit in succession, so that the circuit of the total capital value is successively accomplished in the circuit of its various portions, then it is clear that the longer its aliquot parts remain in the circulation sphere, the smaller must be the part that functions at any time in the production sphere. The expansion and contraction of the circulation time hence acts as a negative limit on the contraction or expansion of the production time, or of the scale on which a capital of a given magnitude can function. The more that the circulation metamorphoses of capital are only ideal, i.e. the closer the circulation time comes to zero, the more the capital functions, and the greater is its productivity and self-valorization. If a capitalist works to order, receives payment on the delivery of his product, and is paid in his own means of production, then his time of circulation approaches zero.

Capital's circulation time generally restricts its production time, and hence its valorization process. Moreover, it restricts this in proportion to its duration. This can increase or decrease very considerably, and hence restrict the production time of capital to a very different degree. But what political economy sees is only the appearance, i.e. the effect of the circulation time on the valorization process of capital in general. It conceives this negative effect as positive, because its results are positive. It sticks all the more firmly to this illusion, as it seems to provide it with the proof that capital possesses a mystical source of self-valorization that is independent of its production process and hence of the exploitation of labour, and derives rather from the sphere of circulation. We shall see later how even scientific economics* let itself be taken in by this illusion, an illusion which, as we shall show, is confirmed by various phenomena: (1) The capitalist way of calculating profit, in which the negative reason appears as positive, in that with capitals in different spheres of investment, in which only the circulation times differ, longer circulation time is the basis for a higher price, in short, is one of the bases in the equalization of profits. (2) The circulation time forms only one moment of the turnover time; but the latter includes the production time or reproduction time. (3) The conversion of commodities into variable capital (wages) is conditioned by their previous transformation into money. In the case of capital accumulation, therefore, the conversion into additional variable capital takes place in the circulation sphere, or during the circulation time. Hence the accumulation arising therefrom appears to be due to the circulation time.

Within the sphere of circulation, capital passes through the two opposing phases *C–M* and *M–C*, in whichever order. Thus its circulation time breaks down into two parts, the time needed for its transformation from commodity into money, and the time that it needs for its transformation from money into commodities. We already know from the analysis of simple commodity circulation (Volume 1, Chapter 3) that *C–M*, the sale, is the most difficult part of its metamorphosis, and thus forms the greater part of the circulation time in normal circumstances. As money, value exists in its ever convertible form. As commodity, it must first receive this form of direct exchangeability and hence constant readiness for action by being transformed into money. What is involved in the circulation process of capital in its phase *M–C* is its transformation into those commodities which form the specific elements of productive capital in a given sphere of investment. The means of produc-

*By this Marx means classical political economy; see Volume 1, Chapter 1, 4, pp. 174–5, note 34.

tion may not be present on the market, needing first to be produced, or they may have to be drawn from distant markets, or there may be dislocations in their normal supply, changes of price, etc., in short, a mass of circumstances that are not recognizable in the simple change of form $M–C$, but require for this part of the circulation phase either less time or more. Just as $C–M$ and $M–C$ are separated in time, so they may also be separated in space, the selling and the buying markets being in different places. In factories, for example, buyers and sellers are frequently even different persons. Circulation is just as necessary for commodity production as is production itself, and thus agents of circulation are just as necessary as agents of production. The reproduction process includes both functions of capital, and thus also the need for these functions to be represented, either by the capitalist himself, or by salaried workers, his agents. But this is just as little a reason for confusing the circulation agents with the production agents as it is a reason for confusing the functions of commodity capital and money capital with those of productive capital. The circulation agents must be paid by way of the production agents. But if capitalists who buy and sell among themselves create by this act neither products nor value, this situation is not altered when the scale of their business enables them to pass this function onto others, and indeed makes it necessary to do so. In many businesses, sellers and buyers are paid in the form of a percentage of the profit. The phrase that they are paid by the consumers is no help at all. The consumers can pay only in so far as they themselves produce, as agents of production, an equivalent in commodities, or alternatively appropriate this from the production agents, whether by a legal title (as their partners, etc.), or through personal services.

There is a distinction between $C–M$ and $M–C$ that has nothing to do with the difference in form between commodities and money, but derives from the capitalist character of production. In and for themselves, both $C–M$ and $M–C$ are mere translations of the given value from one form into the other. But $C'–M'$ is at the same time the realization of the surplus-value contained in C'. Not so $M–C$. Hence the sale is more important than the purchase. $M–C$ is in normal conditions a necessary act for the valorization of the value expressed in M, but it is not a realization of surplus-value; it is a prelude to its production, not an appendix to it.

The very form of existence of commodities, their existence as use-values, sets certain limits to the circulation of the commodity capital $C'–M'$. If they do not enter into productive or individual consumption within a certain interval of time, according to their particular characteristics, in other words if they are not sold within a definite time, then they get spoiled, and lose, together with their use-value, the property of being bearers of exchange-value. Both the capital value contained in them and the surplus-value added to it are lost. Use-values remain the bearers of perennial and self-valorizing capital value only in so far as they are constantly renewed, are replaced by new use-values of the same or another kind. Their sale in their finished commodity form, i.e. their entry, mediated through sale, into productive or individual consumption, is however the constantly repeated condition for their reproduction. They must change their old use form within a certain time, and continue their existence in a new one. It is only through this constant renewal of its body that the exchange-value maintains itself. The use-values of different commodities may decay at different speeds; thus a greater or lesser interval may elapse between their production and their consumption, and they may thus persist for a shorter or longer time in the circulation phase $C-M$ as commodity capital, endure a shorter or longer circulation time as commodities. The limitation of the circulation time of commodity capital imposed by the spoiling of the commodity body itself is the absolute limit of this part of the circulation time, or of the time for which the commodity capital can circulate as commodity capital. The more perishable a commodity, the more directly after its production it must be consumed, and therefore sold, the smaller the distance it can move from its place of production, the narrower therefore is its sphere of spatial circulation, and the more local the character of its market. Hence the more perishable a commodity, the greater are the absolute barriers to its circulation time that its physical properties impose, and the less appropriate it is as an object of capitalist production. Capitalism can only deal in commodities of this kind in populous places, or to the extent that distances are reduced by the development of means of transport. The concentration of the production of an article in a few hands, however, and in a populous place, can create a relatively large market even for an article of this kind, as is the case with the big breweries, dairies, etc.

Chapter 6: The Costs of Circulation

I. PURE CIRCULATION COSTS

(a) Buying and Selling Time

Capital's changes of form from commodity into money and from money into commodity are at the same time business transactions for the capitalist, acts of buying and selling. The time which these changes of form take for their completion exists subjectively, from the standpoint of the capitalist, as selling time and buying time, the time during which he functions as seller and buyer on the market. Just as the circulation time of capital forms a necessary part of its reproduction time, so the time during which the capitalist buys and sells, prowls around the market, forms a necessary part of the time in which he functions as a capitalist, i.e. as personified capital. It forms a part of his business hours.

Since it was assumed that commodities are bought and sold at their values, all that is involved in these acts is the conversion of the same value from one form into another – from the commodity form into the money form, and from the money form into the commodity form – a change of state. If the commodities are sold at their values, then the amounts of value in the hands of both buyer and seller remain unchanged; it is only the form of existence that has altered. If the commodities are not sold at their values, then the sum of converted values remains unaffected; what is a plus for one side is a minus for the other.

But the metamorphoses $C-M$ and $M-C$ are business transactions between buyer and seller; they need time to come to terms, the more so in so far as a struggle is involved here, in which each side seeks to get the better of the other. It is businessmen who face each other here, and 'when Greek meets Greek then comes the tug of war'.* The change of

* Nathanael Lee, 'Rival Queens', in *The Dramatick Works*, Vol. 3, London, 1734, p. 266.

state costs time and labour-power, not to create value, but rather to bring about the conversion of the value from one form into the other, and so the reciprocal attempt to use this opportunity to appropriate an excess quantity of value does not change anything. This labour, increased by evil intent on either side, no more creates value than the labour that takes place in legal proceedings increases the value of the object in dispute. This labour – which is a necessary moment of the capitalist production process in its totality, and also includes circulation, or is included by it – behaves somewhat like the 'work of combustion' involved in setting light to a material that is used to produce heat. This work does not itself produce any heat, although it is a necessary moment of the combustion process. For example, in order to use coal as a fuel, I must combine it with oxygen, and for this purpose transform it from the solid into the gaseous state (for carbon dioxide, the result of the combustion, is coal in this state: F.E.), i.e. effect a change in its physical form of existence or physical state. The separation of the carbon molecules that were combined into a solid whole, and the breaking down of the carbon molecule itself into its individual atoms, must precede the new combination, and this costs a certain expenditure of energy which it not transformed into heat, but rather detracts from the heat. When the commodity owners are not capitalists, but rather independent direct producers, the time they spend on buying and selling is a deduction from their labour time, and they therefore always seek (in antiquity, as also in the Middle Ages: F.E.) to defer such operations to feast days.

The dimensions assumed by the conversion of commodities in the hands of capitalists can naturally not transform this labour, which does not create value, but only mediates a change in the form of value, into value-creating labour. Just as little can such a miracle of transsubstantiation proceed by a transposition, i.e. if the industrial capitalists, instead of themselves performing the 'work of combustion', make this into the exclusive business of third parties paid by them. These third parties will certainly not put their labour-power at the disposal of the capitalists for the sake of their blue eyes. It is similarly immaterial for the rent collector of a landlord or the porter at a bank that their labour does not add one iota to the magnitude of the value of the rent, nor to the gold pieces carried to another bank by the sackful.[1]

For the capitalist who has others to work for him, buying and selling

1. The above three paragraphs are taken from a note at the end of Manuscript VIII.

is a major function. Since he appropriates the product of many people, on a larger social scale, so he has also to sell on such a scale, and later to transform money back again into the elements of production. Now, as before, the time taken up with buying and selling creates no value. An illusion is introduced here by the function of merchant's capital. But, without going into further detail, this much is clear from the start: if we have a function which, although in and for itself unproductive, is nevertheless a necessary moment of reproduction, then when this is transformed, through the division of labour, from the secondary activity of many into the exclusive activity of a few, into their special business, this does not change the character of the function itself. *One* merchant (considered here merely as the agent of the formal transformation of commodities, as mere buyer and seller) may, by way of his operations, shorten the buying and selling time for *many* producers. He should then be considered as a machine that reduces the expenditure of useless energy, or helps to set free production time.[2]

In order to simplify the matter (since we shall only be considering the merchant as capitalist, and merchant's capital, later on), let us assume that this buying and selling agent is a man who sells his labour. He expends his labour-power and his labour time in the operations *C–M* and *M–C*. And hence he lives off this in the same way as someone else might live from spinning or making pills. He performs a necessary function, because the reproduction process itself includes unproductive functions. He works as well as the next man, but the content of his labour creates neither value nor products. He is himself part of the *faux frais** of production. His usefulness does not lie in his transforming an

2. 'The costs of trade, though necessary, must be viewed as a burdensome expenditure' (Quesnay, *Analyse du tableau économique*, in Daire, *Physiocrates*, part I, Paris, 1846, p. 71). According to Quesnay, the 'profit' that arises from competition among the merchants, in so far as this compels them 'to reduce their reward or gain ... is strictly speaking only a *loss avoided* for the original seller and for the purchasing consumer. But this prevention of loss on the costs of trade is not a *real product* or an addition to wealth effected by trade, whether we consider trade in itself, simply as exchange, independently of transport costs, or envisage it in conjunction with these costs' (pp. 145–6). 'The costs of trade are always borne by the sellers of products, who would receive the full price that the buyers pay, if there were no intermediate costs' (p. 163). '*Propriétaires* and *producteurs* are *salariants*, merchants are *salariés*' ['Landlords and capitalist producers are payers of wages, merchants are recipients of wages'] (p. 164, Quesnay, *Dialogues sur le commerce et sur les travaux des artisans*, in Daire, *Physiocrates*, part I, Paris, 1846). [Marx's emphasis]

*Overhead costs.

unproductive function into a productive one, or unproductive labour into productive. It would be a miracle if a transformation of this kind could be brought about by such a transference of functions. He is useful rather because a smaller part of society's labour-power and labour time is now tied up in these unproductive functions. Still more. Let us assume that he is simply a wage-labourer, even if one of the better paid. Whatever his payment, as a wage-labourer he works part of the day for nothing. He may receive every day the value product of eight hours' labour, and function for ten. The two hours' surplus labour that he performs no more produce value than do his eight hours of necessary labour, although it is by means of the latter that a part of the social product is transferred to him. In the first place, both before and after, from the social point of view a person's labour-power is used up for ten hours in this mere circulation function. It is not available for anything else, including productive labour. Secondly, however, society does not count these two hours of surplus labour, although they are spent by the individual who performs them. Society does not appropriate by this means any additional product or value. But the costs of circulation that he represents are reduced by a fifth, from ten hours to eight. Society pays no equivalent for a fifth of this active circulation time whose agent he is. If it is the capitalist who employs these agents, then the circulation costs of *his* capital, which form a deduction from his receipts, are reduced by the non-payment of the two hours. For him, this is a positive profit, because the negative restriction on the valorization of his capital is reduced. As long as small independent commodity producers spend a part of their own time in buying and selling, this simply presents itself as time spent in the intervals between their productive function, or as a loss in their production time.

In all circumstances, the time taken here is a cost of circulation, which does not add anything to the values converted. It is a necessary cost for transferring these from the commodity form into the money form. In so far as the capitalist commodity producer appears as the agent of circulation, he is distinguished from the direct commodity producer only in that he sells and buys on a larger scale, and hence functions as circulation agent to a higher degree. But if the scale of his business forces or enables him to buy (hire) his own circulation agents as wage-labourers, this does not affect the substance of the phenomenon. Labour-power and labour-time must be spent to a certain degree in the circulation process (in so far as this is a mere change of form). But this now appears as an additional outlay of capital; a part of the variable capital must be deployed in acquiring these labour-powers that function only in circulation. This capital advance creates neither products nor value. It proportionately reduces the scale on which the capital advanced functions productively. It is the same as if a part of the product was transformed into a machine that bought and sold the remaining part of the product. This machine means a deduction from the product. It is not involved in the production process, although it can reduce the labour-power, etc. spent on circulation. It simply forms a part of the circulation costs.

(b) Book-keeping

Besides the actual buying and selling, labour-time is spent on book-keeping, which requires pens, ink, paper, desks and other office equipment as well as objectified labour. Thus it is spent in this function both as labour-power and as means of labour. In this connection, the same state of affairs obtains as with buying and selling time.

As a unity within its circuits, as value in process, whether within the production sphere or the two phases of the circulation sphere, it is only ideally that capital exists in the shape of money of account, at first in the head of the commodity producer, capitalist or otherwise. By way of book-keeping, which also includes the determination or reckoning of commodity prices (price calculation), the movement of capital is registered and controlled. The movement of production, and particularly of valorization – in which commodities figure only as bearers of value, as the names of things whose ideal value-existence is set down in money of account – thus receives a symbolic reflection in the imagination. As long as the individual commodity producer either keeps his accounts merely in his head (as the peasant does, for example; only capitalist agriculture produces the book-keeping farmer) or only keeps account of his expenses, receipts, dates of payment, etc. incidentally, outside his production time, it is obvious that this function of his, and the instruments of labour which he may use to perform it, such as paper, etc., represent an additional expenditure of labour-time and instruments of labour, which, although necessary, constitutes a deduction both from the time that he can spend productively, and from the instruments of labour that function in the actual production process and enter into the formation of products and value.[3] The nature of the function itself is in

3. In the Middle Ages agricultural book-keeping was found only in the monasteries. We have seen however (Volume 1, p. 478) that a book-keeper for agriculture

no way changed by the scale that it assumes by being concentrated in the hands of the capitalist commodity producer, and by appearing, not as the function of many small commodity producers, but as that of *one* capitalist, as one function within a large-scale production process; nor is it changed by being torn loose from the productive functions to which it is an adjunct and becoming the independent function of special agents who are exclusively entrusted with it.

The division of labour, with one function becoming independent in this way, does not make this into a product- or value-forming function if it is not so in itself, and thus was already so before it became independent. If a capitalist invests his capital for the first time, then he must invest one part in acquiring a book-keeper, etc. and in means of book-keeping. If his capital is already functioning, in its continuous reproduction process, then he must constantly transform a part of the commodity product, by way of money, into a book-keeper, clerks, and so on. This part of the capital is withdrawn from the production process and belongs to the costs of circulation, as a deduction from the total yield (including the actual labour-power which is exclusively devoted to this function).

There is nevertheless a certain distinction between the costs arising from book-keeping or unproductive expenditure of labour-time on the one hand, and those of mere buying and selling time on the other. The latter arise simply from the particular social form of the production process, from the fact that it is a process of production of commodities. Book-keeping, however, as the supervision and the ideal recapitulation of the process, becomes ever more necessary the more the process takes place on a social scale and loses its purely individual character; it is thus more necessary in capitalist production than in the fragmented production of handicraftsmen and peasants, more necessary in communal production than in capitalist. The costs of book-keeping are however reduced with the concentration of production and in proportion to its increasing transformation into social book-keeping.

already figured in the primitive Indian communities. Here book-keeping gained an independent position as the exclusive function of a communal official. This division of labour saves time, energy and expense, but production and book-keeping of production remain as separate as the cargo of a ship and the bill of lading. In the person of the book-keeper, a portion of the communal labour-power is withdrawn from production, and the costs of its function are replaced, not by his own labour, but by a deduction from the common product. Just as with the book-keeper of the Indian community, so the same applies, *mutatis mutandis*, to the capitalist's book-keeper. (From Manuscript I I.)

We are concerned here simply with the general character of those circulation costs that arise from the merely formal metamorphosis. It would be superfluous to go into all their detailed forms. But how forms pertaining to the merely formal transformation of value, thus arising from the specific social form of the production process, forms which in the case of the individual commodity producer are only evanescent and scarcely noticeable moments that run alongside his production or are dovetailed in with it – how these may strike the eye as massive circulation costs is seen in the simple case of the receipt and dispensing of money, once this has become independent as an exclusive function of banks, etc., or of cashiers in individual businesses, and is concentrated on a large scale. What must be emphasized is that these circulation costs do not change their character with their altered form.

(c) Money

Whether a product is produced as a commodity or not, it is always a material form of wealth, a use-value, destined for individual or productive consumption. As a commodity, its value exists only ideally in the price, which does not affect its actual use form. But the fact that certain commodities, such as gold and silver, function as money and, as such, dwell exclusively in the circulation process (for they also remain in the circulation sphere as hoard, reserve, etc., even if only latently) is purely a product of the particular social form of the production process, as a process of commodity production. Since, on the basis of capitalist production, the commodity is the general form of the product, the great mass of products are produced as commodities and must hence assume the money form; and since the mass of commodities, the part of the social wealth functioning as commodities, is constantly growing, so the quantity of the gold and silver that functions as a means of circulation, means of payment, reserve, etc. also increases. The commodities that function as money go neither into individual nor into productive consumption. They represent social labour fixed in a form in which it serves merely as a machine for circulation. Apart from the fact that a part of the social wealth is confined to this unproductive form, the wear and tear of money requires its steady replacement, or the transformation of more social labour – in the product form – into more gold and silver. These replacement costs are significant in nations where there is a developed capitalism, because the part of the wealth that is confined to the form of money is considerable. Gold and silver, as the money commodities, constitute for society costs of circulation that arise simply from the social form of production. They are *faux frais* of commodity production in general, which grow with the development of this production, and with capitalist production in particular. This is a part of the social wealth which has to be sacrificed to the circulation process.[4]

2. COSTS OF STORAGE

Those circulation costs that proceed from the mere change in form of value, from circulation in its ideal sense, do not enter into the value of commodities. The portions of capital spent on them constitute mere deductions from the capital productively spent, as far as the capitalist is concerned. The circulation costs that we shall deal with now are different in nature. They can arise from production processes that are simply continued in the circulation sphere, and whose productive character is thus merely hidden by the circulation form. They may also be nothing but costs from the social point of view, unproductive expenditure of labour, either living or objectified, but precisely because of this they still have a value-forming effect for the individual capitalist, and form an addition to the selling price of his commodities. This follows from the simple fact that these costs differ between different individual capitals within the same production sphere. The act of adding them to the price of the commodity means that they become distributed in proportion to the degree to which they occur for the individual capitalist. But all labour that adds value can also add surplus-value and will always add surplus-value on the basis of capitalism, since the value that it forms is dependent on its own extent, and the surplus-value that it forms is dependent on the extent to which the capitalist pays for it. Thus while costs that make commodities dearer without increasing their use-value are *faux frais* of production from the social point of view, for the individual capitalist they can constitute sources of enrichment. On the other hand, in so far as what they add to the price of the commodity merely distributes these circulation costs equally, they do not thereby

4. 'The money circulating in a country is a certain portion of the capital of the country, absolutely withdrawn from productive purposes, in order to facilitate or increase the productiveness of the remainder. A certain amount of wealth is, therefore, as necessary in order to adopt gold as a circulating medium, as it is to make a machine, in order to facilitate any other production' (*Economist*, Vol. V, p. 520) [8 May 1847].

cease to be unproductive in character. Insurance companies, for example, divide the losses of individual capitalists among the capitalist class. But this does not prevent the losses thus adjusted from being losses as before, from the standpoint of the total social capital.

(a) Stock Formation in General

During its existence as commodity capital, or its stay on the market, i.e. as long as it finds itself in the interval between the production process from which it emerges and the consumption process which it enters into, the product forms a commodity stock. As a commodity on the market, and hence in the form of a stock, commodity capital figures twice in each circuit, once as the commodity product of the actual capital in process whose circuit is under consideration; the other time as the commodity product of another capital that must be present on the market in order to be sold and transformed into productive capital. It is possible, of course, that this latter commodity capital is produced only to order. There is then an interruption until it has been produced. The flow of the production and reproduction process, however, requires that a mass of commodities (means of production) is constantly present on the market, i.e. forms a stock. Productive capital similarly includes the purchase of labour-power, and the money form is here only the value form of the means of subsistence that the worker must find for the greater part on the market. In the course of this sub-section we shall go into this in more detail. The point, however, is already established. Let us take up the standpoint of the capital value in process, which has been transformed into commodity product and must now be sold or transformed back into money, and which therefore functions for the time being as commodity capital on the market. The state in which it forms a stock is therefore an inexpedient and involuntary stay on the market. The more quickly it is sold, the more fluid the reproduction process. The delay in the formal transformation hinders the material change that must occur in the circuit of capital, and thus its further functioning as productive capital. On the other hand, the constant presence of commodities on the market, the commodity stock, appears for M–C as the condition for the flow of the reproduction process and for the investment of new or additional capital.

The persistence of commodity capital as a commodity stock requires buildings, stores, containers, warehouses, i.e. an outlay of constant capital; it equally requires that payment be made for the labour-power employed in placing the commodities in their containers. Furthermore, commodities decay, and are subject to the damaging influence of the elements. Additional capital must thus be expended to protect them from this, partly in objective form as means of labour, and partly in labour-power.[5]

The existence of capital in its form as commodity capital, and hence as a commodity stock, gives rise to costs that, since they do not pertain to the production sphere, count as costs of circulation. These circulation costs are distinguished from those mentioned under heading 1 in as much as they do enter into the value of commodities to a certain extent, and thus make the commodities dearer. Under all circumstances, capital and labour-power which serve to maintain and store the commodity stock are withdrawn from the direct production process. On the other hand, the capital employed here, including labour-power as a component of the capital, must be replaced out of the social product. Hence this outlay has the same effect as a reduction in the productivity of labour, so that a greater quantity of capital and labour is required to obtain a specific useful effect. These are simply *expenses*.

In so far as the costs of circulation made necessary by the formation of the commodity stock arise solely from the time taken to transform existing values from the commodity form into the money form, i.e. only from the specific social form of the production process (only from the fact that the product is produced as a commodity and must therefore also pass through a transformation into money), they share exactly the same character as the circulation costs enumerated under heading 1. On the other hand, however, the value of the commodities is conserved, or increased, only because the use-value, the product itself, is transferred under certain objective conditions that cost an outlay of capital, and subjected to operations in which additional labour works on the use-values. The calculation of the commodity values (the book-keeping for this process) and the buying and selling, on the contrary, do not operate on the use-value in which the commodity value exists. They are

5. Corbet calculated the costs of storing wheat for a nine-month period in 1841 as $\frac{1}{2}$ per cent loss in quantity, 3 per cent interest on the price, 2 per cent warehouse rental, 1 per cent sifting and drayage, $\frac{1}{2}$ per cent delivery, making a total of 7 per cent, or 3s. 6d. per quarter on a wheat price of 50s. (T. Corbet, *An Inquiry into the Causes and Modes of the Wealth of Individuals*, etc., London, 1841 [p. 140]). According to the evidence given to the Railway Commission by the Liverpool merchants, the (pure) costs of grain storage in 1865 amounted to 2d. per quarter per month, or 9s. 10d. per ton (Royal Commission on Railways, 1867, *Evidence*, p. 19, no. 331).

only concerned with its form. Thus although in the case assumed here these expenses of stock formation (which is here involuntary) arise purely from a delay in the change of form and from the necessity for this change, they are nevertheless distinguished from the expenses under heading 1 in that their actual object is not the formal transformation of value, but the conservation of the value which exists in the commodity as a product, a use-value, and hence can be conserved only by conserving the product, the use-value itself. The use-value is not increased or raised; on the contrary, it declines. But its decline is restricted, and it itself is conserved. The value that is advanced and exists in the commodity is also not increased here. But new labour, both objectified and living, is added to it.

We must now investigate how far these expenses proceed from the particular character of commodity production in general, and how far from commodity production in its universal, absolute form, i.e. capitalist commodity production; how far, too, they are common to all social production and simply assume a particular shape, a specific form of appearance, within capitalist production.

Adam Smith put forward the incredible opinion that the formation of a stock is a phenomenon peculiar to capitalist production.[6] Later economists, e.g. Lalor, stressed on the contrary that with the development of capitalist production, stock formation declines. Sismondi even regarded this as one of the negative features of capitalist production.*

In point of fact, stock exists in three forms: in the form of productive capital, in the form of the individual consumption fund and in the form of the commodity stock or commodity capital. Stock declines relatively in the one form when it increases in the other, although its absolute size may grow simultaneously in all three forms.

It is clear from the start that, where production is oriented directly towards the satisfaction of the producers' own requirements, and only a small portion of goods are produced for exchange or sale, i.e. where the social product does not assume the commodity form, or does so only to a small extent, the stock in the form of commodity, the commodity stock, forms only a small and evanescent part of wealth. Here, however, the consumption fund, i.e. the fund of means of subsistence, is relatively large. One has only to consider the peasant economy of

6. *The Wealth of Nations,* Book Two, Introduction.

*Lalor, *Money and Morals: A Book for the Times,* London, 1852, pp. 43–4; Sismondi, *Études sur l'économie politique,* 3rd edn, Vol. 2, Paris, 1817, p. 433.

antiquity. Here an overwhelming part of the product was transformed directly, without forming a commodity stock, into a stock of means of production or means of subsistence, precisely because it remained in the hands of its possessor. Because it did not assume the form of a commodity stock, Adam Smith held that no stock existed in societies based on this mode of production. Adam Smith thus confused the form of stock with the stock itself, and believed that society previously lived from hand to mouth, abandoning itself to the hazards of the next day.[7] This is a childish misunderstanding.

Stock in the form of productive capital exists as means of production that are already engaged in the production process, or at least in the hands of the producer, i.e. latently already in the production process. We have seen above that as the productivity of labour develops, and thus with the development of the capitalist mode of production – which develops the social productivity of labour more than all previous modes of production – the mass of means of production that are incorporated once and for all in the process in the form of means of labour, and function repeatedly in it over a longer or shorter period (buildings, machines, etc.) constantly grows, and that its growth is both premise and effect of the development of the social productive power of labour. The growth of wealth in this form, which is not only absolute but also relative (cf. Volume 1, Chapter 25, 2), is particularly characteristic of the capitalist mode of production. The material forms of existence of the constant capital, however, the means of production, do not consist only of such means of labour, but also of material for labour at the most varied stages of elaboration, as well as ancillary materials. As the scale

7. Adam Smith believed that the formation of a stock arises only with the transformation of the product into a commodity, and the consumption stock into a commodity stock. The reverse is actually the case: this change of form in the course of the transition from production for the producers' own needs to commodity production gives rise to the most violent crises in the producers' economy. In India, for example, 'the disposition to hoard largely the grain for which little could be got in years of abundance' has been observed right up to this day (*Return. Bengal and Orissa Famine*, House of Commons, 1867, I, pp. 230, 231, no. 74). The sudden increase in demand for cotton, jute, etc. as a result of the American Civil War led to a great limitation of rice cultivation in India, a rise in the price of rice, and the sale of old stocks of rice by the producers. On top of this, there was the unparalleled export of rice to Australia, Madagascar, etc. in 1864–6. Hence the acute character of the famine of 1866, which carried off a million people in Orissa alone (op. cit., pp. 174, 175, 213, 214, and III, *Papers relating to the Famine in Bihar*, pp. 32, 33, in which the 'drain of old stock' is stressed as one of the causes of the famine). (From Manuscript II.)

of production grows, and the productive power of labour grows through cooperation, division of labour, machinery, etc., so does the mass of raw material, ancillaries, etc. that go into the daily reproduction process. These elements must be ready to hand at the place of production. The extent of this stock in the form of productive capital thus grows absolutely. In order for the process to keep flowing – quite apart from whether this stock can be renewed daily or only at definite intervals – there must always be a greater store of raw material, etc. at the place of production than is used up daily or weekly, for example. The continuity of the process requires that the existence of its preconditions should depend neither on the possible interruption of daily purchases, nor on whether the commodity product is sold daily or weekly, and can therefore only irregularly be transformed back into its elements of production. But it is clear that the degree to which productive capital is latent or forms a stock can differ very greatly. It makes a great difference, for example, whether the mill-owner has to have sufficient cotton or coal on hand for three months, or only for one. We can see that this stock can decrease relatively even though it increases in absolute terms.

This depends on various conditions which essentially all derive from the greater speed, regularity and certainty with which the necessary mass of raw material can be constantly supplied in such a way that no interruption arises. The less these conditions are fulfilled, and the less therefore the certainty, regularity and speed of the supply, the greater must be the latent part of the productive capital, i.e. the stock of raw materials, etc. in the hands of the producer and still waiting to be worked up. These conditions stand in inverse proportion to the level of development of capitalist production, and thus of the productive power of social labour. And so too, therefore, does the stock in this form.

But what appears here as a decline in the stock (e.g. with Lalor) is in part only a decline of stock in the form of commodity capital or of commodity stock proper; i.e. a mere change of form of the same stock. For example, if a great mass of coal is produced every day in the country in question, i.e. if the scale and intensity of coal production is large, then the mill-owner does not need a great store of coal in order to secure the continuity of his production. The constant and certain renewal of the coal supply makes this superfluous. Secondly, the speed with which the product of one process can be transferred to another process as means of production depends on the development of the means of transport and communication. The cheapness of transport plays a great role in this connection. The constantly repeated transportation of coal, for example, from the mine to the spinning mill will be dearer than the storage of a larger amount of coal for a longer period, if transport is relatively cheap. The two circumstances considered here proceed from the production process itself. The less dependent the mill-owner is for the renewal of his stocks of cotton, coal, etc. on the direct sale of his yarn – and the more developed the credit system, the smaller this direct dependence – the smaller the relative size of these stocks need be, in order to secure a continuous production of yarn independent of the accidents of its sale. Fourthly, however, many raw materials, semi-finished goods, etc. require lengthy periods of time for their production, and this holds in particular for all raw materials provided by agriculture. If there is to be no interruption of the production process, then a definite stock of these must be present for the whole period of time in which new products cannot replace old. If this stock in the hands of the industrial capitalist declines, this only means that it increases in the form of a commodity stock in the hands of the merchant. The development of the means of transport, for example, permits cotton lying in the import docks to be quickly delivered from Liverpool to Manchester, so that the manufacturer can renew his stocks of cotton in relatively small portions according to his needs. But then the same cotton exists in even greater amounts as a commodity stock in the hands of the Liverpool merchants. There is thus simply a change in the form of the stock, which Lalor and others have overlooked. If we consider the social capital, there is the same quantity of products as before in the form of stock. For an individual country, the scale on which the quantity needed for the year, for example, must be held ready, declines with the development of the means of transport. If there are many steamships and sailing ships plying between America and Britain, then the opportunities for Britain to renew its cotton stock are increased, and thus the average volume of the cotton stock that Britain must keep in store declines. The development of the world market and the consequent multiplication of sources of supply for the same article has the same effect. The article is supplied bit by bit from different countries and at different points in time.

(b) The Commodity Stock Proper

We have already seen how, on the basis of capitalist production, the commodity becomes the general form of the product, and the more so, the more this production develops in scale and depth. Thus a far greater part of the product exists as a commodity, even at the same scale of production, in comparison either with earlier modes of production, or with the capitalist mode of production itself at a less developed stage. But every commodity (and thus also every commodity capital, which is simply a commodity, even if a commodity as the form of existence of capital value), in so far as it does not directly pass from the sphere of its production into productive or individual consumption, and finds itself on the market during the interval, forms an element of the commodity stock. In and for itself – assuming the scale of production is constant – the commodity stock therefore grows with capitalist production. We have already seen that this is only a change of form for the stock, i.e. that the stock increases in commodity form because it decreases in the form of direct production or consumption stock. There is simply a changed social form of the stock. If at the same time there is an increase not only in the relative size of the commodity stock, in relation to the total social product, but also in its absolute size, this is because the volume of the total product increases with capitalist production.

As capitalist production develops, the scale of production is determined to an ever lesser degree by the immediate demand for the product, and to an ever greater degree by the scale of the capital which the individual capitalist has at his disposal, by his capital's drive for valorization and the need of his production process for continuity and extension. The mass of products from every particular branch of production that are on the market as commodities, or seek an outlet, necessarily grows together with this. The mass of capital tied up for a shorter or longer time in the form of commodity capital grows, and hence the commodity stock grows as well.

Ultimately, most members of the society are transformed into wage-labourers, people who live from hand to mouth, who receive their wages by the week and spend them by the day, and must thus find their means of subsistence available as a stock. However rapidly the particular elements of this stock may flow, a part of them must always stand still in order for the stock to remain in motion.

All these moments arise out of the form of production, and the changes of form which are included in it, and which the product must pass through in the circulation process.

Whatever the social form of the stock of products, its storage involves costs: buildings, containers, etc. which form receptacles for the product; similarly means of production and labour, more or less according to the nature of the product, which must be spent to ward off damaging influences. The more these stocks are socially concentrated, the smaller, relatively speaking, are the costs. These outlays always form part of social labour, whether in objectified or living form – thus in the capitalist form they are outlays of capital – which do not go towards the formation of the product itself, and are thus deductions from it. They are necessary expenditures of social wealth, for they are the costs of conserving the social product, whether its existence as an element of the commodity stock arises merely from the social form of production, i.e. from the commodity form and its necessary transformations, or whether we consider the commodity stock simply as a special form of the stock of products common to all societies, even if not in the form of a *commodity* stock, this particular form of stock pertaining to the circulation process.

The question now arises as to what extent these expenses enter into the value of commodities.

If the capitalist has transformed the capital he advanced in means of production and labour-power into products, into a certain mass of commodities ready for sale, and these remain in store unsold, then it is not only the valorization process of his capital that is held up during this time. The expenditures that the conservation of this stock requires in buildings, additional labour, etc. form a positive loss. The eventual purchaser would laugh at the capitalist if he said: 'I could not sell my commodity for six months, and it not only cost me so and so much in idle capital to maintain it for these six months, but also caused expenses *x*.' 'So much the worse for you,' the buyer will say, 'for next to you there is another seller whose commodity was finished only yesterday. Your commodity is evidently a white elephant, and probably more or less damaged by the ravages of time. You must therefore sell cheaper than your rival.' Whether the commodity producer is the real producer of his commodity, or its capitalist producer, and therefore merely the representative of the real producer, in no way affects the conditions of life of the commodity. He has to transform his article into money. The expenses it cost him to maintain it in its commodity form pertain to his own individual experience, and do not interest the buyer of the commodity. The latter does not pay him for the circulation time of his commodity. Even if the capitalist deliberately keeps his commodity off the market, in times of a real or anticipated revolution in values, it depends on whether this revolution actually comes about, on the correctness or incorrectness of his speculation, whether he realizes his additional expenses. The revolution in values is not the result of his expenses. Thus in so far as the formation of a stock is a hold-up in circulation, the expenses occasioned by it add no value to the commodity. On the other hand, there can be no stock without a delay in the circulation sphere, without the capital persisting for a longer or shorter period in its commodity form; thus there can be no stock without a hold-up in circulation, just as no money can circulate without the formation of a money reserve. That is to say, without the commodity stock, no commodity circulation. If the capitalist does not encounter this necessity in $C'-M'$, then he encounters it in $M-C$; not for his own commodity capital, but for the commodity capital of other capitalists, who produce means of production for him and means of subsistence for his workers.

Whether the formation of a stock is voluntary or involuntary, i.e. whether the commodity producer deliberately builds up a stock or whether his commodities form a stock as a result of the resistance that the circumstances of the circulation process itself oppose to their sale, makes no essential difference to the matter. Yet it is useful to know, as a contribution towards solving this question, what it is that distinguishes voluntary from involuntary stock formation. The involuntary formation of a stock arises from, or is identical with, a hold-up in circulation that is independent of the knowledge of the commodity producer and goes against his intentions. What characterizes voluntary stock formation? Here the seller still attempts to get rid of his commodities as fast as possible. He still offers his product for sale as a commodity. If he were to withdraw it from sale, it would form only a potential (δυνάμει) element of the commodity stock, and not an actual (ἐνεργείᾳ) one. The commodity as such is still for him simply the bearer of its exchange-value, and as such it can only have its effect by and through shedding its commodity form and assuming the money form.

The commodity stock must have a certain volume in order to satisfy the scale of demand over a given period. The continual extension of the circle of buyers is taken into account in this connection. In order to last for one day, for example, one part of the commodities on the market must persist in the commodity form, while the other part flows and is transformed into money. Of course the part that stands still in this way steadily declines, as the scale of the stock itself declines, until it is finally all sold. This stagnation of commodities is thus taken into account here as a necessary condition for their sale. Moreover, it must be greater in scale than the average sale or the average demand, otherwise excesses above this average could not be satisfied. On the other hand, the stock must be constantly renewed, because it is constantly disappearing. In the last instance, this renewal can derive only from production, from a supply of the commodity. It is immaterial whether this comes from abroad or not. The renewal depends on the periods that the commodities need for their reproduction. The stock of commodities must be adequate for this length of time. The fact that this stock does not remain in the hands of the original producers, but runs through various reservoirs, from the large-scale merchant to the retail trader, changes only the appearance, and not the thing itself. From the social point of view, a part of the capital still exists in the form of commodity stock, as long as the commodity has not entered into productive or individual consumption. The producer himself attempts to have an inventory adequate for his average demand, in order not to be directly dependent on production, and to secure himself a constant circle of customers. The production periods give rise to dates of purchase, and the commodity forms a stock for a longer or shorter period of time before it can be replaced by new items of the same kind. It is only by way of this stock formation that the permanence and continuity of the circulation process is ensured, and hence that of the reproduction process which includes the circulation process.

We must remember that $C'-M'$ can be completed for the producer of C even though C is still on the market. If the producer himself intended to keep his own commodity in store until it was sold to the final consumer, he would have to set in motion a double capital, once as producer of the commodity, the other time as merchant. As far as the commodity itself is concerned – whether it is considered as an individual commodity or as a component part of the social capital – it makes no difference to the situation whether the expenses of stock formation fall onto its producers or onto a series of merchants from A to Z.

In as much as the commodity stock is nothing more than the commodity form of the stock that would still exist on the given scale of social production either as productive stock (latent production fund) or as a consumption fund (reserve of means of consumption), if it did not exist as a commodity stock, the expenses required to maintain the stock, that is the expenses of stock formation – i.e. the objectified or living labour spent on this – are merely the transposed expenses of maintaining the social production fund and the social consumption fund. The increase in the value of the commodity to which they give rise simply distributes these expenses proportionately between the various commodities, as they are different for different sorts of commodity. The expenses of stock formation continue to be deductions from the social wealth, even though they are a condition of its existence.

It is only in so far as the commodity stock is a condition of commodity circulation and itself a form that has necessarily arisen in commodity circulation, in so far therefore as this apparent stagnation is a form of the flow itself, that it is normal. But once the commodities lingering in their circulation stores fail to make room for the incoming wave of production, and the stores are overfilled, the commodity stock expands as a result of the stagnation of circulation, just as hoards grow if the money circulation stagnates. It is quite immaterial here whether this stagnation takes place in the storeroom of the industrial capitalist or the warehouse of the merchant. The commodity stock is then not a condition of uninterrupted sale, but a consequence of the unsaleability of the commodities. The expenses remain the same, but as they arise purely from the form, i.e. from the necessity of transforming the commodities into money, and the difficulty of this metamorphosis, they do not enter into the value of the commodities, but form deductions, a loss of value in the realization of value. Since the normal and the abnormal forms of the stock are not distinguished in their form, and both are stagnations of circulation, the phenomena can be confused, and may deceive the agents of production themselves all the more, in that it is possible for the producer to feel that the circulation process of his capital is occurring, that it is in flux, even though the circulation of his commodities, which have passed into the hands of the merchants, is stagnating. If the extent of production increases, then, other circumstances remaining the same, so does the volume of the commodity stock. It is then renewed and absorbed just as quickly, but on a greater scale. The rise in the volume of the commodity stock as a result of a stagnation in circulation can thus be mistaken for a symptom of an expansion in the reproduction process, particularly if the real movement is mystified by the development of the credit system.

The expenses of stock formation consist of (1) a quantitative reduction in the mass of the product (e.g. with stocks of flour); (2) a deterioration in quality; (3) the objectified and living labour required to conserve the stock.

3. TRANSPORT COSTS

It is not necessary to go into all the details of the costs of circulation here, such as packing, sorting, etc. The general law is that *all circulation costs that arise simply from a change in form of the commodity cannot add any value to it.* They are simply costs involved in realizing the value or transferring it from one form into another. The capital expended in these costs (including the labour it commands) belongs to the *faux frais* of capitalist production. The replacement of these costs must come from the surplus product, and from the standpoint of the capitalist class as a whole it forms a deduction of surplus-value or surplus product, in just the same way as the time that a worker needs to buy his means of subsistence is lost time for him. Transport costs, however, play too important a role not to be briefly considered here.

Within the circuit of capital and the commodity metamorphoses that form a section of it, the metabolism* of social labour takes place. This metabolism may require a motion of the products in space, their real movement from one location to another. But circulation of commodities can also take place without their physical movement, as can the transport of products without commodity circulation, even without direct exchange of products. A house that is sold by A to B circulates as a commodity, but it does not get up and walk. Movable commodity values, such as cotton or pig-iron, can remain in the same warehouse while they undergo dozens of circulation processes, and are bought and resold by speculators.[8] What actually moves here is the property title to the thing and not the thing itself. In the realm of the Incas, on the other hand, the transport industry played a major role, although the social product neither circulated as a commodity nor was distributed by means of exchange.

If the transport industry therefore appears as a cause of circulation costs on the basis of capitalist production, this particular form of appearance in no way alters the substance of the matter.

The quantity of products is not increased by their transport. The change in their natural properties that may be effected by transport is also, certain exceptions apart, not an intended useful effect, but rather an unavoidable evil. But the use-value of things is realized only in their consumption, and their consumption may make a change of location necessary, and thus also the additional production process of the transport industry. The productive capital invested in this industry thus adds

8. Storch* calls this *circulation factice* [artificial circulation].

*Henri Storch was a Russian vulgarizer of classical political economy, though he wrote in French and his principal work, the *Cours d'économie politique*, was published in Paris in 1823.

*By *Stoffwechsel* or metabolism, Marx means the exchange of matter between man and nature effected by labour. See Volume 1, Chapter 7, p. 283.

value to the products transported, partly through the value carried over from the means of transport, partly through the value added by the work of transport. This latter addition of value can be divided, as with all capitalist production, into replacement of wages and surplus-value.

Within every production process, the change of location of the object of labour and the means of labour and labour-power needed for this plays a major role; for instance, cotton that is moved from the carding shop into the spinning shed, coal lifted from the pit to the surface. The transfer of the finished product as a finished commodity from one separate place of production to another a certain distance away shows the same phenomenon, only on a larger scale. The transport of products from one place of production to another is followed by that of the finished products from the sphere of production to the sphere of consumption. The product is ready for consumption only when it has completed this movement.

As we have already seen, it is a general law of commodity production that the productivity of labour and the value it creates stand in inverse proportion. This holds for the transport industry as much as any other. The smaller the quantity of labour, dead and living, that is required to transport a commodity for a given distance, the greater the productive power of the labour, and vice versa.[9]

9. Ricardo quotes Say,* who saw it as one of the blessings of trade that it increased the transport costs of the products, or raised their value: 'Commerce [says Say] enables us to obtain a commodity in the place where it is to be found, and to convey it to another where it is to be consumed; it therefore gives us the power of increasing the value of the commodity, by the whole difference between its price in the first of these places, and its price in the second.' Ricardo remarks on this: 'True, but how is this additional value given to it? By adding to the cost of production, first, the expenses of conveyance; secondly, the profit on the advances of capital made by the merchant. The commodity is only more valuable, because more labour is expended on its production and conveyance, before it is purchased by the consumer. This must not be mentioned as one of the advantages of commerce' (Ricardo, *Principles of Political Economy*, third edition, London, 1821, pp. 309, 310 [Pelican edition, p. 270n]).

*Jean-Baptiste Say, the French economist, took advantage of the confusion in Adam Smith's theory of the revenues of the three major classes (see below, pp. 454 ff.) to found the vulgar-economic doctrine of the 'factors of production', presenting land, capital and labour as independent sources of rent, profit and wages. This is referred to by Marx as the 'trinity formula'; cf. *Capital* Volume 3, Chapter 48, and the important but seldom read Addendum to *Theories of Surplus-Value* on 'Revenue and its Sources. Vulgar Political Economy' (Part III, pp. 453 ff.). Say's 'law' to the effect that supply creates its own demand, and that there can therefore never be general over-production, reigned supreme in bourgeois economics

The absolute magnitude of value added by the transport of commodities stands in inverse proportion to the productive power of the transport industry and in direct proportion to the distance to be covered, other circumstances remaining the same.

The relative part of value that transport costs add to the price of the commodity, under otherwise equal circumstances, stands in direct proportion to their size and weight. The modifying circumstances are numerous. Transport requires, for example, greater or lesser measures of precaution, hence more or less expenditure of labour and means of labour, according to the relative fragility, perishability and explosiveness of the article. The railway magnates have shown greater genius in inventing fantastic species than have botanists or zoologists. The classification of goods on the British railways, for example, fills volumes, and rests for its general principle on the tendency to transform the variegated natural properties of goods into an equal number of transportation ailments and pretexts for obligatory impositions:

'Glass, which was formerly worth £11 per crate, is now worth only £2 since the improvements which have taken place in manufactures, and since the abolition of the duty; but the rate for carriage is the same as it was formerly, and higher than it was previously, when carried by canal. Formerly, manufacturers inform me that they had glass and glass wares for the plumbers' trade carried at about 10s. per ton, within 50 miles of Birmingham. At the present time, the rate to cover risk of breakage, which we can very rarely get allowed, is three times that amount . . . The companies always resist any claim that is made for breakages.'[10]

Moreover, the fact that the relative share that transport costs add to the value of an article stands in inverse proportion to its value is made by the railway magnates into a special reason for taxing an article in direct proportion to its value. The complaints of the industrialists and merchants on this score are repeated on every page of the evidence in the above-quoted report.

The capitalist mode of production reduces the transport costs for the individual commodity by developing the means of transport and communication, as well as by concentrating transport – i.e. by increasing its

---

from its formulation in 1817 through to the 'Keynesian revolution' – though even Keynes's theory is itself simply one of under-consumption, teaching that the problem of over-production (i.e. the inability of the working class to buy sufficient of the goods produced) can be solved by an increase in the supply of money.

---

10. Royal Commission on Railways [*Evidence*, op. cit.], p. 31, no. 630.

scale. It increases the part of social labour, both living and objectified, that is spent on commodity transport, firstly by transforming the great majority of all products into commodities, and then by replacing local by distant markets.

The 'circulating' of commodities, i.e. their actual course in space, can be resolved into the transport of commodities. The transport industry forms on the one hand an independent branch of production, and hence a particular sphere for the investment of productive capital. On the other hand it is distinguished by its appearance as the continuation of a production process *within* the circulation process and *for* the circulation process.

Part Two

The Turnover of Capital

Chapter 7: Turnover Time and Number of Turnovers

As we have seen, the overall time of circulation of a given capital is the sum of its circulation time proper and its production time. It is the period of time that elapses from the moment that the capital value is advanced in a particular form until the return of the capital value in process in the same form.

The specific purpose of capitalist production is always the valorization of the value advanced, whether this value is advanced in its independent form, i.e. the money form, or in commodities, in which case its value form only possesses an ideal independence in the price of the commodities advanced. In both cases, this capital value passes through different forms of existence in the course of its circuit. Its identity with itself is established in the capitalist's ledger, or in the form of money of account.

Whether we take the form $M \ldots M'$ or the form $P \ldots P$, both these forms include the following facts:

(1) the value advanced functions as capital value and is valorized;

(2) after describing its process, it returns to the form in which this process began.

In $M \ldots M'$, both the valorization of M, the value advanced, and the return of the capital to this form (the money form), are readily apparent. But the same thing also takes place in the second form. For the starting-point of P is the presence of the elements of production, commodities of a given value. This form includes the valorization of this value (C' and M') and its return to its original form, since in the second P the value advanced once again possesses the form of the elements of production in which it was originally advanced.

As we saw in the previous volume:

'If production has a capitalist form, so too will reproduction. Just as in the capitalist mode of production the labour process appears only as a means towards the process of valorization, so in the case of reproduction it appears only as a means of reproducing the value advanced as capital, i.e. as self-valorizing value' (Volume 1, Chapter 23, p. 711).

The three forms (I) $M\ldots M'$, (II) $P\ldots P$, and (III) $C'\ldots C'$ are distinguished in the following ways. In form II ($P\ldots P$) the repetition of the process, the process of reproduction, is expressed as a reality, whereas in form I it is only a possibility. Both of these, however, are distinguished from form III in so far as the capital value advanced – – whether as money, or in the shape of the material elements of production – forms the starting-point and hence also the point of return. In $M\ldots M'$ the return is $M' = M+m$. If the process is repeated on the same scale, then M again forms the starting-point; m does not enter into it, but simply shows us that although M has been valorized as capital and thus created a surplus-value, it has cast this surplus-value off. In the form $P\ldots P$, the capital value P advanced in the form of the elements of production forms the point of departure. The form includes its valorization. In the case of simple reproduction, it is the same capital value that begins its process again in the same form. In the case of accumulation, P' (possessing a value of M' or C') now starts the process as an increased capital value. But the process still begins with capital value advanced in the original form, even if with a greater value than previously. In form III, however, the capital value does not begin the process as capital value advanced, but as capital value already valorized, as the total wealth existing in the form of commodities, of which the capital value advanced forms only a part. This latter form is important for Part Three of the present volume, where the movement of individual capitals will be dealt with in its relationship with the movement of the total social capital. But it cannot be used for the turnover of capital, which always begins with the advance of capital value, in the form either of money or of commodities, and always requires the return of the circling capital value in the form in which it was advanced. Out of circuits I and II, the former will be adhered to in so far as the influence of the turnover on the formation of surplus-value is the main thing under consideration; the latter in so far as its influence on the formation of the product is concerned.

Just as the economists have rarely distinguished between the different forms of the circuit, so too they have rarely considered these separately in connection with the turnover of capital. They have generally concentrated on the form $M\ldots M'$ because it is this that dominates the individual capitalist and is used by him in his calculations, even if money forms the starting-point only in the shape of money of account. Certain others proceed from outlays in the form of elements of production, finishing with the receipt of returns, without even mentioning the form of these returns, whether they are in commodities or money. For example:

'The Economic Cycle . . . [is] the whole course of production, from the time that outlays are made till returns are received. In agriculture, seed-time is its commencement, and harvesting its ending' (S. P. Newman, *Elements of Political Economy*, Andover and New York, p. 81).

Others begin with C' (form III):

'The world of trade may be conceived to revolve in what we shall call an economic cycle, which accomplishes one revolution by business, coming round again, through its successive transactions, to the point from which it set out. Its commencement may be dated from the point at which the capitalist has obtained those returns by which his capital is replaced to him: whence he proceeds anew to engage his workmen; to distribute among them, in wages, their maintenance, or rather, the power of lifting it; to obtain from them, in finished work, the articles in which he specially deals; to bring these articles to market and there terminate the orbit of one set of movements, by effecting a sale, and receiving, in its proceeds, a return for the whole outlays of the period' (T. Chalmers, *On Political Economy*, 2nd edn, Glasgow, 1832, p. 85).*

When the entire capital value that the individual capitalist invests in one branch of production or other has described its cyclical movement, it exists once again in its original form and can then repeat the same process. It has to repeat it, if the value is to be perpetuated and valorized as capital value. In the life of the capital, the individual circuit forms only a section that is constantly repeated, i.e. a period. At the close of the period $M \ldots M'$, the capital exists again in the form of money capital and passes once more through the series of changes of form that constitute its process of reproduction and valorization. At the close of the period $P \ldots P$, the capital exists again in the form of the elements of production which constitute the premise of its repeated circuit. The circuit of capital, when this is taken not as an isolated act but as a periodic process, is called its turnover. The duration of this turnover is given by the sum of its production time and its circulation time. This period of time forms the capital's turnover time. It thus measures the interval between one cyclical period of the total capital value and the

---

*Thomas Chalmers (1780–1847) is described by Marx in *Theories of Surplus-Value* (Part I, p. 290) as 'one of the most fanatical Malthusians'. Like Malthus, he was himself a cleric, and in fact Professor of Divinity at Glasgow University.

next; the periodicity in the capital's life-process, or, if you like, the time required for the renewal and repetition of the valorization and production process of the same capital value.

If we disregard the individual occurrences that may accelerate or shorten the turnover time of an individual capital, the turnover times of capitals differ according to their different spheres of investment.

As the working day forms the natural measuring unit for the function of labour-power, so the year forms the natural measuring unit for the turnovers of capital in process. The natural basis for this measurement is that the most important food crops in the temperate zone, the native ground of capitalist production, are annual products.

If we call the year, as measurement unit of the turnover time, U, the turnover time of a particular capital u, and the number of its turnovers n, then $n = \dfrac{U}{u}$. If the turnover time u is three months, for example, then $n = \frac{12}{3} = 4$; the capital completes four turnovers in a year, or turns over four times. If $u = 18$ months, then $n = \frac{12}{18} = \frac{2}{3}$; the capital only gets through two thirds of its turnover time in one year. If the turnover time amounts to several years, then it is reckoned in terms of multiples of a year.

For the capitalist, the turnover time of his capital is the time for which he has to advance his capital in order for this to be valorized and for him to receive it back in its original shape.

Before we investigate more closely the influence of turnover on the production and valorization process, we have to consider two new forms which capital obtains as a result of the circulation process, and which affect the form of its turnover.

Chapter 8: Fixed Capital and Circulating Capital

I. THE FORMAL DISTINCTIONS

We saw in Volume 1, Chapter 8,* that one part of the constant capital maintains the specific use-form in which it enters the production process, over and against the products that it helps to fashion. It continues to perform the same functions over a shorter or longer period, in a series of repeated labour processes. Examples of this are factory buildings, machines, etc. – in short, everything that we collect together under the description *means of labour*. This part of the constant capital gives up value to the product in proportion to the exchange-value that it loses together with its use-value. The extent to which the value of such a means of production is given up or transferred to the product that it helps to fashion is determined by an average calculation; it is measured by the average duration of its function, from the time that it enters the production process as means of production to the time it is completely used up, is dead, and has to be replaced or reproduced by a new item of the same kind.

The peculiarity of this part of the constant capital, the means of labour in the strict sense, is this:

A part of the capital has been advanced in a form of constant capital, i.e. means of production, which then function as factors of the labour process so long as they maintain the independent use-shape with which they entered it. The finished product, and thus also the elements of its formation, in so far as they are transformed into the product, is ejected from the production process, and passes as a commodity from the sphere of production into that of circulation. The means of labour, on the other hand, never leave the production sphere once they have stepped into it. Their function confines them firmly within it. A part of the capital value advanced is *fixed* in this form, which is determined by the function of the means of labour in the process. As a means of labour functions and is used up, one part of its value passes over to the product,

*p. 311.

while another part remains fixed in the means of labour and hence in the production process. The value fixed in this way steadily declines, until the means of labour is worn out and has therefore distributed its value, in a longer or shorter period, over the volume of products that has emerged from a series of continually repeated labour processes. As long as a means of labour still remains effective, and does not yet have to be replaced by a new item of the same kind, some constant capital value remains fixed in it, while another part of the value originally fixed in it passes over to the product and thus circulates as a component of the commodity stock. The longer the means of labour lasts and the more slowly it wears out, the longer the constant capital value remains fixed in this use-form. But whatever its degree of durability, the proportion in which it gives up value is always in inverse ratio to the overall duration of its function. If two machines are of equal value, but one of them wears out in five years and the other in ten, then the first gives up twice as much value in the same space of time as the second does.

The part of the capital value that is fixed in the means of labour circulates, just like any other part. As we have seen, the whole of the capital value is in constant circulation, and in this sense, therefore, all capital is circulating capital. But the circulation of the part of the capital considered here is a peculiar one. In the first place, it does not circulate in its use form. It is rather its value that circulates, and this does so gradually, bit by bit, in the degree to which it is transferred to the product that circulates as a commodity. A part of its value always remains fixed in it as long as it continues to function, and remains distinct from the commodities that it helps to produce. This peculiarity is what gives this part of the constant capital the form of *fixed capital*. All other material components of the capital advanced in the production process, on the other hand, form, by contrast to it, circulating or *fluid capital*.

There is a further part of the means of production – those ancillaries that are consumed by the means of labour proper as they function, such as coal by the steam engine, or which only support the action, such as gas for lighting, etc., which also do not enter the product in their material form. It is only their value that constitutes part of the value of the product. The product circulates their value in its own circulation, and they have this in common with fixed capital. But they are completely consumed in every labour process that they enter into, and therefore, with each new labour process, they must be completely replaced by new items of the same kind. They do not preserve their independent use-shape as they function. And so no part of the capital value, either, remains fixed in their old use-shape, their natural form. The fact that this part of the ancillaries does not materially enter into the product, but enters the value of the product only according to its own value, and the related fact that the function of these materials is confined within the sphere of production, has misled economists such as Ramsay (who at the same time confuses fixed and constant capital) into applying to them the category of fixed capital.*

The part of the means of production that enters the product materially, i.e. raw materials, etc., thereby receives, to some extent, a form in which it can later enter individual consumption as a means of enjoyment. Means of labour, for their part, the material bearers of fixed capital, are consumed only productively, and cannot enter individual consumption, since they do not enter the product or use-value which they help to fashion, but rather maintain their independent shape vis-à-vis it until they are completely worn out. An exception to this is provided by the means of transport. The use-effect that these produce in their productive function, i.e. during their stay in the sphere of production – the change of location – simultaneously enters individual consumption, e.g. that of the traveller. The latter then pays for their use just as he pays for the use of other means of consumption. As we have seen, the distinction between raw material and ancillaries can become blurred, as in the manufacture of chemicals, for example.† The same is true with the distinction between means of labour on the one hand, and ancillaries and raw materials on the other. In agriculture, for instance, the materials added to improve the soil partly enter the plant product as formative elements. Their effect, however, is spread over a fairly long period, e.g. four to five years. One part of these, therefore, enters the product materially, and thus immediately transfers its value to it, while another part remains fixed in its old use-form, so that its value does too. It continues to exist as means of production and hence receives the form of fixed capital. An ox, as a draught animal, is fixed capital. If it is eaten, however, it no longer functions either as a means of labour, or as fixed capital.

The quality that gives a part of the capital value spent on means of production the character of fixed capital, lies exclusively in the specific

---

* See *Theories of Surplus-Value*, Part III, pp. 326–8. Marx considered Sir George Ramsay (1800–1871) to be one of the last representatives of classical (bourgeois) political economy. His *An Essay on the Distribution of Wealth* was published in Edinburgh in 1836.

† See Volume 1, p. 288.

manner in which this value circulates. This particular manner of circulation arises from the particular way in which the means of labour gives up its value to the product, or acts to form value during the production process. This in turn arises from the special way in which the means of labour function in the labour process.

We know that the same use-value that emerges from one labour process in the shape of a product can enter another labour process as means of production. It is only the function of a product as a means of labour in the production process that makes it fixed capital. It is in no way fixed capital in itself, just as it emerges from a process. A machine that is the product and thus the commodity of a machine-builder is part of his commodity capital. It only becomes fixed capital in the hands of its buyer, the capitalist who employs it productively.

Assuming that all other circumstances remain the same, the degree of fixedness grows with the durability of the means of labour. On this durability depends the size of the difference between the capital value fixed in means of labour, and the part of this value that is given up to the product in repeated labour processes. The more slowly this value is given up – and the means of labour gives up value with each repetition of the same labour process – the greater is the capital still fixed, and the greater the difference between the capital employed in the production process and the capital consumed in it. Once this difference has disappeared, the means of labour has lived out its time, and lost its value together with its use-value. It has ceased to be a bearer of value. Since the means of labour, like every other material bearer of constant capital, gives up value to the product only to the extent that it loses its value together with its use-value, then the longer it lasts out in the production process, the longer is the period for which constant capital remains fixed in it.

If a means of production which is not a means of labour in the strict sense (e.g. ancillaries, raw material, semi-finished goods, etc.) behaves with respect to the way it gives up value and hence to the mode of circulation of its value in the same way as the means of labour, then it is also a material bearer, a form of existence, of fixed capital. This is the case with the already mentioned improvements to the soil, which put into it chemical components whose effect extends over several periods of production or several years. Here, one part of the value continues to exist alongside the product in its independent shape, or in the shape of fixed capital, while another portion of value is given up to the product and hence circulates with it. In a case like this, it is not only a part of the value of the fixed capital that enters the product, but also the use-value, the substance, in which this portion of value exists.

Besides their basic error, their confusion of the categories of fixed and circulating capital with the categories of constant and variable capital, the confusion in the demarcation of concepts made by previous economists rests primarily on the following points:

Firstly, certain properties that characterize the means of labour materially are made into direct properties of fixed capital, e.g. physical immobility, such as that of a house. But it is always easy to show that other means of labour, which are also as such fixed capital, ships for example, have the opposite property, i.e. physical mobility.

Alternatively, the formal economic characteristic that arises from the circulation of value is confused with a concrete [*dinglich*] property; as if things, which are never capital at all in themselves, could already *in themselves* and by nature be capital in a definite form, fixed or circulating. We saw in Chapter 7 of Volume 1* that the means of production in any labour process, irrespective of the social conditions under which it is pursued, are divisible into means of labour and object of labour. It is only within the capitalist mode of production, however, that the two become capital, in fact 'productive capital' as defined in Part One. Here the distinction between means of labour and object of labour which is based in the nature of the labour process itself is reflected in the new form of the distinction between fixed capital and circulating capital. It is only in this way that a thing that functions as means of labour becomes fixed capital. If its material properties also allow it to serve for other functions than that of means of labour, then whether it is fixed capital or not depends on these various functions. Cattle as draught animals are fixed capital; when being fattened for slaughter they are raw material that eventually passes into circulation as a product, and so not fixed but circulating capital.

The mere length of time for which a means of production is fixed in repeated labour processes which are related and continuous, and hence form a production period – i.e. the total production time that is needed in order to complete the product – already involves a longer or shorter advance for the capitalist, just as is the case with fixed capital, but this alone does not make his capital fixed capital. Seed, for example, is not fixed capital, but simply raw material that is fixed in the production process for approximately a year. All capital that functions as productive capital is fixed in the production process, and thus so are all the elements

*pp. 283–8.

of that productive capital, whatever may be their material shape, their function, or the mode of circulation of their value. Whether they are fixed in this way for a longer or shorter time, according to the kind of production process or the intended useful effect, is not what makes the distinction between fixed and circulating capital.[1]

Some of the means of labour, including the general conditions of labour, are held fast in their place once they enter the production process as means of labour and are made ready for their productive function: machines for example. Other means of labour, however, are produced from the start in this static form, tied to the spot, such as improvements to the soil, factory buildings, blast furnaces, canals, railways, etc. The continued attachment of the means of labour to the production process in which it is to function is here simultaneously conditioned by its sensuous mode of existence. On the other hand, a means of labour may constantly change its physical place, i.e. move, and yet be engaged throughout in the production process, as with a locomotive, a ship, draught cattle, etc. Immobility does not give it the character of fixed capital in the one case, nor does mobility remove this character in the other. But the circumstance that some means of labour are fixed in location, with their roots in the soil, gives this part of the fixed capital a particular role in a nation's economy. They cannot be sent abroad or circulate as commodities on the world market. It is quite possible for the property titles to this fixed capital to change; they can be bought and sold, and in this respect circulate ideally. These property titles can even circulate on foreign markets, in the form of shares, for example. But a change in the persons who are the owners of this kind of fixed capital does not change the relationship between the static and materially fixed part of the wealth of a country and the movable part of it.[2]

The peculiar circulation of fixed capital gives rise to a peculiar turnover. The portion of value that it loses in its natural form by wear and tear circulates as a value portion of the product. Through its circulation,

1. The difficulty involved in defining fixed and circulating capital leads Herr Lorenz Stein* to believe that this distinction is made purely for ease of presentation.

*Lorenz von Stein was a Right Hegelian in the 1840s, later an economist and also Professor of Public Law at Kiel University. His book *The Socialism and Communism of Contemporary France*, published in 1842, gave a major impetus to the radical movement among the disaffected German intellectuals of the time, but despite occasional claims to the contrary it had no influence on Marx's own development.

2. Up to here, Manuscript I V. From here on, Manuscript I I.

the product is transformed from a commodity into money, and so is the portion of the value of the means of labour that is circulated by the product; its value trickles from the circulation process as money in the same proportion that this means of labour ceases to be a bearer of value in the production process. Its value thus acquires a dual existence. A part of it remains tied to its use form or natural form, which pertains to the production process, while another part separates off from this form as money. In the course of its function, the part of the value of the means of labour that exists in the natural form steadily declines, while the part of its value converted into the money form steadily increases, until the means of labour eventually expires and its entire value has separated off from its dead body and been transformed into money. Here we can see the peculiarity that this element of the productive capital displays in its turnover. The transformation of its value into money accompanies, step by step, the transmutation into money of the commodity that bears its value. But its transformation back from the money form into the use-form is separate from the transformation of the commodity back into its former elements of production, and is rather determined by its own reproduction period, i.e. by the time for which the means of labour serves until it has to be replaced by another item of the same kind. If a machine with a value of £10,000, say, lasts for ten years, then the turnover time of the value originally advanced in it is ten years. Until this time has elapsed, it does not need to be renewed, but continues to function in its natural form. In the meantime, its value circulates bit by bit as a portion of the value of the commodities that it steadily serves to produce, and is thus gradually converted into money, until finally, at the end of the ten years, it has been completely transformed into money and from money back into a machine, i.e. has completed its turnover. Until this reproduction time arrives, its value is accumulated gradually, in the first instance in the form of a money reserve fund.

The remaining elements of productive capital consist in part of the elements of constant capital existing in the ancillaries and raw materials and in part of variable capital, laid out in labour-power.

In analysing the processes of labour and valorization (Volume 1, Chapter 7), we showed how these different components behave quite differently in the formation of products and value. The value of the part of constant capital that consists of ancillaries and raw materials, just like the value of the part that consists of means of labour, reappears in the value of the product simply as transferred value, while labour-power, through the labour process, adds to the product an equivalent of its value or actually reproduces its value. Furthermore, one part of the ancillary material – coal for heating, gas for lighting, etc. – is consumed in the labour process without physically entering the product, while another part does enter the product bodily and forms the material of its substance. All these differences are irrelevant, however, as far as circulation and hence the mode of turnover are concerned. In so far as ancillary and raw materials are completely consumed in the formation of their product, they transfer their entire value to the product. This value is thus completely circulated via the product, transformed into money and from money back into the elements of production of the commodity. Its turnover is not interrupted, like that of the fixed capital, but passes continuously through the entire circuit of its forms, so that these elements of the productive capital are constantly renewed in kind.

In so far as the variable capital is concerned, i.e. the component part of the productive capital that is spent on labour-power, this labour-power is bought for a definite period of time. Once the capitalist has bought it and incorporated it into the production process, it forms a component of his capital, and in fact precisely its variable component. It functions daily for a certain space of time in which it adds to the product not only its entire daily value, but also an additional surplus-value, which we shall in the first instance ignore. When the labour-power has been bought for one week, for example, and functioned for this time, the purchase must continually be repeated at the customary intervals. The equivalent of its value, which labour-power adds to the product during its function, and which is transformed into money as the product circulates, must constantly be transformed back from money into labour-power, or constantly describe the complete circuit of its forms, i.e. turn over, if the cycle of continuous production is not to be interrupted.

The part of the value of the productive capital that is advanced for labour-power thus completely passes over to the product (we are still ignoring the surplus-value), describes together with it the two metamorphoses pertaining to the circulation sphere, and remains permanently incorporated in the production process by way of this constant renewal. No matter how differently labour-power acts with respect to value-formation from the components of constant capital that do not form fixed capital, this manner of turnover of its value is something that it has in common with the latter, in contrast to the fixed capital. Because of this common characteristic in their turnover, these components of productive capital – the portions of value spent on labour-power and on means of production that do not form fixed capital – confront fixed capital as *circulating* or *fluid* capital.

We saw previously* how the money that the capitalist pays the worker for the use of his labour-power is in fact only the general equivalent form of the worker's necessary means of subsistence. In this respect, the variable capital consists materially of means of subsistence. Here however, in considering the turnover, we are dealing with the form. What the capitalist buys is not the worker's means of subsistence, but his actual labour-power. It is not the worker's means of subsistence that form the variable part of the capitalist's capital, but his active labour-power. What the capitalist consumes productively in the labour process is labour-power and not the worker's means of subsistence. It is the worker himself who converts the money he receives for his labour-power into means of subsistence, so as to transform these back into labour-power and keep alive, just as the capitalist, for example, converts a part of the surplus-value of the commodities that he sells for money into means of subsistence for himself, although no one would be led to say that the buyer of his commodities therefore pays him in means of subsistence. Even if the worker is paid a part of his wages in means of subsistence, in kind, this nowadays forms a second transaction. He sells his labour-power for a definite price, and it is then agreed that he should receive a part of this price in means of subsistence. This only alters the form of the payment, it does not alter the fact that what he actually sells is labour-power. This second transaction is no longer between worker and capitalist as such, but between the worker as buyer of commodities and the capitalist as their seller; whereas in the first transaction it was the worker who was the seller of a commodity (his own labour-power), and the capitalist its buyer. It is just as if the capitalist had had his commodity replaced by another commodity, e.g. as if he replaced the machine that he sells to an iron works by iron. Thus it is not the worker's means of subsistence that acquire the characteristic of fluid capital in contrast to fixed capital. And it is also not his labour-power, but rather the portion of the value of the productive capital that is spent on it, that has this characteristic in the turnover in common with some components of the constant part of the capital, and in contrast with other parts.

The value of the fluid capital – both in labour-power and means of production – is advanced only for the time that it takes to produce the

*Volume 1, pp. 270–80.

product, according to the scale of production which is given by the volume of the fixed capital. This value enters in its entirety into the product, and thus returns again completely from circulation with the sale of the product and can be advanced afresh. The labour-power and means of production in which the fluid component of the capital exists are withdrawn from the circulation sphere in the quantity needed for the formation and sale of the finished product, but they must constantly be replaced and renewed by new purchases, by the transformation from the money form back into the elements of production. They are withdrawn from the market at any one time in smaller quantities than are the elements of fixed capital, but they must be withdrawn again all the more frequently, and the advance of the capital spent on them is repeated at shorter intervals. This regular repetition is mediated by the regular conversion of the product, which circulates their entire value. It is not only their value that continuously describes the whole circuit of metamorphoses, but also their material form; they are constantly transformed back from commodities into the elements of production of those commodities.

Together with its own value, labour-power constantly adds to the product surplus-value, i.e. the embodiment of unpaid labour. This surplus-value is then just as constantly circulated by the finished product and transformed into money as are its other value elements. Here, however, where what we are concerned with in the first instance is the turnover of the capital value, and not that of the surplus-value that is turned over together with it, we shall disregard the latter for the time being.

Our argument so far leads to the following conclusions.

(1) The formal characteristics of fixed and fluid capital arise only from the different turnovers of the capital value or *productive capital* that functions in the production process. This difference in turnover arises for its part from the different ways in which the various components of the productive capital transfer their value to the product, though not from their different share in the production of the product's value or from their characteristic behaviour in the valorization process. The different ways in which value is given up to the product, and hence also the different ways in which this value is circulated by the product and replaced in its original natural form as a result of its metamorphoses, ultimately arise from the different material shapes in which productive capital exists, one part of it being consumed entirely in the course of forming the particular product, while another is used up only gradually. Thus it is only productive capital that can be divided up into

fixed and fluid capital. This antithesis does not exist for the two other modes of existence of industrial capital, neither for commodity capital nor for money capital, nor yet as an antithesis between these two and productive capital. It exists only *for productive capital and only within it.* No matter how much money capital and commodity capital function as capital, and how fluidly they circulate, they can become fluid capital in contrast to fixed only when they have been transformed into the fluid components of productive capital. But because these two forms of capital inhabit the circulation sphere, economists have been misled ever since Adam Smith, as we shall see,* into classing them together with the fluid part of productive capital under the heading of circulating capital. They are certainly capital of circulation in contrast to productive capital, but they are not circulating capital in contrast to fixed capital.

(2) The turnover of the fixed component of capital, and thus also the turnover time needed by it, encompasses several turnovers of the fluid components of capital. In the same time that it takes for the fixed capital to turn over once, the fluid capital turns over several times. The one component of the value of productive capital receives the formal characteristic of fixed capital only in so far as the means of production in which it exists are not used up in the space of time that it takes to produce the product and eject it from the production process as a commodity. A part of its value must remain tied up in the old and persisting use form, while another part is circulated by the finished product; in its circulation, however, the product circulates at the same time the total value of the fluid components of capital.

(3) That part of the value of productive capital that is laid out on fixed capital is advanced all at once in its entirety, for the whole period of functioning of that part of the means of production of which the fixed capital consists. The capitalist thus casts this value into the circulation sphere all at once; but it is withdrawn from circulation again only gradually and bit by bit, by the realization of the value portions that the fixed capital adds bit by bit to the commodities. The actual means of production themselves, however, in which a part of the productive capital is fixed, are withdrawn from circulation all at once, to be incorporated into the production process for the whole of the period during which they function, though they do not need throughout this time to be replaced by new items of the same kind, i.e. to be reproduced. They continue to contribute for a longer or shorter time to the formation of the commodities thrown into circulation, without withdrawing from

* See below, Chapters 10 and 11.

circulation the elements of their own renewal. During this time, therefore, they do not require for their part any new advance on the part of
the capitalist. Finally, while the effective life of the means of production
in which it exists continues, the capital value laid out as fixed capital
does not pass through the circuit of its forms materially, but only in its
value, and this only partially and gradually. That is to say, a part of its
value is continually circulated and transformed into money as a part of
the value of the commodity, without being transformed back from
money into its original natural form. This transformation of money back
into the natural form of the instrument of production takes place only at
the end of the latter's period of functioning, when the instrument of
production has been completely used up.

(4) The elements of fluid capital are just as permanently fixed in the
production process – if this is to be continuous – as are the elements of
fixed capital. But while the elements of the former that are fixed in this
way are steadily renewed in kind (the means of production by new
items of the same kind; labour-power by ever-repeated purchases), the
elements of fixed capital are neither themselves renewed as long as they
last, nor does their purchase have to be repeated. Raw and ancillary
materials are constantly present in the production process, but there are
always new items of the same kind, the old ones having been consumed
in the formation of the finished product. Just as constantly is there
labour-power in the production process, but only in association with a
constant repetition of its purchase, and often with a change in persons.
However the very same buildings, machines, etc. carry on functioning
in the same repeated production processes while the fluid capital turns
over repeatedly.

2. COMPONENTS, REPLACEMENT, REPAIRS AND ACCUMULATION OF THE FIXED CAPITAL

The various elements of fixed capital in a particular investment have
differing lifespans, and hence also different turnover times. In a railway,
for example, the rails, sleepers, earthworks, station buildings, bridges,
tunnels, locomotives and carriages all function for different periods and
have different reproduction times, and so the capital advanced in them
has different turnover times. The buildings, platforms, water tanks,
viaducts, tunnels, cuttings and embankments, in short, all those things
which on the English railways are called 'works of art', do not need to

be renewed for a whole series of years. The things that wear out most quickly are the permanent way and the rolling stock.

When modern railways were first constructed, the general opinion, backed by the most eminent practical engineers, was that a railway would last for centuries, and that the wear and tear of the tracks would be so negligible that it could be ignored for all financial and practical purposes: 100–150 years was considered the lifetime of good rails. It soon transpired, however, that the life of a rail, which of course depends on the speed of the locomotives, the weight and number of trains, the thickness of the rails themselves and a number of secondary circumstances, is no more than twenty years on average. At certain particular stations and centres of heavy traffic, the rails actually wear out each year. Around 1867 steel rails began to be introduced, which, although they cost around twice as much as iron rails, last for more than twice as long. The lifespan of wooden sleepers was between twelve and fifteen years. It also became evident, as far as the rolling stock was concerned, that goods wagons wore out significantly quicker than passenger carriages. In 1867, the life of a locomotive was estimated at between ten and twelve years.

Wear and tear is occasioned in the first place by actual use. As a general rule, the rails wear out in proportion to the number of trains (R. C., no. 17645).[3] The wear and tear also increases by more than the square of the speed; i.e. if the speed of the trains doubles, then the wear and tear increases more than fourfold (R. C., no. 17046).

A further item of wear and tear is that caused by natural forces. Sleepers, for example, do not just deteriorate as a result of actual use, but also suffer from rot:

'The cost of maintaining the road does not depend so much upon the wear and tear of the traffic passing over it, as upon the quality of wood, iron, bricks, and mortar exposed to the atmosphere. A month of severe winter would do more damage to the road of a railway than a year's traffic' (R. P. Williams, *On the Maintenance and Renewal of the Permanent Way*, paper read at the Institute of Civil Engineers, Autumn, 1866).*

3. The quotations marked 'R. C.' are taken from Royal Commission on Railways, *Minutes of Evidence taken before the Commissioners. Presented to both Houses of Parliament*, London, 1867. The questions and answers are numbered as here indicated.

* This paper was published in the *Money Market Review* on 2 December 1867, and this is the source of the quotation.

Finally, as is the case throughout large-scale industry, moral deterioration also plays its part. After ten years have elapsed, it is generally possible to buy the same quantity of carriages and locomotives for £30,000 as previously cost £40,000. A depreciation of 25 per cent on the market price must thus be reckoned with on this material, even if there is no depreciation in the use-value (Lardner, *Railway Economy* [p. 120]).

'Tube bridges will not be replaced in their present form.' (Because there are now better forms for such bridges.) 'Ordinary repairs, taking away gradually, and replacing, are not practicable' (W. B. Adams, *Roads and Rails*, London, 1862 [p. 136]).

The means of labour are for the most part constantly revolutionized by the progress of industry. Hence they are not replaced in their original form, but in the revolutionized form. On the one hand, the volume of fixed capital that is invested in a particular natural form, and has to last out for a definite average lifespan within this, is a reason why new machines, etc. are introduced only gradually, and hence forms an obstacle to the rapid general introduction of improved means of labour. On the other hand, competition forces the replacement of old means of labour by new ones before their natural demise, particularly when decisive revolutions have taken place. Catastrophes, crises, etc. are the principal causes that compel such premature renewals of equipment on a broad social scale.

Depreciation (apart from moral depreciation) is the portion of value that the fixed capital gradually gives up to the product as it is used, according to the average degree of its loss of use-value.

This depreciation in part takes the form that the fixed capital has a certain average lifespan; it is completely advanced for this period of time, and after it has elapsed must be completely replaced. In the case of living means of labour, such as horses, for example, the reproduction time is prescribed by nature itself. Their average life as means of labour is determined by natural laws. Once this period has elapsed, the worn-out items must be replaced by new ones. A horse cannot be replaced bit by bit, but only by another horse.

Other elements of the fixed capital permit periodic or partial renewal. This partial or periodic replacement should be distinguished from the gradual extension of a business.

Fixed capital consists in part of components which are similar but do not all last equally long, and are rather renewed bit by bit at different intervals in time. The rails at a station, for example, have to be replaced more often than rails at other parts of the line. The same is the case with sleepers; Lardner states that in the 1850s, on the Belgian railways, these had to be replaced at the rate of 8 per cent per year, the whole of the sleepers thus being replaced in the course of twelve and a half years. Here the situation is as follows: a sum is advanced, for example, for ten years on a particular kind of fixed capital. This outlay is made all at once. But a certain part of this fixed capital, the value of which has gone into the value of the product and has been converted along with this into money, is replaced each year in kind, while the remainder continues to exist in its original natural form. What distinguishes this fixed capital from fluid capital is precisely this outlay all at once and reproduction only bit by bit in the natural form.

Other items of fixed capital consist of different types of component, which wear out and thus have to be replaced at different intervals of time. This is particularly the case with machines. The same applies here, in connection with the life of these different components of one and the same machine forming an item of fixed capital, as we previously noted with respect to the varying life of different components of a total fixed capital.

The following should be noted in connection with the gradual extension of a business in the course of partial renewal. Even though, as we have seen, the fixed capital continues to function in its natural form in the production process, if a part of its value has circulated with the product, according to the average wear and tear, and been transformed into money, then this forms an element of the money reserve fund for the replacement of the capital when its reproduction in kind falls due. This part of the fixed capital value transformed into money can therefore serve to expand the business or to effect improvements in the machines which increase their effectiveness. Reproduction then occurs, in shorter or longer periods, and from the social point of view this is reproduction on an expanded scale; extensively, if the field of production is extended; intensively, if the means of production are made more effective. This reproduction on an expanded scale does not arise from accumulation – the transformation of surplus-value into capital – but from a re-transformation of the value, which branches into two parts, and in its money form has separated itself off from the body of the fixed capital, into new fixed capital of the same kind, either additional or more effective. Of course it depends in part on the specific nature of the business how far and in what dimensions it is susceptible to a gradual addition of this kind, and thus also in what dimensions a reserve fund has to be built up in order to be reinvested in this way, and in what periods of time this can take place. How far improvements of detail to existing machinery can be brought about, on the other hand, naturally depends on the nature of the improvements and on the construction of the machine itself. Adams shows that this point is borne in mind very strongly, and from the start, in railway investments:

'The whole structure should be set out on the principle which governs the beehive – capacity for indefinite extension. Any fixed and decided symmetrical structure is to be deprecated, as needing subsequent pulling down in case of enlargement' (p. 123).

This in turn depends to a large extent on the space available. In some buildings extra floors can be added, while others require horizontal extension, and thus more land. While capitalist production is marked by the waste of much material, there is also much inappropriate horizontal extension of this kind (partly involving a loss of labour-power) in the course of the gradual extension of a business, since nothing is done according to a social plan, but rather depends on the infinitely varied circumstances, means, etc. with which the individual capitalist acts. This gives rise to a major wastage of productive forces.

The progressive reinvestment of the money reserve fund (i.e. of the part of the fixed capital that is transformed back into money) is most easily effected in agriculture. Here a spatially given field of production is capable of the greatest gradual absorption of capital. The same is true when natural reproduction takes place, as in the case of cattle breeding.

Fixed capital gives rise to special costs of maintenance. A part of the maintenance is effected by the labour process itself; fixed capital spoils if it does not function in the labour process. (See Volume 1, Chapter 8, p. 315, and Chapter 15, p. 528: deterioration of machinery that arises from its non-use.) The English law therefore expressly considers it as waste if land that is farmed out is not cultivated according to custom. (W. A. Holdsworth, Barrister at Law, *The Law of Landlord and Tenant*, London, 1857, p. 96.) This maintenance that results from use in the labour process is a gift of nature provided *gratis* by living labour. In fact the preserving power of labour is of a dual type. On the one hand it preserves the value of the materials of labour, by transferring it to the product, while on the other hand it preserves the value of the means of labour, without transferring this value to the product, by preserving their use-value through their action in the production process.

But fixed capital also requires positive outlays of labour if it is to be kept in good condition. The machinery must be cleaned from time to time. This involves additional labour, without which it becomes unfit for use; this is merely a defence against the damaging influence of the elements that is inseparable from the production process, and is thus keeping it in working order in the most literal sense. The normal life-span of fixed capital is naturally reckoned on the assumption that the conditions under which it can function normally during this time are fulfilled, just as it is assumed, if the average life of a man is taken as thirty years, that he washes himself. What is involved here is not the replacement of the labour contained in the machine, but additional labour that is constantly necessary for it to be used. This is not a matter of labour performed by the machine, but of labour performed on the machine; here it is not an agent of production, but rather raw material. The capital spent on this labour is part of the fluid capital, even though it does not properly enter the actual labour process to which the product owes its origin. The labour must be constantly performed in the course of production, and so its value must also be constantly replaced by the value of the product. The capital spent on it belongs to that part of fluid capital that has to cover the general overheads, and is distributed over the value of the product according to an average annual calculation. As we have seen,* in industry proper this work of cleaning is performed by the workers for nothing during breaks, and for this reason it is often actually done during the production process itself, where it is the major source of accidents. This labour does not count in the price of the product. In this respect the consumer receives it *gratis*. The capitalist, moreover, does not have to pay anything for the maintenance of his machine. The worker pays in his own person, and this forms one of the mysteries of capital's self-preservation, constituting in point of fact a legal claim of the worker on the machinery, and making him a co-owner of this even from the standpoint of bourgeois right.† But in various branches of production where the machinery has to be removed from the production process for cleaning, and the cleaning can therefore not take place on the quiet, as with locomotives, for example, this maintenance work counts as running costs, i.e. as an element of fluid capital. 'A goods engine should not run more than three days without being kept one day in the shed. . . . If

---

*Volume 1, p. 552, note 10.

†'*Bürgerliches Recht*', but 'right' evidently in the philosophical sense of jurisprudence rather than that of positive law. Cf. 'Critique of the Gotha Programme', in *The First International and After*, Pelican Marx Library, pp. 346–7.

you attempt to wash out the boiler before it has cooled down that is very injurious' (R. C., no. 17823).

Repairs proper, the work of patching up, require an outlay of capital and labour which is not contained in the capital originally advanced, and thus cannot always be replaced and covered by the gradual replacement of the fixed capital. If the value of the fixed capital is £10,000, and its overall life is ten years, then this £10,000, when after ten years it is completely transformed into money, replaces only the value of the original capital investment, and does not replace the capital or labour newly added in between times for repairs. This is an additional component of value, which is not advanced all at once, but rather according to need, and its various times of advance are by the nature of the case accidental. All fixed capital requires these later doses of additional capital outlay on means of labour and labour-power.

The damage to which particular parts of the machinery, etc. are exposed are by nature accidental, and hence so are also the repairs necessitated by such damage. However, two kinds of repair works can be singled out here, both having a more or less firm character and falling in different periods of the fixed capital's lifetime: childhood infirmities, and the far more numerous ailments of the years beyond middle age. No matter how perfectly constructed a machine may be when it enters the production process, faults become evident with actual use, and they have to be corrected by subsequent work. Moreover, the more it passes beyond its middle years, and thus the more that normal wear and tear mounts up, and the material it is made of becomes worn out and weak with age, the more frequent and serious becomes the repair work needed to keep the machine going until the end of its average life; just as an old man has more medical expenses than a man in the prime of life, if he is not to die before his time. Despite its accidental character, therefore, the work of repair is distributed unevenly over the various periods of the fixed capital's life.

It follows from this, as well as from the otherwise accidental character of the repair work on a machine:

Firstly, that the actual expenditure on labour-power and means of labour for repair work is accidental, as are the circumstances themselves that make these repairs necessary; the extent of the repairs needed is differentially distributed over the various periods of the fixed capital's life. It is however assumed in assessing the average life of the fixed capital that it is constantly maintained in working condition, partly by cleaning (which includes keeping clean its site), partly by repairs, as often as these are required. The transfer of value through the wear and tear of the fixed capital is calculated over its average period of life, but this average period is itself calculated on the assumption that the additional capital required to keep it in working order is continuously advanced.

Secondly, it is equally clear that the value added by this additional expenditure of capital and labour cannot go into the price of the commodities in step with the actual expenditure itself. A cotton spinner, for instance, cannot sell his yarn dearer this week than last week because he had a wheel broken or a belt snapped. The general costs of spinning are in no way affected by this accident in an individual factory. Experience shows the average extent of such accidents, and the work of maintenance and repair needed during the average life of a fixed capital invested in a certain line of business. This average expenditure is distributed over its average life and added in corresponding aliquot parts to the price of the product, and this is how it is replaced by the product's sale.

The extra capital that is replaced in this way is part of the fluid capital, even though the expenditure is of an irregular kind. Since it is of the utmost importance to treat every ailment of the machinery immediately, every large factory has, in addition to the factory workers proper, a staff of engineer, carpenter, mechanic, fitter, etc. Their wages form part of the variable capital, and the value of their labour is distributed over the product. The expenditure that the means of production require is determined according to this average calculation and always forms a corresponding portion of the value of the product, even though it is in fact advanced at irregular intervals and so also enters the product, i.e. the fixed capital, irregularly. This capital spent on repairs in the strict sense forms in many respects a capital of a peculiar kind; it cannot be properly classed either as fluid or as fixed capital, but, since it is part of the running expenses, it tends more towards the first of the two forms.

The way the books are kept does not of course affect the actual relationships of the things entered in the accounts. But it is important to note that in many lines of business it is customary to calculate the repair costs in conjunction with the actual wear and tear of the fixed capital, in the following way: If the fixed capital advanced is £10,000, its life fifteen years, then the annual depreciation is £666⅔. If the depreciation is now calculated over ten years only, then instead of £666⅔, £1,000 is added annually to the price of the goods produced to compensate for the wearing-out of the fixed capital; i.e. £333⅓ is reserved for repairs, etc. (The figures ten and fifteen are taken only for the sake of example.) This, then, is the amount spent on repairs, on an average, so that the fixed capital may last for fifteen years. The calculation does not of course prevent the fixed capital and the additional capital spent on repairs from forming different categories. On the basis of this way of calculating, it has been assumed, for example, that the lowest cost estimate for the maintenance and replacement of steamships would be 15 per cent per year, i.e. a reproduction time of $6\frac{2}{3}$ years. In the 1860s, the British government compensated the Peninsular and Oriental Co. at an annual rate of 16 per cent, which assumes a reproduction time of $6\frac{1}{4}$ years. In the case of railways, the average life of a locomotive is ten years, but if repairs are included, the depreciation is taken as $12\frac{1}{2}$ per cent, which reduces the lifespan to eight years. For passenger coaches and goods wagons, 9 per cent is reckoned, i.e. a life of $11\frac{1}{9}$ years.

In connection with contracts of rental for houses and other things that are fixed capital for their proprietors and are rented out as such, legislation has always recognized the distinction between normal deterioration, produced by time, the influence of the elements and normal wear and tear, and the occasional repairs that are necessary from time to time for maintenance in the course of the normal life of a house and its normal use. As a rule, the first fall on the landlord, the second on the tenant. Repairs are further divided into ordinary and substantial. The latter represent in part a renewal of fixed capital in its natural form, and also fall on the landlord, unless the contract expressly states the opposite. Thus in English law for example:

'A tenant from year to year, on the other hand, is not bound to do more than keep the premises wind and water tight, when that can be done without "substantial" repairs; and generally to do repairs coming fairly under the head "ordinary". Even with respect to those parts of the premises which are the subject of "ordinary" repairs, regard must be had to their age and general state, and condition, when he took possession, for he is not bound to replace old and worn out materials with new ones, nor to make good the inevitable depreciation resulting from time and ordinary wear and tear' (Holdsworth, *Law of Landlord and Tenant*, pp. 90 and 91).

Something that is quite different both from the replacement of wear and tear and from the work of repair and maintenance is *insurance*, which relates to destruction by way of extraordinary natural events, fire, flood, etc. This must be made good out of surplus-value, and forms a deduction from it. Considered from the standpoint of the whole society, there must be a constant over-production, i.e. production on a greater scale than is needed for the simple replacement and reproduction of the existing wealth – quite apart from any increase in population – for the society to have at its disposal the means of production needed to make good unusual destruction caused by accidents and natural forces.

In actual fact, only a very small part of the capital needed for replacement exists in the money reserve fund. The most significant part exists in the extension of the scale of production itself, which is partly an actual expansion, and partly falls within the normal capacity of the branches of production that produce fixed capital. An engineering works, for example, is organized to take account of both an annual expansion of the factories of all its customers, and the need of part of them for reproduction, as a whole or in part.

When wear and tear and repair costs are determined on a social average, great unevenness necessarily arises, even for equally large capital investments in the same branch of production which are under otherwise similar conditions. In practice a machine, etc. will last one capitalist longer than the average period, and another capitalist not so long. The repair costs of the one are above the average, those of the other below it, etc. But the addition to the price determined by wear and tear and by repair costs is the same in both cases and is determined on the average. Thus the increase in price brings the one more than he actually added, and the other less. This circumstance, like all others that lead the profit of different capitalists in the same line of business to differ, given the same exploitation of labour-power, helps to make insight into the true nature of surplus-value more difficult.

The boundary between what is repair and what is replacement, between costs of maintenance and costs of renewal, is a more or less shifting one. This gives rise to a perpetual struggle – in the railways, for example – as to whether certain expenses are repairs or replacement, whether they are to be met from current expenditure or from the original capital. The transfer of repair costs to the capital account instead of the current account is a well-known device through which railway directors artificially rack up their dividends. Here, too, experience has already provided the most fundamental reference points. The subsequent works undertaken during the early life of a railway, for example, 'ought not to be denominated *repairs*, but should be considered as an essential part of the construction of the railway, and in the financial accounts should be debited to capital, and not to revenue, not being expenses due to wear and tear, or to the legitimate operation of the traffic, but to the original and inevitable incompleteness of the construction of the line' (Lardner, op. cit., p. 40). 'The only sound way is to charge each year's revenue with the depreciation necessarily suffered to earn the revenue whether the amount is actually spent or not' (Captain Fitzmaurice, 'Committee of Inquiry on Caledonian Railway', published in *Money Market Review*, [25 January] 1868).

In agriculture it becomes in practice impossible and meaningless to separate the replacement of the fixed capital from its maintenance, at least in so far as steam power is not yet used.

'Where there is a full, though not excessive stock of implements' (of agricultural and other implements and appliances of all kinds), 'the general rule is to estimate the annual wear and tear *together with* the maintenance of the implements, according to the different conditions obtaining, at 15–25 per cent of the original capital' (Kirchhof, *Handbuch der landwirthschaftlichen Betriebslehre*, Dessau, 1852, p. 137) [Marx's emphasis].

In the case of railway rolling stock it is quite impossible to separate repairs from replacement:

'We maintain our stock by number. Whatever number of engines we have we maintain that. If one is destroyed by age, and it is better to build a new one, we build it at the expense of revenue, of course, taking credit for the materials of the old one as far as they go . . . there is a great deal left; there are the wheels, the axles, the boilers, and in fact a great deal of the old engine is left' (T. Gooch, Chairman of the Great Western Railway Co., R. C. on Railways, p. 858, nos. 17327–17329). '. . . Repairing means renewing; I do not believe in the word replacement . . .; once a railway company has bought a vehicle or an engine, it ought to be repaired, and in that way admit of going on for ever' (no. 17784). '. . . The engines are maintained for ever out of this 8½d. We rebuild our engines. If you purchase an engine entirely it would be spending more money than is necessary . . . yet there is always a pair of wheels or an axle or some portion of the engine which comes in, and hence it cheapens the cost of producing a practically new engine' (no. 17790). 'I am at this moment turning out a new engine every week, or practically a new engine, for it has a new boiler, cylinder, or framing' (no. 17823: Archibald Sturrock, Locomotive Superintendent of the Great Northern Railway, in R. C. 1867).

The same with carriages:

'In the course of time the stock of engines and vehicles is continually repaired. New wheels are put on at one time, and a new body at another. The different moving parts most subject to wear are gradually renewed; and the engines and vehicles may be conceived even to be subject to such a succession of repairs, that in many of them not a vestige of the original materials remains . . . Even in this case, however, the old materials of coaches or engines are more or less worked up into other vehicles or engines, and never totally disappear from the road. The movable capital therefore may be considered to be in a state of continual reproduction; and that which, in the case of the permanent way, must take place altogether at a future epoch, when the entire road will have to be relaid, takes place in the rolling stock gradually from year to year. Its existence is perennial, and it is in a constant state of rejuvenescence' (Lardner, op. cit., pp. 115–16).

The process depicted here by Lardner in the case of the railways does not apply to an individual factory, but it does provide a picture of the constant partial reproduction of the fixed capital, shot through with repairs, that takes place within an entire branch of industry, or generally within production as a whole, considered on the social scale.

Here is some evidence of the broad limits within which clever directors can manipulate the concepts of repairs and replacement in the interest of their dividends. According to the above-quoted paper by R. P. Williams, various English railway companies annually wrote off the following average sums over a number of years for repairs and maintenance of the permanent way and buildings (for each mile of track):

London and North Western	£370
Midland	£225
London and South Western	£257
Great Northern	£310
Lancashire and Yorkshire	£377
South Eastern	£263
Brighton	£266
Manchester and Sheffield	£200

These differences arise only to a very slight degree from variations in actual expenditure; they are almost exclusively due to differing modes of calculation, according to whether items are debited to the capital account or the current account. Williams says in so many words that a lesser charge is put down when this is necessary for a good dividend, and a higher figure when there is a greater revenue able to bear it.

In certain cases, the wear and tear, and thus replacement for it, is in practice of an infinitesimal magnitude, so that it is only repair costs that come into the balance. What Lardner says about 'works of art' in the case of the railways holds good generally for all similarly durable works such as canals, docks, iron and stone bridges, etc. [He refers to]

'that wear and tear which, being due to the slow operation of time acting upon the more solid structures, produces an effect altogether insensible when observed through short periods, but which, after a long interval of time, such, for example, as centuries, must necessitate the reconstruction of some or all even of the most solid structures. These changes may not unaptly be assimilated to the periodical and secular inequalities which take place in the movements of the great bodies of the universe. The operation of time upon the more massive works of art upon the railway, such as the bridges, tunnels, viaducts, etc., afford examples of what may be called the secular wear and tear. The more rapid and visible deterioration, which is made good by repairs or reconstruction effected at shorter intervals, is analogous to the periodic inequalities. In the annual repairs is included the casual damage which the exterior of the more solid and durable works may from time to time sustain; but, independently of these repairs, age produces its effects even on these structures, and an epoch must arrive, however remote it be, at which they would be reduced to a state which will necessitate their reconstruction. For financial and economic purposes such an epoch is perhaps too remote to render it necessary to bring it into practical calculation, and therefore it need here only be noticed in passing' (Lardner, op. cit., pp. 38, 39).

This applies to all similar works with a long span of life, so that the capital advanced in them does not have to be gradually replaced in accordance with its wear and tear, but it is only the annual average costs of maintenance and repair that are transferred to the price of the product.

Even though, as we have seen, a large part of the money that flows back to replace the wear and tear of the fixed capital is transformed back into its natural form annually, or even more frequently, each individual capitalist still needs an amortization fund for the part of the fixed capital that reaches its term of reproduction only after a period of years, and then has to be replaced entirely. A significant component of the fixed capital excludes piecemeal reproduction by its very nature. Apart from the case where reproduction takes place bit by bit in such a way that new stock is added to the depreciated old stock at short intervals, a prior accumulation of money is necessary, of a greater or lesser amount according to the specific character of the branch of production in question, before this replacement can occur. This cannot be just any sum of money whatever; an amount of a certain size is required.

If we consider this exclusively on the assumption of simple money circulation, without any regard to the credit system (this will be brought in later*), then the mechanism of the movement is as follows. In the first volume (Chapter 3, 3, a) it was shown that although part of the money present in a society always lies fallow in the form of a hoard, while another part functions as means of circulation or as an immediate reserve fund of directly circulating money, the proportion in which the total quantity of money is divided between hoard and means of circulation constantly alters. In our present case, money that has to be accumulated on a large scale as a hoard in the hands of a big capitalist is thrown into circulation all at once on the purchase of fixed capital. It is then divided up again in the society between means of circulation and hoard. By way of the amortization fund in which the value of the fixed capital flows back to its starting-point in proportion to the wear and tear, a part of the money in circulation again forms a hoard – for a longer or shorter period of time – in the hands of the same capitalist whose hoard was transformed into means of circulation and separated from him with his acquisition of fixed capital. There is a constantly changing distribution of the hoard existing in a society, which alternately functions as means of circulation, and is then again divided off from the mass of circulating money as a hoard. With the development of the credit system, which necessarily runs parallel with the development of large-scale industry and capitalist production, this money no longer functions as a hoard but as capital, though not in the hands of its proprietor, but rather of other capitalists at whose disposal it is put.

*See Volume 3, Part Five.

Chapter 9: The Overall Turnover of the Capital Advanced. Turnover Cycles

We have seen already that the fixed and the fluid components of productive capital turn over differently and in different periods, just as the various components of fixed capital in the same business also have different turnover periods according to their different lifespans and reproduction times. (On the actual or apparent variations in the turnover of different components of fluid capital in the same business, see heading 6 at the end of this chapter.)

1. The overall turnover of the capital advanced is the average turnover of its different component parts; the mode of calculation is given below. In so far as only different periods of time are involved, it is of course perfectly simple to take their average. However,

2. There are not only quantitative distinctions involved, but also qualitative ones.

The fluid capital entering the production process transfers its whole value to the product, and must therefore be constantly replaced in kind by the sale of the product, if the production process is to continue without interruption. The fixed capital entering the production process transfers only part of its value (the wear and tear) to the product, and continues to function in the production process despite this wear and tear; hence it only needs to be replaced in kind at shorter or longer intervals, in any case not as often as the fluid capital. This necessity of replacement, the reproduction period, does not just differ quantitatively for the different components of the fixed capital. As we have already seen, one part of the fixed capital, of longer durability and fixed for several years, can be replaced annually or at shorter intervals, and the old fixed capital added to in kind; while with fixed capital of a different sort, the replacement can only be effected all at once at the end of its life.

It is necessary therefore to reduce the separate turnovers of the various parts of the fixed capital to a similar form of turnover, so that these differ only quantitatively, in the duration of their turnover.

A qualitative homogeneity of this kind does not exist if we take as the starting-point $P \ldots P$, the form of the continuous production process. For some elements of P have to be constantly replaced in kind, while others do not. Let us take a machine with a value of £10,000, for example, which lasts for ten years, so that one tenth of it, or £1,000, is transformed back into money every year. In the course of one year, this £1,000 has been transformed from money capital into productive capital and commodity capital, and from this back into money capital. It has returned to its original money form, just like the fluid capital, if we consider the latter in this form, and it is immaterial here whether the money capital of £1,000 is transformed back again into the natural form of a machine at the end of the year, or not. In calculating the overall turnover of the productive capital advanced, we therefore take all its elements in the money form, so that the return to the money form concludes the turnover. We always consider the value as advanced in money, even in the case of a continuous production process, where the money form of the value is only that of money of account. We can then take the average.

3. It follows that even if by far the greater part of the productive capital advanced consists of fixed capital whose reproduction time, and therefore turnover time, makes up a cycle of many years, the capital value turned over during the year by way of repeated turnovers of the fluid capital may be greater than the total value of the capital advanced. Let the fixed capital be £80,000 and its reproduction time ten years, so that £8,000 of this annually returns to its money form or completes one tenth of its turnover. Let the fluid capital be £20,000, turning over five times in the year. The total capital is then £100,000. The fixed capital turned over is £8,000, and the fluid capital turned over is 5 times £20,000 = £100,000. The capital turned over in the year is then £108,000, £8,000 greater than the capital advanced. $1\frac{2}{25}$ of the capital has turned over.

4. The *value turnover* of the capital advanced is thus separate from its actual reproduction time, or the real turnover time of its components. Say that a capital of £4,000 turns over five times in the year. The capital turned over is then 5 times £4,000 = £20,000. But what returns at the end of each turnover, to be advanced once again, is the originally advanced capital of £4,000. Its size is not affected by the number of turnover periods in which it functions anew as capital. (We again disregard surplus-value.)

In the example under heading 3, we have assumed that at the end of the year there returns to the capitalist, (a) a value sum of £20,000, which he lays out once again on the fluid components of capital, and (b) a sum of £8,000, which has separated off from the fixed capital advanced as a result of wear and tear; the same fixed capital still continues to exist in the production process, but with the reduced value of £72,000 instead of £80,000. The production process must thus continue for nine years before the fixed capital advanced has come to the end of its life, no longer functions to form products or value, and has to be replaced. The capital value advanced has thus to describe a cycle of turnovers, in the given case for example a cycle of ten annual turnovers, and this cycle is in fact determined by the lifespan, and hence the reproduction time or turnover time, of the fixed capital applied.

To the same extent as the value and durability of the fixed capital applied develops with the development of the capitalist mode of production, so also does the life of industry and industrial capital in each particular investment develop, extending to several years, say an average of ten years. If the development of fixed capital extends this life, on the one hand, it is cut short on the other by the constant revolutionizing of the means of production, which also increases steadily with the development of the capitalist mode of production. This also leads to changes in the means of production; they constantly have to be replaced, because of their moral depreciation, long before they are physically exhausted. We can assume that, for the most important branches of large-scale industry, this life cycle is now on average a ten-year one. The precise figure is not important here. The result is that the cycle of related turnovers, extending over a number of years, within which the capital is confined by its fixed component, is one of the material foundations for the periodic cycle* in which business passes through successive periods of stagnation, moderate activity, over-excitement and crisis. The periods for which capital is invested certainly differ greatly, and do not coincide in time. But a crisis is always the starting-point of a large volume of new investment. It is also, therefore, if we consider the society as a whole, more or less a new material basis for the next turnover cycle.[1]

1. 'Urban production is tied to a cycle of days, rural production to one of years' (Adam H. Müller, *Die Elemente der Staatskunst*, Berlin, 1809, III, p. 178). This is the naïve conception of industry and agriculture held by the Romantic school.

---

* The German text here has the word 'crises'.

5. On the mode of calculation of the turnover we will let an American economist have his say:

'In some trades the whole capital embarked is turned or circulated several times within the year. In others a part is turned oftener than once a year, another part less often. It is the average period which his entire capital takes in passing through his hands, or making one revolution, from which a capitalist must calculate his profits. Suppose for example that a person engaged in a particular business has one half of his capital invested in buildings and machinery; so as to be turned only once in ten years; that one fourth more, the cost of his tools, etc., is turned once in two years; and the remaining fourth, employed in paying wages and purchasing material, is turned twice in one year. Say that his entire capital is $50,000. Then his annual expenditure will be

$$\$25,000 \div 10 \; - \quad \$2,500$$
$$\$12,500 \div 2 \; = \quad \$6,250$$
$$\$12,500 \times \; 2 = \$25,000$$

$$\overline{\;\;\$33,750}$$

... the mean term in which his capital is turned being about eighteen months ... Take another case, ... say that one-fourth of the entire capital circulates in ten years, one-fourth in one year, and one half twice in the year. Then the annual expenditure will be,

$$\$12,500 \div 10 = \quad \$1,250$$
$$\$12,500 \qquad = \$12,500$$
$$\$25,000 \times 2 \; = \$50,000$$

$$\overline{\text{Turned over in 1 year} \quad \$63,750}$$

(Scrope, *Political Economy*, edited by Alonzo Potter, New York, 1841, pp. 142, 143).

6. Actual and apparent variations in the turnover of the various parts of capital. This Scrope says in the same passage [p. 141]:

'The capital laid out by a manufacturer, farmer, or tradesman in the payment of his labourer's wages, circulates most rapidly, being turned perhaps once a week (if his men are paid weekly), by the weekly receipts on his bills or sales. That invested in his materials and stock in hand circulates less quickly, being turned perhaps twice, perhaps four times in the year, according to the time consumed between his purchases of the one and sales of the other, supposing him to buy and sell on equal credits. The capital invested in his implements and machinery circulates still more slowly, being turned, that is, consumed and renewed, on the average, perhaps but once in five or ten years; though there are many tools that are worn out in one set of operations. The capital which is embarked in buildings, as mills, shops, warehouses, barns, in roads, irrigation, etc., may appear scarcely to circulate at all. But, in truth, these things are, to the full, as much as those we have enumerated, consumed in contributing to production, and must be reproduced in order to enable the producer to continue his operations; with this only difference, that they are consumed and reproduced by slower degrees than the rest ... and the capital invested in them may be turned perhaps every twenty or fifty years.'

Here Scrope confuses the difference in the flow of particular parts of the fluid capital brought about by payment periods and credit conditions, with turnovers arising from the nature of the capital. He says that wages must be paid weekly out of the weekly receipts from payment for sales or bills. The first thing to note here is that differences arise with respect to wages themselves, according to the length of the period of payment, i.e. the length of time for which the worker has to give the capitalist credit; thus according to whether the payment of wages is weekly, monthly, three-monthly, half-yearly, etc. Here the law put forward earlier applies, that 'the quantity of the means of payment required' (and thus the quantity of money capital that has to be advanced at one go) 'is in direct proportion to the length of the [payment] periods' (Volume 1, Chapter 3, 3, b, p. 240).

In the second place, it is not only the entire new value added in its production by the week's labour that enters into the weekly product, but also the value of the raw material and ancillaries consumed in it. The value contained in the product circulates together with the product itself. It receives the money form by the sale of the product, and has to be converted once again into the same elements of production. This holds good just as much for labour-power as for raw and ancillary materials. But as we have already seen (Chapter 6, 2, a), the continuity of production requires a stock of means of production, which differs for various lines of business, and in the same line of business differs once again for different components of this element of fluid capital, e.g. for coal and   cotton. Hence although these materials must constantly be replaced in kind, they do not always need to be bought afresh. How often the purchase is repeated depends on the size of the stock invested in, how long it will last until it is exhausted. In the case of labour-power, there is no such storage process. For the portion of the capital that is laid out on labour, the transformation back into money goes hand in hand with that laid out on ancillary and raw materials. But the transformation of the money back into labour-power, on the one hand, and raw materials, on the other, proceeds separately, on account of the particular purchase and payment periods of these two components, one of them being bought at longer intervals, as a productive stock, the other, labour-power, at shorter intervals, e.g. weekly. Besides his production stock, the capitalist must also keep a stock of finished commodities. One way of disregarding the difficulties of sale, etc., is to assume that a certain quantity of goods must be produced to order. Even so, while the latter part of these are being produced, those items already finished lie in store until the time when the others can be completed. Other distinctions in the turnover of the fluid capital arise if particular elements of this have to persist longer than others at a preliminary stage of the production process (drying of wood, etc.).

The credit system, which Scrope refers to here, modifies the turnover of the individual capitalist, and so does commercial capital. At the level of society, however, it modifies this only in so far as it speeds up both consumption and production.

Chapter 10: Theories of Fixed and Circulating Capital. The Physiocrats and Adam Smith

In Quesnay's work, the distinction between fixed and circulating capital appears as one between *avances primitives* and *avances annuelles*.* He is correct in presenting this distinction as one within productive capital, capital incorporated into the immediate production process. Since he considers capital applied in agriculture, i.e. the capital of the farmer, as the only really productive capital, these distinctions in fact only arise for the farmer's capital. What also results from this is the annual turnover time of one part of the capital, and the more than annual (decennial) turnover time of the other. In the course of development, the Physiocrats incidentally transferred these distinctions to other kinds of capital as well, to industrial capital in general. For society as a whole, the distinction between advances for one year and advances for several years remains so important that many economists, even after Adam Smith, have returned to this definition.

The distinction between the two kinds of advance arises only when money advanced has been transformed into the elements of productive capital. It is simply and solely a distinction within productive capital. Thus it did not occur to Quesnay to count money as part of the original advances or the annual advances. As advances for production, i.e. as productive capital, the two contrast both with money and with commodities on the market. Moreover, Quesnay correctly reduced the distinction between these two elements of productive capital to the different ways in which they enter the value of the finished product, hence the different ways in which their value is circulated together with the value of the product, and the different ways in which they are replaced or reproduced, the value of one being completely replaced each year, that of the other bit by bit over a longer period.[1]

1. Cf. for Quesnay the *Analyse du tableau économique* (*Physiocrates*, ed. Daire, part I, Paris, 1846). Quesnay says there for example: 'The annual advances consist

* Original and yearly advances.

The only step forward taken by Adam Smith was to generalize these categories. In his work, they no longer relate just to one special form of capital, farmer's capital, but to every form of productive capital. It follows automatically that in place of the distinction, taken from agriculture, between annual and more than annual turnovers, we have a general distinction between turnovers of varying times, so that a turnover of fixed capital always comprises more than one turnover of circulating capital, whatever the length of turnover of this circulating capital may be – a year, greater than a year, or less than a year. In Smith, therefore, *avances annuelles* are transformed into circulating capital, *avances primitives* into fixed capital. But the progress he made was confined to this generalization of categories. In the development of his presentation, he falls far behind Quesnay.

The crudely empirical way in which Smith opens his investigation immediately introduces an ambiguity:

'There are two different ways in which a capital may be employed so as to yield a revenue or profit to its employer' (*Wealth of Nations*, Book Two, Chapter I, p. 185, edit. Aberdeen, 1848).*

The ways in which value may be employed to function as capital, to yield a surplus-value to its owner, are as varied and manifold as the spheres of investment of capital. This is a question of the various branches of production in which capital can be invested. The question, formulated in this way, goes still further. It includes the problem of how value, even if it is not invested as productive capital, can function as capital for its owner, e.g. as interest-bearing capital, merchant's capital, etc. Here we are already a world away from the real object of the

---

of the expenditures annually made for the work of cultivation; these advances must be distinguished from the original advances which form the fund for the commencement of cultivation' (p. 59). Later Physiocrats were already describing these *avances* much more directly as capital: '*capital* or *avances*', Dupont de Nemours, *Maximes du Docteur Quesnay, ou résumé de ses principes d'économie sociale* (Daire, I, p. 391). Also Le Trosne: 'As a consequence of the longer or shorter lifespan of the instruments of labour, a nation possesses a considerable stock of riches independent of its yearly reproduction; this represents a *capital* accumulated over a long period and originally paid for with products, and it is continually maintained and increased' ([*De l'intérêt Social*,] Daire, II, pp. 928–9) [Marx's emphasis]. Turgot already uses the term 'capital' for the *avances* more regularly, and more closely identifies the *avances* of the *manufacturiers* with those of the farmers (Turgot, *Réflexions sur la formation et la distribution des richesses*, 1766).

* From here on Marx's page references are replaced by references to the Pelican edition, Harmondsworth, 1974, in which this passage appears on p. 374.

analysis, i.e. the question how the division of *productive* capital into its various elements affects the turnover, irrespective of its different spheres of investment.

Adam Smith immediately goes on to say:

'First, it may be employed in raising, manufacturing, or purchasing goods, and selling them again with a profit.'

Here Smith tells us no more than that capital can be applied in agriculture, manufacture or trade. Thus he speaks only of the different spheres of investment of capital, as well as of some in which, as in trade, capital is not incorporated into the immediate production process, and thus does not function as productive capital. He thus already abandons the basis on which the Physiocrats depicted the distinctions within productive capital and their influence on the turnover. In fact he immediately takes merchant's capital as an example in a question where what is at issue is exclusively the differences within *productive* capital in the process of forming products and value, differences which in turn produce differences in its turnover and reproduction.

He continues:

'The capital employed in this manner yields no revenue or profit to its employer, while it either remains in his possession, or continues in the same shape.'

'The capital employed in this manner'! But Smith speaks of capital that is invested in agriculture and industry, and later tells us that the capital thus invested can be divided into fixed and circulating capital! The employment of capital in this manner can thus make the capital neither fixed nor circulating.

Perhaps what Smith has in mind is that capital employed to produce commodities and to sell these commodities at a profit must, after its transformation into commodities, be sold; by way of sale it firstly passes from the possession of the seller into that of the buyer, and, secondly, is converted from its natural form as a commodity into its money form, hence is useless to the possessor 'while it either remains in his possession, or continues in the same shape' – for him. But what emerges then is this: the same capital value that functioned previously in the form of productive capital, in a form pertaining to the production process, now functions as commodity capital and money capital, in the forms pertaining to the circulation process, and thus is no longer either fixed or fluid capital. And this holds just as much for the elements of value that are added by way of raw and ancillary materials, thus by fluid capital, as for those added by the use of means of labour, i.e. by fixed capital. Thus we do not get a step nearer to the distinction between fixed and fluid capital.

Further:

'The goods of the merchant yield him no revenue or profit till he sells them for money, and the money yields him as little till it is again exchanged for goods. His capital is continually going from him in one shape, and returning to him in another, and it is only by means of such circulation, or successive exchanges, that it can yield him any profit. Such capitals, therefore, may very properly be called circulating capitals' [ibid.].

What Adam Smith here calls circulating capital is what I intend to call *capital of circulation*, capital in the form pertaining to the circulation process, pertaining to the change of form mediated by exchange (material change and change of hands), i.e. commodity capital and money capital, in contrast to the form pertaining to the production process, that of productive capital. These are not particular ways in which the industrial capitalist divides his capital, but rather different forms that the same capital value, once advanced, successively assumes and discards throughout its *curriculum vitae*. Adam Smith lumps these together with the distinctions of form that arise within the circulation of the capital value, in its circuit through its successive forms, while the capital value exists in the form of *productive* capital, and this is a great step backward in relation to the Physiocrats. These distinctions arise in fact from the various ways in which the different elements of productive capital participate in the process of value-formation and transfer their value to the product. We shall see more below of the consequences of this basic confusion between productive capital and capital in the circulation sphere (commodity capital and money capital), on the one hand, and fixed capital and fluid capital on the other. The capital value advanced in fixed capital is circulated via the product just as much as that advanced in fluid capital, and it is transformed into money capital through the circulation of the commodity capital every bit as much as the other. The distinction simply arises from the fact that its value circulates bit by bit, and must thus also be replaced bit by bit, in shorter or longer periods, and so be reproduced in this way in its natural form.

The particularly unfortunate example selected by Adam Smith demonstrates that by circulating capital he understands here nothing other than capital of circulation, i.e. capital value in its forms pertaining to the circulation process (commodity capital and money capital). He takes as his example a kind of capital that does not belong to the production process at all, but exclusively inhabits the circulation sphere and consists solely of capital of circulation – merchant's capital.

The absurdity of beginning with an example in which capital does not figure as productive capital at all is immediately indicated by Smith himself:

'The capital of a merchant . . . is altogether a circulating capital.'

The distinction between circulating and fixed capital, however, is supposedly, as we are later told, one arising from basic distinctions within productive capital itself. Adam Smith has in mind, on the one hand, the Physiocratic distinction, on the other hand, the distinctions of form which the capital value undergoes in its circuit. The two are completely jumbled up.

There is no way of seeing how a profit is supposed to arise through the change of form between money and commodity, through a mere transformation of value from one of these forms to the other. Explanation of this is even made absolutely impossible in so far as Smith begins with merchant's capital, which moves solely within the circulation sphere. We shall return to this point; let us first see what he says about fixed capital:

'Secondly, it' (capital) 'may be employed in the improvement of land, in the purchase of useful machines and instruments of trade, or in such-like things as yield a revenue or profit without changing masters, or circulating any further. Such capitals, therefore, may very properly be called fixed capitals. Different occupations require very different proportions between the fixed and circulating capitals employed in them . . . Some part of the capital of every master artificer or manufacturer must be fixed in the instruments of his trade. This part, however, is very small in some, and very great in others . . . The far greater part of the capital of all such master artificers' (such as tailors, shoemakers, weavers), 'however, is circulated, either in the wages of their workmen, or in the price of their materials, and repaid with a profit by the price of the work' [ibid.].

Quite apart from the childish definition of the source of profit, the weakness and confusion are immediately apparent. For a machine-builder, for example, the machine is the product that circulates as his commodity capital, i.e. in Smith's words, 'is parted with, changes masters, circulates further'. The machine would thus not be fixed but circulating capital, even according to his own definition. This confusion also arises from the way that Smith mixes up the distinction between fixed and fluid capital which arises from the different kinds of circulation of the different elements of productive capital, with the distinctions of form that the same capital undergoes in so far as it functions as *productive* capital within the production process, but as capital of circulation, i.e. as commodity capital or money capital, in the circulation sphere. According to the position they assume in the life process of capital, therefore, the same things can function for Adam Smith as fixed capital (as means of labour, elements of productive capital), and as 'circulating' capital, commodity capital (as the product that is ejected from the sphere of production into that of circulation).

But then he suddenly changes the whole basis of his distinction and contradicts what he started the whole investigation with a few lines earlier. Previously he said: 'There are two different ways in which a capital may be employed so as to yield a revenue or profit to its employer', i.e. as circulating or as fixed capital. These were different modes of employment of distinct and independent capitals, so that capital might be employed either in industry or in agriculture, for example. Now, however, he says:

'Different occupations require very different proportions between the fixed and circulating capitals employed in them.'

Fixed and circulating capital are now no longer distinct and independent capital investments, but rather different portions of the same productive capital, which form different shares of the total value in different spheres of investment. They are thus distinctions that arise from the division of *productive* capital itself, as it lies in the facts, and they therefore apply only in relation to this. This is again contradicted, however, when commercial capital is counterposed to fixed capital as simply circulating capital, for Smith himself says:

'The capital of a merchant . . . is altogether a circulating capital.'

What it is in fact is a capital functioning within the circulation sphere; as such it contrasts with productive capital in general, capital incorporated into the production process, and for this very reason it can never be counterposed to the fixed component of productive capital as a fluid (circulating) component of productive capital.

In the examples he provides, Smith defines fixed capital as 'instruments of trade', and circulating capital as the share of capital laid out on wages and raw materials, including ancillaries, which is 'repaid with a profit by the price of the work'. At first, therefore, the starting-point is simply the various components of the labour process, labour-power (labour) and raw materials on the one hand, instruments of labour on the other. But these are components of capital, because a sum of value that is to function as capital is laid out on them. In this respect they are the material elements, modes of existence, of *productive* capital, i.e. capital functioning in the production process. Why then is one part called 'fixed'? Because 'some part of the capital must be fixed in the instruments of trade'. The other part, however, is also fixed, in wages and raw materials. However, machines and

'instruments of trade ... such-like things ... yield a revenue or profit without changing masters, or circulating any further. Such capitals, therefore, may very properly be called fixed capitals'.

Let us take for example mining. Here there is no raw material involved, since the object of labour, e.g. copper, is a natural product that has first to be appropriated by labour. The as yet unappropriated copper, the product of the process that will later circulate as a commodity, as commodity capital, does not form an element of the productive capital. No part of the value is laid out on it. Neither do the other elements of the production process, labour-power and ancillaries such as coal, water, etc., for their part, enter materially into the product. The coal is entirely consumed, and only its value enters the product, just as a part of the value of the machine, etc. enters the product. The worker, finally, still exists just as independently vis-à-vis the product as does the machine. It is only the value that he produces through his labour that is now a component of the value of the copper. In this example, therefore, not a single component of the productive capital changes hands ('masters'): none of these components is circulated further, because none of them materially enters the product. Where then is the circulating capital in this case? According to Smith's own definition, the whole of the capital employed in a copper mine consists solely of fixed capital.

Let us take on the other hand a different industry, which uses raw materials that form the substance of the product, as well as ancillaries that enter the product bodily, and not just in respect of their value, as does coal for heating, for example. Here, when the product, yarn for instance, changes hands, so does the raw material, the cotton, of which it consists, passing from the production process into that of circulation.* But as long as cotton functions as an element of productive capital, its owner does not sell it but works on it, makes yarn out of it. He does not let it go. Or, to use Smith's crudely false and trivial expression, he does not make a profit 'by parting with it, by its changing masters, or by circulating it'. He no more has his materials circulate

---

*The German text has 'consumption', but this would appear to be a slip of Marx's pen that, unlike several others, has so far escaped correction.

than his machines. They are fixed in the production process, just as much as are the spinning machines and factory buildings. Indeed, a part of the productive capital must as constantly be fixed in the form of coal, cotton, etc., as in that of means of labour. The distinction is simply that the cotton, coal, etc. needed for a week's production of yarn, for example, is completely consumed, and must therefore be replaced by new cotton, coal, etc.; thus these elements of productive capital, although they remain identical in kind, always consist of new items, whereas the same individual spinning machine and the same individual factory building continue to serve for a whole series of weeks of production, without being replaced by new items. As elements of productive capital, all its components are constantly fixed in the production process, since this cannot proceed without them. And all elements of productive capital, fixed as well as fluid, are, as productive capital, equally distinct from circulation capital, i.e. from commodity capital and money capital.

It is just the same with labour-power. A part of the productive capital must constantly be fixed in it, and it is generally the very same labour-powers, like the same machines, that are used by the same capitalist for a long period. The distinction between labour-power and machine here does not consist in the fact that the machine is bought once and for all (which is in fact not the case when it is paid for by instalments, for example), while the worker is not, but rather in that the labour that the worker expends enters entirely into the value of the product, while the value of the machine enters only bit by bit.

Smith confuses different characteristics, when he says of circulating capital in contrast to fixed:

'The capital employed in this manner yields no revenue or profit to its employer, while it either remains in his possession, or continues in the same shape.'

He places the merely formal commodity metamorphosis which the product, the commodity capital, undergoes in the circulation sphere and which mediates the commodities' change of hands, on the same level with the bodily metamorphosis which the various elements of the productive capital undergo during the production process. Without further ado, he lumps together the transformation of commodity into money and money into commodity with the transformation of the elements of production into the product. His example of circulating capital is merchant's capital, which is transformed from commodity into money and from money into commodity – the change of form $C–M–C$ that pertains to commodity circulation. The significance that this formal change within the circulation sphere has for functioning industrial capital is that the commodities which money is transformed back into are elements of production (means of labour and labour-power), and so the change of form therefore mediates the continuity of the capital's function, mediates the production process as a continuous one, as a process of reproduction. This entire change of form proceeds in the *circulation* sphere; it is this that mediates the actual transition of commodities from one hand to another. The metamorphoses that productive capital undergoes within its productive process, on the other hand, are metamorphoses pertaining to the *labour process*, which are necessary in order to transform the elements of production into the intended product. Adam Smith confines himself to saying that one part of the means of production (the means of labour proper) serve in the labour process (which he wrongly expresses as 'yield a profit to their master') not by changing their natural form, but simply by being gradually worn out; whereas another part, the materials, are changed, and fulfil their function as means of production precisely through their alteration. This differing behaviour of the elements of productive capital in the labour process, however, forms only the starting-point of the distinction between fixed and non-fixed capital, and not the distinction itself, as is already shown by the fact that it obtains equally for all modes of production, non-capitalist as well as capitalist. Corresponding to this different material role is the *way in which value is surrendered* to the product, to which further corresponds the way in which value is replaced by the sale of the product; and it is only this that constitutes the distinction in question. Thus capital is not fixed capital simply because it is fixed in the means of labour, but rather because a part of the value laid out on means of labour remains fixed in these, while another part circulates as a value component of the product.

'If it' (the stock) 'is employed in procuring further profit, it must procure this profit either by staying with him' (the employer), 'or by going from him. In the one case it is a fixed, in the other it is a circulating capital' (p. 380).

The first thing that strikes one here is the crudely empirical conception of profit, taken from the manner in which it appears to the ordinary capitalist, something that stands in complete contradiction to Smith's own better and esoteric insight*. In the price of the product, the price of both materials and labour-power is replaced, but so, too, is the

*Marx frequently counterposes the falsely superficial or 'exoteric' elements in Adam Smith's writings with the deeper 'esoteric' insights that occasionally emerge.

portion of value transferred from the instruments of labour to the product by wear and tear. Profit can in no case flow from this replacement. Whether a value advanced for the production of the product is replaced completely or bit by bit can alter only the manner and time of the replacement; in no case however can it transform what is common to both – the replacement of value – into a creation of surplus-value. What lies at the bottom of this is the everyday idea that, because surplus-value is only realized by the sale of the product, by its circulation, it therefore arises simply from sale, from circulation. In point of fact, saying that profit arises in 'different ways' is here only an incorrect way of saying that the various elements of productive capital serve or function differently in the labour process as productive elements. Finally, the distinction is not derived from the labour and valorization process itself, from the function of productive capital, but is rather one that simply obtains subjectively for the individual capitalist, to whom one part of capital is useful in this way, another in that.

Quesnay, on the other hand, derived the distinctions from the actual reproduction process and its exigencies. In order for this process to be continuous, the value of the annual advances has to be completely replaced each year out of the value of the annual product, whereas the value of the original investment capital need only be replaced bit by bit, so that it is only completely replaced over a series of e.g. ten years, and only in this way is it entirely reproduced (replaced by new items of the same kind). Thus Adam Smith falls a long way behind Quesnay.

Nothing more remains for Adam Smith to use in defining fixed capital than the fact that it consists of means of labour that do not change their shape in the production process, and continue to serve in production until they are worn out, as opposed to the products which they help to form. He forgets that all elements of productive capital are always distinct from the product, and the product circulating as a commodity, in their natural form (as means of labour, materials and labour-power), and that the distinction between the part consisting of materials and labour-power and the part consisting of means of labour simply lies, in the case of labour-power, in that it is always bought anew (not bought for its duration as with means of labour), and, in the case of the materials, in that it is not the very same ones, but ever new items of the same kind, that function in the labour process. At the same time, the illusion is generated that the value of the fixed capital does not also circulate, although Adam Smith has of course earlier explained that the wear and tear of the fixed capital forms part of the price of products.

When Smith distinguishes circulating capital from fixed capital, what he emphasizes is not that this circulating capital is simply that component of the productive capital that must be *completely* replaced out of the value of the product, and must therefore go through all its metamorphoses together with the latter, whereas this is not the case with fixed capital. Circulating capital is rather lumped together with the shapes that the capital assumes on its transition from the sphere of production to that of circulation, as commodity capital and money capital. These two forms, however, commodity capital and money capital, are bearers of both the fixed and the fluid components of the value of productive capital. Both are capital of circulation, in contrast to productive capital, but not circulating (fluid) capital in contrast to fixed.

Finally, the wholly erroneous explanation that fixed capital makes a profit by remaining in the production process, while circulating capital makes a profit by leaving this and circulating, permits the similarity of form that variable capital and the fluid component of constant capital have in the *turnover* to conceal the basic difference that they have in the *valorization process* and the formation of surplus-value, and in this way the whole secret of capitalist production is still further obscured. The inclusive characterization of both forms as circulating capital abolishes this fundamental distinction, and this was carried still further by later economists, who took the contrast between fixed and circulating capital as the basic and sole distinction, instead of distinguishing between variable and constant capital.

After Adam Smith has firstly described fixed and circulating capital as two specific ways of investing capital, each of which independently yields a profit, he goes on to say:

'No fixed capital can yield any revenue but by means of a circulating capital. The most useful machines and instruments of trade will produce nothing without the circulating capital which affords the materials they are employed upon, and the maintenance of the workmen who employ them' (pp. 378–9).

Here we see what the earlier expressions 'yield a revenue', 'make a profit', etc. really mean, i.e. that both parts of capital serve in the formation of products.

But Smith offers the following as an example:

'That part of the capital of the farmer which is employed in the implements of agriculture is a fixed, that which is employed in the wages and maintenance of his labouring servants is a circulating capital' [p. 375].

(Here the distinction between fixed and circulating capital is correctly related simply to the difference in circulation, to the turnover of different components of the productive capital.)

'He makes a profit of the one by keeping it in his own possession, and of the other by parting with it. The price or value of his labouring cattle is a fixed capital' (here we have the further correct assertion that it is value to which the distinction refers, and not the material element) 'in the same manner as that of the instruments of husbandry. Their maintenance' (that of the labouring cattle) 'is a circulating capital, in the same manner as that of the labouring servants. The farmer makes his profit by keeping the labouring cattle, and by parting with their maintenance.'

(The farmer keeps the cattle's fodder, he doesn't sell it. He needs it as cattle-fodder while he uses the cattle themselves as instruments of labour. The distinction is simply that the cattle-fodder that enters the maintenance of the draught cattle is completely consumed and must be constantly replaced by new cattle-fodder from the agricultural product or its sale, while the cattle themselves are replaced only to the extent that each animal in succession becomes incapable of further work.)

'Both the price and the maintenance of the cattle which are brought in and fattened, not for labour, but for sale, are a circulating capital. The farmer makes his profit by parting with them.'

(Every commodity producer, and thus the capitalist producer as well, sells his product, the result of his production process, but this does not make the product either a fixed or a fluid component of his *productive* capital. It now exists rather in a form in which it has been ejected from the production process and must function as commodity capital. Fattening cattle function in the production process as raw material, not as an instrument like draught cattle. They therefore enter the product as substance, and their entire value enters the product, just as that of the ancillary materials – their fodder. This is why they are a fluid part of the productive capital, and not because the product sold, the fattened cattle, has here the same natural form as the raw material, the not yet fattened cattle. That is a mere accident. At the same time, Smith should have been able to see from this example that it is not the material shape of the element of production that makes the value contained in it fixed or fluid, but rather its function within the production process.)

'The whole value of the seed, too, is properly a fixed capital. Though it goes backwards and forwards between the ground and the granary, it never changes masters, and therefore does not properly circulate. The farmer makes his profit not by its sale, but by its increase' [ibid.].

Here the utter shallowness of Smith's distinction comes into the open. In his conception, the seed is fixed capital because there is no 'change of masters', i.e. the seed is directly replaced out of the annual product, subtracted from it. It would be circulating capital, however, if the entire product were sold and new seed-corn were bought with one part of the product's value. In the one case there is a 'change of masters', in the other case not. Here Smith confuses fluid capital with commodity capital. The product is the material bearer of the commodity capital, but of course only of that part of it that actually enters circulation, and does not directly re-enter the production process from which it emerged as a product.

Whether the seed is directly subtracted from the product, or whether the whole product is sold and a part of its value is replaced by the acquisition of new seed, what occurs in both cases is no more than a replacement, and no profit is made by this replacement. In the one case the seed passes into circulation as a commodity along with the rest of the product, while in the other case it figures only in the book-keeping as a component of the value of the capital advanced. In both cases, however, it remains a fluid component of the productive capital. It is completely consumed in preparing the product, and it must be completely replaced out of this if reproduction is to be made possible.

'Hence raw material and auxiliary substances lose the independent form with which they entered into the labour process. It is otherwise with the actual instruments of labour. Tools, machines, factory buildings and containers are only of use in the labour process as long as they keep their original shape, and are ready each morning to enter into it in the same form. And just as during their lifetime, that is to say during the labour process, they retain their shape independently of the product, so too after their death. The mortal remains of machines, tools, workshops, etc., always continue to lead an existence distinct from that of the product they helped to turn out' (*Capital* Volume 1, Chapter 8, p. 311).

These different ways in which the means of production are used in the formation of the product, some of them maintaining their independent shape vis-à-vis the product, others changing it or even losing it entirely – this distinction, which pertains to the labour process as such, and therefore applies just as much to labour processes oriented simply to the needs of the producers themselves, e.g. the patriarchal family, and devoid of any exchange or commodity production, is falsified by Adam Smith, in that he (1) introduces what is here the quite inapposite characteristic that some means of production bring their owner profit by maintaining their shape, others by losing it; (2) lumps the alterations suffered by one part of the elements of production in the labour process together with the change of form pertaining to the exchange of products, to commodity circulation (buying and selling), which at the same time includes the change of ownership of the commodities in circulation.

Turnover implies that r-production is mediated by circulation, i.e. by the sale of the product, by its transformation into money and transformation back from money into its own elements of production. But in so far as a part of his product again directly serves the same capitalist producer as means of production, the producer appears as selling this to himself; this is how the matter figures in his book-keeping. This part of reproduction is then not mediated by circulation, but directly. The part of the product that serves again in this way as means of production replaces fluid capital, not fixed, in so far as (1) its value goes completely into the product and (2) it is itself replaced completely in kind by a new item from the new product.

Adam Smith then tells us what circulating and fixed capital consist of. He lists the things, the material elements, that constitute fixed capital, and those that constitute circulating capital, as if this characteristic belonged to these things materially, by nature, and did not rather derive from their specific function within the capitalist production process. And yet he notes in the same chapter (Book Two, Chapter I) that although a certain thing, a house for example, which is reserved for direct consumption,

'may yield a revenue to its proprietor, and thereby serve *in the function of a capital* to him, it cannot yield any to the public, nor serve in the function of a capital to it, and the revenue of the whole body of the people can never be in the smallest degree increased by it' (p. 376) [Marx's emphasis].

Here Adam Smith clearly asserts that the property of being capital cannot be attributed to things as such and under all circumstances, but is rather a function with which they are or are not endowed according to the given conditions. But what is true of capital in general is also true of its subdivisions.

The same things may form components of fluid or of fixed capital, according to the different functions they perform in the labour process. Cattle used as draught-cattle (means of labour), for example, form a material mode of existence of fixed capital, while as fattening cattle (raw material) they are a component part of the farmer's circulating capital. The same thing, moreover, can function at one time as a component of productive capital, and at another time form part of the direct consumption fund. A house, for example, when it functions as a place of work, is a fixed component of productive capital; when it functions as a dwelling, it is in no way a form of capital in this capacity. The same means of labour can in many cases function at one time as means of production, at another time as means of consumption.

One of the errors that followed from Smith's conception was that of taking fixed and circulating capital as characteristics attributable to things. Our analysis of the labour process (Volume 1, Chapter 7) has already shown how the determinations of means of labour, material of labour and product change according to the various roles that one and the same thing assumes in the process. The characteristics of fixed and non-fixed capital are in their turn, however, built on the particular roles that these elements play in the labour process and hence in the process of value formation.

Secondly, however, in enumerating the things which fixed and circulating capital consist of, it becomes evident that Smith lumps together the distinction between fixed and fluid components, which is only valid, and only has any meaning, in relation to productive capital (capital in its productive form), with the distinction between productive capital and the forms pertaining to capital in its circulation process: commodity capital and money capital. He says in the same passage (p. 378):

'The circulating capital consists ... of the provisions, materials, and finished work of all kinds that are in the hands of their respective dealers, and of the money that is necessary for circulating and distributing them ...'

When we look more closely, in fact, we find that, in contrast to his earlier assertions, circulating capital is here again equated with commodity capital and money capital, i.e. with two forms of capital that do not belong to the production process at all, which are not circulating (fluid) capital in opposition to fixed, but rather circulation capital in opposition to productive capital. It is only *alongside* these that the components of productive capital advanced in materials (raw material or semi-manufactured goods) and actually incorporated into the production process again figure. He says:

'The third and last of the three portions into which the general stock of the society naturally divides itself, is the circulating capital; of which the characteristic is, that it affords a revenue only by circulating or changing masters. It is composed likewise of four parts: First, of the money . . .'

(But money is never a form of productive capital, capital functioning in the production process. It is never more than one of the forms which capital assumes within its process of circulation.)

'Secondly, of the stock and provisions which are in the possession of the butcher, the grazier, the farmer . . . and from the sale of which they expect to derive a profit . . . Fourthly, and lastly, of the work which is made up and completed, but which is still in the hands of the merchant or manufacturer.' And 'thirdly, of the materials, whether altogether rude, or more or less manufactured, of clothes, furniture, and building, which are not yet made up into any of those three shapes, but which remain in the hands of the growers, the manufacturers, the mercers and drapers, the timber merchants, the carpenters and joiners, the brick-makers etc.' [pp. 377-8].

The second and fourth parts simply contain products that have been ejected from the production process as such and have to be sold; in short, products that now function as commodities and hence as commodity capital, i.e. possess a form and assume a position in the process in which they do not constitute an element of productive capital, whatever may be their eventual destination, i.e. whether their purpose (use-value) finally fits them for individual or for productive consumption. The products in the second part are foodstuffs, those in the fourth part all other finished products, which thus themselves consist only of finished means of labour or articles of consumption (other than the foodstuffs comprised under the second part).

Smith also demonstrates his confusion on this point by the way that he speaks of the merchant. If the producer has sold his product to the merchant, this no longer constitutes capital of his in any form. From the social point of view, however, it is still just as much commodity capital, even if in other hands than those of its producer. But precisely because it is commodity capital, it is neither fixed nor fluid capital.

In every production not directed towards satisfying the producer's own immediate needs, the product must circulate as a commodity, i.e. be sold, not so that a profit may be made on it, but simply so that the producer may live. In the case of capitalist production, the sale of the commodity also realizes the surplus-value contained in it. The product passes out of the production process as a commodity, and is therefore no longer either a fixed or a fluid element of this process.

Here, by the way, Smith actually refutes his own argument. The finished products, whatever may be their material shape or use-value, their useful effect, are all commodity capital, i.e. capital in a form pertaining to the circulation process. Because they exist in this form, they cannot constitute a component of their owner's productive capital; but this in no way prevents them, once they are sold, from *becoming* components of productive capital, whether fluid or fixed, in the hands of their buyer. It is evident here that the same things that enter the market at one time as commodity capital in opposition to productive capital may function as either fluid or fixed components of productive capital, or as neither, once they are withdrawn from the market.

The product of the cotton spinner – yarn – is the commodity form of his capital, commodity capital for him. It cannot function again as a component of his productive capital, either as material of labour or as means of labour. The weaver who buys it, however, incorporates it into his productive capital, as a fluid part of this. For the spinner, on the other hand, the yarn is the bearer of the value of a part of both his fluid and his fixed capital (we ignore surplus-value). Similarly a machine, as the product of the machine-builder, is commodity capital for him, and as long as it persists in this form, it is neither fluid nor fixed capital. When sold to a manufacturer who puts it to use, it becomes a fixed component of a productive capital. Even when the use-form of the product enables it in part to re-enter, as means of production, the process from which it emerged, as when coal re-enters the production of coal, the part of the coal product destined for sale still represents neither fluid nor fixed capital, but rather commodity capital.

The use-form of the product may however render it completely incapable of forming any element of productive capital, either material or means of labour. Any kind of means of subsistence, for example. It is none the less commodity capital for its producer, the bearer of value of both the fixed and the fluid capital; and in the proportion that the capital bestowed on its production must be completely or partially replaced, its value has been transferred wholly or partly to it.

In Smith's third case the raw materials (including semi-finished goods and ancillaries) figure in the first place not as a component already incorporated into productive capital, but in fact only as a special kind of those use-values, the mass of commodities, which the social product consists of in general, alongside the other material components, means of subsistence, etc. listed in the second and fourth cases. Secondly, however, they are also presented as incorporated into productive capital, and hence as elements of the latter in the hands of the producer. The confusion shows itself in the way that they are conceived as functioning both in the hands of the producer ('in the hands of the growers, the manufacturers, etc.') and in the hands of merchants ('mercers, drapers, timber merchants'), where they are mere commodity capital, not components of productive capital.

In listing the elements of circulating capital, in fact, Adam Smith completely forgets the distinction between fixed and fluid capital, which is applicable only to productive capital. Instead he counterposes commodity capital and money capital, i.e. the two forms of capital pertaining to the circulation process, to productive capital, although even this he does unconsciously.

A final striking thing is that Adam Smith forgets labour-power in his list of the components of circulating capital. There are two reasons for this.

We have already seen that, leaving aside money capital, circulating capital is [for Smith] only another name for commodity capital. But in so far as labour-power circulates on the market, it is not capital, and so not a form of commodity capital. It is not capital at all; the worker is not a capitalist, even though he brings a commodity to market, i.e. his own skin. It is only when labour-power has been sold and incorporated into the production process – i.e. after it has ceased to circulate as a commodity – that it becomes a component of productive capital: variable capital as the source of surplus-value, a fluid component of the productive capital in relation to the turnover of the capital value laid out on this. Because Smith confuses fluid capital with commodity capital, he cannot bring labour-power under his heading of circulating capital. Variable capital thus appears here in the form of the commodities that the worker buys with his wages, the means of subsistence. It is in this form that the capital value laid out on wages is supposed to form part of the circulating capital. But what is incorporated into the production process is labour-power, the actual worker, and not the means of subsistence with which the worker maintains himself. We have certainly seen (Volume 1, Chapter 23) that, considered from the society's standpoint, the reproduction of the worker himself by his individual consumption forms part of the reproduction process of the social capital. But this does not hold for the individual production process taken by itself, which is what we are considering here. The 'acquired and useful abilities' (p. 377), which Smith introduces under the heading of fixed capital, form on the contrary components of fluid capital once they are 'abilities' of the wage-labourer, who has sold his abilities together with his labour.

It is a great error on Smith's part that he divides up the whole social wealth into (1) immediate consumption fund, (2) fixed capital and (3) circulating capital. According to this, wealth would be divided into a consumption fund that does not form a part of the functioning social capital, although parts of it *may* always function as capital, and capital. One part of the wealth accordingly functions as capital, the other part as non-capital or a consumption fund. And it appears here as an indispensable necessity for all capital to be either fixed or fluid, just as a mammal is by natural necessity either male or female. We have seen however that the opposition of fixed and fluid is only applicable to the elements of *productive* capital, and that alongside this there is still a very significant amount of capital – commodity capital and money capital – which exists in a form in which it *cannot be* either fixed or fluid.

Since, with the exception of the part of the product that is directly used in its natural form as means of production by the individual capitalist producer himself, without sale or purchase, the entire mass of social production – on the capitalist basis – circulates on the market as commodity capital, it is clear that both fixed and fluid elements of productive capital, and, in addition, all elements of the consumption fund, are drawn from the commodity capital; this is saying no more than that both means of production and means of consumption first appear, on the basis of capitalist production, as commodity capital, even if they are also destined later to serve as means of consumption or production; just as labour-power itself is found on the market as a commodity, even if not as commodity capital.

This leads Adam Smith to a further misunderstanding. He says that 'of these four parts' (of the 'circulating capital', i.e. of capital in its forms of commodity capital and money capital, which pertain to the circulation process – two parts which are transformed into four by Smith when he makes a further distinction, on a material basis, within the components of commodity capital),

'three – provisions, materials, and finished work – are, either annually, or in a longer or shorter period, regularly withdrawn from it, and placed either in the fixed capital or in the stock reserved for immediate consumption. Every fixed capital is both originally derived from, and requires to be continually supported by a circulating capital. All useful machines and instruments of trade are originally derived from a circulating capital, which furnishes the materials of which they are made and the maintenance of the workmen who make them. They require, too, a capital of the same kind to keep them in constant repair' (p. 378).

Always excepting that part of the product directly used again by its producers as means of production, we can make the general statement about capitalist production that all products come onto the market as commodities, and hence circulate for the capitalist as the commodity form of his capital, as commodity capital, whether the natural or use-form of these products means that they can or must function as means of production, and hence as fixed or fluid elements of productive capital, or whether they can serve only as means of individual rather than productive consumption. All products are thrown onto the market as commodities; all means of production and consumption, all elements of productive and individual consumption, must therefore be withdrawn again from the market as commodities, by purchase. This truism is manifestly correct. It therefore holds good equally for the fixed and for the fluid elements of productive capital, for means of labour as well as material of labour in all forms. (It is still overlooked here that there are elements of productive capital which are given by nature, and are not products.) The machine is bought on the market as much as the cotton is. But it in no way follows from this – it follows only from Smith's confusion of circulation capital with circulating or fluid, i.e. non-fixed capital – that every fixed capital originally derives from a fluid one. Moreover, Smith actually refutes his own argument. According to him, machines, as commodities, belong to the fourth part of the circulating capital. That they derive from the circulating capital thus only means that they functioned as commodity capital before they functioned as machines, although materially they derive from themselves; just as cotton as a fluid element of the spinner's capital derives from cotton on the market. But if in his further elaboration Smith derives fixed capital from fluid capital on the ground that labour and raw material are necessary in order to make machines, it is still the case, firstly, that means of labour, i.e. fixed capital, are necessary to make machines, and secondly, too, that fixed capital – machinery, etc. – is necessary in order to make raw materials, since productive capital always includes means of labour, but not always material of labour. He himself goes on to say on this point:

'Lands, mines, and fisheries, require all both a fixed and a circulating capital to cultivate them;' (he thus concedes that fixed capital is needed to produce raw material, as well as circulating capital) 'and' (here a new muddle) 'their produce replaces with a profit, not only those capitals, but *all the others in society*' [p. 379, Marx's emphasis].

This is totally confused. Their product supplies the raw material, ancillaries, etc. for all other branches of industry. But their value does not replace the value of all other social capitals; it replaces only its own capital value (plus surplus-value). Here again Smith is looking back to the Physiocrats.

From the society's standpoint, it is true that the part of commodity capital that consists of products that can only serve as means of labour, also functions sooner or later as means of labour – otherwise the products will have been produced to no avail, will be unsaleable. On the basis of capitalist production, in other words, once they have ceased to be commodities, they must form actual elements of the fixed part of the social productive capital, which they already were prospectively.

There is a distinction here which arises from the natural form of the product.

A spinning machine, for instance, has no use-value if it is not used for spinning, i.e. does not function as an element of production, and thus, from the capitalist standpoint, as a fixed component of a productive capital. But the spinning machine is mobile. It can be exported from the country where it is produced and be sold, directly or indirectly, to a foreign country, whether in exchange for raw materials, etc. or for champagne. In the country where it was produced it then functions only as commodity capital, but never, not even after its sale, as fixed capital.

However, products that have been localized by being incorporated into the earth, and hence can only be used locally, e.g. factory buildings, railways, bridges, tunnels, docks etc., soil improvements, and so on, cannot be exported body and soul. They are immobile. If they are not to be useless, they must function after their sale as fixed capital in the country in which they were produced. For the capitalist producer who builds factories speculatively or improves estates in order to sell them, these things are the form of his commodity capital, and so according to Smith the form of his circulating capital. But from the society's standpoint, they must ultimately function as fixed capital, if they are not to be useless, in the country in question, in a production process fixed by their own location. It in no way follows from this that immobile objects as such are automatically fixed capital; they may be dwelling-houses, etc. that belong to the consumption fund and thus do not form part of the social capital at all, even though they form an element of the social wealth, of which capital is only one part. The producer of these things, to express ourselves in Smith's terms, makes a profit by their sale. So they are circulating capital! The person who puts them to use, their ultimate buyer, can use them only by employing them in the production process. So they are fixed capital!

Property titles to a railway, for instance, can change hands daily, and their owners can even make a profit by selling them abroad. The property titles are thus exportable, but the railway itself is not. It is no less the case, however, that these things must either function as the fixed component of a productive capital in the actual country where they are located, or else lie idle. Similarly, manufacturer A can make a profit by selling his factory to manufacturer B, but this does not prevent the factory from functioning now as before as fixed capital.

The locally fixed means of labour, those inseparable from the soil, even though they may function for their producer as commodity capital, and do not form any element of *his* fixed capital (which consists for him of the means of labour that he needs to build buildings, railways, etc.), must necessarily function prospectively as fixed capital in the country in question. But it in no way follows, conversely, that fixed capital necessarily consists of immovable objects. A ship and a locomotive operate only by moving, yet they function as fixed capital for their users, even if not for their producers. Things on the other hand that are most fully fixed in the production process, live and die in it, and never leave it after they have once entered it, can be fluid components of productive capital. For example, the coal that drives the machine in the production process, the gas consumed in lighting a factory building, etc. These are fluid not because they physically leave the production process along with the product, and circulate as commodities, but rather because their value enters completely into the value of the commodity that they help to produce, and must thus be entirely replaced from the sale of the commodity.

In the passage last quoted, one phrase of Smith's should still be noted: 'A circulating capital, which furnishes . . . the maintenance of the workmen who make them' (machines, etc.).

With the Physiocrats, the portion of capital advanced in wages figured correctly under the heading '*avances annuelles*', as contrasted with '*avances primitives*'. On the other hand, what appears with them as a component of the productive capital applied by the farmer is not labour-power itself, but rather the means of subsistence given to the agricultural workers ('the maintenance of the workmen', as Smith puts it). This is directly related to their specific doctrine. The portion of value which labour adds to the product (like the portion of value added by raw materials, instruments of labour, etc. – in short by the material components of the constant capital) is equal only to the value of the means of subsistence paid to the workers and necessarily consumed by them to maintain their function as labour-powers. The very doctrine of the Physiocrats prohibited them from discovering the distinction between constant capital and variable capital. If it is labour that produces surplus-value (as well as reproducing its own price), then it produces this in industry just as much as in agriculture. But since in the Physiocratic system labour produces surplus-value only in one branch of production, agriculture, surplus-value was not seen as arising from labour, but rather from the special activity (collaboration) of nature in this branch. It was for this reason that they saw agricultural labour as productive labour, in distinction from other kinds of labour.

Adam Smith defines the workers' means of subsistence as circulating capital in opposition to fixed,

(1) because he confuses fluid capital, as opposed to fixed, with the forms of capital pertaining to the circulation sphere, with circulation capital; a confusion which has been uncritically taken over by his successors. He therefore confuses commodity capital with the fluid component of productive capital, and it is then self-evident that, where the social product takes the form of a commodity, the workers' means of subsistence, just like those of the non-workers – not to mention the materials and means of labour themselves – have to be supplied out of commodity capital.

(2) But the Physiocratic conception also creeps in with Smith, although it contradicts the esoteric – genuinely scientific – part of his own theoretical presentation.

All capital advanced is converted into productive capital, i.e. it assumes the shape of elements of production which are themselves the product of earlier labour. (Including labour-power.) Only in this form can it function in the production process. If now we substitute the worker's means of subsistence for the actual labour-power into which the variable part of capital has been transformed, then it is clear that these means of subsistence as such are not different from the other elements of productive capital as far as the formation of value is concerned, not different for example from raw materials and from the means of subsistence of draught cattle, which is why Smith, following the example of the Physiocrats, puts these all on the same level in one of the passages quoted above.* The means of subsistence cannot themselves valorize their value or add to it a surplus-value. Their value, like that of the other

*p. 279 above.

elements of productive capital, can reappear only in the value of the product. They cannot add more value to it than they themselves possess. They are only distinguished from the fixed capital, which consists of means of labour, in the same way as are raw material, semi-finished goods, etc., namely in that they are completely consumed in the product that they help to form (at least as far as the capitalist who pays for them is concerned), and their value must thus be completely replaced, whereas replacement occurs only gradually, bit by bit, in the case of fixed capital. The part of productive capital advanced in labour-power (or the means of subsistence of the worker) is thus distinguished here only materially, and not with regard to the labour and valorization process, from the remaining material elements of the productive capital. It is only distinguished in that it falls into the category of circulating capital, along with one part of the objective elements of product formation ('materials' is Smith's general term for them), in opposition to another part of the objective elements that falls into the category of fixed capital.

Although the part of capital spent on wages belongs to the fluid part of productive capital, and has this fluidity in common with a portion of the objective elements of product formation, the raw materials, etc., as opposed to the fixed component of productive capital, this has absolutely nothing to do with the role that this variable part of capital plays in the valorization process as opposed to the constant part. It is simply related to how this part of the capital value advanced has to be replaced, renewed, and thus reproduced out of the value of the product, by way of circulation. The purchase and re-purchase of labour-power pertains to the circulation process. But it is only within the production process that the value laid out on labour-power is transformed (not for the worker, but for the capitalist) from a definite, constant quantity into a variable one, and the value advanced in capital value, in capital, is thereby transformed for the first time into self-valorizing value. But because it is not the value laid out on labour-power that Smith defines as a fluid component of the productive capital, but rather the value laid out on the worker's means of subsistence, it is impossible for him to understand the distinction between variable and constant capital, and thus the capitalist production process in general. The characteristic of this part of capital as variable capital in opposition to the constant capital laid out on the objective elements of product formation is buried underneath the characteristic that the part of capital laid out on labour-power belongs to the fluid part of the productive capital with respect to the turnover. This burial is made complete in so far as in place of labour-power it is the worker's means of subsistence that are counted as an element of productive capital. Whether the value of the labour-power is advanced in money or in means of subsistence is immaterial, even though the latter can of course only be the exception on the basis of capitalist production.[2]

Because Adam Smith fixed in this way upon the characteristic of circulating capital as the decisive one for capital value laid out on labour-power – the Physiocratic definition without the premises of the Physiocrats – he managed to make it impossible for his successors to perceive that the part of capital laid out on labour-power was variable capital. The profound and correct explanation that he himself offered elsewhere did not prevail, whereas this blunder did. Indeed, later writers went even further, and not only made it the decisive characteristic of the part of capital laid out on labour-power to be circulating capital in opposition to fixed, but also made it the fundamental characteristic of circulating capital to be laid out on means of subsistence for the worker. This naturally linked up with the doctrine of the labour fund* of necessary means of subsistence as a given magnitude, which on the one hand physically restricts the share of the workers in the social product, but on the other hand has to be spent to its full extent on the acquisition of labour-power.

2. How much Adam Smith barred his own way to an understanding of the role of labour-power in the valorization process is shown by the following sentence, which puts the labour of the worker on the same level as that of draught cattle, in the Physiocratic manner: 'Not only his' (the farmer's) 'labouring servants, but his labouring cattle, are productive labourers' (Book Two, Chapter V, p. 462).

---

*See Volume 1, pp. 758–61.

Chapter 11: Theories of Fixed and Circulating Capital. Ricardo

Ricardo introduces the distinction between fixed and circulating capital only in order to present the exceptions to the law of value, i.e. those cases in which the rate of wages affects prices. We shall only come to speak of these in Volume 3.*

The basic confusion is however evident from the start in the following juxtaposition:

'This difference in the degree of durability of fixed capital, *and* this variety in the proportions in which the two sorts of capital may be combined...'[1]

If we now ask what the two sorts of capital are, we are told:

'The proportions, too, in which the capital that is to support labour, and the capital that is invested in tools, machinery, and buildings, may be variously combined.'[2]

Fixed capital thus = means of labour, and circulation capital = capital laid out on labour. 'Capital that is to support labour' is itself an absurd expression taken over from Adam Smith. Here circulation capital is on the one hand lumped together with variable capital, i.e. with the part of productive capital laid out on labour. On the other hand, however, because the opposition is not derived from the valorization process – constant and variable capital – but rather from the circulation process (the old Smithian confusion), two misconceptions arise.

Firstly, the differences in the degree of durability of the fixed capital, and the variations in the composition of capital in terms of constant and variable, are taken as equivalent. The latter distinction, however, deter-

---

1. *Principles*, p. 25. [All Marx's quotations from Ricardo in this chapter are to be found on pp. 72–3 of the Pelican edition of Ricardo's *Principles*, Harmondsworth, 1971. The emphasis here is Marx's.]

2. [ibid.].

---

*Chapter 11 of that volume.

mines the variation in the production of surplus-value; the former, on the other hand, in so far as the valorization process is concerned, is simply related to the manner in which a given value of means of production is transferred to the product. As far as the circulation process is concerned, it affects only the period of renewal of the capital laid out, in other words the time for which this is advanced. If, instead of penetrating through to the inner mechanism of the capitalist production process, you adopt the standpoint of the phenomena in their finished form, these distinctions do in fact coincide. When the social surplus-value is distributed between the capitals invested in different branches of industry, differences in the various times for which the capital is advanced (for example, varying lifespans in the case of fixed capital) and different organic compositions of capital (thus also the different circulations of constant and variable capital) have similar effects in the equalization of the general rate of profit and the transformation of values into prices of production.*

Secondly, from the standpoint of the circulation process, we have on the one hand the means of labour: fixed capital, on the other hand material of labour and wages: fluid capital. From the standpoint of the labour and valorization process, however, we have on the one hand means of production (means and material of labour): constant capital, on the other hand labour-power: variable capital. As far as the organic composition of capital is concerned (Volume 1, Chapter 25, 2, p. 772), it is quite immaterial whether the same value of constant capital consists of more means of labour and less material of labour, or of more material of labour and less means of labour, whereas everything depends on the relation between the capital laid out on means of production and that laid out on labour-power. Conversely, from the standpoint of the circulation process, the distinction between fixed and circulating capital, it is just as immaterial in what proportion a given value of circulating capital is divided between material of labour and wages. From the one standpoint, the material of labour is ranked in the same category as the means of labour, as opposed to the capital value laid out on labour-power. From the other standpoint, the part of capital laid out on labour-power is ranked together with that laid out on material of labour, as opposed to the part of capital laid out on means of labour.

In Ricardo, therefore, the part of capital value laid out on material of labour (raw materials and ancillaries) is not found on either side. It

* These themes are covered in Volume 3, Part Two of *Capital*.

completely vanishes. It does not fit on the side of fixed capital, because it completely coincides in its mode of circulation with the part of capital laid out on labour-power. And it cannot be put on the side of circulating capital, because this would be a self-refutation of the equation taken over from Adam Smith and still silently running through Ricardo's writings between the antithesis: fixed and circulating capital, and the antithesis: constant and variable capital. Ricardo has far too great an instinct for logic not to be sensitive to this, and he therefore just lets this part of the capital disappear.

It should be noted here that the capitalist 'advances' the capital laid out on wages, to use the mode of speech peculiar to political economy, for different periods, according to whether he pays wages by the week, by the month or every three months. In point of fact, the opposite happens. The worker advances the capitalist his labour for a week, a month or three months, according to the intervals at which he is paid. If the capitalist did actually buy labour, instead of simply paying for it later, i.e. if he paid the worker his wages for the day, week, month or three months in advance, then we could speak of an advance for these periods. But since he pays only after the labour *has* lasted for days, weeks or months, instead of buying it and paying for the time that it *is* to last, the whole thing is a capitalist *quid pro quo*, and the advance that the worker makes to the capitalist in the form of labour is transformed into an advance that the capitalist makes to the worker in money. This in no way alters the fact that the capitalist gets the product back from circulation, or realizes its value (together with the surplus-value incorporated into it), only after a shorter or longer period of time – according to the varying time that its production requires, or alternatively according to the varying time needed for its circulation. What the buyer of a commodity might want to do with it is completely immaterial to the seller. The capitalist does not get a machine any cheaper because he has to advance its entire value all at once, while the same value flows back to him from the circulation sphere only gradually and bit by bit; nor does he pay more for cotton because its value enters completely into the value of the product made from it, and is thus completely replaced at one stroke when this is sold on the market.

Let us then return to Ricardo.

1. The characteristic feature of variable capital is that a definite, given (i.e. in this sense constant) part of capital, a given sum of value (assumed to be equal to the value of the labour-power, although it is immaterial here whether the wage is the same as, or more or less than,

the value of the labour-power), is exchanged for a force that valorizes itself and creates value – labour-power, which not only reproduces the value paid to it by the capitalist, but also produces a surplus-value, a value that did not previously exist and is not bought for an equivalent. This characteristic property of the portion of value laid out on wages, which distinguishes it fundamentally from constant capital as variable capital, disappears as soon as this portion of capital laid out on wages is considered simply from the standpoint of the circulation process and thus appears as circulation capital as against the fixed capital laid out on means of labour. This happens as soon as it is placed together under a single heading (that of circulating capital) with a component of the constant capital, that laid out on material of labour, and counterposed to another component of the constant capital laid out on means of labour. Here surplus-value, i.e. the very circumstance which transforms the sum of value laid out into capital, is completely ignored. It is similarly ignored that the portion of value that the capital laid out on wages adds to the product is freshly produced (and thus actually repro- duced), while the portion of value that the raw material adds to the product is not freshly produced, and not really reproduced, but is simply maintained and conserved in the value of the product, and hence merely reappears as a component of the product's value. As the distinc- tion is presented from the standpoint of the antithesis between fluid and fixed capital, it simply consists in the fact that the value of the means of labour applied in the production of a commodity goes only partly into the value of the commodity, and hence is only partly replaced by the sale of the commodity, i.e. only bit by bit and gradually. On the other hand, the value of the labour-power and objects of labour (raw materials etc.) applied in the production of a commodity goes into the commodity completely, and is therefore completely replaced by its sale. In this respect one part of the capital presents itself as fixed in regard to the circulation process, and the other as fluid or circulating. What is involved in both cases is a transfer of given, previously advanced values to the product, and their replacement when the product is sold. The sole distinction here is whether the transfer of value, and therefore the replacement of value, proceeds bit by bit and gradually, or all at once. The all-important distinction between variable and constant capital is thereby obliterated, and with it the whole secret of surplus-value forma- tion and of capitalist production, namely the circumstances that trans- form certain values and the things in which they are represented into capital. The components of capital are distinguished from one another simply by the mode of circulation (and the circulation of commodities has of course only to do with already existing, given values); the capital laid out on wages has a particular mode of circulation in common with the portion of capital laid out on raw materials, semi-finished goods and ancillaries, in contrast to that laid out on means of labour.

We can thus understand why bourgeois political economy held instinctively to Adam Smith's confusion of the categories 'fixed and circulating capital' with the categories 'constant and variable capital', and uncritically echoed it from one generation down to the next for a whole century. It no longer distinguished at all between the portion of capital laid out on wages and the portion of capital laid out on raw material, and only formally distinguished the former from constant capital in terms of whether it was circulated bit by bit or all at once through the product. The basis for understanding the real movement of capitalist production, and thus of capitalist exploitation, was thus submerged at one blow. All that was involved, on this view, was the reappearance of values advanced.

Ricardo's uncritical reception of Smith's confusion is more surprising, not only than that of the later apologists, among whom the confusion of concepts is rather something unsurprising, but also than that of Adam Smith himself, since Ricardo, in contrast to Smith, presented value and surplus-value consistently and clearly, and in point of fact upheld the esoteric Adam Smith against the exoteric.

Among the Physiocrats, there is none of this confusion. The distinction between *avances annuelles* and *avances primitives* is related solely to the different reproduction periods of the different components of capital, agricultural capital in particular; while their views on the production of surplus-value constitute a part of their theory which is independent of these distinctions, a part in fact that they held up as its culminating point. The formation of surplus-value is not explained in terms of capital as such, but ascribed simply to one specific sphere of capitalist production, agriculture.

2. The essential feature of the definition of variable capital – and hence of the transformation of any sum of values at all into capital – is that the capitalist exchanges a definite, given (and in this sense constant) value for value-creating power; a magnitude of value for the production of value, for self-valorization. Whether the capitalist pays the worker in money or in means of subsistence does not affect this fundamental characteristic. It affects only the mode of existence of the value advanced by him, which exists in one case in the form of money,

with which the worker himself buys his means of subsistence on the market, in the other case in the form of means of subsistence that he consumes directly. Developed capitalist production in fact assumes that the worker is paid in money, just as it assumes in general that the production process is mediated by the circulation process, i.e. a money economy. But the creation of surplus-value, and hence the capitalization of the sum of value advanced, arises neither from the money form nor from the natural form of wages, i.e. of the capital laid out on the acquisition of labour-power. It arises from the exchange of value for value-creating power, from the conversion of a constant quantity into a variable one.

The more or less fixed character of the means of labour is a function of their degree of durability, i.e. of a physical property. According to their durability, they are worn out more quickly or more slowly, conditions remaining otherwise the same, and thus function for a longer or shorter time as fixed capital. But it is in no way simply this physical property of durability which leads them to function as fixed capital. In metal works, the raw material is just as durable as the machines with which it is processed, and more durable in fact than many components of these machines – leather, wood, etc. But the metal serving as raw material does not form any the less a part of the circulating capital, while the functioning means of labour that may be constructed of the same metal form part of fixed capital. Thus it is not its material, physical nature, its greater or lesser propensity to perish, which makes the same metal in one case fixed capital and in the other case circulating capital. This distinction rather arises from the role that it plays in the production process, in one case as object of labour, in the other case as means of labour.

The function of a means of labour in the production process generally requires it to serve over and over again in repeated labour processes for a longer or shorter period of time. Its function thus prescribes a greater or lesser degree of durability for its material. But the durability of the material from which it is made does not make it in and for itself fixed capital. The same material becomes circulating capital if it is used as raw material, and for those economists who confuse the distinction between commodity capital and productive capital with the distinction between circulating and fixed capital, the same material or the same machine is circulating capital as a product, and fixed capital as a means of labour.

Even though it is not the durable material of which the means of labour is made that makes it fixed capital, its role as means of labour does require it to consist of a more or less durable material. The durability of its material is thus a condition for its function as means of labour, hence also a material basis of the mode of circulation that makes it fixed capital. Other things being equal, the greater or lesser perishability of its material imprints it to a lower or higher degree with the stamp of fixedness, and is thus very fundamentally bound up with its quality as fixed capital.

If the portion of capital laid out on labour-power is considered exclusively from the standpoint of circulating capital, i.e. in contrast to fixed capital, and if the distinction between constant and variable capital is therefore lumped together with the distinction between fixed and circulating capital, it is then natural, as the material reality of the means of labour is an essential basis for its character as fixed capital, also to derive the opposite character of the capital laid out on labour-power as circulating capital from the material reality of this capital, and then to define circulating capital in terms of the material reality of variable capital.

The real material of the capital laid out on wages is labour itself, self-acting, value-creating labour-power, living labour, which the capitalist has exchanged for dead, objectified labour, and incorporated into his capital, this being the way that the value existing in his hands is first transformed into a self-valorizing value. But the capitalist does not sell this power of self-valorization. It forms throughout simply a component of his productive capital, just like his means of labour, and is never a component of his commodity capital, like the finished product that he sells, for instance. Within the production process, the means of labour, as components of productive capital, are not distinguished from labour-power as fixed capital, any more than the material of labour and ancillaries coincide with it as circulating capital. From the standpoint of the labour process, both of these confront labour-power as the personal factor, they themselves being the objective factors. From the standpoint of the valorization process, both are distinct from labour-power, variable capital, as constant capital. Alternatively, if we are to speak of a material difference that affects the circulation process, this is simply that it follows from the nature of value, which is nothing other than objectified labour, and from the nature of self-acting labour-power, which is nothing other than self-objectifying labour, that labour-power constantly creates value and surplus-value as long as it continues to function; that what presents itself on its side as movement, as the creation of value, presents itself on the side of its product in a motionless form, as created value. If the labour-power has performed its function, then the capital no longer consists of labour-power on the one hand and means of production on the other. The capital value that was laid out on labour-power is now value which has been added to the product (together with surplus-value). In order to repeat the process, the product must be sold, and with the money released by this, labour-power has constantly to be bought afresh and incorporated into the productive capital. This then is what gives the portion of capital laid out on labour-power the character of circulating capital in contrast to the capital that remains fixed in the means of labour.

But if the secondary characteristic of circulating capital, which labour-power has in common with a part of the constant capital (raw materials and ancillaries), is made into the fundamental one – i.e. the fact that the value laid out on it is transferred in its entirety to the product in whose production it is consumed, and not gradually and bit by bit, as in the case of fixed capital, that it must therefore also be replaced in its entirety by the sale of the product – then the portion of capital laid out on wages must also consist materially not of self-acting labour-power, but of the material elements that the worker buys with his wages, i.e. of the part of the social commodity capital that enters the worker's consumption, the means of subsistence in other words. The fixed capital then consists of the means of labour, which perish more slowly and need only be replaced more slowly, while the capital laid out on labour-power consists of the means of subsistence, which have to be replaced more rapidly.

The boundary between quicker and slower perishability, however, tends to get blurred:

'The food and clothing consumed by the labourer, the buildings in which he works, the implements with which his labour is assisted, are all of a perishable nature. There is however a vast difference in the time for which these different capitals will endure: a steam-engine will last longer than a ship, a ship than the clothing of the labourer, and the clothing of the labourer longer than the food which he consumes.'[3]

Ricardo forgets here the house in which the worker lives, his furniture, his tools of consumption such as knives, forks, dishes, etc., all of which possess the same character of durability as do the means of labour. The same things and the same classes of things thus appear now as means of consumption, now as means of labour.

The distinction, as expressed by Ricardo, is this:

3. op. cit., p. 26 [Pelican edn, p. 72].

'According as capital is rapidly perishable, and requires to be frequently reproduced, or is of slow consumption, it is classed under the heads of circulating, or of fixed capital.'[4]

He notes below this:

'A division not essential, and in which the line of demarcation cannot be accurately drawn.'[5]

Thus we have happily ended up once again back with the Physiocrats, where the distinction between *avances annuelles* and *avances primitives* was a distinction in the times of consumption, and hence also in the varying reproduction times, of the capital applied. It is simply that what in their case expressed a phenomenon of importance for social production, and is depicted in [Quesnay's] *Tableau économique* in connection with the circulation process, here becomes a subjective distinction, and one that Ricardo himself says is superfluous.

As soon as the part of capital laid out on labour is distinguished from that laid out on means of labour only by its reproduction period and thus its term of circulation, as soon as the one part consists of means of subsistence, the other of means of labour, so that the former is distinguished from the latter only by its more transient character, then every pertinent difference between the capital laid out on labour-power and that laid out on means of production is obviously destroyed.

This completely contradicts Ricardo's doctrine of value, as well as his theory of profit, which is in point of fact a theory of surplus-value. He only ever considers the distinction between fixed and circulating capital in so far as different proportions of the two, in the case of capitals of equal size in different branches of industry, influence the law of value, and particularly the degree to which a rise or fall in wages affects prices as a result of these circumstances. Yet even within this restricted investigation, he commits very great errors, as a result of confusing fixed and circulating with constant and variable capital, and in fact he starts his investigation on a completely false basis. Thus (1) in so far as the portion of capital value laid out on labour-power is subsumed under the heading of circulating capital, the characteristics of circulating capital are themselves falsely presented, and so in particular are the circumstances which subsume the portion of capital laid out on labour under this heading. (2) There is a confusion between the quality that makes the part of capital laid out on labour variable, and the quality that makes it circulating in contrast to fixed.

4. ibid. [Pelican edn, pp. 72–3].   5. ibid.

It is clear from the start that the definition of the capital laid out on labour-power as circulating or fluid is a secondary one, which glosses over its specific difference in the production process. Firstly, in this definition the capitals laid out on labour and on raw materials, etc. are equivalent; and a classification that identifies one part of the constant capital with the variable capital does not come to grips with the specific difference of variable capital as opposed to constant. Secondly, although the portions of capital laid out on labour and on means of labour are counterposed to one another, this is in no way with respect to the fact that they are involved in the production of value in completely different ways, but simply with respect to the different periods of time during which the given value of both is transferred to the product.

What is at issue in all these cases is *how* a given value which is invested in the production process of a commodity, whether as wages, the price of raw materials or the price of means of labour, is transferred to the product, hence circulated by the product and brought back to its starting-point or replaced by its sale. The only distinction here consists in the '*how*', in the particular way in which this value is transferred and thus circulates.

Whether the price of labour-power, which in any case is previously determined by contract, is paid in money or in means of subsistence, in no way changes its character of being a definite and given price. However, in the case of wages paid in money, it is obvious that it is not the money itself that enters the production process, in the same way that it is not just the value but also the material of the means of production that enters this process. But if the means of subsistence that the worker buys with his wage are directly placed under one heading together with the raw materials, etc., as the material shape of circulating capital, and the means of labour counterposed to them, then this gives the matter a different appearance. If the value of one lot of things, the means of production, is transferred to the product in the labour process, then the value of the other lot of things, the means of subsistence, reappears in the labour-power that consumes them, and is similarly transferred to the product by the labour-power's activity. What is involved in all these cases is similarly the mere reappearance in the product of the values advanced during production. (The Physiocrats took this seriously and denied that industrial labour created surplus-value.) Thus, in the passage from Wayland already quoted:

'It matters not in what form capital reappears . . . The various kinds of food, clothing, and shelter, necessary for the existence and comfort of the human being, are also changed. They are consumed from time to time, and their value reappears . . .' (*Elements of Political Economy*, pp. 31, 32.)*

The capital values advanced to production in the shape of means of production and means of subsistence here both equally reappear in the value of the product. The capitalist production process is thus successfully transformed into a complete mystery, and the origin of the surplus-value present in the product completely withdrawn from view.

What is also brought to fulfilment here is the fetishism peculiar to bourgeois economics, which transforms the social, economic character that things are stamped with in the process of social production into a natural character arising from the material nature of these things.†

Means of labour, for instance, are fixed capital – a scholastic definition which leads to contradictions and confusion. Just as we have shown how, in the labour process (Volume 1, Chapter 7), it depends entirely on the role which the objective components play at the time in a particular labour process, on their function, whether they function as means of labour, material of labour or product, so, in precisely the same way, means of labour are fixed capital only where the production process is in fact a capitalist production process and the means of production are thus actually capital, i.e. possess the economic determination, the social character, of capital; secondly, they are fixed capital only if they transfer their value to the product in a particular way. If this is not the case, then they remain means of labour without being fixed capital. In the same way, ancillaries such as fertilizer, if they give up their value in the same particular way as do the greater part of means of labour, are fixed capital, although they are not means of labour. What is at issue here is not a set of definitions under which things are to be subsumed. It is rather definite functions that are expressed in specific categories.

If it is the destiny of the means of subsistence in themselves, a property devolving on them under all circumstances, to be capital laid out on wages, then it also becomes the character of this 'circulating' capital 'to support labour' (Ricardo, p. 25 [Pelican edn, p. 72]). If the means of subsistence were not 'capital', then they would not support labour-

---

*See Volume 1, p. 316. Francis Wayland (1796–1865) was an American economist, and the author of a popular manual *The Elements of Political Economy*, Boston, 1843. Like the Britons Malthus and Chalmers, Wayland, too, combined the professions of economist and parson.

†See Volume 1, Chapter 1, 4.

power; though it is in fact precisely their character as capital that gives them the property of supporting *capital* by the labour of others.

If means of subsistence are inherently circulating capital – after this has been transformed into wages – then it further results that the size of the wage depends on the ratio between the number of workers and the given mass of circulating capital – a favourite proposition of the economists – whereas in point of fact the quantity of means of subsistence that the worker withdraws from the market, and the quantity which the capitalist has at his disposal for his own consumption, depend rather on the ratio between surplus-value and the price of labour.

Ricardo, like Barton,[6] constantly confuses the ratio between variable and constant capital with the ratio between circulating and fixed capital. We shall see later on how this vitiates his investigation of the rate of profit.*

Ricardo further equates the distinctions that arise in the turnover for reasons other than the distinction between fixed and circulating capital, with the latter distinction itself:

'It is also to be observed that the circulating capital may circulate, or be returned to its employer, in very unequal times. The wheat bought by a farmer to sow is comparatively a fixed capital to the wheat purchased by a baker to make into loaves. One leaves it in the ground, and can obtain no return for a year; the other can get it ground into flour, sell it as bread to his customers, and have his capital free to renew the same, or commence any other employment in a week' (pp. 26, 27 [Pelican edn, p. 73]).

It is characteristic here that wheat, although as seed-corn it serves not as means of subsistence but as raw material, is firstly circulating capital, because it is inherently means of subsistence, and secondly fixed capital, because its return stretches over a year. But it is not just the slower or more rapid return that makes a means of production into fixed capital, but rather the specific manner in which it gives up value to the product.

The confusion created by Adam Smith has led to the following results:

1. The distinction between fixed and fluid capital is confused with the distinction between productive capital and commodity capital. Thus the same machine is circulating capital, for example, when it exists on

---

6. *Observations on the Circumstances which Influence the Condition of the Labouring Classes of Society*, London, 1817. A striking passage from this work is quoted in Volume 1, p. 783, note 13.

*See Volume 3, Chapters 1 to 3.

the market as a commodity, and fixed capital when it is incorporated into the production process. It is impossible to see here why one particular kind of capital should be more fixed or more circulating than another.

2. All circulating capital is identified with capital laid out or to be laid out on wages. This is the case with John Stuart Mill* among others.

3. The distinction between variable and constant capital, which Barton, Ricardo and others already confused with that between circulating and fixed capital, is eventually reduced completely to the latter distinction, as with Ramsay for example, who takes not only means of labour, but all means of production, raw materials etc. as fixed capital, and only the capital laid out on wages as circulating capital. But because the reduction is accomplished in this way, the real distinction between constant and variable capital is not grasped.

4. The most recent English economists, and even more so the Scottish ones, who view everything from the unutterably narrow standpoint of a bank clerk – such as MacLeod, Patterson† and others – transform the distinction between fixed and circulating capital into that between 'money at call' and 'money not at call' (that is to say, between deposit money that can be withdrawn without prior notification, and money whose withdrawal requires such notification).

*The work that Marx refers to here is Mill's *Essays on Some Unsettled Questions of Political Economy*, London, 1844. This is criticized in detail by Marx in *Theories of Surplus-Value*, Part III, pp. 190 ff. In his Postface to the second German edition of *Capital*, Volume 1, Marx described Mill's general theoretical position as follows: 'The Continental revolution of 1848 also had its reaction in England [i.e. on economic thought]. Men who still claimed some scientific standing and aspired to be something more than mere sophists and sycophants of the ruling classes tried to harmonize the political economy of capital with the claims, no longer to be ignored, of the proletariat. Hence a shallow syncretism, of which John Stuart Mill is the best representative' (Pelican edn., pp. 97–8).

† Henry Dunning MacLeod was the author of *The Elements of Political Economy*, London, 1858. Robert Hogard Patterson wrote *The Science of Finance*, Edinburgh and London, 1868.

Chapter 12: The Working Period

Let us take two lines of business each with the same working day, say a labour process of ten hours: e.g. cotton spinning and the manufacture of locomotives. In one case a definite quantity of the finished product, cotton yarn, is turned out every day and every week; in the other, the labour process must be repeated for perhaps three months in order to produce a finished product, one locomotive. In the one case the product is discrete in nature, and the same work begins afresh each day or each week. In the other case the labour process is continuous, and stretches over a large number of daily labour processes, which supply a finished product only after a protracted interval, through the connectness and continuity of their operations. Even though the duration of the daily labour process is the same in both cases, there is a very significant difference in the duration of the act of production, i.e. in the duration of the repeated labour processes that are required in order to turn out the product in its finished form, to send it onto the market as a commodity, and thus to transform it from productive capital into commodity capital. The distinction between fixed and circulating capital has nothing to do with this. The distinction made here would obtain even if exactly the same proportions of fixed and circulating capital were applied in the two lines of business.

These differences in the duration of the act of production do not just occur between different branches of production, but also within the same branch, according to the size of the product to be supplied. An ordinary dwelling-house is built in a shorter time than a large factory, and hence requires a smaller number of continuous labour processes. If the building of a locomotive takes three months, that of a battleship takes a year, if not several. The production of grain demands almost a year, that of horned cattle several years, while it can take anything from twelve to 100 years to raise timber. A road can be built in a few months, while a railway requires years; an ordinary carpet perhaps

one week, while a Gobelin takes years, etc. The differences in length of
the act of production are thus of infinite variety.

The differing duration of the act of production must obviously produce a difference in the speed of turnover where capital outlays of
equal size are involved, i.e. in the periods of time for which a given
capital is advanced. Let us assume that the spinning mill and the locomotive works apply equal capitals, with the same division between
constant and variable, and between the fixed and fluid components of
capital; finally that the working day is equally long and there is the same
division between necessary and surplus labour. So as to set aside, too,
all circumstances arising from the circulation process and external to the
present case, we shall assume that both yarn and locomotive are produced to order and paid for on delivery of the finished product. At the
end of the week, when the finished yarn is delivered, the spinner receives back his outlay of circulating capital as well as the wear and tear
of the fixed capital contained in the value of the yarn (we ignore the
surplus-value). He can now repeat the same circuit again with the same
capital. He has completed his turnover. The locomotive manufacturer,
on the other hand, must lay out fresh capital on wages and raw material
week after week for three months, and only after three months, when
the locomotive is delivered, does the circulating capital laid out bit by
bit during this time for one and the same act of production, to produce
one and the same commodity, exist again in a form in which it can begin its circuit once more; the wear and tear of the machinery during
these three months is also replaced only now. One business has an outlay for one week, the other the same weekly outlay multiplied by
twelve. All other circumstances being assumed equal, the one must
have twelve times as much circulating capital at its disposal as the other.

The fact that the capitals advanced each week are equal, however, is a
matter of indifference here. Whatever may be the size of the capital
advanced, in the one case it is advanced only for one week, in the other
for twelve, before it can be used for a new operation, before the same
operation can be repeated with it, or one of a different kind begun.

The difference in the speed of turnover or the length of time for
which the individual capital must be advanced before the same capital
value can serve again for a new labour or valorization process, arises
here from the following circumstances:

Let us assume that the building of the locomotive, or any other
machine, takes 100 working days. As far as the workers occupied in
machine-building are concerned, just as in spinning, the 100 working

days form a discontinuous (discrete) quantity; according to our assumption they consist of 100 successive and separate ten-hour labour processes. But in relation to the product – the machine – the 100 working days form a continuous quantity, a working day of 1,000 working hours, a single related act of production. A working day of this kind, which is formed by the succession of more or less numerous interrelated working days, I call a *working period*. If we speak of the working day, then we mean the length of time for which the worker must daily expend his labour-power, must work. If we speak of the working period, on the other hand, this means the number of inter-related working days that are required, in a particular line of business, to complete a finished product. The product of each working day is here only a partial product, which is taken a step further day by day and receives its finished shape, is a finished use-value, only at the close of a longer or shorter period of working time.

Interruptions and disturbances of the social production process, as a result of crises, for example, thus have a very different effect on those products of labour that are discrete in nature, and those whose production requires a longer connected period. In the former case, one day's production of a particular quantity of yarn, coal, etc. is simply not followed the next day by a fresh production of yarn or coal. It is otherwise with ships, buildings, railways, etc. Here it is not only work that is interrupted, but an inter-connected act of production. If the job is not carried any further, then the means of production and the labour already consumed in its production have been spent to no avail. Even if it is taken up again, deterioration will always have taken place in the meantime.

The portion of value that the fixed capital surrenders every day to the product, until the latter is ready, builds up in layers throughout the whole duration of the working period. Here we can also see the practical importance of the distinction between fixed and circulating capital. The fixed capital is advanced to the production process for a longer period of time; it does not need to be renewed until an interval of perhaps several years has elapsed. The fact that a steam engine gives up some value bit by bit each day to the yarn, the product of a discrete labour process, while it gives up value over three months to a locomotive, the product of a continuous act of production, in no way alters the outlay of capital needed to acquire the steam engine. In the one case, its value flows back in small doses, e.g. weekly, in the other case in large amounts, e.g. every three months. But in both cases, the steam engine is renewed only after some twenty years, say. As long as the individual period in which its value flows back bit by bit with the sale of the product is always shorter than its own period of existence, the same steam engine continues to function in the production process for several working periods.

It is otherwise with the circulating components of the capital advanced. The labour-power bought for this week is used up during the week, and has objectified itself in the product. It must be paid for at the end of the week. And this capital outlay on labour-power is repeated weekly over the three months, although the expenditure of this portion of capital in the one week does not enable the capitalist to cover the acquisition of labour in the next week. New, additional capital must be spent each week in payment for labour-power, and if we set aside all credit relations the capitalist must be able to lay out wages for the whole period of three months, even though he pays them only in weekly doses. It is the same with the other part of circulating capital, the raw materials and ancillaries. One layer of labour after the other is deposited on the product. It is not only the value spent on labour-power that is steadily transferred to the product during the labour process, but also surplus-value; however all this is transferred to an unfinished product that does not yet have the shape of a finished commodity, and is thus not capable of circulation. The same applies to the capital value transferred to the product layer upon layer in raw materials and ancillaries.

According to the longer or shorter duration of the working period that the specific nature of the product or the useful effect to be attained demands for its production, a steady additional expenditure of circulating capital is required (wages, raw materials and ancillaries), no part of which exists in a form capable of circulation, such that it could serve to repeat the same operation; each part is rather successively tied up within the production sphere as a component of the developing product, tied up in the form of productive capital. The turnover time of capital, however, is the sum of its production time and its circulation time. A lengthening of the production time thus reduces the speed of turnover as much as a lengthening of the circulation time. In the present case however there are two points to be noted:

Firstly, the lengthened stay in the production sphere. The capital advanced in the first week on labour, raw materials etc., for instance, as well as the portions of value given up by the fixed capital to the product, remains confined to the production sphere for the entire term of three months, and as it is incorporated only into a product in formation, as yet unfinished, it cannot pass into circulation as a commodity.

Secondly, since the working period necessary for the act of production lasts three months, and in actual fact simply forms a single interrelated labour process, every week a new dose of circulating capital must be added to the preceding one. The quantity of additional capital successively advanced thus grows with the length of the working period.

We have assumed that equal capitals are invested in the spinning and machine-building businesses, that these capitals are divided equally into constant and variable capital, ditto into fixed and circulating capital, and that the working day is of the same length in each – in short, that all conditions are the same except for the duration of the working period. In the first week, the outlay is the same for both, but the product of the spinner can then be sold and new labour-power, raw materials, etc. bought with the proceeds, in short, production can be continued on the same scale. The machine-builder, on the other hand, can transform the circulating capital spent in the first week back into money, and use it for a fresh operation, only after three months, when his product has been completed. There is thus firstly a difference in the reflux of the same quantity of capital laid out. Secondly, however, the same amount of productive capital is applied both in the spinning mill and the machine factory over a three-month period, but the amount of capital laid out is completely different for the spinner and the machine-builder, since in the one case the same capital is quickly renewed and the same operation can thus be repeated afresh, while in the other case the capital is renewed only relatively slowly, and new amounts of capital must therefore be steadily added to the old until its renewal period arrives. Thus the length of time in which specific portions of the capital are renewed – or the length of the time during which capital is advanced – differs according to the length of the labour process, and so too does the amount of capital that has to be advanced, even though the capital applied daily or weekly is the same. This circumstance needs to be noted, for the time of advance can grow, as in the cases to be considered in the following chapter, without the amount of capital advanced growing in proportion to this length of time. The capital has to be advanced for longer, and a larger amount of capital is tied up in the form of productive capital.

At the less developed stages of capitalist production, enterprises that require a long working period, and thus a large capital outlay for a longer time, particularly if they can be conducted only on a large scale, are often not pursued capitalistically at all. Roads, canals, etc., for example, were built at the cost of the municipality or state (in earlier periods mostly by forced labour, in so far as labour-power is concerned). Alternatively, products which require a long working period for their fabrication are manufactured only to a very minor extent with the financial means of the capitalist himself. In the construction of houses, for instance, the private individual for whom the house is being built pays advances to the builder in successive portions. He thus pays for the house bit by bit, in proportion to the progress of its production process. In the era of developed capitalism, however, where on the one hand massive capitals are concentrated in the hands of individuals, and on the other hand the associated capitalist (joint-stock companies) steps onto the scene alongside the individual capitalist – where credit, too, is developed – it is only in exceptional cases that a capitalist builder still builds houses to order for individual clients. He makes a business out of building rows of houses and whole districts of towns for the market, just as individual capitalists make a business out of building railways as contractors.

How capitalist production has revolutionized house building in London can be seen from the evidence given by a builder to the Bank Acts Committee of 1857. In his youth, he said, houses were generally built to order, and the price was paid to the contractor in instalments as stages of the construction were completed. There was little speculative building; contractors would resort to this p..ncipally just to keep their workers regularly occupied and hold their labour force together. In the last forty years all that has changed. There is now little building to order. If someone wants a new house, he looks for one that has already been built on speculation, or is already in the process of being built. Today the contractor no longer works directly for a client, but rather for the market; just like any other industrialist, he has to have finished goods for sale. Whereas previously a contractor might have built three or four houses at a time on speculation, he now has to buy an extensive piece of land (in the Continental sense, he leases it, usually for ninety-nine years), erect on it up to 100 or 200 houses, and thus involve himself in an undertaking that exceeds his own means some twenty to fifty times over. Funds are procured by taking out a mortgage, and this money is put at the contractor's disposal bit by bit as the building of the houses progresses. If a crisis breaks out, bringing the payment of these instalments to a halt, then the whole undertaking generally collapses; in the best case, the houses remain uncompleted until better times, while in the worst they are auctioned off at half price. It is impossible nowadays for any contractor to get along without speculative building, and on a large scale at that. The profit on the actual construction is extremely slight; the main source of profit comes from raising the ground rent, and from the clever selection and exploitation of the building land. Almost the whole of Belgravia, Tyburnia and the countless thousands of villas around London have been built in this way, by speculative anticipation of the demand for houses. (Abbreviated from *Report from the Select Committee on Bank Acts*, part I, 1857, Evidence, nos. 5413–5418, 5435–5436.)

Large-scale jobs needing particularly long working periods are fully suitable for capitalist production only when the concentration of capital is already well advanced, and when the development of the credit system offers the capitalist the convenient expedient of advancing and thus risking other people's capital instead of his own. It is self-evident, however, that whether the capital advanced for production belongs to the person who uses it or not has no effect on the speed and time of turnover.

Circumstances that increase the product of the individual working day, such as cooperation, division of labour, application of machinery, also shorten the working period for inter-connected acts of production. Thus machinery shortens the building time of houses, bridges, etc.; reaping and threshing machines, etc. shorten the working period required to transform ripened corn into a finished commodity. Improved ship-building techniques, resulting in greater speed, shorten the turnover time of the capital invested in shipping. These improvements, which shorten the working period and hence the time for which circulating capital has to be advanced, are generally bound up with an increased outlay of fixed capital. The working period, however, can be shortened in some branches simply by an extension of cooperation; the completion of a railway is hastened by setting afoot great armies of workers and tackling the job from many different points in space. Here the turnover time is shortened by the growth of the capital advanced. More means of production and more labour-power have to be united under the capitalist's command.

If the shortening of the working period is thus generally bound up with an increase in the capital advanced for this shorter time, so that the amount of capital advanced increases to the degree that the time of advance is shortened, we should remember that, apart from the total volume of social capital available, it comes down to a question of the extent to which the means of production and subsistence, i.e. disposal over them, are fragmented, or united in the hands of individual capitalists, i.e. the extent reached by the concentration of capital. In so far as credit mediates, accelerates and intensifies the concentration of capital in a single hand, it contributes to shortening the working period, and with this also the turnover time.

In branches of production where the working period, whether it is continuous or interrupted, is prescribed by specific natural conditions, no shortening can take place by the means described above:

'In regard to quicker returns, this term cannot be made to apply to corn crops, as one return only can be made per annum. In respect to stock, we will simply ask, how is the return of two- and three-year-old sheep, and four- and five-year-old oxen to be quickened?' (W. Walter Good, *Political, Agricultural, and Commercial Fallacies*, London, 1866, p. 325).

The need to have ready cash as soon as possible (e.g. to pay fixed obligations such as taxes, ground-rent, etc.) solves this question in so far as cattle, for instance, are sold and slaughtered before they have reached the normal economic age, to the great detriment of agriculture; this also leads, moreover, to a rise in meat prices.

'Men who have mainly reared cattle for supplying the pastures of the Midland counties in summer, and the yards of the eastern counties in winter . . . have become so crippled through the uncertainty and lowness in the prices of corn that they are glad to take advantage of the high prices of butter and cheese; the former they take to market weekly to help to pay current expenses, and draw on the other from some factor, who takes the cheese when fit to move, and, of course, nearly at his own price. For this reason, remembering that farming is governed by the principles of Political Economy, the calves which used to come south from the dairying counties for rearing, are now largely sacrificed, at times at a week and ten days old, in the shambles of Birmingham, Manchester, Liverpool, and other large neighbouring towns. If, however, malt had been free from duty, not only would farmers have made more profit and therefore been able to keep their stock till it got older and heavier, but it would have been substituted for milk and rearing by men who did not keep cows, and thus the present alarming scarcity of young cattle which has befallen the nation would have been largely averted. What these little men now say, in reply to recommendations to rear, is, "We know very well it would pay to rear on milk, but it would first require us to put our hands in our purse, which we cannot do, and then we should have to wait a long time for a return, instead of getting it at once by dairying"' (ibid., pp. 11, 12).

If the lengthening of turnover can have consequences like this even among the smaller English farmers, it is easy to understand what disturbances it must provoke among the small peasants of the Continent.

According to the duration of the working period, and thus also the period till a commodity ready for circulation is completed, the portion of value that the fixed capital surrenders layer by layer to the product mounts up, and the reflux of this portion of value is delayed. This delay, however, does not necessitate a renewed outlay of fixed capital. The machine continues to operate in the production process whether replacement for its wear and tear flows back quicker or more slowly in the money form. It is different with circulating capital. Here not only must capital be tied up for a longer time, in proportion to the duration of the labour process, but new capital must continually be advanced for wages, raw and ancillary materials. The delayed reflux thus has a different effect in the two cases. Whether the reflux is slower or quicker, the fixed capital continues to operate. The circulating capital, on the contrary, becomes unable to function when the reflux is delayed, if it is tied up in the form of unsold, or unfinished and not yet saleable products, and there is no additional capital to renew it in kind.

'While the peasant farmer starves, his cattle thrive. Repeated showers had fallen in the country, and the forage was abundant. The Hindoo peasant will perish by hunger beside a fat bullock. The prescriptions of superstition, which appear cruel to the individual, are conservative for the community; and the preservation of the labouring cattle secures the power of cultivation, and the sources of future life and wealth. It may sound harsh and sad to say so, but in India it is more easy to replace a man than an ox' (*Return, East India. Madras and Orissa Famine*, no. 4, p. 44).

We can compare this with a passage from the *Manava Dharma Sastra*:*

'Desertion of life, without reward, for the sake of preserving a priest or a cow . . . may cause the beatitude of those base-born tribes' (Chapter X, 62).

It is impossible, of course, to deliver a five-year-old animal before the end of five years. But what is possible within certain limits is to prepare animals for their fate more quickly by new modes of treatment. This was precisely what Bakewell managed to do. Previously, British sheep, just like French sheep as late as 1855, were not ready for slaugh-

* This text is the classical Hindu code of conduct ascribed to Manu as the progenitor of mankind. Marx quotes the English translation by Graves Chamney Haughton (third edition), published in Madras in 1863.

ter before the fourth or fifth year. In Bakewell's system, one-year-old sheep can already be fattened, and in any case they are fully grown before the second year has elapsed. By careful selective breeding, Bakewell, farmer of Dishley Grange [North Leicestershire], reduced the bone structure of his sheep to the minimum necessary for their existence. These sheep are called the New Leicesters:

'The breeder can now send three to market in the same space of time that it formerly took him to prepare one; and if they are not taller, they are broader, rounder, and have a greater development in those parts which give most flesh. Of bone, they have absolutely no greater amount than is necessary to support them, and almost all their weight is pure meat' (Lavergne, *The Rural Economy of England, etc.*, 1855, p. 20).

The methods that shorten the working period differ greatly in the extent to which they can be applied in different branches of industry, and they do not cancel out the differences in length of the different working periods. To stick to our example, the application of new machine-tools may, in absolute terms, shorten the working period necessary for the production of a locomotive. But if improved processes in spinning increase the finished product turned out daily or weekly here to an even greater extent, then the length of the working period in machine-building will still have increased relatively, compared with that in spinning.

Chapter 13: Production Time

Working time is always production time, i.e. time during which capital is confined to the production sphere. But it is not true, conversely, that the entire time for which capital exists in the production process is necessarily therefore working time.

What is at issue here are not interruptions in the labour process conditioned by the natural limits of labour-power itself, even though we have seen the extent to which the mere fact that fixed capital – factory buildings, machinery, etc. – lies idle during the pauses in the labour process became one of the motives for the unnatural extension of the labour process, and for working day and night.* What is involved is rather an interruption independent of the length of the labour process, an interruption conditioned by the nature of the product and its production, during which the object of labour is subjected to natural processes of shorter or longer duration, and has to undergo physical, chemical or physiological changes while the labour process is either completely or partially suspended.

After grapes have been pressed, for instance, the wine must go through a period of fermentation, and then also rest for a while before it reaches a certain degree of readiness. In many branches of industry the product must undergo a process of drying, as in pottery, or else be exposed to certain conditions in order to change its chemical properties, as with bleaching. Winter corn needs nine months or so to ripen. Between seed-time and harvest, the labour process is almost completely interrupted. In the raising of timber, once planting and the preliminary work connected with this is completed, the seed may need 100 years to be transformed into a finished product; during this whole time, only a relatively very insignificant intervention of labour is needed.

In all these cases, additional labour is added only occasionally for a large part of the production time. The situation described in the pre-

*See Volume 1, Chapter 10, 4.

vious chapter, where additional capital and labour has to be added to capital already tied up in the production process, occurs here only with interruptions of a greater or lesser extent.

In all these cases, therefore, the production time of the capital advanced consists of two periods: a period in which the capital exists in the labour process, and a second period in which its form of existence – that of an unfinished product – is handed over to the sway of natural processes, without being involved in the labour process. This situation is not altered if the two periods of time occasionally cut across one another or are interspersed. Here the working period and the production period do not coincide. The production period is longer than the working period. But it is only after the production period has been left behind that the product is finished and mature, and can thus be transformed from the form of productive capital into that of commodity capital. The turnover period is then extended according to the length of that part of the production time that does not consist of working time. In so far as this time of production over and above the labour time is not determined by natural laws given once and for all, as with the ripening of corn, the growth of an oak, etc., the turnover period can often be shortened to a greater or lesser extent by the artificial shortening of the production time. Examples of this are the introduction of chemical in place of open-air bleaching, and more effective drying apparatus in the drying processes. In tanning, the penetration of tannic acid into the skins, which used to take between six and eighteen months with the old method, only takes one and a half to two months with the new method involving the use of the air-pump (J. D. Courcelle-Seneuil, *Traité théorique et pratique des entreprises industrielles*, etc., Paris, 1857, 2nd edn [p. 49]). The most far-reaching example of artificial shortening of a production time made up exclusively of natural processes is given by the history of iron production over the last 100 years, from the invention of puddling in 1780 to the modern Bessemer process and the latest procedures introduced since then. The production time has been enormously curtailed, but the application of fixed capital has also increased to the same extent.

A peculiar example of the divergence between production time and working time is provided by the American manufacture of shoe-lasts. Here a significant part of the expense arises from the wood having to dry out in store for up to eighteen months, so that the finished lasts do not warp. During this time, the wood does not undergo any other labour process. The turnover period of the capital applied is therefore not only determined by the time required to produce the lasts themselves, but also by the time for which the capital has to lie idle in the shape of wood which is being dried out. The capital exists in the production process for eighteen months before it can enter the labour process proper. This example also shows how the turnover times of various parts of the total circulating capital may differ as a result of circumstances that arise from the production sphere and not from the circulation sphere.

The distinction between production time and working time is particularly important in agriculture. In our temperate climates, the land brings forth grain once a year. The shortening or lengthening of the production period (an average of nine months for winter sowing) is itself dependent on the alternation of good and bad years, and hence cannot be precisely determined in advance and controlled, as in industry proper. Only subsidiary products such as milk, cheese, etc. can be produced and sold continuously in short periods. But the working time is in the following quite different situation:

'The number of working days for the three main working periods is assumed to be as follows in the different districts of Germany, with respect to the climatic and other conditions involved: the spring period from mid-March or the beginning of April up to the middle of May, 50–60 days; the summer period from early June to late August, 65–80 days; the autumn period from early September to the end of October or middle or late November, 55–75 days. As far as winter goes, there is simply the work suited to that period, such as haulage of fertilizer, wood, goods for market, building materials, etc.' (F. Kirchhof, *Handbuch der landwirtschaftlichen Betriebslehre*, Dessau, 1852, p. 160).

Thus the more unfavourable the climate, the more the agricultural working period, and hence the outlay of capital and labour, is compressed into a short interval, as for example in Russia. 'In some of the northern districts, field labour is only possible during from 130 to 150 days in the course of the year, and it may be imagined what a loss Russia would sustain, if out of 65,000,000 of her European population, 50,000,000 remained unoccupied during six or eight months of winter, when all agricultural labour is at a standstill.' Besides the 200,000 peasants who work in Russia's 10,500 factories, particular cottage industries have grown up everywhere in the villages. 'There are villages, for instance, in Russia in which all the peasants have been for generations either weavers, tanners, shoemakers, locksmiths, cutlers, etc.'; this is particularly the case in the gubernias of Moscow, Vladimir, Kaluga, Kostroma and St Petersburg. These cottage industries, incidentally, are already being pressed more and more into the service of capitalist production; for example, merchants supply the weavers with warps and weft, either directly, or by intermediate agents. (Abbreviated from *Reports by H.M. Secretaries of Embassy and Legation, on the Manufactures, Commerce etc.*, no. 8, 1865, pp. 86, 87.) We see here how the distinction between production period and working period, with the latter forming only a part of the former, constitutes the natural basis for the unification of agriculture with rural subsidiary industries, just as these, in turn, are points of vantage for the capitalist, who first intrudes in his capacity as merchant. In so far as capitalist production later manages to complete the separation between manufacture and agriculture, the rural worker becomes ever more dependent on merely accidental subsidiary employments and his condition thereby worsens. As far as capital is concerned, as we shall see later on, all these differences in the turnover balance out. Not so for the worker.

In most branches of industry proper, as well as in mining, transport, etc., production proceeds evenly and the same working time is worked year in year out; apart from fluctuations of price, disturbances of business, etc. and abnormal interruptions, the outlay of capital going into the daily circulation process is evenly distributed. While market conditions remain the same, therefore, the reflux or renewal of circulating capital is distributed over the whole year in equal portions. However, in those investments of capital where working time forms only one part of the production time, there is great unevenness in the outlay of circulating capital in the course of the different periods of the year, in as much as the reflux only follows, at one stroke, at a time prescribed by natural conditions. On a given scale of business, therefore, i.e. with the same volume of circulating capital advanced, this must be advanced in larger amounts at once, and for a longer time, than in those businesses with continuous working periods. The life of fixed capital is significantly different here from the time in which it actually functions productively. With this difference between working time and production time, the time during which the fixed capital is utilized is of course constantly interrupted for a longer or shorter interval; in agriculture for instance, with the use of draught cattle, implements and machines. In so far as this fixed capital consists of draught animals, it continues to require the same or almost the same outlay on fodder, etc. as during the time in which it operates. In the case of dead means of labour, non-use also gives rise to a certain depreciation. The product thus always becomes dearer, since the transfer of value to the product is not calculated according to the time for which the fixed capital functions, but rather according to the time in which it loses value. In these branches of production it is a condition of normal use that fixed capital should lie idle, whether or not this still involves running costs, just as in spinning a condition of normal use is the loss of a certain quantity of cotton; and in the same way, in every labour process, the labour-power expended unproductively, but unavoidably so under normal technical conditions, counts just as much as the productive. Every improvement that reduces the unproductive expenditure of means of labour, raw materials and labour-power also reduces the value of the product.

In agriculture the two things are combined, the long duration of the working period and a great difference between working time and production time. Hodgskin correctly notes on this point:

'The difference of time' (although he does not differentiate here between working time and production time) 'required to complete the products of agriculture, and of other species of labour' is 'the main cause of the great dependence of the agriculturists. They cannot bring their commodities to market in less time than a year. For that whole period they are obliged to borrow of the shoemaker, the tailor, the smith, the wheelwright, and the various other labourers, whose products they cannot dispense with, but which are completed in a few days or weeks. Owing to this natural circumstance, and owing to the more rapid increase of the wealth produced by other labour than that of agriculture, the monopolizers of all the land, though they have also monopolized legislation, have not been able to save themselves and their servants, the farmers, from becoming the most dependent class of men in the community' (Thomas Hodgskin, *Popular Political Economy*, London, 1827, p. 147, note).

All methods in agriculture which on the one hand distribute expenditure on wages and means of labour more evenly over the whole year, and on the other hand shorten the turnover, by diversifying the products and thus making different crops possible during the year, require an increase in the circulating capital laid out on production, on wages, fertilizer, seed, etc. This is the case with the transition from the three-field system (with fallow) to the system of crop rotation without fallow. Also with the *cultures dérobées* [undersowing system] in Flanders.

'The root crops are planted by undersowing; the same field first bears corn, flax or rape-seed for human requirements, and then after the harvest root crops are sown for the maintenance of cattle. This system, which enables the horned cattle to remain permanently in the stall, produces a considerable amount of manure and is thus the cornerstone of crop rotation. More than a third of the cultivated area in the sandy districts is undersown in this way; it is just as if the cultivated land had been extended by a third.'

Besides root crops, clover and other fodder is also used here:

'Agriculture, being thus carried to the point at which it is transformed into horticulture, understandably requires a relatively considerable capital investment. In England the sum reckoned with is 250 francs of investment capital to the hectare.* In Flanders our farmers will probably find an investment capital of 500 francs per hectare* far too low' (*Essais sur l'économie rurale de la Belgique*, par Émile de Laveleye, Brussels, 1863, pp. 59, 60, 63).

Let us finally consider timber-raising:

'The production of timber is fundamentally different from most others in that here natural forces work independently, and the power of men or capital is not required for natural growth. Even where forests are artificially cultivated, the amount of human and capital power expended in comparison with the action of natural forces is only slight. Furthermore, forests will thrive in types of soil and places where grain cannot grow, or where it no longer pays to produce it. Forest culture, however, requires a greater surface area than the cultivation of grain, if it is to be conducted on a regular commercial basis. Since small plots do not allow proper forestry methods, the secondary uses are abandoned, and forest protection is made more difficult, etc. The production process is also tied to such a long period of time that it extends beyond the plans of a private undertaking, and sometimes even beyond a single human life. Capital invested in the acquisition of forest land' (in communal production this capital disappears and the question is simply how much land the community can withdraw from arable and grazing land for timber production) 'only bears fruit after a comparatively long period of time, and turns over only partially, taking up to 150 years in the case of many types of wood. Moreover, effective timber production actually requires a reserve stock of growing timber amounting to between ten and forty times the annual yield. Thus someone who does not have other income or possess substantial areas of forest cannot pursue regular forestry' (Kirchhof, p. 58).

The long production time (which includes a relatively slight amount

* Approximately £4 and £8 per acre respectively at the currency values of the time.

of working time), and the consequent length of the turnover period, makes forest culture a line of business unsuited to private and hence to capitalist production, the latter being fundamentally a private operation, even when the associated capitalist takes the place of the individual. The development of civilization and industry in general has always shown itself so active in the destruction of forests that everything that has been done for their conservation and production is completely insignificant in comparison.

Particularly worthy of note in the quotation from Kirchhof is the following passage:

'Moreover, effective timber production actually requires a reserve stock of timber amounting to between ten and forty times the annual yield.'

Thus the turnover takes from ten years up to forty and more.

It is the same with cattle-raising. Part of the herd (cattle stock) remains in the production process, while another part is sold as the annual product. Here only one part of the capital turns over each year, just as in the case of the fixed capital – machinery, draught cattle, etc. Even though this capital is fixed for a longer time in the production process, and thus lengthens the turnover of the total capital, it does not constitute fixed capital in the categorical sense.

What is referred to here as a stock – a definite quantity of growing wood or cattle – exists partially in the production process (both as means of labour and material of labour); depending on the natural conditions of its reproduction, a significant part must always exist in this form in the case of regular cultivation.

A further kind of stock has a similar effect on the turnover, a stock that forms only potential productive capital, but has to be accumulated in larger or smaller amounts as a result of the nature of agriculture, and must be advanced to production for a relatively long time even though it enters the active production process only bit by bit. This includes manure, for example, before it is carted to the field, as well as corn, hay, etc. and any stocks of feed that go into the production of cattle.

'A considerable part of the working capital is contained in the stocks of the business. These can lose their value to a greater or lesser extent if the appropriate measures of protection required for their maintenance in good order are not taken; a part of the production stock can even be completely lost to the business by lack of attention. What is principally required in this connection is painstaking attention to the barns, fodder and grain lofts and cellars; the storage places must always be kept well closed, and also kept clean, ventilated, etc.; the grain and other crops kept in store must be thoroughly turned over from time to time, and potatoes and beets protected against frost, water and rot' (Kirchhof, p. 292).

'In calculating one's own requirements, particularly for cattle, in which connection a division must be made according to the measure of the product and the intended use, attention must be paid not only to covering requirements, but also to having a sufficient stock left over for unforeseen contingencies. As soon as it appears that the need cannot be fully met by one's own production, it is necessary to take into consideration whether this lack cannot be covered by other products (substitutes), or whether these cannot be procured more cheaply in place of the missing products. If there should be a lack of hay, for example, this can be made up by root crops with added straw. In general, the material value and market price of the different products must be constantly borne in mind, and consumption regulated accordingly; if oats are dearer, for instance, while peas and rye are relatively cheap, then it will be advantageous to replace some of the oats for the horses with peas and rye, and sell the superfluous oats' (ibid., p. 300).

In considering the formation of stock,* we have already noted that a greater or lesser quantity of potential productive capital is required, i.e. a quantity of means of production destined for production, which has to be held in reserve in a greater or lesser amount in order to go into the production process bit by bit. We noted in this connection that with a capital investment of a given scale, the size of this production stock depends on the greater or lesser difficulty of its replacement, its relative proximity to the supplying markets, the development of means of transport and communication, etc. All these circumstances affect the minimum capital that must exist in the form of productive stock, and thus the period of time for which advances of capital have to be made, and the volume of capital that has to be advanced at once. This volume, which also has an effect on the turnover, is determined by the longer or shorter time for which circulating capital is tied up in the form of productive stock, as only potentially productive capital. On the other hand, in so far as the extent of this stagnation depends on the greater or lesser possibility of rapid replacement, on market conditions, etc., it itself arises from the circulation time, from circumstances that pertain to the circulation sphere.

'Moreover, a stock of all these implements or accessories, working

* See above, pp. 215–20.

tools, sieves, baskets, ropes, axle grease, nails, etc. is all the more necessary for replacement at any moment, the less opportunity there is of procuring them quickly in the vicinity. Finally, the entire inventory should be carefully inspected each winter, and the necessary additions and repairs immediately put in hand. Whether a larger or smaller stock of implements is generally needed is principally determined by local conditions. Where there are no craftsmen or shops in the vicinity, a greater stock must be kept than where these are to be found in the locality or very close by. If the requisite stocks are procured in greater quantities at once, under otherwise similar conditions, the advantage in cheap purchase is generally obtained, provided that a suitable point of time has been chosen; but of course a greater sum is then withdrawn at once from the current capital, which cannot always be dispensed with in the business' (Kirchhof, p. 301).

The difference between production time and working time, as we have seen, permits a wide range of possibilities. The circulating capital can be in its production time before it enters the actual labour process (manufacture of lasts); it may still be in production time after it has undergone the actual labour process (wine, seed-corn); the production time may be occasionally interrupted by labour time (field crops, timber); or a large part of the product in a condition ready for circulation may remain incorporated in the active production process, while a much smaller part enters into the annual circulation (timber and cattle-growing); the greater or lesser length of time, thus the greater or lesser measure in which circulating capital has to be laid out all at once in the form of potential productive capital, partly arises from the kind of production process (agriculture) and partly depends on the proximity of markets, etc., in short, on circumstances that belong to the circulation sphere.

We shall see later on (in Volume 3) what nonsensical theories MacCulloch, James Mill* etc. were led to in their attempts to identify this production time diverging from working time with working time, attempts which in their turn arose from an incorrect application of the theory of value.

*

*On MacCulloch see above, p. 94. James Mill, the Utilitarian philosopher, was in economics a disciple of Ricardo, his main economic work *Elements of Political Economy* being published in 1821. It is not in Volume 3 of *Capital*, as published, but rather in *Theories of Surplus-Value*, that Marx's discussion of the elder Mill's 'futile attempts to resolve the contradictions of the Ricardian system' is to be

sive days of the week, and goods trains run at different hours of the day from Manchester to London. Admittedly, the last-mentioned development does not alter the absolute speed, and so neither this part of the circulation time, if the effectiveness of the means of transport remains at a given level. But successive quantities of goods can now start their journey at more closely spaced intervals, and thus arrive on the market one after the other without accumulating in great masses as potential commodity capital until they are actually dispatched. Hence the reflux is distributed over shorter successive periods of time, so that one part is steadily being transformed into money capital while another part circulates as commodity capital. By this distribution of the reflux over several successive periods, the total circulation time is shortened, and hence also the turnover. At first the greater or lesser frequency with which the means of transport function, e.g. the number of trains on a railway, develops with the degree to which a place of production more, and becomes a major centre of production, and this is a development in the direction of the already existing market, i.e. towards the major centres of production and population, towards export ports, etc. On the other hand, however, and conversely, this particular ease of commerce and the consequent acceleration in the turnover of capital (in as much as this is determined by the circulation time) gives rise to an accelerated concentration of both the centre of production and its market. With this accelerated concentration of people and capital at given points, the concentration of these masses of capital in a few hands makes rapid progress. There is simultaneously a further shift and displacement as a result of the change in the relative situation of production and market places which itself results from the changes in the means of communication. A place of production which possessed a particularly advantageous position through being situated on a main road or canal now finds itself on a single railway branch line that operates only at relatively long intervals, while another point, which previously lay completely off the major traffic routes, now lies at the intersection of several lines. The second place rises, the first declines. The changes in the means of transport therefore bring about local variations in the circulation time of commodities, in the opportunities to buy and sell, etc., or else they alter the distribution of already existing local variations. The importance of this factor in the turnover of capital is evinced by the disputes between the mercantile and industrial representatives of different places and the directors of railways. (See for example the above quoted Blue Book of the Railway Committee.)

The turnover cycle that we considered previously is a function of the durability of the fixed capital advanced to the production process. Since this encompasses a greater or smaller number of years, it also encompasses a series of turnovers of the fixed capital, repeated either yearly or within a year.

In agriculture, a turnover cycle of this kind arises from the system of crop rotation:

'The duration of the lease must in any case not be shorter than the time taken to complete the system of crop rotation that is introduced, and hence with the three-field system it is always reckoned in terms of 3, 6, 9, etc. If we assume the three-field system with complete fallow, the field is cultivated only four times in six years, and in the years cultivated, with both winter and summer grain; the properties of the soil also require or permit this to be alternated between wheat and rye, barley and oats. Each kind of grain grows on the same soil better or worse than the others, each has a different value and is also sold at a different price. The yield of the land thus varies with the years of cultivation; it is different in the first half of the cycle' (in the first three years) 'and in the second. Even the average yield over the whole cycle is not the same in one case as in the other, since fertility does not just depend on the quality of the soil, but also on the year's weather, the price also depending on many different conditions. If the yield is calculated on the basis of the average years of the entire cycle of six years, and of the average prices in these years, then the total yield for one year can be arrived at for either period of the rotation. But this is not the case if the yield is only calculated for half of the rotation, i.e. for three years, since then the total yields would not be the same. It is evident from this that the duration of the lease in the three-field system must be fixed at at least six years. It is always far more desirable for both landlord and tenant that the lease should run for a multiple of the lease (*sic*: F.E.) and thus instead of six years in the case of the three-field system, it should be twelve or eighteen years or more, and in the case of the seven-field system not seven but fourteen or twenty-eight' (Kirchhof, pp. 117, 118).

(The manuscript states here: 'The English system of crop rotation. A note on this to be given.' – F.E.)

found (Part III, pp. 84 ff.), a discussion of MacCulloch coming later on in the same chapter, 'The Disintegration of the Ricardian School' (pp. 168 ff.).

Chapter 14: Circulation Time

All the circumstances so far considered as differentiating the circulation periods of different capitals invested in different branches of industry, and hence also the times for which capital has to be advanced, such as the distinction between fixed and fluid capital, the difference in working periods, etc., arise within the production process itself. But the turnover time of capital is the sum of its production time and its circulation or rotation time. It is self-evident, therefore, that circulation times of varying length make for different times of turnover and thus different turnover periods. This becomes most readily apparent either when we compare two different capital investments in which all other circumstances modifying the turnover are equal and only the times of circulation are different, or when a given capital is taken with a given composition in terms of fixed and fluid capital, a given working period etc., and only the circulation time is hypothetically varied.

One section of circulation time – and relatively the most decisive one – consists of selling time, the period in which the capital exists in the state of commodity capital. According to the relative extent of this interval, the circulation time in general, and hence also the turnover period, is lengthened or shortened. An additional outlay of capital may also be necessary for costs of storage etc. It is clear from the start that the time required for the sale of the finished product may be very different for individual capitalists in one and the same line of business; i.e. not only for the quantities of capital that are invested in different branches of production, but also for the various independent capitals invested in a particular sphere of production, which in actual fact simply constitute bits of the total capital which have attained an independent position. With other circumstances remaining the same, the selling period required by the same individual capital changes with the general fluctuations in market conditions, or with fluctuations in the particular line of business in question. We shall not deal any further here with this point. We need only establish the simple fa circumstances that generally produce a variation in the turnov of capital invested in different lines of business may operate ind (e.g. if one capitalist has the occasion to sell more quickly competitor, if one applies more methods that shorten the w period than the other does, etc.), and effect a similar variation turnover of the various capitals inhabiting the same line of business

A permanently effective cause of differentiation in the selling t and hence in the turnover time in general, is the distance of the mar where the commodities are sold from their place of production. For whole period of its journey to the market, capital is confined to tl state of commodity capital; if it is produced to order, then there i added to the time of the journey to the market the time in which the commodity is up for sale on the market. Improvement in the means of communication and transport shortens absolutely the period in which commodities migrate in this way, but it does not abolish the relative difference in the circulation time of different commodity capitals arising from the migration, or even that of different bits of the same commodity capital that migrate to different markets. Improved sailing ships and steamships, for instance, which shorten the journey, shorten it just as much for nearby ports as for distant ones. The relative difference remains, even though it is often reduced. The relative differences n however be displaced by the development of the means of communi tion and transport in a way that does not correspond to the natu distances. For instance, a railway leading from the place of producti to a major inland centre of population may lengthen the distance to nearer inland point which is not served by a railway, absolutely relatively, in comparison to the one naturally more distant; similar the relative distances of places of production from the major mark outlets may be altered as a result of the same circumstances, whic explains the demise of old centres of production and the emergence new ones with changes in the means of transport and communication (In addition to this there is the relatively cheaper cost of transport fo longer distances as compared to shorter.) With the development of th means of transport, the speed of movement in space is accelerated, an spatial distance is thus shortened in time. In addition to this, the mas of means of communication develops, so that for instance many ship depart for the same port at the same time, several trains run betwee the same two points along different railways, and, above all, freigh ships leave Liverpool for New York, for example, on different succes

All branches of production which, owing to the nature of their product, are oriented principally to local outlets, such as breweries, thus develop to their largest dimensions in the major centres of population. Here the rapid turnover of capital partly balances out the increase in the cost of many conditions of production, building land, etc.

If the progress of capitalist production and the consequent development of the means of transport and communication shortens the circulation time for a given quantity of commodities, the same progress and the opportunity provided by the development of the means of transport and communication conversely introduces the necessity of working for ever more distant markets, in a word, for the world market. The mass of commodities in transit grows enormously, and hence so does the part of the social capital that stays for long periods in the stage of commodity capital, in circulation time – both absolutely and relatively. A simultaneous and associated growth occurs in the portion of social wealth that, instead of serving as direct means of production, is laid out on means of transport and communication, and on the fixed and circulating capital required to keep these in operation.

Merely the relative length of the journey of commodities from their place of production to their outlet gives rise to a difference not only in the first part of the circulation time, the selling time, but also in the second part, the transformation of money back into the elements of productive capital, the purchasing time. Say that the commodity is sent to India. This takes maybe four months. Let us take the selling time as zero, i.e. assume that the commodity is shipped to order and paid for on delivery to the producer's agent. A further four months is required to send back the money (the form in which it is remitted is immaterial here). It is thus altogether eight months before the same capital can function once again as productive capital, and can be used to renew the same operation. The variations in turnover brought about in this way form one of the material bases for differing periods of credit, just as overseas trade in general, in Venice and Genoa, for instance, formed one of the original sources of the credit system in its true sense.

'The crisis of 1847 enabled the banking and mercantile community of that time to reduce the India and China usance' (time allowed for the currency of bills of exchange between there and Europe) 'from ten months' date to six months' sight, and the lapse of twenty years with all the accelerations of speed and establishment of telegraphs ... renders necessary ... a further reduction' – from six months' sight to four months' date as a first step to four months' sight. 'The voyage of a sailing vessel via the Cape from Calcutta to London is on the average under 90 days. An usance of four months' sight would be equal to a currency of say 150 days. The present usance of six months' sight is equal to a currency of say 210 days' (*Economist*, 16 June 1866).

On the other hand:

'The Brazilian usance remains at two and three months' sight, bills from Antwerp are drawn' (on London) 'at three months' date, and even Manchester and Bradford draw upon London at three months and longer dates. By tacit consent, a fair opportunity is afforded to the merchant of realizing the proceeds of his merchandise, not indeed before, but within a reasonable time of, [when] the bills drawn against it fall due. In this view, the present usance for Indian bills cannot be considered excessive. Indian produce for the most part being sold in London with three months' prompt, and allowing for loss of time in effecting sales, cannot be realized much within five months, while another period of five months will have previously elapsed (on average) between the time of purchase in India and of delivery in the English warehouse. We have here a period of ten months, whereas the bill drawn against the goods does not live beyond seven months' (ibid., 30 June 1866).

On 2 July 1866, five big London banks dealing mainly with India and China, and the Paris Comptoir d'Escompte, gave notice that 'from the 1st January 1867, their branches and agencies in the East will only buy and sell bills of exchange at a term not exceeding four months' sight' (ibid., 7 July 1866). However this reduction miscarried, and had to be abandoned. (Since then the Suez Canal has revolutionized all this.)

It is clear that with the longer circulation time of commodities, the risk of a change of price on the selling market rises, owing to the lengthening of the period in which this price change can occur.

A difference in circulation time, both individually between different capitals in the same branch of industry, and between different branches of industry according to the different usances, when payment is not immediately made in cash, arises from the different terms of payment in purchase and sale. We shall not dwell any longer on this point here, although it is important for the credit system.

The size of delivery contracts, which grows with the volume and scale of capitalist production, also gives rise to differences in the turnover time. The contract of delivery, as a transaction between buyer and seller, is an operation pertaining to the market, to the sphere of circulation. The differences in turnover time arising from it thus arise from the circulation sphere, but they react directly back on the production sphere, quite apart from all terms of payment and credit conditions, i.e. even with cash payment. Coal, cotton, yarn, etc. are discrete products. Each day provides its quantity of finished product. But if the spinner or mine-owner agrees to deliver quantities of products which require, say, a four week or six-week period of successive working days, it is just the same, with respect to the length of time for which capital has to be advanced, as if a continuous working period of four to six weeks was introduced into his labour process. It is of course assumed here that the entire quantity of products ordered is to be delivered at once, or at least is paid for only after it has all been delivered. Each day, then, considered in isolation, has provided its particular quantity of finished products. But this finished quantity is still only a part of the quantity contracted for. If the already finished part of the commodities ordered is no longer in the production process, it is still merely lying in the warehouse as potential capital.

We come now to the second stage of the circulation time, the time of purchase, or the period in which the capital is transformed back from the money form into the elements of productive capital. In the course of this period it must persist for a shorter or longer time in its state of money capital, and thus a certain part of the total capital advanced always exists in the state of money capital, although this part consists of constantly changing elements. In a particular business, for instance, $n \times £100$ of the total capital advanced has to be present in the form of money capital; this is continuously being transformed into productive capital, but just as constantly being added to again by the influx from circulation, from the realized commodity capital. Thus a definite portion of the capital value advanced always exists in the state of money capital, i.e. in a form pertaining not to its sphere of production but rather to its sphere of circulation.

We have already seen how, when the time in which capital is confined to the form of commodity capital is prolonged, by the greater distance of the market, this directly gives rise to a delayed reflux of money, and thus also delays the transformation of capital from money capital into productive capital.

We also saw (Chapter 6), with respect to the purchase of commodities, how the time of purchase, and the greater or lesser distance from the major sources of raw material, makes it necessary to buy raw materials for longer periods and keep them available in the form of productive stock, latent or potential productive capital; how this increases the mass of capital that must be advanced at one stroke, and the time for which it must be advanced, the scale of production being otherwise the same.

In different branches of industry, the shorter or longer periods for which large quantities of raw materials are thrown onto the market have a similar effect. In London, for instance, major auctions of wool take place every three months, and these dominate the wool market, whereas the cotton market is on the whole supplied continuously from harvest to harvest, even if not always evenly. Periods of this kind determine the major terms of purchase for these raw materials, and particularly affect speculative purchases, making necessary longer or shorter advances in these elements of production, just as the nature of the commodities produced affects the speculative and deliberate withholding of products from the market for longer or shorter periods in the form of potential commodity capital.

'The agriculturalist must therefore also be a speculator to a certain extent, and hold back the sale of his products according to the conditions of the time...'

(A few general rules follow: F.E.)

'Marketing the products, however, mostly depends on the person, the product itself and the locality. Someone who, besides being skilful and fortunate (!), is endowed with sufficient operating capital, is not to be blamed if he sometimes lets the crops he has obtained lie for a year when prices are unusually low; someone who has insufficient operating capital, on the other hand, or who completely lacks the spirit of speculation (!), will seek to obtain the current average price, and will thus have to sell as soon and as often as he has the opportunity. To let wool lie for longer than a year will almost always involve a loss, while corn and oil-seed can be kept for a few years without any detriment to their quality and properties. Products that are generally subject to a substantial rise and fall in price over short periods of time, such as for example oil-seed, hops, teasels and the like, are rightly left to lie in the years when their prices stand far below the prices of production. One should least delay the sale of such objects as give rise to daily costs of maintenance, such as fattened cattle, or are liable to spoil, such as fruit, potatoes, etc. In many districts, a product generally has at certain times of the year its lowest price, at other times its highest; grain, for instance, is in many places generally lower in price at Martinmas than between Christmas and Easter. There are also many products in several districts that are only good for sale at certain times, as is the case with wool in the wool markets of those districts where at other times the wool trade is generally dull, etc.' (Kirchhof, p. 302).

In considering the second half of the circulation time, during which money is transformed back into the elements of productive capital, it is not only this conversion alone that is involved, nor only the time in which the money flows back, according to the distance of the market where the product is sold. What is also and especially involved is the extent to which a part of the capital advanced must always exist in the money form, in the state of money capital.

If we leave out of consideration all speculative activities, the scale of purchases of those commodities that must be constantly present as a productive stock depends on the latter's periods of renewal, i.e. on circumstances that in turn depend on market conditions, and hence vary for different raw materials, etc. Here, therefore, money must from time to time be advanced in large amounts at once. But whether it flows back quicker or more slowly, according to the turnover of the capital, it always flows back bit by bit. One part of it is just as regularly spent again at short intervals, i.e. the part transformed back into wages. Another part, however, that transformed back into raw materials, etc., has to be accumulated for a longer period of time as a reserve fund, either for purchase or for payment. It therefore exists in the form of money capital, although the extent to which it exists in this form changes.

We shall see in the next chapter how other circumstances, arising both from the production and the circulation processes, require this presence of a definite portion of the capital advanced in the money form. It should generally be noted, however, that the economists are much inclined to forget not only that a part of the capital needed in a business is constantly passing alternately through the three forms of money capital, productive capital and commodity capital, but that it is always different portions of this that possess these forms alongside each other, even if the relative magnitudes of these portions are in constant flux. It is particularly the part always present as money capital that the economists forget, although precisely this circumstance is very necessary for the understanding of the bourgeois economy, and makes itself felt as such in practice as well.

Chapter 15: Effect of Circulation Time on the Magnitude of the Capital Advanced

In this chapter and the one following, we deal with the influence of circulation time on the valorization of capital.

[First example.] Let us consider a commodity capital that is the product of a working period of nine weeks, for example. We abstract for the time being both from the portion of the product's value that is added to it by the average wear and tear of the fixed capital, and from the surplus-value added to it during the production process, so that the value of this product can be taken as equal to the value of the fluid capital advanced for its production, i.e. the value of the wages and of the raw and ancillary materials consumed in its production. Let this value be £900, so that the weekly outlay amounts to £100. The periodic production time, which coincides here with the working period, is nine weeks. It is immaterial in this connection whether we assume a working period for a continuous product or a continuous working period for a discrete product, as long as the quantum of the discrete product that is put on the market at one stroke simply takes nine weeks' labour. Let the circulation time be three weeks. The total turnover period is then twelve weeks. After nine weeks have elapsed, the productive capital advanced is transformed into commodity capital, but it now has to spend three weeks in the circulation period. Thus the new cycle of production can begin again only at the start of the thirteenth week, and production is at a standstill for three weeks, or a quarter of the total circulation period. It is also immaterial whether we suppose that this is the average time that it takes to sell the commodity, or whether the time is determined by the distance of the market, or, alternatively again, by the date of payment for the commodity sold. In every three months, production is at a halt for three weeks, i.e. for $4 \times 3 = 12$ weeks $= 3$ months of the year, or a quarter of the annual turnover period.

Hence if production is to be continuous, pursued on the same scale week in, week out, there are only two possibilities.

One possibility is that the scale of production is cut back, so that the sum of £900 is now sufficient to keep work going during the circulation time of the first turnover as well as during the working period. A second working period is then begun in the tenth week – and thus a new turnover period as well – before the first turnover period is at an end, since the turnover period is a twelve-week one, while the working period is nine weeks. £900 divided by 12 weeks gives £75 per week. It is clear straight away that a cut of this kind in the scale of business presupposes different dimensions for the fixed capital, and thus a reduced investment in general. It is questionable, however, whether this reduction can always be made, since the development of production in the various branches of industry sets a normal minimum of capital investment below which the business in question will cease to be competitive. This normal minimum itself grows steadily with the development of capitalist production, and so it is in no way fixed. Between the normal minimum at any time and the normal maximum, which is itself continuously on the increase, there are several intermediate levels – a middle range that permits varying degrees of capital investment. Within the bounds of this middle range, therefore, there can be a reduction in scale, the limits to this being fixed by the normal minimum at the time. In the case of a hold-up of production, over-supply of markets, increase in prices of raw materials, etc., the limitation of the normal outlay of circulation capital in relation to a given basis of fixed capital takes the form of a limitation of working hours, for example only half the day being worked, just as in periods of prosperity there is an abnormal extension of the circulating capital on the given basis of fixed capital – partly by the prolongation of working hours, partly by their intensification. With businesses that have always to reckon with fluctuations of this kind, these are coped with partly by the above means, and partly also by the employment of a larger number of workers, combined with a reserve of fixed capital, e.g. reserve locomotives on the railways, etc. Here we leave such abnormal fluctuations out of account, as we are assuming normal conditions.

For production to be continuous, the same circulating capital must be distributed in this case over a longer period of time, over twelve weeks instead of nine. In any given interval of time, therefore, the productive capital function is reduced; the fluid part of the productive capital is reduced from 100 to 75, i.e. by a quarter. The total sum by which the productive capital functioning during the nine-week working period is reduced is $9 \times 25 = £225$, or a quarter of the £900. But the ratio of the circulation time to the turnover period is also $\frac{3}{12} = \frac{1}{4}$. It follows therefore that if production is not to be interrupted during the circulation time of the productive capital that has been transformed into commodity capital, if it is rather to be continued simultaneously and continuously week by week, and there is no special circulating capital available for this purpose, the goal can only be attained by reducing the scale of the productive operations, by diminishing the fluid component of the functioning productive capital. The portion of fluid capital thus set free for production during the circulation time is related to the total fluid capital advanced as the circulation time is to the turnover period. As already noted, this applies only to branches of production in which the labour process is continued week in, week out on the same scale, and where the amounts of capital that have to be laid out do not vary between the different working periods, as in agriculture.

If, however, we assume the reverse of this, namely that the nature of the investment excludes a reduction in the scale of production and hence also in the fluid capital to be advanced each week, then the continuity of production can be maintained only by an additional fluid capital, in the above case one of £300. During the turnover period of twelve weeks, £1,200 is successively advanced, of which £300 makes a quarter, as does three weeks out of twelve. After the working period of nine weeks, the capital value of £900 is transformed from the form of productive capital into that of commodity capital. Its working period is concluded, and this cannot immediately be repeated with the same capital. During the three weeks for which the capital exists in the circulation sphere, functioning as commodity capital, it is the same for the production process as if it did not exist at all. We are abstracting here from all credit relations, and assume therefore that the capitalist operates only with his own capital. But while the capital advanced for the first working period spends three weeks in the circulation process after completing its production process, an additional capital outlay of £300 now functions, so that the continuity of production is not interrupted.

The following must now be noted in this connection:

Firstly, the working period of the capital of £900 originally advanced is ended after nine weeks, and yet the capital does not return for another three weeks, until the beginning of the thirteenth week. A new working period, however, is immediately opened with the additional capital of £300. This is precisely how the continuity of production is maintained.

Secondly, the functions of the original capital of £900, and of the capital of £300 newly advanced at the close of the first nine-week working period, which opens the second working period without interruption on the close of the first, are completely separate in the first turnover period, or can at least be separated, whereas in the course of the second turnover period they cut across one another.

We can represent the matter more clearly in the following way:

First turnover period of twelve weeks. First nine-week working period; the turnover of the capital advanced in this period is completed by the start of the thirteenth week. During the last three weeks the additional capital of £300 functions, opening the second nine-week working period.

Second turnover period. At the start of the thirteenth week, £900 has returned and is available to begin a new turnover. But the second working period has already opened in the tenth week with the additional £300; by the beginning of the thirteenth week, a third of this working period has been completed by means of this capital, and £300 has been transformed from productive capital into products. Since there are only six weeks more to go till the end of the second working period, only two thirds of the returned capital of £900, i.e. only £600, can enter the production process of the second working period. £300 of the original £900 is set free, to play the same role that the capital of £300 played in the first working period. At the end of the sixth week of the second turnover period, the second working period is concluded. The capital of £900 laid out on it flows back three weeks later, i.e. at the end of the ninth week of the second twelve-week turnover period. During the three weeks of its circulation time the capital of £300 that was set free enters the scene. This begins the third working period of a capital of £900 in the seventh week of the second turnover period, or the nineteenth week of the year.

Third turnover period. The end of the ninth week of the second turnover period brought a new reflux of £900. But the third working period had already begun in the seventh week of this turnover period, and six weeks of this have already elapsed [by the start of the third turnover]. Thus it has only three more weeks to run. Of the £900 that returned, only £300 therefore goes into the production process. The fourth working period comprises the remaining nine weeks of this turnover period, and thus the fourth turnover period and the fifth working period begin together with the thirty-seventh week of the year.

[Second example.] In order to simplify the example for purposes of calculation, we shall assume a working period of five weeks and a circulation time of five weeks, making a turnover period of ten weeks;

fifty weeks to the year; and a capital outlay of £100 per week. Thus the working period requires a fluid capital of £500, and the circulation time of the additional capital a further £500. Working periods and turnover times can now be represented as follows:

Working Period	Weeks	Commodities in £	Returning
1	1–5	500	end of week 10
2	6–10	500	„ „ „ 15
3	11–15	500	„ „ „ 20
4	16–20	500	„ „ „ 25
5	21–25	500	„ „ „ 30
			etc.

If the circulation time was zero, so that the turnover period was the same as the working period, the number of turnovers would simply equal the number of working periods in the year, hence with a five-week working period, $50 \div 5 = 10$; the value of the capital turned over would be $500 \times 10 = £5,000$. In the above table, where a circulation time of five weeks is assumed, a value of £5,000 in commodities is still produced each year, but one tenth of this, i.e. £500, is always in the shape of commodity capital, and returns only after five weeks' delay. At the end of the year, therefore, the product of the tenth working period (weeks 46–50) has only completed half its turnover time, since its circulation time falls into the first five weeks of the ensuing year.

[Third example.] We now take a third example: working period six weeks, circulation time three weeks, weekly advance for the labour process £100.

First working period: weeks 1–6. At the end of the sixth week a commodity capital of £600, returning at the end of week 9.

Second working period: weeks 7–12. £300 additional capital advanced during weeks 7–9. A return of £600 at the end of week 9. £300 of this advanced in weeks 10–12, so that £300 is free at the end of week 12, and £600 present in commodity capital, returning at the end of week 15.

Third working period: weeks 13–18. Advance of the above £300 in weeks 13–15, then return of £600, of which £300 is advanced for weeks 16–18. At the end of week 18, £300 is free in money; £600 is present in commodity capital, and returns at the end of week 21. (For a more detailed presentation of this case see heading 2 below.)

$600 \times 9 = £5,400$ worth of commodities are thus produced in nine working periods ($= 54$ weeks). At the end of the ninth working period, the capitalist has £300 in money, and £600 in commodities which have not yet completed their circulation time.

When we compare these three examples, we find, firstly, that only in the second example do capital 1 of £500 and additional capital II, also £500, successively replace one another, so that the two portions of capital perform their movements separately, and this is simply because the assumption is made that the case is the highly exceptional one in which the working period and the circulation time form two equal halves of the turnover period. In all other cases, no matter what the discrepancy between the two sections of the turnover period may be, the movements of the two capitals intersect, as in the first and third examples, right from the second turnover period onwards. The capital functioning in the second turnover period is then formed by the additional capital II together with a part of capital I, while the remainder of capital I is set free for the original function of capital II. The capital active during the circulation time of the commodity capital is no longer identical with the capital II originally advanced for this purpose, but it is equal to it in value and forms the same aliquot part of the total capital advanced.

Secondly, the capital which has functioned during the working period lies idle during the circulation time. In the second example, the capital functions for a working period of five weeks and is idle for a circulation period of five weeks. Thus the overall time during which capital I is idle amounts to half of every year. However, the additional capital required to maintain the continuity of production during the circulation time is not determined by the total sum of circulation time within the year, but simply by the ratio of circulation time to turnover period. (We assume here of course that all the turnovers take place under the same conditions.) Hence it is an additional capital of £500 that is needed in the second example, and not one of £2,500. This simply follows from the fact that the additional capital enters the turnover just as much as that originally advanced, and so is replaced after a number of turnovers just as the former was.

Thirdly, it in no way alters the circumstances considered here if the production time is longer than the working time. The total turnover period is certainly extended by this factor, but this extended turnover does not require any additional capital for the labour process. The additional capital simply has the job of filling up the gaps in the labour process that are due to the circulation time, and so it has to protect production only from disturbances that arise as a result of this circulation time; disturbances that arise from the specific conditions of production are taken care of in another way, which is not under consideration here. There are however businesses where work is done only spasmodically, to order, and in which there can be interruptions between the working periods for this reason. In such cases the need for additional capital is proportionately reduced. In most types of seasonal work, moreover, there is also a certain limit for the reflux. The same work cannot be repeated the next year with the same capital, if this capital has not meanwhile completed its circulation time. The circulation time may however be less than the interval between one production period and the next. In this case the capital lies idle unless it is applied in the meantime in another manner.

. Fourthly, the capital advanced for one working period, e.g. the £600 in the third example, is laid out partly on raw and ancillary materials, i.e. in a productive stock for the working period, in constant circulating capital, and partly in variable circulating capital, in payment for labour itself. Not all of that part of the capital laid out on constant circulating capital need exist for the same length of time in the form of productive stock; e.g. raw material may not be stored for the whole working period, or coal may be procured every two weeks. None the less, if we again exclude credit here, this part of the capital, in so far as it is not present in the form of a productive stock, must still remain available in the money form, in order to be transformed into productive stock according to need. This in no way alters the value of the constant circulating capital advanced for six weeks. Wages, on the other hand – quite apart from the money for unforeseen expenses, the specific reserve fund to cope with disturbances – are paid at shorter intervals, mostly weekly. So except where the capitalist forces the worker to make particularly long advances of his labour, the capital needed for wages must be present in the money form. When capital returns, therefore, one part must be kept in the form of money for payment of labour, while another part can be transformed into productive stock.

The additional capital is divided up just like the original capital. But what distinguishes it from capital I is that it must already be advanced for the entire duration of the first working period of capital I, which it is not involved in, in order to be available for its own working period (this is again abstracting from credit relations). During this time it can be at least partially transformed already into constant circulating capital. The extent to which it assumes this last form, or else persists in the form of additional money capital until the time that this transformation is necessary, will depend partly on the particular production conditions of the specific lines of business involved, partly on local circumstances, and partly on fluctuations in the price of raw materials, etc. If we consider the total social capital, then a more or less significant part of this additional capital exists for a prolonged time in the state of money capital. As far as the part of capital II advanced for wages is concerned, however, it is only gradually transformed into labour-power, in as much as the working periods that elapse and are paid for are relatively short. This part of capital II is thus present in the form of money capital for the whole duration of the working period, until it is transformed into labour-power and thus embarks on the function of productive capital.

This intervention of the additional capital required for the conversion of capital I's circulation time into production time thus not only increases the size of the capital advanced and the length of time for which the total capital has to be advanced, but it also specifically increases that part of the capital advanced that exists as a money reserve, i.e. exists in the state of money capital and possesses the form of potential money capital.

The same thing occurs (as concerns both an advance of capital in the form of productive stock and that in the form of a money reserve) if the division of the capital into two parts that is required by the circulation time – capital for the first working period and replacement capital for the circulation time – is brought about not by an increase in the capital laid out, but instead by a reduction in the scale of production. In relation to the scale of production, the capital confined to the money form increases here still further.

What is always attained by this division of the capital into original productive capital and additional capital is the uninterrupted succession of working periods, the steady functioning of an equal-sized part of the capital advanced as productive capital.

Let us consider the second example. The capital existing in the production process at any one time is £500. Since the working period is five weeks, this capital operates ten times in every fifty weeks (taken as a year). If we disregard surplus-value, the product therefore amounts to $10 \times 500 = £5,000$. From the standpoint of the capital functioning directly and uninterruptedly in the production process – a capital value of £500 – the circulation time thus appears to have disappeared completely. The turnover period coincides with the working period; the circulation time is assumed to be zero.

But if the capital of £500 were to be regularly inhibited in its productive activity by the circulation time of five weeks, so as to be only ready for production once again after completing the entire turnover period of ten weeks, we should have, in the fifty-week year, five ten-week turnovers; these would include five five-week production periods, i.e. a total of twenty-five weeks' production with a total product of $5 \times 500 =$ £2,500; and five five-week circulation times, i.e. a total circulation time of also twenty-five weeks. If we say in this case that the capital of £500 has turned over five times in the year, then it is perfectly clear that for half of each turnover period this capital of £500 has not functioned as productive capital at all, and that, all things considered, it has functioned only for half the year, and not during the other half.

In our example, the replacement capital of £500 enters the scene for the duration of these five circulation times, and in this way the turnover is raised from £2,500 to £5,000. But the capital advanced is now £1,000 instead of £500. 5,000 divided by 1,000 is 5. Thus instead of ten turnovers we have five. But because it is then said that the capital of £1,000 has turned over five times in the year, the memory of the circulation time vanishes from the empty heads of the capitalists, and the confused idea is formed that this capital has functioned constantly in the production process throughout the five successive turnovers. However, when we say that the capital of £1,000 has turned over five times, we include in this the circulation time as well as the production time. In fact, if £1,000 really had been continuously active in the production process, then the product would have been £10,000, on the basis of our assumptions, instead of £5,000. And in order to have £1,000 continuously in the production process, a capital of £2,000 would have had to be advanced. The economists, who have never produced a clear account of the turnover mechanism, constantly overlook this basic aspect, i.e. the fact that only a part of the industrial capital can be actually engaged in the production process, if production is to proceed without interruption. In other words, one part can function as productive capital only on condition that another part is withdrawn from production proper in the form of commodity or money capital. Since this is overlooked, so also is the importance and role of money capital in general.

What we now have to investigate is the difference in the turnover that arises according to whether the two sections of the turnover period – working period and circulation period – are equal, or whether the working period is longer or shorter than the circulation period; further, how this affects the tying-up of capital in the form of money capital.

We assume here that the capital advanced each week is in all cases £100, and the turnover period nine weeks, so that the capital that has to be advanced for each turnover period is £900.

I. WORKING PERIOD AND CIRCULATION PERIOD EQUAL

This case, though in reality it is only a chance exception, must serve as the starting-point for the discussion, since it is here that conditions are present in their simplest and most palpable form.

The two capitals (capital I, which is advanced for the first working period, and additional capital II, which functions during the circulation period of capital I) relieve one another in their movements without crossing each other's path. With the exception of the first period, therefore, each of the two capitals is advanced only for its own turnover period. If the turnover period is nine weeks, as in the following examples, then the working period and circulation period are accordingly both four and a half weeks. We then have the following schema for a complete year [Table I].

In the fifty-one weeks that we take here as the year, capital I has concluded six full working periods, and thus produced commodities to the value of $6 \times 450 = £2,700$; capital II has produced commodities for five full working periods, $5 \times 450 = £2,250$. Capital II has also produced a further £150 in the final one and a half weeks of the year (midweek 50 to end of week 51) – a total product of £5,100 in fifty-one weeks. As far as the direct production of surplus-value is concerned, and this is produced only during the working period itself, the total capital of £900 has turned over $5\frac{2}{3}$ times ($5\frac{2}{3} \times 900 = 5,100$). But if we consider the real turnover, then capital I has turned over $5\frac{2}{3}$ times, since at the end of week 51 it has only three weeks of its sixth turnover period still to complete: $5\frac{2}{3} \times 450 = £2,550$; while capital II has turned over $5\frac{1}{6}$ times, since it has only completed one and a half weeks of its sixth turnover period, and a further seven and a half weeks of this fall in the coming year: $5\frac{1}{6} \times 450 = £2,325$; real amount turned over $= £4,875$.

We may treat capital I and capital II as two quite independent capitals. In their movements they are completely autonomous; these movements are complementary only in so far as their working and circulation periods directly relieve one another. They can be considered as two completely independent capitals, belonging to different capitalists.

TABLE I¹

Capital I

	Turnover Period (weeks)	Working Period (weeks)	Advance in £	Circulation Period (weeks)
I	1–9	1–first half week 5	450	second half week 5–9
II	10–18	10– ,, ,, 14	450	,, ,, ,, 14–18
III	19–27	19– ,, ,, 23	450	,, ,, ,, 23–27
IV	28–36	28– ,, ,, 32	450	,, ,, ,, 32–36
V	37–45	37– ,, ,, 41	450	,, ,, ,, 41–45
VI	46–(54)	46– ,, ,, 50	450	,, ,, ,, 50–(54)

Capital II

	Turnover Period (weeks)	Working Period (weeks)	Advance in £	Circulation Period (weeks)
I	second half week 5–first half week 14	second half week 5–9	450	10–first half week 14
II	,, 14– ,, ,, 23	,, ,, 14–18	450	19– ,, ,, 23
III	,, 23– ,, ,, 32	,, ,, 23–27	450	28– ,, ,, 32
IV	,, 32– ,, ,, 41	,, ,, 32–36	450	37– ,, ,, 41
V	,, 41– ,, ,, 50	,, ,, 41–45	450	46– ,, ,, 50
VI	,, 50–(,, ,, 59)	,, ,, 50–(54)	450	55–(,, ,, 59)

1. The weeks falling in the second turnover year are put in parentheses. [Despite Engels's adjustments of Marx's figures (see below, pp. 359–60), this Table I remains ambiguous in the German edition, and the presentation here has accordingly been further modified slightly.]

Capital I has gone through five complete turnover periods and two thirds of its sixth. It exists at the end of the year in the form of commodity capital, requiring a further three weeks for its normal realization. It functions as commodity capital and circulates. As far as its last turnover goes, it has completed only two thirds of it. This is expressed by saying that it has turned over only two thirds of a time; only two thirds of its total value has turned over completely. We say that £450 completes its turnover in nine weeks, and therefore £300 does so in six weeks. By expressing it in this way, we leave aside the organic relations between the two specific and different components of the turnover time, since the exact sense of the statement that the capital of £450 advanced has made $5\frac{2}{3}$ turnovers is simply that it has made five turnovers and only completed two thirds of its sixth. Nevertheless, the expression that the capital turned over is $5\frac{2}{3}$ the capital advanced, thus in the above case $5\frac{2}{3} \times 450 = £2,550$, is correct in the sense that, if this capital of £450 were not supplemented by another capital of £450, then one part of it would have to exist in the production process, and another part in the circulation process. If the turnover time is to be expressed in terms of the quantity of capital turned over, it can only ever be expressed in a quantity of existing value (in fact, of finished products). The circumstance that the capital advanced does not exist in a state in which it can reopen the production process once again is expressed in the form that only one part of it exists in a state suitable for production, or that, in order to exist in a state of continuous production, the capital must always be divided into one part that is in the production period and another part in the circulation period, according to the ratio between these two periods. This is the same law as that which determines the mass of productive capital functioning at one time by the ratio of circulation time to turnover time.

Of capital II, at the end of week 51, which we take here as the close of the year, £150 is advanced in the production of unfinished products. A further part exists in the form of fluid constant capital – raw material, etc. – i.e. in a form in which it can function as productive capital in the production process. But a third part exists in the money form, a quantity at least as great as the amount of wages for the remainder of the working period (three weeks), which are paid only at the end of each week. Even though this part of the capital does not exist in the form of productive capital at the beginning of the new year, i.e. of a new turnover cycle, but rather in the form of money capital in which it is incapable of entering the production process, the new turnover nevertheless opens with fluid variable capital, i.e. living labour-power, active in the production process. This phenomenon comes about because although labour-power is bought and used at the beginning of the working period, say weekly, it is paid for only at the end of the week. Here money functions as means of payment. It therefore exists on the one hand as money still in the hands of the capitalist, while on the other hand labour-power, the commodity into which it is converted, is already active in the production process, and thus the same capital value here appears two-fold.

If we consider simply the working periods, then

$$\text{Capital I has produced} \quad 6 \times 450 = \text{£2,700}$$
$$\text{,,} \quad \text{II ,,} \quad \text{,,} \quad 5\tfrac{1}{3} \times 450 = \text{£2,400}$$

$$\text{i.e. together} \quad 5\tfrac{2}{3} \times 900 = \text{£5,100}$$

The money capital of £900 advanced has thus functioned as productive capital $5\tfrac{2}{3}$ times in the year. As far as the production of surplus-value is concerned, it is all the same whether £450 in the production process always functions alternately with £450 in the circulation process, or whether £900 functions for four and a half weeks in the circulation process.

If we consider the turnover periods, on the other hand, then

$$\text{Capital I has turned over} \quad 5\tfrac{2}{3} \times 450 = \text{£2,550}$$
$$\text{,,} \quad \text{II ,,} \quad \text{,,} \quad \text{,,} \quad 5\tfrac{1}{6} \times 450 = \text{£2,325}$$

$$\text{i.e. the total capital turned over is} \quad 5\tfrac{5}{12} \times 900 = \text{£4,875}$$

This is because the turnover of the total capital is equal to the amounts of capitals I and II turned over, divided by the sum of capitals I and II.

It should be noted here that capitals I and II, if they really were independent of one another, would still only form different independent parts of the social capital advanced in the same branch of production. If the social capital in this branch of production consisted *only* of I and II, the same calculation would hold for the turnover of the social capital in this branch as holds here for the two components I and II of the same private capital. Any portion of the total social capital in a particular branch of production can be calculated in this way by extension. Finally, the number of turnovers of the total social capital equals the sum of the capital turned over in the various branches of production, divided by the sum of the capital advanced in these branches.

It should further be noted that, just as here, in the same private business, the two capitals I and II have, in the strict sense, different turnover years (in as much as the turnover cycle of capital II begins four and a half weeks later than that of capital I, and I's year therefore comes to a close four and a half weeks earlier than that of II), so too the various private capitals in the same branch of production begin business at quite different points in time and hence complete their annual turnover at different times of the year. The same average calculation that we applied above to I and II also serves here to reduce the turnover years of the various independent parts of the social capital to a uniform turnover year.

2. WORKING PERIOD LONGER THAN CIRCULATION PERIOD

In this case the working and turnover periods of capitals I and II cut across one another, instead of following on from each other. We also find capital set free, which was not the position in the case considered previously.

This is in no way altered by the fact that now, as previously, (1) the number of working periods of the total capital advanced is equal to the value of the annual product of the two parts of the capital advanced, divided by the total capital advanced, and (2) the number of turnovers of the total capital is equal to the sum of the two amounts turned over, divided by the sum of the two capitals advanced. Here, too, we must consider the two portions of capital as if they performed their turnover movements in complete independence of one another.

*

We assume once again that £100 has to be advanced each week in the labour process. The working period lasts for six weeks, and therefore requires an advance of £600 (capital I). The circulation period is three weeks, and so the turnover period, as above, is nine weeks. A capital II of £300 enters the scene during the three-week circulation period of capital I. If we consider the two as independent capitals, then the annual turnover presents itself according to the following schema [Table II].

The production process proceeds uninterruptedly on the same scale throughout the whole year. Here we have kept the two capitals I and II completely separate. But in order to present them separately in this

TABLE II

Capital I, £600

	Turnover Period (weeks)	Working Period (weeks)	Advance in £	Circulation Period (weeks)
I	1–9	1–6	600	7–9
II	10–18	10–15	600	16–18
III	19–27	19–24	600	25–27
IV	28–36	28–33	600	34–36
V	37–45	37–42	600	43–45
VI	46–(54)	46–51	600	(52–54)

Additional Capital II, £300

	Turnover Period (weeks)	Working Period (weeks)	Advance in £	Circulation Period (weeks)
I	7–15	7–9	300	10–15
II	16–24	16–18	300	19–24
III	25–33	25–27	300	28–33
IV	34–42	34–36	300	37–42
V	43–51	43–45	300	46–51

way, we have had to cut through their actual intersections and entanglements. According to the above table, for instance, the amounts turned over would be:

$$\text{capital I} \quad 5\tfrac{2}{3} \times 600 = £3,400$$
$$\text{capital II} \quad 5 \times 300 = £1,500$$

for the total capital, $5\tfrac{4}{9} \times 900 = £4,900$

This is not correct, however, since, as we shall see, the actual production and circulation periods do not entirely coincide with those in the above table, in which the important thing was to exhibit the two capitals I and II in complete independence from one another.

In reality, for instance, capital II does not have working and circulation periods separate from those of capital I. The working period is six weeks, the circulation period three weeks. Since capital II is only £300, it can serve for only part of a working period. This is in fact the case. At the end of week 6, a product to the value of £600 steps out into circulation, and at the end of week 9 this value returns in money. Capital II thus moves into action at the beginning of week 7, and covers the needs of the next working period for weeks 7–9. According to our assumption, however, the working period is only half finished by the end of week 9. The capital I of £600 that has just returned therefore moves into action once more, and £300 of it meets the advance needed for weeks 10–12. The second working period is thus taken care of. A product to the value of £600 is in circulation and will return at the end of week 15; on top of this, however, £300, the amount of the original capital II, is set free and can function in the first half of the following working period, i.e. weeks 13–15. After this has elapsed, the £600 then returns once again; £300 of it suffices until the close of the working period, while £300 remains free for the following period.

The matter now stands as follows:

Turnover period I: weeks 1–9

First working period: weeks 1–6. Capital I of £600 functions.

First circulation period: weeks 7–9. At the end of week 9, £600 returns.

Turnover period II: weeks 7–15

Second working period: weeks 7–12.

first half: weeks 7–9. Capital II of £300 functions. At the end of week 9, £600 returns in money (capital I).

second half: weeks 10–12. £300 of capital I functions. The other £300 of capital I remains free.

Second circulation period: weeks 13–15.

At the end of week 15, £600 returns in money (formed half from capital I, half from capital II).

Turnover period III: weeks 13–21

Third working period: weeks 13–18.

first half: weeks 13–15. The £300 set free begins to function. At the end of week 15, £600 returns in money.

second half: weeks 16–18. Of the £600 that has returned, £300 functions, the other £300 again remains free.

Third circulation period: weeks 19–21. At its close, £600 again returns in money; in this £600, capital I and capital II have now merged indistinguishably together.

In this way we have eight full turnover periods of a capital of £600 up till the end of the fifty-first week (I: weeks 1–9; II: 7–15; III: 13–21; IV: 19–27; V: 25–33; VI: 31–39; VII: 37–45; VIII: 43–51). But since weeks 49–51 fall in the eighth circulation period, the £300 of capital set free must enter production and keep it going during this time. The turnover thus presents itself as follows at the end of the year: £600 has completed its circuit eight times, making £4,800 turned over. On top of this there is the product of the final three weeks (49–51), but this has accomplished only a third of its nine-week circuit, and thus counts only for a third of its total amount, i.e. £100, in the sum turned over. So if the annual product of fifty-one weeks is £5,100, the capital turned over is only 4,800+100 = £4,900; the total capital advanced was £900, and this has therefore turned over 5⅘ times, i.e. slightly less than in case I.

In the present example, we assumed a case in which the working time was two thirds of the turnover period, and the circulation time one third, i.e. the working time was a simple multiple of the circulation time. The question arises whether the setting-free of capital noted above also occurs when this is not the case.

Let us take a working period of five weeks and a circulation time of four weeks, with a capital advance of £100 per week.

Turnover period I: weeks 1–9

First working period: weeks 1–5. Capital I of £500 functions.

First circulation period: weeks 6–9. At the end of week 9, £500 returns in money.

Turnover period II: weeks 6–14

Second working period: weeks 6–10.

first section: weeks 6–9. Capital II of £400 functions. At the end of week 9, capital I of £500 returns in money.

second section: week 10. £100 out of the returned £500 functions. The remaining £400 stays free for the following working period.

Second circulation period: weeks 11–14. At the end of week 14, £500 returns in money.

Up till the end of week 14 (weeks 11–14), the £400 that has been set free functions; £100 of the £500 that has then returned meets the remaining needs of the third working period (weeks 11–15), so that a further £400 is set free for the fourth working period. The same phenomenon is repeated in each working period. At its beginning, there is £400 available, which suffices for the first four weeks. At the end of the fourth week, £500 returns in money, and only £100 of this is needed for the final week, the remaining £400 being free until the next working period.

Let us now take a working period of seven weeks, with capital I of £700, and a circulation time of two weeks with capital II of £200.

The first turnover period then lasts from week 1 to week 9, and out of this period the first working period comprises weeks 1–7, with an advance of £700, while the first circulation period comprises weeks 8–9. At the end of the ninth week, the £700 returns in money.

The second turnover period, weeks 8–16, includes the second working period of weeks 8–14. The needs of weeks 8 and 9 are met by capital II. At the end of the ninth week, the above £700 returns; £500 of this is used up by the end of the working period (weeks 10–14). There remains £200, which is set free for the next working period. The second circulation period covers weeks 15–16; at the end of week 16, a further £700 returns. The same phenomenon is now repeated in each working period. The capital needs of the first two weeks are met by the £200 set free at the close of the previous working period; at the end of the second week, £700 returns, but the working period now has only a further five weeks to run, so that only £500 can be used, and there is always £200 set free for the next working period.

It emerges, therefore, that in our present example, where the working period is taken as greater than the circulation period, there is always set free at the close of each working period, under all circumstances, a money capital of the same magnitude as the capital II, which was advanced for the circulation period. In our three examples, capital II was £300 in the first, £400 in the second and £200 in the third, and the capital set free at the close of the working period was accordingly £300, £400 and £200.

3. WORKING PERIOD SHORTER THAN CIRCULATION PERIOD

We again start with a turnover period of nine weeks; the working period is now three weeks, the capital I required for this being £300. The circulation period is six weeks. For these six weeks an additional capital of £600 is needed, which we can however divide up again into two capitals of £300, each of these catering for one working period. We then have three capitals of £300 each, with £300 always occupied in production, while £600 circulates [Table III].

Here we have the exact counterpart of case I, with the simple distinction that three capitals now relieve one another instead of two. There is no intersection or entanglement between the capitals; each individual capital can be separately traced right through to the end of the year. Just as little as in case I, therefore, is any capital set free at the close of a working period. Capital I is completely laid out by the end of week 3,

TABLE III

Capital I

	Turnover Period (weeks)	Working Period (weeks)	Circulation Period (weeks)
I	1–9	1–3	4–9
II	10–18	10–12	13–18
III	19–27	19–21	22–27
IV	28–36	28–30	31–36
V	37–45	37–39	40–45
VI	46–(54)	46–48	49–(54)

Capital II

	Turnover Period (weeks)	Working Period (weeks)	Circulation Period (weeks)
I	4–12	4–6	7–12
II	13–21	13–15	16–21
III	22–30	22–24	25–30
IV	31–39	31–33	34–39
V	40–48	40–42	43–48
VI	49–(57)	49–51	(52–57)

Capital III

	Turnover Period (weeks)	Working Period (weeks)	Circulation Period (weeks)
I	7–15	7–9	10–15
II	16–24	16–18	19–24
III	25–33	25–27	28–33
IV	34–42	34–36	37–42
V	43–51	43–45	46–51

completely returns at the end of week 9, and begins to function again at the start of week 10. Similarly with capitals II and III. The even and complete replacement of the capitals excludes the setting free of any part of them.

The overall turnover is calculated as follows:

$$\text{turned over by capital} \quad \text{I} \quad £300 \times 5\tfrac{2}{3} = £1,700$$
$$\text{,,} \quad \text{,,} \quad \text{,,} \quad \text{,,} \quad \text{II} \quad £300 \times 5\tfrac{1}{3} = £1,600$$
$$\text{,,} \quad \text{,,} \quad \text{,,} \quad \text{,,} \quad \text{III} \quad £300 \times 5 = £1,500$$

$$\text{turned over by the total capital} \quad £900 \times 5\tfrac{1}{3} = £4,800$$

We shall now take an example in which the circulation period is not an exact multiple of the working period, i.e. a working period of four weeks, a circulation period of five weeks. The corresponding sums of capital are thus capital I = £400, capital II — £400, capital III — £100. The table only gives the first three turnovers.

TABLE IV

Capital I

	Turnover Period (weeks)	Working Period (weeks)	Circulation Period (weeks)
I	1–9	1–4	5–9
II	9–17	9, 10–12	13–17
III	17–25	17, 18–20	21–25

Capital II

	Turnover Period (weeks)	Working Period (weeks)	Circulation Period (weeks)
I	5–13	5–8	9–13
II	13–21	13, 14–16	17–21
III	21–29	21, 22–24	25–29

Capital III

	Turnover Period (weeks)	Working Period (weeks)	Circulation Period (weeks)
I	9–17	9	10–17
II	17–25	17	18–25
III	25–33	25	26–33

Here the capitals are intertwined in so far as the working period of capital III, which does not have an independent working period of its own, since it is sufficient only for one week, coincides with the first working week of capital I. For this reason, however, a capital of £100, equal to capital III, is set free at the close of the working periods of both capitals I and II. If, for instance, capital III serves for the first week of the second and all subsequent working periods of capital I, and at the close of this first week the entire capital I of £400 returns, then the remainder of the working period of capital I amounts only to three weeks, and the corresponding capital outlay is £300. The £100 set free in this way then suffices for the first week of the directly following working period of capital II; at the close of this week the entire capital II of £400 returns; but since the working period which is in progress can absorb only £300, there remains at its close, once again, £100 set free;

and so on. Capital is thus set free at the close of the working period whenever the circulation time is not a simple multiple of the working period; and this capital that is set free is moreover equal to the portion of capital which has to fill in for the excess of the circulation period over a working period or over a number of working periods.

It has been assumed in all the cases investigated that both working time and circulation time remain the same throughout the year in the business under consideration, whatever it may be. This assumption was necessary, if we wished to establish the influence of the circulation time on the turnover and on the capital advanced. It is beside the point here that this is not unconditionally the case in reality, and often not at all so.

In this whole Part, we are considering only the turnovers of circulating capital, and not those of fixed capital. This is for the simple reason that the matter under consideration does not involve the fixed capital. The means of labour, etc. that are applied in the production process only form fixed capital to the extent that the time during which they are in use extends longer than the turnover period of the fluid capital; in so far as the time during which these means of labour endure and serve for constantly repeated labour processes is greater than the turnover period of the fluid capital, i.e. covers a number – n – of turnover periods of this fluid capital. Whether the overall interval which is formed by these n turnover periods of the fluid capital is longer or shorter, the part of the productive capital that is advanced for this time in the form of fixed capital is not advanced again within the same interval. It goes on functioning in its old use form. The difference is simply that, according to the differing length of the individual *working period* in each turnover period of the fluid capital, the fixed capital surrenders a greater or smaller part of its original value to the product of this working period, and, according to the duration of the circulation time in each turnover period, this portion of the value of the fixed capital that is given up to the product returns more quickly or more slowly in the money form. The nature of the object of investigation in this Part – the turnover of the circulating part of the productive capital – arises from the nature of this portion of the capital itself. The fluid capital applied in one working period cannot be applied in a new working period before it has completed its turnover, i.e. has been transformed into commodity capital, from the latter into money capital, and then back again into productive capital. In order to follow the first working period directly with a second, therefore, new capital must be advanced, and in sufficient quantity to fill the gaps that arise as a result of the circulating period of the fluid capital that is advanced for the first working period. Hence the influence of the length of the working period of the fluid capital on the scale of the labour process and on the division of the capital advanced, or on the addition of new portions of capital. This however is precisely what we are considering in this Part.

4. RESULTS

The above investigation leads to the following results:

A. The various portions in which the capital has to be divided, so that one part of it can always be in its working period while other parts are in their circulation period, relieve each other, like independent private capitals, in two cases: (1) If the working period is equal to the circulation period, and the turnover period is thus divided into two equal sections; (2) if the circulation period is longer than the working period, but is a simple multiple of it, so that 1 circulation period $= n$ working periods, where n must be a whole number. In these cases, no part of the capital successively advanced is set free.

B. However, in all cases where (1) the circulation period is greater than the working period, without forming a simple multiple of it, or (2) the working period is greater than the circulation period, a part of the overall fluid capital is always periodically set free at the close of each working period. This capital that is set free, moreover, is equal to the portion of the total capital that is advanced for the circulation period, if the working period is greater than the circulation period; and equal to the portion of capital which has to stand in for the excess of the circulation period over a working period or a whole number of working periods, if the circulation period is greater than the working period.

C. It follows from this that as far as the total social capital is concerned, considering the fluid part of this, the setting-free of capital is the rule, while the simple mutual replacement of portions of capital functioning successively in the production process must form the exception. For the equality of working period and circulation period, or the equality of circulation period and a whole number of working periods, in other words a regular proportion between the two components of the turnover period, has nothing at all to do with the nature of the case, and can therefore occur, by and large, only exceptionally.

A very significant portion of the social circulating capital, which is turned over several times in the year, will thus periodically exist in the course of the annual turnover cycle in the form of capital set free.

It is also evident that, assuming that all other circumstances remain the same, the magnitude of this capital set free will grow with the extent of the labour process or the scale of production, and thus with the development of capitalist production in general. In case B (2), simply because the overall capital advanced grows; in B (1), [for the same reason, and] because the length of the circulation period also grows with the development of capitalist production, while the circulation period is not a simple multiple of the working period.

In the first case, for example, there was £100 to be laid out each week. This made £600 for a six-week working period, and £300 for a three-week circulation period, making a total of £900. Here, £300 was always set free. If however £300 was laid out each week, then this would make £1,800 for the working period and £900 for the circulation period; and so £900 would be periodically set free instead of £300.

D. The total capital of e.g. £900 must be divided up into two portions, in the above case £600 for the working period, and £300 for the circulation period. The portion that is actually laid out in the labour process will therefore diminish by a third, from £900 to £600, and hence the scale of production will also be reduced by a third. The £300, on the other hand, only functions to make the working period continuous, so that in each week of the year £100 can be laid out in the labour process.

Taken abstractly, it is all the same whether £600 operates for $6 \times 8 = 48$ weeks (product = £4,800), or whether the entire capital of £900 is laid out for six weeks in the labour process and then lies idle for a circulation period of three weeks; in the latter case it would operate for thirty-two weeks ($=5\frac{1}{3} \times 6$) out of a total of forty-eight (product = $5\frac{1}{3} \times 900$ = £4,800), and lie idle for sixteen weeks. But apart from the greater waste of fixed capital during the idle period of sixteen weeks, and the increased cost of labour, which has to be paid for the whole year even if only a part of this is worked, a regular interruption of this kind in the production process would be incompatible with the running of modern large-scale industry. Continuity is itself a productive force of labour.

If we now look more closely at the capital that is set free, or in actual fact suspended, it is clear that a significant part of this must always possess the form of money capital. Let us stick to the example of the working period of six weeks and the circulation period of three weeks, weekly outlay £100. In the middle of the second working period, at the end of week 9, £600 returns, of which only £300 has to be laid out dur-

ing the remainder of the working period. At the end of the second working period, therefore, £300 of this is set free. In what state does this
£300 now exist? We shall assume that one third of it is laid out on
wages, and two thirds on raw and ancillary materials. Of the £600 that
has returned, £200 thus exists in the money form for wages, and £400
in the form of a productive stock, i.c. as elements of the constant
circulating productive capital. But since only half of this productive
stock is required for the second half of working period II, the other half
exists for three weeks in the form of surplus productive stock, i.e.
surplus to the needs of one working period. The capitalist, however,
knows that, out of the portion of capital that has returned to him (£400),
he needs only one half for the current working period. It will therefore
depend on the market conditions whether he immediately transforms
this £200 completely or partially back into surplus productive stock,
or hangs onto it wholly or partly as money capital, in the expectation
of more favourable market conditions. It is self-evident, on the other
hand, that the part to be laid out on wages (£200) is kept in the money
form. The capitalist cannot dispose of labour-power, once he has
bought it, as he can the raw material in his storeroom. He has to incorporate it into the production process and pay for it at the end of the
week. Of the capital of £300 that has been set free, therefore, this £100
will in any case possess the form of money capital that has been set
free, i.e. is not needed for the working period. The capital set free in the
form of money capital must therefore at least be equal to the variable
portion of the capital, that laid out on wages; at the maximum, it can
include the whole of the capital set free. In reality, it constantly fluctu-
ates between the minimum and the maximum.

This money capital that is set free simply by the mechanism of the
turnover movement (together with the money capital set free by the
successive reflux of the fixed capital and that needed for variable capital
in every labour process) must play a significant role, as soon as the
credit system has developed, and must also form one of the foundations
for this.

Let us assume in our example that the circulation time is cut from
three weeks to two. This is not a normal occurrence, but may be an
effect of a good period for business, shortened terms of payment, etc.
The capital of £600 that was laid out during the working period returns
one week earlier than needed, and is therefore set free for this week.
£300 (part of that £600) is again set free, as before, in the middle of the
working period, but for four weeks now instead of three. Hence £600

exists on the money market for one week, and £300 for four weeks instead of three. Since this does not just affect one single capitalist, but rather several, and occurs at different periods in different branches of industry, a greater quantity of disposable money capital is thereby brought onto the market. If this state of affairs lasts a long time, production will be expanded, where circumstances permit; capitalists who operate with borrowed capital will exert less demand on the money market, which relieves it as much as does increased supply; alternatively the sums that have become superfluous for the turnover mechanism will eventually be definitively thrown out onto the money market.

As a result of the contraction of the circulation time from three to two weeks, and hence of the turnover period from nine weeks to eight, one ninth of the total capital advanced becomes superfluous; the six-week working period can now be kept going just as steadily with £800 as it could before with £900. A portion of the commodity capital, £100, therefore, once it is turned back into money, persists in this state as money capital, and no longer functions as a part of the capital advanced for the production process. While production is continued on the same scale and with conditions such as prices, etc. remaining otherwise the same, the value of the capital advanced declines from £900 to £800; the remaining £100 of the value originally advanced is precipitated out in the form of money capital. As such it enters the money market and forms an additional part of the capital functioning there.

We can see from this how a surfeit of money capital can arise – and not only in the sense that the supply of money capital is greater than the demand for it; the latter is never more than a relative surplus, which is found for instance in the depressed period that opens the new business cycle after the crisis is over. It is rather in the sense that a definite part of the capital advanced is superfluous for the overall process of social reproduction (which includes the circulation process), and is therefore precipitated out in the form of money capital; it is thus a surplus which has arisen with the scale of production and prices remaining the same, simply by a contraction in the turnover period. The mass of money in circulation, whether this is larger or smaller, does not have the slightest influence on this.

Let us assume, inversely, that the circulation period is extended, say from three weeks to five. Then, when the next turnover takes place, the reflux of the capital advanced is already two weeks too late. The last part of the production process of this working period cannot be completed simply through the turnover mechanism of the capital originally advanced. If the situation continues for much longer, there will be a contraction of the production process (i.e. a reduction of the scale on which it is conducted), just as in the previous case there was an expansion. In order to continue the process on the same scale, the capital advanced would have to be increased by $\frac{2}{9}$ (=£200) for the entire duration, to cope with this prolongation of the circulation period. This additional capital can be obtained only from the money market. If the prolongation of the circulation period affects one or more major lines of business, then it may exert pressure on the money market, if this effect is not cancelled out by a counter-effect from another direction. In this case too, it is manifestly evident that this pressure, just like the surplus in the previous case, has nothing to do with a change either in the prices of commodities or in the quantity of the available means of circulation.

(The preparation of this chapter for publication has involved no small difficulties. Despite Marx's firm grasp of algebra, he was never at ease in reckoning with figures, i.e. in commercial calculations, even though there is a thick sheaf of notebooks in which he worked through all the various kinds of commercial calculation in several examples. But knowledge of the proper rules of calculation is not at all the same thing as exercise in the everyday practical calculations of the trader, and in his turnover calculations Marx became confused, with the result that, apart from being incomplete, they contain many errors and contradictions. In the tables reproduced above I have retained only the simplest and the arithmetically correct calculations, mainly for the following reason.

The uncertain results of this tiresome calculation business led Marx to ascribe an undeserved significance to what in my opinion is in fact a matter of little importance. I refer to what he calls the 'setting-free' of money capital. The real question involved, on the assumptions made above, is this:

No matter what the ratio between the length of the working period and the circulation time may be, and thus between capital I and capital II, once the first turnover has occurred there returns to the capitalist, at regular intervals equal in length to the working period, the capital needed for one such working period – thus a sum equal to capital I.

If the working period is five weeks, the circulation time four weeks, and capital I £500, then a sum of £500 flows back each time, at the end of weeks 9, 14, 19, 24, etc.

If the working period is six weeks, the circulation time three weeks, and capital I £600, then £600 flows back at the end of weeks 9, 15, 21, 27, 33, etc.

Finally, if the working period is four weeks, the circulation time five weeks, capital I £400, then the reflux of £400 follows at the end of weeks 9, 13, 17, 21, 25, etc.

Whether and to what degree this capital that has returned is super-fluous for the current working period, and is thus set free, makes no difference. It is assumed that production proceeds uninterruptedly on the existing scale, and, for this to occur, money must be present, and thus flow back, whether it is 'set free' or not. If production is inter-rupted, then this setting-free comes to an end.

In other words, there is in any case a release of money, i.e. a formation of latent, only potential capital, in the money form; but this happens in all circumstances, and not only under those particular conditions specified in the text; it happens, moreover, to a greater extent than that assumed in the text. In relation to circulating capital I, the industrial capitalist finds himself, at the end of each turnover, in precisely the same situation as when he set up his business; he has this capital completely in his hands once more, and at one go, while he can only gradually transform it again into productive capital.

The main thing in the text is the proof that a considerable part of in-dustrial capital is always present in the money form, while a still more considerable part must assume this form from time to time. This proof is reinforced, if anything, by these additional remarks of mine. – F.E.)

5. EFFECT OF CHANGES IN PRICE

We have so far assumed that prices and the scale of production stay the same, while there is a contraction or expansion in the circulation time. Let us now assume, by way of contrast, a constant turnover period and a constant scale of production, but a change in price, i.e. a fall or rise in the price of raw materials, ancillaries and labour, or of the first two of these elements. Let us say that the price of raw materials and ancillaries falls by a half. In our example, only £50 would then be needed each week instead of £100, and £450 for the nine-week turnover period in-stead of £900. £450 of the capital value advanced will at first be preci-pitated out as money capital, but the production process will be con-tinued on the same scale, with the same turnover period and the same division within this. The annual product will remain the same in volume, but its value will fall by one half. It is neither an accelerated circulation that has led to this, nor a change in the quantity of money in circulation, but it is still accompanied by a change in the supply of and demand for money capital. The converse is also true. The initial effect of a fall of a half in the value or price of the elements of productive capital would be that the capital value that has to be advanced for business *X*, continued on the same scale as before, would be reduced by a half, and so business *X* would also have to cast only half as much money into the market, since it is in the form of money, i.e. as money capital, that business *X* originally advances this capital value. The quantity of money cast into circulation would decline, because the price of the elements of production had fallen. This would be the first effect.

Secondly, however, half of the capital value of £900 originally advanced, i.e. £450, which either (a) alternately passed through the forms of money capital, productive capital and commodity capital, or (b) existed simultaneously and contiguously partly in the form of money capital, partly as productive capital and partly as commodity capital, would be precipitated out from the circuit of business *X* and would therefore enter the money market as additional money capital, and function there as an additional component. This £450 set free in money functions as money capital not because it is money that has become superfluous for the conduct of business *X*, but rather because it is a component of the original capital value, hence continues to operate as capital and is not spent as a mere means of circulation. The most direct form in which it can be made to operate as capital is if it is placed on the money market as money capital. Alternatively, the scale of production could be doubled (ignoring the fixed capital). A production process of double the scale could then be conducted with the same capital advance of £900.

If the prices of the fluid elements of the productive capital were to rise by a half, on the other hand, so that, instead of £100 a week, £150 was necessary, and thus £1,350 instead of £900, then £450 of additional capital would be needed in order to carry on business on the same scale, and this would exert a proportionate pressure on the money market, greater or less according to its condition. If all capital available on it was already taken up, then there would be increased competition for available capital. If a part of it lay idle, then it would be proportionately called into action.

But there can also be a third case, when, with a given scale of production, given velocity of turnover and given prices of the elements of fluid productive capital, the price of the products of business X falls or rises. If the price of the commodities supplied by business X falls, then the price of its commodity capital of £600, which it is constantly casting into circulation, sinks to £500, for example. Thus a sixth of the value of the capital advanced does not return from the circulation process (the surplus-value concealed in the commodity capital is left out of consideration here); it is lost in it. But since the value or price of the elements of production remains the same, this reflux of £500 is only sufficient to replace five sixths of the capital of £600 engaged in the production process. £100 of additional money capital must be advanced, therefore, if production is to be continued on the same scale.

Conversely, if the price of the products of business X rose, then the price of the commodity capital would rise from £600 to, say, £700. A seventh of its price, £100, does not derive from the production process, was not advanced to it, but rather flows in from the circulation process. But still only £600 is needed to replace the productive elements, and so £100 is set free.

The reason why in the first case the turnover period is reduced or prolonged, and in the second case the prices of raw materials and labour, in the third case the prices of the products supplied, rise or fall, does not belong within the orbit of our investigation so far.

What does belong here, however, is this:

Case I. Scale of production remaining the same, constant prices of elements of production and products; change in the period of circulation and hence in the turnover period.

On the assumptions of our example, one ninth less total capital is needed as a result of the reduction in the circulation period, so that this capital is reduced from £900 to £800, and £100 in money capital is precipitated out.

Business X continues to supply the same six-weekly product with the same value of £600, and, since work continues uninterruptedly throughout the year, it turns out in fifty-one weeks the same quantity of products, with a value of £5,100. Thus as far as the quantity and price of the product that the business casts into circulation is concerned, no change takes place, and so neither is there a change in the terms on which it is put on the market. But £100 is precipitated, since by reducing the circulation period the process can be completed with a capital advance of £800, instead of £900 as previously. The £100 of capital that has been precipitated exists in the form of money capital. But this is in no way the same part of the capital advanced that always had to function in the form of money capital. Let us suppose that, of the fluid capital I = £600 that was advanced, four fifths was always laid out on materials of production, making £480, and $\frac{1}{5}$ = £120 on wages. Capital II = £300 must therefore be similarly divided into $\frac{4}{5}$ = £240 for material elements of production and $\frac{1}{5}$ = £60 for wages. The capital laid out on wages must always be advanced in the money form. As soon as the commodity product, to the sum of £600, has been transformed back into the money form, has been sold, £480 of it can be transformed into material elements of production (into a productive stock), but £120 maintains its money form, to serve for six weeks' payment of wages. This £120 is the minimum part of the returned capital of £600 which must always be replaced and renewed in the form of money capital, and hence must always be present as a part of the capital advanced which functions in the money form.

Now if, of the £300 that is periodically set free for three weeks, and is also divisible into a productive stock of £240 and wages of £60, £100 is precipitated out in the form of money capital as a result of the reduced circulation time, being completely withdrawn from the turnover mechanism, the question arises: where does the money for this £100 money capital come from? Only a fifth part of it consists of the money capital periodically set free within the turnovers. The remaining $\frac{4}{5}$, =£80, has already been replaced by additional productive stock of the same value. By what means is this additional productive stock transformed into money, and where does the money for this conversion come from?

If the reduction in the circulation time has already taken place, then only £400 out of the above £600, instead of £480, is transformed back into a production stock. The remaining £80 is kept in its money form and composes, together with the above £20 for wages, the £100 of capital precipitated. Even though this £100 is derived from the circulation sphere by the sale of the £600 commodity capital, and is now withdrawn from this, in so far as it is not laid out again on wages and materials of production, it should not be forgotten that, in the money form, it is once more in the same form as that in which it was originally cast into circulation. At the beginning, £900 in money was laid out on production stock and wages. In order to keep the same production process going, only £800 is now needed. The £100 thus precipitated out in the money form now constitutes a new money capital seeking investment, a new element on the money market. Certainly, it already existed periodically in the form of money capital set free, and in the form of superfluous productive capital, but these latent states were themselves conditions for the accomplishment of the process, as preconditions of its continuity. Now they are no longer needed, and therefore form new money capital and a component of the money market, even though they are in no way either a superfluous element of the existing social money stock (since they existed at the start of the business and were cast into circulation by it) or a newly accumulated hoard.

This £100 now really is withdrawn from circulation, in as much as it is a part of the money capital advanced that is no longer applied in the same business. But this withdrawal is only possible because the transformation of commodity capital into money and of this money into productive capital, $C'-M-C$, has been accelerated by a week, so that the circulation of the money engaged in this process is also similarly accelerated. It has been withdrawn from circulation because it is no longer needed for the turnover of capital X.

It is assumed here that the capital advanced belongs to the person who uses it. It would however in no way change things if it were borrowed. With the reduction in the circulation time, only £800 of borrowed capital would be needed instead of £900. If £100 were repaid to its lender, this would once again form additional money capital, only it would be in Y's hands instead of X's. Furthermore, if capitalist X receives his material elements of production, to the value of £480, on credit, so that all he has to advance himself in money is £120 for wages, he would now have to obtain on credit an amount of the material elements of production to the value of £80 less, which is therefore so much additional commodity capital for the credit-giving capitalist, while capitalist X has also precipitated out £20 in money.

The additional production stock is now reduced by one third. It was previously £240, four fifths of £300, the additional capital II; it is now only £160, i.e. additional stock for two weeks instead of three. It is now replaced every two weeks instead of every three, but this is stock only for two weeks instead of for three. Purchases, on the cotton market, for instance, are repeated more frequently and in smaller quantities. The same amount of cotton is withdrawn from the market, since the quantity produced remains the same. But the withdrawal is differently distributed in time, and over a longer period. Let us assume, for instance, that there was originally a renewal of the production stock every three months and a subsequent reduction of the renewal time to two months; the annual consumption of cotton is 1200 bales. In the first case, sales were as follows:

1 January	300 bales, leaving 900 bales in the warehouse
1 April	300 ,,	,,	600 ,,	,, ,,	,,
1 July	300 ,,	,,	300 ,,	,, ,,	,,
1 October	300 ,,	,,	— ,,	,, ,,	,,

In the second case, on the other hand, we have:

1 January	200 bales sold, leaving 1,000 in the warehouse
1 March	200 ,,	,,	,,	800 ,,	,,	,,
1 May	200 ,,	,,	,,	600 ,,	,,	,,
1 July	200 ,,	,,	,,	400 ,,	,,	,,
1 September	200 ,,	,,	,,	200 ,,	,,	,,
1 November	200 ,,	,,	,,	— ,,	,,	,,

The money invested in cotton, therefore, only completes its return one month later, in November instead of in October. Thus if, as a result of the reduction in the circulation time, and hence in the turnover, one ninth of the capital advanced, i.e. £100, is precipitated out in the form of money capital, and this £100 is composed of £20 that was a periodic excess money capital for the payment of wages, and £80 that previously existed as a periodic excess production stock for one week, then, corresponding to this £80 reduction in the surplus production stock on the part of the manufacturer, there will be an increased commodity stock in the hands of the cotton broker. The same cotton lies as much longer in the broker's warehouse as a commodity, as it exists for a shorter time as a production stock in the stores of the manufacturer.

We previously assumed that the reduction in circulation time in X's business depended on X selling his commodity more quickly, or else being paid for it more quickly, i.e. on a reduction in the length of credit. Such a reduction is based on reducing the time for the sale of the commodity, i.e. for the transformation of commodity capital into money capital, $C'-M$, the first phase of the circulation process. It could also arise, however, from the second phase $M-C$, i.e. from a simultaneous alteration either in the working period or in the circulation time of capitals Y, Z, etc., which supply capitalist X with the elements of production of his fluid capital.

If cotton, coal, etc., for instance, took three weeks with the old means of transport to travel from their place of production or their depot to the site of capitalist X's place of production, then the minimum productive stock that X had to hold pending the arrival of new stocks had to be sufficient for at least three weeks. As long as cotton and coal are in transit, they cannot serve as means of production. They form instead the object of labour for the transport industry and the capital employed in it, and commodity capital in circulation for the coal producer or the cotton broker. Now let improved means of transport reduce the journey to two weeks. The production stock can then be transformed from a three-week supply to one of two weeks. An additional capital of £80 that was advanced is now set free, and so is £20 for wages, because the capital of £600 completes its turnover and returns one week sooner.

If on the other hand the working period of the capital that supplies the raw material is reduced (as in the examples given in the previous chapters), then it also becomes possible to replace the raw material in less time. This then permits a reduction in the productive stock, and a shortening in the time between one replacement period and the next.

If, inversely, the circulation time and hence the turnover period is prolonged, an advance of additional capital is needed. This comes from the pockets of the capitalist himself, if he possesses extra capital. But this will have been invested in some form or other as part of the money market; in order to make it available, it must be prised out from its old form, e.g. shares sold, deposits withdrawn, so that here too there is an indirect effect on the money market. Alternatively, the capitalist has to raise the capital. As far as the part of the capital needed for wages is concerned, in normal circumstances this is always advanced as money capital, and to this extent capitalist X exerts his share of direct pressure on the money market. For the part to be invested in raw materials etc., this is only indispensable if he has to pay cash. If he can get it on credit, then he does not exert a direct influence on the money market, as the additional capital is then advanced directly as a productive stock, and not in the first instance as money capital. In so far as his creditor directly puts the bill received from X back into the money market, has it discounted, etc., this has an indirect, second-hand effect on the money market. But if he uses this bill to meet a debt that he has later to settle, then this additionally advanced capital has neither a direct nor an indirect effect on the money market.

Case II. Change in price of the materials of production, all other circumstances being unchanged

We have just assumed that, of the total capital of £900, $\frac{4}{5}$ = £720 is laid out on material elements of production, and $\frac{1}{5}$ = £180 on wages.

If the price of raw materials etc. falls by half, then these require only £240 for the six-week working period, instead of £480, and only £120 in additional capital II, instead of £240. Capital I is now reduced from £600 to 240+120 = £360, and capital II from £300 to 120+60 = £180. The total capital of £900 is reduced to 360+180 = £540. £360 is thus precipitated.

This precipitated money capital, which is now unoccupied and is therefore seeking investment on the money market, is simply a fragment of the capital of £900 originally advanced as money capital which has now become superfluous owing to the fall in price of the elements of production into which it is periodically transformed; that is if the business is not expanded, but rather continued on the old scale. If this fall in price was not due to accidental circumstances (a particularly good harvest, over-supply, etc.), but to an increased productivity in the branch of industry that supplies the raw material, then the unoccupied money capital would be an absolute addition to the money market, an absolute addition to the capital available in the form of money capital, because it has ceased to form an integral component of the capital already invested.

Case III. Change in the market price of the product itself

In the case of a fall in price, a part of the capital is lost and has therefore to be replaced by a new advance of money capital. This loss for the seller may be recouped by the buyer. Directly, if the market price of the product has been affected only by accidental conjunctures, and the price subsequently rises again to its normal level. Indirectly, if the change in price has been brought about by a change in value reacting on the old product, and if this product again enters another sphere of production as an element of production, and sets free a proportionate amount of capital there. In both cases, the capital lost by X, capital which he endeavours to replace by exerting pressure on the money market, can be supplied by his business friends as new additional capital. There is then only a transfer.

If the price of the product rises, on the other hand, then a portion of capital that was not advanced is appropriated from the circulation sphere. This is not an organic part of the capital advanced in the production process, and if production is not extended it forms precipitated money capital. Though it is assumed here that the prices of the elements of the product were given before the latter entered the market as commodity capital, this price increase could still have been caused by a real change in value, to the extent that this had a retroactive effect, e.g. if raw materials had subsequently risen in value. In this case capitalist *X* would have profited both on his product, circulating as commodity capital, and on his existing production stock. This profit would then supply him with the additional capital he now needs to carry on his business as a result of the increased prices of the elements of production.

Alternatively, the price rise might be only transitory. What one capitalist then needs as extra capital is precipitated out elsewhere to the extent that his product forms an element of production for other branches of business. What the one lost, the other has gained.

Chapter 16: The Turnover of Variable Capital

I. THE ANNUAL RATE OF SURPLUS-VALUE

Let us take a circulating capital of £2,500, with four fifths of this, £2,000, being constant capital (material elements of production) and one fifth, £500, being variable capital, capital laid out on wages.

Let the turnover period be five weeks: the working period four weeks and the circulation period one week. Capital I is then £2,000, consisting of £1,600 constant capital and £400 variable capital; capital II is £500, of which £400 is constant capital and £100 variable. In each working week, a capital of £500 is laid out. In a year of fifty weeks, an annual product of $50 \times 500 = £25,000$ is produced. The capital I of £2,000 that is applied in each working period thus turns over $12\frac{1}{2}$ times. $12\frac{1}{2}$ times 2,000 = £25,000. Of this £25,000, $\frac{4}{5}$, = £20,000, is constant capital, laid out on means of production, and $\frac{1}{5}$, = £5,000, is variable, laid out on wages. The total capital of £2,500, on the other hand, turns over

$$\frac{25,000}{2,500} = 10 \text{ times.}$$

The variable circulating capital expended in the course of production can serve again in the circulation process only to the extent that the product in which its value is reproduced is sold, transformed from commodity capital into money capital, so that it can be laid out anew in payment for labour-power. But this is just the same for the constant circulating capital laid out in production (on materials), whose value also reappears as a portion of the value of the product. What these two parts of the circulating capital – the constant and the variable – have in common, and what distinguishes them from fixed capital, is not that the value they have transferred to the product is circulated by commodity capital, i.e. circulates through the circulation of the product as a commodity. A portion of the product's value, and hence of the product itself circulating as a commodity, of the commodity capital, always consists of the wear and tear of the fixed capital, or the part of the fixed capital's value that it has transferred to the product in the course of production. The difference is rather that the fixed capital continues to function in the productive process in its old shape through a longer or shorter cycle of turnover periods of the circulating capital (= circulating constant+circulating variable capital), while any single turnover has as its precondition the replacement of the entire circulating capital that enters the circulation sphere from the production sphere in the shape of commodity capital. The first phase of circulation $C'-M'$ is common to both fluid constant and fluid variable capital. In the second phase these separate. The money into which the commodity is transformed back is partly converted into a production stock (circulating constant capital). According to the different terms of purchase of the components of this stock, one part of the money may be converted into materials of production earlier, another part later, but eventually it goes into these completely. A further part of the money released by the sale of the commodity remains in the form of a money reserve, to be spent bit by bit in payment for the labour-power incorporated into the production process. It forms the circulating variable capital. None the less, the entire replacement of one or the other part derives each time from the turnover of the capital, its transformation into a product, from product into commodity, and from commodity into money. This is the reason why, in the previous chapter, we could treat the turnover of both constant and variable capital together as a separate theme, without regard to the fixed capital.

For the question that we have to deal with now, we must go one step further and treat the variable part of the circulating capital as if it alone formed the circulating capital, in other words we shall disregard here the constant circulating capital that turns over together with the variable capital.

£2,500 has been advanced, and the value of the annual product is £25,000. But the variable part of the circulating capital is £500; hence the variable capital contained in the £25,000 is £5,000. If we divide the £5,000 by £500, then we get the number of turnovers, ten, just as with the total capital of £2,500.

This average calculation, in which the value of the annual product is divided by the value of the capital advanced and not by the value of that part of this capital that is constantly applied in a particular working period (i.e. in this case not by 400 but by 500, not by capital I, but rather by capital I+capital II), is here, where only the production of surplus-value is at issue, absolutely exact. We shall see later on, though, that from another point of view it is inexact, just as this average calculation in general is not quite exact. It is sufficient for the practical purposes of the capitalist, but it does not adequately or precisely express all the real circumstances of the turnover.

Up to now we have completely left out of account one part of the value of the commodity capital, i.e. the surplus-value contained in it, which is produced during the production process and has been incorporated into the product. This is what we have now to turn our attention to.

Let us assume that the variable capital of £100 laid out each week produces a surplus-value of 100 per cent = £100. Then the variable capital of £500 laid out in the course of the turnover period of five weeks produces a surplus-value of £500, i.e. half of the working day consists of surplus labour.

But if a variable capital of £500 produces £500, then 5,000 produces a surplus-value of $10 \times 500 = £5,000$. The variable capital advanced, however, is £500. The ratio of the total surplus-value annually produced to the value of the variable capital advanced, we call the annual rate of surplus-value. In the present case this is $\dfrac{5,000}{500} = 1,000$ per cent.

If we analyse this rate more closely, it is clear that it is equal to the rate of surplus-value that the variable capital advanced produces during one turnover period, multiplied by the number of turnovers of the variable capital (which is the same as the number of turnovers of the total circulating capital).

The variable capital advanced in one turnover period is £500 in the present case, and the surplus-value produced in it is also £500. The rate of surplus-value in one turnover period is therefore $\dfrac{500s}{500v} = 100$ per cent. This 100 per cent multiplied by ten, the number of turnovers in the year, gives $\dfrac{5,000s}{500v} = 1,000$ per cent.

This holds for the annual rate of surplus-value. But as far as the mass of surplus-value obtained during a particular turnover period is concerned, this is equal to the value of the variable capital advanced during this period, here £500, multiplied by the rate of surplus-value; here $500 \times \dfrac{100}{100} = 500 \times 1 = £500$. If the capital advanced was £1,500, with the same rate of surplus-value, then the mass of surplus-value would be $1,500 \times \dfrac{100}{100} = £1,500$.

The variable capital of £500 which turns over ten times in the year, producing an annual surplus-value of £5,000, its annual rate of surplus-value thus being 1,000 per cent, we shall call capital A.

Let us now suppose that another variable capital B of £5,000 is advanced for a whole year (i.e. here for fifty weeks), and hence turns over only once in the year. We further assume that the product is paid for at the end of the year on the same day that it is finished, so that the money capital into which it is transformed returns the same day. The circulation period here is now zero; the turnover period is the same as the working period, i.e. one year. As in the previous case, a variable capital of £100 is in the labour process each week, hence £5,000 in fifty weeks. The rate of surplus-value is also the same, 100 per cent; i.e., with a working day of the same length, half of this consists of surplus labour. If we take five weeks, then the variable capital applied is £500, the rate of surplus-value 100 per cent, and the mass of surplus-value created during the five weeks is therefore £500. The amount of labour-power that is exploited, and the degree of its exploitation, are exactly the same here, on the assumptions made, as in capital A.

In any one week, the variable capital of £100 that is applied produces a surplus-value of £100, and so in fifty weeks the capital of 50×100, $=$£5,000, produces a surplus-value of £5,000. The mass of surplus-value annually produced is the same as in the previous case, £5,000, but the annual rate of surplus-value is quite different. Here the surplus-value produced during the year divided by the variable capital advanced

is $\dfrac{5,000s}{5,000v} = 100$ per cent, whereas for capital A it was 1,000 per cent.

In the case of both capital A and capital B, we have the expenditure of £100 variable capital each week; the degree of valorization or the rate of surplus-value is the same, 100 per cent, and the magnitude of the variable capital is also the same, £100. The same amount of labour-power is exploited, and the degree and scale of exploitation are in both cases the same; the working days are equal, and similarly divided into necessary labour and surplus labour. The sum of variable capital applied during the year is equally large, £5,000, and sets the same amount of labour in motion, while the same mass of surplus-value is extracted from the labour-power set in motion by the two equal capitals, £5,000. Yet there is a difference of 900 per cent in the annual rate of surplus-value between A and B.

This phenomenon makes it appear, moreover, as if the rate of surplus-value did not depend only on the amount of variable capital and the rate of exploitation of the labour-power set in motion by it, but also on inexplicable influences deriving from the circulation process; and in fact the phenomenon has been interpreted in this way, if not in this pure form, then at least in its more complicated and concealed form (that of the annual rate of profit). Since the beginning of the 1820s, this phenomenon has led to the complete destruction of the Ricardian school.*

However, its strangeness immediately disappears if we really do place capitals A and B in exactly the same conditions, and do not just appear to do so. The same conditions obtain only if the variable capital B is wholly spent on payment of labour-power in the same interval of time as capital A.

The £5,000 of capital B is then paid out in five weeks, £1,000 per week, giving an outlay of £50,000 over the year. The surplus-value is now also £50,000, under our assumptions. The capital turned over, £50,000, divided by the capital advanced, £5,000, gives the number of turnovers, ten. The rate of surplus-value, $\frac{5,000s}{5,000v} = 100$ per cent, multiplied by the number of turnovers, ten, gives the annual rate of surplus-value, $\frac{50,000s}{5,000v} = \frac{10}{1} = 1,000$ per cent. The annual rates of surplus-value for A and B are now the same, i.e. 1,000 per cent, but the mass of surplus-value is, for B: £50,000; for A: £5,000; the masses of surplus-value produced are now in the same ratio as the capital values B and A that were advanced, i.e. 5,000:500 = 10:1. This is the reason why capital B could set ten times as much labour-power in motion in the same time as capital A.

It is only the capital actually operating in the labour process which creates surplus-value and to which all the laws given for surplus-value apply, including the law that, with a given rate of surplus-value, the mass of surplus-value is given by the relative magnitude of the variable capital.†

The labour process itself is measured by time. The length of the working day being given (as it is here, where we assume equality between capital A and capital B in all circumstances, in order to present the difference in the annual rate of surplus-value in a clear light), the

---

* See *Theories of Surplus-Value*, Part III, Chapter XX.
† See Volume 1, Chapter 13.

working week consists of a definite number of working days. Alternatively, we can treat each working period, e.g. here a five-week one, as a single working day – of 300 hours, for example, if the working day is ten hours and the week six working days. We must then multiply this figure by the number of workers who are employed alongside one another each day in the same labour process. If this number was ten, for example, then the weekly total would be $60 \times 10 = 600$ hours, and a five-week working period would amount to $600 \times 5 = 3,000$ hours. Variable capitals of the same size are thus applied if, with the same rate of surplus-value and the same length of working day, equal amounts of labour-power (one labour-power of the given price multiplied by the given number of workers) are set in motion in the same interval of time.

Let us now return to our original examples. In both cases, *A* and *B*, equal variable capitals, £100 per week, are applied each week of the year. The variable capitals that are applied and actually function in the labour process are therefore the same, but the variable capitals advanced are quite unequal. With *A*, £500 is advanced every five weeks, and £100 of this is applied each week. With *B*, £5,000 has to be advanced for the first five-week period, but out of this only £100 per week, and thus in these five weeks only £500 = $\frac{1}{10}$ of the capital advanced, is actually applied. In the second five-week period, £4,500 has to be advanced, but only £500 is applied, and so on. The variable capital advanced for a certain period of time is transformed into applied, i.e. really functioning and effective, variable capital, only to the degree that it actually does enter those sections of the period of time in question that are filled by the labour process, and really does function in this labour process. In the intervening period in which a part of it is advanced for application only at a later date, this part is as good as non-existent for the labour process, and thus does not have any influence on the formation of either value or surplus-value. Take capital *A* of £500, for instance. It is advanced for five weeks, but each week only £100 of it successively enters the labour process. In the first week, one fifth of it is applied; four fifths is advanced without being applied, although since it must be on hand for the labour process of the four following weeks it must certainly be advanced.

The circumstances that differentiate the ratio between the advanced and the applied variable capital affect the production of surplus-value – at a given rate of profit – only in so far as they differentiate the amount of variable capital which can actually be applied in a definite period of time, e.g. in one week, five weeks, etc. The variable capital advanced functions as variable capital only to the extent that it is actually applied, and during the time for which it is applied; not during the time in which it remains advanced in reserve without being applied. But all circumstances that differentiate the ratio between advanced and applied variable capital can be summed up in the difference in turnover periods (determined by a difference either in working periods or in circulation periods, or in both). The law of surplus-value production is that, with the same rate of surplus-value, equal amounts of functioning variable capital create equal masses of surplus-value. So if equal amounts of variable capital are applied by capitals A and B for the same space of time at the same rate of surplus-value, then they must produce equal amounts of surplus-value in this time, no matter how different may be the ratio between the variable capital applied in the time in question and the variable capital advanced during the same time, and hence how different also the ratio between the mass of surplus-value produced and the total variable capital advanced, rather than that actually applied. The variation of this ratio, instead of contradicting the laws put forward for the production of surplus-value, rather confirms these and is an inescapable consequence of them.

Let us consider the first five-week production period of capital B. At the end of week 5, £500 has been applied and consumed. The value produced is £1,000; $\frac{500s}{500v} = 100$ per cent. It is just the same with capital A. The fact that capital A has realized its surplus-value along with the capital advanced, while B has not, is of no importance to us here, where the issue is simply the production of surplus-value and its ratio to the variable capital advanced during its production. If on the other hand we calculate the ratio of the surplus-value in B to the total capital of £5,000 advanced, and not to the part of this capital that is applied during its production and hence consumed, then we get $\frac{500s}{5,000v} = \frac{1}{10} = 10$ per cent. That is, 10 per cent for capital B as against 100 per cent, ten times as much, for capital A. If it be said here that this difference in the rate of surplus-value for capitals of equal magnitude, which have set in motion an equal quantity of labour, and moreover labour that is divided into the same portions of paid and unpaid labour, contradicts the laws of surplus-value production, the answer is simple, and given by a mere glance at the factual relations. For A it is the actual rate of surplus-value that is expressed here, i.e. the ratio of the surplus-value produced during five weeks by a variable capital of £500 to this variable capital of £500. For *B*, on the other hand, the mode of reckoning is one that has nothing to do with either the production of surplus-value or the corresponding determination of the rate of surplus-value. The £500 surplus-value which has been produced by the variable capital of £500 is in fact not calculated on the basis of the £500 variable capital that is advanced during its production, but rather on a capital of £5,000, nine tenths of which – i.e. £4,500 – has nothing at all to do with the production of this surplus-value of £500, but is rather designed to function gradually over the course of the following forty-five weeks, and does not exist at all as far as the production of the first five weeks goes, which is all that we are concerned with here. In this case, therefore, the difference in the rate of surplus-value between *A* and *B* is no problem at all.

Let us now compare the annual rates of surplus-value for capitals *A* and *B*. For capital *B* we have $\frac{5,000s}{5,000v} = 100$ per cent; for capital *A*, $\frac{5,000s}{500v} = 1,000$ per cent. The ratio of the surplus-value rates, however, is still the same as before. Then we had

$$\frac{\text{surplus-value rate for capital } B}{\text{surplus-value rate for capital } A} = \frac{10 \text{ per cent}}{100 \text{ per cent}},$$

and now we have

$$\frac{\text{annual rate of surplus-value for capital } B}{\text{annual rate of surplus-value for capital } A} = \frac{100 \text{ per cent}}{1,000 \text{ per cent}};$$

but

$$\frac{10 \text{ per cent}}{100 \text{ per cent}} = \frac{100 \text{ per cent}}{1,000 \text{ per cent}},$$

the same ratio as before.

For all that, the problem has now been turned round the other way. The annual rate for capital *B*: $\frac{5,000s}{5,000v} = 100$ per cent, does not present the slightest divergence – not even the shadow of a divergence – from the laws of surplus-value production which we already knew, and the rate of surplus-value corresponding to these. $5,000_v$ has been advanced during the year and productively consumed, having produced $5,000_s$. The rate of surplus-value is thus the above fraction $\frac{5,000s}{5,000v} = 100$ per cent. The annual rate of surplus-value agrees with the actual rate. This time it is not capital B that presents the anomaly to be explained, as it did last time, but rather capital A.

Here we have the rate of surplus value $\dfrac{5,000s}{500v} = 1,000$ per cent. But if in the first case 500_s, the product of five weeks, was calculated on a capital advance of £5,000, nine tenths of which was not applied in its production, now $5,000_s$ is calculated on the basis of 500_v, i.e. on only one tenth of the variable capital that was really applied in the production of $5,000_s$; for the $5,000_s$ is the product of a variable capital of £5,000 that is productively consumed over fifty weeks, and not of the capital of £500 used during one single five-week period. In the first case, the surplus-value produced during five weeks was calculated on the capital that was advanced for fifty weeks, i.e. a capital ten times greater than that used during the five weeks. Now the surplus-value produced in fifty weeks is calculated on the capital which was advanced for five weeks, and which is thus ten times smaller than that used during the fifty weeks.

Capital A of £500 is not advanced for any longer than five weeks. At the end of this period it returns, and can repeat the same process ten times in the course of the year by turning over ten times. Two things follow from this.

Firstly, the capital advanced in case A is only five times greater than the portion of capital applied in any one week's production process. Capital B, on the other hand, which turns over only once in fifty weeks, must therefore also be advanced for fifty weeks, and is fifty times greater than the part of the capital that can ever be applied in one week. The turnover time thus modifies the ratio between the capital advanced for the production process during the year and the capital applied for any given production period, e.g. a week. And this gives us the first case, in which the surplus-value of five weeks is reckoned, not on the capital applied during these five weeks, but rather on the ten times greater capital that is applied over fifty weeks.

Secondly, the turnover period of capital A, five weeks, comprises only one tenth of the year; the year therefore includes ten such turnover periods, in which capital A of £500 is each time applied afresh. The capital applied here is equal to the capital advanced for five weeks, multiplied by the number of turnover periods in the year. The capital applied during the year is $500 \times 10 = £5,000$. The capital advanced during the year is $5,000 \div 10 = £500$. In point of fact, even though the

£500 is always applied afresh, never more than the same £500 is applied every five weeks. In the case of capital *B*, it is still only £500 that is applied and advanced for these five weeks. But since the turnover period is now fifty weeks, the capital applied during the year is the same as the capital advanced not for every five weeks, but for fifty. The mass of surplus-value produced annually, however, is governed, at a given rate of surplus-value, by the capital applied during the year, and not by that advanced. Thus it is no greater for this capital of £5,000 that turns over once than it is for the capital of £500 that turns over ten times, and the only reason why it is the size it is, is that the capital that turns over once in the year is itself ten times greater than that turning over ten times.

The variable capital turned over during the year – i.e. the part of the annual product or the annual expenditure equal to this part – is the variable capital actually applied and productively consumed in the course of the year. It follows therefore that, if the variable capital *A* turned over annually and the variable capital *B* turned over annually are the same, and they are applied under the same conditions of valorization, the rate of surplus-value must be the same for both; and since the masses of capital applied are the same, so must be the annually reckoned rate of surplus-value, as long as it is expressed as:

$$\frac{\text{mass of surplus-value annually produced}}{\text{annual turnover of variable capital}}.$$

To express it more generally, whatever may be the relative magnitudes of the variable capitals turned over, the rate of surplus-value that they produce in the course of a year is determined by the rate of surplus-value at which the respective capitals have operated in average periods (e.g. on a weekly or even daily average).

This is the only possible result that follows from the laws of surplus-value production and those determining the rate of surplus-value.

Let us now look once again at what the ratio

$$\frac{\text{annual turnover of capital}}{\text{capital advanced}}$$

expresses. (We are dealing here only with the variable capital, as already stated.) The quotient gives the number of turnovers of the capital advanced in one year.

For capital *A* we have: $\dfrac{\text{£5,000 capital annually turned over}}{\text{£500 capital advanced}}$; for capital B: $\dfrac{£5,000 \text{ capital annually turned over}}{£5,000 \text{ capital advanced}}$.

In both ratios, the numerator expresses the capital advanced multiplied by the *number* of turnovers; for A, 500×10, for B, $5,000 \times 1$. Alternatively, the capital is multiplied by the reciprocal of the turnover *time*, reckoned in terms of a year. The turnover time for A is $\frac{1}{10}$ year; the reciprocal of this is $\frac{10}{1}$, and $500 \times \frac{10}{1} = 5,000$; for B, $5,000 \times \frac{1}{1} = 5,000$. The denominator expresses the capital turned over multiplied by the reciprocal of the *number* of turnovers; for A, $5,000 \times \frac{1}{10}$, for B, $5,000 \times \frac{1}{1}$.

The respective quantities of labour (the sum of the paid and the unpaid labour) that are set in motion are the same here, since the capitals turned over are the same, and so are their rates of valorization.

The ratio between the variable capital annually turned over and that advanced indicates, firstly, the ratio in which the capital to be advanced stands to the variable capital applied in a certain working period. If the number of turnovers is ten, as under A, and the year is taken as fifty weeks, then the turnover time is five weeks. This five weeks is the time for which variable capital has to be advanced, and the capital advanced for five weeks must be five times larger than the variable capital applied during one week. That is to say, only one fifth of the capital advanced (here £500) can be applied in the course of a week. In the case of capital B, on the other hand, where the number of turnovers is $\frac{1}{1}$, the turnover time is 1 year $= 50$ weeks. The ratio of the capital advanced to that applied week by week is therefore 50:1. If the situation was the same for B as for A, then B would have to apply £1,000 each week instead of £100.

Secondly, it follows that B has applied a capital ten times as great as A, i.e. £5,000, in order to set in motion the same amount of variable capital, thus, with a given rate of surplus-value, the same quantity of labour (both paid and unpaid), and thus to produce the same mass of surplus-value in the course of the year. The real rate of surplus-value expresses nothing more than the ratio of the variable capital applied in a given period of time to the surplus-value produced in the same period; or the mass of unpaid labour that the variable capital applied during this time sets in motion. It has absolutely nothing to do with the portion of variable capital that is advanced during the time in which it is not applied, and hence just as little to do with the ratio between the part of it advanced for a definite period of time and that applied during the same period, a ratio which is modified and differentiated by the turnover period.

It rather follows from what has already been developed that the annual rate of surplus-value coincides with the real rate of surplus-value, that which expresses the degree of exploitation of labour, only in a single case; namely when the capital advanced turns over only once in the year, so that the capital advanced is equal to the capital turned over during the year, and the ratio of the mass of surplus-value produced during the year to the capital applied during the year for the purpose of this production coincides and is identical with the ratio between the mass of surplus-value produced during the year and the capital advanced for the year.

(A) The annual rate of surplus-value is:

$$\frac{\text{mass of surplus-value produced during the year}}{\text{variable capital advanced}}.$$ But the mass of surplus-value produced during the year equals the real rate of surplus-value multiplied by the variable capital applied in its production. The capital applied for the production of the annual mass of surplus-value is equal to the capital advanced multiplied by the number of its turnovers, which we shall call n. The formula (A) is thus transformed into:

(B) The annual rate of surplus-value is:

$$\frac{\text{real rate of surplus-value} \times \text{variable capital advanced} \times n}{\text{variable capital advanced}},$$ e.g. for capital

B, $\dfrac{100 \text{ per cent} \times 5{,}000 \times 1}{5{,}000}$ or 100 per cent. Only if $n = 1$, i.e. if the variable capital advanced turns over only once in the year, and is thus equal to the capital applied or turned over in the year, is the annual rate of surplus-value equal to the real rate of surplus-value.

Let us call the annual rate of surplus-value S', the real rate of surplus-value s', the variable capital advanced v and the number of turnovers n. Then $S' = \dfrac{s'vn}{v} = s'n$; i.e. $S' = s'n$, and only $= s'$ if $n = 1$, when $S' = s' \times 1 = s'$.

It follows that the annual rate of surplus-value is always $s'n$, i.e. the real rate of surplus-value produced in a turnover period by the variable capital consumed during this period, multiplied by the number of turnovers of this variable capital during the year, or (what is the same thing) multiplied by the reciprocal of its turnover *time*, reckoned on the basis of a year. (If the variable capital turns over ten times in the year, then its turnover time is one tenth of a year; the reciprocal of this is therefore $\frac{10}{1} = 10$.)

It follows further that $S' = s'$ if $n = 1$. S' is greater than s' if n is greater than 1; i.e. if the capital advanced turns over more than once in the year, so that the capital turned over is greater than that advanced.

Finally, S' is smaller than s' if n is less than 1; i.e. if the capital turned over during the year is only one part of the capital advanced, and the turnover period thus lasts for longer than a year.

Let us pause a moment to consider this last case.

We keep all the assumptions made in our earlier example, but simply extend the turnover period to fifty-five weeks. The labour process demands £100 in variable capital each week, and thus £5,500 for the turnover period, and each week it produces 100_s; s' is thus 100 per cent, as before. The number of turnovers is now $\frac{50}{55} = \frac{10}{11}$, since the turnover time is $1 + \frac{1}{10}$ years (the year taken as fifty weeks), $= \frac{11}{10}$ years.

$$S' = \frac{100\% \times 5,500 \times \frac{10}{11}}{5,500} = 100 \times \frac{10}{11} = \frac{1,000}{11} = 90\frac{10}{11} \text{ per cent, i.e.}$$

less than 100 per cent. In point of fact, if the annual rate of surplus-value were 100 per cent, then $5,500_v$ would have to produce $5,500_s$ in a year, whereas it actually now takes $\frac{11}{10}$ years for this. The $5,500_v$ produces only $5,000_s$ in the course of the year, giving an annual rate of surplus-value of $\dfrac{5,000s}{5,500v} = \dfrac{10}{11} = 90\frac{10}{11}$ per cent.

The annual rate of surplus-value, or the comparison between the surplus-value produced during the year and the total variable capital *advanced* (as distinct from the variable capital *turned over* during the year), is therefore not something merely subjective, but a comparison produced by the actual movement of capital itself. For the owner of capital A receives back at the end of the year his variable capital of £500 together with a surplus-value of £5,000. What expresses the size of the capital he has advanced is not the quantity of capital that he has applied during the year, but that which periodically flows back to him. That the capital may exist at the end of the year partly as a production stock, and partly as commodity or money capital, adds nothing to the question in hand. Nor does the ratio in which it is divided between these various portions. The owner of capital B receives back £5,000, his capital advanced, together with £5,000 surplus-value. The owner of capital C (that of £5,500 last introduced) has produced £5,000 surplus-value during the year (£5,000 outlay with a rate of surplus-value of 100 per cent), but his capital advanced has not yet returned to him, and so neither has the surplus-value it has produced.

$S' = s'n$ expresses the fact that the rate of surplus-value on the variable capital applied during a turnover period:

$$\frac{\text{mass of surplus-value produced during a turnover period}}{\text{variable capital applied during a turnover period}}$$

has to be multiplied by the number of turnover periods or reproduction periods of the variable capital advanced, the number of periods in which it repeats its circuit.

We have already seen in Volume 1, Chapter 4 ('The General Formula for Capital'), and again in Chapter 23 ('Simple Reproduction'), how the capital value is always advanced and not genuinely spent, in that once this value has gone through the various phases of its circuit, it returns again to its starting-point, and, moreover, it does so enriched with surplus-value. This is what characterizes it as advanced. The time that elapses between its point of departure and its point of return is the time for which it is advanced. The entire circuit which the capital value undergoes, measured by the time from its advance to its reflux, forms its turnover, and the duration of this turnover is a turnover period. Once this period has elapsed, the circuit is at an end, and the same capital value can begin the same circuit afresh, and thus also valorize itself afresh and again produce surplus-value. If the variable capital turns over ten times in the year, as A does, then the mass of surplus-value produced in the course of the year will be ten times that corresponding to one turnover period.

The nature of the advance must now be investigated from the standpoint of capitalist society as a whole.

Capital A, which turns over ten times during the year, is advanced ten times in the course of the year. It is advanced afresh for each new turnover period. But at the same time, all that the owner of A ever advances during the year is the same capital value of £500, and all that he ever has at his disposal for the production process we are considering is £500. Once this £500 has completed a circuit, he lets the same circuit begin anew; capital by its very nature only maintains its capital character precisely by functioning as capital in ever repeated production processes. It is never advanced for longer than five weeks. If the turnover lasts for longer, this capital is not sufficient. If it is reduced, then a part of the capital is superfluous. It is not ten capitals of £500 that are advanced, but *one* capital of £500 advanced ten times in succession at different intervals of time. Hence the annual rate of surplus-value is not calculated on a capital of £500 advanced ten times, i.e. on £5,000, but rather on a capital of £500 advanced once; just as, when a shilling circulates ten times, there is still only one shilling in circulation, even though it performs the functions of ten shillings. However, no matter in whose hand it exists for the moment, it remains as always the same identical value of one shilling.

Capital A shows in just the same way, each time it returns, including its return at the end of the year, that its owner has always operated simply with the same capital value of £500. All that he receives back each time is £500. The capital he advances is therefore never more than £500. The capital of £500 that is advanced forms the denominator of the fraction that expresses the annual rate of surplus-value. We already had for this the formula $S' = \dfrac{s'vn}{v} = s'n$. Since the real rate of surplus-value $s' = \dfrac{s}{v}$, the mass of surplus-value divided by the variable capital that produced it, we can substitute in $s'n$ the equivalent of s', i.e. $\dfrac{s}{v}$, and arrive at the further formula: $S' = \dfrac{sn}{v}$.

However, by turning over ten times, and hence repeating its advance ten times, the capital of £500 performs the function of a capital ten times as great, a capital of £5,000, just as 500 shilling pieces that turn over ten times in the year perform the same function as 5,000 turning over only once.

2. THE TURNOVER OF AN INDIVIDUAL VARIABLE CAPITAL

'Whatever the social form of the production process, it has to be continuous, it must periodically repeat the same phases ... When viewed, therefore, as a connected whole, and in the constant flux of its incessant renewal, every social process of production is at the same time a process of reproduction ... As a periodic increment of the value of the capital, or a periodic fruit borne by capital-in-process, surplus-value acquires the form of a *revenue* arising out of capital' (Volume 1, Chapter 23, pp. 711–12).

We have ten five-week turnover periods for capital A. In the first turnover period, £500 variable capital is advanced; i.e. £100 is converted each week into labour-power, so that at the end of the first turnover period, £500 has been spent on labour-power. This £500, originally part of the total capital advanced, has ceased to be capital. It has been paid out in wages. The workers, for their part, pay it out again in purchasing their means of subsistence, and consume means of subsistence to the value of £500. A mass of commodities amounting altogether to this value is thereby annihilated (what the worker may save as money, etc. is also not capital). This mass of commodities is consumed unproductively, as far as the worker is concerned, except in as much as he thereby maintains his labour-power, which is an indispensable instrument for the capitalist, in working condition. In the second place, however, this £500 is converted, for the capitalist, into labour-power of the same value (or price). He consumes the labour-power productively in the labour process. At the end of the five weeks, a value product of £1,000 has been brought into existence. Half of this, £500, is the reproduced value of the variable capital spent as payment for labour-power. The other half, £500, is newly produced surplus-value. But the five weeks' labour-power, by conversion into which a part of capital has been transformed into variable capital, is also spent or consumed, even if productively. The labour active yesterday is not the same labour as is active today. Its value, together with the surplus-value created by it, now exists as the value of a thing distinct from labour-power, the product. But because the product is transformed into money, the part of its value equal to the value of the variable capital advanced is converted once more into labour-power and hence functions afresh as variable capital. The fact that the capital value that is not only reproduced, but also transformed back into the money form, may engage the same workers, i.e. the same bearers of labour-power, is beside the point. It is quite possible for the capitalist to employ new workers in place of the old ones in the second turnover period.

In fact, therefore, in the course of the ten five-week turnover periods a capital of £5,000 is successively spent on wages, and not one of £500, these wages being spent again by the workers on means of subsistence. The capital of £5,000 advanced in this way is consumed. It no longer exists. On the other hand, it is labour-power to the value of £5,000, and not just £500, that is successively incorporated into the production process, not only reproducing its own value of £5,000, but producing in addition to this a surplus-value of £5,000. The variable capital of £500 that is advanced in the second turnover period is not the identical capital of £500 advanced in the first turnover period. The latter has been consumed, spent on wages. But it has been *replaced* by a new variable capital of £500, which was produced in the first turnover period in the commodity form and was then transformed back into the money form. This new money capital of £500 is therefore the money form of the mass of commodities newly produced in the first turnover period. The fact that an identical money sum of £500 exists once more in the hands of the capitalist – i.e. if we disregard the surplus-value, the same amount of money capital as he originally advanced – conceals the fact that he is operating with a newly produced capital. (As far as the other value components of the commodity capital are concerned, those that replace the constant parts of the capital, their value is not newly produced; it is only the form in which the value exists that is changed.) Let us take the third turnover period. Here it is evident that the variable capital of £500 advanced for the third time is not an old capital, but one newly produced, for it is the money form of the mass of commodities produced in the second turnover period and not in the first turnover period, i.e. the money form of that mass of commodities whose value is equal to the value of the variable capital advanced. The part of their value that equals the variable part of the capital advanced was converted into the new labour-power for the second turnover period, and produced a new mass of commodities; this was again sold, and a part of their value forms the capital of £500 advanced in the third turnover period.

The same thing happens for all ten turnover periods. Every five weeks, newly produced masses of commodities (whose value, in so far as it replaces variable capital, is also newly produced, and does not simply reappear, as with the constant circulating capital) are thrown on the market, so that ever new labour-power can be incorporated into the production process.

What is attained by the ten-fold turnover of the variable capital advanced, therefore, is not that this capital of £500 can be productively consumed ten times over or that a variable capital that suffices for five weeks can be applied for fifty. In fact, $10 \times £500$ of variable capital is applied in the fifty weeks; the capital of £500 is only ever sufficient for five weeks, and must be replaced at the end of these five weeks with a newly produced capital of £500. This occurs just as much for capital *A* as for capital *B*. But now comes the difference.

At the close of the first section of five weeks, a variable capital of £500 has been advanced and spent both in case *B* and in case *A*. For *B* just as for *A*, its value has been converted into labour-power and replaced by a part of the value of the product newly produced by this labour-power equal in value to the advanced variable capital of £500. For both *B* and *A*, the labour-power has not just replaced the value of the variable capital expended, £500, with a new value to the same amount, but also added to it a surplus-value – one of the same size, according to our assumption.

In case *B*, however, the value product which replaces the variable capital advanced and adds to its value a surplus-value does not exist in the form in which it can function once again as productive capital, i.e. as variable capital. This is the form in which it does exist for *A*. For *B*, however, through to the end of the year, while the variable capital spent in the first five weeks, and then successively every five weeks again, is replaced by newly produced value and surplus-value, it does not exist in the form in which it can function as productive capital or in particular variable capital. Its *value* has certainly been replaced by a new value, and thus renewed, but the *form* of its value (in this case the absolute value form, its money form) has not been renewed.

For the second period of five weeks (and successively for every five weeks during the year), a further £500 must be on hand, just as for the first period. If we ignore credit, then £5,000 must be on hand at the beginning of the year, and exist as latent money capital advanced, even though it is only actually spent and converted into labour-power bit by bit in the course of the year.

In case *A*, on the other hand, since the circuit or turnover of the capital advanced has been completed, the replacement value already exists, after five weeks have elapsed, in the form in which it can set in motion new labour-power for five weeks: in its original money form.

In both cases, *A* and *B*, new labour-power is consumed in the second five-week period, and a new capital of £500 spent in payment for this labour-power. The workers' means of subsistence, which were paid for with the first £500, have disappeared, or at any rate the value of these has vanished from the hands of the capitalist. The second £500 serves to buy new labour-power, to withdraw new means of subsistence from the market. In short, a new capital of £500 is spent, not the old one. But in case *A*, this new capital is the money form of the newly produced replacement value for the £500 spent previously. In case *B*, the replacement value exists in a form in which it cannot function as variable capital. It does exist, but not in the form of variable capital. An additional capital of £500 must therefore be available in the money form, which is here unavoidable, to continue the production process for the next five weeks, and it must be advanced as such. Thus the same amount of variable capital is spent in fifty weeks in case B as in case A; the same amount of labour-power paid for and used. But in B this has to be paid for with a capital advance equal to its entire value, £5,000. In A, however, it is paid for successively by the ever renewed money form of the replacement value that is produced every five weeks for the capital of £500 advanced for each five weeks. In this case, therefore, the money capital advanced is never greater than that needed for five weeks, i.e. never greater than the capital of £500 advanced for the first five weeks. This £500 is sufficient for the whole year. It is clear, therefore, that with the same degree of exploitation of labour, i.e. the same real rate of surplus-value, the annual rates in cases A and B must stand in inverse proportion to the magnitudes of the variable money capitals that have had to be advanced in order to set in motion the same quantity of labour-power over the year. $A : \dfrac{5,000s}{500v} = 1,000$ per cent, and

$B : \dfrac{5,000s}{5,000v} = 100$ per cent. But $500_v : 5,000_v = 1:10 = 100$ per cent $:1,000$ per cent.

The distinction arises from the divergence in the turnover periods, i.e. the intervals at which the replacement value of the variable capital applied in a certain period of time can function afresh as capital, and therefore as new capital. With both B and A, we find the same replacement value for the variable capital applied during the same period. There is also the same additional surplus-value produced during the same period. But with B, even though every five weeks there is a replacement value of £500, plus £500 surplus-value, this replacement value does not yet form any new capital, since it does not exist in the money form. In case A, the old capital value is not only replaced by a new one, but is re-established in its money form, and hence replaced as new capital capable of performing its function.

The earlier or later transformation of the replacement value into money, and hence into the form in which the variable capital is advanced, is evidently a circumstance quite immaterial to the production of surplus-value. The latter depends on the magnitude of the variable capital applied, and on the level of exploitation of labour. But the circumstance mentioned above does modify the size of the money capital that has to be advanced in order to set in motion a definite amount of labour-power in the course of the year, and in this way it does affect the annual rate of surplus-value.

3. THE TURNOVER OF VARIABLE CAPITAL CONSIDERED FROM THE SOCIAL POINT OF VIEW

Let us consider the matter for a moment from the whole society's standpoint. A worker costs, say, £1 per week; the working day is ten hours. Both with capital *A* and capital *B* 100 workers are employed throughout the year (£100 per week for 100 workers, making £500 for five weeks and £5,000 for fifty weeks), and each of these works for sixty hours in a six-day week. 100 workers perform 6,000 hours' labour per week and therefore 300,000 hours' labour in fifty weeks. This labour-power is requisitioned by *A* and *B*, and cannot be spent by the society on anything else. In this respect, the matter is the same, from the social standpoint, for both *A* and *B*. Moreover, in both cases, each 100 workers receive a yearly wage of £5,000 (thus the 200 together receive £10,000), and withdraw from society means of subsistence to this value. In this respect, too, the matter is equivalent in both cases, from the social standpoint. Since the workers are in both cases paid by the week, they also withdraw means of subsistence from society each week, and each week they cast into circulation in return their money equivalent. But now comes the difference.

Firstly. The money that the workers under capital *A* cast into circulation is not only, as for the workers under capital *B*, the money form of the value of their labour-power (in actual fact a means of payment for labour already performed); right from the second turnover period onward, reckoning from the opening of the business, it is the money form of *their own value product* (=price of labour-power plus surplus-value) in the first turnover period which pays for their labour during the second turnover period. With capital *B* the position is different. Here, too, the money is certainly a means of payment for labour that the workers have already performed, but this labour is not paid for with their own value product turned into money (the money form of the value they themselves have produced). This can only start to happen from the second year onwards, when the workers under capital *B* are paid with their own value product of the previous year, converted into money.

The shorter the turnover period of the capital – and hence the shorter the intervals at which its reproduction period is repeated in the course of the year – the sooner is the variable part of the capital originally advanced by the capitalist in the money form transformed into the money form of the value product created by the worker as a replacement for this variable capital (this product also including surplus-value); the shorter, too, is the time for which the capitalist has to advance money from his own funds, and the smaller the total capital that he advances in relation to the given scale of production; the relatively greater, therefore, is the mass of surplus-value that the capitalist extracts in the course of the year, at a given rate of surplus-value, since he can buy the workers all the more often, and set their labour in motion, with the money form of their own value product.

At a given scale of production, the absolute size of the variable money capital advanced (and so of the circulating capital in general) is reduced in proportion to the brevity of the turnover period, and the annual rate of surplus-value correspondingly grows. With a given volume of capital advanced, the scale of production grows, and hence, with a given rate of surplus-value, the absolute mass of the surplus-value produced in one turnover period also grows, and there occurs, simultaneously with this, a rise in the annual rate of surplus-value caused by the reduction in the reproduction period. The preceding investigation has led us to the result that, according to the varying magnitudes of the turnover period, money capitals of very different scale have to be advanced, in order to set in motion the same volume of productive circulating capital and the same amount of labour, given the same level of exploitation of labour.

Secondly – and this is related to the first distinction – in both cases the workers pay for the means of subsistence that they buy with the variable capital that is transformed in their hands into means of circulation. They not only withdraw wheat from the market, for example, but also replace it with an equivalent in money. But since the money with which the workers employed by capital *B* pay for their means of subsistence and withdraw them from the market is not the money form of their own value product cast into the market in the course of the year, as is the case with the workers employed by capital *A*, it follows that although they supply the seller of their means of subsistence with money, they do not supply any commodity – either means of production or means of subsistence – which he could buy with the money provided, which is the position however with *A*. Hence labour-power, means of subsistence for this labour-power, fixed capital in the form of the means of labour applied under capital *B*, and production materials, are all withdrawn from the market, and an equivalent in money is cast into the market to replace them with; but no product is cast into the market during the year in question to replace the material elements of productive capital withdrawn from it. If we were to consider a communist society in place of a capitalist one, then money capital would immediately be done away with, and so too the disguises that transactions acquire through it. The matter would be simply reduced to the fact that the society must reckon in advance how much labour, means of production and means of subsistence it can spend, without dislocation, on branches of industry which, like the building of railways, for instance, supply neither means of production nor means of subsistence, nor any kind of useful effect, for a long period, a year or more, though they certainly do withdraw labour, means of production and means of subsistence from the total annual product. In capitalist society, on the other hand, where any kind of social rationality asserts itself only *post festum*,* major disturbances can and must occur constantly. On the one hand there is pressure on the money market, while conversely the absence of this pressure itself calls into being a mass of such undertakings, and therefore the precise circumstances that later provoke a pressure on the money market. The money market is under pressure because large-scale advances of money capital for long periods of time are always needed here. This is quite apart from the fact that industrialists and merchants throw the money capital they need for the carrying on of their businesses into railway speculations, etc., and replace it with loans from the money market.

The other side of the coin is pressure on the society's available productive capital. Since elements of productive capital are constantly being withdrawn from the market and all that is put into the market is an equivalent in money, the effective demand rises, without this in itself providing any element of supply. Hence prices rise, both for the means of subsistence and for the material elements of production. During this time, too, there are regular business swindles, and great transfers of capital. A band of speculators, contractors, engineers, lawyers, etc. enrich themselves. These exert a strong consumer demand on the market, and wages rise as well. As far as foodstuffs are concerned, agriculture is given a boost by this process. But since these foodstuffs cannot be suddenly increased within the year, imports grow, as well as the import of exotic foods (coffee, sugar, wine, etc.) and objects of luxury. Hence over-supply and speculation in this part of the import trade. On the other hand, in those branches of industry in which production can be increased more quickly (manufacture proper, mining,

*Literally 'after the feast'; a favourite expression of Marx's, in the sense of 'too late to have any effect'.

etc.), the price rise leads to sudden expansion, soon followed by collapse. The same effect occurs on the labour market, drawing great numbers of the latent relative surplus population, and even workers already employed, into the new lines of business. Undertakings of this kind, such as railways, generally withdraw from the labour market on a large scale a certain quantity of force, which can derive only from branches such as agriculture, etc. where only strong lads are needed. This still occurs even after the new undertakings have already become an established branch of industry and the migrant working class needed for them has already been formed e.g. when railway construction is temporarily pursued on a scale greater than the average. A part of the reserve army of workers whose pressure keeps wages down is absorbed. Wages generally rise, even in the formerly well employed sections of the labour market. This lasts until, with the inevitable crash, the reserve army of workers is again released and wages are pressed down once more to their minimum and below it.[1]

In as much as the greater or lesser length of the turnover period depends on the working period in the strict sense, i.e. the period needed to prepare the product for the market, it depends on the material conditions of production in the various spheres of capital investment, as these are given at the time. In agriculture these have more the character of natural conditions of production; in manufacture, and for the most part in the extractive industries too, they change with the social development of the productive process itself.

In as much as the length of the working period depends on the size of deliveries (on the quantitative scale on which the product is generally thrown onto the market), this has a conventional character. But the convention itself has as its material basis the scale of production, and is therefore accidental only if considered in isolation.

Finally, in as much as the length of the turnover period is dependent

1. The following note for future elaboration is here inserted in the manuscript: 'Contradiction in the capitalist mode of production. The workers are important for the market as buyers of commodities. But as sellers of their commodity – labour-power – capitalist society has the tendency to restrict them to their minimum price. Further contradiction: the periods in which capitalist production exerts all its forces regularly show themselves to be periods of over-production; because the limit to the application of the productive powers is not simply the production of value, but also its realization. However the sale of commodities, the realization of commodity capital, and thus of surplus-value as well, is restricted not by the consumer needs of society in general, but by the consumer needs of a society in which the great majority are always poor and must always remain poor. This however belongs rather to the next Part.'

on the length of the circulation period, this is partly conditioned by the constant change in market conditions, the greater or lesser ease of selling, and the necessity, which arises from this, of casting the product partly on nearer and partly on more distant markets. Apart from the scale of demand in general, the movement of prices plays a major role here. Sales are deliberately restricted when prices are falling, while production goes ahead; and the converse occurs when prices are rising, when production and sale keep in step, or selling even takes place in advance. However the actual distance of the place of production from the market outlet should be considered as a specific material basis.

English cotton cloth or yarn, for instance, is sold to India. The export merchant has to pay the English cotton manufacturer. (He does this willingly only when the situation on the money market is favourable. As soon as the manufacturer himself replaces his money capital by credit operations, things start to go wrong.) The exporter later sells his cotton goods on the Indian market, from where the capital he has advanced is remitted. Until this reflux, the situation is just the same as one in which the length of the working period requires a new advance of money capital in order to keep the production process going on the same scale. The money capital with which the manufacturer pays his workers and replaces the other elements of his circulating capital is not the money form of the yarn that he produced. This can only be the case after the value of this yarn has returned to England in money or products. It is additional money capital, as before. The distinction is simply that instead of the manufacturer it is the merchant who advances it, and he may well have obtained it himself by credit operations. Similarly, until this money has been cast into the market, no additional product has been put on the English market that could be bought with this money and enter the sphere of production or individual consumption. If this condition sets in for a long while and on a large scale, then it must lead to the same results as the prolonged working period did previously.

It is also possible that the yarn is sold on credit in India itself. With this credit, products are bought in India and sent as a return shipment to England, or else drafts are remitted to this amount. If this process is delayed, then pressure builds up on the Indian money market, which may react on England to produce a crisis here. This crisis, in its turn, even if it is combined with the export of precious metals to India, provokes a new crisis in that country, on account of the bankruptcy of English firms and their Indian branches, who were given credit by Indian banks. Thus a simultaneous crisis arises both on the market for which the trade balance is unfavourable, and on that for which it is favourable. This phenomenon can be still more complicated. England may have sent silver bullion to India, but India's English creditors now press their demands here, and in a short while India will have to send its silver back to England.

It can happen that the export trade to India and the import trade from India are in approximate balance, even though the size of the latter (with the exception of special circumstances such as an increase in cotton prices, etc.) is determined by the former, and stimulated by it. The balance of trade between England and India may appear in equilibrium, or exhibit only weak fluctuations on one side or the other. But once the crisis breaks out in England, it becomes clear that unsold cotton goods are being stored up in India (goods which have therefore not been transformed from commodity capital into money capital – over-production on this side) and that on the other hand there are not only unsold stocks of Indian products in England, but a major part of stocks sold and consumed have not yet been paid for. Thus what appears as a crisis on the money market in actual fact expresses anomalies in the production and reproduction process itself.

Thirdly, in relation to the actual circulating capital applied (both variable and constant), the length of the turnover period, in so far as it derives from the length of the working period, leads to the distinction that, with a greater number of turnovers in the course of the year, an element of the variable or constant circulating capital can be supplied by way of its own product, as with the production of coal, of ready-made clothes, etc. In other situations this is not the case, at least not within the year.

Chapter 17: The Circulation of Surplus-Value

We have already seen how the variation in the turnover period produces a variation in the annual rate of surplus-value, even with the mass of surplus-value annually produced remaining the same.

There is however a further necessary variation in the capitalization of surplus-value, in *accumulation*, and in this respect also in the mass of surplus-value produced during the year even with the rate of surplus-value remaining the same.

We note first of all that capitalist *A* (in the example of the preceding chapter) has a steady periodic revenue, and so, if we except the turnover period with which he starts business, he meets his own consumption during the year out of his production of surplus-value, and does not have to advance anything for this out of his own funds. This is the position however with *B*. Capitalist *B* produces the same amount of surplus-value in the same time as *A* does, but the surplus-value is not realized and can therefore be consumed neither individually nor productively. So far as individual consumption is concerned, surplus-value is anticipated. Funds for this must be advanced.

A part of the productive capital which it is difficult to categorize, i.e. the extra capital needed for repair and maintenance of the fixed capital, now presents itself in a new light.*

In case *A*, this part of the capital is either not advanced at the start of production, or is only advanced to a small extent. It does not need to be available, let alone actually present. It arises from the business itself, by the direct transformation of surplus-value into capital, i.e. its direct application as capital. A part of the surplus-value that is not only produced periodically in the course of the year, but also realized, can cover the expenses necessary for repairs, etc. In this way a part of the capital needed to conduct the business on its original scale is produced by the business itself, in the course of business, by the capitalization of a part

*See above, p. 255.

of the surplus-value. This is impossible for capitalist *B*. The portion of capital in question must in his case form part of the capital originally advanced. In both cases, this part of the capital figures in the capitalist's books as capital advanced, which indeed it is, since on our assumption it forms part of the productive capital needed to carry on business on the given scale. But it makes a great difference whose funds it is advanced out of. In case *B*, it is an actual part of the capital that has to be originally advanced or kept available. In case *A*, on the other hand, it is a portion of the surplus-value applied as capital. This latter case shows us how not only the capital accumulated, but also a part of the capital originally advanced, can be simply capitalized surplus-value.

Once the development of credit intervenes, the relation between the capital originally advanced and the capitalized surplus-value becomes still more intricate. For example, *A* may borrow part of the productive capital with which he begins his business, or carries it on during the year, from banker *C*. At the start, therefore, he lacks sufficient capital of his own to conduct the business. Banker *C* lends him a sum that simply consists of surplus-value deposited with him by industrialists *D*, *E*, *F*, etc. From *A*'s standpoint, it is still not accumulated capital. In point of fact, however, for *D*, *E*, *F*, etc., *A* is no more than an agent who capitalizes the surplus-value that they have appropriated.

In Chapter 24 of Volume 1 we saw how the real content of accumulation, the transformation of surplus-value into capital, is the reproduction process on an expanded scale, whether this expansion expresses itself extensively in the form of the addition of new factories to old ones, or intensively in the enlargement of the former scale of operations.*

The expansion of the scale of production can proceed in relatively small doses, if a part of the surplus-value is applied to improvements which either simply raise the productive power of the labour applied, or allow it simultaneously to be more intensively exploited. Alternatively, when the working day is not restricted by law, an additional outlay of circulating capital (in production materials and wages) permits an expansion of the scale of production without any increase in the fixed capital, since the time during which the latter is used is thus simply prolonged, while its turnover period is correspondingly shortened. Alternatively, again, the capitalized surplus-value, given favourable market conjunctures, may permit speculation in raw materials, operations for which the capital originally advanced would have been insufficient, and so on.

* See Volume 1, pp. 725–34.

It is clear, however, that where a relatively large number of turnover periods brings about a more frequent realization of surplus-value in the course of the year, periods do occur in which the working day cannot be extended, nor can individual improvements be brought about; while, on the other hand, extension of the whole business on a proportional scale, partly by expanding the entire plant, the buildings, for example, partly by increasing the labour fund, as in agriculture, is possible only within certain limits, which may be broader or narrower, and requires a volume of additional capital that can only be supplied by several years' accumulation of surplus-value.

Besides real accumulation, or the transformation of surplus-value into productive capital (and, correspondingly, reproduction on an expanded scale), there is thus accumulation of money, scraping together a part of the surplus-value as latent money capital, which is only to function as additional active capital later on, when it has attained a certain volume.

This is how the matter appears from the standpoint of the individual capitalist. With the development of capitalist production, however, there occurs a simultaneous development in the credit system. The money capital that the capitalist cannot yet apply in his own business is employed by others from whom he receives interest. It functions for him as money capital in the specific sense that it is a kind of capital distinct from productive capital. But it is in someone else's hands that it actually operates as capital. It is clear that, with the more frequent realization of surplus-value and the rising scale on which it is produced, a growth occurs in the proportion in which new money capital or money as capital is placed on the money market, and at least a large part of this is absorbed again from the money market for the expansion of production.

The simplest form which this extra latent money capital can assume is that of a hoard. This hoard may be additional gold or silver received directly or indirectly in exchange with the countries producing precious metals. It is only in this way, moreover, that the money hoard within a country grows in absolute terms. It is possible on the other hand, however – and this is the position in the majority of cases – that this hoard is nothing more than money withdrawn from domestic circulation which has assumed the form of a hoard in the hands of individual capitalists. It is also possible that this latent money capital consists simply of value tokens – we are still leaving credit money out of account here – or else of mere claims (titles) of the capitalist on third parties established by legal documents. In all these cases, whatever may be the form of existence of the extra money capital, it represents, in as much as it is prospective capital, no more than extra legal titles to the future additional production of the society that the capitalists hold in reserve.

'The mass of real accumulated wealth, in point of magnitude ... is so utterly insignificant when compared with the powers of production of the same society in whatever state of civilization, or even compared with the actual consumption for even a few years of that society, that the great attention of legislators and political economists should be directed to "productive powers" and their future free development, and not, as hitherto, to the mere accumulated wealth that strikes the eye. Of what is called accumulated wealth, by far the greater part is only nominal, consisting not of any real things, ships, houses, cottons, improvements on land, but of mere demands on the future annual productive powers of society, engendered and perpetuated by the expedients or institutions of insecurity ... The use of such articles (accumulations of physical things or actual wealth) as a mere means of appropriating to their possessors the wealth to be created by the future productive powers of society, being that alone of which the natural laws of distribution would, without force, gradually deprive them, or, if aided by co-operative labour, would in a very few years deprive them.' (William Thompson, *An Inquiry into the Principles of the Distribution of Wealth*, London, 1850, p. 453. This book originally appeared in 1824.)

'It is little thought, by most persons not at all suspected, how very small a proportion, either in extent or influence, the actual accumulations of society bear to human productive powers, even to the ordinary consumption of a few years of a single generation. The reason is obvious; but the effect very pernicious. The wealth that is annually consumed, disappearing with its consumption, is seen but for a moment, and makes no impression but during the act of enjoyment or use. But that part of wealth which is of slow consumption, furniture, machinery, buildings, from childhood to old age stand out before the eye, the durable monuments of human exertion. By means of the possession of this fixed, permanent, or slowly consumed, part of national wealth, of the land and materials to work upon, the tools to work with, the houses to shelter whilst working, the holders of these articles command for their own benefit the yearly productive powers of all the really efficient productive labourers of society, though these articles may bear ever so small a proportion to the recurring products of that labour. The population of Britain and Ireland being twenty millions, the average consumption of each individual, man, woman, and child, is probably about twenty pounds, making four hundred millions of wealth, the product of labour annually consumed. The whole amount of the accumulated capital of these countries, it has been estimated, does not exceed twelve hundred millions, or three times the year's labour of the community; or, if equally divided, sixty pounds capital for every individual. 'Tis with the proportions, rather than with the absolute accurate amount of these estimated sums, we are concerned. The interest of this capital stock would support the whole population in the same comfort in which they now exist, for about two months of one year, and the whole accumulated capital itself would maintain them in idleness (could purchasers be found) for three years! at the end of which time, without houses, clothes, or food, they must starve, or become the slaves of those who supported them in the three years' idleness. As three years to the life of one healthy generation, say forty years, so is the magnitude and importance of the actual wealth, the accumulated capital of even the wealthiest community, to the productive powers of only one generation; not of what, under judicious arrangements of equal security, they might produce, particularly with the aid of co-operative labour, but of what, under the defective and depressing expedients of insecurity, they do absolutely produce! . . . The seeming mighty mass of existing capital to maintain and perpetuate which (or rather the command of the products of yearly labour which it serves as the means of engrossing) . . . in its present state of forced division, are all the horrible machinery, the vices, crimes, and miseries of insecurity, sought to be perpetuated. As nothing can be accumulated without first supplying necessaries, and as the great current of human inclination is to enjoyment; hence the comparatively trifling amount of the actual wealth of society at any particular moment. 'Tis an eternal round of production and consumption. From the amount of this immense mass of annual consumption and production, the handful of actual accumulation would hardly be missed; and yet it is to this handful, and not to the mass of productive powers that attention has chiefly been directed. This handful, however, having been seized upon by a few, and been made the instrument of converting to their use the constantly recurring annual products of the labour of the great majority of their fellow-creatures; hence, in the opinion of these few, the paramount importance of such an instrument . . . About one third part of the annual products of the labour of these countries is now abstracted from the producers, under the name of public burdens, and unproductively consumed by those who give no equivalent, that is to say, none satisfactory to the producers ... With the accumulated masses, particularly when held forth in the hands of a few individuals, the vulgar eye has been always struck. The annually produced and consumed masses, like the eternal and incalculable waves of a mighty river, roll on and are lost in the forgotten ocean of consumption. On this eternal consumption, however, are dependent, not only for almost all gratifications, but even for existence, the whole human race. The quantity and distribution of these yearly products ought to be the paramount objects of consideration. The actual accumulation is altogether of secondary importance, and derives almost the whole of that importance from its influence on the distribution of the yearly productions. . . Actual accumulations and distributions have been always considered' (in Thompson's works) 'in reference, and subordinate, to the power of producing. In almost all other systems, the power of producing has been considered in reference, and subordinate, to actual accumulations, and to the perpetuating of the existing modes of distribution. In comparison to the preservation of this actual distribution, the ever-recurring misery or happiness of the whole human race has been considered as unworthy of regard. To perpetuate the results of force, fraud, and chance, has been called security; and to the support of this spurious security, have all the productive powers of the human race been unrelentingly sacrificed.' (ibid., pp. 440–43.)

As far as reproduction is concerned, only two normal cases are possible, leaving aside disturbances which inhibit reproduction even on the existing scale.

Either reproduction occurs on a simple scale;

Or alternatively, there is capitalization of surplus-value, accumulation.

I. SIMPLE REPRODUCTION

In the case of simple reproduction, the surplus-value that is periodically produced and realized, either annually or by several turnovers within the year, is consumed individually, i.e. unproductively, by its owners, the capitalists.

The fact that the value of products consists partly of surplus-value, and partly of the portion of value formed by the variable capital reproduced in it together with the constant capital consumed, does not change in the least either the volume or the value of the total product which enters circulation at any given time as commodity capital and is similarly withdrawn from it to go into productive or individual consumption, i.e. to serve as means of production or means of consumption. Leaving aside the constant capital, it is only the distribution of the annual product between workers and capitalists that is thereby affected.

Even supposing simple reproduction, one part of the surplus-value must always exist in money and not in products, because it cannot otherwise be transformed from money into products for the needs of consumption. This transformation of surplus-value from its original commodity form into money must now be investigated further. To simplify the matter, we take the problem in its simplest form, i.e. the exclusive circulation of metallic money, of money that is a real equivalent.

According to the laws developed for simple commodity circulation (Volume 1, Chapter 3), the mass of metallic money existing in a country cannot just be enough to circulate the commodities. It must be sufficient to cope with fluctuations in the circulation of money, which arise partly from fluctuations in the speed of circulation, partly from changes in the price of commodities, and partly from the different and changing proportions in which the money functions as means of payment and as means of circulation proper. The ratio in which the existing mass of money is divided into a hoard and into money in circulation constantly changes, but the mass of money is always equal to the sum of money present as a hoard and as money in circulation. This quantity of money (the quantity of precious metal) is a social hoard accumulated bit by bit. In as much as a part of this hoard is consumed by wear and tear, it must be replaced each year, as with any other product. This happens in reality by the direct or indirect exchange of a part of the annual product of the country in question with the product of the gold- and silver-producing countries. The international character of this transaction conceals its simple course. In order to reduce the problem to its simplest and most perceptible expression, we must therefore assume that there is production of gold and silver in the country itself, i.e. that gold and silver production forms a part of the total social production of any country.

Ignoring the gold and silver produced for luxury articles, the minimum annual production of these metals must be equal to the wear and tear of the money metals occasioned by the annual monetary circulation. Moreover, if the value of the mass of commodities annually produced and circulated grows, then the annual production of gold and silver must also grow, in so far as the increased value of the commodities in circulation and the quantity of money required for this circulation (and for the corresponding hoard formation) is not compensated for by a greater velocity of monetary circulation and by the more comprehensive function of money as means of payment, i.e. by more mutual settlement of sales and purchases without the intervention of actual money.

A part of the social labour-power and a part of the social means of production must therefore be spent each year in the production of gold and silver.

The capitalists who pursue the production of gold and silver – and since we are here assuming simple reproduction, they pursue it only within the bounds of the average annual wear and tear and the average annual consumption of gold and silver necessitated by that wear and tear – directly cast their surplus-value, which according to our supposition they consume each year without capitalizing any of it, into the circulation sphere in the money form, which is for them the natural form of their product, not, as with the other branches of production, its transformed form.

Furthermore, as far as wages are concerned – the money form in which the variable capital is advanced – here too they are not replaced by the sale of the product, its transformation into money, but rather by a product whose natural form is money from the very beginning.

Finally, this also applies to the part of the total precious metal product that is equal in value to the whole of the constant capital periodically consumed, including both the constant circulating capital and the constant fixed capital consumed during the year.

Let us firstly consider the circuit or turnover of the capital invested in the production of precious metals in the form $M–C\ldots P\ldots M'$. In so far as the C in $M–C$ does not consist only of labour-power and means of production, but also of fixed capital, only a part of whose value is used up in P, it is evident that M' – the product – is a sum of money equal to the variable capital laid out on wages, plus the circulating constant capital laid out on means of production, plus the portion of value of the fixed capital used up, plus the surplus-value. If the sum were smaller, with the general value of the gold unchanged, then the mines in question would be unprofitable, or – if this is generally the case – the value of gold would in future rise, compared with commodities whose value was unchanged; i.e. the prices of commodities would fall, so that the sum of money laid out in $M–C$ would in future be less.

Let us start by considering only the circulating part of the capital advanced in *M*, the starting-point of $M-C...P...M'$. In this case a certain sum of money is advanced and cast into circulation in payment for labour-power and in order to purchase materials of production. The money is not withdrawn again from circulation by the circuit of *this* capital, and then cast in afresh. The product in its natural form is already money, it does not need to be first transformed into money by exchange, by a process of circulation. It moves from the production process into the circulation sphere not in the form of commodity capital that has to be transformed back into money capital, but rather as money capital that has to be transformed back into productive capital, i.e. has to buy new labour-power and materials of production. The money form of the circulating capital, that consumed in labour-power and means of production, is replaced not by the sale of the product, but rather by the natural form of the product itself, i.e. not by withdrawing its value again from circulation in the money form, but rather by adding money newly produced.

Let us assume that this circulating capital is £500, and the turnover period five weeks: a four-week working period, with the circulation period only one week. Right from the start, money has in part to be advanced for five weeks in a production stock, and in part kept on hand to be paid out bit by bit as wages. At the beginning of the sixth week, £400 has returned and £100 been set free. This is continually repeated. Here, as before, £100 always exists in the released form for a certain section of the turnover. But this consists of additional money newly produced, just like the other £400. Here we have ten turnovers in the year, and the annual product is £5,000 in gold. (The circulation period here does not arise from the time taken to transform commodities into money, but rather that taken to transform money into elements of production.)

For any other capital of £500, turning over under the same conditions, the constantly renewed money form is the changed form of the commodity capital produced, a capital which is cast into circulation every four weeks and always receives this money form afresh by its sale – i.e. by the periodic withdrawal of the sum of money in the shape of which it originally entered the process. Here, on the contrary, in every turnover period a new additional sum of £500 in money is cast into circulation by the production process, so as to keep withdrawing materials of production and labour-power from circulation. The money thus cast into the circulation sphere is not withdrawn from it again by the circuit of this capital, but rather by the increased quantity of new gold that is constantly produced.

If we consider the variable part of this circulating capital and take it to be £100, as above, then this £100 would in ordinary commodity production be sufficient to pay labour-power through a ten-fold turnover. Here, in money production, the same sum is also sufficient; however the five-weekly reflux of £100 with which the labour-power is paid is not the changed form of its product, but rather a part of its ever new product itself. The gold producer pays his workers directly with a part of the gold they have themselves produced. Thus the £1,000 that is laid out each year on labour-power and thrown into circulation by the workers does not return via circulation to its starting-point.

As far as the fixed capital is concerned, moreover, the initial establishment of the business requires the expenditure of a relatively large money capital, which is thus cast into the circulation sphere. Like all fixed capital, this only returns back bit by bit over a number of years. But it flows back as a direct fragment of the product, the gold, not by the sale of the product and its consequent conversion into monetary form. Thus it does not receive its money form by a withdrawal of money from circulation, but rather by the accumulation of a corresponding part of the product. The money capital thus re-established is not a sum of money gradually withdrawn from circulation to balance the sum of money originally cast into it for fixed capital. It is an additional quantity of money.

Finally, as far as the surplus-value is concerned, this is also equal to a part of the new gold product that is cast into circulation in each new turnover period, to be spent unproductively, according to our assumption, and paid out for means of subsistence and luxury articles.

According to our assumption, however, this entire annual gold production – through which labour-power and materials of production, though not money, are steadily withdrawn from the market, and additional money is steadily supplied to it – only replaces the money worn out during the year, and thus simply keeps intact the social money stock which always exists in the two forms of hoard and money in circulation, though in varying proportions.

According to the law of commodity circulation, the total quantity of money must be equal to the quantity of money required for circulation plus a sum of money existing in the hoard form which increases or decreases according to the contraction or expansion of circulation, and serves in particular for the formation of the reserve fund of means of payment that is needed. What has to be paid in money – in so far as there is no direct balancing of accounts – is the value of the commodities. The fact that part of this value consists of surplus-value, i.e. has cost the seller of the commodity nothing, does not change this situation in any way. If the producers all possessed their means of production independently, there would then be circulation between the direct producers themselves. Ignoring the constant part of their capital, we could divide their annual surplus product, by analogy with the situation under capitalism, into two parts: part (a), which simply replaces their necessary means of subsistence, and part (b), which they partly consume as luxury products, and partly apply to the expansion of production. Part (a) then represents the variable capital, part (b) the surplus-value. But this division would still have no effect on the quantity of money required to circulate their total product. With circumstances otherwise remaining the same, the value of the mass of commodities in circulation would be the same, and so would the quantity of money required by it. They would also have to have the same money reserves as before, given a similar division of the turnover period – i.e. the same part of their capital would always have to be in the money form – on our continued supposition that their production was commodity production. Thus the circumstance that a part of the commodity value consists of surplus-value does not alter in the least the quantity of money needed to carry on the business.

An opponent of Tooke, who supports the form $M–C–M'$, asked him how the capitalist always managed to withdraw more money from circulation than he cast into it. Let us be clear that what is involved here is not the *formation* of surplus-value. This, the only real secret, is taken for granted by the capitalists. The sum of value invested would not be capital if it did not enrich itself with a surplus-value. Hence surplus-value is assumed from the outset. Its existence is a matter of course.

Thus the question is not: where does surplus-value come from? But rather: where does the money come from which it is turned into?

In bourgeois economics, the existence of surplus-value is taken for granted. Thus not only is it presupposed, but it is also presupposed at the same time that a part of the mass of commodities cast into circulation consists of surplus product, and thus represents a value that the capitalist did not cast into circulation with his capital; that the capitalist therefore casts into circulation an excess over and above his capital, and withdraws this excess from it again.

The commodity capital that the capitalist casts into circulation is of greater value (why this should be so is not explained or understood from the capitalist's standpoint, but it is a fact for all that) than the productive capital he has withdrawn in labour-power and means of production from the circulation sphere. On this assumption, it is therefore clear why not only capitalist *A*, but also *B, C, D,* etc. can always withdraw from circulation, by exchanging their commodities, more value than the value of their original capital, which is always advanced anew. *A, B, C, D,* etc. always cast a greater commodity value into circulation in the form of commodity capital (an operation which has as many sides to it as there are independently functioning capitals) than they withdraw from it in the form of productive capital. Thus they always have a value sum to share among themselves (i.e. each of them can withdraw from circulation a productive capital) equal to the value of the productive capitals they have respectively advanced, and can just as regularly share out a value sum which they cast into circulation from just as many sides in the commodity form, as a respective surplus of commodity value over the value of their commodity's elements of production.

But before the commodity capital is transformed back into productive capital and the surplus-value contained in it is spent, it must be turned into money. Where does the money for this come from? This question appears difficult at first glance, and neither Tooke nor anyone else has yet answered it.

Assume that the circulating capital of £500 advanced in the form of money capital, whatever may be its turnover period, is the total circulating capital of society, i.e. of the capitalist class. The surplus-value is £100. How then can the entire capitalist class continue extracting £600 from the circulation sphere, if it only ever puts £500 into it?

Once the money capital of £500 has been transformed into productive capital, this is transformed within the production process into a commodity value of £600, and there now exists in the circulation sphere not only a commodity value of £500, equal to the money capital originally advanced, but also a newly produced surplus-value of £100.

This extra surplus-value of £100 is cast into circulation in the commodity form. There is no doubt about that. But the extra money needed for the circulation of this additional commodity value is not provided by the same operation.

This difficulty should not be circumvented by plausible subterfuges.

For example: as far as concerns the constant circulating capital, it is clear that not all of it is laid out at the same time. While capitalist A is selling his commodities, and thus the capital he has advanced is assuming the money form, the capital of buyer B, which is present in the money form, is assuming the form of B's means of production, and it is A himself who produces these. By the same act through which A gives back its money form to the commodity capital he has produced, B gives his capital back its productive form, transforming it from the money form into means of production and labour-power; the same sum of money functions in the two-way process just as in every simple sale $C-M$. On the other hand, if A transforms his money into means of production again, he buys from C, and this latter thereby pays B, etc. The transaction might thus appear to have been explained.

However, none of the laws put forward with respect to the quantity of money circulating for the purpose of commodity circulation (Volume 1, Chapter 3) are in any way altered by the capitalist character of the production process.

Therefore, when it is said that the circulating capital advanced by society in the money form amounts to £500, it has already been taken into account that this is not only the sum which was advanced at the same time, but that this sum also sets more productive capital than £500 in motion, since it serves alternately as the money fund for different productive capitals. This mode of explanation already presupposes that the money exists, whereas it is precisely its existence that is to be explained.

It might further be said that capitalist A produces articles that capitalist B consumes individually and unproductively. B's money thus turns A's commodity capital into money, and so the same sum of money serves to turn into money both B's surplus-value and A's circulating constant capital. But here the solution to the question that is to be answered is presupposed even more directly. Namely, where does B get this money to meet his revenue? How did he himself manage to convert into money this part of his product's surplus-value?

It might be said, again, that the part of the circulating variable capital that A advances at any one time to his workers constantly flows back to him from the circulation sphere; only a changing part of it is kept back by him for the payment of wages. Between the outlay and the reflux there is however a certain interval, in the course of which the money paid out in wages can serve among other things to convert his surplus-value into money.

However, we know, firstly, that the greater this interval, the greater must be the quantity of money in reserve which capitalist *A* must constantly retain in his possession. Secondly, if the workers pay the money out and buy commodities with it, the surplus-value contained in these commodities is also proportionately converted into money. Thus the same money that is advanced in the form of variable capital also serves to that extent to convert the surplus-value into money. Without going any deeper into the question here, it is at least clear that the consumption of the entire capitalist class and the unproductive persons dependent on it keeps even pace with that of the working class; thus, on top of the money cast into circulation by the workers, money must be cast into circulation by the capitalists, if they are to spend their surplus-value as revenue; and so money for this must be withdrawn from circulation. The explanation just given would only reduce the quantity needed, and not obviate the need.

It might be said, finally: a large amount of money is always cast into circulation on the first investment of the fixed capital, and this is withdrawn from circulation again only gradually, bit by bit, in the course of several years, by whoever threw it in. Is this sum not sufficient to convert the surplus-value? The answer to this is that the sum of £500 (which also includes hoard formation for the necessary reserve fund) may well already imply the investment of this sum as fixed capital, if not by the person who cast it in, then at least by someone else. Besides, it is already presupposed, in connection with the sum that is spent on the acquisition of products serving as fixed capital, that the surplus-value in these commodities is also paid for, and the question precisely arises: where does this money come from?

The general answer has already been given: if a mass of commodities of *x* times £1,000 is to circulate, it in no way affects the quantity of money needed for this circulation whether the value of this commodity mass contains surplus-value or not, or whether the mass of commodities is produced under capitalist conditions or not. *Thus the problem itself does not exist.* With conditions otherwise given, such as the velocity of circulation of the money, etc., a definite sum of money is required to circulate the commodity value of *x* times £1,000, quite irrespective of how much or how little of this value accrues to the direct producers of these commodities. In as much as a problem does exist here, it coincides with the general problem: where does the sum of money needed in a country for the circulation of commodities come from?

However there does exist, from the standpoint of capitalist production, the *semblance* of a special problem. For here it is the capitalist, the man who casts the money into circulation, who appears as the point of departure. The money that the worker spends in payment for his means of subsistence existed previously as the money form of the variable capital, and was therefore originally cast into circulation by the capitalist as means of purchase or payment for labour-power. Moreover, the money that the capitalist casts into circulation originally constituted the money form of his constant fixed and fluid capital; he spends it as means of purchase or payment for means of labour and production materials. Beyond this, however, the capitalist no longer appears as the point of departure for the quantity of money that exists in circulation. All that exist now are two starting-points, the capitalist and the worker. All third parties either must receive money from these two classes for the performance of services, or, in so far as they receive money without providing services in return, they are co-proprietors of surplus-value in the forms of rent, interest, etc. If the surplus-value does not all remain in the pockets of the industrial capitalist, but has to be shared by him with other persons, this has nothing to do with the question at issue. What was asked is how he converts his surplus-value into money, not how the money obtained for it is then divided up. For the present case, therefore, we can still consider the capitalist as the sole owner of surplus-value. As far as the workers are concerned, it has already been said that they are only a secondary point of departure, whereas the capitalist is the primary point of departure for the money cast into circulation by the workers. The money that is first advanced as variable capital is already performing its second circulation when the worker spends it in payment for means of subsistence.

Thus the capitalist class remains the sole starting-point of the money circulation. If it needs £400 for payment for means of production, and £100 for payment of labour-power, then it casts £500 into circulation. But the surplus-value contained in the product, given a rate of surplus-value of 100 per cent, makes up a value of £100. How can the capitalist class continue to extract £600 from circulation, if it only ever puts £500 in? Out of nothing, nothing comes. The entire capitalist class cannot extract anything from the circulation sphere that was not put into it already.

We disregard here the fact that the sum of £400 in money may be sufficient, given a ten-fold turnover, to circulate means of production to a value of £4,000 and labour to a value of £1,000, while the remaining £100 may suffice for the circulation of £1,000 surplus-value. This ratio between the sum of money and the commodity value circulated by it contributes nothing to the matter in hand. The problem remains the same. If the same piece of money did not undergo several circulations, then £5,000 would have to be cast into circulation as capital, and £1,000 would be needed to convert the surplus-value into money. The question is where this money comes from, whether it is £1,000 or £100. In either case, it is additional money capital cast into circulation.

In point of fact, paradoxical as it may seem at the first glance, the capitalist class itself casts into circulation the money that serves towards the realization of the surplus-value contained in its commodities. But note well: it does not cast this in as money advanced, and therefore not as capital. It spends it as means of purchase for its individual consumption. Thus the money is not advanced by the capitalist class, even though this class is the starting-point of its circulation.

Let us take a particular capitalist who sets up a business, a farmer for example. During the first year he advances a money capital of £5,000, let us say, in payment for means of production (£4,000) and for labour-power (£1,000). If the rate of surplus-value is 100 per cent, then the surplus-value he appropriates is £1,000. The above £5,000 includes all the money that he advances as money capital. But the man must also live, and he does not take in any money until the end of the year. Say that his consumption comes to £1,000. He must then have this in hand. He admittedly tells us that he has to advance this £1,000 for the first year. But this is an advance only in the subjective sense, and means nothing more than that he has to cover his individual consumption for the first year out of his own pocket, instead of using the product produced for nothing by his workers. He does not advance this money as capital. He spends it, i.e. pays it out for an equivalent in means of subsistence which he then consumes. This value is spent by him in money, cast into circulation, and withdrawn from it in commodity values. These commodity values are consumed by him. Thus he has ceased to stand in any relationship to their value. The money with which he pays for it exists as a component of the circulating money stock. But he has withdrawn the value of this money from circulation in products, and the value of these products is destroyed together with the products in which it existed. It has all gone. At the end of the year, then, he throws into circulation a commodity value of £6,000 and sells this. There returns to him as a result (1) the money capital of £5,000 that he advanced; (2) his converted surplus-value of £1,000. He advanced £5,000 as capital, cast this into circulation, and he withdraws from circulation £6,000; £5,000 as capital and £1,000 for surplus-value. The final £1,000 is converted into money with the money that he threw into circulation not as capitalist, but as consumer, i.e. did not advance, but actually spent. It now returns to him as the money form of the surplus-value produced by him. And from now on this operation is repeated annually. From the second year, however, the £1,000 that he spends is always the changed form, the money form, of the surplus-value he produced. He spends this annually, and it returns to him at the same interval.

If his capital were to turn over several times in the course of the year, this would not change things in any way, even though it would affect the length of time for which he had to cast into circulation, over and above the money capital he advanced, this sum for his individual consumption, and hence also the magnitude of the sum involved.

This money is not cast into circulation by the capitalist as capital. However, it certainly pertains to the character of the capitalist that he should be capable of living off the means of subsistence in his possession until the reflux of his surplus-value.

It was assumed in this case that the sum of money that the capitalist casts into circulation to cover his individual consumption until the first reflux of his capital is exactly equal to the surplus-value that he produces and hence has to convert into money. This is obviously an arbitrary assumption in relation to the individual capitalist. But it must be correct for the capitalist class as a whole, on the assumption of simple reproduction. It simply expresses the same thing as this assumption implies, namely that the entire surplus-value is unproductively consumed (but no more than this, i.e. no fraction of the original capital stock).

It was assumed above that the entire production of precious metals (taken as £500) was just sufficient to replace the wear and tear of the money.

The gold-producing capitalists possess their entire product in gold, including the part of it which replaces constant capital, the part which replaces variable capital, and the part which consists of surplus-value. One part of the society's surplus-value thus consists of gold, and not of products that are turned into money only in the course of circulation. It consists of gold from the start, and is cast into the circulation sphere in order to withdraw products from this. The same applies here to wages, the variable capital, and to the replacement of the constant capital advanced. Thus if one section of the capitalist class casts into circulation a commodity value greater (by the surplus-value) than the money capital they advanced, another section of capitalists casts into circulation a greater money value (greater by the surplus-value) than the commodity value that they constantly withdraw from circulation for the production of gold. If one group of capitalists constantly pump more money out of the circulation sphere than they put into it, the gold-producing group constantly pump more money in than they withdraw from it in means of production.

Now even though a part of the £500 gold product is surplus-value for the gold producers, the entire sum is still simply determined by the replacement of the money needed for the circulation of commodities; how much of this converts the surplus-value of the commodities into money, and how much the other component parts of their value, is immaterial here.

If gold production is transferred from the country in question to other countries, this does not alter the situation in any way. A part of the social labour-power and social means of production in country *A* is transformed into a product, e.g. linen, to the value of £500, and this is exported to country *B* in order to buy gold there. The productive capital thus applied in country *A* no more throws commodities onto the market in country *A*, as opposed to money, than if it had been directly applied in gold production. This product of *A* is represented by £500 in gold, and comes into circulation in country *A* only as money. The part of the social surplus-value that this product contains exists directly in money and, as far as country *A* goes, never in any other form. Although, for the gold-producing capitalists, only one part of their product is surplus-value, while another represents the replacement of capital, the question as to how much of this gold, besides the circulating constant capital, replaces variable capital, and how much represents surplus-value, depends exclusively on the respective ratios of wages and surplus-value to the value of the commodities in circulation. The part that forms surplus-value is divided between the various members of the capitalist class. Even though it is continuously paid out for their individual consumption, and taken in again by the sale of new products – and it is precisely this buying and selling that circulates among them the money needed for the conversion of surplus-value – a part of the social surplus-value still exists in the form of money in the pockets of the capitalists, even if in changing portions, just as a part of the workers' wages remains in their pockets in the form of money for at least part of the week. And this part is not restricted by the part of the gold product that originally forms the surplus-value of the gold-producing capitalists, but rather, as we have already said, by the proportion in which the above product of £500 is divided between capitalists and workers in general, and in which the commodity value consists of surplus-value and the other components of value.

Still, the part of the surplus-value that does not exist in other commodities, but rather alongside these other commodities in money, only consists of a part of the gold annually produced in so far as a part of the annual gold production circulates in order to realize surplus-value. The other part of the money which exists in ever changing portions in the hands of the capitalist class as the money form of their surplus-value is not an element of the gold annually produced, but rather of the quantity of money previously accumulated in the country.

On our supposition, the annual gold production of £500 is just sufficient to replace the money annually worn down. Thus if we simply bear in mind this £500, and abstract from the part of the mass of commodities annually produced which circulate by means of the money previously accumulated, then the surplus-value produced in the form of commodities already finds in circulation money for its conversion, because, at another point, surplus-value is annually being produced in the form of gold. The same applies to the other parts of the gold product of £500 that replace the money capital advanced.

There are two points to be noted here.

It follows, firstly, that the surplus-value spent by the capitalists in money, as well as the variable and other productive capital which they advance in money, is in fact the product of the workers, in particular of those workers occupied in gold production. These produce afresh both the part of the gold product that is 'advanced' to them as wages, and the part of the gold product in which the surplus-value of the capitalist gold producers is directly represented. Finally, as far as concerns the part of the gold product that simply replaces the constant capital value advanced for its production, this reappears in the gold form (or in any kind of product) only as a result of the annual labour of the workers. At the start of the business it was originally given out by the capitalist in money which was not newly produced but formed a part of the social quantity of money in circulation. However, in so far as it is replaced by a new product, additional gold, it is the annual product of the workers. The advance on the part of the capitalist appears here, too, only as a form deriving from the fact that the worker is neither the proprietor of his own means of production, nor does he have at his disposal during the course of production the means of subsistence produced by other workers.

Secondly, however, as far as concerns the quantity of money that exists independently of this annual replacement of £500, partly in the form of a hoard, partly in the form of a quantity of money in circulation, the same must apply to it, i.e. the same must originally have applied, as still applies to this annual £500. We shall return to this point at the conclusion of this section. In the meantime, some other points must be noted.

*

In considering the turnover, we have already seen that, with circumstances otherwise remaining the same, changes in the length of the turnover periods make different amounts of capital necessary in order to continue production on the same scale. The monetary circulation must thus be elastic enough to adapt to this alternate expansion and contraction.

If we further assume that other circumstances remain the same – and therefore that there is no change in the size, intensity or productivity of the working day – but that there is an *altered division of the value product* between wages and surplus-value, so that either the former rises and the latter falls, or vice versa, then the quantity of money in circulation is not affected. This change can come about without any kind of expansion or contraction in the quantity of money in circulation. If we consider for instance the case of a general rise in wages, and – on the conditions here assumed – a consequent general fall in the rate of surplus-value, there would not be, again on the assumptions made here, any change in the value of the mass of commodities in circulation. In this case, moreover, the money capital that has to be advanced as variable capital would grow, and so would the quantity of money that serves for this function. But this being the case, surplus-value would decline by the same amount as the increase in the quantity of money required for the function of variable capital, and thus so would the quantity of money needed for its realization. The quantity of money needed to realize the commodity value is therefore no more affected than is this commodity value itself. The cost price of the commodities rises for the individual capitalist, but their social price of production remains unaltered. What is changed is the ratio in which, leaving aside the constant portion of the value, the production price of the commodities is divided between wages and profit.

It will be said, however, that a greater outlay of variable money capital means a correspondingly greater quantity of monetary means in the hands of the workers. (The value of the money is of course assumed to be constant here.) This gives rise to a greater demand for commodities on the part of the workers. A further consequence is a rise in the price of commodities. Alternatively, it is said that, if wages rise, the capitalists will increase the prices of their commodities. In both cases, the general rise in wages leads to a rise in the prices of commodities. Thus a greater quantity of money must be needed to circulate the commodities, whether the price rise is explained in one way or the other.

The reply to the first of these conceptions is that as a result of rising wages the demand of the workers for necessary means of subsistence will grow. Their demand for luxury articles will increase to a smaller degree, or else a demand will arise for articles that previously did not enter the area of their consumption. The sudden and large-scale rise in demand for necessary means of subsistence will certainly cause a temporary rise in their prices. The result of this is that a greater part of the social capital will be applied to the production of necessary means of subsistence, and a smaller part to the production of luxury goods, since the latter will have fallen in price on account of the decline in surplus-value and the resulting diminished demand for them from the capitalists. To the extent that the workers themselves buy luxury goods, however, the rise in their wages does not lead to a rise in the prices of necessary means of subsistence, but simply displaces the buyers of luxury goods. More luxury goods than before are consumed by the workers, and relatively fewer are consumed by the capitalists. That is all. After a few oscillations, the mass of commodities in circulation is the same in value as before. As for these temporary oscillations, moreover, they can have no other result than to cast into domestic circulation, as unoccupied money capital, capital which formerly sought employment in speculative undertakings on the stock exchange or abroad.

The reply to the second conception is this. If it were within the capacity of the capitalist producers to increase the prices of their commodities at will, then they could and would do so even without any rise in wages. Nor would wages rise with a fall in commodity prices. The capitalist class would never oppose trade unions, since they would always and in all circumstances be able to do what they now do exceptionally under certain particular and so to speak local conditions – i.e. use any increase in wages to raise commodity prices to a far higher degree, and thus tuck away a greater profit.

The contention that the capitalists can raise the prices of luxury articles because the demand for these declines (as a result of the reduced demand of the capitalists, whose means of purchasing them have diminished) would be an extremely original application of the law of supply and demand. In as much as there is not just a shift in the buyers, workers replacing capitalists – and to the extent that this displacement occurs, the workers' demand does not operate to raise the price of the necessary means of subsistence, since the part of their additional wages that the workers spend on articles of luxury cannot be spent by them on necessary means of subsistence – the prices of luxury goods fall as a consequence of the reduced demand. As a result, capital is withdrawn from their production, until their supply is reduced to the extent that corresponds with their changed role in the social production process. With this reduction in production, they rise again to their normal prices, given that their values are unchanged. While this contraction or balancing process is taking place, the same amount of additional capital will be supplied for the production of means of subsistence, whose prices are rising, as is withdrawn from the other branch of production, until demand is satisfied. There is then once again an equilibrium, and the conclusion of the whole process is that the social capital, and hence also the money capital, is divided between the production of necessary means of subsistence and that of luxury goods in changed proportions.

The entire objection is a red herring brought in by the capitalists and their economic sycophants.

The facts that provide the pretext for this diversion are of three kinds.

(1) It is a general law of monetary circulation that, if the sum of the prices of goods in circulation rises – whether this increase is for the same volume of commodities or for an increased volume – with other circumstances remaining the same, the quantity of money in circulation grows. The effect is then taken for the cause. However, wages rise (even if seldom, and proportionately only in exceptional cases) with the increased price of the necessary means of subsistence. Their rise is the result of the rise in commodity prices, and not the cause of this.

(2) Given a partial or local rise in wages – i.e. a rise in just a few branches of production – it is possible that a local rise in prices for the products of this branch may result. But even this depends on many circumstances. For example, that wages were not abnormally depressed here, and hence the rate of profit abnormally high, that the market for these commodities was not constricted by a rise in price (and thus that a rise in their prices does not depend on a preceding contraction in their supply), etc.

(3) With a general rise in wages, the price of the goods produced in

branches of industry in which variable capital is predominant rises, whereas prices fall in those branches in which constant or fixed capital predominates.

*

In the case of simple commodity circulation (Volume 1, Chapter 3, 2) we showed that even if the money form is only transient in the circulation of a particular quantity of commodities, yet the money transiently in the hands of one person in the commodity metamorphosis still necessarily finds its way into the hands of someone else, and so not only are commodities exchanged on all sides, replacing each other, but this replacement is also mediated and accompanied by a precipitation of money on all sides. 'When one commodity replaces another, the money commodity always sticks to the hands of some third person. Circulation sweats money from every pore' (Volume 1, p. 208). The very same fact is expressed on the basis of capitalist commodity production by the constant retention of a part of capital in the form of money capital, and the constant presence of a part of the surplus-value similarly in the money form in the hands of its proprietor.

Apart from this, the *circuit of money* – i.e. the *return* of the money to its starting-point – in as much as this forms a moment of the turnover of capital, is a phenomenon completely different from and even opposed to the *circulation of money*,[1] which expresses its constant *removal* from its starting-point through a series of hands (Volume 1, p. 210). However, an accelerated turnover involves by its very nature an accelerated circulation.

To take the case of variable capital first. If for example a money

1. If the Physiocrats still lumped the two phenomena together, they were at least the first to have stressed the return of money to its point of departure as an essential form of the circulation of capital, as a form of the circulation that mediates reproduction. 'If you take a look at the *Tableau économique*, you will see that the productive class gives out the money with which the other classes come to buy its products, and that these return this money to it the following year in coming back to make the same purchases again . . . The sole cycle that you see here is therefore that of expenditure followed by reproduction, and reproduction followed by expenditure; a cycle which is described by the circulation of the money that measures expenditure and reproduction' (Quesnay, *Dialogues sur le commerce et sur les travaux des artisans,* in *Physiocrates,* ed. Daire, I, pp. 208–9).

'It is this continuous advance and return of capitals that must be called the circulation of money, this useful and fertile circulation which animates all the works of society, sustaining the movement and life of the body politic in a way that may well be compared with the circulation of blood in the animal body' (Turgot, *Réflexions,* etc., *Œuvres,* ed. Daire, I, p. 45).

capital of £500 turns over ten times a year in the form of variable capital, it is clear that this aliquot part of the quantity of money in circulation circulates ten times its sum of values. It circulates ten times in the year between capitalist and worker. The worker is paid – and himself pays – ten times in the year with the same aliquot part of the quantity of money in circulation. If this variable capital were to turn over once in the year, with the same scale of production, then there would only be one circulation of £5,000.

Furthermore, the constant part of the circulating capital is £1,000. If the capital turns over ten times, then the capitalist sells his commodity ten times in the year, and thus also the constant circulating part of its value with it. The same aliquot part of the money quantity in circulation (£1,000) passes ten times in the year from the hands of its owner to those of the capitalist. There are ten changes of place from one hand to another. Secondly, the capitalist buys means of production ten times in the year; these are again ten circulations of money from one hand to another. With money to the total of £1,000, commodities for £10,000 are sold by the industrial capitalist, and other commodities of £10,000 are bought. By a twenty-fold circulation of the £1,000 of money, a commodity stock of £20,000 is circulated.

Finally, accelerated turnover also leads to a quicker circulation of the portion of money that realizes surplus-value.

Conversely, however, a more rapid monetary circulation does not necessarily involve a more rapid turnover of capital, and hence also of money, i.e. there is not necessarily a shortening and more rapid renewal of the reproduction process.

More rapid monetary circulation takes place whenever a greater volume of transactions is completed with the same quantity of money. This can also be the case without a change in the reproduction period of the capital, as a result of changed technical arrangements for monetary circulation. Further, the volume of transactions in which money circulates can increase without this expressing a real replacement of commodities (speculation in futures on the stock exchange etc.). On the other hand, certain monetary circulations can completely disappear. Where the agriculturist is his own landlord, for example, there is no monetary circulation between farmer and landlord; where the industrial capitalist is himself the owner of his capital, there is no circulation between him and a creditor.

As for the question of the original formation of a money hoard in a country, as well as the appropriation of it by a few people, it is not necessary to go into this in detail here.

The capitalist mode of production – since its basis is wage-labour, and therefore also the payment of the worker in money and the general transformation of services in kind into money payments – can develop on a large scale and penetrate deeply only when there is a quantity of money in the country in question sufficient for circulation and for the hoard formation (reserve fund, etc.) conditioned by this circulation. This is a historical precondition, even if the situation should not be conceived in such a way that a sufficient hoard has first to be formed before capitalist production can begin. The latter rather develops simultaneously with the development of its preconditions, and one of these preconditions is a sufficient supply of precious metals. Hence the increased supply of precious metals from the sixteenth century onwards was a decisive moment in the historical development of capitalist production. In so far as we are dealing with the further supply of money material needed on the basis of the capitalist mode of production, we can say that on the one hand surplus-value is cast into circulation in the product without the money for its conversion, while on the other hand surplus-value in gold is cast into circulation without its previous transformation from product into money.

The additional commodities that have to be transformed into money find the sums of money needed available because on the other hand additional gold (and silver) is cast into circulation by production itself, not by exchange, and has to be transformed into commodities.

2. ACCUMULATION AND EXPANDED REPRODUCTION

The case in which accumulation takes place in the form of reproduction on an expanded scale clearly does not offer any new problems with respect to money circulation.

As far as the additional money capital is concerned, that required for the function of the increased productive capital, this is supplied by the portion of realized surplus-value that is cast into circulation by the capitalists as money capital, instead of as the money form of revenue. The money is already in the hands of the capitalists. It is simply its application that differs.

Now, however, as a result of the addition to the productive capital, an additional mass of commodities is cast into circulation as its product. Together with the extra mass of commodities, a part of the extra money needed for their realization is also cast in, to the extent that the value of this mass of commodities contains the value of the productive capital consumed in their production. This additional quantity of money is advanced precisely as additional money capital, and hence returns to the capitalist with the turnover of his capital. Here the same question comes up again as before. Where does the extra money come from to realize the extra surplus-value that now exists in the commodity form?

The general reply is again the same. The total price of the mass of commodities in circulation has increased, not because the price of a given mass of commodities has risen, but rather because the mass of commodities now in circulation is greater than that of the commodities circulating earlier, without this having been balanced by any fall in prices. The additional money required for the circulation of this increased commodity mass of a greater value must be created either by a more economic use of the quantity of money in circulation – whether by directly balancing payments, etc., or by means that accelerate the circulation of the same pieces of money – or alternatively by the transformation of money from the hoard form into the circulating form. This does not just imply that idle money capital begins to function as means of purchase or payment, or that money capital already functioning as a reserve fund, while continuing to perform the function of a reserve fund for its owners, circulates actively for the society (as with deposits in banks, which are constantly lent out), and thus performs a double function. It also means that stagnant reserves of coin are used more economically.

'So that money as coin may flow continuously, coin must continuously congeal into money. The continual movement of coin implies its perpetual stagnation in larger or smaller amounts in reserve funds of coin which arise everywhere within the framework of circulation and which are at the same time a condition of circulation. The formation, distribution, dissolution and re-formation of these funds constantly changes; existing funds disappear continuously and their disappearance is a continuous fact. This unceasing transformation of coin into money and of money into coin was expressed by Adam Smith when he said that, in addition to the particular commodity that he sells, every commodity-owner must always keep in stock a certain amount of the general commodity with which he buys. We have seen that *M–C*, the second member of the circuit *C–M–C*, splits up into a series of purchases, which are not effected all at once but successively over a period of time, so that one part of *M* circulates as coin, while the other part remains at rest as money. In this case, money is in fact only *suspended coin* and the various component parts of the coinage in circulation appear, constantly changing, now in one form, now in another. The first transformation of the medium of circulation into money constitutes therefore merely a technical aspect of the circulation of money' (Karl Marx, *Zur Kritik der politischen Ökonomie*, 1859, pp. 105–6. [*A Contribution to the Critique of Political Economy*, London, 1971, p. 126.] 'Coin', as opposed to money, is used here to denote money in its function as mere means of circulation, as opposed to its other functions.)

To the extent that all these means together are not enough, there must be additional production of gold, or, what comes to the same thing, a part of the additional product must be exchanged either directly or indirectly for gold – the product of those countries that produce precious metals.

The sum of labour-power and social means of production that is spent in the annual production of gold and silver as instruments of circulation forms a heavy item of *faux frais** for the capitalist mode of production, or more generally for a mode of production based on commodity circulation. It withdraws from social use a corresponding sum of possible additional means of production and consumption, i.e. of real wealth. To the extent that the costs of this expensive machinery of circulation are reduced, with the scale of production remaining the same, i.e. at a given level of its extension, the productive forces of social labour are correspondingly heightened. Thus in as much as the auxiliary means that develop with credit have this effect, they directly increase capitalist wealth, whether this is because a greater part of the social production and labour process is thereby accomplished without the intervention of real money, or because the capacity of the actually functioning quantity of money to fulfil its function is thereby increased.

This also disposes of the pointless question of whether capitalist production on its present scale would be possible without credit (even considered from *this* standpoint alone), i.e. with a merely metallic circulation. It would clearly not be possible. It would come up against the limited scale of precious-metal production. On the other hand, we should not get any mystical ideas about the productive power of the

---

* Overhead costs.

credit system, just because this makes money capital available or fluid. But the further development of this point does not belong here.

*

We must now consider the case where there is not actual accumulation, i.e. direct expansion of the scale of production, but where a part of the surplus-value realized is stored up over a longer or shorter time as a monetary reserve fund, so as later to be transformed into productive capital.

In so far as the money thus accumulated is extra money, the situation is very clear. This money can only be a part of the additional gold supplied by the gold-producing countries. It should be noted in this connection that the domestic products in return for which this gold is imported no longer exist in the country in question. They have been dispensed abroad in exchange for gold.

If we assume on the other hand that there is the same quantity of money in the country as before, then the money that has been stored away or is being stored away has flowed in from circulation; it is simply its function that has changed. It has been transformed from circulating money into a gradually formed latent money capital.

The money that is stored up here is the money form of commodities that have been sold, and moreover, of that portion of their value that represents surplus-value for their owner. (The credit system is assumed here to be non-existent.) The capitalist who stores up money has to that extent sold without buying.

If we look upon this process simply as a partial phenomenon, there is nothing in it that needs explaining. One group of capitalists keep back part of the money they obtain from the sale of their products, instead of using it to withdraw products from the market. Another group, on the other hand, transform their money into products, with the exception of the constantly recurring money capital needed to carry on production. A part of the product thrown onto the market as a bearer of surplus-value consists of means of production, or of the real elements of variable capital, the necessary means of subsistence. It can therefore immediately serve to expand production. For it is in no way assumed that one group of capitalists accumulate money capital, while the other group completely consume their surplus-value, but simply that one group carry out their accumulation in the money form, and build up latent money capital, while the others really do accumulate, i.e. expand the scale of production, actually expand their productive capital. The quantity of money present remains sufficient for the needs of circulation, even if it is alternately one group of capitalists who store up money, while the other group expand their scale of production, and vice versa. The storing up of money on the one side can proceed even without cash, simply through the piling up of credit notes.

But difficulties start to arise when we assume not partial accumulation of money capital but general accumulation within the capitalist class. Outside this class, on our assumption – that of the universal and exclusive domination of capitalist production – there is no other class except the working class. The total purchases of the working class are equal to the sum of their wages, i.e. the sum of the variable capital advanced by the entire capitalist class as a whole. This money flows back to the latter through the sale of their product to the working class. Their variable capital thereby receives its money form. If the sum of variable capital is x times £100, this is not the total variable capital advanced in the year, but only that applied; whether this variable capital value is advanced with more money or less during the year, according to the speed of turnover, does not affect the question at present under discussion. With this capital of x times £100, the capitalist class buys a certain quantity of labour-power, or pays wages to a certain number of workers – first transaction. The workers use this sum to buy a certain value of commodities from the capitalists, and in this way the sum of x times £100 returns to the hands of the capitalists – second transaction. This process is constantly repeated. The sum of x times £100 can therefore never enable the working class to buy the part of the product which contains the constant capital, let alone the surplus-value which belongs to the capitalists. The workers can buy with x times £100 only a portion of the value of the social product equal to the portion of value which represents the value of the variable capital advanced.

Apart from the case in which this all-round monetary accumulation simply expresses the division, in whatever proportions, between the various individual capitalists of the additional precious metal which has been brought in – how else is the entire capitalist class to accumulate money?

They would all have to have sold a part of their product without buying again. It is nothing mysterious that they all possess a certain money fund which they cast into the circulation sphere as means of circulation for their consumption, and of which each receives a certain part back again from the circulation sphere. But this monetary fund is then precisely a circulation fund, acquired by the conversion into money of surplus-value, and does not consist at all of latent money capital.

If we consider the way things happen in real life, we can say that the latent money capital that is stored up for later use consists of:

(1) Bank deposits; and the money that the banks really dispose of is a relatively small sum. Here it is only nominally stored up as money capital. What is really stored up are monetary claims which are only convertible (to the extent that they ever are converted) because there is a balance between the money drawn out and the money put in. The money that exists in the hands of the bank is relatively only a small sum.

(2) Government papers. These are not capital at all, but simply outstanding claims on the nation's annual product.

(3) Shares. Leaving aside the fraudulent ones, these are titles of ownership to a real capital belonging to a corporate body, and drafts on the surplus-value that flows in from this each year.

In all these cases, there is no storage of money, and what appears on the one hand as storage of money capital appears on the other hand as the continuous real expenditure of money. Whether the money is spent by the person it belongs to, or by other people, by people in debt to him, does not affect the situation.

On the basis of capitalist production, the formation of a hoard as such is never a purpose, but rather a result, a result either of a stagnation in circulation – in that greater quantities of money than usual assume the hoard form – or of the storage required by the turnover. The hoard can also, finally, be simply a formation of money capital, in the latent form for the time being, but destined to function as productive capital.

If on the one hand, therefore, a part of the surplus-value realized in money is withdrawn from circulation and stored up as a hoard, at the same time a further part of the surplus-value is always transformed into productive capital. With the exception of the division of additional precious metal among the capitalist class, storage in the money form never occurs simultaneously at all points.

The same applies to that part of the annual product which represents surplus-value in the commodity form, as applies to the rest of the annual product. A certain sum of money is required for its circulation. This sum of money belongs just as much to the capitalist class as does the annually produced mass of commodities that represents surplus-value. It was originally cast into circulation by the capitalist class itself. It is continuously divided among them afresh by circulation. Just as with the circulation of coin in general, a part of this monetary surplus-value is held up, at ever changing points, while a further part is always circulating. Whether some of this storage is deliberate, in order to form money capital, does not affect the situation in any way.

Here we have disregarded the vicissitudes of circulation, in which one capitalist seizes for himself a piece of another's surplus-value, and even of his capital, and there is therefore a one-sided accumulation and centralization of both money capital and productive capital. A part of the extorted surplus-value that *A* stores up as money capital may thus be a fragment of *B*'s surplus-value that has failed to return to him.

Part Three

The Reproduction and Circulation of the Total Social Capital

Chapter 18: Introduction[1]

I. THE OBJECT OF THE INQUIRY

The immediate production process of capital is its process of labour and valorization, the result of this process being the commodity product, and its determining motive the production of surplus-value.

The process of capital's reproduction includes, on top of this immediate production process, the specific process of circulation with its two phases; it is the overall circuit forming the turnover of capital, a periodic process that is constantly repeated afresh at definite intervals.

Whether we consider the circuit in the form $M \ldots M'$ or that of $P \ldots P$, the immediate production process, P, never forms more than one term in this circuit. In one form it appears as the mediator of the circulation process, while in the other form it is the circulation process that appears as mediating production. The constant repetition of the circuit, the perpetual re-emergence of the capital as productive capital, is conditioned in both cases by its transformations in the circulation process. On the other hand, the constant repetition of the process of production is the condition for the transformations that the capital undergoes over and again in the circulation sphere, for its alternately presenting itself as money capital and as commodity capital.

But each individual capital forms only a fraction of the total social capital, a fraction that has acquired independence and been endowed with individual life, so to speak, just as each individual capitalist is no more than an element of the capitalist class. The movement of the social capital is made up of the totality of movements of these autonomous fractions, the turnovers of the individual capitals. Just as the metamorphosis of the individual commodity is but one term in the series of metamorphoses of the commodity world as a whole, of com-

1. From Manuscript II.

modity circulation, so the metamorphosis of the individual capital, its turnover, is a single term in the circuit of the social capital.

This overall process involves both productive consumption (the immediate production process) together with the changes of form that mediate it (which considered in their material aspect are exchanges), and individual consumption, with the changes of form or exchanges which mediate this. It involves on the one hand the conversion of variable capital into labour-power and the consequent incorporation of labour-power into the capitalist production process. In this aspect, the worker enters the scene as the seller of his commodity, labour-power, and the capitalist as its buyer. On the other hand, however, the sale of commodities involves their purchase by the working class, i.e. the workers' individual consumption. Here, the working class appears as a buyer of commodities, and the capitalists as sellers of commodities to the workers.

The circulation of the commodity capital involves the circulation of surplus-value, and therefore the purchases and sales by way of which the capitalists mediate their individual consumption, the consumption of surplus-value.

The circuits of the individual capitals, therefore, when considered as combined into the social capital, i.e. considered in their totality, do not encompass just the circulation of capital, but also commodity circulation in general. In its fundamentals, the latter can consist of only two components: (1) the specific circuit of capital, and (2) the circuit of those commodities that go into individual consumption, i.e. the commodities on which the workers spend their wages and the capitalists their surplus-value (or part of it). The circuit of capital, in fact, itself comprises the circulation of surplus-value, in as much as this forms part of the commodity capital, and it similarly includes the transformation of variable capital into labour-power, the payment of wages. But the expenditure of this surplus-value and wages on commodities does not form any part of the circulation of capital, even though the spending of wages, at least, depends on this circulation.

In Volume 1, the capitalist production process was analysed both as an isolated event and as a process of reproduction: the production of surplus-value, and the production of capital itself. The formal and material changes undergone by capital in the circulation sphere were assumed, and no attempt was made to consider their details. It was therefore assumed both that the capitalist sells the product at its value and that he finds in the circulation sphere the material means of production that he needs to begin the process anew or to continue it without a break. The only act within the circulation sphere which we had to dwell on in that volume was the purchase and sale of labour-power as the basic condition of capitalist production.

In Part One of the present Volume 2, we considered the various forms that capital assumes in its circuit, and the various forms of this circuit itself. In addition to the working time considered in Volume 1, we now dealt with the circulation time.

In Part Two, we considered the circuit as a periodic one, i.e. as a turnover. It was shown, on the one hand, how the various components of capital (fixed and circulating) complete the circuit of their forms at different intervals and in different ways; the circumstances which gave rise to differing lengths of working period and circulation period were also investigated. We indicated the influence of the circuit's periodicity and of the varying ratio of its component parts on the scale of the production process itself, and on the annual rate of surplus-value. In point of fact, if what was principally considered in Part One were the successive forms that capital constantly assumes and discards in the course of its circuit, what was considered in Part Two was principally how, within this flux and succession of forms, a capital of given size is simultaneously divided, even if to a changing extent, into the various forms of productive capital, money capital and commodity capital, so that not only do these alternate with each other, but also different parts of the total capital value exist and function in these different states alongside each other at any one time. Money capital, in particular, presented specific features that were not indicated in Volume 1. Certain laws were discovered, according to which major components of a given capital, varying according to the conditions of the turnover, must constantly be advanced and renewed in the form of money capital, in order to keep a productive capital of a given size in constant functioning.

What we were dealing with in both Parts One and Two, however, was always no more than an individual capital, the movement of an autonomous part of the social capital.

However, the circuits of individual capitals are interlinked, they presuppose one another and condition one another, and it is precisely by being interlinked in this way that they constitute the movement of the total social capital. Just as, in the case of simple commodity circulation, the overall metamorphosis of a single commodity appeared as but one term in the series of metamorphoses of the commodity world as a whole, now the metamorphosis of the individual capital appears as one term in the series of metamorphoses of the social capital. But if simple commodity circulation in no way necessarily involved the circulation of capital – since it can proceed quite well on the basis of non-capitalist production – the circuit of the total social capital, as already noted, also involves a commodity circulation that does not fall within the circuit of any individual capital, i.e. the circulation of those commodities that do not form capital.

What we now have to consider is the circulation process of the individual capitals as components of the total social capital, i.e. the circulation process of this total social capital. Taken in its entirety, this circulation process is a form of the reproduction process.

2. THE ROLE OF MONEY CAPITAL

(The following subject, i.e. money capital considered as a component of the total social capital, really belongs in a later section of this Part. However, we intend to investigate it here.)

In connection with the turnover of the individual capital, we saw that money capital displays two aspects.

Firstly, it provides the form in which each individual capital steps onto the scene and commences its process as capital. Hence it appears as prime mover, giving the first impulse to the whole process.

Secondly, according to the varying lengths of the turnover period and the varying ratio of its two components – working period and circulation period – the component of the capital value advanced that must be advanced and renewed at any one time in the money form stands in a different ratio to the productive capital that it sets in motion, i.e. to the continuous scale of production. But whatever this ratio may be, the portion of the capital value in process that can function at any one time as productive capital is always restricted by the part of the capital value advanced that must always exist alongside the productive capital in the money form. What is involved here is simply the normal turnover, an abstract average. We therefore disregard any additional money capital required to cope with delays in circulation.

On the first point. Commodity production presupposes commodity circulation, and commodity circulation presupposes the representation of commodities in money, monetary circulation; the duplication of commodities into commodities and money is a law of the emergence of the product as a commodity.* Capitalist commodity production, for its part, whether we consider it socially or individually, similarly presupposes capital in the money form, or money capital, both as the prime mover for each business when it first begins, and as a permanent driving force. Circulating capital, especially, presupposes the constantly repeated appearance, at short intervals, of the motor of money capital. The entire capital value advanced, i.e. all components of the capital that consist of commodities – labour-power, means of labour and materials of production – must always first be bought with money and later on purchased again. What holds here for the individual capital, holds also for the social capital, which operates only in the form of many individual capitals. But, as we already showed in Volume 1, it in no way follows from this that the field of operation of capital, the scale of production, even on the capitalist basis, has its *absolute* limits determined by the volume of money capital in operation.

The elements of production that are incorporated into capital are independent in extent, within certain limits, of the magnitude of the money capital advanced. Labour-power with a certain rate of payment may be more or less severely exploited, both extensively and intensively. If the amount of money capital increases with severer exploitation, i.e. if wages rise, they still do not rise in relation to the degree of exploitation, i.e. not at all proportionately.

The natural materials which are exploited productively (and which do not form an element of the capital's value), i.e. soil, sea, mineral ores, forests, etc. may be more or less severely exploited, in extent and intensity, by greater exertion of the same amount of labour-power, without an increase in the money capital advanced. In this way the real elements of productive capital can be increased without the need for additional money capital. In so far as the latter is needed for additional ancillaries, then the money capital in which the capital value is advanced is not increased in relation to the increased effectiveness of the productive capital, i.e. again not at all proportionately.

The same means of labour, i.e. the same fixed capital, may be used more efficiently without an additional outlay of money for fixed capital, either by prolonging their daily use or by raising the intensity of their application. There is then only a more rapid turnover of the fixed capital, but this also means that the elements of its reproduction are supplied more quickly.

Apart from natural materials, natural forces that cost nothing may

* See Volume 1, Chapter 2, 'Exchange'.

also be incorporated more or less effectively as agents in the production process. Their level of effectiveness depends on methods and scientific advances that cost the capitalist nothing.

The same applies to the social combination of labour-power in the production process, and to the accumulated skills of the individual worker. Carey* reckons that the landowner never receives his due rent, since he is not paid for all the capital and labour that has been put into the soil from time immemorial to give it its present productive capacity. (There is no mention, of course, of the productive capacity that is taken out of the soil.) According to this conception, the individual worker should be paid according to the work that it cost the entire human race to build him up from a savage into a modern engineer. What actually happens is quite the reverse. If all the unpaid labour put into the soil to the profit of the landowners and capitalists is counted up, then this capital contained in the soil has been repaid over and over again at an extortionate rate of interest, so that landed property has long since been redeemed by society, and redeemed time and again at that.

The increase in the productive forces of labour, in so far as this does not rest on any additional outlay of capital value, increases in the first instance only the quantity of products, and not their value, except to the extent that it enables more constant capital to be reproduced, and its value thus maintained, with the same amount of labour. However, it also forms extra material for capital, and thus provides the basis for an increased capital accumulation.

In as much as the organization of social labour, and therefore the heightening of the social productivity of labour, itself requires production on a large scale and hence the advance of money capital in great quantities by individual capitalists, we have already shown in Volume 1 how this happens partly as a result of the centralization of capitals in a few hands, without any absolute growth in the volume of capital values in operation, and nor therefore in the volume of money capital through which they are advanced. The size of individual capitals can grow by way of centralization in a few hands, without any growth in their social sum. There is then simply a redistribution of individual capitals.

Finally, it was shown in the previous Part how a reduction in the turnover period enables either the same productive capital to be set in motion with less money capital, or more productive capital to be set in motion with the same money capital.

* Henry Charles Carey was an American 'vulgar economist' and champion of the 'harmony of interests' between opposing classes.

All this clearly has nothing to do with the specific question of money capital as such. It simply indicates that the capital advanced – a given sum of value which, in its free form, its value form, consists of a certain sum of money – contains, once it has been transformed into productive capital, productive powers whose limits are not given by the bounds of its own value, but, within a given field of action, can operate differently, both in extent and intensity. Once the prices of the elements of production (means of production and labour-power) are given, the size of the money capital required to buy a certain quantity of these elements of production, present as commodities, is also determined. In other words, the capital value that has to be advanced is determined. However, the scale on which this capital operates to form values and products is elastic and variable.

On the second point. It is self-evident that the portion of social labour and means of production that has to be spent each year on the production or acquisition of money, in order to replace worn-down coins, involves a proportionate reduction in the scale of social production. But as for the money value already functioning partly as means of circulation and partly as a hoard, this has already been obtained, and exists alongside the labour-power, the produced means of production, and the natural sources of wealth. It cannot be considered as a restriction on these. If it is transformed into elements of production, or exchanged with other nations, the scale of production may be expanded. But this presupposes that the money continues to play, as before, its role of world money.*

According to the length of the turnover period, a greater or lesser quantity of money capital is needed to set the productive capital in motion. We have also seen how the division of the turnover period into working time and circulation time gives rise to an increase in the capital that is latent or suspended in the money form.

To the extent that the turnover period is governed by the length of the working period, it is determined by the material character of the production process, conditions remaining otherwise the same, and not by the specific social character of this production process. On the basis of capitalist production, however, extended operations of long duration require greater advances of money capital for a longer time. Production in these branches is therefore dependent on the extent of the money capital which the individual capitalist has at his disposal. This limit is overcome by the credit system and the forms of association related to it, e.g. joint-stock companies. Disturbances in the money market there-

*Cf. Volume 1, Chapter 3, 3, c, 'World Money'.

fore bring such businesses to a halt, while those same businesses, for their part, induce disturbances in the money market.

On the basis of social production, it would be necessary to determine to what extent it was possible to pursue these operations, which withdraw labour-power and means of production for a relatively long period without providing any product or useful effect during this time, without damaging those branches of production that not only withdraw labour-power and means of production continuously or several times in the course of a year, but also supply means of subsistence and means of production. With social production just as with capitalist production, workers in branches of industry with short working periods will withdraw products only for a short time without giving other products back in return, while branches of industry with long working periods will continue to withdraw products for a long time before they give anything back. This circumstance arises from the material conditions of the labour process in question, and not from its social form. With collective production, money capital is completely dispensed with. The society distributes labour-power and means of production between the various branches of industry. There is no reason why the producers should not receive paper tokens permitting them to withdraw an amount corresponding to their labour time from the social consumption stocks. But these tokens are not money; they do not circulate.

We see that in so far as the need for money capital arises from the length of the working period, this is conditioned by two factors. Firstly, that money is the general form in which each individual capital must enter the scene (leaving aside credit), in order to be transformed into productive capital; this arises from the nature of capitalist production, and of commodity production in general. Secondly, the size of the money advance needed arises from the circumstance that labour-power and means of production are withdrawn from society for a long period without the return of a product that can be transformed back into money. The first factor, that the capital has to be advanced in the form of money, is not abolished by the form this money takes, whether it is metallic money, credit money, tokens of value, etc. The second factor is not affected in any way either by the monetary medium or by the form of production in which labour, means of subsistence and means of production are withdrawn, without an equivalent being cast back into circulation.

Chapter 19: Former Presentations of the Subject[1]

I. THE PHYSIOCRATS

Quesnay's *Tableau économique* shows in a few broad lines how the annual result of national production, defined in terms of value, is distributed by circulation in such a way that, with other circumstances remaining the same, simple reproduction can take place, i.e. reproduction on the same scale. From the material standpoint, it is always the previous year's harvest that forms the starting-point of the production period. The numberless individual acts of circulation are thereby immediately grouped together in their characteristic social movement as a mass circulation between major economic classes of society that are defined by their functions. What is of interest for us here is that one part of the total product – which as an object of use, just like any other part, is the fresh result of the past year's labour – is also just a bearer of old capital value reappearing in the same natural form. It does not circulate, but rather remains in the hands of its producers, the class of farmers, to begin its service as capital there once again. Quesnay in fact includes in this constant capital part of the annual product, elements that do not belong there, but he comes to grips with the main question, thanks to the very narrowness of his mental horizon, in which agriculture is the only sphere of application of human labour that produces surplus-value, and is therefore the only one that is really productive from the capitalist standpoint. The process of economic reproduction, whatever its specific social character may be, is in this area (agriculture) always intertwined with a process of natural reproduction. The readily apparent conditions of the latter illuminate those of the former, and keep at bay those confusions which are only introduced by the illusions of circulation.

The label of a system of ideas is distinguished from that of other

1. This is the start of Manuscript VIII.

articles, among other things, by the fact that it deceives not only the buyer, but often the seller as well. Quesnay himself, and his closest disciples, believed in their feudal signboard. Our academic pedants do the same to this very day. In point of fact, however, the Physiocratic system is the first systematic conception of capitalist production. The representatives of industrial capital *– the class of farmers – lead the whole economic movement. Agriculture is pursued on a capitalist footing, i.e. as the large-scale undertaking of the capitalist farmer; the immediate tillers of the soil are wage-labourers. Production does not just produce articles of use, but their value as well; its driving motive is to obtain surplus-value, and the birthplace of surplus-value is the sphere of production, not that of circulation.† In the three classes that figure as bearers of the process of social reproduction, mediated by circulation, the direct exploiter of 'productive' labour, i.e. the producer of surplus-value, the capitalist farmer, is distinguished from the mere appropriator of this surplus-value.‡

The capitalist character of the Physiocratic system already provoked opposition during its heyday, on the one hand from Linguet and Mably,§ on the other from the defenders of free small-scale property in land.

*

The retrogression[2] in Adam Smith's analysis of the reproduction process is all the more striking, in that he not only elaborated on Quesnay's correct analyses, e.g. generalizing Quesnay's '*avances primitives*' and '*avances annuelles*' into 'fixed' and 'circulating' capital,[3] but in places

---

2. Cf. *Capital* Volume 1, p. 738, note 20.

3. Even here, certain Physiocrats had prepared the ground for him, in particular Turgot. Turgot already used the term '*capital*' for '*avances*' more frequently than did Quesnay and the other Physiocrats, and more closely identified the *avances* or *capitaux* of the manufacturers with those of the farmers. For example, 'Just like the latter' (the *entrepreneurs-manufacturiers*), 'these too' (the farmers, i.e. the capitalist farmers) 'must receive in addition to the capitals that return to them', etc. (Turgot, *Œuvres*, ed. Daire, Paris, 1844, vol. I, p. 40).

---

* See above, p. 133, for Marx's definition of 'industrial capital'.

† i.e. not merchant's capital. Cf. Volume 3, Chapter 20, 'Historical Facts About Merchant's Capital'.

‡ i.e. the landlord.

§ Simon-Nicolas-Henri Linguet, a French historian and economist, used the Physiocratic presentation of the capitalist economy as the basis of a criticism of the position of the working class in bourgeois society, in his work *Théories des lois civiles*, London, 1767. This was however a reactionary criticism, confined to contrasting the present condition of the working class with its supposedly superior

fell back completely into the errors of the Physiocrats. In order to show, for instance, that the farmer produces greater value than any other kind of capitalist, he says:

'No equal capital puts into motion a greater quantity of productive labour than that of the farmer. Not only his labouring servants, but his labouring cattle, are productive labourers.' (A charming compliment for the labouring servants!) 'In agriculture, too, nature *labours* along with man; and though *her labour costs no expense*, its produce has its *value, as well as that of the most expensive workmen*. The most important operations of agriculture seem intended not so much to increase, though they do that too, as to direct the fertility of nature towards the production of the plants most profitable to man. A field overgrown with briars and brambles may frequently produce as great a quantity of vegetables as the best cultivated vineyard or corn field. Planting and tillage frequently regulate more than they animate the active fertility of nature; and after all their labour, a great part of the work always remains to be done by her. The labourers and labouring cattle (!), therefore, employed in agriculture, not only occasion, like the workmen in manufactures, the reproduction of a value equal to their own consumption, or to the capital which employs them, together with its owners' profits; but of a much greater value. Over and above the capital of the farmer and all its profits, they regularly occasion the reproduction of the rent of the landlord. This rent may be considered as the produce of those powers of nature, the use of which the landlord lends to the farmer. It is greater or smaller according to the supposed extent of those powers, or in other words, according to the supposed natural or improved fertility of the land. It is the work of nature which remains after deducting or compensating everything which can be regarded as the work of man. It is seldom less than a fourth, and frequently more than a third of the whole produce. No equal quantity of productive labour employed in manufactures can ever occasion so great a reproduction. In them nature does nothing; man does all; and the reproduction must always be in proportion to the strength of the agents that occasion it. The capital employed in agriculture, therefore, not only puts into motion a greater quantity of productive labour than any equal capital employed in manufactures, but in proportion, too, to the

---

position in pre-capitalist society. See *Theories of Surplus-Value*, Part I, Chapter VII, 'Linguet'.

Gabriel-Bonnot de Mably, a French philosopher and historian, was an early representative of utopian communism.

quantity of productive labour which it employs, it adds a much greater value to the annual produce of the land and labour of the country, to the real wealth and revenue of its inhabitants.' (Book Two, Chapter V, pp. 462–3). [Marx's emphases. Here, as above, the page references to *The Wealth of Nations* are given according to the Pelican edition.]

Adam Smith says in Book Two, Chapter I:

'The whole value of the seed, too, is properly a fixed capital.'

Here, therefore, capital = capital value; this exists in a 'fixed' form.

'Though it goes backwards and forwards between the ground and the granary, it never changes masters, and therefore does not properly circulate. The farmer makes his profit, not by its sale, but by its increase' (p. 375).

The narrowness of this conception lies in Smith's failure to see what Quesnay had already seen, namely the reappearance of the value of constant capital in a renewed form. Instead, he saw here only a further illustration, and moreover a false one, of his distinction between fixed and circulating capital; hence he missed an important aspect of the reproduction process. The progress in Smith's translation of '*avances primitives*' and '*avances annuelles*' into 'fixed capital' and 'circulating capital' consists in the word 'capital', this concept being generalized and freed from its special reference to the Physiocratic, 'agricultural' sphere of application; the retrogression consists in the acceptance and the perpetuation of the concepts 'fixed' and 'circulating' as the decisive distinctions.

2. ADAM SMITH

(a) Smith's General Perspectives

In Book One, Chapter VI (p. 153), Smith says:

'In every society the price of every commodity finally resolves itself into some one or other, or all of those three parts' (wages, profit and rent) 'and in every improved society, all the three enter more or less, as component parts, into the price of the far greater part of commodities.'[4]

4. So that the reader may not be deceived as to the meaning of the phrase 'the price of the far greater part of commodities', Smith explains himself with the following example. No rent, for instance, enters into the price of sea fish, but only wages and profit. The price of Scotch Pebbles includes only wages: 'In some parts of Scotland a few poor people make a trade of gathering, along the sea-shore, those little variegated stones commonly known by the name of Scotch Pebbles. The price which is paid to them by the stone cutter is altogether the wages of their labour; neither rent or profit make any part of it [p. 154].'

He goes on to say (p. 155):

'Wages, profit, and rent, are the *three original sources* of all revenue as well as *of all exchangeable value*' [Marx's emphases].

Later we shall investigate in more detail this doctrine of Adam Smith's as to the 'component parts of the price of commodities' and of 'all exchangeable value'. He goes on to say:

'Since this is the case, it has been observed, with regard to every particular commodity, taken separately, it must be so with regard to all the commodities which compose the *whole annual produce* of the land and labour of every country, taken complexly. The *whole price of exchangeable value* of that annual produce must *resolve itself* into the same three parts, and *be parcelled out* among the different inhabitants of the country, either as the *wages* of their labour, the *profits* of their stock, or the *rent* of their land (Book Two, Chapter II, pp. 381–2) [Marx's emphases].'

After Adam Smith has thus resolved both the price of all commodities taken separately and 'the whole price or exchangeable value . . . of the annual produce of the land and labour of every country' into three sources of revenue, for wage-labourer, capitalist and landlord, into wages, profit and rent, he has to smuggle in a fourth element by an indirect route, namely the element of capital. He does this by his distinction between gross and net revenue:

'The *gross* revenue of all the inhabitants of a great country comprehends the *whole annual produce* of their land and labour; the *net revenue, what* remains free to them *after deducting the expense of maintaining* – first, their *fixed,* and, secondly, their *circulating capital*; or what, without encroaching upon their capital, they can place in their stock reserved for immediate consumption, or spend upon their subsistence, conveniences, and amusements. Their real wealth, too, is in proportion, not to their gross, but to their net revenue' (p. 382) [Marx's emphases].

On this the following points must now be made:

1. Adam Smith is expressly dealing only with simple reproduction, not with reproduction on an expanded scale, or with accumulation; he speaks only of the expense of 'maintaining' the functioning capital. The 'net' revenue is that part of the annual product, whether of the whole society or the individual capitalist, that can go into the 'consumption fund', but the scale of this fund must not be such as to 'encroach upon capital'. One part of the value of both individual and social product, therefore, is neither resolved into wages nor into profit or rent, but into capital.

2. Adam Smith escapes from his own theory by means of a play on words, the distinction between 'gross' and 'net' 'revenue'. Both the individual capitalist and the entire capitalist class, the so-called 'nation', receive, in place of the capital used up in production, a commodity product. The value of this – which can be depicted in proportionate parts of this product itself – on the one hand replaces the capital value used up, and hence forms income and in the most literal sense 'revenue' (*revenu*, past participle of *revenir* [French], to return), but, let it be noted, capital revenue or capital income; on the other hand it comprises components of value that are 'parcelled out among the different inhabitants of the country, either as the wages of their labour, the profits of their stock, or the rent of their land' – i.e. what is understood by income in everyday life. The value of the whole product, whether that of the individual capitalist or that of the country as a whole, accordingly forms income for someone, but on the one hand capital income, on the other hand a 'revenue' distinct from this. Thus, what was eliminated when the value of commodities was analysed into its component parts is introduced again through the back door by the ambiguity of this word 'revenue'. But only the components of the product's value that already exist in the product can be 'taken in'. If *capital* is to come in as revenue, then capital must previously have been spent.

Adam Smith goes on to say:

'The lowest ordinary rate of profit must always be something more than what is sufficient to compensate the occasional losses to which every employment of stock is exposed. It is this surplus only which is net or clear profit.' (What capitalist sees profit as including necessary outlays of capital?) 'What is called gross profit comprehends frequently, not only this surplus, but what is retained for compensating such extraordinary losses' (Book One, Chapter IX, pp. 198–9).

But this means no more than that a part of the surplus-value, treated here as part of the gross profit, has to form an insurance fund for production. This insurance fund is created by a part of the surplus labour, which thereby directly produces capital, i.e. the fund set aside for reproduction. As far as the outlay for the 'maintenance' of the fixed capital, etc. is concerned (see the passages quoted above), the replacement of the fixed capital consumed by new capital in no way constitutes a new investment of capital, but is simply a replacement of the old capital value in new form. As far as the repair of the fixed capital goes, however, something that Adam Smith also counts together with the maintenance costs, its cost forms part of the price of the capital advanced.

If the capitalist invests this only gradually and according to need, while his capital is already functioning, and can invest it out of profit already tucked away, instead of having to invest it all at once, this in no way changes the source of this profit. The component of value from which it derives simply indicates that the workers provide surplus labour for the repair fund as well as for the insurance fund.

What Adam Smith's explanation of fixed capital actually boils down to is that it is the part of the industrial capital advanced that is fixed in the production process, or, as he says on p. 377, 'affords a revenue or profit without circulating or changing masters', or, according to p. 374, 'either remains in his possession, or continues in the same shape'.*

Adam Smith now tells us that not only should the whole fixed capital be excluded from the net revenue, i.e. from revenue in its specific sense, but so should that entire part of the circulating capital required to maintain, repair and replace the fixed capital, in point of fact all capital that does not exist in a natural form destined for the consumption fund.

'The whole expense of maintaining the fixed capital must evidently be excluded from the net revenue of the society. Neither the materials necessary for supporting their useful machines and instruments of trade, their profitable buildings, etc., nor the produce of the labour necessary for fashioning those materials into the proper form, can ever make any part of it. The *price* of that labour may indeed make a part of it; as the workmen so employed may place the whole value of their wages in their stock reserved for immediate consumption. But in other sorts of labour, both the *price*' (i.e. the wage paid for this labour) 'and the *produce*' (in which this labour is embodied) 'go to this stock, the price to that of the workmen, the produce to that of other people, whose subsistence, conveniences, and amusements, are augmented by the labour of those workmen' (Book Two, Chapter II, pp. 382–3) [Marx's emphases].

Here Adam Smith has stumbled upon a very important distinction, between the workers involved in the production of *means of production*, and those involved in the direct production of *means of consumption*. The commodity product of the former contains, in its value, a component equal to the sum of the wages paid, i.e. to the portion of capital laid out on the purchase of labour-power; this portion of value exists bodily as an aliquot part of the means of production produced by these workers. The money they receive as wages forms revenue for them, and yet their labour has not produced consumable products, either for

*This paragraph is omitted in Engels's second edition and most subsequent ones.

themselves or for others. These products therefore do not themselves form any element of the portion of the annual product that is designed to supply the social consumption fund, in which alone 'net revenue' can be realized. Adam Smith forgets to add that what holds here for wages holds equally for the value component of the means of production that forms the revenue of the industrial capitalists (in the first instance), as surplus-value under the headings of profit and rent. This component of value also exists in means of production, non-consumables; only after it is converted into money can it withdraw a certain amount of the means of consumption produced by the second type of worker, corresponding to its own price, and transfer this into the individual consumption fund of its proprietors. All the more should Adam Smith have seen that the portion of the annually produced means of production equal in value to the means of production functioning within this sphere of production – the means of production with which means of production are made – and therefore a portion equal in value to the constant capital applied here is absolutely excluded, not only by the natural form in which it exists, but also by its capital function, from being any component of value that constitutes revenue.

In relation to the second type of worker – who directly produces means of consumption – Adam Smith's definitions are not quite exact. He says in particular that, in these types of labour, both the price of labour and the product 'go to' the direct consumption fund: 'the *price*' (i.e. the money received as wages) 'to that of the *workmen*, the *product* to that of other people, whose subsistence, conveniences, and amusements, are augmented by the labour of those workmen'.

But the worker cannot live off the 'price' of his labour, the money in which his wages are paid; he realizes his money by using it to buy means of consumption, and these may consist partly of types of commodities which he has himself produced. However, his own product may be one that is only consumed by the exploiters of labour.

After Adam Smith has thus completely excluded the fixed capital from the 'net revenue' of a country, he continues:

'But though the whole expense of maintaining the fixed capital is thus necessarily excluded from the net revenue of the society, it is not the same case with that of maintaining the circulating capital. Of the four parts of which this latter capital is composed – money, provisions, materials, and finished work – the three last, it has already been observed, are regularly withdrawn from it, and placed either in the fixed capital of the society, or in their stock reserved for immediate consumption. Whatever portion of those consumable goods is not employed in maintaining the former,' (the fixed capital) 'goes all to the latter,' (to the stock reserved for immediate consumption) 'and makes a part of the net revenue of the society. The maintenance of those three parts of the circulating capital, therefore, withdraws no portion of the annual produce from the net revenue of the society, besides what is necessary for maintaining the fixed capital' (Book Two, Chapter II, p. 384).

All this is simply the tautology that the part of circulating capital that does not serve for the production of means of production goes into the production of means of consumption, i.e. into the part of the annual product that is destined to form the society's consumption fund. But what is important is the immediately following passage:

'The circulating capital of a society is in this respect different from that of an individual. That of an individual is totally excluded from making any part of his net revenue, which must consist altogether in his profits. But though the circulating capital of every individual makes a part of that of the society to which he belongs, it is not upon that account totally excluded from making a part likewise of their net revenue. Though the whole goods in a merchant's shop must by no means be placed in his own stock reserved for immediate consumption, they may [be placed] in that of other people, who, from a revenue derived from other funds, may regularly replace their value to him, together with its profits, without occasioning any diminution either of his capital or of theirs' (ibid.).

We learn here, then:

1. Just like the fixed capital, and that circulating capital needed for its reproduction and maintenance (he forgets its functioning), so the circulating capital of each individual capitalist involved in the production of means of consumption is also totally excluded from *his* net revenue, which can consist only of his profits. The part of his commodity product that replaces his capital cannot therefore be resolved into components of value that form revenue for him.

2. The circulating capital of each individual capitalist forms part of the circulating capital of the society, just as with each individual fixed capital.

3. The circulating capital of the society, even though it is only the sum of the individual circulating capitals, possesses a character distinct from the circulating capital of an individual capitalist. The latter can never form a part of *his revenue*; but, as against this, a section of the

former (i.e. that consisting of means of consumption) can simultaneously form part of the *society's revenue*, or in other words, as he previously said, the net revenue of the society is not necessarily reduced by this part of the annual product. In actual fact, what Adam Smith here calls circulating capital is the annually produced commodity capital that the capitalists who produce means of consumption annually cast into circulation. This, their entire annual commodity product, consists of consumable articles, and therefore constitutes the fund in which the net revenues of the society (including wages) are realized or on which they are spent. Instead of selecting as his example the goods in the retail shop, Adam Smith should have chosen the stocks amassed in the storehouses of the industrial capitalists.

If Adam Smith had now, in discussing what he calls circulating capital, fitted together the fragmentary ideas that impressed themselves on him previously, while he was contemplating the reproduction of what he calls fixed capital, he would have arrived at the following result:

1. The annual social product consists of two departments; the first comprises the means of production, the second the means of consumption; the two have to be treated separately.

2. The total value of the part of the annual product that consists of *means of production* is divided as follows. One portion is simply the value of the means of production consumed in the creation of these means of production, and therefore only the capital value reappearing in a new form; a second part is equal to the value of the capital laid out on labour-power, or the sum of the wages paid out by the capitalists in this sphere of production. A third portion of value, finally, forms the source of profits for the industrial capitalists in this category, including rent of land.

The first portion, according to Adam Smith the reproduced fixed capital component of all the individual capitals occupied in this first department, is 'totally excluded from making any part' of the 'net revenue', either that of the individual capitalist or that of the society. It always functions as capital, and never as revenue. In this respect, the 'fixed capital' of each individual capitalist is in no way distinguished from the fixed capital of the society. However, the other value components of the society's annual output of means of production – value components that also exist, therefore, as aliquot parts of this total mass of means of production – do indeed form at the same time *revenues for all agents involved in this production*, i.e. wages for the workers, profits and rents for the capitalists. For the *society*, however, they do not form revenue, but *capital*, even though the annual social product simply consists of the sum of the products of its individual capitalist members. Most of the products in the first department can by their very nature function only as means of production, and even those that could function as means of consumption, if need be, are designed to serve as raw or ancillary material for new production. [The revenue-forming value components of the first department] function as means of production, and therefore as capital, not in the hands of their producers, however, but rather in those of their users, who are:

3. The capitalists in the second department, the direct producers of *means of consumption*. They replace the capital the capitalists in the first department used up in the production of means of consumption (except in so far as this capital is converted into labour-power, and represents the sum of the wages of the workers in this second department), while this used-up capital, which now exists in the hands of the capitalists producing it in the form of means of consumption, forms for its part – from the social standpoint, that is – *the consumption fund in which the capitalists and workers in the first department realize their revenue.*

If Adam Smith had pursued his analysis as far as this, little more would be required for the solution of the entire problem. He almost hit the nail on the head, for he had already noted that certain portions of value of *one* particular kind (means of production) of the commodity capital in which the total annual product of the society exists, although they formed revenue for the individual workers and capitalists engaged in their production, were not a component of the society's revenue; while a value component of the *other* kind of product (means of consumption), although it formed capital value for its individual owners, the capitalists engaged in this sphere of investment, was however simply a part of the social revenue.

This much is already clear from the investigation so far:

Firstly, even though the social capital is simply the sum of the individual capitals, and therefore the annual commodity product (or commodity capital) of the society is equal to the sum of the commodity products of these individual capitals; and although, therefore, the same analysis of the commodity value into its components that holds for each individual commodity capital must also hold for the society as a whole and in the last analysis actually does hold, yet the form of appearance which these components assume in the overall process of social reproduction is a *different* one.

Secondly, even on the basis of simple reproduction, we find not only the production of wages (variable capital) and surplus-value, but also the direct production of new constant capital value; this is true even though the working day consists of only two parts, one in which the worker replaces the variable capital, and the other in which he produces surplus-value (profit, rent, etc.). In other words, the daily labour that is spent in reproducing the means of production – whose value breaks down into wages and surplus-value – is realized in new means of production which also replace the constant capital component expended in the production of the means of consumption.

The main difficulties arise not in the treatment of accumulation, but already in that of simple reproduction, although the greater part of these have already been resolved in what was said above. This is why both Adam Smith ([*Wealth of Nations,*] Book Two) and before him Quesnay (*Tableau économique*) started with simple reproduction, whenever they had to deal with the movement of the annual social product and its reproduction by way of circulation.

(b) Smith's Resolution of Exchange-Value into v+s

Adam Smith's dogma that the price or 'exchangeable value' of every single commodity – and thus of all the commodities comprising the annual social product (he correctly assumes capitalist production everywhere) – is composed of, or 'resolves itself into', the three 'component parts' wages, profit and rent, can be reduced to the thesis that commodity value $= v+s$, i.e. the value of the variable capital advanced, plus the surplus-value. As the following quotation shows, we have Smith's express permission to reduce profit and rent to a common unit which we call s; we leave aside for the time being all secondary factors, and in particular all apparent or actual divergences from the dogma that the value of commodities consists exclusively of the elements that we designate as $v+s$.

In manufacture:

'The value which the workmen add to the materials ... resolves itself ... into two parts, of which the one pays their wages, the other the profits of their employer upon the whole stock of materials and wages which he advanced' (Book One, Chapter VI, p. 151). 'Though the manufacturer' (i.e. the manufacturing worker) 'has his wages advanced to him by his master, he, in reality, costs him no expense, the value of those wages being generally restored, together with a profit, in the improved value of the subject upon which his labour is bestowed' (Book Two, Chapter III, p. 430).

The part of 'stock' that is laid out 'in maintaining productive hands', 'after having served in the function of a capital to him' (the employer) ... 'constitutes a revenue to them' (the workers). (Book Two, Chapter III, p. 432.)

In the same chapter, Adam Smith expressly states:

'. . . the whole annual produce of the land and labour of every country ... naturally divides itself into two parts. One of them, and frequently the largest, is, in the first place, destined for replacing a capital, or for renewing the provisions, materials, and finished work, which had been withdrawn from a capital; the other for constituting a revenue either to the owner of this capital, as the profit of his stock, or to some other person, as the rent of his *land*' (p. 431) [Marx's emphasis].

Only one part of the capital, as Adam Smith has just told us, also forms revenue for someone, namely the part invested in the purchase of productive labour. This part – the variable capital – firstly performs 'the function of a capital' in the hands of the employer, and for him, and then it 'constitutes a revenue' for the productive worker himself. The capitalist transforms one part of his capital value into labour-power, and precisely in this way into variable capital; but as a result of this transformation it is not only this part of the capital, but his entire capital, that functions as industrial capital. The worker – the seller of labour-power – receives its value in the form of his wage. In his hands, labour-power is simply a saleable commodity, the commodity from whose sale he lives, and which therefore forms the only source of his revenue; it is only in the hands of its buyer, the capitalist, that the labour-power functions as variable capital, and in fact the capitalist only appears to advance the purchase price of the labour-power, for its value has already been supplied to him by the worker.

After Adam Smith has shown us that the value of the product in manufacture $= v+s$ (where s is the profit of the capitalist), he tells us that in agriculture the workers, besides 'the reproduction of a value equal to their own consumption, or to the' (variable) 'capital which employs them, together with its owners' profits' – 'over and above the capital of the farmer and all its *profits*, they regularly occasion the reproduction of the *rent* of the landlord' (Book II, Chapter V, p. 463) [Marx's emphases].

The fact that the rent goes into the hands of the landlord is quite beside the point for the question we are dealing with here. Before it passes into his hands, it must first exist in the hands of the farmer, i.e. of the industrial capitalist. It must form a value component of the product, before it becomes revenue for anyone. Thus for Smith rent and profit are both only components of the surplus-value that the productive worker constantly reproduces together with his own wages, i.e. with the value of the variable capital. Rent and profit are parts of the surplus-value s, and in this way Smith resolves the price of all commodities into $v+s$.

The dogma that the prices of all commodities (and therefore of the annual commodity product) can be resolved into wages plus profit plus rent of land, assumes the form, even in the intermittent esoteric* part of Smith's work, that the value of any commodity, and thus of the society's annual commodity product, $=v+s$, i.e. the capital value laid out on labour-power and constantly reproduced by the workers, plus the surplus-value added by the workers through their labour.

Smith's end result reveals to us at the same time the source of his one-sided analysis of the components into which commodity value is divisible (for more on this, see below). For the fact that these components also form the various sources of revenue for classes with different functions in production has nothing to do with the quantitative determination of each of these components, and the limits of their total values.

When Adam Smith says:

'Wages, profit, and rent, are the three original sources of all revenue as well as of all exchangeable value. All other revenue is ultimately derived from some one or other of these' (Book One, Chapter VI, p. 155), all kinds of confusion are heaped together.

1. All members of society who do not figure directly in the reproduction process, whether as workers or not, can receive their share of the annual commodity product – i.e. their means of consumption – in the first instance only from the hands of those classes to whom this product firstly accrues – productive workers, industrial capitalists and landlords. To this extent, their revenues are, in a material sense, derived from wages (the wages of the productive workers), profit, and ground-rent, and hence appear, in contrast to these original revenues, as derivative. On the other hand, however, the recipients of these derivative revenues, in the sense just given, draw them by way of their social functions as king, priest, professor, prostitute, mercenary, etc.,

* On Marx's frequent distinction between the 'esoteric' and 'exoteric' aspects of Adam Smith's theoretical work, see above, p. 276, note.

and they can therefore view these functions of theirs as the original source of their revenue.

2. (and this is the high point of Smith's stupid blunder:) After he has begun by correctly defining the value components of the commodity and the total value product embodied in them, and then by showing how these components form an equal number of different sources of revenue;[5] thus after he has derived revenues from value, he proceeds in the reverse direction – and this remains the predominant idea in his work – and makes these revenues, instead of just 'component parts', into '*original sources* of all exchangeable value', thereby throwing the doors wide open to vulgar economics. (Cf. our Roscher.*)

(c) The Constant Capital Component

We shall now see how Adam Smith tries to conjure the constant part of capital out of commodity value.

'In the price of corn, for example, one part pays the rent of the landlord . . .'

The origin of this component of value has as little to do with the circumstance that it is paid to the landlord and forms revenue for him in the form of rent, as the origin of the other value components has with the fact that they form sources of revenue as profit and wages.

'Another [part] pays the wages or maintenance of the labourers' ('and labouring cattle', he adds) 'employed in producing it, and the third pays the profit of the farmer. These three parts seem' (they 'seem' indeed) 'either immediately or ultimately to make up the whole price of corn.'[6]

This whole price, i.e. its quantitative determination, is absolutely independent of its distribution among three kinds of person.

5. I have reproduced this sentence literally, as it stands in the manuscript, even though it seems in its present context to contradict both what precedes it and what directly follows. This apparent contradiction is resolved below in subsection (d): 'Capital and Revenue in Adam Smith'. – F.E.

6. We leave completely aside here the fact that our Adam was particularly unfortunate in his choice of example. The value of corn can be resolved into wages, profit and rent only by depicting the feed consumed by the draught cattle as their wages, and the draught cattle as wage-labourers – hence depicting the wage-labourer in his turn as a draught animal. (From Manuscript II.)

---

*Wilhelm Roscher was a German vulgar economist and founder of the 'historical school' of economics. The work to which Marx alludes here is *Die Grundlagen der Nationalökonomie*, published in 1858.

'A fourth part, it may perhaps be thought, is necessary for replacing the stock of the farmer, or for compensating the wear and tear of his labouring cattle, and other instruments of husbandry. But it must be considered that the price of any instrument of husbandry, such as a labouring horse, is itself made up of the same three parts; the rent of the land upon which he is reared, the labour of tending and rearing him, and the profits of the farmer who advances both the rent of this land, and the wages of this labour. Though the price of the corn, therefore, may pay the price as well as the maintenance of the horse, the whole price still resolves itself either immediately or ultimately into the same three parts of rent, labour,' (he means wages) 'and profit' (Book One, Chapter VI, p. 153).

This is literally all that Adam Smith has to say in support of his astonishing doctrine. His proof consists simply in the repetition of the same assertion. He concedes, by way of example, that the price of corn not only consists of $v+s$, but also of the price of the means of production consumed in the production of corn, i.e. that it consists of a capital value that the farmer did not invest in labour-power. Nevertheless, he says, the prices of all these means of production can themselves be decomposed, just like the price of corn itself, into $v+s$. Smith simply forgets to add: as well as into the price of the means of production used up in their own creation. He refers us from one branch of production to another, and from this again to a third. The statement that the entire price of commodities is either 'immediately' or 'ultimately' resolvable into $v+s$ would only cease to be an empty subterfuge if Smith could demonstrate that the commodity products whose price is immediately resolved into c (the price of the means of production consumed) $+v+s$ are finally compensated for by commodity products which entirely replace these 'consumed means of production', and which are for their part produced simply by the outlay of variable capital, i.e. capital laid out on labour-power. The price of these latter commodities would then immediately be $v+s$. And in this way the price of the former, too, $c+v+s$, where c stands for the component of constant capital, would be ultimately resolvable into $v+s$. Adam Smith himself did not believe he had given such a proof with his example of the Scotch Pebble collectors, who according to him (1) do not supply any kind of surplus-value, but simply produce their own wages; (2) do not employ any means of production. (Though in fact they do, in the form of baskets, sacks and other containers for carting off the pebbles.)

We have already seen above how Adam Smith refutes his own theory without even becoming aware of its contradictions. The source of these, however, is to be sought precisely in his own scientific premises. The capital converted into labour produces a value greater than its own. How? Because, says Smith, the workers impart to the things on which they work, during the production process, a value that, besides the equivalent for their own purchase price, forms a surplus-value accruing to their employers (profit and rent). This they do indeed, and they can do no other. What applies to the industrial labour of a single day, however, applies also to the labour set in motion by the entire capitalist class in the course of a whole year. The society's total annual value product, therefore, can be broken down only into $v+s$, into an equivalent with which the workers replace the capital value spent on their own purchase price, and the additional value that they have to provide for their employers over and above this. These two elements of the commodity value, however, also form sources of revenue for the different classes involved in the reproduction process: the first wages, the revenue of the workers; the second surplus-value, of which the industrial capitalist keeps one part for himself in the form of profit, while another is deducted as rent, the revenue of the landlord. How can there be any other component of value, if the annual value product contains no other elements besides $v+s$? Here we are concerned with simple reproduction. Since the total annual labour is resolved into labour needed for the reproduction of the capital value laid out on labour-power, and labour needed for the creation of a surplus-value, where can still more labour come from to produce a capital value not laid out on labour-power?

The matter stands as follows.

1. Adam Smith defines the value of a commodity by the amount of labour that the wage-labourer 'adds' to the object of labour. He says in fact, 'to the materials', as he is dealing with manufacture, which works up what are already products of labour; but this in no way affects the matter in hand. The value that the worker adds to a thing (and this 'adds' is our Adam's own expression) is quite independent of whether the object to which the value is added already has value *before* this addition, or whether it does not. The worker therefore creates a value in the commodity form. According to Adam Smith this is on the one hand an equivalent for his wages, this part being therefore determined by the value of the wage; depending on whether this is higher or lower, the value he has added here by his labour is in this respect that needed to produce or reproduce his wages. Another part, however, is added by

the worker by further labour above this limit, and forms surplus-value for his capitalist employer. Whether this surplus-value remains entirely in the hands of the capitalist, or is partially taken off him by third parties, does not in the least affect either the qualitative determination of the surplus-value added by the wage-labourer (that it is all surplus-value), or its quantitative determination (the amount). It is value just the same as any other value component of the product, simply distinguished by the fact that the worker has not received any equivalent for it, and does not receive one subsequently, for this value is instead appropriated by the capitalist without an equivalent. The overall value of the commodity is determined by the amount of labour that the worker has spent in its production. One part of this total value is characterized as being equal to the value of the wage, i.e. an equivalent for wages. The second part, therefore, the surplus-value, is necessarily characterized, by the same token, as being equal to the total value of the product minus the value component that is the equivalent for the wage; i.e. equal to the excess value created in the production of the commodity over the value component contained in it that is the equivalent for wages.

2. What holds for a commodity produced in a single capitalist business by some individual worker holds also for the annual product of all branches of industry taken together. What applies to the day's labour of an individual productive worker applies also to the annual labour performed by the entire class of productive workers. This class 'fixes' (Smith's expression) in the annual product a total value determined by the amount of labour annually expended, and this total value breaks down into one part determined by that portion of the annual labour in which the working class creates an equivalent for its annual wage, in point of fact this wage itself, and another part determined by the additional annual labour in which the workers create a surplus-value for the capitalist class. The annual value product contained in the annual product thus consists of only two elements, the equivalent for the annual wage received by the working class and the surplus-value annually supplied to the capitalist class. But the wage forms the revenue of the working class, and the annual sum of surplus-value the revenue of the capitalist class; the two therefore represent (and this viewpoint is correct where it is a matter of depicting simple reproduction) the relative shares in the annual consumption fund, and are realized in it. There is therefore no room left for the constant capital value, for the reproduction of the capital functioning in the form of means of production.

However, Adam Smith expressly says in the Introduction to his work that the parts of the commodity value that function together as revenue coincide with the annual product destined for the social consumption fund:

'To explain in what has consisted the revenue of the great body of the people, or what has been the nature of those funds which . . . have supplied their annual consumption, is the object of these Four first Books' (p. 106).

And in the very first sentence of this Introduction he states:

'The annual labour of every nation is the fund which originally supplies it with all the necessaries and conveniences of life which it annually consumes, and which consists always either in the immediate produce of that labour, or in what is purchased with that produce from other nations' (p. 104).

Smith's first error, then, is to equate the *value of the annual product* with the annual *value product*. The latter is simply the product of the current year's labour; the former includes, on top of this, all those elements of value that were used in the production of this annual product, *but which were produced in the previous year and partly in still earlier years*: means of production whose value only *re-appears* – and which, as far as their value is concerned, have been neither produced nor reproduced by the labour spent during the current year. This confusion enables Adam Smith to juggle away the constant component in the value of the annual product. The confusion is itself based on a further error in his fundamental conception. He does not distinguish the twofold character of labour itself: labour that creates value, by the expenditure of labour-power, and labour that creates objects of use (usevalues), as concrete useful labour. The total sum of commodities annually produced, i.e. the *total annual product*, is the product of the *useful* labour operating in the current year; it is only by the social application of labour in an intricate system of varieties of useful labour that all these commodities have come into being; it is only in this way that the value of the means of production used up in their production is retained in their total value, and reappears in a new natural form. The total *annual product* is thus the result of the *useful* labour expended during the year; but only one part of the *value of this product* has been created during the year; this part is the annual *value product*, which represents the amount of labour actually performed during the year itself.

When, therefore, Smith says in the passage just quoted:

'The annual labour of every nation is the fund which originally supplies it with all the necessaries and conveniences of life which it annually consumes, etc.',

he one-sidedly adopts the standpoint of useful labour. It is this, to be sure, that has brought all these means of subsistence into their consumable form. He forgets here, however, that this would have been impossible without the collaboration of means of labour and objects of labour handed down from earlier years, and that the 'annual labour', therefore, in as much as it forms value, has in no way created the entire value of the products prepared by it; that the value produced is smaller than the value of the product.

If we cannot reproach Adam Smith for going no further in this analysis than his successors (even if an approach to the correct conception was already available with the Physiocrats), we can say that he fell increasingly into confusion, and the principal reason for this was that his 'esoteric' conception of commodity value was constantly being thwarted by the exoteric ideas which on the whole prevail in his work, even though his scientific instinct did permit the esoteric standpoint to reappear from time to time.

(d) Capital and Revenue in Adam Smith

That component of a commodity's value (and therefore also of the annual product's) which simply forms an equivalent for the wage is equal to the capital advanced by the capitalist in wages, i.e. to the variable component of the total capital he advances. The capitalist receives back this component of the capital value advanced in the form of a newly produced value component of the commodities supplied by the wage-labourers. Whether the variable capital is advanced in the sense that the capitalist pays in money the share accruing to the worker of a product which is not yet ready for sale, or which, although finished, has not yet been sold by the capitalist, whether he pays the worker with money that he has already received from the sale of the commodity that the worker supplied, or whether he has anticipated this money by credit in all of these cases, the capitalist spends variable capital which accrues to the workers as money, and he possesses in return the equivalent of this capital value in that portion of his commodities' value with which the worker newly produces the share in the total value of these that accrues to him; with which, in other words, he has produced the value of his own wages. Instead of giving him this portion of value in the natural form of his own product, the capitalist pays him the same in money. For the capitalist, therefore, the variable component of the capital value he has advanced now exists in the commodity form, while the worker has received in the form of money the equivalent for the labour-power he has sold.

Thus, while the part of the capital advanced by the capitalist that has been transformed into variable capital by the purchase of labour-power functions as active labour-power within the production process itself, and is newly produced, i.e. reproduced, by the expenditure of this power as new value in the commodity form – i.e. reproduction, the new production of the capital value originally advanced! – the worker spends the value or price of the labour-power he has sold on means of subsistence, on the means to reproduce his labour-power. A sum of money equal to the variable capital forms his income, in other words his revenue, which he receives only so long as he can sell his labour-power to the capitalist.

The wage-labourer's commodity – his own labour-power – functions as a commodity only in so far as it is incorporated into the capitalist's capital, and functions as capital; on the other hand, the capital spent as money capital on the purchase of labour-power functions as revenue in the hands of the seller of labour-power, the wage-labourer.

Different processes of circulation and production are intertwined here, and Adam Smith does not distinguish between them.

Firstly, acts belonging to the *circulation* process. The worker sells his commodity – labour-power – to the capitalist; the money with which the capitalist buys it is for him money invested for the purpose of valorization, i.e. money capital; it is not spent, but merely advanced. (This is the real sense of the 'advance' – the Physiocrats' *avance* – quite independently of where the capitalist acquires the money itself. What is advanced, for the capitalist, is every value that he pays for the purpose of the production process, whether this is done in advance or after the event; it is advanced to the production process itself.) All that happens here is what happens in any sale of commodities: the seller hands over a use-value (in this case labour-power) and receives the value of it in money (realizes its price); the buyer hands over his money and receives in return the commodity itself – in this case labour-power.

Secondly. In the *production* process, the labour-power that has been bought now forms part of the functioning capital, and the worker himself functions here simply as a special natural form of this capital, as distinct from the elements of capital that exist in the natural form of means of production. During the process, the worker adds value to the means of production that he transforms into a product by spending his labour-power to the value of this labour-power (leaving aside surplus-value). In this way, he reproduces for the capitalist, in the commodity form, the part of the former's capital advanced to him in wages, or due to be advanced; produces for him an equivalent for this capital. He produces for the capitalist, in other words, the capital that the capitalist can 'advance' afresh in the purchase of labour-power.

Thirdly. With the sale of the commodity, therefore, a part of its sale price replaces for the capitalist the variable capital that he advanced, and therefore enables him to buy labour-power afresh, just as it enables the worker to sell it again.

With all commodity purchases and sales – in as much as these transactions are simply considered by themselves – it is completely immaterial what happens in the hands of the seller to the money received for his commodity, and what happens in the hands of the buyer to the item of use that he purchased. It is also completely immaterial, therefore, in so far as it is simply the circulation process that is under consideration, that the labour-power bought by the capitalist reproduces capital value for him, while the money paid as the purchase price of this labour-power forms revenue for the worker. The value of the worker's item of trade, his labour-power, is affected neither by the fact that this forms 'revenue' for him, nor by the fact that the use of his commodity by the buyer reproduces capital value for the buyer.

Because the value of labour-power – i.e. the adequate sale price of this commodity – is determined by the amount of labour needed to reproduce it, and this amount of labour is itself determined by that needed to produce the means of subsistence that the worker needs, i.e. the amount of labour needed to maintain his life, the wage becomes the revenue from which the worker has to live.

Adam Smith is completely wrong to say (p. 432) that the part of capital employed 'in maintaining productive hands', 'after having served in the function of a capital to him' (the capitalist), 'constitutes a revenue for them' (the workers).

The *money* with which the capitalist pays for the labour-power that he buys 'serves in the function of a capital to him', in as much as he thereby incorporates labour-power with the material components of his capital and hence for the first time puts his capital in a position in which it can function as productive capital. The difference is that labour-power is a *commodity* in the hands of the worker, and not capital, and it constitutes a revenue for him in so far as he can regularly repeat its sale; it functions as capital *after* the sale, in the hands of the capitalist, during the production process itself. What serves two purposes here is labour-power. In the hands of the worker, it is a commodity sold at its value; in the hands of the capitalist who has bought it, it is a power producing both value and use-value. The money, however, that the worker receives from the capitalist, he receives only after he has given him the use of his labour-power, after this has already been realized in the value of the product of labour. The capitalist has this value in his hand before he pays for it. So it is not the money that functions twice: first as money form of the variable capital, then as wages. It is rather the labour-power that has functioned twice; first as a *commodity*, when the labour-power is sold (when the wage to be paid is stipulated, the money operates merely as an ideal measure of value, and it in no way needs to be in the capitalist's hands yet); secondly in the production process, where it functions as *capital*, i.e. as an element creating both use-value and value in the hands of the capitalist. It has already supplied the equivalent to be paid to the worker, in the commodity form, before the capitalist pays this to the worker in the money form. The worker therefore himself creates the payment fund from which the capitalist pays him. But this is not all.

The worker spends the money he receives on maintaining his labour-power, and thus – if we consider the capitalist class and the working class as a whole – on maintaining for the capitalist the only instrument by means of which he can remain a capitalist.

On the one hand, therefore, the constant purchase and sale of labour-power perpetuates the position of labour-power as an element of capital, and in this way capital appears as the creator of commodities, articles of use that have a value; this is also how the portion of capital that buys labour-power is regularly restored by the product of labour-power itself, so that the worker himself constantly creates the capital fund out of which he is paid. On the other hand, the constant sale of labour-power becomes a source of maintaining the worker's life that he perpetually has to repeat, and his labour-power thus appears as the means by which he draws the revenue from which he lives. Revenue, here, means nothing more than the appropriation of values effected by the constantly repeated sale of a commodity (labour-power), and in this connection these values themselves serve only towards the constant reproduction of the commodity to be sold. To this extent, Adam Smith is correct to say that the value component of the product created by the worker for which the capitalist pays an equivalent in the form of the wage becomes a source of revenue for the worker. But this affects the nature and the size of this portion of commodity value just as little as the value of the means of production is affected by the fact that they function as capital values, or the nature and length of a straight line by the fact that it functions as the base of a triangle or the axis of an ellipse. The value of labour-power remains just as independently determined as that of any means of production. This component of commodity value does not *consist of* revenue as an autonomous factor constituting it, nor does this component of value *resolve itself* into revenue. This new value constantly reproduced by the worker forms a source of revenue for him, but it does not follow from this, inversely, that his revenue forms a component of the new value he has produced. What determines the volume of his revenue is the share in the new value he creates that is paid to him, and not the other way round. If this portion of the new value forms revenue for him, this simply shows what becomes of it, how it is used, and has as little to do with its formation as with the formation of any other value. If my income is 10 shillings per week, then the circumstances of this weekly income affect neither the nature of the 10 shillings' value nor its *magnitude*. Just as with any other commodity, so in the case of labour-power, too, its value is determined by the amount of labour needed to reproduce it; the fact that this amount of labour is determined by the value of the means of subsistence needed by the worker, and is thus the labour needed for the reproduction of these means of subsistence, is a characteristic of this particular commodity (labour-power), but it is no more peculiar to it than the fact that the value of draught cattle is determined by the means of subsistence needed for their maintenance, and thus by the amount of human labour needed to produce the latter, is peculiar to these draught cattle.

The category of 'revenue' is the root cause of Smith's whole trouble. For him the different types of revenue form the 'component parts' of the commodity value annually produced, newly created, whereas in actual fact it is the other way round; it is the two parts into which this commodity value is divided *for the capitalist* – the equivalent for the variable capital that he advanced in the money form for the purchase of labour, and the other portion of value that belongs to him although it has cost him nothing, the surplus-value – that form sources of revenue. The equivalent of the variable capital is advanced once again in labour-power, and to this extent forms a revenue for the worker in the form of his wage; the other part – the surplus-value – since it does not have to replace for the capitalist any of the capital advanced, can be spent by him on means of consumption (both necessities and luxuries), can be consumed as revenue, instead of forming capital of any kind. The precondition for this revenue is the commodity value itself, and its components are distinguished for the capitalist only to the extent that they form either an equivalent *for*, or a surplus *over*, the variable capital that he has advanced. Both of these consist of nothing but labour-power spent in the course of commodity production, set flowing as labour. They do not consist of income or revenue, but rather of expenditure – expenditure of labour.

After this *quid pro quo*, in which revenue is made into the source of commodity value, instead of this commodity value being the source of revenue, commodity value now appears to be 'composed' of the various kinds of revenues; these are determined independently of one another, and the total value of the commodity is determined by adding together the values of these revenues. But now this question arises: how can we determine the value of each of these revenues from which the commodity value is supposed to derive? In the case of wages, this can in fact be done, because wages are the value of the commodity labour-power, and the latter can be determined (like the value of any other commodity) by the labour needed for its reproduction. But as for surplus-value, or in Adam Smith's case its two forms, profit and rent, how are these to be determined? Here we are left with empty prattle. At some points Adam Smith depicts wages and surplus-value (or wages and profit) as components out of which the commodity value or price is put together, while at others, and often almost in the same breath, he depicts them as parts into which the commodity value 'resolves itself'; the latter, however, means that the commodity value is given first and that various parts of this given value accrue to different persons involved in the production process in the form of different revenues. This is in no way identical with the composition of value from these three 'components'. If I define the lengths of three straight lines independently, and then make these three lines 'components' of a fourth straight line equal in length to their sum, this is in no way the same procedure as if I start with a given straight line and divide this for some purpose or other – 'resolve' it, so to speak – into three parts. The length of the line in the first case invariably changes with the length of the three lines whose sum it forms; in the latter case the length of the three segments is limited from the beginning by their forming parts of a line of a given size.

In point of fact, if we stick to what is correct in Smith's presentation, i.e. that that value contained in the society's annual commodity product which is *newly created by the year's labour* is equal (just as with any single commodity or the product of a day, week, etc.) to the sum of the variable capital advanced (i.e. to that value component destined to serve again for the purchase of labour-power), plus the surplus-value, which the capitalist can realize in items for his individual consumption (in the case of simple reproduction and with other conditions remaining the same); if we bear in mind moreover that Smith lumps together labour in its value-creating capacity, as expenditure of labour-power, with labour in its capacity of creating use-value, i.e. labour spent in useful, purposive form – then the whole conception boils down to this: The value of any commodity is the product of labour; so too, therefore, is the value of the product of a year's labour or the value of the society's annual commodity product. Since however all labour can be resolved into (1) necessary labour-time, in which the worker simply reproduces an equivalent for the capital advanced in purchasing his labour-power, and (2) surplus labour, by which he supplies the capitalist with a value for which the latter pays no equivalent, i.e. a surplus-value, all commodity value can then be resolved simply into these two different components, and in the last analysis it forms, as wages, the revenue of the working class, and as surplus-value, that of the capitalist class. As far as the constant capital value is concerned, however, i.e. the value of the means of production consumed in the production of the annual product, there is no way of telling how this value comes into the value of the new product (except in the mere phrase that the capitalist charges it to the buyer when he sells his commodity), but 'ultimately', since the means of production are themselves the product of labour, this portion of value can in turn consist only of an equivalent for the variable capital and the surplus-value; that is, it can consist only of the product of necessary labour and surplus labour. If the values of these means of production function in the hands of their employers as capital values, this does not hinder them from being divisible 'originally' (and if one goes to the root of it, in other people's hands, even though earlier) into the same two portions of value, i.e. into two different sources of revenue.

A correct point in all this is that in the movement of the social capital – i.e. of the totality of individual capitals – things look different from the way they do when each individual capital is taken separately, i.e. from the standpoint of each individual capitalist. For the latter, commodity value can be resolved into (1) a constant element (a fourth element, as Smith says) and (2) the sum of wages and surplus-value, i.e. wages, profit and rent. From the social standpoint, however, Smith's fourth element, the constant capital value, simply vanishes.

(e) Summary

The absurd formula that the three revenues of wages, profit and rent form three 'components' of commodity value, derives in Smith's case from the more plausible formula that commodity value 'resolves itself' into these three components. This too is false, even on the assumption that commodity value can be divided simply into the equivalent for the labour-power used up and the surplus-value created by the latter. This error, however, is based in turn on a deeper and true foundation. Capitalist production rests on the fact that the productive worker sells his own labour-power as a commodity to the capitalist, in whose hands it then functions simply as an element of his productive capital. This transaction (the sale and purchase of labour-power) does not just introduce the production process, but implicitly determines its specific character. The production of a use-value, and even of a commodity (something that can also be undertaken by independent productive workers), is here only a means for the production of absolute and relative surplus-value for the capitalist. In analysing the production process, therefore, we saw how the production of absolute and relative surplus-value determines (1) the duration of the daily labour process, and (2) the whole social and technical shape of capitalist production. It is within this process that the distinction emerges between the mere maintenance of value (of the constant capital value), the actual reproduction of value advanced (the equivalent for labour-power), and the production of surplus-value, i.e. of value for which the capitalist neither advanced a previous equivalent, nor advances one after the event.

The appropriation of surplus-value (of a value over and above the equivalent of the value advanced by the capitalist), even though it is introduced by the purchase and sale of labour-power, is an act performed within the production process itself, and forms an essential moment of the latter.

The introductory act of circulation, the purchase and sale of labour-power, itself depends in turn on a distribution of the social *elements* of production which is the presupposition and premise of the distribution of social *products*, viz. the separation between labour-power as a commodity for the worker, and the means of production as the property of non-workers.

At the same time, however, this appropriation of surplus-value, the separation of value production into the reproduction of the value advanced and the production of a new value that does not replace any equivalent (a surplus-value), in no way affects the substance of value itself and the nature of value production. The substance of value is and remains nothing more than expended labour-power – labour independent of its particular useful character – and value production is nothing but the process of this expenditure. If the feudal serf, for example, expends his labour-power for six days of the week, i.e. works for these six days, it makes no difference to the fact of this expenditure of labour-power as such that he may work for three of these days on his own field and three others on his lord's field and for his lord. Both his voluntary labour for himself and his forced labour for his lord are equally labour; in as much as this is considered as labour in relation to the values – or even the useful products – created by it, there is no distinction between these six days' labour. The distinction is solely related to the different situations which have given rise to the expenditure of his labour-power in the two halves of the six-day working period. It is just the same with the necessary and surplus labour of the wage-labourers.

The process of production disappears in the finished commodity. The fact that labour-power was expended to create it now appears in the form that the commodity has the following concrete property: it possesses value. The magnitude of this value is measured by the amount of labour expended; the commodity value cannot be resolved into anything further, and consists of nothing more. If I draw a straight line of a certain length, I have, in the first place, 'produced' a straight line (only symbolically, of course, as I am aware from the start) by my manner of drawing, practised in accordance with certain rules (laws) that are independent of me. If I divide this line into three segments (which may be required for a certain problem), then each of these three pieces remains a straight line, as before, and this division does not resolve the line whose parts they are into anything other than a straight line, e.g. a curve of some kind. Just as little can I divide this line of a given length in such a way that the sum of these parts is greater than the undivided line itself; the length of the undivided line in other words is not determined by the lengths of the segments into which it is divided. It is rather the relative lengths of the latter that are limited in advance by the limits of the line of which they are parts.

In this respect, the commodity produced by the capitalist is in no way distinguished from a commodity produced by an independent worker, by a community of workers, or by slaves. In our case, however, the entire product of labour and its entire value belongs to the capitalist. Just like any other producer, he has first to transform the commodity into money by selling it, before he can manipulate it any further; he must convert it into the form of the universal equivalent.

Let us consider the commodity product as it is before it is transformed into money. It belongs completely to the capitalist. But while, as the product of useful labour – as a use-value – it is in every respect the product of the labour process just completed, the same is not true of its value. A part of this value is merely the value of the means of production used up to produce the commodity, which reappears in a new form. This value has not been produced in the process of producing the commodity, for the means of production already possessed this value before the production process in question and independently of it. They entered this process as the bearers of this value, and all that has been replaced and changed is simply its form of appearance. For the capitalist, this part of the commodity value forms an equivalent for the portion of the constant capital value he advanced that has been consumed in the commodity's production. It previously existed in the form of means of production, it now exists as a value component of the newly produced commodity. Once the latter has been converted into money, this value now existing in money must be transformed back again into means of production, into its original form as determined by the production process and by its own function within this. The value character of a commodity is in no way changed by the function of this value as capital.

A second portion of the commodity's value is the value of the labour-power that the worker sells to the capitalist. This is determined, just like the value of the means of production, independently of the production process which the labour-power is to enter, and is fixed in an act of circulation, the purchase and sale of labour-power, before this goes into the production process. In the course of his function – the expenditure of his labour-power – the wage-labourer produces a commodity value equal to the value that the capitalist has to pay him for the use of his labour-power. He gives the capitalist this value in commodities, and the capitalist pays him the same in money. If this part of the commodity value is for the capitalist only an equivalent for the variable capital that he has to advance in wages, this makes absolutely no difference to the fact that it is a commodity value newly created during the production process, consisting exactly like the surplus-value of past expenditure of labour-power. Just as little is this affected by the fact that the value of labour-power, paid by the capitalist to the worker in the form of wages, assumes for the worker the form of a revenue, and that in this way not only is the labour-power continuously reproduced, but also the class of wage-labourers as such, and with it the basis of capitalist production as a whole.

However, there is more to the commodity's value than the sum of these two components. Over and above them both, there is still the surplus-value. This has in common with the value component that replaces the variable capital advanced in wages that it is a value newly created by the workers – congealed labour. It is just that it does not cost anything to the owner of the total product, the capitalist. This circumstance is what enables the capitalist to consume it completely as revenue, as long as he does not have to deduct parts of it for others with a stake in it – e.g. rent for the landlords – in which case these portions then constitute the revenues of third parties of this kind. This same circumstance was also the driving motive for our capitalist to concern himself with commodity production at all. But neither his original benevolent intention to hunt out surplus-value, nor the subsequent spending of this as revenue by himself and others, affects the surplus-value as such. It in no way alters the fact that it is unpaid congealed labour, nor does it alter its size, which is determined by quite other factors

Given that Adam Smith already wanted to concern himself in dealing with commodity value with the roles that the various parts of this play in the overall process of reproduction, it should have been evident that, if certain portions function as revenue, others must just as constantly function as capital – and on his logic, this means that these should also have been described as constituent parts of the commodity value, or parts into which it is resolved.

Adam Smith identifies commodity production in general with capitalist commodity production; the means of production are 'capital' from the beginning, labour is wage-labour, and hence:

'The number of useful and productive labourers . . . is everywhere in proportion to the quantity of capital stock which is employed in setting them to work' (Introduction, p. 105).

In short, the various factors of the labour process – objective and personal – appear from the start in the character masks of the era of capitalist production. The analysis of commodity value therefore directly coincides with the question as to how far this value is, on the one hand, simply the equivalent for the capital laid out, and how far, on the other hand, it constitutes 'free' value that does not replace any capital value advanced, i.e. is surplus-value. The portions of commodity value compared from this standpoint are thereby transformed surreptitiously into its independent 'component parts', and ultimately into the 'sources of all value'. A further conclusion is that commodity value is composed of revenues of various kinds, or alternatively is 'resolved into' these revenues, so that it is not the revenues that consist of commodity value, but rather the commodity value that consists of 'revenues'. But just as it scarcely affects the nature of a commodity value as commodity value, or of money as money, whether it functions as capital value or not, so equally a commodity value is scarcely altered by the fact that it goes on to function as revenue for this person or that. The commodities Smith is dealing with here are commodity capital from the start (and therefore include surplus-value as well as the capital value consumed in their production), i.e. they are commodities produced in the capitalist manner, the result of the capitalist production process. This last should therefore have been the object of prior analysis, together with the process of valorization and value formation that it involves. And since the very presupposition of this is in turn commodity circulation, its presentation also requires, therefore, an independent and prior analysis of the commodity.* Even when Smith in his 'esoteric' aspect occasionally comes up with something correct, he takes account of value formation only in connection with the analysis of commodities, i.e. the analysis of commodity capital.

3. LATER WRITERS[7]

Ricardo reproduces Adam Smith's theory almost verbatim:

'It must be understood that all the productions of a country are consumed; but it makes the greatest difference imaginable whether

7. The passage which extends from here to the end of this chapter is an addition from Manuscript II.

*This is of course Marx's own procedure in *Capital*, Volume 1 of which commences with the analysis of 'Commodities and Money' (Part One), and continues with the all-round analysis of the capitalist production process. The separate text on 'The Results of the Immediate Process of Production', published in the present edition as an appendix to Volume 1, analyses commodities produced in the capitalist manner as this 'result', and this lays the basis for the analysis of capital circulation in Volume 2.

they are consumed by those who reproduce, or by those who do not reproduce another value. When we say that revenue is saved, and added to capital, what we mean is, that the portion of revenue, so said to be added to capital, is consumed by productive instead of unproductive labourers' (*Principles*, p. 169, note [Pelican edition]).

In point of fact Ricardo completely accepted Smith's theory of the resolution of commodity price into wages and surplus-value (or variable capital and surplus-value). What he takes issue with Smith over are (1) the components of surplus-value: he eliminates ground-rent as a necessary element of it; (2) Ricardo *breaks down* commodity price into these components. The magnitude of value thus comes first. He takes the sum of the components as a given magnitude, rather than deriving the magnitude of value of the commodity after the event by adding together its components, as Smith often does, even against his own better judgement.

Ramsay remarks against Ricardo:

'He seems always to consider the whole produce as divided between wages and profits, forgetting the part necessary for replacing fixed capital' (*An Essay on the Distribution of Wealth*, Edinburgh, 1836, p. 174).

What Ramsay understands by fixed capital is what I call constant capital:

'Fixed capital exists in a form in which, though assisting to raise the future commodity, it does not maintain labourers' (ibid., p. 59).

Adam Smith baulked at the logical conclusion of his resolution of commodity value, and thus of the value of the annual social product, into wages and surplus-value, i.e. simply into revenue: the conclusion that the total annual product could then be entirely consumed. It is never the original thinkers who draw the absurd conclusions. They rather leave this for the Says and MacCullochs.

Say certainly has an easy time of it. What is for one person an advance of capital is for the other revenue and net product, or was so at least; the distinction between gross and net product is purely subjective, and

'thus the entire value of all products has been distributed in society as revenue' (*Traité d'économie politique*, 1817, II, p. 64). 'The total value of any product is composed of the profits of the landlords, the capitalists and the artisans' (thus wages figure here as *profits des industrieux* [artisans' profits]!) 'who have contributed to its production. This means that the society's revenue is equal to the *gross value produced*, and not as the sect of economists' (the Physiocrats) 'believed, only equal to the net product of the soil' (p. 63) [Marx's emphasis].

This discovery of Say's was taken over by Proudhon, among others.

Storch also accepts Adam Smith's doctrine in principle, but finds the application made of it by Say to be untenable.

'If it is held that the revenue of a nation is equal to its gross product, i.e. that no capital' (he should say no constant capital) 'needs to be deducted, it must also be conceded that this nation can consume the entire value of its annual product unproductively, without making the least inroad on its future revenue ... The products that compose the' (constant) 'capital of a nation are not consumable' (Storch, *Considérations sur la nature du revenu national*, Paris, 1842, pp. 147, 150).

Storch has forgotten to tell us how the existence of this constant portion of capital fits in with the analysis of prices that he has taken over from Smith, in which commodity value contains only wages and surplus-value, but no portion of constant capital. It is only through Say that he realizes that this price analysis leads to absurd results, and his own last word on it is 'that it is impossible to resolve the necessary price into its simplest elements' (*Cours d'économie politique*, Petersburg, 1815, II, p. 141).

Sismondi, who deals particularly with the relation between capital and revenue, and in actual fact makes his particular conception of this relationship the *differentia specifica* of his *Nouveaux Principes*, did not utter a single scientific word or contribute one jot or tittle to the explanation of the problem.

Barton, Ramsay and Cherbuliez* make attempts to go beyond Smith's conception. They fail because they pose the problem one-sidedly from the start, by not clearly separating the distinction between constant and variable capital from the distinction between fixed and circulating capital.

John Stuart Mill, too, reproduces the doctrine handed down by Adam Smith to his successors, with his customary air of self-importance.

The result is that Smith's confusion persists to this day, and his dogma forms an article of orthodox belief in political economy.

* Antoine-Elise Cherbuliez, a Swiss economist influenced by both his compatriot Sismondi, and Ricardo. See *Theories of Surplus-Value*, Part III, Chapter XXIII.

Chapter 20: Simple Reproduction

I. FORMULATION OF THE PROBLEM[1]

If we consider the result of the annual functioning of the social capital – that is of the total capital of which the individual capitals are only fractions, their movement being both an individual movement and at the same time an integral link in the movement of the total capital – if we consider therefore the commodity product which the society supplies in the course of the year, we shall necessarily be able to see how the reproduction of the social capital proceeds, what characteristics distinguish this reproduction process from the reproduction process of an individual capital, and what characteristics are common to both. The annual product includes both the parts of the social product that replace capital, social reproduction, and the parts that accrue to the consumption fund and are consumed by workers and capitalists: i.e. both productive and unproductive consumption. This consumption thus includes the reproduction (i.e. maintenance) of the capitalist class and the working class, and hence too the reproduction of the capitalist character of the entire production process.

The form of circulation that we have to analyse is evidently

$$C' - \begin{cases} M-C\ldots P\ldots C', \\ m-c \end{cases}$$

and consumption necessarily plays a role in this; for the starting-point $C' = C + c$, the commodity capital, includes not only constant and variable capital value, but also surplus-value. This movement thus encompasses both individual consumption and productive consumption. In the circuits $M-C\ldots P\ldots C'-M'$ and $P\ldots C'-M'-C\ldots P$, the movement of *capital* is both the starting-point and the concluding point, and this certainly also involves consumption, for the commodity, the product, has to be sold. But once this is assumed to have happened, it is

1. From Manuscript II.

immaterial, for the movement of the individual capital, what later becomes of this commodity. With the movement of $C' \ldots C'$, on the other hand, the preconditions for social reproduction can be immediately recognized from the fact that it is necessary to demonstrate what becomes of each portion of the value of this overall product C'. The overall process of reproduction here includes the consumption process mediated by circulation, just as much as the reproduction of capital itself.

For our present purpose, in fact, the process of reproduction has to be considered from the standpoint of the replacement of the individual components of C' both in value and in material. We can no longer content ourselves, as with the value analysis of the product of the individual capital, with the *assumption* that the individual capitalist first converts the components of his capital into money by selling his commodity product, and can then transform this back into productive capital by repurchasing his elements of production on the commodity market. These elements of production, in so far as they are of the objective kind, form as much a component of the social capital as the individual finished product that is exchanged for them and replaced by them. On the other hand, the movement of the part of the social commodity product that is consumed by the worker in spending his wage, and by the capitalist in spending surplus-value, not only forms an integral link in the movement of the total product, but is also interwoven with the movements of the individual capitals, so that its course, too, cannot be explained by being simply presupposed.

The immediate form in which the problem presents itself is this. How is the *capital* consumed in production replaced in its value out of the annual product, and how is the movement of this replacement intertwined with the consumption of surplus-value by the capitalists and of wages by the workers? What we are dealing with first of all is reproduction on a simple scale. Moreover, we assume not only that products are exchanged at their values, but also that no revolution in values takes place in the components of the productive capital. In as much as prices diverge from values, this circumstance cannot exert any influence on the movement of the social capital. The same mass of products is exchanged afterwards as before, even though the value relationships in which the individual capitalists are involved are no longer proportionate to their respective advances and to the quantities of surplus-value produced by each of them. As far as revolutions in value are concerned, they change nothing in the relations between the value components of the total annual product, as long as they are generally and evenly distributed. In so far as they are only partially and unevenly distributed, they represent disturbances which, *firstly*, can be understood only if they are treated as *divergences* from value relations that remain unchanged; *secondly*, however, given proof of the law that one part of the value of the annual product replaces constant capital, and another variable capital, then a revolution, either in the value of the constant capital or in that of the variable, would in no way affect this law. It would alter only the relative magnitudes of the portions of value that function in one or the other capacity, because different values would have appeared in place of the original values.

As long as we were dealing with capital's value production and the value of its product individually, the natural form of the commodity product was a matter of complete indifference for the analysis, whether it was machines or corn or mirrors. This was always simply an example, and any branch of production whatever could equally serve as illustration. What we were dealing with then was the actual immediate process of production, which presented itself at each turn as the process of an individual capital. In so far as the reproduction of capital came into consideration, it was sufficient to assume that the opportunity arose within the circulation sphere for the part of the product that represented capital value to be transformed back into its elements of production, and therefore into its shape as productive capital, just as we could assume that worker and capitalist found on the market the commodities on which they spent their wages and surplus-value. But this purely formal manner of presentation is no longer sufficient once we consider the total social capital and the value of its product. The transformation of one portion of the product's value back into capital, the entry of another part into the individual consumption of the capitalist and working classes, forms a movement within the value of the product in which the total capital has resulted; and this movement is not only a replacement of values, but a replacement of materials, and is therefore conditioned not just by the mutual relations of the value components of the social product but equally by their use-values, their material shape.

[2] Simple reproduction on the same scale seems to be an abstraction, both in the sense that the absence of any accumulation or reproduction on an expanded scale is an assumption foreign to the capitalist basis, and in the sense that the conditions in which production takes place do

2. From Manuscript VIII.

not remain absolutely the same in different years (which is what is assumed here). The supposition is that a social capital of a given value supplies the same mass of commodity values and satisfies the same quantity of needs in both the current year and the previous year, even if the forms of the commodities may change in the reproduction process. But since, when accumulation takes place, simple reproduction still remains a part of this, and is a real factor in accumulation, this can also be considered by itself. Moreover, the value of the annual product may decrease, even though the volume of use-values remains the same; the value may remain the same, even though the volume of use-values declines; the value and volume of the use-values reproduced may decrease simultaneously. What emerges from all this is that reproduction either takes place under more favourable circumstances than previously, or under more difficult ones, and the latter may result in an incomplete – defective - reproduction. All this can affect only the quantitative aspect of the various elements of reproduction, and not the role that they play in the total process as capital reproducing itself or as reproduced revenue.

2. THE TWO DEPARTMENTS OF SOCIAL PRODUCTION[3]

The society's total product, and thus its total production process, breaks down into two great departments:

I. *Means of production*: commodities that possess a form in which they either have to enter productive consumption, or at least can enter this.

II. *Means of consumption*: commodities that possess a form in which they enter the individual consumption of the capitalist and working classes.

In each of these departments, all the various branches of production belonging to it form a single great branch of production, one of these being that of means of production, the other that of means of consumption. The total capital applied in each of these two branches of production forms a separate major department of the social capital.

In each department, the capital has two components:

(1) *Variable capital*. As far as its *value* goes, this is equal to the value of the social labour-power applied in this branch of production, i.e. the

3. Mainly from Manuscript II. The schema from Manuscript VIII.

sum of the wages paid for it. Considered in its material aspect, it consists of self-acting labour-power itself, i.e. of living labour set in motion by this capital value.

(2) *Constant capital.* This is the value of all the means of production applied to production in this branch. It breaks down in turn into *fixed* capital: machines, instruments of labour, buildings, draught animals, etc.; and *circulating* constant capital: materials of production, such as raw and ancillary materials, semi-finished goods, etc.

The value of the total annual product created in each of these two departments with the aid of this capital breaks down into a component that represents the constant capital *c* consumed in its production, only its value being transferred to the product, and the portion of value that is added by the overall annual labour. This last breaks down again into the replacement of the variable capital *v* advanced and the excess over it that forms the surplus-value *s*. Just as with the value of any individual commodity, so that of the total annual product of each department also breaks down into $c+v+s$.

The value component *c*, which represents the constant capital *consumed* in the course of production, is not the same thing as the value of the constant capital *applied* in production. The materials of production are certainly completely consumed, and their value is therefore entirely transferred to the product. But only a part of the *fixed* capital is entirely consumed, its value thereby being transferred to the product. Another part of the fixed capital in machines, buildings, etc. continues to exist and to function just as before, even if its value is diminished by the annual wear and tear. This part of the fixed capital that continues to function does not exist for us when we consider the value of the product. It forms a part of the capital value that is independent of this newly produced commodity value and is present alongside it. This was already shown when we considered the value of the product of an individual capital (Volume 1, Chapter 8, pp. 311–12). Here, however, we must set aside for the time being the mode of consideration used there. We saw in dealing with the product of an individual capital how the value subtracted from the fixed capital by wear and tear is transferred to the commodity product created during the period of this depreciation, irrespective of whether or not a part of this fixed capital is replaced in kind during this period out of this transferred value. Here, however, in dealing with the total social product and its value, it is necessary to abstract at least provisionally from the portion of value transferred to the annual product during the year by the wear and tear of the fixed capital, in as much as this fixed capital is not replaced again in kind in the course of the year. In a later section of this chapter [section 9], we shall discuss this point separately.

*

For our investigation of simple reproduction, we intend to use the following schema, in which c — constant capital, v = variable capital, s = surplus-value, and the rate of valorization $\frac{s}{v}$ is taken as 100 per cent.

The figures may be in millions of marks, francs or pounds sterling.

I. Production of means of production:

Capital $4,000_c + 1,000_v = 5,000$.

Commodity product $4,000_c + 1,000_v + 1,000_s = 6,000$, existing in the form of means of production.

II. Production of means of consumption:

Capital $2,000_c + 500_v = 2,500$.

Commodity product $2,000_c + 500_v + 500_s = 3,000$, existing in means of consumption.

The total annual commodity product, taken together, is thus:

I. $4,000_c + 1,000_v + 1,000_s = 6,000$ means of production.

II. $2,000_c + 500_v + 500_s = 3,000$ means of consumption.

The total value is 9,000, the fixed capital that continues to function in its natural form being excluded by our assumption.

If we now investigate the transactions necessary on the basis of simple reproduction, i.e. where the whole surplus-value is unproductively consumed, and ignore in the first instance the monetary circulation that mediates these, we gain from the outset three important clues towards further developments.

1. The 500_v of workers' wages in department II, and the 500_s surplus-value of the capitalists in the same department, must be spent on means of consumption. But their value exists in the means of consumption to a value of 1,000 that restore to the capitalists of department II the 500_v they advanced, and represent besides this their 500_s. The wages and surplus-value in department II are thus converted within department II into the product of department II. $(500_v + 500_s)$ II $= 1,000$ in means of consumption thereby drops out of the total product.

2. The $1,000_v + 1,000_s$ in department I must likewise be spent on means of consumption, i.e. on the products of department II. It must therefore be exchanged for the remaining part of this product, representing constant capital, to the equal amount of $2,000_c$. Department II

receives for this an equal sum in means of production, the product of department I, which embodies the value of $1,000_v + 1,000_s$ in department I. In this way, 2,000 II_c and $(1,000_v + 1,000_s)I$ drop out of the account.

3. There still remains 4,000 I_c. This consists of means of production that can only be used in department I and serve to replace the constant capital consumed there; they are therefore disposed of by mutual exchange among the individual capitalists of department I, just as the $(500_v + 500_s)II$ is disposed of by exchange between workers and capitalists, or between individual capitalists, in department II.

This is simply temporary, for the better understanding of what follows.

3. EXCHANGE BETWEEN THE TWO DEPARTMENTS: $I_{(v+s)}$ AGAINST II_c[4]

We begin with the major exchange between the two departments. $(1,000_v + 1,000_s)I$, values that exist in the hands of their producers in the natural form of means of production, are exchanged for 2,000 II_c, values that exist in the natural form of means of consumption. The capitalist class in department II thereby converts its constant capital of 2,000 from the form of means of consumption back into that of means of production for these means of consumption, into a form in which it can function afresh as a factor of the labour process and as a constant capital value for the process of valorization. On the other hand, the equivalent for labour-power in department I (1,000 I_v) and for the surplus-value of the capitalists in this department (1,000 I_s) is thereby realized in means of consumption; both of these are converted from their natural form of means of production into a natural form in which they can be consumed as revenue.

This mutual exchange is brought about by a money circulation, which both mediates it and makes it harder to comprehend, even though it is of decisive importance, since the component of variable capital must always reappear in the money form, as money capital which is converted from the money form into labour-power. Variable capital must be advanced in the money form in all the branches of production simultaneously pursued alongside one another across the entire surface of the society, irrespective of whether these belong to departments I or II.

4. From here on, again Manuscript VIII.

The capitalist buys labour-power before it enters the production process, but pays for it only at a prearranged date, after it has already been spent in the production of use-values. Just like the remaining portion of the product's value, so the part of this that is simply an equivalent for the money spent in payment for labour-power, the value portion of the product that represents the variable capital value, also belongs to the capitalist. In this particular portion of value, the worker has supplied the capitalist with the equivalent for his wage. However, it is the transformation of the commodity back into money, its sale, that again restores to the capitalist his variable capital as money capital, which he can advance once more in order to purchase labour-power.

In department I, the collective capitalist has already paid the workers £1,000, i.e. $1,000_v$ (I say '£' simply to denote that this is value in the *money form*), for the v-component of the value of a product of department I, i.e. of the value of the means of production produced by those workers. The workers use this £1,000 to purchase means of consumption of the same value from the capitalists in department II, and thereby transform half of department II's constant capital into money. The capitalists in department II, for their part, use this £1,000 to buy means of production to the value of 1,000 from the capitalists in department I; as a result of this, the variable capital value, $= 1,000_v$, which existed as a part of department I's product in the natural form of means of production, is transformed back again into money, and can now function once more in the hands of the department I capitalists as money capital to be converted into labour-power, i.e. into the most essential element of productive capital. In this way, through the realization of one part of their commodity capital, their variable capital flows back to them in the money form.

As far as money is concerned, i.e. the money needed to exchange the s-component of department I's commodity capital for the second half of department II's constant capital component, it may be advanced in various ways. In actual fact, this circulation comprises countless individual purchases and sales by individual capitalists in the two departments, and the money for this must in all circumstances originate from these capitalists, since we have already accounted for the money cast into circulation by the workers. At one time, a capitalist in category II may use the money capital that he has alongside his productive capital to purchase means of production from the capitalists of category I, while on another occasion a capitalist from category I may buy means of consumption from the capitalists of category II with the part of his money fund that is ear-marked for personal expenses, rather than for capital expenditure. As we have already shown in Parts One and Two, certain reserves of money – whether for capital advance, or for expenditure of revenue – must always be taken as present in the hands of the capitalists alongside their productive capital. Let us assume that half the money is advanced by the capitalists in department II, on the purchase of means of production to replace their constant capital, the other half spent by the capitalists in department I on consumption – the proportions are quite immaterial for our present purpose. Then department II advances £500 and uses this to purchase means of production from department I, so that, including the above £1,000 coming from department I's workers, it has replaced three quarters of its constant capital in kind; department I uses the £500 received in this way to buy means of consumption from department II, so that half of that part of its commodity capital that consists of s has gone through the circulation $c-m-c$ and this, its product, has been realized in a consumption fund. By this second process, the £500 returns to the hands of the department II capitalists as money capital which department II possesses alongside its productive capital. On the other hand, department I anticipates the sale of half the part of its commodity capital that is still in store as a product, with a money expenditure to the sum of £500 for the purchase of means of consumption from department II. The same £500 enables department II to buy further means of production from department I and thereby replace its entire constant capital $(1,000 + 500 + 500 = 2,000)$ in kind, while department I has realized its entire surplus-value in means of consumption. All in all, an exchange of commodities amounting to £4,000 has taken place with a monetary circulation of £2,000, this latter sum only being as high as it is because the entire annual product is depicted as having been exchanged all at once in a few large amounts. All that is important here is the fact that department II does not only convert the constant capital, reproduced by it in the form of means of consumption, back into the form of means of production, but, on top of this, the £500 that it advances to the circulation sphere to acquire means of production returns to it; in the same way, department I not only recovers possession of its variable capital, which it reproduced in the form of means of production, in the money form, as money capital which is directly convertible back into labour-power, but besides this, the £500 that it spent before the sale of the surplus-value part of its capital, on purchasing means of consumption in anticipation, also flows back to it. However, it does not flow back through this actual expenditure, but rather through the subsequent sale of the part of its commodity product that bears half its surplus-value.

In these two cases, not only is the constant capital of department II converted from the product form back into the natural form of means of production, in which alone it can function as capital; and similarly not only is the variable component of capital in department I converted into the money form and the surplus-value part of the means of production in department I converted into a form consumable as revenue. Besides all this, the £500 of money capital that department II advanced on the purchase of means of production, before it had sold the compensating part of the value of its constant capital – present in the form of means of consumption – flows back to it; and there flows back to department I the £500 that it had spent in anticipation on the purchase of means of consumption. If the money that department II advanced on the account of the constant part of its commodity product, and department I on the account of a part of the surplus-value in its commodity product, flows back to them, this is simply because the one class of capitalists casts into circulation, besides its constant capital existing in the commodity form of department II, £500 in money, and the other class £500 over and above its surplus-value existing in the commodity form of department I. Ultimately, the two departments pay one another fully by the exchange of their respective commodity equivalents. The money that they cast into circulation over and above the total value of their commodities, as a means for exchanging these commodities, returns to each of them from the circulation sphere to the exact amount that each of the two cast into it. Neither has become a farthing richer from all this. Department II had a constant capital of 2,000 in the form of means of consumption, and 500 in money; it now has 2,000 in the form of means of production, and 500 in money as before. Similarly department I has, as before, a surplus-value of 1,000 (now transformed from its own commodities, means of production, into a consumption fund), and 500 in money. The general conclusion that follows, as far as concerns the money that the industrial capitalists cast into circulation to mediate their own commodity circulation, is that whether this is advanced on the account of the constant value portion of their commodities, or on the account of the surplus-value existing in these commodities in so far as it is spent as revenue, the same amount flows back to the respective capitalists as they themselves advanced for the monetary circulation.

As far as the re-transformation of department I's variable capital into the money form is concerned, this exists for the capitalists in department I, after they have laid it out on wages, firstly in the commodity form in which their workers have supplied it to them. They have paid it out to the workers in the money form as the price of their labour-power. They have in this way paid out the value component of their commodity product that is equal to the variable capital laid out in money. This is why they are also the owners of this part of the commodity product. But the section of the working class that they employ is not the buyer of the means of production they have themselves produced. The variable capital advanced in money for the payment of labour-power thus does not directly return to the capitalists of department I. It is transferred by the purchases of the workers into the hands of the capitalist producers of the commodities needed by and generally accessible to the working-class milieu, i.e. into the hands of the capitalists of department II, and it is only by this detour, by being first employed by these for the purchase of means of production, that it returns to the hands of the department I capitalists.

The result of all this is that, in the case of simple reproduction, the value components $v+s$ of the commodity capital in department I (and therefore a corresponding proportionate part of department I's total commodity product) must be equal to the constant capital II_c similarly precipitated out by department II as a proportionate part of its total commodity product; in other words, $I_{(v+s)} = II_c$.

4. EXCHANGE WITHIN DEPARTMENT II. NECESSARY MEANS OF SUBSISTENCE AND LUXURY ITEMS

Of the value of the commodity product in department II, we still have to investigate the components $v+s$. This does not bear on the most important question we are dealing with here: the extent to which the breakdown of the value of each individual capitalist commodity product into $c+v+s$ holds also for the value of the total annual product, even if mediated by a different form of appearance. That question is resolved by the exchange of $I_{(v+s)}$ against II_c, on the one hand, and by the reproduction of I_c in the annual commodity product of department I on the other, something that will be left for later investigation. [See section 6 below.] Since $II_{(v+s)}$ exists in the natural form of items of consumption, since the variable capital advanced to the workers in payment for labour-power must be spent by them by and large on means of consumption, and since, on the supposition of simple reproduction, the *s*-component of commodity values is also spent as revenue on means of consumption, it is evident at first glance that the workers in department II use the wages received from the department II capitalists to buy back a part of their own product – a part corresponding in extent to the money value they receive as wages. In this way, the capitalist class of department II re-transform the money capital they have advanced in payment for labour-power into the money form; it is just as if they had paid the workers in mere tokens of value. As soon as the workers realize such tokens by purchasing a part of the commodity product produced by them and belonging to the capitalists, these value tokens return to the hands of the capitalists; in our case, however, the tokens not only represent value, but actually possess value in their material existence as gold or silver. We shall later investigate more closely this particular kind of reflux of the variable capital advanced in the money form, which takes place through the process in which the working class appears as buyer and the capitalist class as seller. [See section 5 below.] What matters here is a different point which must be dealt with in discussing this reflux of the variable capital back to its starting-point.

Department II of the annual commodity production consists of the most diverse branches of industry, but as far as its products go these may be broken down into two major subdivisions:

(*a*) Those means of consumption that enter the consumption of the working class, and, in so far as they are necessary means of subsistence, also form part of the consumption of the capitalist class, even if this part is different in both quality and value from that of the workers. This whole subdivision can be classified for our present purpose under the heading: *necessary* means of consumption, and in this connection it is quite immaterial whether a product such as tobacco, for example, is from the physiological point of view a necessary means of consumption or not; it suffices that it is such a means of consumption by custom.

(*b*) *Luxury* means of consumption, which enter the consumption only of the capitalist class, i.e. can be exchanged only for the expenditure of surplus-value, which does not accrue to the workers.

As far as the first category goes, it is evident that the variable capital advanced in the production of the kinds of commodities pertaining to it has to flow directly back in the money form to the section of capitalists in department II (i.e. the capitalists in II*a*) who produce these necessary means of subsistence. They sell these to their own workers to the amount of the variable capital paid the latter in wages. This reflux is a *direct* one for subdivision (*a*) of the capitalist class in department II as a whole, no matter how numerous may be the transactions between the capitalists in the various component branches of industry by which this reflux of variable capital is proportionately distributed. These are processes of circulation in which the means of circulation are directly supplied by the money spent by the workers. It is different, however, with subdivision II*b*. The component of the value product with which we are dealing here, $IIb_{(v+s)}$, exists entirely in the natural form of luxury items, i.e. items that the working class can as little buy as they can buy the commodity value I_v existing in the form of means of production; even though these luxury items are, like the means of production, products of the workers concerned. The reflux by which the variable capital advanced in this subdivision returns to the capitalist producers in its money form cannot be a direct one, therefore, but has to be mediated in a similar way to the case of I_v.

Let us assume, as above, that for department II as a whole, $v = 500$, $s = 500$; but that the variable capital and the surplus-value corresponding to it is distributed as follows:

Subdivision (*a*), necessary means of subsistence: $v = 400$, $s = 400$; i.e. a quantity of commodities in the form of necessary means of consumption to the value of $400_v + 400_s = 800$, or $IIa\,(400_v + 400_s)$.

Subdivision (*b*), luxury items to the value of $100_v + 100_s = 200$, or $IIb\,(100_v + 100_s)$.

The workers in II*b* have received 100 in money in payment for their labour-power, let us say £100 sterling; they use this to buy means of consumption to the sum of 100 from the capitalists in II*a*. This class of capitalists then buys 100 worth of commodities II*b*, and in this way the variable capital of the capitalists in II*b* flows back to them.

The capitalists in II*a* already have their 400_v back in the money form, as a result of exchange with their own workers; of the part of their product that represents surplus-value, moreover, a quarter has been passed to the workers in II*b*, and, in exchange for this, II*b* (100_v) in luxury goods have been withdrawn.

If we now suppose that the capitalists in II*a* and II*b* divide their expenditure of revenue in the same proportions between necessary means of subsistence and luxury items, i.e. if we assume that both of them spend $\frac{3}{5}$ of their revenue on necessary means of subsistence and $\frac{2}{5}$ on luxuries, then this means that the capitalists in subdivision II*a* spent $\frac{3}{5}$ of their surplus-value revenue of 400_s on their own products, necessary means of subsistence, i.e. 240; and $\frac{2}{5} = 160$ on luxury articles. The capitalists of subdivision IIb divide their surplus-value $= 100_s$ in a similar way: $\frac{3}{5} = 60$ on necessities and $\frac{2}{5} = 40$ on luxuries, these latter being produced and exchanged within their own subdivision.*

We shall now see how the 160 of luxury items received for $(IIa)_s$ flows to the capitalists in IIa. Out of $(IIa)400_s$ in the form of necessary means of subsistence, we already saw how 100 was exchanged for an equal sum of $(IIb)_v$ existing in luxury articles; a further 60 has then to be exchanged for $(IIb)60_s$ in luxuries. The whole account at the start is IIa: $400_v + 400_s$; IIb: $100_v + 100_s$.

1. $400_v(a)$ is consumed by the workers in IIa, whose product (necessary means of subsistence) it forms part of; the workers buy this from the capitalist producers in their own subdivision. In this way £400 in money flows back to these capitalists, the variable capital value of 400 that they paid to their own workers; this can now be used to buy labour-power again.

2. A part of the $400_s(a)$ equal to the $100_v(b)$, i.e. one quarter of the surplus-value (a), is realized in luxury items in the following way. The workers in (b) receive £100 as wages from the capitalists in their own subdivision; they use this to buy one quarter of $_s(a)$, i.e. commodities that exist in the form of necessary means of subsistence. The capitalists of (a) use this money to buy luxury articles to the same amount, $100_v(b)$, i.e. half of the total luxury production. In this way, the variable capital of the capitalists (b) flows back to them in the money form, and they are able to begin their reproduction afresh by renewing the purchase of labour-power, since the total constant capital of the entire department II has already been converted by the exchange of $I_{(v+s)}$ for II_c. Thus the luxury workers can sell their labour-power once again only because the part of their own product that they created as an

* Since the whole $v+s$ of subdivision IIb is consumed by the capitalists, and the workers of the two subdivisions together consume the equivalent of IIa_v+IIb_v in the form of necessities (the product of subdivision IIa), the consumption fund for the capitalists of the two subdivisions, IIa_s+IIb_s is composed of:

IIa (necessities): II$a_{(v+s)}$−(IIa_v+IIb_v) (workers' consumption) $=$ IIa_s−IIb_v;
IIb (luxuries): II$b_{(v+s)}$;

which in this case comes to 300 IIa+200 IIb.

The ratio in which the department II capitalists as a whole divide their revenue expenditure between necessities and luxuries is thus already determined, once the relative production of the two subdivisions and the rates of surplus-value obtaining in them are given; the only additional supposition that Marx makes here, therefore, is that the two subdivisions taken separately each divide their expenditure according to this already given overall average.

equivalent for their wages has been drawn by the capitalists IIa into their consumption fund, turned into cash. (The same applies to the sale of labour-power in department I, since the II_c against which $I_{(v+s)}$ is exchanged consists of both luxury goods and necessary means of subsistence, while what is renewed by $I_{(v+s)}$ are the means of production both for luxury goods and for necessary means of subsistence.)

3. We come now to that exchange between (a) and (b) which is simply an exchange between the capitalists of the two subdivisions. We have already disposed of the variable capital 400_v and a part of the surplus-value 100_s in (a), as well as of the variable capital 100_v in (b). We further assumed that the capitalists in both cases divide their expenditure of revenue in the average ratio of $\frac{2}{5}$ for luxuries and $\frac{3}{5}$ for necessary provisions. Besides the 100 paid out for luxuries, which has already been spent, subdivision (a) as a whole still has a further 60 for luxuries to come and, in the same ratio, (b) has a total of 40.

$(IIa)_s$ is therefore divided into 240 for means of subsistence and 160 for luxuries; $240 + 160 = 400_s$ (IIa).

$(IIb)_s$ is divided into 60 for means of subsistence and 40 for luxuries: $60 + 40 = 100_s$ (IIb). The latter 40 is consumed by this class out of their own product ($\frac{2}{5}$ of their surplus-value); the 60 for means of subsistence they receive by exchanging 60 of their own surplus product for $60_s(a)$.

We have therefore the following equations for the capitalist class of department II, seen as a whole (where $v+s$ exists for subdivision (a) in necessary means of subsistence, for (b) in luxury articles):

IIa $(400_v + 400_s) + IIb (100_v + 100_s) = 1,000$; through the above-described movement, $500_v(a+b)$ is realized in $400_v(a)$ and $100_s(a)$, and $500_s(a+b)$ is realized in $300_s(a) + 100_v(b) + 100_s(b)$; a total of 1,000.

For (a) and (b), each considered by itself, we obtain the realizations:

$$(a)\ \frac{v}{400_v(a)} + \frac{s}{240_s(a) + 100_v(b) + 60_s(b)} = 800$$

$$(b)\ \frac{v}{100_s(a)} + \frac{s}{60_s(a) + 40_s(b)} = 200$$

$$\overline{1,000}$$

If we stick for simplicity's sake to the same ratio between variable and constant capital in the two subdivisions (although this is in no way necessary), then we obtain for $400_v(a)$ a constant capital of 1,600, and for $100_v(b)$ a constant capital of 400. The subdivisions of department II are then as follows:

$$(IIa) \quad 1,600_c + 400_v + 400_s = 2,400$$
$$(IIb) \quad 400_c + 100_v + 100_s = 600$$

altogether: $\quad 2,000_c + 500_v + 500_s = 3,000.$

Out of the 2,000 II_c in means of consumption that are exchanged for 2,000 $I_{(v+s)}$, we accordingly have 1,600 exchanged for means of production of necessary means of subsistence, and 400 for means of production of luxuries.

The 2,000 $I_{(v+s)}$ is thus itself broken down into $(800_v + 800_s)I$ for (a), or 1,600 in means of production for necessary means of subsistence, and $(200_v + 200_s)I$ for (b), or 400 in means of production for luxuries.

An important part, not only of the means of labour proper, but also of the raw and ancillary materials, etc., is the same for both subdivisions. But as far as the exchanges of the various value components of the total product $I_{(v+s)}$ are concerned, any division along these lines would be completely irrelevant. Both the above 800 I_v and the 200 I_v are realized through the spending of wages on means of consumption 1,000 II_c, so that the money capital advanced for wages is distributed evenly on the reflux between the capitalist producers of department I, and proportionately converts the variable capital they advanced back again into money; on the other hand, as far as the realization of the 1,000 I_s is concerned, here too the capitalists uniformly draw 600 IIa and 400 IIb in means of consumption from the entire second half of II_c — 1,000 (in proportion to the size of their s). I.e. those who replace the constant capital of IIa draw:

480 ($\frac{3}{5}$) from 600_c (IIa) and 320 ($\frac{2}{5}$) from 400_c (IIb) = 800;

those who replace the constant capital of IIb draw:

120 ($\frac{3}{5}$) from 600_c (IIa) and 80 ($\frac{2}{5}$) from 400_c (IIb) = 200;

a total of 1,000.

What is arbitrarily chosen here, for both departments I and II, is the ratio of variable capital to constant capital; arbitrary also is the identity of this ratio between the departments and their subdivisions. This identity is assumed here only for the sake of simplification, and the assumption of different ratios would not change anything at all in the conditions of the problem or its solution. The necessary result, however, on the assumption of simple reproduction, is as follows.

(1.) The new value product of the year's labour that is created in the natural form of means of production (which can be broken down into $v+s$) is equal to the constant capital value c in the product of the other section of the year's labour, reproduced in the form of means of consumption. If it were smaller than II_c, then department II could not completely replace its constant capital; if it were larger, then an unused surplus would be left over. In both cases, the assumption of simple reproduction would be destroyed.

(2.) In the annual product reproduced in the form of means of consumption, the variable capital v advanced in the money form can be realized only by those of its recipients who are workers in the luxury trades in the part of the necessary means of subsistence that at first sight embodies surplus-value for its capitalist producers; i.e. the v that is laid out on luxury production is equal to a part of s corresponding to it in value which is produced in the form of necessary means of subsistence, and must thus be smaller than the total $s - (IIa)_s$, that is – and it is only by realizing this v in part of s that the variable capital advanced by the capitalist producers of luxury articles returns to them in the money form. This is a phenomenon quite analogous to the realization of $I_{(v+s)}$ in II_c; only that in the second case, $(IIb)_v$ is realized in a *part* of $(IIa)_s$ equal to it in value. These ratios remain qualitatively decisive in every distribution of the annual social product, in as much as this actually goes into the process of annual reproduction mediated by circulation. $I_{(v+s)}$ can be realized only in II_c, just as II_c can be renewed only in its function as a component of the productive capital by way of this realization; $(IIb)_v$, similarly, can be realized only in a part of $(IIa)_s$, and only in this way can $(IIb)_v$ be transformed back into its form as money capital. It goes without saying that this applies only to the extent that all this is really a result of the reproduction process itself, i.e. in as much as the capitalists in IIb do not for instance obtain their v on credit from another source. Quantitatively, however, the exchange between the various parts of the annual product only takes place in the proportionate way depicted above to the extent that the scale of production and the value ratios involved in it remain constant, and these fixed ratios are not altered by foreign trade.

If it is now said, in the manner of Adam Smith, that $I_{(v+s)}$ is resolved into II_c, and II_c resolved into $I_{(v+s)}$, or alternatively, as he often and still more absurdly likes to say, $I_{(v+s)}$ form components of the price (or as he says 'value in exchange') of II_c, and II_c forms the entire component of the value $I_{(v+s)}$, then one could say and one would in fact have to say as well that $(IIb)_v$ can be resolved into $(IIa)_s$, or $(IIa)_s$ into $(IIb)_v$, or that $(IIb)_v$ forms a component of the surplus-value of IIa, and vice versa; in this way the surplus-value would be resolved into wages or variable capital, and this variable capital would form a 'component' of the surplus-value. This piece of absurdity is actually to be found in Smith, in as much as he sees wages as determined by the value of the necessary means of subsistence, and these commodity values as determined in turn by the value of the wages (variable capital) and surplus-value contained in them. He is so absorbed in the fractions into which the value product of a working day breaks down on the capitalist basis (i.e. into $v+s$) that he completely forgets that it is quite immaterial, in simple commodity exchange, whether the equivalents that exist in various natural forms consist of paid or unpaid labour, since in both cases they need the same amount of labour for their production; and that it is equally immaterial whether A's commodity is a means of production and B's a means of consumption, whether after its sale the one commodity has to function as a component of capital, and the other to go into the consumption fund and be (according to Adam) consumed as revenue. The use that the individual buyer makes of his commodity does not fall into the sphere of commodity exchange, of circulation, and does not affect the value of the commodity. This is in no way altered by the fact that analysis of the circulation of the total annual social product must deal with the specific destination in terms of use, the consumption aspect, of the different components of that product.

In connection with the exchange, noted above, of $(IIb)_v$ for an equal valued portion of $(IIa)_s$, and the further exchanges between $(IIa)_s$ and $(IIb)_s$, it is in no way assumed, whether we are dealing with the capitalists of IIa and IIb individually or in the aggregate, that they divide their surplus-value between necessary consumption and luxuries in the same ratio. One person may spend more on one kind of consumption, another person on something else. All that is presupposed on the basis of simple reproduction is that a sum of value equal to the total surplus-value is realized in a consumption fund. The limits of this are thus given. Within each department, one person may spend more on (a), another person more on (b); though these may compensate for one another in such a way that the capitalist class in both (a) and (b), taken as a whole, share in each in the same proportion. The value relations, however – the proportionate shares in the total value of the products of department II for the two kinds of producers (a) and (b) – and therefore also a definite quantitative ratio between the branches of production that supply those products – are necessarily given in each concrete case. It is only the ratio taken by way of example that is hypothetical; if a different one is taken, then this in no way alters the qualitative aspects; it is only the quantitative determinations that change. If any circumstances lead to a change in the proportionate magnitudes of (a) and (b), then the conditions of simple reproduction alter accordingly.

*

Since $(IIb)_v$ is realized in an equivalent portion of $(IIa)_s$, it follows that as the luxury part of the annual product grows, and a rising quota of labour-power is absorbed in luxury production, the re-transformation of the variable capital advanced in $(IIb)_v$ into money capital that can function anew as the money form of variable capital, and with it the existence and reproduction of the part of the working class engaged in II*b* – their supply of necessary means of consumption – is conditioned by the prodigality of the capitalist class, the conversion of a significant part of their surplus-value into luxury items.

Every crisis temporarily decreases luxury consumption; it delays and slows down the re-transformation of $(IIb)_v$ into money capital, so that only a partial transformation is possible and a section of the luxury workers are thrown onto the streets; this leads in turn to a stagnation and restriction in the sale of necessary means of consumption. And this quite apart from the unproductive workers who are discharged at the same time, workers who receive for their services a part of the luxury expenditure of the capitalists (they are themselves to this extent a luxury item), and who also participate very substantially in the consumption of necessary means of subsistence, etc. The reverse is the case in periods of prosperity, and particularly during the phase of hyper-activity, when the relative value of money (as expressed in commodities) already falls for other reasons (without a real revolution in values taking place), and so the prices of commodities rise independently of their own value. It is then not only the consumption of necessary means of subsistence that rises; the working class (in which the entire reserve army of labour has now been enrolled) also takes a temporary share in the consumption of luxury articles that are otherwise for the most part 'necessary' only for the capitalists. This phenomenon also provokes a rise in prices.

It is a pure tautology to say that crises are provoked by a lack of effective demand or effective consumption. The capitalist system does not recognize any forms of consumer other than those who can pay, if we exclude the consumption of paupers and swindlers. The fact that commodities are unsaleable means no more than that no effective buyers have been found for them, i.e. no consumers (no matter whether the commodities are ultimately sold to meet the needs of productive or individual consumption). If the attempt is made to give this tautology the semblance of greater profundity, by the statement that the working class receives too small a portion of its own product, and that the evil would be remedied if it received a bigger share, i.e. if its wages rose, we need only note that crises are always prepared by a period in which wages generally rise, and the working class actually does receive a greater share in the part of the annual product destined for consumption. From the standpoint of these advocates of sound and 'simple' (!) common sense, such periods should rather avert the crisis. It thus appears that capitalist production involves certain conditions independent of people's good or bad intentions, which permit the relative prosperity of the working class only temporarily, and moreover always as a harbinger of crisis.[5]

We saw just now how the proportional relation between the production of necessary items of consumption and the production of luxuries gives rise to the division of $II_{(v+s)}$ into IIa and IIb – and so also of II_c into $(IIa)_c$ and $(IIb)_c$. It thereby affects the character and the quantitative ratios of production right at the roots, and is an essential determining factor of their overall pattern.

Simple reproduction is oriented by nature to consumption as its aim. Even though the squeezing out of surplus-value appears as the driving motive of the individual capitalist, this surplus-value – no matter what its proportionate size – can be used here, in the last analysis, only for his individual consumption.

In so far as simple reproduction is also part of any annual reproduction on an expanded scale, and the major part at that, this motive remains alongside the motive of enrichment as such and in opposition to it. In the real world the matter appears more intricate, since the partners who share the loot – the surplus-value of the capitalist – figure independently of him as consumers.

5. THE MEDIATION OF THE EXCHANGES BY MONETARY CIRCULATION

As we have analysed it up to the present, circulation takes place between the different categories of producer according to the following schema.

1. Between departments I and II:

I. $4,000_c + 1,000_v + 1,000_s$

II. $ 2,000_c + 500_v + 500_s.$

This disposes of the circulation of $II_c = 2,000$, which is exchanged for $I(1,000_v + 1,000_s)$.

5. This should be noted by prospective supporters of Rodbertus's theory of crises. – F.E.

There remains the circulation of $v+s$ within department II (we leave aside for the time being the 4,000 I_c). This $II_{(v+s)}$ is divided between the subdivisions IIa and IIb as follows:

2. II. $500_v + 500_s = a(400_v + 400_s) + b(100_v + 100_s)$.

The $400_v(a)$ circulates within its own subdivision; the workers paid with it use it to buy necessary means of subsistence that they have themselves produced from their employers, the capitalists in IIa.

Since the capitalists of both subdivisions spend their surplus-value $\frac{3}{5}$ on products of IIa (necessary means of subsistence) and $\frac{2}{5}$ on products of IIb (luxuries), $\frac{2}{5}$ of the surplus-value of (a), i.e. 240, is consumed within subdivision IIa itself; similarly $\frac{2}{5}$ of the surplus-value in (b) (which was produced and is present in luxuries) is consumed within subdivision IIb.

There still remains to be exchanged between IIa and IIb:

On the part of IIa, 160_s.

On the part of IIb, $100_v + 60_s$.

These cancel each other out. With the 100 they receive in money as wages, the workers in IIb buy necessary means of subsistence from IIa. The capitalists in IIa thereby receive the money they require in order to invest $\frac{2}{5}$ of their surplus-value, $= 160_s$, in the luxuries produced by IIb (100_v that remains in the hands of the capitalists of IIb as the product replacing the wages they paid, and 60_s). The schema for this is thus:

3. IIa. $(400_v) + (240_s)$ $+160_s$
     b. $\overline{100_v + 60_s}$ $(+40_s)$,

where the items in parentheses are those that circulate and are consumed only within their own subdivision.

The direct reflux of the money capital advanced in variable capital, which takes place for the capitalists only in subdivision IIa producing necessary means of subsistence, is simply a manifestation, modified by special conditions, of the general law already explained that the money that commodity producers advance returns to them in the normal course of commodity circulation. What also follows from this, incidentally, is that wherever there is a money capitalist behind the commodity producers, and it is he who first advances the money capital to the industrial capitalist (money capital in the strict sense of the word, i.e. capital value in the money form), the actual point of return of this money is the pocket of the money capitalist. In this way, even if the money circulates through the hands of more or less all concerned, the mass of the circulating money belongs to the department of money capital organized and concentrated in the form of banks, etc.; the way in which this department advances its capital determines that the final reflux in the money form is always to it, even if this is mediated by the transformation of the industrial capital back into money capital.

Two things are always required for commodity circulation: commodities have to be cast into circulation, and so has money.

'The process of circulation, therefore, unlike the direct exchange of products, does not disappear from view once the use-values have changed places and changed hands. The money does not vanish when it finally drops out of the series of metamorphoses undergone by a commodity. It always leaves behind a precipitate at a point in the arena of circulation vacated by the commodities' (Volume 1, Chapter 3, p. 208).

In the circulation between II_c and $I_{(v+s)}$, for example, we assumed that £500 was advanced for this circulation by department II. In the countless circulation processes which the circulation between major social groups of producers is resolved into, it is now one of this group and now one of that who first appears as a buyer and casts money into circulation. Quite apart from individual circumstances, this is already determined by the difference in the production periods and hence the turnovers of the various commodity capitals. Department II uses £500 to buy means of production to this amount from department I, but the latter uses the £500 to buy means of consumption from II; the money simply flows back to department II, which is not made any the richer by this reflux. Department I first cast £500 into circulation in money and withdrew commodities to the same value; it then sold commodities for £500 and extracted from circulation the same amount in money. In this way, the £500 flows back. In point of fact, department II has cast into circulation £500 in money and £500 in commodities, a total of £1,000; it withdraws from circulation £500 of commodities and £500 in money. The circulation sphere needs only £500 in money for the conversion of both £500 in commodities (I) and £500 in commodities (II), so whoever advanced the money for the purchase of someone else's commodity receives it back again in the sale of his own. If it had been department I that first bought commodities worth £500 from department II, and later sold £500 of commodities to department II, this £500 would return to department I instead of to department II.

In department I, the money invested in wages, i.e. advanced as variable capital in the money form, does not return directly in this form, but indirectly by a detour. In department II, on the other hand, the £500 for wages returns directly from the workers to the capitalists, since this reflux is always direct where sale and purchase are repeated between the same persons in such a way that they regularly face one another alternately as buyer and seller of commodities.* The capitalist in department II pays for his labour-power in money; he thereby incorporates the labour-power into his own capital, and it is only by this process of circulation, which for him is simply the transformation of money capital into productive capital, that he, as industrial capitalist, confronts the worker as his wage-labourer. But after this the worker, who was in the first instance the seller, the dealer in his own labour-power, now, in the second instance, confronts the capitalist, the seller of commodities, as the possessor of money; in this way the money laid out by the capitalist on wages flows back to him. In so far as the sale of these commodities does not involve swindling, etc., but equivalents are exchanged in commodities and money, this is not a process by which the capitalist can enrich himself. Nor does he pay the worker twice over, first in money and then in commodities; his money returns to him when the worker exchanges it with him for commodities.

This money capital transformed into variable capital, i.e. the money advanced as wages, plays a major role in actual monetary circulation. Since the working class has to live from hand to mouth, i.e. since it cannot give the industrial capitalists any long-term credit, variable capital has to be advanced at the same time in money at countless different points in society, and at definite and short intervals, such as a week, etc. These periods are repeated fairly rapidly, no matter how different the turnover periods of capitals in the various branches of industry; though the shorter the intervals, the smaller need be the relative size of the total sum of money cast into circulation at one stroke through these channels. In every country of capitalist production, the money capital advanced in this way forms a relatively decisive share in the total circulation, and all the more so in that the same money flows through the most varied channels and functions as means of circulation for a myriad other businesses, before returning to its starting-point.

*

Let us now consider the circulation between $I_{(v+s)}$ and II_c from a different point of view.

The capitalists in department I advance £1,000 as payment for wages; the workers use this to buy £1,000 worth of means of subsistence from

---

*This does of course apply when department II is taken as a whole, in contrast to department I. But as Marx has just explained, within department II it properly applies only to subdivision IIa, producing means of subsistence that enter the consumption of the working class.

the capitalists in department II, and these in turn use it to buy means of production from the capitalists in department I. The variable capital advanced by the latter has now returned to them in its monetary form, while the capitalists in department II have transformed half of their constant capital from the form of commodity capital back into productive capital. The capitalists in department II advance a further £500 in money to get means of production from department I. The capitalists in department I spend this money on means of consumption from department II; this £500 thus flows back to the capitalists in department I, who advance it afresh in order to transform the last quarter of the constant capital they previously transformed into commodities back into its productive natural form. This money again flows back to department I and once more withdraws from department II means of consumption to the same amount; the capitalists in department II are now as before in possession of £500 in money and £2,000 in constant capital, though this has been newly converted from the form of commodity capital back into that of productive capital. With £1,500 in money, a commodity mass of £5,000 has been circulated.

To recapitulate:

(1) Department I pays its workers £1,000 for labour-power of the same value;

(2) these workers use this £1,000 to buy means of subsistence from department II;

(3) department II buys means of production with the same money from department I, thereby restoring department I's variable capital in its money form;

(4) department II uses £500 to buy means of production from department I;

(5) department I buys means of consumption from department I with the same £500;

(6) department II buys means of production from department I with this £500;

(7) department I buys means of consumption from department II with the £500. As a result, the £500 which department II cast into circulation on top of its £2,000 in commodities, and for which it did not withdraw any equivalent in commodities, has flowed back to it.[6]

6. The presentation here departs somewhat from that given previously (p. 476). There department I also cast its own £500 into circulation. Here department II alone supplies the additional money material needed for circulation. This however in no way alters the principle involved. – F.E.

The exchange process thus takes the following course:

(1) Department I pays £1,000 for labour-power, i.e. for a commodity of £1,000.

(2) Its workers use their wages to buy means of consumption from department II to the amount of £1,000; i.e. commodities of £1,000.

(3) With the £1,000 received from these workers, department II buys means of production to the same value from department I; i.e. commodities of £1,000. With this, £1,000 in money, as the money form of the variable capital, has flowed back to department I.

(4) Department II buys means of production from department I for £500; i.e. commodities of £500.

(5) Department I uses the same £500 to buy means of consumption from department II; i.e. commodities of £500.

(6) Department II uses the £500 to buy means of production from department I; i.e. commodities of £500.

(7) Department I uses the £500 to buy means of consumption from department II; i.e. commodities of £500.

The sum of the commodity values exchanged is £5,000.

The £500 that department II advanced for its purchases has returned to it.

As a result:

(1.) Department I possesses variable capital in the money form to the sum of £1,000, which is what it originally advanced to the circulation sphere. It has also spent £1,000 on individual consumption – from its own commodity product; i.e. it has spent the money that it received for the sale of means of production, amounting to the total of £1,000.

On the other hand, the natural form into which the variable capital existing in the money form has to be converted – i.e. labour-power – has to be maintained, reproduced by consumption, and be present once again as the only article of trade of its proprietors, who have to sell this if they want to live. In this way, the relationship between wage-labourers and capitalists is also reproduced.

(2.) The constant capital of department II is replaced in kind, and the £500 advanced to circulation by department II has returned to it.

For the workers in department I, the circulation is the simple one of $C–M–C$: $C^{(1)}$(labour-power)–$M^{(2)}$ (£1,000, the money form of the variable capital in department I)–$C^{(3)}$ (necessary means of subsistence to the sum of £1,000); this £1,000 converts into money the same value of constant capital in department II, existing in the commodity form as means of subsistence.

For the capitalists in department II, the process is $C-M$, the transformation of a part of their commodity product into the money form, from which it is transformed back into components of their productive capital – i.e. into a part of the means of production that they need.

In the advance of M (£500) which the capitalists in department II make in order to purchase the remaining components of their means of production, they anticipate the money form of that part of II_c that is still in the commodity form (means of consumption). In the act $M-C$, in which department II buys with M and department I sells C, department II's money is transformed into a part of its productive capital, while I's commodity undergoes the act $C-M$ and is transformed into money, although it does not represent any component of capital value, but rather realized surplus-value which is simply spent on means of consumption.

In the circulation $M-C...P...C'-M'$, the first act $M-C$ of one capitalist is the final act $C'-M'$ of another (or part of it); it is completely immaterial for the commodity circulation itself whether this C, by which M is transformed into productive capital, represents for its seller (who thereby converts this C into money) the constant component of his capital, the variable component, or surplus-value.

As far as the department I capitalists are concerned, with respect to the component $v+s$ of their commodity product they withdraw more money from the circulation sphere than they cast into it. Firstly, their £1,000 of variable capital returns to them; secondly, they sell means of production for £500 (see above, exchange no. 4), and this enables them to convert half their surplus-value into cash; then they again sell a further £500 of means of production (exchange no. 6), the second half of their surplus-value, and as a result their entire surplus-value has been withdrawn from circulation in the money form. We have therefore, in succession, (1) variable capital transformed back into money, £1,000; (2) half of the surplus-value realized, £500; the other half of the surplus-value, £500; a total realized of $1,000_v+1,000_s = £2,000$. Even if department I cast only £1,000 into circulation (we leave aside here the circumstances that mediate the reproduction of I_c, which will be considered later), it has withdrawn twice the amount. Of course, the s that has been realized (transformed into money) immediately vanishes again into someone else's hands (department II), because the money is exchanged for means of consumption. The capitalists of department I have withdrawn only as much in *money* as they cast in in *commodities*. The fact that this value is surplus-value, and costs the capitalists nothing, in no way alters the value of the commodities themselves; it is therefore completely immaterial, as far as the exchange of values in commodity circulation is concerned. The realization of the surplus-value in money is naturally temporary, just like all other forms that the capital advanced passes through in its conversions. It lasts only so long as the interval between the transformation of department I's commodities into money and the subsequent transformation of I's money into II's commodities.

If the turnovers are assumed to be shorter – or, from the standpoint of simple commodity circulation, the velocity of monetary circulation is assumed to be greater – then still less money would be needed in order to circulate the commodity values to be exchanged. This sum is always determined – once the number of successive exchanges is given – by the sum of the prices or values of the circulating commodities. The proportion in which this sum of values consists of surplus-value on the one hand and capital value on the other is completely irrelevant here.

Say that in our example wages are paid four times a year in department I. $4 \times 250 = 1,000$, and so £250 in money would be sufficient for the circulation of $I_v - \frac{1}{2}II_c$, and for the circulation between the variable capital I_v and the labour-power of department I. In the same way, if the circulation between I_s and II_c consisted of four turnovers, then £250 would be sufficient for it, and therefore a total sum of money or a money capital of £500 would be enough for the circulation of commodities to the sum of £5,000. A quarter of the surplus-value would then be realized four times a year, instead of half of it twice.

If in exchange no. 4 it was department I instead of department II that appeared as the buyer, i.e. £500 in money was spent on means of consumption to the same value, department II would then buy means of production with the same £500 in exchange no. 5; in exchange no. 6, department I would use this £500 to buy means of consumption, and in no. 7, department II would use it again to buy means of production. Thus the £500 would ultimately return to department I, instead of department II as before. The surplus-value is realized here by the money spent by its capitalist producers themselves on their private consumption, which represents anticipated revenue, anticipated income from the surplus-value contained in the commodities still to be sold. The realization of surplus-value does not take place through the reflux of the £500; for alongside the £1,000 in commodities I_v, department I has cast £500 of money into circulation in connection with exchange no. 4, and this was an additional sum, not – as far as we know – the proceeds of the sale of the commodities. When this money flows back to department I, I has simply recovered its additional money, and not realized its surplus-value. The monetary realization of department I's surplus-value simply involves the sale of the commodities I_s in which it is contained, and each time it lasts only as long as the money released by the sale of these commodities is not spent again on means of consumption.

Department I uses its additional money (£500) to buy means of consumption from department II; this money is spent by department I, which gets the equivalent for it in commodities from department II; the money flows back the first time through the purchase by department II of £500 of commodities from department I. It flows back therefore as the equivalent for the commodities sold by department I, but these commodities cost department I nothing, they are part of its surplus-value, so that *it is the money that department I itself cast into circulation that realizes its own surplus-value*. Similarly, on its second purchase (no. 6), department I again receives its equivalent in commodities from department II. Suppose that department II does not buy means of production from department I (no. 7). Then department I would in fact have paid £1,000 for means of consumption, and consumed its entire surplus-value as revenue, i.e. paid £500 in its own commodities (means of production) and £500 in money; it would still have £500 of its own commodities (means of production) in stock on the other hand, but would have got rid of its £500 of money.

Department II, on the contrary, would have transformed three quarters of its constant capital from the form of commodity capital back into productive capital; but it would have one quarter left in the form of money capital (£500), this being in fact idle money or money whose functioning has been interrupted and which is held in abeyance. If this situation lasts too long, then department II will have to reduce the scale of its reproduction by a quarter. However the £500 in means of production which department I is still saddled with is not surplus-value in the commodity form; it is there in place of the £500 advanced in money, which department I possessed alongside its surplus-value of £1,000 in the commodity form. As money, this exists in an ever realizable form; in the commodity form, it is temporarily unsaleable. This much is evident, that simple reproduction – in which each element of productive capital in both department I and department II has to be replaced – remains possible only if the 500 golden birds return to department I, which first sent them flying.

Once a capitalist spends his money on means of consumption, he is then done with it, it has gone the way of all flesh. (Here we are still concerned only with industrial capitalists, who stand as the representatives for all others.) If the money flows back to him again, this can happen only in so far as he fishes it out of the circulation sphere in exchange for commodities – i.e. by way of his commodity capital. Just as the value of his total annual commodity product (his commodity capital) can be broken down into constant capital value, variable capital value and surplus-value, so too can every element of this, i.e. the value of every individual commodity. The realization of each of his individual commodities (the elements of his commodity product) is therefore at the same time the realization of a certain quota of the surplus-value contained in the total commodity product. It is therefore literally correct, in the present case, that the capitalist himself cast into circulation the money into which he converts his surplus-value, i.e. by means of which he realizes it, and, what is more, by spending this on means of consumption. What we have here of course are not the identical pieces of money, but rather a given quantity of hard cash equal to the money cast into circulation to cover his personal needs, or to the part of the money needed for that purpose.

In practice this occurs in two ways. If the business was started only within the current year, then it takes a good while, at best a few months, before the capitalist can spend money for his personal consumption out of his income from this actual business. He does not on this account suspend his consumption for a moment. He advances himself money against the surplus-value that he still has to hunt out (whether this is advanced from his own pocket or from someone else's by way of credit). But this money is also a circulating medium in which he can later realize his surplus-value. In the other case, where the business has already been in regular operation for some time, payments and receipts take place at different times of the year, but the capitalist's consumption, which anticipates his receipts and the level of which is fixed as a certain proportion of his customary receipts or those estimated, still continues without interruption. With each portion of commodities sold, one part of the surplus-value to be made in the year is realized. But if, out of the commodities produced in the year, no more is sold than is needed to replace the constant and variable capital value contained in them, or if prices fall so that the sale of the entire annual product realizes only the capital value advanced in it, then the anticipatory character of the money spent against future surplus-value clearly emerges. If our capitalist goes bankrupt, then his creditors and the courts investigate whether his anticipated private spending stood in due proportion to the state of his business and the customary or normal receipts of surplus-value corresponding to it.

In relation to the capitalist class as a whole, however, the proposition that it must itself cast into circulation the money needed to realize its surplus-value (and also to circulate its capital, constant and variable) is not only far from paradoxical, it is in fact a necessary condition of the overall mechanism. For here there are just two classes: the working class, which only disposes of its labour-power, and the capitalist class, which has the monopoly of the means of social production, and of money. It would rather be a paradox if, instead, it was the working class that initially advanced the money required to realize the surplus-value contained in commodities, out of its own resources. The individual capitalist, however, effects this advance only by acting as buyer, *spending* money on the purchase of means of consumption or *advancing* money on the purchase of elements of his productive capital, either labour-power or means of production. He only ever parts with the money in exchange for an equivalent. He advances money to circulation only in the same way that he advances commodities to it. In both cases, he acts as the starting-point of their circulation.

The real course of events is obscured by two circumstances.

1. The appearance of *commercial capital* (the primary form of which is always money, since the merchant as such does not produce any 'product' or 'commodity') and of *money capital*, as the object of manipulation of a special kind of capitalist, in the circulation process of industrial capital.

2. The division of surplus-value – which must always exist initially in the hands of the industrial capitalist – into different categories, the bearers of which appear alongside the industrial capitalist as the landlord (for ground-rent), the money-lender (for interest), etc., as well as the government and its officials, rentiers, etc. These fellows face the industrial capitalist as buyers, and to this extent realize his commodities in money; they too cast their share of 'money' into the circulation sphere, and he receives this from them. What is always forgotten in connection with this are the sources from which they originally obtained this money, and continue to obtain it.

6. THE CONSTANT CAPITAL IN DEPARTMENT I[7]

It still remains for us to investigate the constant capital in department I, $4,000_c$. This is equal in value to the means of production consumed in the production of this mass of commodities, a value which reappears in the commodity product of department I. This reappearing value, which was not produced in the production process of department I, but entered it the year before as constant value, as the given value of its means of production, now exists in that entire part of the commodity mass of department I that is not absorbed by department II; moreover, the value of this commodity mass remaining in the hands of the department I capitalists is two thirds of the value of their entire annual commodity product. If we were dealing with the individual capitalist producing one particular means of production, we could say: He first sold his commodity product, transformed it into money. By transforming it into money, he also transformed the constant value component of his product back into money. With this value portion transformed into money, he then bought his means of production again from other commodity sellers, or transformed the constant value component of his product into a natural form in which it could once more function as productive constant capital. Now, however, this assumption becomes untenable. The capitalist class in department I comprises the totality of capitalists who produce means of production. Moreover, the commodity product of 4,000 that remains in their hands is a part of the social product that cannot be exchanged against any other, for there is no such other part of the annual product. With the exception of this 4,000, all the remainder has been disposed of. One part of it has been absorbed by the social consumption fund, and another part has to replace the constant capital of department II, which has already exchanged everything it has available for exchange with department I.

The difficulty is very simply resolved, when we remember that the entire commodity product of department I consists in its natural form of means of production, i.e. of the material elements of constant capital itself. The same phenomenon is displayed here as previously with department II, only under a different aspect. In department II, the entire commodity product consists of means of consumption; one part of these, measured by the wages plus surplus-value contained in this commodity product, can therefore be consumed by its own producers. Here in department I, the entire commodity product consists of means

7. From here on , Manuscript II.

of production – buildings, machinery, containers, raw and ancillary materials, etc. One part of these, that which replaces the constant capital used up in this sphere, can therefore immediately function in its natural form once again as a component of the productive capital. In so far as it steps into the circulation sphere, it circulates within department I. In department II, one part of the commodity product is individually consumed in kind by its own producers; in department I, on the other hand, a part of the product is productively consumed in kind by its own capitalist producers.

In the $4,000_c$ part of the commodity product of department I there reappears the constant capital value consumed in this department, and it reappears moreover in a natural form in which it can immediately function again as productive constant capital. In department II, the part of the commodity product of 3,000 whose value equals wages plus surplus-value $(=1,000)$ goes directly into the individual consumption of the capitalists and workers, while the constant capital value of this commodity product, on the other hand $(=2,000)$, cannot go back into the productive consumption of the capitalists in department II, but has to be replaced by exchange with department I. In department I, on the contrary, the part of its commodity product of 6,000 whose value is equal to wages plus surplus-value $(=2,000)$ does not go into the individual consumption of its producers, and it is also unable to do this owing to its natural form. Instead it must first be exchanged with department II. However, the constant portion of this product's value $(=4,000)$ does exist in a natural form in which – taking the capitalist class of department I as a whole – it can directly function again as their constant capital. In other words, the entire product of department I consists of use-values which by virtue of their natural form can serve only as elements of constant capital – given the capitalist mode of production. Out of this product, which has a value of 6,000, one third (2,000) therefore replaces the constant capital of department II, and the remaining two thirds replace the constant capital of department I.

The constant capital of department I consists of a number of different groups of capitals, invested in the various branches of production of means of production – so much in iron works, so much in coalmines, etc. Each of these capital groups, or, in other words, each of these social group capitals, is again composed of a larger or smaller number of independently functioning individual capitals. Firstly, the capital of the society, e.g. 7,500 (this may stand for millions, etc.) is broken down into different capital groups. The social capital of 7,500 is broken down into particular portions, each invested in a particular branch of production; the part of the social capital value invested in each particular branch of production consists, in its natural form, partly of the means of production for each special sphere of production, partly of the labour-power necessary and appropriately qualified for the industry in question, modified in various ways by the division of labour, according to the specific kind of labour that it has to perform in the sphere of production in question. The part of the social capital applied in each particular branch of production consists once again of the sum of individual capitals invested and independently functioning in it. This obviously applies to both departments, I and II.

As far as concerns the constant capital value reappearing in department I in the form of its commodity product, part of this goes back once again as means of production into the particular branch of production (or even the individual business) from which it emerged as a product; e.g. corn into the production of corn, coal into coal production, iron in the form of machines into iron production etc.

But to the extent that the partial products of which the constant capital value in department I consists do not go directly back into their particular or individual spheres of production, they simply change their place. They go in their natural form into another sphere of production of department I, while the product of these other spheres of production of department I replaces them in kind. These products merely experience a change of position. They all go back in again as factors that replace the constant capital in department I, only instead of entering one group of department I they go into another. In as much as there is exchange here between the individual capitalists of department I, this is exchange of one natural form of constant capital against another natural form of constant capital, one kind of means of production against other kinds of means of production. It is mutual exchange between the different individual constant portions of capital in department I. These products, in as much as they do not directly serve as means of production in their own branch of production, are thus displaced from their own point of production to another one, and mutually replace each other in this way. In other words (as happens similarly for surplus-value in department II), each capitalist in department I withdraws the appropriate means of production needed by him from this commodity mass in the proportion to which he is a joint owner of this constant capital of 4,000. If production were social instead of capitalist, it is evident that these products of department I would be no less constantly redistributed among the branches of production in this department as means of production, according to the needs of reproduction; one part directly remaining in the sphere of production from which it emerged as a product, another part being shifted to other points of production, and so there would be a constant to and fro between the various points of production in this department.

7. VARIABLE CAPITAL AND SURPLUS-VALUE IN THE TWO DEPARTMENTS

The total value of the means of consumption annually produced is equal to the variable capital value reproduced in the course of the year plus the surplus-value newly produced, in department II (i.e. the value actually produced during the year in department II), together with the variable capital value reproduced in the year and the surplus-value newly produced in department I (i.e. the value produced during the year in department I).

On the premise of simple reproduction, therefore, the total value of the means of consumption annually produced is equal to the annual value product, i.e. equal to the total value produced by the labour of the society in the course of the year, and the reason why this must be the case is that with simple reproduction this entire value is consumed.

The total social working day breaks down into two parts: (1) necessary labour – this creates a value of 1500_v in the course of the year; (2) surplus labour – this creates an additional value or surplus-value of 1500_s. The sum of these values is 3,000, equal to that of the means of consumption annually produced. The total value of the means of consumption produced during the year is therefore equal to the total value that the entire social working day produces during the year, i.e. equal to the value of the social variable capital plus the social surplus-value, or equal to the total new annual product.

We know however that even if these two value magnitudes are equal, this in no way means that the total value of the commodities in department II, the means of consumption, has been produced in this department of social production. They are equal because the constant capital value that reappears in department II is equal to the value newly produced in department I (variable capital value plus surplus-value); hence $I_{(v+s)}$ can purchase the part of the product that represents constant capital value for its producers in department II. This explains why even though, for the capitalists in department II, the value of their product breaks down into $c+v+s$, yet, considered from the social point of view, the value of this product can be broken down into $v+s$. This is the case, in fact, only because II_c is equal here to $I_{(v+s)}$, and these two components of the social product exchange their natural forms with one another by way of their commodity exchange. After this conversion, therefore, II_c exists once again in means of production, and $I_{(v+s)}$ in means of consumption.

It is this circumstance that led Adam Smith to maintain that the value of the annual product resolves itself into $v+s$. This (1) applies only to the part of the annual product consisting of means of consumption, and (2) does not apply in the sense that this total value is produced in department II and the value of the product is therefore the variable capital value advanced in department II plus the surplus-value produced in this department. It holds rather in the sense that

$$II_{(c+v+s)} = II_{(v+s)} + I_{(v+s)},$$
or because $II_c = I_{(v+s)}$.

It also follows that even if the social working day (i.e. the labour spent by the entire working class over a whole year), just like each individual working day, can be simply broken down into two parts, i.e. into necessary labour plus surplus labour, and even though the value produced by this working day can therefore be similarly broken down into two parts, i.e. the portion of value with which the worker buys his own means of reproduction, and the surplus-value that the capitalist can spend for his individual consumption – yet, from the social standpoint, one part of the social working day is spent exclusively on the *production of fresh constant capital*, i.e. of products that are exclusively destined to function in the labour process as means of production, and therefore as constant capital in the accompanying process of valorization. On our assumption, the total social working day is represented by a money value of 3,000, of which one third ($=1,000$) is produced in department II, which produces means of consumption, i.e. the commodities in which the entire variable capital value and the entire surplus-value of the society is ultimately realized. On this supposition, therefore, two thirds of the social working day is applied in the production of new constant capital. Even if, from the standpoint of the individual capitalists and workers in department I, this two thirds of the social working day serves merely to produce variable capital value and surplus-value, just like the other third of the social working day in department II, considered from the social standpoint – and also from the standpoint of the use-value of the product – this two thirds of the social working day still produces only a replacement for the constant capital consumed in the process of productive consumption, or in the process of being consumed. Even taken by itself, this two thirds of the working day, although the total value it produces for its producers is equal simply to variable capital value plus surplus-value, does not produce any use-value of such a kind that either wages or surplus-value could be spent on it; its product is a means of production.

The first thing to note is that no part of the social working day, whether in department I or department II, serves to produce the value of the constant capital applied and functioning in these two great spheres of production. All that is produced here is additional value, $2,000\ I_{(v+s)} + 1,000\ II_{(v+s)}$, an addition to the constant capital value of $4,000\ I_c + 2,000\ II_c$. The new value that has been produced in the form of means of production is not yet constant capital. It is simply destined to function as such in the future.

The entire product of department II – means of consumption – is from the use-value standpoint, i.e. concretely, considered in its natural form, the product of concrete forms of labour such as weaving, baking, etc. which have been employed in this department. It is the product of this labour in as much as the labour functions as the subjective element of the labour process. As far as the constant value component of this product of department II is concerned, however, it simply reappears in a new use-value, in a new natural form, the form of means of consumption, whereas it earlier existed in the form of means of production. Its value has been transferred by the labour process from its old natural form to its new one. But the *value* of this two thirds of the value of the product, 2,000, has not been produced by department II in the current year's valorization process.

Just as, considered from the standpoint of the labour process, the product of department II is the result of newly functioning living labour and its given presupposed means of production, labour realizing itself in these as its objective conditions, so from the standpoint of the valorization process the value of the product, 3,000, is composed of the new value produced by the one third of the social working day newly added ($500_v + 500_s = 1,000$), and a constant value in which there is objectified two thirds of a past working day, which took place before the production process of department II at present under consideration. This value component of the product of department II can be represented by a portion of the product itself. It exists in a quantity of means of consumption to the value of 2,000 = two thirds of a social working day. This is the new use form in which it reappears. The exchange of one part of the means of consumption, $=2,000 \text{ II}_c$, for means of production from department I, $=\text{I}(1,000_v + 1,000_s)$, is therefore in point of fact the exchange of two thirds of a total working day which does not form part of this year's labour, but was performed prior to the current year, for two thirds of the social working day newly added in the present year. Two thirds of this year's social working day could not both be applied in the production of constant capital and yet at the same time form variable capital value and surplus-value for its own producers, if it were not exchanged with a value component of the means of consumption annually consumed that contains two thirds of a working day performed and realized prior to the present year. This is an exchange of two thirds of this year's working day for two thirds of a working day spent prior to this year, an exchange between labour-time of this year and labour-time of a previous year. It therefore explains the riddle as to how the value product of the entire social working day can be resolved into variable capital value plus surplus-value, even though two thirds of this working day was not spent on the production of objects in which variable capital or surplus-value could be realized, but rather on the production of means of production to replace the capital used up during the current year. This is explained by the simple fact that, considered from the point of view of its value, the two thirds of department II's product in which the capitalists and workers of department I realize the variable capital value plus the surplus-value produced by them (making two ninths of the total value of the annual product) is the product of two thirds of a social working day spent before the current year.

The total social product of departments I and II, means of production and means of consumption, is certainly, looked at from the point of view of its use-value, its concrete, natural form, the product of this year's labour, but only in so far as this labour is considered simply as useful, concrete labour, not in so far as it is viewed as the expenditure of labour-power, as value-forming labour. And it is only useful, concrete labour in the sense that the means of production have been transformed into new products, the products of the current year, by the living labour added to them and operating on them. The labour of this year, however, could not have been transformed into products without means of production, i.e. means of labour and production materials, independent of it.

8. THE CONSTANT CAPITAL IN BOTH DEPARTMENTS

As far as concerns the value of the total product, 9,000, and the categories into which it breaks down, its analysis does not offer any greater difficulty than that of the value of the product of an individual capital; it is in fact identical with this.

The annual social product, taken as a whole, contains three one-year social working days. The value expression of each of these working days is 3,000, so that the value expression of the total product is $3 \times 3,000 = 9,000$.

Furthermore, of the labour-time that has been spent *prior* to the production process of the year whose product we are analysing, four thirds of a working day was spent in department I (value product 4,000) and two thirds of a working day in department II (value product 2,000). Taken together, this is two social working days, whose value product is 6,000. Thus $4,000 \text{ I}_c + 2,000 \text{ II}_c = 6,000_c$ figures as the value of the means of production, or constant capital value, reappearing in the value of the overall product.

Besides, out of the one-year working day that the society has newly added, one third is necessary labour or labour that replaces the value of the variable capital $1,000 \text{ I}_v$ in department I, and pays the price of the labour applied in this department. One sixth of the social working day is similarly necessary labour in department II, to a value of 500. Thus $1,000 \text{ I}_v + 500 \text{ II}_v = 1,500_v$, the value expression of half a social working day, is the value expression of that half of the total working day added in the year which consists of necessary labour.

Finally, one third of the total working day, a value product of 1,000, is surplus labour in department I; in department II, this surplus labour is one sixth of a working day, a value product of 500. Together these make up the other half of the total working day added. Thus the total surplus-value produced $= 1,000 \text{ I}_s + 500 \text{ I}_s = 1,500_s$.

In other words:

Constant capital component of the value of the social product (*c*):

Two working days, spent prior to the current production process, a value expression of 6,000.

Necessary labour spent during the year (*v*):

Half the working day spent in the year's production, a value expression of 1,500.

Surplus labour spent during the year (*s*):

Half the working day spent in the year's production, a value expression of 1,500.

The value product of the year's labour $(v+s) = 3,000$.

The value of the total product $(c+v+s) = 9,000$.

Thus the difficulty does not lie in analysing the value of the social product itself. It arises when the *value* components of the social product are compared with its *material* components.

The constant portion of value, that simply reappearing, is equal to the value of the part of the social product that consists of means of *production*, and is embodied in this part.

The new year's value product $= v+s$ is equal to the value of the part of the annual product that consists of means of *consumption*, and is embodied in this.

But, with exceptions that are of no consequence here, means of production and means of consumption are totally different kinds of commodities, products quite different in their natural or use form, and therefore products of totally different varieties of concrete labour. The labour that uses machines for the production of means of subsistence is quite different from the labour that makes machines. The total annual working day, whose value expression is 3,000, seems to be spent on the production of means of consumption $= 3,000$ in which no portion of constant capital value reappears, since this 3,000, $= 1,500_v + 1,500_s$, is simply resolved into variable capital value plus surplus-value. On the other hand, the constant capital value of 6,000 reappears in a kind of product that is completely different from the means of consumption, i.e. the means of production, while no part of the social working day seems to be spent in the production of this new product; the whole working day, rather, seems to consist simply of the kinds of labour that do not result in means of production, but rather in means of consumption. The riddle is already solved. The value product of the annual labour is equal to the value of the product of department II, the total value of the newly produced means of consumption. But the value of this product is three times greater than the part of the annual labour that is spent on the production of means of consumption (department II). Only one third of the annual labour is spent on producing these. Two thirds of the annual labour is spent on producing means of production, i.e. in department I. The value product created in this period in department I, equal to the variable capital value reproduced in department I plus the surplus-value, is equal to the constant capital value of department II that reappears in department II in means of consumption. These can therefore be exchanged for one another and replace one another in kind. The total value of the means of consumption in department II is therefore equal to the sum of the new value product in departments I and II together, or

$$II_{(c+v+s)} = I_{(v+s)} + II_{(v+s)},$$

i.e. the total new value produced by the annual labour in the form of $v+s$.

On the other hand, the total value of the means of production (I) is equal to the sum of the constant capital values reappearing in the forms of means of production (I) and means of consumption (II), i.e. equal to the total constant capital value reappearing in the society's total product. This total value is, in department I, the value expression of four thirds of a working day performed before the current production process, and two thirds in department II, making a total of two complete working days.

The difficulty with the annual social product, therefore, comes from the fact that the constant portion of value is represented in a kind of product – means of production – completely different from the means of consumption in which the new value $v+s$ added to this constant portion of value is represented. It seems, therefore, as if two thirds of the mass of products consumed – in value terms – exist once again in a new form, as new product, without any kind of labour having been expended by the society on their production. This is not the case with the individual capital. Each individual capitalist applies a definite concrete kind of labour, which transforms the means of production peculiar to it into a product. Say for example that the capitalist is involved in engineering, the constant capital spent during the year $6,000_c$, the variable capital $1,500_v$ and the surplus-value $1,500_s$; the product is then 9,000, and we can take it as a product of eighteen machines, each worth 500. The entire product there exists in the same form, that of machines. (If he produces different kinds, then each of these must be dealt with separately.) The total commodity product is the product of the labour expended during the year in engineering, the combination of this concrete kind of labour with its specific means of production. The various parts of the product's value are therefore represented in this same natural form: twelve machines contain $6,000_c$, three machines $1,500_v$, three machines $1,500_s$. It is evident here that if the value of the twelve machines that comprise the constant capital is equal to $6,000_c$, this is not because the labour embodied in these machines took place before the engineering stage was reached and was not spent in it. The value of the means of production for eighteen machines has not been transformed of itself into twelve machines, it is rather the value of these twelve machines (which itself consists of $4,000_c+1,000_v+1,000_s$) that is equal to the total value of the constant capital value contained in the eighteen machines. The capitalist engineer must therefore sell twelve of the eighteen machines in order to replace the constant capital he has spent, that needed for the reproduction of eighteen new machines. What would be inexplicable, rather, would be a situation in which, although the labour applied consisted simply of engineering labour, its result was on the one hand six machines $= 1,500_v+1,500_s$, and on the other hand iron, copper, screws, belts, etc. to a value of $6,000_c$, i.e. the means of production of the machines in their natural form, which the individual capitalist engineer obviously does not produce himself, but must replace by way of the circulation process. And yet it seems at first glance as if the reproduction of the annual social product does proceed in such a contradictory way.

The product of an individual capital, i.e. each independently functioning fraction of the social capital endowed with its own life, may have any natural form whatsoever. The only condition is that it really should have a use form, a use-value, that stamps it as a member of the commodity world capable of circulation. It is completely immaterial and accidental whether or not it can go back as a means of production into the same production process from which it emerged as a product, i.e. whether the part of the product's value that represents the constant capital component possesses a natural form in which it can actually function once again as constant capital. If not, then this part of the product's value is transformed again by sale and purchase into the material elements of its production, and thereby reproduces the constant capital again in its natural form, the form in which it is capable of fulfilling its function.

It is different with the product of the total social capital. All material elements of the reproduction must be parts of this product in their natural form. The portion of constant capital consumed can be replaced by the overall production only if the entire re-appearing constant portion of capital reappears in the product in the natural form of new means of production that actually can function as constant capital. On the assumption of simple reproduction, therefore, the value of the portion of the product that consists of means of production must be equal to the [consumed] constant portion of the value of the social capital.

Moreover, considered individually, all that the capitalist produces in the value of his product, by the labour newly added to it, is his variable capital and his surplus-value, while the constant capital component is transferred to the product by the concrete character of the labour newly added.

Socially considered, however, the portion of the social working day that produces means of production, both adding new value to them and transferring to them the value of the means of production consumed while they were being produced, produces nothing but new *constant capital*, destined to replace that consumed in the form of the old means of production, the constant capital consumed in both departments I and II. It only produces a product destined for productive consumption. The entire value of this product is therefore only value that functions anew as constant capital, which can only buy back constant capital in its natural form, and which is therefore from the social point of view resolved neither into variable capital nor into surplus-value. On the other hand, the part of the social working day that produces means of consumption does not produce any part of the social replacement capital. It produces only products that, in their natural form, are destined to realize the value of the variable capital and the surplus-value in departments I and II.

In speaking of the social point of view, i.e. in considering the total social product, which includes both the reproduction of the social capital and individual consumption, it is necessary to avoid falling into the habits of bourgeois economics, as imitated by Proudhon, i.e. to avoid looking at things as if a society based on the capitalist mode of production lost its specific historical and economic character when considered *en bloc*, as a totality. This is not the case at all. What we have to deal with is the collective capitalist. The total capital appears as the share capital of all individual capitalists together. This joint-stock company has in common with many other joint-stock companies that everyone knows what they put into it, but *not* what they will get out of it.

9. A LOOK BACK AT ADAM SMITH, STORCH AND RAMSAY

The total value of the social product is $9,000 = 6,000_c + 1,500_v + 1,500_s$; in other words, 6,000 reproduces the value of the means of production and 3,000 the value of the means of consumption. The value of the social revenue $(v+s)$ thus amounts to only one third of the value of the total product, and the totality of consumers, both workers and capitalists, can withdraw commodities, i.e. products, from the total social product and incorporate them into their consumption fund only to the amount of this one third part of value. 6,000, two thirds of the product's value, on the other hand, is the value of the constant capital that has to be replaced in kind. Means of production to this amount must therefore be reincorporated into the production fund. This is something that Storch realizes is necessary, without being able to prove it:

'It is clear that the value of the annual product is divided in part into capital and in part into profit, and that each of these parts of the annual value of the product regularly goes to buy the products that the nation needs, both to maintain its capital and to replace its consumption fund ... the products that constitute the *capital* of a nation *can in no way be consumed*' (Storch, *Considérations sur la nature du revenu national*, Paris, 1824, pp. 134–5, 150 [Marx's emphases]).

Yet Adam Smith put forward this fanciful dogma, which is still believed to this day, in the form already discussed, according to which the entire value of the social product resolves itself into revenue, i.e. into wages plus surplus-value, or as he expresses it, into wages plus profit (interest) plus rent. He also put it forward in the still more popular form that the *consumers* must ultimately pay the producers for the *entire value of the products*. Right to the present, this remains one of the most well-loved platitudes, or rather eternal truths, of the so-called science of political economy. It is demonstrated in the following plausible way. Take an article of some kind, e.g. linen shirts. First the spinner of linen yarn has to pay the flax-grower the entire value of the flax, i.e. flax seed, manure, animal fodder, etc., together with the portion of value that the flax-grower's fixed capital, such as buildings, agricultural instruments, etc., surrenders to this product; the wages paid in the production of the flax; the surplus-value (profit, ground-rent) that is contained in the flax; finally the freight costs of the flax from its point of production to the spinning mill. The weaver then has to reimburse the spinner of linen yarn not only with this price of the flax, but also with the portion of value in the machinery, buildings, etc., in other words, of the fixed capital, that is transferred to the flax, as well as that of all ancillary materials consumed during the spinning process, the wages of the spinners, surplus-value, etc.; and this is then taken a stage further with the bleacher, the transport costs of the finished linen, and finally the shirt manufacturer, who has to pay the whole price of all the earlier producers who have only supplied him with his raw material. In his hands, a further addition of values takes place, partly through the constant capital value that is consumed in the form of means of labour, ancillaries, etc. in the manufacture of shirts, and partly through the labour spent in this process, which adds the value of the shirt-maker's wages plus the surplus-value of the shirt manufacturer. Let the entire shirt product now cost £100, and say that this is the share in the total value of the annual product that the society spends on shirts. The consumers of shirts pay £100, i.e. the value of all the means of production contained in the shirts together with the wages plus surplus-value of the flax-grower, spinner, weaver, bleacher, shirt manufacturer and all transporters as well. This is completely correct. And this is in fact what any child can see. But then it is further said: This is how things stand with the value of *all means of consumption*, with the value of the part of the social product that goes into the consumption fund, i.e. with the part of the value of the social product that can be spent as revenue. The value sum of all these commodities is moreover equal to the value of all the means of production consumed in them (the constant capital components) plus the value that the labour last added to them has created (wages plus surplus-value). The totality of consumers can pay this whole value, because although the value of each individual commodity certainly consists of $c + v + s$, the value sum of all the commodities that enter into the consumption fund taken together, at its maximum, can only be equal to the portion of the value of the social product that is resolved into $v + s$, i.e. equal to the value that the labour spent during the year has added to the means of production available – to the constant capital value. As far as the constant capital value is concerned, however, we have seen that it is replaced in two ways from the social product. Firstly by exchange between the capitalists in department II who produce means of consumption and those in department I who produce the means of production for them. Here is the source of the phrase that what is capital for one is revenue for another. But this is not how things are at all. The 2,000 II_c that exists in means of consumption to the value of 2,000 forms constant capital value for the capitalists in department II. These cannot therefore consume it themselves, even though the product has to be consumed [individually], on account of its natural form. The 2,000 $I_{(v+s)}$, on the other hand, is the wages and surplus-value produced by the capitalists and workers in department I. It exists in the natural form of means of production, as things in which their own value cannot be [individually] consumed. We have here, therefore, a value sum of 4,000, of which half simply replaces constant capital, and half simply forms revenue, both before and after the exchange.

Secondly, however, the constant capital of department I is replaced in kind, partly by exchange among the capitalists in department I, partly by replacement in kind in each particular business.

The phrase that the entire value of the annual product must finally be paid by the consumers would be correct only if the expression 'consumers' were taken to include two quite different kinds of consumer, individual consumers and productive ones. But if a part of the product has to be consumed *productively*, this means nothing more than that it has to *function as capital* and cannot be *consumed as revenue*.

If we divide the value of the total product of 9,000 into $6,000_c + 1,500_v + 1,500_s$, and consider the $3,000_{(v+s)}$ simply in its capacity as revenue, then it is the variable capital that seems to vanish, and capital considered from this standpoint seems to consist only of constant capital. For what originally appeared as $1,500_v$ has resolved itself into a part of the social revenue, into wages, the revenue of the working class, and its character as capital has therewith vanished. This conclusion is in fact drawn by Ramsay. According to him, capital consists, from the social standpoint, of fixed capital alone, and by fixed capital he means constant capital, the mass of values consisting of means of production, whether these means of production are means of labour or materials of labour, such as raw material, work in progress, ancillaries, etc. He calls the variable capital 'circulating':

'Circulating capital consists only of subsistence and other necessities advanced to the workmen, previous to the completion of the produce of their labour ... Fixed capital alone, not circulating, is properly speaking a source of national wealth ... Circulating capital is not an immediate agent in production, nor essential to it at all, but merely a convenience rendered necessary by the deplorable poverty of the mass of the people ... Fixed capital alone constitutes an element of cost of production in a national point of view' (Ramsay, op. cit., pp. 23–6 passim).

This fixed capital, by which he means constant capital, Ramsay explains in more detail as follows:

'The length of time during which any portion of the product of that labour' (i.e. 'labour bestowed on any commodity') 'has existed as fixed capital, i.e. in a form in which, though assisting to raise the future commodity, *it does not maintain labourers*' (p. 59).

Here we see once again the confusion that Adam Smith wrought by submerging the distinction between constant and variable capital in the distinction between fixed and circulating capital. Ramsay's constant capital consists of means of labour, his circulating capital of means of subsistence; both of these are in fact commodities of a fixed value – the one is just as incapable of producing a surplus-value as the other.

10. CAPITAL AND REVENUE: VARIABLE CAPITAL AND WAGES[8]

The overall annual reproduction, the entire product of the current year, is the product of the useful labour of this year. But the value of this total product is greater than the portion of its value which embodies the annual labour, i.e. the labour-power spent during this year. The *value product* of the current year, the value newly created during the year in the commodity form, is smaller than the *value of the product*, the total value of the mass of commodities produced during the year. The difference which we obtain when we subtract from the total value of the annual product the value that was added to it by the labour of the current year is not value really reproduced, but simply value that reappears in a new form of existence; value transferred to the annual product from value that existed beforehand, of an earlier or later date depending on the durability of the constant capital component involved in the current year's social labour process. This value may derive from the value of a means of production which came into the world in the preceding year or in one of a series of earlier years. It is at all events value transferred from the means of production of previous years to the product of the current year.

If we take our schema, we have after exchange of the elements already dealt with between departments I and II, and within department II:

I. $4,000_c + 1,000_v + 1,000_s$ (the latter 2,000 realized in means of consumption II_c) $= 6,000$.

II. $2,000_c$ (reproduced by exchange with $I_{(v+s)}$) $+500_v + 500_s = 3,000$. Sum of values 9,000.

Value newly produced during the year is to be found only in v and s. The value product of the current year is thus equal to the sum of $v+s$, $=2,000\ I_{(v+s)} + 1,000\ II_{(v+s)} = 3,000$. All other value components of this year's product are simply value transferred from the value of earlier means of production that have been consumed in the current year's production. Besides this value of 3,000, the current year's labour has produced nothing more; this is its entire annual value product.

8. From here on, Manuscript VIII.

As we have seen, however, the 2,000 $I_{(v+s)}$ restores to department II its 2,000 II_c in the natural form of means of production. The two thirds of the annual labour spent in department I has thus newly produced the constant capital for department II, both in its entire value and in its natural form. Considered from the social standpoint, therefore, two thirds of the labour spent during the year creates new constant capital value, realized in the natural form appropriate for department II. The greater part of the annual social labour is therefore spent on the production of new constant capital (capital value existing in means of production) to replace the constant capital value spent on the production of means of consumption. What distinguishes capitalist society from the savages in this respect is not, as Senior[9] thinks, that it is the privilege and the characteristic of the savage to spend part of his labour in a way that procures him nothing in revenue, i.e. in proceeds that can be resolved into (exchanged for) means of consumption. The distinction rather consists in this:

(a) Capitalist society spends more of its disposable annual labour on the production of means of production (therefore of constant capital), which cannot be resolved into revenue in the form of wages or of surplus-value, but can function only as capital.

(b) If the savage makes bows, arrows, stone hammers, axes, baskets, etc., he knows well enough that he has not spent the time thus employed on the production of means of consumption, i.e. that he has met his need for means of production and nothing else. Besides, the savage commits a serious economic sin by his complete indifference to the use of his time, and may often spend a whole month, as Tyler tells us, on preparing a single arrow.[10]

The current notion by which one group of political economists seek to rid themselves of the theoretical difficulty – i.e. to avoid understanding the real relationship – the idea that what is capital for one person is revenue for another, and vice versa, is partially correct, but becomes

9. 'When the savage makes bows, he exercises an industry, but he does not practise abstinence' (Senior, *Principes fondamentaux de l'économie politique*, trans. Arrivabene, Paris, 1836, pp. 342–3.) 'The more society progresses, the more abstinence is demanded' (ibid., p. 342). Cf. *Capital* Volume 1, Chapter 24, 3, p. 744. [Nassau Senior was one of the principal representatives of 'vulgar economics' in England, and particularly notorious for his opposition to the legal restriction of working hours, on the basis of his theory of the 'last hour'. See Volume One, Chapter 9, 3.]

10. E. B. Tyler, *Researches into the Early History of Mankind, etc.*, London, 1865, pp. 198–9.

completely false as soon as it is put forward as a general rule (i.e. it involves a complete misunderstanding of the whole process of exchange that occurs in conjunction with annual reproduction, and also therefore a misunderstanding of the actual reason why the notion is partially correct).

We shall now summarize the factual relationships on which the partial correctness of this notion rests, and in so doing we shall also demonstrate how false is the current conception of these relationships.

1. The variable capital functions as capital in the hands of the capitalist and as revenue in the hands of the wage-labourer.

The variable capital first exists in the hands of the capitalist as *money capital*; it functions as *money capital* in so far as he buys labour-power with it. As long as it persists in his hands in the money form, it is nothing more than given value existing in that form, i.e. a constant and not a variable magnitude. It is only potentially variable capital, and it is that precisely because it is capable of being converted into labour-power It only becomes actual variable capital after shedding its money form, after it has been converted into labour-power and when this begins to function as a component of productive capital in the capitalist process.

The *money* that functions firstly as the money form of variable capital for the capitalist now functions in the hands of the worker as the money form of his wage which he converts into means of subsistence; i.e. as the money form of the *revenue* that he receives from the ever repeated sale of his labour-power.

We have here the simple fact that the *money* of the buyer, here the capitalist, passes from his hands into those of the seller, in this case the seller of labour-power, the worker. It is not the variable *capital* that functions twice over, as capital for the capitalist and as revenue for the worker, but simply the same *money*, which exists first in the hands of the capitalist as the money form of his variable capital, hence as potential variable capital, and which, once the capitalist has converted it into labour-power, serves in the hands of the worker as the equivalent for the labour-power he has sold. However, the fact that the same money serves one purpose in the hands of the seller and another in the hands of the buyer is simply a phenomenon inherent in all purchases and sales of commodities.

Apologetic economists present the matter wrongly, as is best shown if we look simply at the act of circulation $M - L \, (= M-C)$, the conversion of money into labour-power on the part of the capitalist buyer, and

$L-M$ ($=C-M$), the conversion of the commodity labour-power into money on the part of the seller, the worker, without troubling ourselves for the moment with any of its further consequences. They say that the same money here realizes two capitals: the buyer – the capitalist – converts his money capital into living labour-power, which he incorporates into his productive capital; on the other hand, the seller – the worker – converts his commodity – labour-power – into money that he spends as revenue, which is precisely what enables him to sell his labour-power over and over again and thus to maintain himself; his labour-power is thus actually his capital in the commodity form, from which he constantly draws his revenue. In point of fact, labour-power is his capacity (ever renewing and reproducing itself), not his capital. It is the only commodity that he can constantly sell, and he has to sell it in order to live, but it operates as capital (variable capital) only in the hands of the buyer, the capitalist. If a man is perpetually forced to sell his labour-power over and over again, i.e. to sell himself, to someone else, this proves, according to these economists, that he is a capitalist, because he always has a 'commodity' (himself) for sale. In this sense even a slave would be a capitalist, even though he is sold once and for all as a commodity by a third person; for the nature of this commodity, the working slave, not only requires that its buyer put it to work each day, but also that he give it the means of subsistence that it needs in order to be able to work again. (Compare on this point Sismondi, and Say in the letters to Malthus.)

2. In the exchange of $1,000 \text{ I}_v + 1,000 \text{ I}_s$ for $2,000 \text{ II}_c$, therefore, what is constant capital for some people ($2,000 \text{ II}_c$) becomes variable capital and surplus-value, and thus completely revenue, for others; and what was variable capital and surplus-value ($2,000 \text{ I}_{(v+s)}$), i.e. entirely revenue for some, becomes constant capital for others.

Let us firstly consider the exchange of I_v for II_c, and initially from the standpoint of the worker.

The collective worker in department I has sold his labour-power to the collective capitalist of department I for 1,000; he receives this value paid in money in the form of a wage. With this money, he buys means of consumption to the same amount from department II. The capitalist in department II confronts him simply as a seller of commodities and nothing else, which is even the case when the worker buys from his own capitalist, as above, for example (p. 481) in the exchange of the 500 II_v. The form of circulation that his commodity, labour-power, undergoes, is that of simple commodity circulation: C (labour-power)

–M–C (means of consumption, the commodity of department II), oriented to consumption, i.e. simply to the satisfaction of needs. The result of this act of circulation is that the worker has maintained himself as labour-power for the department I capitalist, and in order to carry on maintaining himself in this way, he has perpetually to repeat the process L(C)–M–C over again. His wage is realized in means of consumption, it is spent as revenue, and taking the working class as a whole, it goes on being spent as revenue continuously.

Let us now consider the same exchange of I_v for II_c from the standpoint of the capitalist. The entire commodity product of department II consists of means of consumption, i.e. of things designed to go into the annual consumption, to serve as the realization of someone or other's revenue, in the present case the collective worker of department I. For the collective capitalist of department II, however, a part of his commodity product, 2,000, is now the form of the constant capital value of his productive capital, and must be transformed back again from this commodity form into the natural form in which it can operate anew as the constant part of the productive capital. So far, capitalist II has managed to transform half (1,000) of his constant capital value, reproduced in the commodity form (that of means of consumption), back into the money form by selling it to the workers of department I. Thus it is not the variable capital I_v that has been converted into this first half of the constant capital value II_c, but rather the money that functioned for department I as money capital in exchange for labour-power and hence came into the possession of the seller of labour-power, for whom it did not represent capital but rather revenue in the money form, i.e. was spent as a means of purchase on items of consumption. The 1,000 in money that flowed to the capitalists in department II from the workers of department I can not function as a constant element of department II's productive capital. It is only the money form of its commodity capital, and still has to be converted into fixed or circulating components of constant capital. Department II therefore uses the money received from the workers of department I, the buyers of its commodities, to buy means of production from department I. In this way, half of department II's constant capital value is renewed in the natural form in which it can function once again as an element of productive capital in department II. The form of circulation here was C–M–C: means of consumption to a value of 1,000 – money (1,000) – means of production to a value of 1,000.

Here, however, C–M–C is a movement of capital. C, sold to the workers, is transformed into M, and this M is converted into means of production; it is a transformation from commodities back into the material elements of the formation of these commodities. On the other hand, just as the collective capitalist of department II functions for department I only as buyer of commodities, so the collective capitalist of department I functions for department II here only as a seller of commodities. Department I originally bought labour-power to the value of 1,000 with 1,000 of money which was destined to function as variable capital; it thereby received an equivalent for the $1,000_v$ spent in the money form; the money now belongs to the worker, who spends it on purchases from department II; department I can get back this money, which has flowed into department II's cash-box, only if it fishes it out again by selling commodities to the same total value.

Department I first had a certain sum of money, 1,000, destined to function as variable capital; this sum functions as variable capital by being converted into labour-power of the same value. As a result of the production process, however, the worker has provided a quantity of commodities (means of production) to the value of 6,000, of which one sixth or 1,000 is an equivalent value for the variable portion of capital advanced in money. The variable capital no more functions as variable capital in its commodity form than it did in its previous money form. As money, the variable capital value was only potentially variable capital, though it did exist in a form in which it could be directly converted into labour-power. As a commodity, however, this same variable capital value is still only potentially money value; it is restored to its original money form only by the sale of the commodity, i.e. here by the purchase by department II of 1,000 of commodities from department I. The movement of circulation is now: 1,000 (money) – labour-power to a value of 1,000 – 1,000 in commodities (equivalent for the variable capital) – $1,000_v$ (money); i.e. $M–C...C–M (=M–L...C–M)$. The production process that falls between $C...C$ does not itself pertain to the circulation sphere; it does not appear in the mutual exchange of the various elements of annual reproduction, even though this exchange includes the reproduction of all elements of the productive capital, not only its constant element but also its variable element, labour-power. All agents in this exchange simply appear as buyers or sellers, or both; the workers appear in it simply as commodity buyers; the capitalists alternately as buyers and sellers; and within certain limits simply as unilateral buyers or sellers.

The result of all this is that department I once more possesses the variable portion of its capital in the money form, the only form from which it is directly convertible back into labour-power; i.e. it possesses it again in the only form in which it can actually be advanced as the variable element of its productive capital. On the other hand, in order to reappear as a buyer of commodities, the worker must firstly reappear as the seller of a commodity, as the seller of his own labour-power.

As far as the variable capital in department II is concerned ($5,000\,\mathrm{II}_v$), the circulation process between capitalists and workers in this department of production takes an unmediated form, in as much as we consider it as taking place between the collective capitalist in department II and the collective worker there.

The collective capitalist in department II advances 500_v for the purchase of labour-power to the same value; the collective capitalist is here the buyer, the collective worker the seller. The worker then appears with the money received for his labour-power, as the buyer of a part of the commodities that he himself produced. Here, therefore, the capitalist is a seller. The worker has replaced the money the capitalist advanced to him for the purchase of his labour-power with a part of the commodity capital produced in department II, i.e. 500_v in commodities. The capitalist now possesses, in the commodity form, the same v that he possessed in the money form before converting it into labour-power; the worker for his part has realized the value of his labour-power in money, and realizes this money in turn by spending it, as revenue to meet his consumption, on acquiring a part of the means of consumption that he himself produced. This is an exchange of the worker's revenue, in money, for the capitalist's commodity component 500_v that the worker himself reproduced in the commodity form. This money thereby returns to capitalist II as the money form of his variable capital. An equal value of revenue in the money form here replaces variable capital value in the commodity form.

The capitalist does not get any richer by taking back the money that he paid the worker for the purchase of labour-power when he sells the worker an equivalent quantity of commodities. He would in fact be paying the worker twice over if he first paid him 500 for the purchase of his labour-power and then gave him for nothing, on top of this, the quantity of commodities to the value of 500 that he has had the worker produce. Conversely, if the worker did not produce anything more for him than an equivalent of 500 in commodities for the price of his labour-power of 500, then the capitalist would be in exactly the same position after the operation as before it. However, the worker has reproduced a product of 3,000; he has maintained the constant value portion of the product, i.e. the value of the means of production = 2,000 used up in transforming it into a new product, and he has added to this given value a further value of $1,000_{(v+s)}$. (The notion that the capitalist gets rich and obtains surplus-value by this reflux of 500 in money is put forward by Destutt de Tracy, and is dealt with in more detail in section 13 of this chapter.)

The value of 500 II_v which the department I capitalist still possesses in commodities returns to him in the form in which he originally advanced it by the purchase of means of consumption to the value of 500 on the part of the department II worker. The immediate result of this transaction, as with every other sale of commodities, is the conversion of a given value from the commodity form into the money form. The reflux of money to its starting-point that this brings about is also nothing unique. If capitalist II had bought commodities from capitalist I for 500 in money, then 500 in money would also have flowed back to him. The 500 in money would have served simply to exchange a quantity of commodities of 1,000, and according to the general law put forward above it would have flowed back to whoever it was that cast the money into circulation for the exchange of this mass of commodities.

But the 500 that has flowed back to capitalist II in money is at the same time renewed potential variable capital in the money form. Why is this? Money, and this of course includes money capital, is potential variable capital only because and in so far as it is convertible into labour-power. The return of the 500 in money to capitalist II is accompanied by the return of department II's labour-power to the market. The return of both of these at opposite poles – i.e. the reappearance of the 500 in money, not just as money, but also as variable capital in the money form – is conditioned by one and the same procedure. The 500 in money flows back to capitalist II because he has sold worker II means of consumption to the value of 500, i.e. because the worker has spent his wage, and in this way has maintained not only himself and his family, but also his labour-power. In order to carry on living and to reappear as a buyer of commodities, he must sell his labour-power afresh. The return of the 500 in money to capitalist II is thus simultaneously the return – or the preservation – of labour-power as a commodity available for purchase with 500 in money, and hence the return of the 500 in money as potential variable capital.

As far as subdivision II*b*, the production of luxury goods, is concerned, the same thing takes place with its v (in this case $(IIb)_v$) as with I_v. The money that renews the IIb capitalists' variable capital in the money form flows to them via a detour through the hands of capitalists IIa. It still makes a difference, for all that, whether the workers buy their means of subsistence directly from the capitalist producers to whom they sell their labour-power, or whether they buy them from another category of capitalists, so that the money flows back to the first category only by a detour. Since the working class lives from hand to mouth, it buys as long as it is able to. It is different with the capitalists, for instance in the exchange of 1,000 II_c for 1,000 I_v. The capitalist does not live from hand to mouth. His driving motive is the greatest possible valorization of his capital. Hence if circumstances of any kind intervene which make it appear more advantageous to the capitalist in department II to retain at least part of his constant capital in the money form for a longer time, instead of directly replacing it all, the reflux of the 1,000 II_c (in money) to department I is then delayed; so too, therefore, is the restoration of the $1,000_v$ in its money form, and capitalist I can only continue operating on the same scale if he has some reserve money available, just as reserve capital in money is generally necessary in order to be able to continue operations without interruption, regardless of whether the reflux of the variable capital value in money is quicker or slower.

Besides investigating the exchange of the various elements of current annual reproduction, we must also investigate the results of the previous year's labour, the labour of the year that has already come to a close. The production process that resulted in this annual product lies behind us; it is past and has disappeared into its product. This is ever more the case with the circulation process that preceded this production process or ran parallel with it, the conversion of potential into actual variable capital, i.e. the purchase and sale of labour-power. The labour market no longer forms any part of the commodity market we are dealing with here. The worker has not only already sold his labour-power, he has also supplied in commodities, besides the surplus-value, an equivalent for the price of his labour-power; he has on the other hand got his wages in his pocket and figures in the exchange only as a buyer of commodities (means of consumption). However the annual product must contain all the elements of reproduction, and restore all the elements of the productive capital, including in particular the latter's most important element, the variable capital. And we have in fact already seen that as far as the variable capital is concerned the result of the exchange is as follows: the worker, as buyer of commodities, maintains and reproduces his labour-power, as the only commodity that he has for sale, by spending his wage and consuming the commodities bought; just as the money advanced by the capitalist on the purchase of labour-power returns to him, so the labour-power, too, returns to the labour market as a commodity exchangeable for this money. The result we obtain for the particular case of the 1,000 I_v is 1,000$_v$ in money on the side of the department I capitalists, and on the other hand labour-power to the value of 1,000 on the side of the department I workers, so that the entire process of reproduction in department I can begin afresh. This is one result of the exchange process.

By spending their wages, on the other hand, the workers in department I have withdrawn means of consumption to the sum of 1,000$_c$ from department II, and thereby transformed these from the commodity form into the money form; department II has transformed its constant capital back from this money form into its natural form, by the purchase of commodities $= 1,000_v$ from department I, and in this way department I's variable capital value flows back to it again in the money form.

The variable capital in department I undergoes three changes of form, which do not appear at all in the exchange of the annual product, or do so only by intimation.

1. Its first form is that of 1,000 I_v in money, which is converted into labour-power to the same value. This conversion does not itself appear in the commodity exchange between departments I and II, although its result appears in the fact that the working class of department I faces the commodity seller of department II with 1,000 in money, just as the working class of department II faces the commodity seller of 500 II_v in the commodity form with 500 in money.

2. The second form, the only one in which the variable capital actually varies, i.e. actually functions as variable capital, where value-creating power appears in place of the value given in exchange for it, pertains exclusively to the production process that lies behind us.

3. The third form, in which the variable capital has demonstrated its quality of being variable in the result of the production process, is the annual value product, which in the case of department I is 1,000$_v$ + 1,000$_s$ $= 2,000$ $I_{(v+s)}$. In place of its original value of 1,000 in money, twice this value has appeared in commodities. The variable capital value of 1,000 in commodities thus forms only half of the value product created by the variable capital as an element of the productive capital. The

1,000 I_v in commodities is the exact equivalent of the part of the total capital originally advanced by department I with the 1,000$_v$ in money, and ear-marked as the variable part; in the commodity form, however, it is only potentially money (it actually becomes money only by its sale), and so still less directly is it variable money capital. Ultimately, it will become so by the sale of the commodities 1,000 I_v for II_c and by the rapid reappearance of labour-power as a purchaseable commodity, as material into which the 1,000$_v$ in money can be converted.

During all these changes, capitalist I constantly keeps in hand his variable capital, (1) originally as money capital; (2) then as an element of his productive capital; (3) later as a value component of his commodity capital, i.e. in commodity value; (4) finally in money again, and once more standing face-to-face with the labour-power into which it is convertible. During the labour process, the capitalist has the variable capital in his hands as self-acting, value-creating labour-power, but not as value of a given magnitude; however, since he pays the worker only after his power has already operated for a definite period of time, whether longer or shorter, he already has the replacement value that labour-power creates for itself in his hands before he pays, as well as the surplus-value.

Since this variable capital always remains in one form or other in the hands of the capitalist, it can in no way be said to be converted into revenue for anyone. 1,000 I_v in commodities is rather converted into money by its sale to department II, for which it replaces half of its constant capital in kind.

What is resolved into revenue is not department I's variable capital of 1,000$_v$ in money; the money has ceased to function as the money form of department I's variable capital as soon as it is converted into labour-power, just as the money of any other commodity seller has ceased to represent anything belonging to him once he has exchanged it for a commodity being sold. The conversions undergone by the money drawn in wages in the hands of the working class are not conversions of variable capital, but rather of the value of their labour-power transformed into money, just as the conversion of the value product created by the worker (2,000 $I_{(v+s)}$) is simply the conversion of a commodity belonging to the capitalist, and does not affect the worker. It is however very difficult for the capitalist, and still more so for his theoretical interpreter, the political economist, to rid himself of the idea that the money paid to the worker is still the capitalist's money. If the capitalist is a producer of gold, then the variable portion of value – i.e. the equivalent in commodities that compensates him for the purchase price of labour – directly appears in the money form, and can therefore function anew as variable money capital without the detour of a reflux. As far as the department II worker is concerned, however – ignoring here the luxury worker – 500_v actually exists in commodities that are destined for the worker's consumption, commodities which he buys, considered as the collective worker, directly from the same collective capitalist to whom he has sold his labour-power. The variable value portion of department II's capital consists of means of consumption, as far as its natural form is concerned, destined for the most part to be consumed by the working class. But it is not the variable capital that is spent by the worker in this form; it is the wage, the worker's money, that re-establishes for the capitalist his variable capital $500 \, II_v$ in its money form, precisely through its realization in these means of consumption. The variable capital II_v is reproduced in means of consumption, just as is the constant capital $2,000 \, II_c$; the one is no more resolved into revenue than the other. What is resolved into revenue is in both cases the wage.

But if $1,000 \, II_c$, and by the same detour $1,000 \, I_v$ and $500 \, II_v$, i.e. both constant capital and variable, are restored as money capital by the expenditure of wages as revenue, this is an important fact in the exchange of the annual product. (In the case of the variable capital this is partly by a direct reflux and partly by an indirect one.)

II. REPLACEMENT OF THE FIXED CAPITAL

A major problem in depicting the conversions involved in the annual reproduction is the following. If we take the simplest form in which the matter presents itself, we have:

$$(I) \ 4,000_c + 1,000_v + 1,000_s +$$
$$(II) \ 2,000_c + 500_v + 500_s = 9,000,$$

which is ultimately resolved into

$$4,000 \, I_c + 2,000 \, II_c + 1,000 \, I_v + 500 \, II_v + 1,000 \, I_s + 500 \, II_s$$
$$= 6,000_c + 1,500_v + 1,500_s$$
$$= 9,000.$$

One portion of the constant capital value, that which consists of means of labour in the strict sense (as a distinct division of the means of production), is transferred from the means of labour to the product of labour (the commodity) while these means of labour still continue to function as elements of the productive capital, and moreover in their old natural form; what is transferred from the instrument to the product of labour, and reappears as an element of the value of the commodities that these means of labour produce, is their wear and tear, the loss of value that they suffer bit by bit in the course of their function over a certain period. As far as the annual reproduction is concerned, therefore, only those components of the fixed capital whose life is longer than a year come into consideration. If they expire in the course of the year, then they have to be completely replaced and renewed by the annual reproduction, and the point at issue here in no way concerns them. In the case of machines and other more long-lasting forms of fixed capital, it may happen – and more often than not does happen – that certain partial organs of the same have to be entirely replaced within the year, even though the building or machine as a whole has a longer life. These partial organs fall into the same category of elements of fixed capital that have to be replaced within the year.

This element of commodity value should in no way be confused with the costs of repair.* When the commodity is sold, this value element is realized and transformed into money like the others; it is only after this transformation that its difference from the other elements of value comes into view. The raw materials and ancillaries consumed in the production of commodities have to be replaced in kind so that the reproduction of the commodities can begin (and generally so that the process of commodity production can be continuous); the labour power spent on them must similarly be replaced by fresh labour-power. The money received from the commodity must therefore be constantly converted back into these elements of productive capital, from the money form into the commodity form. This is in no way changed by the fact that raw materials and ancillaries may be bought at certain dates on a relatively large scale, so that they form production reserves, and for a certain interval, therefore, these means of production do not need to be bought anew; as long as they last, the money received from the sale of the commodities can be collected, in so far as it serves this purpose, and this part of the constant capital temporarily appears as money capital whose active function is suspended. The means of production must always be renewed, even if the form of this renewal may differ, as far as its circulation is concerned. The new purchase, the circulation opera-

* On the repair costs, and the specific way this part of constant capital expenditure goes into the value of the product, see above, p. 255.

tion by which the means of production are renewed or replaced, can proceed at longer intervals: then large investments of money are made at a time, compensated for by corresponding production reserves; alternatively it takes place at closely following dates, in which case small doses of money expenditure follow each other more quickly, and there are smaller production stocks. This in no way alters the matter itself. The same is the case with labour-power. Where production is continuously carried on at the same level throughout the year, there is a constant replacement of the labour-power consumed with new labour-power; where labour is seasonal, or different amounts of labour are applied in different periods, as in agriculture, there is a corresponding purchase of quantities of labour-power of varying magnitude. But the part of the money received from the sale of commodities that represents the realized value component of the commodities, which is equal to the wear and tear of the fixed capital, is no transformed back again into the component of productive capital whose loss of value it replaces. It settles down alongside the productive capital and persists in its money form. This precipitation of money is repeated until the reproduction period during which the fixed element of the constant capital continues to function in the production process in its old natural form, and which consists of a greater or lesser number of years, has elapsed. Once the fixed element – buildings, machinery, etc. – has expired, and can no longer function in the production process, its value exists alongside it completely converted into money, as the sum of the money precipitated, the sum of the values which were gradually transferred from the fixed capital to the commodities in whose production it collaborated, and which passed over into the money form when these commodities were sold. This money then serves to replace the fixed capital in kind (or elements of it, as the various elements have different lifespans), and thus really to replace this component of the productive capital. It is therefore the money form of a part of the constant capital value, of the fixed part of it. This hoard formation is therefore itself an element of the capitalist reproduction process, the reproduction and storage – in the money form – of the value of the fixed capital or its individual elements, until such a time as the fixed capital has expired and consequently surrendered the whole of its value to the commodities produced, when it has to be replaced in kind. This money, however, gives up its hoard form and again steps actively into the reproduction process of capital mediated by circulation only after it has been transformed back into new elements of fixed capital to replace the dead ones.

The reconversion of the annual commodity product can no more be resolved into the mere unmediated mutual exchange of its various components than simple commodity circulation is identical with the direct exchange of products. Money plays a specific role in it, one which is expressed in the very manner in which the fixed capital value is reproduced. (Later, we shall go on to investigate how different things would look if it were assumed that production was collective and did not have the form of commodity production.)

If we return to our basic schema, we had for department II: $2,000_c + 500_v + 500_s$. The total means of consumption produced in the course of the year amount here to a value of 3,000; and each of the various elements which this sum of commodities consists of can be broken down, as far as its value goes, into $\frac{2}{3}_c + \frac{1}{6}_v + \frac{1}{6}_s$, or in percentages, $66\frac{2}{3}_c + 16\frac{2}{3}_v + 16\frac{2}{3}_s$. The various kinds of commodity in department II may contain different proportions of constant capital; the fixed parts of the constant capital may similarly differ, and so too may the lifespans of the fixed portions of capital, and thus the annual wear and tear or the portion of value that they proportionately transfer to the commodities in whose production they participate. This is all immaterial here. As far as the social reproduction is concerned, all that is involved is the exchange between departments II and I. These departments face each other here in their mass social relations; the proportionate magnitude of the value component c in the commodity product of department II (which is alone decisive in the question now being considered) is therefore the average when all branches of production that are subsumed under department II are taken together.

Each of those kinds of commodity whose total value is summarized as $2,000_c + 500_v + 500_s$ (and they are for the most part similar kinds) is thus similarly equal in its value in percentages to $66\frac{2}{3}_c + 16\frac{2}{3}_v + 16\frac{2}{3}_s$. This holds for each 100 commodities, whether these figure under c, v or s.

The commodities in which the $2,000_c$ is embodied can be broken down, as far as their value goes, into:

1. $1,333\frac{1}{3}_c + 333\frac{1}{3}_v + 333\frac{1}{3}_s = 2,000_c$;

similarly the 500_v into:

2. $333\frac{1}{3}_c + 83\frac{1}{3}_v + 83\frac{1}{3}_s = 500_v$;

and finally the 500_s into:

3. $333\frac{1}{3}_c + 83\frac{1}{3}_v + 83\frac{1}{3}_s = 500_s$.

If we now add the c's of 1, 2, and 3 together, we have $1,333\frac{1}{3}_c + 333\frac{1}{3}_c + 333\frac{1}{3}_c = 2,000$. Similarly $333\frac{1}{3}_c + 83\frac{1}{3}_v + 83\frac{1}{3}_s = 500$, and the same under s; the sum results in the total value of 3,000, as above.

The entire constant capital value in the mass of commodities in department II, with a total value of 3,000, is thus contained in $2,000_c$, and neither 500_v nor 500_s contain a single atom of it. The same applies for v and s in their turn.

In other words, the quota of department II's commodities that represents constant capital value, and is therefore reconvertible into this, whether in its natural or in its money form, is $2,000_c$. Everything relevant to the reconversion of the constant value of the commodities in department II is therefore confined to the movement of $2,000$ II_c; and this reconversion can proceed only by exchange with $I(1,000_v + 1,000_s)$.

Similarly, everything relevant to the reconversion of the constant value in department I can be restricted to consideration of the $4,000$ I_c.

(a) Replacement of the Depreciation Component in the Money Form

Let us take to start with:

I. $4,000_c + \underbrace{1,000_v + 1,000_s}$

II. $2000_c + 500_v + 500_s.$

If the commodities $2,000$ II_c are exchanged for commodities of the same value $I(1,000_v + 1,000_s)$, this assumes that $2,000$ II_c is completely reconverted in kind into the natural components of department II's constant capital that are replaced by department I; however, the commodity value of $2,000$ in which II_c exists contains an element for depreciation of its fixed capital, which cannot be immediately replaced in kind, but has to be transformed into money, its total sum accumulating bit by bit until the time falls due for the renewal of this fixed capital in its natural form. Each year is a mortal one for fixed capital that has to be replaced in this or that particular business or even this or that branch of industry; for a single individual capital, this or that part of its fixed capital has to be replaced (since its parts are of varying life). If we consider the annual reproduction – even on the same scale, i.e. abstracting from all accumulation – then we do not begin *ab ovo*; this is one year in the course of many, not capitalist production's year of birth. The various capitals invested in the manifold branches of production in department II are therefore of different ages, and just as each year people functioning in these branches of production die, so each year do quantities of fixed capital reach the end of their life and have to be renewed in kind from the accumulated money fund. To this extent, the exchange of 2,000 II_c for 2,000 $I_{(v+s)}$ involves the reconversion of 2,000 II_c from its commodity form (as means of consumption) back into the natural elements of constant capital that consist not only of raw materials and ancillaries, but also of the natural elements of fixed capital – machines, instruments, buildings, etc. The wear and tear that has to be replaced in *money* in the value of the 2,000 II_c thus in no way corresponds to the total scale of the fixed capital that is functioning, since each year a part of this has to be replaced *in kind*; this presupposes however that in earlier years the money needed for this replacement was accumulated in the hands of the department II capitalists. Precisely this assumption, however, holds just as much for the current year as it is assumed to hold for the previous years.

In the exchange between $I(1,000_v+1,000_s)$ and 2,000 II_c, the first thing to note is that the sum of values $I_{(v+s)}$ does not contain any element of constant value, and thus no value element for the wear and tear to be replaced, i.e. for value that was transferred from the fixed component of the constant capital to the commodities in whose natural form $v+s$ exists. This element does exist on the other hand in II_c, and it is precisely a part of this value element attributable to the fixed capital that does not have to be directly transformed from the money form into the natural form, but has first rather to persist in the money form. The exchange between $I(1,000_v+1,000_s)$ and 2,000 II_c thus immediately presents the apparent difficulty that the means of production I, the natural form in which the $2,000_{(v+s)}$ exists, have to be replaced to the entire amount of their value of 2,000 by an equivalent in means of consumption II, whereas the means of consumption 2,000 II_c cannot be exchanged to their full value for the means of production $I(1,000_v+1,000_s)$, since an aliquot part of their value – equal to the wear and tear or loss of value of the fixed capital – must first be precipitated out into money that does not function again as means of circulation within the current period of annual reproduction, which is all that is under consideration. But the money through which the element of wear and tear contained in the commodity value of 2,000 II_c is realized can derive only from department I, since department II does not itself have to pay out, but is paid precisely by the sale of its commodities, and since according to our assumption $I_{(v+s)}$ buys the entire sum of commodities 2,000 II_c; department I must therefore realize this wear and tear for department II by way of this sale. However, according to the law developed earlier, money advanced to circulation returns to the capitalist producer when he later casts the same amount into circulation in commodities. It is evidently impossible for department I, in purchasing II_c, to give department II commodities worth 2,000, and to give it once and for all, on top of that, an extra amount of money (without any return of this money to it by the reconversion operation). Otherwise the quota of commodities II_c would be sold above its value. If department II does in fact exchange its $2,000_c$ for $I(1,000_v + 1,000_s)$, it cannot demand anything more from department I, and the money circulating in this exchange returns to department I or II depending on which of the two it was that cast it into circulation, i.e. which one first appeared as the buyer. At the same time, in this case, department II would have transformed its commodity capital, to its full value, back into the natural form of means of production, whereas the assumption is that there is an aliquot part of this that it does not transform, after its sale, from money back into the natural form of fixed components of its constant capital, during the current annual reproduction period. Thus a balance in money could accrue to department II only if II sold to department I for 2,000, but bought from I for less than 2,000, e.g. only 1,800; department I would then have to make good the deficit by 200 in money, which would not flow back to it, because it would not in turn have withdrawn this money advanced to circulation by throwing into circulation commodities to the value of 200. In this case, department II would have a money fund against the wear and tear of its fixed capital; on the other side, however, that of department I, there would be an overproduction of means of production to the sum of 200, and in this way the whole basis of the schema would be destroyed, i.e. reproduction on the same scale, which presupposes complete proportionality between the various systems of production. One difficulty would have only been displaced by another much more inconvenient one.

Since this problem offers difficulties all its own, and has not been dealt with at all by the political economists up to now, we intend to consider in succession all possible (at least seemingly possible) solutions of the problem, or rather formulations of it.

To start with, we just supposed that department II sells 2,000 to department I, but only buys from department I commodities for 1,800. The commodity value of 2,000 II_c then contains 200 for replacement of wear and tear, which is hoarded up in money; the value of 2,000 II_c would thus be broken down into 1,800, which is to be exchanged against means of production from department I, and 200 for the replacement of wear and tear, which is to be kept in money (after the sale of $2,000_c$ to department I). As far as its value goes, the 2,000 II_c would be $1,800_c + 200_c$ (d), where *d* stands for *déchet* (depreciation).

We would then have to consider the exchange

I. $\underbrace{1,000_v + 1,000_s}$

II. $1,800_c$ $+ 200_c(d)$.

Department I buys 1,000 II_c means of consumption from department II with £1,000 that its workers have received for their labour-power in payment of wages. The capitalists in department I thereby receive their variable capital back in its money form, so that they can use it to buy labour-power again next year for the same amount, i.e. replace the variable part of their productive capital in kind. Department II also advances £400, say, to buy means of production I_s, and department I uses the same £400, in which it has realized part of its surplus-value, to buy means of consumption II_c. The £400 advanced to the circulation sphere by department II has thus returned to the capitalists in department II, but only as the equivalent for the commodities they have sold. Department I now advances £400 to buy means of consumption; department II buys means of production for £400 from department I, and this £400 thereby flows back to department I. The account up to now is as follows:

Department I has cast into circulation $1,000_v + 800_s$ in commodities, and also casts into circulation in money £1,000 in wages and £400 for exchange with department II. After the exchange is completed, department I has $1,000_v$ in money, 800_s converted into 800 II_c (means of consumption) and £400 in money.

Department II casts into circulation $1,800_c$ in commodities (means of consumption) and £400 in money; after the exchange, it has 1,800 in commodities I (means of production) and £400 in money.

We then still have on I's side 200_s (in means of production), and on II's side $200_c(d)$ (in means of consumption).

According to our assumption, department I buys means of consumption $_c(d)$ to the value of 200 with £200 in money; this £200, however, department II holds on to, since it represents $200_c(d)$ wear and tear, and is not to be directly converted back into means of production. 200 I_s is therefore unsaleable; one fifth of the surplus-value that department I has to convert cannot be realized, or converted from its natural form of means of production into that of means of consumption.

This does not only contradict the assumption of reproduction on the same scale; it is in and of itself not the kind of hypothesis that could explain the realization of $200_c(d)$; it says rather that this is inexplicable. Since there is no way of showing how the $200_c(d)$ is to be realized, we have to suppose that department I is obliging enough to realize it, precisely because department I is not in a position to realize its own remnant of 200_s. To conceive this as a normal operation of the exchange mechanism would be the same as supposing that each year £200 rained down from heaven to realize the $200_c(d)$.

The absurdity of such a hypothesis, however, does not directly leap to the eye if I_s, instead of appearing, as here, in its original mode of existence – i.e. as a value component of means of production, a component of the value of commodities that their capitalist producers have to realize in money by selling them – appears in the hands of the capitalist's co-partners, e.g. as ground-rent in the hands of the landlord or as interest in the hands of the money-lender. If the part of the surplus-value in commodities that the industrial capitalist has to deduct as ground-rent or interest for other persons with a claim on surplus-value cannot be realized in the long run by the sale of the commodities themselves, there is then an end to the payment of rent and interest, and the landlords or the recipients of interest cannot serve as *dei ex machina* for the arbitrary realization of certain portions of annual reproduction. It is just the same with the expenditures of all so-called unproductive workers, state officials, doctors, lawyers, etc., and others who, in the form of the 'general public', perform 'services' for the political economists by explaining what they leave unexplained.

It helps just as little if, instead of direct exchange between departments I and II – between the two great departments of capitalist production itself – the merchant is brought in as mediator to remove all difficulties with his 'money'. In the given case, for example, $200 I_s$ must finally be disposed of to the industrial capitalists of department II. It may go through the hands of a whole series of merchants, but the last of these still finds himself in the same position vis-à-vis department II – according to our hypothesis – as the capitalist producers of department I did at the beginning, i.e. they cannot sell the $200 I_s$ to department II; and as this sum of purchases has thus stuck fast, it prevents department I from repeating the process.

We see here how, apart from our specific purpose of considering the reproduction process in its fundamental form – setting aside all obscuring circumstances that intervene – it is necessary throughout to do away with the false subterfuges that provide a semblance of 'scientific' explanation, if the process of social reproduction in its intricate concrete form is to become the object of our analysis.

The law that, in the normal course of reproduction (whether simple or on an expanded scale), the money advanced to circulation by the capitalist producer must return to its starting-point (it being immaterial here whether the money belongs to him or is borrowed) thus excludes once and for all the hypothesis that the 200 $II_c(d)$ can be realized by the money advanced by department I.

(b) Replacement of the Fixed Capital in Kind

After setting aside the hypothesis dealt with above, there still remain those possibilities which, besides the replacement of the wear and tear component in money, also bring in the replacement of the defunct fixed capital in kind.

We assumed in the previous case:

(a) that £1,000 was paid by department I in wages, and spent by the department I workers on II_c to the same amount, i.e. that they used this to buy means of consumption.

That the £1,000 was advanced by department I in money is no more than a simple statement of fact. Wages are paid by the relevant capitalist producers in money; this money is then spent by the workers on means of subsistence, and serves the sellers of these means of subsistence in turn as means of circulation for the conversion of their constant capital from commodity capital into productive capital. It certainly runs through several channels (shopkeepers, landlords of dwelling-houses, tax collectors, unproductive workers such as doctors, etc. that the worker himself needs), and it therefore flows only in part directly from the hands of the workers in department I into those of the capitalist class of department II. The flow may to a greater or lesser extent stagnate, and new reserves of money may thus be needed on the part of the capitalists. All this can be omitted in considering the fundamental form.

(b) It was also assumed that at one point department I advances a further £400 in money for purchases from department II, which later flows back to it, and at another point department II advances £400 for purchases from department I, which similarly flows back to department II. This assumption must be made, since the opposite assumption, that only the capitalists in either department I or II unilaterally advanced to circulation the money needed for the exchange of commodities, would be arbitrary. Since we showed in sub-section (a) that the hypothesis according to which department I casts additional money into circulation in order to realize the 200 $II_c(d)$ has to be rejected as absurd, we have left only the apparently still more absurd hypothesis that department II itself casts into circulation the money with which that value component of commodities is realized which has to replace the wear and tear of its fixed capital. The portion of value that Mr X's spinning machine loses in the course of production, for example, re-appears as a part of the value of his yarn. The loss that his spinning machine suffers in value he thus collects on the other side as money. X might now for example buy cotton from Y for £200, and in this way advance £200 to the circulation sphere; Y buys yarn from him with the same £200, and this £200 now serves X as a fund for replacing the wear and tear of his spinning machine. What this boils down to is simply that X, apart from his production, its product, and the sale of this, keeps a further £200 stacked away in order to pay himself for the spinning machine's loss of value, i.e. that besides the £200 loss of value of his spinning machine, he has to add a further 200 in money each year from his own pocket, so as finally to be in a position to buy a new spinning machine.

The absurdity of this, however, is only apparent. Department II consists of capitalists whose fixed capital is at different points in its reproduction. For some, it has reached the point at which it has to be completely replaced in kind. For others, it is still more or less distant from this stage; what is common to all members of the latter division is that their fixed capital is not really reproduced, i.e. not renewed in kind or replaced by a new item of the same variety, but that its value is successively collected up in money. The first group of capitalists is in exactly the same situation as when they began their business (or almost so, it is all the same here), i.e. when they appeared on the market with a money capital in order to transform this on the one hand into constant capital (fixed and circulating), on the other hand into labour-power, into variable capital. Just as at that time, they now have to advance this money capital once more to the circulation sphere, i.e. the value of the constant fixed capital as well as that of the circulating and that of the variable capital.

If we assume, therefore, that, out of the £400 that the capitalist class in department II casts into circulation for the purpose of exchange with department I, half derives from those capitalists in department II who not only have to renew in kind, by the sale of their commodities, those of their means of production that form their circulating capital, but also have to renew, with their money, their fixed capital, while the other half of these capitalists in department II renew only the circulating part of their constant capital in kind, with their money, and do not renew their fixed capital, there is nothing contradictory in the fact that the £400 that flows back (and it flows back as soon as department I buys means of consumption with it) is now divided differently between these two sections of department II. It flows back to department II; however, it does not flow back into the same hands, but is rather differently distributed within this class, passing from one section of it to the other.

The first section of department II has, besides the portion of means of production ultimately covered by its commodities, converted a further £200 in money into new elements of fixed capital in kind. The money it has spent in this way flows back to it from the circulation sphere only bit by bit over a series of years – just as at the start of business – in the shape of the depreciation component of the commodities to be produced with this fixed capital.

The other section of department II, on the other hand, did not obtain any commodities from department I with its £200. Instead department I pays it with the money with which the first section of department II bought elements of fixed capital. One section of department II has its fixed capital back in its renewed natural form, the other is still engaged in collecting it up in the money form, so as to replace its fixed capital in kind later on.

The position from which we have to proceed, after the earlier exchanges, is the remnant of commodities to be exchanged on both sides: department I's 400_s, and department II's 400_c.[11] We assume that department II advances £400 in money for the exchange of these commodities to the amount of 800. Half of this £400 (=£200) must under all circumstances be laid out by the section of II_c that accumulates the £200 in money as the value of wear and tear, and which then has to transform this back again into the natural form of its fixed capital.

Just as the constant capital value, variable capital value and surplus-value into which the value of both departments' commodity capital breaks down can be represented in proportionate quotas of the respective departments' commodities, so too can one represent, within the constant capital value itself, the portion of value that does not yet have

11. Once again, the figures here do not agree with earlier assumptions. This is immaterial, however, since it is only the relationships that are important here. – F.E.

to be converted into the natural form of fixed capital, but has for the time being to be gradually hoarded up in the money form. A certain quantity of department II's commodities (in our case, half of the remainder, $=200$) are here no more than the bearers of this wear-and-tear value, which has to be precipitated out by conversion into money. (The first group of capitalists in department II, who renew their fixed capital in kind, may have already realized a part of their wear-and-tear value in this way with the depreciation component of their total mass of commodities, of which we have here only the remnant; but there still remains 200 to be realized in money.)

As for the second half ($=£200$) of the £400 cast into circulation by department II in connection with this residual operation, this buys circulating components of constant capital from department I. Part of this £200 may be cast into circulation by each section of department II, or all by that section which does not renew its fixed value component in kind.

The £400 is thus now used to withdraw from department I: (1) commodities to the total of £200, which consist simply of elements of fixed capital; (2) commodities to the total of £200, which simply replace in kind elements of the circulating part of the constant capital. Department I has now sold its entire annual commodity product, to the extent that this has to be sold to department II. The value of a fifth of it, £400, exists in its hands in the money form, but this money is realized surplus-value and has to be spent as revenue on means of consumption. Department I therefore uses this £400 to buy the remaining commodity value of department II $= 400$. The money flows back to department II by removing commodities from that department.

We shall now assume three different cases. Let us call the section of capitalists in department II who replace their fixed capital in kind 'section 1', and those who store up the wear-and-tear value of their fixed capital in the money form 'section 2'. The three cases are as follows: (a) out of the 400 that still remains as a residue of commodities in department II, a certain quota has to replace the quota of circulating parts of the constant capital for sections 1 and 2 (say half each); (b) section 1 has already sold its entire commodity, so that section 2 still has 400 to sell; (c) section 2 has sold all except the 200 that carries the wear-and-tear value.

We then have the following distributions:

(a) Of the commodity value of 400_c that department II still has in hand, section 1 has 100 and section 2 300; out of this 300, 200 repre-

sents the wear and tear. In this case, out of the £400 that department I
sends back to obtain commodities from department II, section 1
originally laid out £300, i.e. £200 in money with which it drew elements
of fixed capital in kind from department I, and £100 in money to mediate its commodity exchange with department I; section 2, on the other
hand, advanced only a quarter of the £400, i.e. £100, also for the mediation of its commodity exchange with department I.

Out of the £400 in money, section 1 advanced £300 and section 2 £100.
This £400 however flows back as follows:

To section 1: £100, i.e. only a third of the money it advanced. It
possesses, however, for the other two thirds, fixed capital to a value of
200. In return for this element of fixed capital to the value of 200 it
has given money to department I, but not subsequently any commodity.
As far as this 200 is concerned, department II confronts department I
simply as a buyer, and not subsequently again as a seller. This money
cannot then flow back to section 1; otherwise this would have received
its elements of fixed capital from department I for nothing. As far as the
last third of the money it advanced is concerned, section 1 first appeared
as a buyer of the circulating components of its constant capital. With
the same money, department I buys from it the remainder of its commodities to the value of 100. The money thus flows back to section 1 of
department II because this section appears as a seller of commodities
directly after having appeared as a buyer. If the money did not flow
back to it, then section 1 would firstly have given £100 in money to
department I for commodities to a value of 100, and then a further 100
in commodities into the bargain, i.e. it would have given its commodities away as a present.

Section 2, on the other hand, which laid out £100 in money, receives
a reflux of £300; £100, because it firstly cast £100 in money into the
circulation sphere as a buyer, and receives this back as a seller; and
£200, because it functions only as a seller of commodities to the
amount of £200, and not also as a buyer to this amount. Thus the
money cannot flow back to department I. The wear and tear of the
fixed capital is therefore paid for by the money cast into circulation by
department II, section 1, in the purchase of elements of fixed capital;
but it does not come into section 2's hands as the money of section 1,
but rather as money belonging to department I.

(b) On this assumption, the remnant of II_c is distributed in such a
way that section 1 has [only] £200 in money, and section 2 the 400 in
commodities.

Section 1 has sold all its commodities, but the £200 in money is the changed form of the fixed component of its constant capital, which it has to renew in kind. It appears here, therefore, simply as a buyer, and, in place of its money, receives commodities from department I to the same amount in the natural elements of fixed capital. Section 2 has, as a maximum, to cast into circulation only £200, since for half the value of its commodities it only sells to department I, and does not buy from it. (If no money is advanced by department I for the commodity exchange between departments I and II.)

£400 then returns to section 2 from the circulation sphere; £200, because it advanced this as a buyer and receives it back as a seller of commodities to the value of £200; and £200, because it sold commodities to department I to the value of 200, without withdrawing an equivalent in value for these from department I.

(c) Section I possesses £200 in money and 200_c in commodities; section 2 has 200 (d) in commodities.

On this assumption, section 2 does not have to advance anything in money, because it no longer functions at all as a buyer vis-à-vis department I, but rather only as a seller, and thus has to wait until its goods are bought.

Section 1 advances £400 in money; £200 for mutual commodity exchange with department I, £200 as a mere buyer from it. With this latter £200 in money, it buys its elements of fixed capital.

Department I uses £200 to buy 200 in commodities from section 1, and it is therefore to section 1 that the £200 advanced in money for this commodity exchange returns; department I uses the other £200 – which it has also obtained from section 1 – to buy commodities worth 200 from section 2, which thereby has the wear and tear of its fixed capital precipitated out in money.

The situation would in no way be changed if it were assumed that in case (c) it was department I instead of department II, section 1, that advanced the £200 in money for the exchange of the existing values. If department I first buys commodities from department II, section 2, for £200 (we have assumed that this section only has to sell this remnant of its commodities), then the £200 does not return to department I, since department II, section 2, no longer appears as a buyer; but department II, section 1, then has £200 in money to buy with and a further 200 in commodities to be exchanged, thus a total of 400 to be exchanged with department I. £200 in money then returns to department I from department II, section 2. If department I lays this out again in order to buy the 200 in commodities from department II, section 1, then this returns to it when department II, section 1, receives the second half of department I's 400 commodities. Section 1 of department II has laid out £200 in money simply as the buyer of elements of fixed capital; this does not return to it, but rather serves to realize in money the residual 200_c of commodities from department II, section 2, while the money laid out for commodity exchange, £200, flows back to department I not via department II, section 2, but rather via II section 1. For its commodities of 400, an equivalent in commodities to the sum of 400 has returned to it; the £200 in money it advanced for the conversion of the 800 commodities has similarly returned to it, and so everything is in order.

*

The difficulty that emerged in connection with the exchange:

I. $\underbrace{1{,}000_v + 1{,}000_s}$

II. $2{,}000_c$

was reduced to the difficulty in converting the remnants:

I. 400_s

II.   (1) 200 money $+ 200_c$ commodities $+$ (2) 200_c commodities,

or to make the matter still clearer:

I. $200_s + 200_s$

II.   (1) 200 money $+ 200_c$ commodities $+$ (2) 200_c commodities.

Since 200_c in commodities in department II, section 1, is exchanged for $200\ I_s$ (commodities), and since all the money that circulates for this exchange of 400 in commodities between departments I and II returns to the department which advanced it, whether I or II, this money, as an element of the exchange between departments I and II, is in fact not an element of our present problem. To put it another way, if we assume that in this exchange between $200\ I_s$ (commodities) and $200\ II_c$ (commodities of department II, section 1), the money functions as means of payment, and not as means of purchase, and thus not as a 'means of circulation' in the strictest sense, then it is evident that, since the commodities $200\ I_s$ and $200\ II_c$ (section 1) are of equal value, and means of production to a value of 200 are exchanged for means of consumption to a value of 200, the money functions here only ideally, and no money really has to be cast into the circulation sphere to settle the balance, either by one side or the other. The problem therefore emerges in its pure form only if we cancel out the commodities $200\ I_s$ on the side of department I, and their equivalent, commodities $200\ II_c$ (section 1) on the side of department II.

After eliminating these two amounts of commodities of the same value (I and II) that mutually balance each other, the remnant to be exchanged, in which the problem emerges in its pure form, remains as follows:

I. 200_s commodities

II. (1) 200_c (money) + (2) 200_c (commodities).

It is clear here that department II, section 1, buys the components of its fixed capital 200 I_s with £200 in money; the fixed capital of department I, a value of 200, is transformed from the commodity form (as means of production, and indeed as elements of fixed capital) into the money form. With this money, department I buys means of consumption from department II, section 2, and the result, for department II, is that section 1 has been able to renew a fixed component of its constant capital in kind; and that section 2 has another component (which replaces the wear and tear of its fixed capital) precipitated out in money. This continues each year, until this component too is due to be replaced in kind.

The precondition here is evidently that the fixed component of department II's constant capital which in any given year has been transformed back into money to its full value and thus has to be renewed in kind (section 1) has to be equal to the annual wear and tear of the other fixed component of the constant capital in department II which still goes on functioning in its old natural form, and whose wear and tear, the loss of value that it transfers to the commodities in whose production it is involved, has first to be replaced in money. Such a balance accordingly appears as a law of reproduction on the same scale; which means in other words that the proportionate division of labour in department I, where means of production are produced, must remain unaltered, in so far as it supplies on the one hand circulating, and on the other hand fixed components of the constant capital of department II.

Before we investigate this more closely, we must first see how the matter stands if the residual amount of $II_c(1)$ is not equal to the remnant of $II_c(2)$. It may be greater or less, so we shall examine each case separately.

First Case

I. 200_s.

II. (1) 220_c (in money) + (2) 200_c (in commodities).

Here $II_c(1)$ buys commodities 200 I_s for £200 in money, and department I uses the same money to buy commodities 200 $II_c(2)$, i.e. the component of fixed capital that has to be precipitated out in money; the latter is thereby realized. But 20 $II_c(1)$ in money cannot be transformed back into fixed capital in kind.

It might seem that this unfortunate state of affairs can be rectified if we take the remnant of I_s as 220 instead of 200, so that, out of the 2,000 I, only 1,780 instead of 1,800 have been disposed of by earlier exchange. In this case, then, we have:

    I. 220_s.

    II. (1) 220_c (in money)$+$(2) 200_c (in commodities).

Department II section 1 buys the 220 I_s for £220 in money, and I then buys the 200 II_c (2) in commodities for £200. But there is still £20 on the side of department I, a piece of surplus-value that it can only hold onto in money, and cannot spend on means of consumption. The difficulty is only shifted from II_c (section 1) to I_s.

If we now assume on the other hand that II_c (section 1) is smaller than II_c (section 2), then we have:

    Second Case

    I. 200_s (in commodities).

    II. (1) 180_c (in money)$+$(2) 200_c (in commodities).

Department II, section 1, buys commodities 180 I_s for £180 in money; department I uses this money to buy commodities to the same value from department II, section 2, i.e. 180 $II_c(2)$. There remains an unsaleable 20 I_s on one side, and similarly 20 $II_c(2)$ on the other; commodities to the value of 40 that cannot be transformed into money.

It would not be any use to take the remnant in department I as 180; there would certainly not be any longer a surplus in department I, but there would still be an unsaleable surplus in II_c (section 2), one which could not be transformed into money.

In the first case, where II(1) is bigger than II(2), there remains on the side of $II_c(1)$ a surplus in money which cannot be transformed into fixed capital, or if the remnant I_s is taken as $=II_c(1)$, the same surplus in money on the part of I_s, which cannot be transformed into means of consumption.

In the second case, where $II_c(1)$ is smaller than $II_c(2)$, there remains a monetary deficit on the part of both the 200 I_s and the $II_c(2)$, and the same surplus in commodities on the two sides; or if the remnant I_s is taken as $=II_c(1)$, a deficit in money and a surplus in commodities on the part of $II_c(2)$.

If we take the remnant I_s as always equal to $II_c(1)$ – since production is determined by orders, and it does not alter the reproduction in any way if this year more components of fixed capital, and next year more components of circulating capital, are produced by department I for department II's constant capital – then in the first case I_s could be transformed back into means of consumption only if department I bought with it a part of the surplus-value of department II, so that, instead of being consumed, this was accumulated by department II as money; in the second case, it would only help if department I spent the money itself, i.e. the hypothesis that we rejected.

If $II_c(1)$ is bigger than $II_c(2)$, then an import of foreign commodities is needed in order to realize the monetary surplus in I_s. If $II_c(1)$ is less than $II_c(2)$, then conversely an export of commodities II (means of consumption) is needed to realize the wear and tear component in II_c in means of production. In both cases, foreign trade is necessary.

Even if we assume, in considering reproduction on a constant scale, that the productivity of all branches of industry, and thus also the proportionate value ratios of their commodity products, remains constant, the two cases last mentioned, in which $II_c(1)$ is greater or less than $II_c(2)$, would still be of interest for production on an expanded scale, where they will inevitably arise.

(c) Results

As far as the replacement of the fixed capital is concerned, the following general points can be made:

Suppose that all other circumstances remain the same, i.e. not only the scale of production, but also and particularly the productivity of labour. Then if a greater part of the fixed element of II_c becomes defunct than it did the previous year, and therefore a greater part has to be renewed in kind, that portion of fixed capital that is as yet only *en route* to its demise, and has to be replaced in money for the time being, until it actually does expire, must decline in the same proportion, since, according to our assumption, the sum (including the value sum) of the portion of fixed capital functioning in department II remains the same. This however brings about the following situation: Firstly, if a greater part of department I's commodity capital consists of elements of the fixed capital of II_c, then the circulating component for II_c is so much the less, since the total amount that department I produces for II_c remains unchanged. If one part increases, then the other must decline, and vice versa. On the other hand, however, the total production of department II also remains the same. But how is this possible if its raw materials, work in progress and ancillary materials decrease (i.e. the circulating elements of constant capital in department II)? Secondly, a greater part of the fixed capital II_c, restored in the money form, flows to department I to be changed back from the money form into the natural form. Thus additional money accrues to department I, besides the money that circulates simply to exchange commodities between I and II: money that does not mediate reciprocal commodity exchange, but appears in its unilateral function as a means of purchase. At the same time, however, the quantity of commodities II_c that bears the replacement value of the wear and tear would be proportionately reduced, i.e. the quantity of commodities in department II that does not have to be exchanged against commodities from department I, but only against department I's money. More money from department II would flow to department I as mere means of purchase, and there would be fewer commodities from department II towards which department I had to function merely as a buyer. A greater part of I_s – for I_v has already been converted into department II commodities – would thus not be convertible into commodities II, and would be held fast in the money form.

We do not need here to go any further into the opposite case, where the reproduction of the defunct fixed capital in department II was less in one year and the wear and tear component greater.

There would be a crisis – a crisis of production – despite reproduction on a constant scale.

In short, if in the case of simple reproduction and with other circumstances remaining the same – i.e. particularly with the productivity, overall amount and intensity of labour remaining unchanged – a constant proportion is not assumed between the defunct fixed capital (that needing renewal) and the fixed capital which continues to operate in the old natural form (merely adding value to its products to replace its wear and tear), then in one case the amount of circulating components to be reproduced remains the same, but the amount of fixed components to be replaced will have increased; the total production of department I therefore has to grow, or else there would be an insufficient amount of reproduction, quite independent of the monetary relations.

In the other case, if the proportionate size of the fixed capital in department II that has to be reproduced in kind declines, then the amount of constant capital II's circulating components that have been reproduced by department I remains unchanged, while the fixed components to be reproduced have declined. There is thus either a reduction in the total production of department I, or alternatively a surplus (as previously a deficit), a surplus that cannot be realized.

The same labour can certainly supply in the first case a greater product, with increased productivity, extension or intensity, and in this way the deficit in the first case could be covered; but a change of this kind could not occur without a shift of labour and capital from one branch of production in department I to another, and any displacement of this kind would produce momentary dislocations. Secondly, however, in so far as extension and intensification of labour increase, department I would have more value to exchange for less value from department II, i.e. department I's product would depreciate.

The reverse happens in the second case, where department I has either to contract its production, which means a crisis for the workers and capitalists engaged in it, or to supply a surplus, which again leads to crisis. Of themselves, these surpluses are no evil, rather an advantage; in capitalist production however, they are an evil.

Foreign trade could help in both cases, in the first to exchange for means of consumption the commodities from department I which are held fast in the money form, in the second to dispose of the surplus commodities. But foreign trade, in so far as it does not just replace elements (and their value), only shifts the contradictions to a broader sphere, and gives them a wider orbit.

Once we dispense with the capitalist form of reproduction, then the whole problem boils down to the fact that the magnitude of the part of fixed capital that becomes defunct and has therefore to be replaced in kind varies in successive years (here we are dealing simply with the fixed capital functioning in the production of means of consumption). If it is very large one year (if the mortality is above the average, just as with human beings), then in the following years it will certainly be so much the less. The mass of raw materials, work in progress, and ancillaries needed for the annual production of means of consumption – assuming that other circumstances remain the same – does not diminish on this account; and so the total production of the means of production would have to increase in one case, and decrease in the other. This can only be remedied by perpetual relative over-production; on the one hand a greater quantity of fixed capital is produced than is directly needed; on the other hand, and this is particularly important, a stock of raw materials etc. is produced that surpasses the immediate annual need (this is particularly true of means of subsistence). Over-production of this kind is equivalent to control by the society over the objective means of its own reproduction. Within capitalist society, however, it is an anarchic element.

This example of fixed capital – in the context of reproduction on a constant scale – is a striking one. A disproportionate production of fixed and circulating capital is a factor much favoured by the economists in their explanation of crises. It is something new to them that a disproportion of this kind can and must arise from the mere *maintenance* of the fixed capital; that it can and must arise on the assumption of an ideal normal production, with simple reproduction of the social capital already functioning.

12. THE REPRODUCTION OF THE MONEY MATERIAL

One factor has so far been completely disregarded, namely the annual reproduction of gold and silver. As the mere raw material for luxury articles, for gold and silver plating, etc., these would no more need special mention here than any other products. However, they play an important role as money material and hence as potential money. For the sake of simplification, we take gold as the sole money material here.

According to earlier figures, the world's total annual gold production amounted to some 800,000–900,000 lb., i.e. between 1,100 and 1,250 million marks. According to Soetbeer,[12] however, the average for the years between 1871 and 1875 was only 170,674 kilograms, or a value of approximately 476 million marks. Australia supplied around 167 million marks worth, the USA 166 million and Russia 93 million. The remainder was divided between various countries in amounts of less than 10 million marks each. The annual silver production, during the same period, amounted to something under 2 million kilos, with a value of 354½ million marks, of which Mexico supplied about 108 million marks worth, the USA 102, South America 67, Germany 26 million, etc.*

Of the countries in which capitalist production is dominant, only the USA is a producer of gold and silver; the European capitalist countries receive almost all their gold and by far the greater portion of their silver from Australia, the USA, Mexico, South America and Russia.

12. Adolf Soetbeer, *Edelmetall-Produktion*, Gotha, 1879 [p. 112].

---

*The value of a German mark in 1871 was approximately 11·7d. in the English money of the time, or 20·43 to the £.

However, we propose to put gold mines into the country of capitalist production whose annual reproduction we are analysing here, for the following reason:

Capitalist production never exists without foreign trade. If normal annual reproduction on a given scale is presupposed, then it is also supposed together with this that foreign trade replaces domestic articles only by those of other use or natural forms, without affecting value ratios, and therefore without affecting either the value ratios in which the two categories, means of production and means of consumption, mutually exchange for one another, or the ratios between the constant capital, variable capital and surplus-value into which the value of the product of each of these categories can be broken down. Bringing foreign trade into an analysis of the value of the product annually reproduced can therefore only confuse things, without supplying any new factor either to the problem or to its solution. We therefore completely abstract from it here, and treat gold as a direct element of the annual reproduction, not as a commodity imported from abroad by exchange.

The production of gold belongs, along with metal production in general, to department I, the category which comprises the production of means of production. We intend to assume that the annual gold product $= 30$ (for convenience only, as this is in fact far too high in relation to the other figures in our schema); this value can be broken down into $20_c + 5_v + 5_s$; the 20_c is to be exchanged against other elements of I_c, and this will be considered below [see p. 548, note 14]; the $5_v + 5_s$, however, has to be exchanged against elements of II_c, i.e. means of consumption.

As far as the 5_v is concerned, every gold-producing business first begins by buying labour-power; not with the gold it has itself produced, but with an aliquot part of the money already in stock in the country. The workers use this v to withdraw means of consumption from department II, and department II uses it to buy materials of production from department I. Let us say that department II buys gold worth 2 from department I as a commodity material, etc. (a component of its constant capital), so that 2_v flows back to the gold producers in department I in money that already belonged earlier to the circulation sphere. If department II buys nothing more in gold material from department I, the gold producers there still buy from II, in as much as they cast their gold into the circulation here as money, since gold can buy every commodity. The difference is simply that department I does not appear here as a seller, but only as a buyer. The gold-diggers in department I can always get rid of their commodity, which always exists in a directly exchangeable form.

Let us assume that a cotton spinner has paid his workers 5_v, and that these supply him – leaving aside his surplus-value – with spun yarn equal to 5; the workers then buy II_c to the value of 5, and department II buys yarn from department I for 5 in money, so that the 5_v flows back in money to the cotton spinner. In the case assumed here, on the other hand, Ig (as we shall denote the gold producers) advances 5_v to its workers, in money which already belonged earlier to the circulation sphere; these spend the money on means of subsistence, but out of this 5, only 2 returns from department II back to Ig. Ig, however, can begin the reproduction process again just as well as the cotton-spinner can, as its workers have supplied it with 5 in gold. 2 of this has been sold, and it still has 3 left in gold, which therefore only has to be coined,[13] or transformed into banknotes, for its whole variable capital to exist again in its hands in the money form, without any further mediation by department II.

Even in this first process of annual reproduction, however, a change has taken place in the quantity of money actually or virtually belonging to the circulation sphere. We assumed that II_c bought $2_v(Ig)$ as material, and that Ig laid out 3 again in department II as the money form of variable capital. Thus the value of 3 that remained within department II, and did not flow back to department I, comes from the sum of money supplied by the new gold production. According to our assumption, department II has satisfied its need for gold material. The 3 remains in its hands as a gold hoard. It cannot form any element of its constant capital, and department II already had sufficient money capital to purchase labour-power; furthermore, with the exception of the wear and tear element, this additional $3g$ has no function to perform within II_c, for a part of which it was exchanged (it could only serve to meet a proportionate part of the wear and tear element if $II_c(1)$ were smaller than $II_c(2)$, which would be accidental). On the other hand, however, even with the exception of the wear and tear element, the entire commodity product II_c has to be exchanged for means of production $I_{(v+s)}*$ – hence this money must be completely transferred from II_c to II_s, whether this exists in necessary means of subsistence or in luxury

13. 'A considerable quantity of gold bullion . . . is taken direct to the mint in San Francisco by the owners.' *Reports of H.M. Secretaries of Embassy and Legation,* 1879, Part III, p. 337.

* See above, pp. 474–8.

items, and the corresponding commodity value must be transferred, conversely, from II_s to II_c. The result is that a part of the surplus-value is stored away as a money hoard.

In the second year's reproduction, if the same proportion of the gold annually produced continues to be used as money, 2 will once again flow back to Ig and 3 will be replaced in kind, i.e. will be set free again in department II as a hoard, etc.

As far as the variable capital is concerned, we can say generally that capitalist Ig, just like any other, always has to advance this capital in money for the purchase of labour-power. As far as this v is concerned, it is not he but his workers who have to buy from department II; thus the case in which he appears as buyer and casts gold into department II can never arise unless the latter takes the initiative. But in so far as department II buys material from him, and needs to convert its constant capital II_c into gold material, part of $(Ig)_v$ flows back to him from department II in the same way as to other capitalists in department I; to the extent that this is not the case, he directly replaces his v in gold from his own product. But in the proportion to which the v advanced as money does not flow back to him from department II, a part of it that has already been advanced to the circulation sphere is transformed into a hoard (this part is the money that flowed to him from department I and did not return there), and a part of his surplus-value is therefore not spent on means of consumption. As new gold mines are constantly opened, or old ones reopened, so a definite proportion of the money that Ig has to lay out on v is always part of the quantity of money in existence before the new gold production; it was cast into department II by way of its workers, and, to the extent that it does not return to Ig from department II, it forms an element of hoard formation there.

As far as $(Ig)_s$ is concerned, Ig can always appear here as a buyer; it casts its s into the circulation sphere as gold, and correspondingly withdraws means of consumption II_c; here the gold is partly used as material, and hence functions as a real element of the constant component c of department II's productive capital; and in as much as this is not the case, it again becomes an element of hoard formation as a part of II_s that persists in money. It is clear – even leaving aside the I_c, which will be considered later[14] – that even simple reproduction, which excludes accumulation in the strict sense of the term, i.e. reproduction on an expanded scale, necessarily involves the storage of money, or hoard

14. No investigation of the exchange of the newly produced gold within the constant capital of department I is to be found in the manuscript. – F.E.

formation. And since this is repeated anew each year, it explains the assumption from which we proceeded in considering capitalist production, namely that at the beginning of the reproduction process, the capitalists in departments I and II must each already possess a quantity of the monetary medium which corresponds to the amount of commodity exchange. There is even storage of this kind after deduction of the gold lost by the abrasion of the money in circulation.

It is self-evident that the greater the maturity of capitalist production, the greater is the quantity of money accumulated on all sides, and the smaller therefore the proportion that the new gold production of each year adds to this quantity, even though this addition may be quite significant in absolute terms. We come back once again, then, in general terms, to the objection made against Tooke [see p. 404 above]: how is it possible for each capitalist to withdraw a surplus-value from the annual product in money, i.e. to withdraw more money from the circulation sphere than he cast into it, since in the final analysis the capitalist class itself must be seen as the origin of all money in circulation?

We note on this point, by way of summary of what has already been developed earlier (Chapter 17):

1. The only assumption required here is that there should always be sufficient money to convert the various elements of the commodity mass annually reproduced. This is in no way affected by the fact that a part of the commodity value consists of surplus-value. If the whole of production belonged to the workers themselves, then their surplus labour would be surplus labour for themselves, not for the capitalists, but the mass of commodity value in circulation would be the same and would require, given that other circumstances also remained the same, the same amount of money for its circulation. The question in both cases is simply: where does the money come from to convert this total commodity value? It is not: where does the money come from to realize the surplus-value?

Moreover, to come back to this once again, each individual commodity consists of $c+v+s$, and so a certain sum of money is necessary for the circulation of the capital $c+v$, and another sum of money is needed for the circulation of the capitalists' revenue, the surplus-value s. Just as for the individual capitalist, so for the class as a whole, the money in which it advances capital is different from the money in which it spends revenue. Where does this latter money come from? Simply from the fact that of the mass of money that exists in the hands of the capitalist class, which is by and large the total quantity of money that exists in the society, one part circulates the capitalists' revenue. We already saw above how each capitalist who sets up a new business fishes back the money that he spends on means of consumption for his own maintenance, once the business is under way, in the shape of money which serves to realize his surplus-value. Generally speaking, however, the whole difficulty arises from two sources, as follows:

Firstly, if we consider simply the circulation sphere and the turnover of capital, i.e. consider the capitalist simply as the personification of capital – not also as capitalist consumer and man of the world – then although we certainly see him constantly casting surplus-value into circulation as a component of his commodity capital, we never see money in his hands as a form of revenue, we never see him casting money into circulation for the consumption of his surplus-value.

Secondly, if the capitalist class casts a certain sum of money into circulation in the shape of revenue, it appears as if it paid an equivalent for this part of the total annual product, and that this has thereby ceased to represent surplus-value. But the surplus product in which the surplus-value is represented costs the capitalist class nothing. As a class, it possesses it and enjoys it free of charge, and the monetary circulation cannot alter this in any way. The change that this brings about simply consists in the fact that each capitalist, instead of consuming his own surplus product in kind, for which in most cases it would not be suitable, withdraws commodities of all kinds from the total stock to the amount of the surplus-value that he appropriated, and appropriates these. The circulation mechanism, however, has shown that if the capitalist class casts money into circulation to be spent as revenue, it withdraws this same money again from circulation, and so the same process can always begin anew; considered as a capitalist class, therefore, it remains now as before in possession of this sum of money needed for the realization of its surplus-value. If the capitalist not only withdraws surplus-value from the commodity market in the form of commodities for his consumption fund, but at the same time the money with which he buys these commodities flows back to him, he has evidently withdrawn the commodities from circulation without an equivalent. They cost him nothing, even though he pays for them with money. If I buy commodities for £1 sterling, and the seller of these commodities gives me back my £1 in exchange for a surplus product that cost me nothing, then I have obviously received the commodities for nothing. The constant repetition of this operation in no way alters the fact that I constantly withdraw commodities and constantly remain in possession of the £1, even though I part with it temporarily in order to obtain these commodities. The capitalist constantly receives this money back as the realization of surplus value that cost him nothing.

We saw that for Adam Smith the entire value of the social product resolved itself into revenue, into $v+s$, and that the value of the constant capital was therefore taken as zero. It necessarily follows from this that the money required for the circulation of the annual revenue would also be sufficient for the circulation of the entire annual product; and that in our case, therefore, the money needed for the circulation of means of consumption to the value of 3,000 would be sufficient for the circulation of a total annual product to the value of 9,000. This was in fact Adam Smith's opinion, and it is repeated by Thomas Tooke. This false conception of the ratio between the quantity of money needed to realize revenue and the quantity of money that circulates the total social product is a necessary result of the uncomprehending, thoughtless manner in which they view the reproduction and annual replacement of the different material and value elements of the total annual product. It is therefore already refuted.

Let us listen to Smith and Tooke themselves.

Smith says, in Book Two, Chapter II:

'The circulation of every country may be considered as divided into two different branches: the circulation of the dealers with one another, and the circulation between the dealers and the consumers. Though the same pieces of money, whether paper or metal, may be employed sometimes in the one circulation and sometimes in the other, yet as both are constantly going on at the same time, each requires a certain stock of money of one kind or another to carry it on. The value of the goods circulated between the different dealers, never can exceed the value of those circulated between the dealers and the consumers; whatever is bought by the dealers, being ultimately destined to be sold to the consumers. The circulation between the dealers, as it is carried on by wholesale, requires generally a pretty large sum for every particular transaction. That between the dealers and the consumers, on the contrary, as it is generally carried on by retail, frequently requires but very small ones, a shilling, or even a halfpenny, being often sufficient. But small sums circulate much faster than large ones. . . . Though the annual purchases of all the consumers, therefore, are at least' (this 'at least' is a good one!) 'equal in value to those of all the dealers, they can generally be transacted with a much smaller quantity of money', etc. [p. 421].

On this passage of our Adam's, Thomas Tooke remarks (*An Inquiry into the Currency Principle*, London, 1844, pp. 34–6 passim):

'There can be no doubt that the distinction here made is substantially correct ... the interchange between dealers and consumers including the payment of wages, which constitute the principal means of the consumers ... All the transactions between dealers and dealers, by which are to be understood all sales from the producer or importer, through all the stages of intermediate processes of manufacture or otherwise to the retail dealer or the exporting merchant, are resolvable into movements or transfers of capital. Now transfers of capital do not necessarily suppose nor do actually as a matter of fact entail, in the great majority of transactions, a passing of money, that is, bank-notes or coin – I mean bodily, and not by fiction – at the time of transfer ... The total amount of the transactions between dealers and dealers must, in the last resort, be determined and limited by the amount of those between dealers and consumers.'

If we took this last sentence by itself, we might believe Tooke was simply claiming that there was a certain ratio between the 'transactions between dealers' and 'those between dealers and consumers', in other words between the value of the total annual revenue and the value of the capital with which it is produced. But this is not the case. He expressly endorses the Smithian conception. A special criticism of his circulation theory would thus be superfluous.

2. Every industrial capital, at its outset, casts money into circulation all at once for the entire fixed component of its capital, and it recovers this only gradually over a series of years by the sale of its annual product. It therefore casts more money into the circulation sphere at first than it withdraws from this. This is repeated each time that the entire capital is renewed in kind; it is repeated each year for a certain number of businesses, those whose fixed capital has to be renewed in kind; it is repeated partially with each repair, with each fractional renewal of the fixed capital. If at one point more money is withdrawn from circulation than is cast in, the reverse is the case at another point.

In all branches of industry whose production periods (as distinct from their working periods) extend over a relatively long time, money is constantly cast into circulation by the capitalist producers during this period, partly in payment for the labour-power applied, partly for purchasing the means of production that are to be used. Means of production are therefore withdrawn from the commodity market directly, and means of consumption in part indirectly, by the workers when they spend their wages, and in part also directly by the capitalists themselves, who in no way suspend their consumption, even though they do not cast into the market at the same time an equivalent in commodities. During this period, the money that the capitalists cast into circulation serves to realize commodity value, including the surplus-value contained in it. This factor becomes very important in developed capitalist production, in connection with long-drawn-out enterprises undertaken by joint-stock companies, etc. such as the building of railways, canals, docks, large municipal buildings, the construction of iron ships, the draining of land on a large scale, etc.

3. While the other capitalists, apart from their outlay on fixed capital, withdraw more money from the circulation sphere than they cast into it for the purchase of labour-power and the circulating elements, the gold- and silver-producing capitalists cast only money into circulation (leaving aside the portion of precious metal serving as raw material), while they withdraw only commodities from it. Their constant capital (with the exception of the wear and tear component), the greater part of their variable capital and their entire surplus-value (with the exception of a certain hoard that is accumulated in their own hands) is cast into the circulation sphere as money.

4. It is certainly true that all kinds of things circulate as commodities that were not produced within the year: plots of land, houses, etc., as well as products whose production period extends over longer than a year, such as cattle, wood, wine, etc. It is important to establish, for these and other phenomena, that besides the sum of money required for direct circulation, there is always a certain quantity in a latent and non-functioning state, which can come out and function on a given impulse. The value of these products also often circulates bit by bit and gradually: for example the value of houses circulates in rent over a series of years.

On the other hand, not all the motions of the reproduction process are mediated by money circulation. The entire production process falls outside it, once its elements have been procured. So do all products that the producer directly consumes himself – whether individually, or productively – including the provisions paid in kind to agricultural workers.

Thus the quantity of money that circulates the annual product is present in society and has been accumulated bit by bit. It does not form part of the value product of the present year, with the possible exception of the gold that replaces worn-out coins.

In this presentation we have presupposed the exclusive circulation of precious metals as money, and, together with this, the simplest form of cash purchases and sales; though even on the basis of simple metallic circulation money can function also as a means of payment, and actually has functioned in this way historically, and a system of credit and certain aspects of the credit mechanism have developed on this basis.

This assumption was made not simply for methodological reasons, although the importance of these is shown by the simple fact that both Tooke and his school, and their opponents, were constantly forced in their controversies over the circulation of bank notes to come back again to the hypothesis of pure metallic circulation. They were forced to do this *post festum*,* but then they did so very superficially, and necessarily so, since this starting-point fulfilled only an incidental function in their analysis.

However, the simplest consideration of monetary circulation in the form in which it *developed spontaneously* – and this monetary circulation is here an immanent moment of the annual process of reproduction – shows the following:

(a) On the assumption of developed capitalist production, i.e. the domination of the system of wage-labour, money capital evidently plays a major role, in as much as it is the form in which variable capital is advanced. To the degree that the wage system develops, all products are transformed into commodities, and all – with a few important exceptions – must therefore jointly undergo the transformation into money as a phase in their development. The quantity of money in circulation must be sufficient for the realization of the commodities, and the greater part of this is supplied in the form of wages, of money that is advanced by industrial capitalists in payment of labour-power and mainly functions in the hands of the workers only as a means of circulation (means of purchase). This is in complete contrast to natural economy,† such as predominates on the basis of every form of personal bondage (including serfdom), and still more so on the basis of more or less primitive communities, whether or not these involve relations of bondage or slavery.

In the slave system, the money capital laid out on the purchase of labour-power plays the role of fixed capital in the money form, and is only gradually replaced as the active life of the slave comes to an end. This is why in Athens the profit that a slave-owner drew, either directly

*See above, p. 390.
†'Natural economy' in the sense of the relative absence of commodity exchange; see above, pp. 194–6.

from the industrial use of his slave or indirectly by renting the slave to other industrial users (e.g. for work in the mines), was simply considered as interest (together with amortization), just as in capitalist production the industrial capitalist puts a portion of his surplus-value down in his accounts together with the wear and tear of his fixed capital, as interest and replacement for the fixed capital; this is also the rule with capitalists who rent out fixed capital (houses, machines etc.). Mere domestic slaves, whether they are used to perform necessary services or simply as a display of luxury, are not considered here; they correspond to our servant class. But even the slave system – in as much as it was the dominant form of productive labour in agriculture, manufacture, ship-building, etc., as in the developed Greek states and in Rome – retains an element of natural economy. The slave market itself constantly receives supplies of the commodity labour-power from war, piracy, etc., and this pillage is not mediated by a process of circulation, but is rather the appropriation in kind of other people's labour-power by direct physical compulsion. Even in the USA, after the border area between the wage-labour states of the North and the slave states of the South had been transformed into a slave-breeding zone for the South, and where the slave thrown onto the market had therefore himself become an element of the annual reproduction, this was for a long while insufficient, and the African slave trade had to be carried on for as long as possible in order to fill the requirements of the market.

(b) The fluxes and refluxes of money which take place on the basis of capitalist production, for the reconversion of the annual product, and which have grown up spontaneously; the advances of fixed capital at a single stroke, to its entire value, and the progressive withdrawal of this value from circulation by a process that extends over a period of many years, i.e. its gradual reconstitution in the money form by annual hoard formation, a hoard formation that is completely different in nature from the hoard formation based on the new gold production of each year that accompanies it; the different lengths of time for which money has to be advanced, which vary according to the length of the production periods of the commodities, and for which there has to be in each case a prior formation of a hoard before the money can be withdrawn from circulation by the sale of the commodity involved; the varying times of advance that arise simply from differences in the distance of the point of production from the market outlet; as well as the variation in the size and period of the reflux according to the condition or the relative size of the production stocks in different businesses and for the different individual capitalists in the same line of business, i.e. the dates of purchase of the elements of constant capital, and all this during the year's reproduction – all these different aspects of the spontaneous movement had only to be noted and brought to light by experience, in order to give rise both to a methodical use of the mechanical aids of the credit system and to the actual fishing out of available loan capital.

On top of all this, there is still the distinction between businesses whose production proceeds continuously on the same scale, as long as conditions remain otherwise the same, and those that employ labourpower in different degrees at different periods of the year, such as agriculture.

13. DESTUTT DE TRACY'S THEORY OF REPRODUCTION [15]

The 'great logician' Destutt de Tracy* (cf. Volume 1, p. 266, note 17) will serve as an example of the confused and at the same time boastful incomprehension shown by the political economists in dealing with the social reproduction. Here is a man whom even Ricardo took seriously, calling him 'a very distinguished writer' (*Principles*, p. 287 [Pelican edition]).

This 'distinguished writer' presents the following explanations of the overall process of social reproduction and circulation:

'I shall be asked how it is that these industrial entrepreneurs make such great profits, and from whom they can draw them. My reply is that they do so because they sell everything they produce dearer than it cost them to produce it; they sell:

'(1) to one another for the whole of that part of their consumption which is destined to satisfy their own needs, and which they pay for with a part of their profits;

'(2) to the wage-labourers, both those that they pay themselves and those that the idle† capitalists pay; in this way they receive back from

15. From Manuscript II.

---

*Antoine-Louis-Claude, comte Destutt de Tracy, sought to base his economic theory directly on a sensualist philosophy. His *Traité de la volonté* which Marx criticizes here (later reprinted as *Traité de l'économie politique*) forms parts 4 and 5 of a larger work, *Élémens d'idéologie*.

†For Destutt de Tracy's conception of a 'sterile class' or 'class of idlers' who simply live off the labour of others, see the discussion in *Theories of Surplus-Value*, Part I, pp. 269–81.

the wage-labourers their entire wages, with the exception of their small savings;

'(3) to the idle capitalists, who pay them with the part of their revenue that they have not already handed over to the workers directly employed by them; so that the entire rent that they pay these idle capitalists each year flows back to them in one of these ways or another' (Destutt de Tracy, *Traité de la volonté et de ses effets*, Paris, 1826, p. 239).

The capitalists, therefore, get rich firstly by taking advantage of each other in exchanging the part of the surplus-value that they devote to their private consumption or consume as revenue. If this part of their surplus-value or profits is £400, then this £400 becomes £500 if each party to the £400 sells his share to another party 25 per cent too dear. Since all of them do the same thing, the outcome is the same as if they had sold to each other at the right price. It is simply that they need a quantity of money of £500 to circulate a commodity value of £400, and this would seem rather a method of impoverishing than enriching them, in as much as they would have to hold a large part of their total wealth unproductively in the useless form of means of circulation. The whole thing comes down to the fact that the capitalist class, despite the all-round nominal price increase of their commodities, have to distribute among themselves, for their private consumption, a commodity stock of only £400, but that they do each other the favour of circulating this £400 in commodity value with a quantity of money that is required for £500 of commodity value.

In saying this, we entirely disregard the fact that 'a part of their profits' here, and thus generally, is assumed to be a stock of commodities in which profit is represented. But what Destutt intends is precisely to explain the origin of this profit. The quantity of money needed to circulate it is a completely subordinate question. The mass of commodities in which the profit is represented therefore appears to stem from the fact that the capitalists not only sell this mass of commodities to one another, which is already very fine and profound, but also all sell it to each other too dear. Thus we now know one source of capitalist enrichment. It comes to the same thing as the secret of 'Inspector Bräsig',* that great poverty derives from great *pauvreté*.

2. The same capitalists also sell 'to the wage-labourers, both those that they pay themselves and those that the idle capitalists pay; in this way they receive back from the wage-labourers their entire wages, with the exception of their small savings'.

* A comic character in stories by Fritz Reuter.

The reflux of money capital to the industrial capitalists, capital which was advanced in this form by the capitalists as wages to the workers, constitutes, for M. Destutt, the second source of enrichment of these capitalists.

So if the capitalist class pays £100 to the workers in wages, say, and these workers can therefore buy from the capitalist class commodities to the same value of £100, so that the sum of £100 that the capitalists advanced as buyers of labour-power flows back to them on the sale of commodities of £100 to the workers, the capitalists are supposed to *enrich* themselves by this. It would appear, from the standpoint of ordinary common sense, that by means of this procedure the capitalists would simply find themselves once more in possession of the £100 that they previously possessed. At the beginning, they had £100 in money, and they used this to buy £100 worth of labour-power. For this £100 in money, the labour that is bought produces commodities of a value that, as far as we know up to now, is £100. By selling this £100 of commodities to the workers, the capitalists receive back £100 in money. The capitalists therefore again have £100 in money, and the workers have £100 in commodities that they themselves produced. How the capitalists are supposed to get rich in this way is anybody's guess. If the £100 in money did not flow back to them, then they would first have paid the workers £100 in money for their labour, and would secondly have had to give them the product of this labour, £100 worth of means of consumption, for nothing. The reflux might explain why the capitalists do not become any the poorer by this operation, but in no way how they become richer.

A further question, moreover, is how the capitalists come to possess this £100 in money, and why the workers, instead of producing commodities on their own account, are forced to exchange their labour-power for this £100. But this is something that a thinker of Destutt's calibre takes as self-explanatory.

Destutt would not be quite satisfied with this solution. After all, he did not actually tell us that one can get rich by spending a sum of £100 and then receiving back an equal sum of £100, i.e. by the reflux of £100 in money. What he told us is that the capitalists get rich 'because they sell everything they produce dearer than it cost them to buy it'.

So the capitalists must additionally get rich in their transactions with the workers, by selling to them too dear. Excellent!

'They pay wages . . . and all this flows back to them by the spending of all these people, who pay dearer for them' (for the products) 'than they cost them' (the capitalists) 'in wages' (p. 240).

Do the capitalists thus pay the workers £100 in wages, and then sell the workers their own product for £120, so that both the £100 has flowed back to them, and a further £20 has been obtained in addition? This is impossible. The workers can pay only with the money that they receive in the form of wages. If they receive £100 in wages from the capitalists, they can buy only for £100, and not for £120. This would not work at all. But there is still another way. The workers buy commodities from the capitalists for £100, but receive in actual fact only commodities to the value of £80. They have therefore been cheated out of £20. And the capitalist has certainly got £20 richer, because he paid for labour-power 20 per cent below its value, or indirectly made a deduction of 20 per cent from the nominal wage.

The capitalist class would achieve the same end if they paid the workers only £80 in wages from the beginning, and subsequently supplied them with £80 in commodity value for this £80 in money. This would appear the normal way – taking the class as a whole – since according to M. Destutt himself the working class must receive 'sufficient wages' (p. 219), i.e. their wages must at least be sufficient to maintain their existence and working ability, 'to procure them the barest subsistence' (p. 180). If the workers do not receive this sufficient wage, then this spells 'the death of industry' (p. 208), as Destutt himself says, and is therefore, it would appear, not a means of enrichment for the capitalists. But whatever may be the wage that the capitalist class pays the working class, this has a definite value, e.g. £80. If the capitalist class pays £80 to the workers, it has to supply them with £80 in commodity value, and the reflux of the £80 does not enrich them. If it pays them £100 in money, and sells them a commodity value of £80 for £100, then it pays them 25 per cent in money above their normal wages but supplies them that much less than this in commodities.

In other words, the entire fund from which the capitalist class draws its profit is formed by a deduction from the normal wage, by payment of labour-power below its value, i.e. below the value of the means of subsistence that are needed for the normal reproduction of the wage-labourers. If the normal wage is paid, therefore, and this according to Destutt is what should happen, then there does not exist any fund for profit, neither for the industrial capitalists nor for the idle capitalists.

M. Destutt would thus have to reduce the entire secret of how the capitalist gets rich to this: deduction from wages. The other funds of surplus-value which he refers to under headings (1) and (3) would then not exist.

In all countries therefore where the money wage of the workers is reduced to the value of the means of consumption necessary for their subsistence as a class, there does not exist either a consumption fund or an accumulation fund for the capitalists, and so no fund for the existence of the capitalist class, and no capitalist class at all. And this would certainly be the case, according to Destutt, in all rich and developed, long-civilized countries, for here, 'in our old-established societies, the fund from which wages are met . . . is almost a constant quantity' (p. 202).

Even given this deduction from wages, therefore, the capitalists are not enriched because they first pay the workers £100 in money and subsequently supply them with £80 worth of commodities for this £100 – i.e. in fact circulate £80 worth of commodities by means of a sum of money of £100, 25 per cent more than needed – but rather because they appropriate besides the surplus-value – the part of the product in which surplus-value is represented – a further 20 per cent* of that part of the workers' product that should fall to them in the form of wages. In Destutt's foolish conception, the capitalist class would not gain any profit at all. They pay £100 for wages, and in return for this £100 give the workers £80 worth of commodities from their own product. In the next operation, however, they must again advance £100 for the same procedure. Thus they achieve only the useless satisfaction of advancing £100 in money and supplying in return £80, instead of advancing £80 and supplying £80 worth of commodities for it. I.e. they constantly advance, to no avail, a money capital 25 per cent greater than is needed for the circulation of their variable capital. This would indeed be a quite peculiar method of enrichment.

3. Finally, the industrial capitalist class sells 'to the idle capitalists, who pay them with the part of their revenue that they have not already handled over to the workers directly employed by them, so that the entire rent that they pay these idle capitalists each year flows back to them again in one of these ways or another'.

We have already seen that the industrial capitalists pay 'with a part of their profits' for 'the whole of that part of their consumption which is destined to satisfy their own needs'.

Let us take it that their profits are £200. They consume £100, say, for

---

* Marx has '25 per cent' here. But the £20 worth of commodities of which the workers are supposedly cheated, in the example Marx sets up for Destutt, is of course 20 per cent of the £100 worth which the workers 'should' get, even though the extra £20 in money which allegedly enables the capitalists to sell the workers £80 worth of commodities for £100 is, as Marx says, 25 per cent more than needed.

their individual consumption. But the other half, a further £100, does not belong to them, but to the idle capitalists, i.e. the recipients of ground-rent and the capitalists who lend money at interest. They must therefore pay these people £100. Let us say that out of this money, the latter need £80 for their own consumption and £20 for the hire of servants, etc. They therefore buy means of consumption for £80 from the industrial capitalists. The latter thereby receive back, by parting with £80 worth of products, £80 in money, or four fifths of the £100 that they paid to the idle capitalists under the headings of rent, interest, etc. Moreover, the class of servants, the direct wage-labourers of the idle capitalists, has received £20 from its masters. It too uses this to buy means of consumption from the industrial capitalists, to the tune of £20. The latter thereby receive back £20 in money, while they have parted with £20 in products, and this is the last fifth of the £100 that they paid to the idle capitalists as rent, interest, etc.

At the close of the transaction, the industrial capitalists have received back the £100 in money that they remitted to the idle capitalists in payment of rent, interest, etc., while half of their surplus product, or £100, has been transferred from their hands into the consumption fund of the idle capitalists.

It is evidently entirely superfluous, therefore, for the question we are dealing with here, to bring in the division of the £100 between the idle capitalists and their immediate wage-labourers. The situation is quite simple: their rent and interest, in short the share of the surplus-value of £200 that accrues to them, is paid them by the industrial capitalists in money, £100. With this £100, they buy means of consumption directly or indirectly from the industrial capitalists. They therefore pay back to them £100 in money and take means of consumption in exchange for £100.

This is how the reflux of the £100 paid by the industrial capitalists to the idle capitalists has taken place. Is this reflux of money, as Destutt imagines, a means of enrichment for the industrial capitalists? Before the transaction, they had a sum of values of £200; £100 in money and £100 in means of consumption. After the transaction they have only half of the original sum of values. They again have £100 in money, but they have lost the £100 in means of consumption that has been transferred to the hands of the idle capitalists. They are therefore £100 poorer instead of £100 richer. If, instead of this detour of first paying £100 in money and then receiving this £100 back again in payment for £100 worth of means of consumption, they had directly paid rent, interest, etc. in the natural form of their product, then they would not receive any money back from the circulation sphere, as they would not have cast £100 of money into it. Payment in kind would have simply presented the matter in such a way that half the value of the surplus product of £200 was retained by the industrial capitalists themselves and the other half given away to the idle capitalists without an equivalent. Even Destutt would not have tried to present this as a means of enrichment.

The land and the capital that the industrial capitalists borrow from the idle capitalists, and for which they have to pay them a part of the surplus-value in the form of rent, interest, etc., is of course profitable for them, for it is one of the conditions of production, both of the product in general, and of the part of the product that forms surplus product or in which surplus-value is represented. But this profit derives from the use of the borrowed land and capital, and not from the price that is paid for this. This price is rather a deduction from it. It would otherwise be necessary to maintain that the industrial capitalists would become not richer, but poorer, if they could keep the other half of the surplus-value for themselves, instead of giving it away. But this is the confusion that we are led into if phenomena of circulation, such as the reflux of money, are lumped together with the distribution of the product that is simply mediated by these phenomena of circulation.

Despite all this, Destutt is still shrewd enough to note:

'Where do the revenues of these idle people come from? Do they not come from the rents that are paid to them out of the profit of those who make the idlers' capital work, i.e. those who use the funds of the former to pay a labour that produces more than it costs – in short, the industrialists? It is to these that one must always go, therefore, to find the source of all wealth. It is these who actually feed the wage-labourers employed by the others.'

The payment of these rents, etc. is now a deduction from the profit of the industrialists. Previously it was a means for them to get rich.

But our Destutt has one consolation left. These brave industrialists handle the idle capitalists just as they treat one another and the workers. They sell them all commodities too dear, e.g. 20 per cent too dear. Only two things are possible now. Either the idle capitalists have, besides the £100 that they annually receive from the industrialists, further monetary resources, or they do not. In the first case, the industrialists sell them commodities and values of £100 at a price, say, of £120. They receive back for the sale of their commodities not only the £100 that they paid the idlers, but also a further £20 that actually forms new value for them. How does the account now stand? They have given £100 worth of commodities away for nothing, for the £100 in money with which part of it was paid for was their own money. A loss of £100. But they have received, besides this, £20 as an addition to the price above its value. This profit of £20, together with the loss of £100, makes a loss of £80, which is still a loss and can never be a profit. The cheating practised towards the idle capitalists has reduced the industrialists' loss, but it has in no way transformed their loss into a means of enrichment. This method will not work in the long run, however, as the idle capitalists cannot pay out £120 each year if they receive only £100 in money.

The other method, therefore, is that the industrialists sell commodities worth only £80 for the £100 in money that the idle capitalists pay them. In this case, as before, they give £80 away for nothing, in the form of rents, interest, etc. By way of this cheating, they have reduced the tribute to the idle capitalists, but it still exists, and the idle capitalists are in a position – according to the same theory, in which prices depend on the good will of the sellers – to obtain £120 in future as rent, interest, etc. for their land and capital, instead of £100 as previously.

This striking development is completely worthy of the profound thinker who on the one hand copies from Adam Smith the phrase that 'labour is the source of all wealth', that the industrial capitalists 'employ their capital in order to pay labour that reproduces it with a profit' (p. 246), and on the other hand concludes that these industrial capitalists 'feed all the other people, alone increase the public wealth and create all our means of enjoyment' (p. 242), that it is not the capitalists who are fed by the workers, but the workers by the capitalists, and moreover for the brilliant reason that the money with which the workers are paid does not remain in their hands, but always returns to the capitalists in payment for the goods that the workers produced.

'They merely receive with one hand and give back with the other. Their consumption must therefore be seen as produced by those who pay them' (p. 253).

After this exhaustive presentation of social reproduction and consumption, mediated as it is by money circulation, Destutt continues:

'It is this that perfects the *perpetuum mobile* of wealth, a movement that, although badly understood,' (*mal connu* – indeed!) 'has rightly been called circulation; for it is in fact a circuit and always comes back to its point of departure. This is the point at which production is completed (pp. 239, 240).'

Destutt, that 'very distinguished writer', 'member of the Institut de France and the Philosophical Society of Philadelphia', and certainly a genuine luminary among vulgar economists, finally begs his readers to marvel at the wondrous clarity with which he depicts the course of the social process, the flood of light that he has shone on the object, and is even condescending enough to inform the reader where all this light emanates from. This must be read in the original:

'On remarquera, j'espère, combien cette manière de considérer la consommation de nos richesses est concordante avec tout ce que nous avons dit à propos de leur production et de leur distribution, et en même temps *quelle clarté elle repand sur toute la marche de la société*. D'où viennent cet accord et cette *lucidité*? De ce que nous avons rencontré la vérité. Cela rappelle l'effet de ces miroirs où les objets se peignent nettement et dans leur justes proportions, quand on est placé dans leur vrai point-de-vue, et où tout parait confus et désuni, quand on en est trop près ou trop loin' (pp. 242, 243).

Voilà le crétinisme bourgeois dans toute sa béatitude!*

* 'It will be remarked, I trust, how this manner of considering the consumption of our wealth is in harmony with everything that we have said on the subject of its production and distribution, and at the same time *what a clear light it casts on the whole course of society*. Where does this harmony and this *lucidity* come from? From the fact that we have encountered the truth. This recalls the effect of those mirrors in which objects are reflected accurately and in their true proportions when we place ourselves at their correct focal point, but where everything appears confused and disjointed when one is too close or too far away' (pp. 242–3). Here you have bourgeois cretinism in its ultimate state of bliss!

Chapter 21: Accumulation and Reproduction on an Expanded Scale[1]

We showed in Volume 1 how accumulation proceeds for the individual capitalist. The realization of his commodity capital also brings with it the realization of the surplus product in which his surplus-value is represented. The surplus-value that is transformed into money in this way is then transformed back by the capitalist into additional natural elements of his productive capital. In the next production circuit, the increased capital supplies an increased product. But what occurs in the case of an individual capital must also occur in the overall annual reproduction, just as we have seen that what in the case of the individual capital is the successive precipitation of its worn-out fixed components in money that is hoarded up, also finds its expression in the annual social reproduction.

If an individual capital is $400_c + 100_v$, and the year's surplus-value 100, then its commodity product is $400_c + 100_v + 100_s$. This 600 is transformed into money. Of this money, 400_c is converted back into the natural form of constant capital, 100_v into labour-power and – if the entire surplus-value is accumulated – the remaining 100_s transformed into additional constant capital by conversion into the natural elements of productive capital.* It is assumed here: (1) that this sum is sufficient under the given technical conditions, either for the extension of the constant capital already functioning, or for the installation of a new industrial business. It may be necessary, however, to transform surplus-value into money and hoard this money for a much longer time before this process takes place, i.e. before real accumulation, an expansion of production, can occur. (2) It is presupposed that there has in

1. From here to the end, Manuscript VIII.

* As Marx later postulates, the accumulation of capital must generally involve an increased outlay for variable capital as well as for constant. However, because 'on the basis of capitalist production, labour-power is always on hand' (p. 577), Marx 'leaves this out of consideration for the time being' (p. 575).

fact already been reproduction on an expanded scale, for in order to be able to transform the money (the surplus-value hoarded up in money) into elements of productive capital, these elements must be available on the market as commodities; and it makes no difference here if they are not bought as ready-made commodities, but are produced to order. They are paid for only when they are ready, and in any case only after real reproduction on an expanded scale, the extension of what was formerly normal production, has already taken place as far as they are concerned. They had to exist potentially, i.e. in their elements, since it only needed the impulse of the order, i.e. of a purchase of the commodities preceding their existence and their anticipated sale, for their production actually to take place. The money on one side calls into being expanded reproduction on the other only because the possibility of this already exists *without* the money; for money in itself is not an element of real reproduction.

If capitalist A, for example, sells the quantities of commodity product that he successfully produced in the course of a year or a number of years, then he thereby successively transforms that part of his commodity product that is the bearer of surplus-value – the surplus product – i.e. the surplus-value that he produced in the commodity form, into money, stores this away bit by bit, and in this way forms for himself potential new money capital; potential on account of its capacity and its destiny, which is to be converted into elements of productive capital. In fact, however, he only performs simple hoard formation, which is not an element of real reproduction. His activity in this connection consists first of all simply in the successive withdrawal of circulating money from the circulation sphere, and it is of course not excluded here that the circulating money that he puts under lock and key was itself – before its entry into circulation – part of another hoard. This hoard of A's, which is potentially new money capital, is not an addition to the social wealth any more than if it had been spent on means of consumption. Money that is withdrawn from currency, and which therefore was previously in the circulation sphere, may before that have either been already stored up once as a similar hoard, may have been the money form of wages, may have realized means of production or other commodities, or may have circulated constant capital components or revenue for some capitalist or other. It is no more new wealth than money considered from the standpoint of simple commodity circulation is the bearer, not just of its actual value, but of ten times its value, simply because it has turned over ten times in a day, and realized ten different commodity values. The commodities still exist without it, and it remains the same (or even becomes less by wear and tear) in one turnover or in ten. Only in gold production – in so far as the gold product contains or is a bearer of surplus-value – is new wealth (potential money) created, and it is only to the extent that the whole of the new gold product steps into circulation that it increases the money material for potential new money capitals.

But even though it is not additional new social wealth, this surplus-value hoarded up in the money form does represent new potential money capital, on account of the function for which it is stored. (We shall see later that new money capital can also arise by another path than that of the gradual realization of surplus-value.)

Money is withdrawn from circulation and stored up as a hoard by the sale of commodities without subsequent purchase. If this operation is conceived as taking place on all sides, it seems impossible to explain where the buyers are to come from, since in this process – and it must be conceived as a general one, in as much as every individual capital may be simultaneously engaged in the act of accumulation – everyone wants to sell in order to hoard, and no one wants to buy.

If the circulation process between the various parts of the annual reproduction were conceived as rectilinear – which would be incorrect, since, with few exceptions, it always consists of mutually opposing movements – then we would have to begin with the gold (or silver) producer, who buys without selling, and assume that all others sell to him. The total annual social surplus product (which is the repository of the entire surplus-value) would therefore be transferred to him, and all the other capitalists would divide up his surplus product among themselves in due proportion in its natural gold form, the realization in kind of his surplus-value; for the part of the gold producer's product that has to replace his functioning capital is already tied up and disposed of. The surplus-value of the gold producer, produced in gold, would then be the only fund from which all the other capitalists drew the material with which to realize their annual surplus product. It would thus have to be equal in value to the entire annual surplus-value of the society, which first has to be transmogrified into the form of a hoard. These assumptions are so absurd that they are only helpful towards explaining the possibility of a general simultaneous hoard formation, and do not take reproduction itself, except that of the gold producers, a single step forwards.

Before we clear up this apparent difficulty, we have to distinguish between accumulation in department I (production of means of production) and accumulation in department II (production of means of consumption). We start with department I.

I. ACCUMULATION IN DEPARTMENT I

(a) Hoard Formation

It is evident that both capital investment in the several branches of industry that department I consists of, and the various individual capital investments within each of these branches of industry, are to be found at different stages in the process of their successive transformation of surplus-value into potential money capital. This holds whether this money capital is to serve for the expansion of the functioning capital or for the installation of new industrial businesses – the two forms of expansion of production. One section of capitalists, therefore, at any given time, is transforming its potential money capital, which has grown to an appropriate size, into productive capital, i.e. using the money it has hoarded up by the realization of surplus-value to buy means of production, additional elements of constant capital; while another section is still occupied with hoarding up its potential money capital. Capitalists belonging to these two categories thus relate to one another as buyers and sellers respectively, and each of the two in this exclusive role.

Let A sell 600 ($=400_c+100_v+100_s$) to B (who may represent more than one buyer). He has sold commodities for 600 in exchange for 600 in money, of which 100 represents surplus-value that he withdraws from circulation and hoards up; this 100, however, is only the money form of a surplus product that was the bearer of a value of 100. Hoard formation is in no case production, and thus from the start not an increment to production. The action of the capitalist here consists in simply withdrawing from circulation the money he obtained by selling his surplus product, holding on to it and impounding it. This operation is not just performed by A, but at numerous points on the circulation surface by other capitalists A', A'', A''' etc., who all work equally zealously at this kind of hoard formation. These several points at which money is withdrawn from circulation and accumulated in individual hoards or potential money capitals appear as an equal number of obstacles to circulation, because they immobilize the money and deprive it of its capacity for circulation for a longer or shorter time. It must be borne in mind, however, that with simple commodity circulation, long before this is founded on capitalist commodity production, there is already hoard formation; the quantity of money present in the society is always greater than the part of this that is in active circulation, even if the latter rises and falls according to circumstances. It is the same hoards and the same hoard formation that are found with capitalist production too, but now as an immanent moment of the capitalist production process.

It is easy to understand the satisfaction evinced when the credit system concentrates all these potential capitals in the hands of banks, etc., makes them into disposable capital – 'loanable capital' – i.e. money capital, no longer passive and, as it were, a castle in the air, but active, usurious, proliferating capital.

However *A* can bring about this hoard formation only in so far as he appears – as far as his surplus product goes – simply as a seller, and not also subsequently as a buyer. The precondition for his hoard formation is thus his successive production of surplus product – the repository of his surplus-value that is to be realized. In the given case, where we are considering only circulation within department 1, the natural form of the surplus product, like that of the whole product of which it forms part, is the natural form of an element of constant capital in department I, i.e. it belongs to the category of means of production of means of production. What becomes of this, i.e. what function it serves in the hands of the buyers *B*, *B'*, *B''*, etc., we shall soon see.

What has first to be established is this. Even though *A* withdraws money from circulation for his surplus-value, and hoards it, he casts commodities into circulation, on the other hand, without withdrawing other commodities for these; this enables *B*, *B'*, *B''*, etc. for their part simply to cast money into circulation and withdraw commodities. In the present case, these commodities are suited by their natural form to enter the constant capital of *B*, *B'*, etc. as a fixed or fluid element, and are in fact destined to this end. We shall have more to say on this as soon as we have finished with the buyers of the surplus product, *B*, *B'*, etc.

*

We must note here in passing that, just as previously when we were considering simple reproduction, so we find here again that the reconversion of the various components of the annual product, i.e. their circulation (which must also include the reproduction of capital, and moreover its restoration in its different determinations, as constant, variable, fixed, circulating, money or commodity capital), in no way presupposes simply the purchase of commodities supplemented by a subsequent sale, or a sale supplemented by a subsequent purchase, so that there would just be a simple exchange of one commodity for another, as the free trade school have assumed from the Physiocrats and Adam Smith onwards. We know that the fixed capital, once the outlay on it has been made, is not renewed for the whole of the period during which it functions, but continues to operate in its old form, while its value is gradually precipitated out in money. We see now that the periodic renewal of the fixed capital portion of II_c (the entire capital value II_c being exchanged for elements to the value of $I_{(v+s)}$), presupposes on the one hand a *one-sided purchase* of that fixed part of II_c which is transformed back from the money form into the natural form and to which corresponds a one-sided sale of I_s; on the other hand it presupposes a *one-sided sale* on the part of II_c, the sale of that fixed value component (wear and tear) which is precipitated out in money and to which corresponds a one-sided purchase of I_s. In order that the exchange should take place normally, it has to be assumed that the one-sided purchase by II_c is equal in value to its one-sided sale, and similarly that the one-sided sale of I_s to II_c, section 1, is equal to its one-sided purchase from II_c, section 2 (p. 540). Otherwise, simple reproduction would be disrupted; the one-sided purchase at one point must be covered by a one-sided sale at another. It has similarly to be assumed in the present case that the one-sided sales by the hoard-forming section of I_s, A, A', A'', balance the one-sided purchases by section B, B', B'' of I_s, which transform their hoards into elements of additional productive capital.

To the extent that the balance is restored by the fact that the buyer subsequently appears as a seller, and vice versa, to the full amount of value involved, there is a reflux of money to the side that advanced it for the purchase, that which first sold before purchasing again. The real balance, however, as far as the actual commodity exchange is concerned, i.e. the reconversion of the various parts of the annual product, requires that equal values of commodities are reciprocally exchanged.

In as much as one-sided conversions take place, a number of mere purchases on the one hand, and isolated sales on the other – and as we have seen, the normal exchange of the annual product on the capitalist basis requires these one-sided metamorphoses – this balance exists only on the assumption that the values of the one-sided purchases and the one-sided sales cover each other. The fact that the production of commodities is the general form of capitalist production already implies that money plays a role, not just as means of circulation, but also as money capital within the circulation sphere, and gives rise to certain conditions for normal exchange that are peculiar to this mode of production, i.e. conditions for the normal course of reproduction, whether simple or on an expanded scale, which turn into an equal number of conditions for an abnormal course, possibilities of crisis, since, on the basis of the spontaneous pattern of this production, this balance is itself an accident.

We have seen, similarly, that in the exchange of I_v for a corresponding value of II_c, commodities II are ultimately replaced for II_c by the same value of commodities I, and therefore that on the part of collective capitalist II, a sale of his own commodity is subsequently supplemented by a purchase of commodities I to the same amount. This replacement actually does take place; but in this mutual conversion of their reciprocal commodities, there is no direct exchange between capitalists I and II. Capitalist II sells his commodities II_c to the working class of department I, which faces him one-sidedly as a buyer of commodities, with him facing it similarly as simply a seller of commodities; with the money received for these, II_c one-sidedly faces the collective capitalist I as a buyer of commodities, and the latter faces him one-sidedly in turn as a seller of commodities to the value of I_v. It is only by this sale of commodities that department I finally reproduces its variable capital in the form of money capital. If department I's capital one-sidedly faces that of department II as a seller of commodities to the amount of I_v, similarly it faces the department I working class as a buyer of commodities with the purchase of its labour-power; the department I working class one-sidedly faces the capitalists in class II as a buyer of commodities (i.e. as a buyer of means of subsistence), and it faces the capitalists in department I one-sidedly as a seller of commodities, i.e. as a seller of its labour-power.

The continuous supply of labour-power on the part of the working class in department I, the transformation of one part of department I's commodity capital back into the money form of variable capital, the replacement of a part of department II's commodity capital by natural elements of constant capital II_c – these necessary preconditions all mutually require one another, but they are mediated by a very complicated process which involves three processes of circulation that proceed independently, even if they are intertwined with one another. The very complexity of the process provides many occasions for it to take an abnormal course.

(b) *The Additional Constant Capital*

The surplus product, the repository of surplus-value, does not cost anything to its appropriators, here the capitalists in department I. They do not have to advance either money or commodities, in any form, in order to receive it. The advance (*avance*) already meant for the Physiocrats simply the general form of value realized in the elements of productive capital. What the capitalists advance, therefore, is nothing more than their constant and variable capital. The worker does not merely maintain their constant capital for them by way of his labour, and replace their variable capital by way of a corresponding portion of value newly created in the form of commodities; he also supplies them, by his surplus labour, with a surplus-value existing in the form of a surplus product. By their subsequent sale of this surplus product, the capitalists form their hoard, additional potential money capital. In the case considered here, this surplus product consists from the start of means of production of means of production. It is only in the hands of B, B', B'', etc. (department I) that this surplus product functions as additional constant capital; but it is already virtually this, even before it is sold, in the hands of the hoard formers A, A', A'' (department I). If we simply consider the level of reproduction on the part of department I in value terms, then we still find ourselves within the limits of simple reproduction, for no additional capital has been set in motion in order to create this virtual excess of constant capital (the surplus product), and no more surplus labour than was performed on the basis of simple reproduction. The distinction here lies only in the form of the surplus labour applied, the concrete character of its particular useful mode. It has been spent on means of production for I_c instead of II_c, on means of production for means of production instead of on means of production for means of consumption. In the case of simple reproduction, it was assumed that the whole of the surplus-value in department I was spent as revenue, i.e. on commodities from department II; it consisted only of those means of production needed to replace the constant capital II_c in its natural form. Thus in order to make the transition from simple reproduction to expanded reproduction, production in department I must be in a position to produce fewer elements of constant capital for department II, but all the more for department I. This transition, which can never be achieved without difficulty, is made easier by the fact that a number of the products of department I can serve as means of production in both departments.

It follows therefore that – simply considering the values involved – the material substratum for expanded reproduction is produced in the course of simple reproduction. It is simply the surplus labour of the working class in department I that is spent directly in the production of means of production, in the creation of virtual extra capital in department I. The formation of virtual additional money capital on the part of A, A', A'' (department I) – by the subsequent sale of their surplus product, which has been formed without any monetary expenditure by the capitalists involved – is thus here simply the money form of extra production of means of production in department I.

Thus the production of virtual additional capital in the present case (for, as we shall see, it can be formed quite differently) expresses nothing but a phenomenon of the production process itself, the production, in a particular form, of elements of productive capital.

The large-scale production of additional virtual money capital – at numerous points on the surface of circulation – is therefore nothing more than the result and expression of the many-sided production of virtual additional productive capital, whose genesis does not itself presuppose any additional monetary expenditure on the part of the industrial capitalists.

The successive transformation of this virtual additional productive capital into virtual money capital (a hoard) on the part of A, A', A'', etc. (department I), which is conditioned by the successive sale of their surplus product – i.e. by the repeated one-sided sale of commodities without a complementary purchase – results in the repeated withdrawal of money from circulation and a corresponding hoard formation. This hoard formation – except in the case where the buyer is a gold producer – in no way implies additional wealth in precious metals, but only a different function for the money that was already in circulation previously. It formerly functioned as a means of circulation, and now it functions as a hoard, as virtual new money capital in the course of formation. The formation of additional money capital and the quantity of precious metal existing in a country thus do not stand in any causal connection with one another.

It also follows from this that the greater the productive capital already functioning in a country (including the labour-power incorporated into it, the creator of the surplus product), and the more developed the productive power of labour and so also the technical means of rapid expansion of the production of means of production – the greater, accordingly, the mass of surplus product, both in value terms and in the quantity of use-values in which it is represented – the greater, then, is:

(1) the additional virtual productive capital in the form of surplus product in the hands of A, A', A'', etc., and

(2) the quantity of this surplus product transformed into money, i.e. the quantity of the additional virtual money capital in the hands of A, A', A''. Thus if Fullarton,* for instance, does not want to recognize over-production in the customary sense, but does recognize the over-production of capital, in particular of money capital, this proves once again how utterly unable even the best bourgeois economists are to understand the mechanism of their system.

If the surplus product directly produced and appropriated by the capitalists A, A', A'' (department I) is the real basis for capital accumulation, i.e. for expanded reproduction, even though it actually functions in this capacity only in the hands of B, B', B'', etc. (department I), it is however absolutely unproductive in its monetary metamorphosis – as a hoard and as virtual money capital that is formed bit by bit. In this form it runs parallel with the production process but lies outside it. It is a 'dead weight' on capitalist production. The attempt to make use of this surplus-value that is being hoarded up as virtual money capital, either for profit or for revenue, culminates in the credit system and 'papers'. In this way money capital maintains an enormous influence in another form on the course of the capitalist system of production and its prodigious development.

The surplus product converted into virtual money capital becomes quantitatively greater, the greater the total sum of capital already functioning, from the functioning of which it emerged. This absolute increase in the virtual money capital annually reproduced, however, also makes its segmentation more easy to achieve, so that it can be invested more quickly in a particular business, whether in the hands of the same capitalist, or in others (e.g. members of the family, with inheritances, etc.). By segmentation of money capital we mean here that it is completely separated from its parent capital, in order to be invested as new money capital in an independent business.

If the sellers of the surplus product, A, A', A'', etc. (department I) themselves received this as the direct outcome of the production process, which, apart from the advance in constant and variable capital that is required even in the case of simple reproduction, does not presuppose any further act of circulation if it is also to supply the real

*John Fullarton, an English opponent of the quantity theory of money.

basis for reproduction on an expanded scale, in actual fact to create virtual additional capital, it is different for B, B', B'', etc. (department I). (1) It is only in their hands that the surplus product of A, A', A'', etc. actually functions as additional constant capital (the other element of the productive capital, the additional labour-power, i.e. the additional variable capital, we leave out of consideration for the time being). (2) In order for it to come into their hands, an act of circulation is required; they have to buy the surplus product.

On point (1), it must be noted here that a major part of the surplus product (additional virtual constant capital) produced by A, A', A'' (department I), even though it is produced in the current year, can actually function only in the hands of B, B', B'' (department I) as industrial capital in the following year or even later; on point (2), the question arises as to the origin of the money needed for this circulation process.

In so far as the products that B, B', B'', etc. (department I) produce go back again into their production process in kind, it is self-evident that a part of their own surplus product is proportionately transferred directly into their productive capital, and functions here as an extra element of constant capital. To this extent, however, these cannot realize the surplus product of A, A', etc. (department I). But in other cases, where does the money come from? We know that B, B', B'', etc. have formed their hoards just like A, A', A'', etc. by the sale of their respective surplus products, and have now reached the point at which their money capital, which is simply virtual money capital accumulated as a hoard, is supposed to function effectively as additional money capital. But now we are going round in circles. There is still the question as to the origin of the money that the B's (department I) have earlier withdrawn from circulation and accumulated.

We already know, however, from considering simple reproduction, that a certain quantity of money must exist in the hands of the capitalists in departments I and II so that they may exchange their surplus product. There the money whose only use was to be spent as revenue on means of consumption returns to the capitalists to the extent that they advanced it for the exchange of their respective commodities; here the same money similarly reappears, but with its function changed. The A's and B's (department I) supply one another with the money for transforming their surplus products into additional virtual money capital, and alternately cast the newly formed money capital into the circulation sphere as a means of purchase.

The only thing that is presupposed here is that the quantity of money existing in the country (the velocity of circulation etc. taken as constant) is sufficient both for active circulation and for the reserve hoards – i.e. the same condition that, as we already saw previously, has to be fulfilled for simple commodity circulation. It is just that the function of the hoards is different here. The quantity of money present must also be larger, (1) because, in the case of capitalist production, all products (with the exception of newly produced precious metal and the few products used by their own producers) are produced as commodities, and must therefore undergo a metamorphosis into money; (2) because the mass of commodity capital and its value is not only absolutely greater on the capitalist basis, but grows with incomparably greater speed; (3) because the variable capital that has to be converted into money capital is ever more extensive; and (4) because, as production expands, the formation of new money capital keeps in step with this expansion, and so the material for its hoarded form has also to be present. If this is true absolutely for the early phase of capitalist production, where the credit system is accompanied by a predominantly metallic circulation, it is just as true, too, for the most developed phase of the credit system, which still has metallic circulation as its basis. On the one hand, the extra production of precious metals, according to whether this makes them abundant or scarce, can now exert a disturbing influence on the price of commodities, not only in the long term, but also within very short periods; on the other hand, the whole credit mechanism must constantly be engaged in restricting the actual circulation of metal by all kinds of operations, methods, technical devices, to what is relatively an ever decreasing minimum – though this also increases in the same proportion the artificial character of the entire machinery and the chances of its normal course being disturbed.

The various *B*'s (department I) whose virtual new money capital comes into active operation may reciprocally buy their products (parts of their surplus product) from one another, and sell to one another. To this extent, the money advanced for the circulation of the surplus product flows back to the different *B*'s – in the normal course of events – in the same measure to which they advanced this for the circulation of their respective commodities. If the money circulates as a means of payment, then there are only balances to be settled, in so far as the reciprocal sales and purchases do not cover one another. It is important above all, however, to start by assuming metal circulation in its most simple original form, since in this way the flux or reflux, settlement of balances, in short all those aspects that appear in the credit system as consciously regulated processes, present themselves as existing independently of the credit system, and the thing appears in its spontaneous form, instead of the form of subsequent reflection.

(c) The Additional Variable Capital

Since we have so far dealt only with the additional constant capital, we now have to turn to consider the additional variable capital.

In Volume 1, we explained at considerable length how, on the basis of capitalist production, labour-power is always on hand, and how, if necessary, more labour can be extracted without an increase in the number of workers employed, or the mass of labour-power. We do not have to go into this any further here, therefore, but can simply assume that the portion of the newly formed money capital that is convertible into variable capital always finds available the labour-power into which it is to be transformed. We also considered in Volume 1 how a given capital can within certain limits expand its scale of production without accumulation. What we are dealing with now, however, is capital accumulation in the specific sense, where the expansion of production is conditioned by the transformation of surplus-value into extra capital, and therefore by the expanded capital basis of production.

The gold producer can accumulate a part of his golden surplus-value as virtual money capital; once it attains the level needed, he can convert it directly into new variable capital, and in the same way convert it into elements of constant capital. In the latter case, however, he must find these material elements of his constant capital available; whether, as was assumed in the former presentation, each producer works to fill his stocks and then brings his finished commodities to the market, or whether he simply works to order. The real expansion of production, i.e. the surplus product, is presupposed in both cases, once as actually present, the other time as virtually present, capable of being supplied.

2. ACCUMULATION IN DEPARTMENT II

We have assumed up to now that A, A', A'' (department I) sell their surplus products to B, B', B'', etc. who belong to the same department I. Say however that A (department I) converts his surplus product into money by selling it to a B belonging to department II. This can only happen if A (I), after he has sold means of production to B (II), does not go on to buy means of consumption; i.e. only by a unilateral sale on his part. Now in as much as the conversion of II_c from the form of commodity capital back into the natural form of productive constant capital involves not only the exchange of I_v, but also of at least a part of I_s for part of II_c, this II_c existing in the form of means of consumption – whereas A now realizes his I_s in money in a way that does not involve this exchange, but our A instead withdraws from circulation the money received from department II by the sale of his I_s, rather than exchanging it in the purchase of means of consumption II_c – then although the formation of additional virtual money capital takes place on A's part, on the other side an equal part of B (II)'s constant capital is tied up in the form of commodity capital, incapable of conversion into the natural form of productive, constant capital. In other words, a part of B (II)'s commodities, and at first sight a part without selling which he cannot transform his constant capital completely back into the productive form, has become unsaleable; in this respect there is overproduction, which also inhibits B (II)'s reproduction – even on the same scale.

In this case, therefore, although the additional virtual money capital on the part of A (I) is the realized form of surplus product (surplus-value), surplus product (surplus-value) considered as such is here a phenomenon of simple reproduction, and not yet of reproduction on an expanded scale. $I_{(v+s)}$, at least a part of s being included here, must ultimately be exchanged against II_c, so that the reproduction of II_c can proceed on the same scale. A (I), by selling its surplus product to B (II), has supplied the latter with a corresponding portion of constant capital in the natural form, but at the same time made an equal portion of B(II)'s commodity value unsaleable. If we bear in mind the total social reproduction – which includes both capitalists I and II – then the transformation of A(I)'s surplus product into virtual money capital expresses the non-transformability of a portion of commodity capital equal to this in value back into productive (constant) capital; i.e. not virtual production on an expanded scale, but rather a restriction of simple reproduction, i.e. a shortfall in simple reproduction. Since the formation and sale of A(I)'s surplus product are themselves normal phenomena of simple reproduction, we have here, even on the basis of simple reproduction, the following mutually conditioning phenomena: formation of virtual extra money capital in department I (hence under-consumption from department II's standpoint); piling up of commodity stocks in department II which cannot be transformed back into productive capital (i.e. relative over-production in department I I); surplus money capital in department I and a shortfall in reproduction in department I I.

Without delaying any longer on this point, we simply note that it was presupposed in our presentation of simple reproduction that the entire surplus-value in departments I and II was spent as revenue. In point of fact, however, one portion of surplus-value is spent as revenue, and another portion transformed into capital. Only with this precondition does real accumulation take place. But the idea that accumulation is achieved at the expense of consumption – considered in this general way – is an illusion that contradicts the essence of capitalist production, in as much as it assumes that the purpose and driving motive of this is consumption, and not the grabbing of surplus-value and its capitalization, i.e. accumulation.

*

Let us now consider accumulation in department II somewhat more closely.

The first problem in relation to II_c, i.e. its transformation back from a component of commodity capital II into the natural form of department II's constant capital, concerns simple reproduction. Let us take the previous schema:

$(1,000_v + 1,000_s)I$ is exchanged for
$2,000 II_c$.

If half the surplus product of department I, i.e. $\dfrac{1,000}{2}s$ or $500 I_s$ is now reincorporated into department I as constant capital, then this part of the surplus product that is retained in department I cannot replace any part of II_c. Instead of being converted into means of consumption (and in this section of the circulation between departments I and II there is genuine mutual exchange, i.e. a bilateral change of place by the commodities, as distinct from the replacement of $1,000 II_c$ by $1,000 I_v$ which was mediated by the workers in department I), it is to serve as additional means of production in department I itself. It cannot perform this function simultaneously in both department I and department II. The capitalist cannot spend the value of his surplus product on means of consumption, and at the same time himself productively consume the surplus product, i.e. incorporate it into his productive capital. Thus instead of $2,000 I_{(v+s)}$, only 1,500, i.e. $(1,000_v + 500_s)$ I is available for conversion into $2,000 II_c$; and so $500 II_c$ can in fact not be transformed from its commodity form into productive (constant) capital II. There would thus be an overproduction in department II, corresponding in value precisely to the expansion of production that took place in department I. The over-production in department II might in fact react so strongly on department I that even the reflux of the 1,000 spent by the department I workers on means of consumption II would take place only partially, so that this 1,000 would not return to the hands of the department I capitalists in the form of variable money capital. The latter would thus be inhibited even in their reproduction on the same scale, and inhibited, moreover, by the very attempt to expand it. It should also be mentioned in this connection that all that has taken place in department I is in fact simple reproduction, the elements merely being grouped together differently from the above schema, in accordance with the needs of future expansion, say in the coming year.

One might endeavour to circumvent this difficulty in the following way. The 500 II_c lying in the capitalists' stores, which cannot be directly converted into productive capital, is so far removed from being over-production that it actually represents a necessary element of reproduction which we have up to now neglected. We saw how the piling up of money takes place at several points, so that money has to be withdrawn from circulation, partly to make possible the formation of new money capital in department I itself, partly to maintain the value of the fixed capital that is gradually being consumed, for the time being, in the money form. But since in this schema all money and all commodities are from the start exclusively in the hands of the capitalists I and II, and there are neither merchants nor money-dealers involved, nor bankers nor any classes that merely consume and are not directly involved in commodity production, it follows that the constant formation of commodity stocks is indispensable, in the hands of their respective producers themselves, in order to keep the machinery of reproduction going. The 500 II_c lying in the stores of the department II capitalists thus represents the commodity stock in means of consumption that ensures the continuity of the consumption process involved in reproduction, and therefore the transition from one year to the other. The consumption fund that is here still in the hands of its sellers, who are also its producers, cannot sink to nothing in the current year, to begin again from nothing the next year, any more than this can be the case in the passage from one day to the next. Since there must be a constant new formation of these commodity stocks, even if they change in extent, our capitalist producers in department II must have a money reserve capital that enables them to continue their production process even though one part of their productive capital is temporarily tied up in the commodity form. Our assumption is that these capitalists combine the whole business of trading with that of producing. They must therefore also have at their disposal the additional money capital which exists in the hands of the merchants once the individual functions of the reproduction process are made the independent functions of different sorts of capitalist.

(1) The objection could be made that this stock formation and the need for it holds for all capitalists, in both departments. Considered simply as sellers of commodities, these are distinguished only by the different kinds of commodities they sell. A stock of commodities in department II implies a previous stock of commodities in department I. If we ignore this stock on one side, we must also ignore it on the other. But if we bring both sides into consideration, the problem is in no way changed. (2) Just as the current year concludes on the side of department II with a commodity stock for the next, so it began with a commodity stock on the same side left over from the previous year. In analysing the annual reproduction – reduced to its most abstract expression – we must thus cancel out the stock on both sides. If we leave the year in question with the whole of its production, and thus also that which it transfers as a commodity stock to the next year, we must deduct from this on the other side the commodity stock that it receives from the year before, and we thus have the total product of an average year as the object of our analysis. (3) The simple fact that we did not come up against the difficulty that has now to be overcome in considering simple reproduction shows that we are dealing here with a specific phenomenon that is due merely to the different arrangement of the elements of department I (as far as reproduction is concerned), an arrangement without which there could be no reproduction on an expanded scale at all.

3. SCHEMATIC PRESENTATION OF ACCUMULATION

We shall now consider reproduction according to the following schema:

Schema (a):
$$\left. \begin{array}{ll} \text{I.} & 4{,}000_c + 1{,}000_v + 1{,}000_s = 6{,}000 \\ \text{II.} & 1{,}500_c + 376_v + 376_s = 2{,}252 \end{array} \right\} \text{Total} = 8{,}252.$$

It will be seen immediately that the total sum of the annual social product, 8,252, is smaller than in our original schema, where it was 9,000.

We might just as well take a much larger sum, multiply it by ten, say, for all the difference it makes. The reason why a smaller sum has been chosen than in the earlier schema is precisely to draw attention to the fact that reproduction on an expanded scale (which is conceived here simply as production pursued with a greater investment of capital) has nothing to do with the absolute size of the product, that for a given volume of commodities it simply assumes a different arrangement or a different determination of the functions of the various elements of the given product, and is thus in the first instance only simple reproduction, as far as its value goes. It is not the quantity, but the qualitative character of the given elements of simple reproduction that is changed, and this change is the material precondition for the ensuing reproduction on an expanded scale.[2]

We could alternatively take a different schema, with different proportions between variable and constant capital, as for example:

$$\text{Schema }(b)\text{:} \quad \left.\begin{array}{l} \text{I. } 4,000_c + 875_v + 875_s = 5,750 \\ \text{II. } 1,750_c + 376_v + 376_s = 2,502 \end{array}\right\} \text{Total} = 8,252.$$

In this way it would be arranged for reproduction on the same scale, with the surplus-value being spent completely as revenue and not accumulated. In both case (a) and case (b) we have an annual product of the same value, simply that in case (b) there is a functional arrangement of its elements such that reproduction begins again on the same scale, whereas in case (a) this forms the material basis for reproduction on an expanded scale. In case (b), in particular, $(875_v + 875_s)\text{I} = 1,750 \text{ I}_{(v+s)}$ is exchanged without a surplus for 1,750 II$_c$, while in case (a) $(1,000_c + 1,000_s)\text{I} = 2,000 \text{ I}_{(v+s)}$ leaves behind, when exchanged for 1,500 II$_c$, a surplus of 500 I$_s$ for accumulation in department I.

We must now analyse schema (a) more closely. Let us suppose that both in department I and department II half the surplus-value, instead of being spent as revenue, is accumulated, i.e. is transformed into elements of additional capital. Since half of 1,000 I$_s$ = 500 is accumulated in one form or another, to be invested as additional money capital, i.e. to be transformed into extra productive capital, it follows that only $(1,000_v + 500_s)\text{I}$ is spent as revenue. Hence the normal size of II$_c$ is now only 1,500. The exchange between 1,500 I$_{(v+s)}$ and 1,500 II$_c$ needs

2. This puts an end once and for all to the conflict over the accumulation of capital between James Mill and S. Bailey, which we discussed from a different angle in Volume 1 (Chapter 24, 5, p. 759, note 52), i.e. the dispute over whether it is possible to extend the operation of an industrial capital without any alteration in its size. We shall come back to this later.

no further investigation, since it has already been presented as a process of simple reproduction; just as little does the 4,000 I_c come into consideration, since its rearrangement for the reproduction newly beginning (which takes place this time on an expanded scale) was similarly explained as a process of simple reproduction.

All that remains to be investigated here, therefore, are the 500 I_s and $(376_v + 376_s)$II, which involves both the internal relations in the two departments and the movement between them. Since it is assumed that in department II, also, half of the surplus-value is to be accumulated, it follows that 188 has here to be transformed into capital, one quarter of this or 47 into variable capital, say 48 for the sake of a round number, leaving 140 to be transformed into constant capital.

Here we come up against a new problem, the very existence of which must appear remarkable for the current view that commodities of one kind are customarily exchanged for commodities of another kind, ditto commodities for money and the same money once again for commodities of a different kind. The 140 II_s can be transformed into productive capital only by being replaced by a portion of commodities I_s to the same value. It is self-evident that the part of the I_s that is to be exchanged for II_s must consist of means of production, able to go either into the production of both departments, or exclusively into that of department II. This exchange can take place only by a unilateral purchase on the part of department II, since the surplus product 500 I_s, which has still to be considered, is destined to serve for accumulation within department I, and cannot therefore be exchanged for commodities II. In other words, department I cannot at the same time both accumulate and consume the surplus product. Department II must therefore buy 140$_s$ for cash, without this money flowing back to it by the subsequent sale of its commodities to department I. And this is moreover a constant and repeated process for each new year's production, in so far as this is reproduction on an expanded scale. Where then in department II is the source of money for this?

Department II seems, on the contrary, a completely unprofitable field for the formation of new money capital that accompanies actual accumulation and is a necessary condition for this in the case of capitalist production, where this accumulation actually presents itself at first as mere hoarding.

We have, to start with, 376 II_v; the money capital of 376, advanced for labour-power, constantly returns to the department II capitalists as variable capital in the money form, with the purchase of department

II's commodities. This constantly repeated removal from and return to the starting-point – the capitalist's pocket – in no way increases the amount of money driving round this circuit. So this is not a source of monetary accumulation; nor can this money be withdrawn from this circulation and hoarded up to form virtual new money capital.

But wait a minute! Isn't there a little profit to be made here?

We must not forget that department II has the advantage over department I that the workers it employs have to buy back again from it the commodities they have themselves produced. Department II is not only a buyer of labour-power but at the same time a seller of commodities to the possessors of labour-power it employs. Department II, therefore, can:

(1) (and it has this in common with the capitalists in department I) simply reduce wages below their normal average level. In this way, a part of the money that functions as the money form of variable capital is set free, and this could, if the process is constantly repeated, become a normal source of hoard formation, and also therefore of the formation of virtual extra money capital in department II. Of course we are not referring here to an occasional swindle, but rather to a normal process of capital formation. It should not be forgotten, however, that the normal wage which is actually paid (and which determines the size of the variable capital, other things being equal) is in no way paid out of the good will of the capitalists, but is what has to be paid under the given conditions. This mode of explanation is thereby dispensed with. If we take 376_v as the variable capital to be spent by department II, we cannot suddenly insert the hypothesis that department II advances only 350_v and not 376_v, simply in order to solve the new problem that has just arisen.

(2) On the other hand, however, department II, considered as a totality, has the advantage over department I, as we already said, that it not only buys labour-power but resells its commodities to its own workers. As to how this fact can be exploited, there are the most palpable data in every industrial country. Even if the normal wage is nominally paid, a part of it can in actual fact be grabbed back without a corresponding equivalent, in other words stolen; this is achieved partly by way of the truck system, and partly by falsification of the circulating medium (even if possibly in a way that circumvents the law). This is what happens in England and the USA, for example. (The opportunity should be taken to expand on this somewhat with a few nice examples.) However this is the same operation as that in case (1),

only disguised and executed in a devious way. It must therefore be rejected here just like the previous case. What we are talking about here is the real wage, not that nominally paid.

We see here that in an objective analysis of the capitalist mechanism, certain blemishes that still stick to it, and with extraordinary tenacity, cannot be used as subterfuges for getting round theoretical difficulties. But strange though this seems, the great majority of my bourgeois critics complain that I do the capitalist an injustice by assuming – in Volume 1 of *Capital*, for example – that he pays the real value of labour-power, which in most cases he does not! (Here I might quote Schäffle*, with the magnanimity he attributes to me.)

The 376 II_v, therefore, does not get us any nearer the goal we have mentioned.

However, the 376 II_s seems to stand in an even more dubious position. Here it is only capitalists in the same department who confront one another, selling and buying from each other the means of consumption that they have produced. The money needed for this exchange functions simply as a means of circulation, and in the normal course it must flow back to the parties involved in the same degree to which they first advanced it to circulation, so it can tread the same path once again.

The withdrawal of this money from circulation for the formation of virtual additional money capital seems possible only in two ways. Firstly, one section of capitalists in department II might swindle the others and rob them of their money. As we know, no preliminary expansion of the medium in circulation is necessary for the formation of new money capital; all that is needed is for money to be withdrawn at certain points and stored up as a hoard. The fact that the money can be stolen and that the formation of additional money capital by one section of the capitalists in department II can therefore be combined with a positive loss of money by another section has absolutely no bearing on the matter. T' e defrauded section of department II capitalists would have to live a little less extravagantly, but that would be all.

Alternatively, a portion of II_s that represents necessary means of subsistence is directly transformed into new variable capital in department II. How this happens will be investigated at the close of the present chapter (section 4).

* See above, p. 88.

(a) First Example

(A) Schema of simple reproduction

$$\left.\begin{array}{ll}\text{I.} & 4,000_c+1,000_v+1,000_s = 6,000 \\ \text{II.} & 2,000_c+500_v+500_s = 3,000\end{array}\right\} \text{Total} = 9,000.$$

(B) Initial schema for reproduction on an expanded scale

$$\left.\begin{array}{ll}\text{I.} & 4,000_c+1,000_v+1,000_s = 6,000 \\ \text{II.} & 1,500_c+750_v+750_s = 3,000\end{array}\right\} \text{Total} = 9,000.$$

If we assume that in schema (B) half the surplus-value in department I is accumulated, i.e. 500, then we get in the first place $(1,000_v+500_s)$I or $1,500\,\text{I}_{(v+s)}$ to be replaced by $1,500\,\text{II}_c$; there then remains in department I, $4,000_c+500_s$, the latter having to be accumulated. The replacement of $(1,000_v+500_s)$I by $1,500\,\text{II}_c$ is a process of simple reproduction and has already been examined in connection with the latter.

Let us assume that 400 of the 500 I_s to be accumulated has to be transformed into constant capital, and 100 into variable capital. The exchange within department I of the 400_s that has to be capitalized has already been explained; so this can be annexed to I_c without any more ado, and we then get the following capitalization for department I:

I. $4,400_c+1,000_v$ [in money]$+100_s$ (to be converted into 100_v).

Department II, for its part, buys from department I, for the purpose of accumulation, the 100 I_s (existing in means of production), which now forms extra constant capital for department II, while the 100 in money that it pays for it is transformed into the money form of department I's extra variable capital. We then have, for department I, a capital of $4,400_c+1,100_v$ (the latter in money) $= 5,500$.

Department II now has $1,600_c$ in constant capital; a further 50_v has to be added for the purchase of new labour-power for working this up, and so its variable capital grows from 750 to 800. This extension of both department II's constant and variable capital is met out of its own surplus-value; of the 750 II_s, therefore, there only remains 600_s as a consumption fund for the department II capitalists, whose annual product is now distributed as follows:

II. $1,600_c+800_v+600_s$ ([capitalists'] consumption fund)
$= 3,000$.

The 150_s produced in means of consumption that is converted here into (100_c+50_v)II goes completely into the workers' consumption in its natural form; 100 is consumed by the workers in department I (100 I_v) and 50 by the workers in department II (50 II_v), as elaborated above. In point of fact the portion of surplus-value that has to be reproduced in the form of *necessary* means of consumption in department II is 100 greater when its total product is produced in the form needed for accumulation. When reproduction on an expanded scale gets under way, then department I's extra 100 variable money capital flows back to department II through the hands of department I's working class; department II in turn transfers 100_s to department I in a commodity stock, and at the same time 50 in a commodity stock to its own working class.

The arrangement as changed for the purpose of accumulation now stands as follows:

$$\text{I.} \quad 4,400_c + 1,100_v + 500$$
$$\text{[capitalists'] consumption fund} = 6,000$$
$$\text{II.} \quad 1,600_c + 800_v + 600$$
$$\text{[capitalists'] consumption fund} = 3,000$$
$$\text{total} \quad = 9,000 \text{ as above.}$$

The capital in this is:

$$\left.\begin{array}{l} \text{I.} \quad 4,400_c + 1,100_v \text{ (money)} = 5,500 \\ \text{II.} \quad 1,600_c + 800_v \text{ (money)} = 2,400 \end{array}\right\} = 7,900,$$

whereas production began with:

$$\left.\begin{array}{l} \text{I.} \quad 4,000_c + 1,000_v = 5,000 \\ \text{II.} \quad 1,500_c + 750_v = 2,250 \end{array}\right\} = 7,250.$$

If real accumulation now proceeds on this basis, i.e. if production actually takes place with this increased capital, then we have at the end of the following year:

$$\left.\begin{array}{l} \text{I.} \quad 4,400_c + 1,100_v + 1,100_s = 6,600 \\ \text{II.} \quad 1,600_c + 800_v + 800_s = 3,200 \end{array}\right\} = 9,800.$$

Let accumulation now continue in department I in the same proportions; i.e. 550_s is spent as revenue, and 550_s accumulated. To start with, then, $1,100 \text{ I}_v$ is replaced by $1,100 \text{ II}_c$, and 550 I_s remains to be realized in an equal amount of commodities II; i.e. altogether $1,650 \text{ I}_{(v+s)}$. But the constant capital in department II that has to be exchanged is only 1,600, so that the remaining 50 must be supplemented from the 800 II_s. If we initially leave aside the money here, then the result of this transaction is:

I. $4,400_c + 550_s$ (to be capitalized); as well as $1,650_{(v+s)}$ in the consumption fund for capitalists and workers, realized in commodities II_c.

II. $1,650_c$ (with 50 being added as above from II_s) $+ 800_v + 750_s$ (capitalists' consumption fund).

But if the former ratio of v to c in department II remains unchanged, then a further 25_v must be laid out for 50_c; this has to be taken from the 750_s; we therefore get:

II. $1,650_c + 825_v + 725_s$.

In department I, 550_s has to be capitalized; if the earlier ratio remains the same, then 440 of this forms constant capital and 110 variable capital. This 110 is ultimately obtained from the 725 II_s, so that means of consumption to the value of 110 are consumed by the workers in department I instead of by the capitalists in department II, the latter being forced to capitalize this 110_s instead of consuming it. This leaves 615 II_s over out of the 725 II_s. But if department II transforms this 110 into additional constant capital, it needs a further additional variable capital of 55. This has again to come out of its surplus-value; deducted from the 615 II_s it leaves 560 for the consumption of the capitalists in department II, and we now get, after the completion of all actual and potential transfers, the following capital value:

I. $(4,400_c + 440_c) + (1,100_v + 110_v) = 4,840_c + 1,210_v = 6,050$
II. $(1,600_c + 50_c + 110_c) + (800_v + 25_v + 55_v)$
$$= 1,760_c + 880_v = 2,640;$$
$$\text{a total of} \quad 8,690.$$

If things are to proceed normally, accumulation in department II must take place quicker than in department I, since the part of $I_{(v+s)}$ that has to be exchanged for commodities II_c would otherwise grow more quickly than II_c, which is all that it can be exchanged for.

If reproduction continues on this basis, and other conditions remain the same, then we get at the end of the following year:

I. $4,840_c + 1,210_v + 1,210_s = 7,260$ ⎫
II. $1,760_c + 880_v + 880_s = 3,520$ ⎬ $= 10,780.$

If the surplus-value is partitioned in the same ratio, then department I first has $1,210_v$ plus half of s, $=605$, to spend as revenue, a total of 1,815. This consumption fund is 55 greater again than II_c. The 55 has to be deducted from the 880_s. The transformation of 55 II_s into I_c presupposes a further deduction from II_s for a corresponding variable capital of $27\frac{1}{2}$; there remains $797\frac{1}{2}$ II_s to be consumed.

There is now 605_s to be capitalized in department I, 484 of this for constant and 121 variable; the latter has to be deducted from II_s, which is still $797\frac{1}{2}$, leaving $676\frac{1}{2}$. Thus department II transforms a further 121 into constant capital and needs for this purpose a further variable capital of $60\frac{1}{2}$; this similarly comes out of the $676\frac{1}{2}$, leaving 616 for consumption.

We then have in capital:

I. Constant $4,840+484 = 5,324$
 Variable $1,210+121 = 1,331$.
II. Constant $1,760+55+121 = 1,936$
 Variable $880+27\frac{1}{2}+60\frac{1}{2} = 968$
 Together: I. $5,324_c+1,331_v = 6,655$ $\Big\} = 9,559$;
 II. $1,936_c+968_v = 2,904$

and in products at the end of the year:

I. $5,324_c+1,331_v+1,331_s = 7,986$ $\Big\} = 11,858$.
II. $1,936_c+968_v+968_s = 3,872$

Repeating the same calculation and rounding off the fractions, we get at the end of the following year a product of:

I. $5,856_c+1,464_v+1,464_s = 8,784$ $\Big\} = 13,043$.
II. $2,129_c+1,065_v+1,065_s = 4,259$

and at the close of the year after that:

I. $6,442_c+1,610_v+1,610_s = 9,662$ $\Big\} = 14,348$.
II. $2,342_c+1,172_v+1,172_s = 4,686$

In the course of five years' reproduction on an expanded scale, the total capital of departments I and II has risen from $5,500_c+1,750_v = 7,250$, to $8,784_c+2,782_v - 11,566$, i.e. in a ratio of 100:160. The total surplus-value was originally 1,750, it is now 2,782. The surplus-value consumed was originally 500 for department I and 600 for department II, a total of 1,100; in the final year it is 732 for department I and 745 for department II, altogether 1,477. It has thus grown in the ratio of 100:134.

(b) Second Example

Let us now take an annual product of 9,000 existing entirely as commodity capital in the hands of the industrial capitalist class, in a form in which the general average ratio of variable to constant capital [in both departments] is 1:5. This already presupposes a significant development of capitalist production and, accordingly, of the productivity of social labour as well; a significant prior expansion of the scale of production; and finally a development of all the circumstances that produce in the working class a relative surplus population. The annual product will then be divided up as follows, after rounding off the fractions:*

$$\left.\begin{array}{ll} \text{I.} & 5,000_c+1,000_v+1,000_s = 7,000 \\ \text{II.} & 1,430_c+285_v+285_s = 2,000 \end{array}\right\} = 9,000.$$

Let us again take it that the capitalist class in department I consumes half its surplus-value, or 500, and accumulates the other half. In this case, $(1,000_v+500_s)\,\text{I} = 1,500$ would need to be exchanged with $1,500\,\text{II}_c$. But since II_c is here only 1,430, 70 of surplus-value has to be added; and this, when deducted from the $285\,\text{II}_s$, leaves $215\,\text{II}_s$. We thus get:

    I. $5,000_c+500_s$ (to be capitalized)$+1,500_{(v+s)}$ in the consumption fund for capitalists and workers.

    II. $1,430_c+70_s$ (to be capitalized)$+285_v+215_s$.

Since $70\,\text{II}_s$ has been directly annexed here to the II_c, a variable capital of $\frac{70}{5} = 14$ is required to set this extra constant capital in motion; this 14 has to come out of the $215\,\text{II}_s$, leaving $201\,\text{II}_s$, and we have:

    II. $(1,430_c+70_c)+(285_v+14_v)+201_s$.

The exchange of $1,500\,\text{I}_{(v+\frac{1}{2}s)}$ against $1,500\,\text{II}_c$ is a process of simple reproduction, and nothing further need be said about it. In so far as there are still some peculiarities to be noted here, these stem from the fact that with accumulating reproduction, $\text{I}_{(v+\frac{1}{2}s)}$ is not just replaced by II_c alone, but rather by II_c plus a part of II_s.

It is self-evident that, on the assumption of accumulation, $\text{I}_{(v+s)}$ is greater than II_c, and not equal to it as in simple reproduction; since (1) department I incorporates a part of its surplus product into its own productive capital and transforms five sixths of this into constant capital, so that it cannot simultaneously exchange this five sixths for means of consumption II; and (2) department I has to supply the material for the constant capital needed for accumulation within department II out of its surplus product, just as department II has to supply department I with the material for the variable capital that is to set in motion the portion of its surplus product that department I itself applies as extra constant capital. We know that variable capital actually consists of labour-power, and so too therefore does this additional capital. It is not the capitalists in department I who buy or store up means of subsistence from department II for the additional labour-

---

*The division of the social product between departments I and II here is an arbitrary ratio, selected presumably for arithmetical convenience.

power that they need to employ, as the slave-owners had to do. It is the workers themselves who deal with department II. But this does not prevent the means of consumption for this additional labour-power from being viewed by the capitalist as only so many means of production and maintenance for his potential additional labour-power. His own immediate operation, in this case that of department I, simply consists in storing up the new money capital needed, that needed for the purchase of additional labour-power. Once he has incorporated this labour-power, the money becomes for the workers a means of purchase of commodities II, and they must therefore find their means of consumption to hand.

*

Incidentally, Mr Capitalist, as well as his press, is frequently discontented with the way in which labour-power spends its money, and with the commodities II in which it realizes this. On this occasion he philosophizes, waxes cultural and philanthropizes, as for example Mr Drummond, the British Secretary of Embassy in Washington. *The Nation* carried an interesting article last October, 1879, in which is said among other things:

'The working-people have not kept up in culture with the growth of invention, and they have had things showered on them which they do not know how to use, and thus make no market for.' (Every capitalist naturally wants the worker to buy his particular commodities.) 'There is no reason why the working man should not desire as many comforts as the minister, lawyer, and doctor, who is earning the same amount as himself.' (These particular ministers, lawyers and doctors will certainly have to be satisfied merely with desiring many comforts.) 'He does not do so, however. The problem remains, how to raise him as a consumer by rational and healthful processes, not an easy one, as his ambition does not go beyond a diminution of his hours of labour, the demagogues rather inciting him to this than to raising his condition by the improvement of his mental and moral powers' (*Reports of H.M.'s Secretaries of Embassy and Legation on the Manufactures, Commerce etc. of the Countries in which they reside*, Part III, London, 1879, p. 404.).

Long hours of labour seem to be the secret of these 'rational and healthful processes', which are to raise the condition of the worker by improving his 'mental and moral powers' and making a rational consumer out of him. In order to become a rational consumer of the capitalists' commodities, he must before all else – but the demagogues prevent him – begin by letting his own labour-power be consumed irrationally and in a way contrary to his own health, by the capitalist who employs him. What the capitalist understands by rational consumption is shown when he is condescending enough to take a direct interest in the consumer behaviour of his workers – i.e. in the truck system, which even includes the supply of housing to the workers involved, so that the capitalist is simultaneously their landlord – one line of business among many others.

The same Drummond whose fine soul enthuses for capitalist attempts at raising the level of the working class tells us in this report, among other things, about the model cotton factories of Lowell and Lawrence Mills. The boarding and lodging houses for the factory girls here belong to the joint-stock company that owns the factory; the stewardesses of these houses are in the employment of the same company, which prescribes to them certain rules of conduct. No girl may return home after 10 p.m. A particular gem is that a special police force patrols the area to prevent this regulation from being transgressed. After 10 p.m., no girl is allowed in or out. No girl may lodge anywhere but on the company's land, and each house brings in some 10 dollars a week in rent. We now see the rational consumer in all his or her glory:

'As the ever-present piano is, however, to be found in many of the best appointed working girls' boarding-houses, music, song, and dance come in for a considerable share of the operatives' attention, at least among those who, after ten hours' steady work at the looms, need more relief from monotony than actual rest' (p. 412).

But the chief clue as to how to make the workers into rational consumers only comes at the end. Mr Drummond visits the cutlery factory at Turner's Falls (Connecticut River), and Mr Oakman, the company secretary, after telling him how American cutlery beats English in quality, continues:

'The time is coming that we will beat England as to prices also; we are ahead in quality now, that is acknowledged, but we must have lower prices and shall have it the moment we get our steel at lower prices and have our labour down!' (p. 427).

Reduction in wages and long working hours, this is the kernel of the 'rational and healthful process' that is to raise the workers to the dignity of rational consumers, so that they 'make a market' for the 'things showered on them' by civilization and the progress of invention.

*

Just as department I has to supply the additional constant capital for department II out of its surplus product, so department II supplies in the same way the extra variable capital for department I. Department II accumulates both for department I and for itself, as far as the variable capital is concerned, in as much as it reproduces a larger portion of its total production, and of its surplus product in particular, in the form of necessary means of consumption.

With production on an increasing capital basis, $I_{(v+s)}$ must be equal to II_c, plus the part of the surplus product that is reincorporated as capital, plus the extra portion of constant capital needed to expand production in department II, and the minimum for this expansion is that without which genuine accumulation, i.e. the actual extension of production in department I, cannot be carried out.

Let us now return to the case last considered, which has the peculiarity that II_c is smaller than $I_{(v+\frac{1}{2}s)}$, i.e. smaller than the part of the product of department I that is spent as revenue on means of consumption, so that a part of the surplus product of department II ($=70$) has to be realized in order to convert the 1,500 $I_{(v+s)}$. As far as $II_c = 1,430$ is concerned, with circumstances remaining otherwise the same, it must be replaced by the same amount from $I_{(v+s)}$ for simple reproduction to take place in department II, and to this extent it does not need further consideration. It is different for the supplementary 70 II_s. What is for department I simply the exchange of revenue for means of consumption, merely a commodity exchange oriented to consumption, is now for department II not just (as with simple reproduction) the transformation of its constant capital back from the form of commodity capital into its natural form, but rather the actual process of accumulation itself, the transformation of a part of its surplus product from the form of means of consumption into that of constant capital. If department I uses £70 in money (its money reserve for the exchange of surplus-value) to buy the 70 II_s, and department II does not use this money to buy the 70 I_s, but accumulates the £70 as money capital, this latter is certainly still the expression of an extra product (precisely of the surplus product of department II, of which it is an aliquot part), even if not of a product that goes back again into the production sphere; but then this money accumulation on the part of department II would be at the same time the expression of an unsaleable 70 I_s in means of production. There would thus be relative over-production, corresponding to this simultaneous non-expansion of reproduction on the part of department II.

But apart from this, during the time in which the £70 in money that came from department I has not yet returned, or only partly returned to department I by the purchase of 70 I_s on the part of department II, this £70 in money figures completely or in part as additional virtual money capital in the hands of department II. This holds for each transaction between the two departments, until the mutual replacement of commodities on both sides has effected the reflux of the money to its starting-point. In the normal course of events, however, the money figures only temporarily here in this role. In the credit system, where all additional money temporarily set free can immediately function actively as additional money capital, this money capital that is only released temporarily may get stuck, and be used for new enterprises in department I, for example, whereas it ought to be used to set in motion surplus products still held down in other enterprises. It should also be noted that the annexation of 70 I_s to the constant capital of department II also requires an expansion of 14 in department II's variable capital. This presupposes – similarly to the case of the direct incorporation of the surplus product I_s into capital I_c in department I – that reproduction in department I is already proceeding with the tendency to further capitalization; and that it therefore involves the expansion of that part of the surplus product that consists of necessary means of subsistence.

*

As we already saw, the product of 9,000 in the second example must be divided as follows for the purpose of reproduction, if 500 I_s is to be capitalized. Here we simply consider the commodities, and ignore the monetary circulation.

I. $5,000_c + 500_s$ (to be capitalized)$+ 1,500_{(v+s)}$ consumption fund $= 7,000$ in commodities.

II. $1,500_c + 299_v + 201_s = 2,000$ in commodities.

A total of 9,000 in commodity product.

The capitalization now proceeds as follows:

The 500$_s$ that is capitalized in department I is divided into $\frac{5}{6} = 417_c$ $+ \frac{1}{6} = 83_v$. The 83$_v$ withdraws an equal amount from II$_s$, which buys elements of constant capital, added to II$_c$. An increase of 83 in II$_c$ necessitates an increase of $\frac{1}{5}$ of 83 or 17 in II$_v$.

We then have after the exchange:

I. $(5,000_c + 417_s)_c + (1,000_v + 83_s)_v = 5,417_c + 1,083_v = 6,500$
II. $(1,500_c + 83_s)_c + (299_v + 17_s)_v = 1,583_c = 316_v = 1,899$

Altogether: 8,399.

The capital in department I has grown from 6,000 to 6,500, i.e. by one twelfth. In department II it has grown from 1,715 to 1,899, i.e. by almost one ninth.

Reproduction on this basis for a second year produces at the end of the year a capital of:

I. $(5,417_c + 452_s)_c + (1,083_v + 90_s)_v = 5,869_c + 1,173_v = 7,042$

II. $(1,583_c + 42_s + 90_s)_c + (316_v + 8_s + 18_s)_v$

$$= 1,715_c + 342_v = 2,057;$$

and at the end of the third year a product of:

I. $5,869_c + 1,173_v + 1,173_s$

II. $1,715_c + 342_v + 342_s$.

Here, as before, department I accumulates half its surplus-value, so that $I_{(v+\frac{1}{2}s)}$ equals $1,173_v + 587_{(\frac{1}{2}s)} = 1,760$, bigger by 45 than the total II_c. This must again be balanced with II_c by transferring an equal amount of means of production to II_c. II_c thus grows by 45, which requires an increase of $\frac{1}{5} \times 45 = 9$ in II_v. The capitalized 587 I_s then divides into $\frac{5}{6}$ and $\frac{1}{6}$, 489_c and 98_v; this 98 requires a new addition of 98 to department II's constant capital, and this in turn an increase in department II's variable capital of $\frac{1}{5} \times 98 = 20$. We now have:

I. $(5,869_c + 489_s)_c + (1,173_v + 98_s)_v = 6,358_c + 1,271_v = 7,629$

II. $(1,715_c + 45_s + 98_s)_c + (342_v + 9_s + 20_s)_v$

$$= 1,858_c + 371_v = 2,229$$
$$\text{total capital} = 9,858.$$

In three years of increased reproduction, therefore, the total capital of department I has grown from 6,000 to 7,629, that of department II from 1,715 to 2,229, and the total social capital from 7,715 to 9,858.

(c) *The Exchange of II_c in the Case of Accumulation*

There are several different cases in the exchange between $I_{(v+s)}$ and II_c.

In the case of simple reproduction, the two must be equal and replace one another, otherwise, as we have seen above, simple reproduction cannot proceed undisturbed.

In the case of accumulation, the principal thing to be considered is the rate of accumulation. In the above examples we assumed that the rate of accumulation in department I was $\frac{1}{2}I_s$, and that it remained constant in different years. We simply changed the proportions according to which this accumulated capital was divided into variable and constant. This gave us three examples:

1. $I_{(v+\frac{1}{2}s)} = II_c$, which is thus smaller than $I_{(v+s)}$. (In fact, it must always be smaller or else department I cannot accumulate.)

2. $I_{(v+\frac{1}{2}s)}$ is greater than II_c. In this case, the replacement is effected

by a corresponding portion of II_s being added to II_c, so that this sum $= I_{(v+\frac{1}{2}s)}$. Here the exchange is not for department II the simple reproduction of its constant capital, but already accumulation, the increase of its constant capital by a part of its surplus product which it exchanges for means of production from department I; this increase also means that department II correspondingly enlarges its variable capital out of its own surplus product.

3. $I_{(v+\frac{1}{2}s)}$ is smaller than II_c. In this case, department II has not completely reproduced its constant capital by the exchange, and must therefore make up the deficiency by purchase from department I. But this does not require any further accumulation of variable capital in department II, since its constant capital is fully reproduced in magnitude by this operation. On the other hand, the section of capitalists in department I that is simply storing up additional money capital has already accomplished one part of this kind of accumulation by this exchange.

The precondition for simple reproduction, that $I_{(v+s)} = II_c$, is incompatible with capitalist production from the start, although this does not rule out the possibility that in one year of the industrial cycle of ten to eleven years there may be a smaller total production than the preceding, i.e. that even simple reproduction fails to take place in relation to the previous year. Secondly, however, given the natural annual growth of the population, simple reproduction would mean that a proportionately greater number of unproductive servants had to share in the 1,500 that represents the total surplus-value. Accumulation of capital, i.e. genuine capitalist production, would be impossible in this way. The existence of capitalist accumulation accordingly excludes the possibility that II_c may be equal to $I_{(v+s)}$. Yet even with capitalist accumulation, the case could arise in which, as a result of the accumulation achieved in the previous run of production periods, II_c was not only equal to $I_{(v+s)}$, but in fact even greater. This would mean over-production in department II, and could only be balanced out by a major crash, as a result of which capital would be transferred from department II to department I. Nothing is altered in the relation between $I_{(v+s)}$ and II_c if a section of the constant capital in department II is reproduced there – as in agriculture for example, with the employment of home-grown seed. This part of II_c is then as little involved in the exchange between departments I and II as is I_c. It also makes no difference if some of the products of department II are capable of entering department I as means of production. This is covered by a part of the means of production supplied by department I, and this part must be deducted from both sides at the outset, if we want to investigate the exchange between the two great departments of social production, the producers of means of production and the producers of means of consumption, in its pure and unadulterated form.

In the case of capitalist production, therefore, $I_{(v+s)}$ cannot be equal to II_c, i.e. the two cannot balance one another in the exchange. It is possible, on the other hand, if $I_{s/x}$ is the part of I_s that is spent by the capitalists of department I as revenue, for $I_{(v+s/x)}$ to be equal to, greater or less than II_c; however, $I_{(v+s/x)}$ must always be smaller than $II_{(c+s)}$, and indeed smaller by the part of II_s that the capitalist class in department II must itself under all circumstances consume.

We have to note here that in this presentation of accumulation, the value of the constant capital is not depicted exactly in so far as this is a portion of the value of the commodity capital in whose production it collaborates. The fixed part of the newly accumulated constant capital only goes gradually and periodically into the commodity capital, according to the differential nature of these fixed elements; the commodity capital therefore consists, in those cases in which raw materials and semi-finished goods, etc. are involved in commodity production on a large scale, for the most part of replacements for the circulating constant components and for the variable capital. (However, we were able to proceed in this manner on account of the turnover of the circulating components. The assumption was thereby made that the circulating part, together with the portion of value of the fixed capital surrendered to it, turns over within the year with such a frequency that the total sum of commodities supplied is the same as the value of the whole of the capital that goes into the annual production.) But where, as with the construction of machinery, it is only ancillaries that are involved, and not raw material, the labour element $= v$ must again appear as the larger component of the commodity capital. For the rate of profit, the surplus-value is calculated on the total capital, independently of whether the fixed components surrender a great deal of value to the product in a given period or only a little. But for the value of any commodity capital periodically produced, the fixed part of the constant capital has only to be taken into account to the extent that it actually gives up value to the product by its average wear and tear.

4. SUPPLEMENTARY REMARKS

The original source of money for department II is the $v+s$ of the gold production in department I, exchanged against part of II_c; it is only to the extent that the gold producers store up surplus-value or transform it into means of production in department I, i.e. extend their production, that their $v+s$ does not go into department II; on the other hand, as far as accumulation of money by the gold producers themselves finally leads to expanded reproduction, a portion of the surplus-value from gold production that is not spent as revenue goes into department II for the gold producers' additional variable capital, and either requires a new hoard formation here or provides new means for buying from department I without directly selling to it again. From the money that stems from this $I_{(v+s)}$ in gold production, a part of the gold is deducted that is needed by certain branches of production in department II as raw material, etc., in short as a replacement element of their constant capital. In the exchange between departments I and II, there is an element for provisional hoard formation, for the purpose of future expanded reproduction, as follows: in department I, only if a part of I_s is unilaterally sold to department II without a purchase from the other side, and serves here as additional constant capital for department II; in department II, if department I buys unilaterally for additional variable capital; furthermore, if a part of the surplus-value spent by department I as revenue is not covered by department II, so that a part of II_s is bought with it and thereby transformed into money. If $I_{(v+s/x)}$ is greater than II_c, then II_c, for its simple reproduction, does not have to replace, in commodities from department I, what I consumed from II_s. The question then arises as to how far hoard formation can take place in exchange among the capitalists of department II themselves – an exchange that can consist only of the mutual exchange of II_s. We know that within department II there is only direct accumulation in so far as a part of II_s is directly transformed into variable capital (just as, in department I, a part of I_s is directly transformed into constant capital). Given the different ages of accumulation within the various lines of business in department II, and within each particular line of business for the individual capitalists involved there, the matter is explained, *mutatis mutandis*, just as in department I. Some of these capitalists are still at the stage of hoard formation, selling without buying, while others, at the point of actual expansion of reproduction, buy without selling. The additional variable money capital is certainly laid out at first on additional labour-power, but this is used to buy means of subsistence from the hoard-forming proprietors of the extra means of consumption that go into the workers' consumption. In proportion to their hoard formation, this money does not return from these proprietors to its starting-point; they store it up.

Quotations in Languages other than English and German

p. 100, n. 3 'Ainsi donc, par la concentration des fortunes entre un petit nombre de propriétaires, le marché intérieur se resserre toujours plus, et l'industrie est toujours plus réduite à chercher ses débouchés dans les marchés étrangers, où de plus grandes révolutions les attendent.'

p. 209, n. 2 'Les frais de commerce, quoique nécessaires, doivent être regardés comme une dépense onéreuse.'

'. . . à mettre leur rétribution ov leur gain au rabais . . . n'est sérieusement parlant qu'une *privation de perte* pour le vendeur de la première main et pour l'acheteur-consommateur. Or, une privation de perte sur les frais du commerce n'est pas un *produit réel* ou un accroît de richesses obtenu par le commerce, considéré en lui-même simplement comme échange, indépendemment des frais de transport, ou envisagé conjointement avec les frais de transport.'

'Les frais du commerce sont toujours payés aux dépens des vendeurs des productions qui jouiraient de tout le prix qu'en payent les acheteurs, s'il n'y avait point de frais intermédiares. Les propriétaires et producteurs sont "salariants", les commerçants sont "salariés".'

pp. 268–9, n. 1 'Les avances annuelles consistent dans les dépenses qui se font annuellement pour le travail de la culture; ces avances doivent être distinguées des avances primitives, qui forment le fonds de l'établissement de la culture.'

'Au moyen de la durée plus ou moins grande des ouvrages de main-d'œuvre, une nation possède un fonds considérable de richesses, indépendant de sa réproduction annuelle, qui forme un capital accumulé de longue main et originairement payé avec des productions, qui s'entretient et s'augmente toujours.'

p. 416, n. 1 . . . 'Jetez les yeux sur le Tableau Économique, vous verrez que la classe productive donne l'argent avec lequel les autres classes viennent lui acheter des productions, et qu'elles lui rentrent cet argent en revenant l'année suivante faire chez elle les mêmes achats . . . Vous ne voyez donc ici d'autre cercle que celui de la dépense suivie de la réproduction, et de la réproduction suivie de la dépense; cercle qui est parcouru par la circulation de l'argent qui mesure la dépense et la réproduction.'

'C'est cette avance et cette rentrée continuelle des capitaux qu'on doit appeler la circulation de l'argent, cette circulation utile et féconde qui anime tous les travaux de la société, qui entretient le mouvement et la vie dans le corps politique et qu'on a grande raison de comparer à la circulation du sang dans le corps animal.'

p. 436, n. 2 '... Comme eux' (les entrepreneurs-manufacturiers), 'ils' (les fermiers) 'doivent recueillir, outre la rentrée des capitaux etc.'

Index of Authorities Quoted

[*Titles as given here may differ in detail from those in the text, since the latter follow Marx's own versions.*]

I. BOOKS BY NAMED OR ANONYMOUS AUTHORS

Adams, William Bridges, *Roads and Rails and Their Sequences, Physical and Moral*, London, 1862, 250–52

Bailey, Samuel, *A Critical Dissertation on the Nature, Measures, and Causes of Value; Chiefly in Reference to the Writings of Mr Ricardo and His Followers. By the Author of Essays on the Formation and Publication of Opinions*, London, 1825, 186

Barton, John, *Observations on the Circumstances which Influence the Condition of the Labouring Classes of Society*, London, 1817, 304

Chalmers, Thomas, *On Political Economy in Connection with the Moral State and Moral Prospects of Society*, 2nd edn, Glasgow, 1832, 235

[Chuprov] Чупров, А[лександр Иванович]: Желѣзнодорожное хозяйство. Его экономическія особенности и его отношенія къ интересамъ страны. Moscow, 1875. 134–5

Corbet, Thomas, *An Inquiry into the Causes and Modes of the Wealth of Individuals; or the Principles of Trade and Speculation Explained*, in two parts, London, 1841, 216

Courcelle-Seneuil, Jean-Gustave, *Traité théorique et pratique des entreprises industrielles, commerciales et agricoles ou Manuel des affaires*, 2nd edn, revue et augmentée, Paris, 1857, 317

Destutt de Tracy, Antoine-Louis-Claude comte de, *Élémens d'idéologie*, Parts 4 and 5, *Traité de la volonté et de ses effets*, Paris, 1826, 556–64

Dupont de Nemours, Pierre-Samuel, *Maximes du docteur Quesnay, ou résumé de ses principes d'économie sociale*, in *Physiocrates. Quesnay, Dupont de Nemours, Mercier de la Rivière, Baudeau, Le Trosne, avec une introd. sur la doctrine des physiocrates, des commentaires et des notices historiques, par Eugène Daire*, Part 1, Paris, 1846, 269

Good, William Walter, *Political, Agricultural and Commercial Fallacies; or, the Prospect of the Nation after Twenty Years' 'Free-Trade'*, London, [1866], 313

Turgot, Anne-Robert-Jacques, de L'Aulne, *Réflexions sur la formation et la distribution des richesses*, in *Oeuvres. Nouv. éd . . . par Eugène Daire*, Vol. 1, Paris, 1844, 269, 416, 436

Tyler, Edward Burnett, *Forschungen über die Urgeschichte der Menschheit und die Entwickelung der Civilisation*, trans. by H. Müller, Leipzig, n.d., 514

Wayland, Francis, *The Elements of Political Economy*, Boston, 1843, 302–3

Williams, Richard Price, 'On the Maintenance and Renewal of Permanent Way', in *Minutes of Proceedings of the Institution of Civil Engineers; with Abstracts of the Discussions*, Vol. 25, Session 1865/66, ed. James Forrest, London, 1866, 249, 259

2. PARLIAMENTARY REPORTS AND OTHER OFFICIAL PUBLICATIONS

East India (*Bengal and Orissa famine*). *Papers and correspondence relative to the famine in Bengal and Orissa, including the report of the Famine Commission and the minutes of the Lieutenant Governor of Bengal and the Governor General of India.* (*Presented to Parliament by Her Majesty's command.*) Ordered, by the House of Commons, to be printed, 31 May 1867, 218

East India (*Bengal and Orissa famine*). *Papers relating to the famine in Behar, including Mr F. R. Cockerell's report.* (*Presented to Parliament by Her Majesty's command.*) Part III. Ordered, by the House of Commons, to be printed, 31 May 1867, 218

East India (*Madras and Orissa famine*). *Return to an address of the Honourable the House of Commons, dated 4 July 1867.* Ordered, by the House of Commons, to be printed, 30 July 1867, 314

Report from the select committee on bank acts; together with the proceedings of the committee, minutes of evidence, appendix and index. Part I. Report and evidence. Ordered, by the House of Commons, to be printed, 30 July 1857, 311–12

Reports by Her Majesty's secretaries of embassy and legation, on the manufactures, commerce &c., of the countries in which they reside. No. 8. Presented to both Houses of Parliament by command of Her Majesty, 1865, London [1865], 318–19

Reports by Her Majesty's secretaries of embassy and legation, on the manufactures, commerce &c., of the countries in which they reside. Part III. Presented to both Houses of Parliament by command of Her Majesty, May 1879, London, 1879, 547, 591–2

Royal commission on railways. Report of the commissioners. Presented to both Houses of Parliament by command of Her Majesty, London, 1867, 216, 249, 253, 258, 328

3. NEWSPAPERS AND PERIODICALS

Economist, London, 8 May 1847, 214
  16 June 1866, 329–30
  30 June 1866, 330
  7 July 1866, 330

Money Market Review, London, 2 December 1867, 249
  25 January 1868, 257

Neue Rheinische Zeitung. Organ der Demokratie, Cologne, 24 June 1848, 89
  4 July 1848, 89
  26 July 1848, 89
  10 September 1848, 89
  12 September 1848, 89
  9 November 1848, 89
  5 April 1849, 90
  6 April 1849, 90
  7 April 1849, 90
  8 April 1849, 90
  11 April 1849, 90

Zeitschrift für die gesammte Staatswissenschaft, ed. von Fricker, Schäffle und A. Wagner, Vol. 35, Tübingen, 1879, 88–9

General Index

Abstinence, theory of, 514
Abstract labour, 214, 453–4, 460, 504
Accumulation, rate of, 579, 582, 586–9, 592–5
Accumulation fund, 164–5, 188, 587–9
Accumulation of capital, 158–60, 251, 394–6, 399, 565, 577–9; and consumption, 578–9; and hoard formation, 158, 162–3, 199, 565–76 *passim*, 598–9; and productivity, 432, 574, 589; as expanded reproduction, 418; embraces simple reproduction, 471; in department I, 573–6, 581–2; in department II, 577–98; necessity of, 160, 199, 596. *See also* Reproduction on an expanded scale
Accumulation of money, 162–6, 188, 396, 418–26
Adams, William Bridges, 250–51
Advances of capital, 382, 455; annual and less frequent, 268; different forms, 340–41, 412; effect of turnover time on, 334–68; minimum required, 162–3, 187; Physiocratic conception, 178, 268–9, 289–90, 297, 454–5, 572
Africa, 555
Agriculture, and cottage industries, 318–19; and manufacture, 319; book-keeping in, 211–12; capital in, 268–9, 297; in England, 313–15; in Germany, 318; in India, 212, 314; in Russia, 117, 318–19; production and working time in, 316–24 *passim*; reproduction in, 252, 435; storage in, 322–3; turnover time and cycle in, 312–15, 320 325. *See also* Working class, in agriculture
Alembert, Jean-Baptiste d', 158
America, South, 545
America, United States of, 218, 220, 545, 547, 555

Amortization fund, 260–61
Amortization of fixed capital, 198, 242–51, 263, 524–6, 528–36, 552–3, 570
Anarchy of capitalist production, 252, 545. *See also* Disproportions; Crises
Ancillaries, 218, 238–9, 243–4, 274–5, 280, 309
Arabs, 120
Argentina, 52
Arrivabene, Jean (Giovanni), comte de, 514
Athens, 554–5
Australia, 218, 545

Bailey, Samuel, 186, 582
Bakewell, Robert, 314–15
Balances, 192
Banknotes, 547, 554
Banks, 164, 199, 329–30, 392, 419, 422–3, 488, 569; their function, 213
Baran, Paul, 53
Barton, John, 304–5, 467
Bauer, Otto, 21, 27, 65
Belgium, 251, 320–21
Benedikt, O., 65–6
Bernstein, Eduard, 88
Bessemer, Sir Henry, 317
Bills, 164, 329–30, 366
Bismarck, Otto, Prince von, 11
Bleaching, 316–17
Bondage, 554
Book-keeping, 141, 211–12, 216, 233, 355–6, 395; its function, 211–12
Brewing, 206, 329
Britain, *see* England
Building industry, 148, 311–12
Bukharin, Nikolai, 21, 27
Bulganov, S., 9

Note on Previous Editions of the Works of Marx and Engels

Until recently there existed no complete edition of the works of Marx and Engels in any language. The Marx-Engels Institute, under its director D. Riazanov, began to produce such an edition in the late 1920s. For reasons never since made clear, the project did not survive the mid-1930s. However, eleven indispensable volumes did emerge between 1927 and 1935, under the title *Karl Marx – Friedrich Engels: Historisch-Kritische Gesamtausgabe*, commonly referred to as the *MEGA* edition. The *MEGA* contains the works of both men down to 1848, and their correspondence, but nothing more. For the next thirty years, the field was held by the almost inaccessible Russian edition, the Marx-Engels *Sochineniya* (twenty-nine volumes, 1928–46).

Only in 1968 did the East Germans complete the first definitive edition in the German language, the forty-one volume *Marx-Engels Werke* (*MEW*). Until then, the works of Marx and Engels existed only in separate editions and smaller collections on specific themes. For this reason, the translations into English have followed the same pattern – the only general selection being the *Marx-Engels Selected Works* (*MESW*), now expanded to a three-volume edition. Recently, however, the major gaps in the English translations have begun to be filled up. Lawrence and Wishart have produced a complete translation of *Theories of Surplus-Value*, as well as the first adequate translation of *A Contribution to the Critique of Political Economy* and Marx's book on *The Cologne Communist Trial*. They plan to issue a complete English-language edition of even greater scope than the *MEW*, though this will inevitably take many years to complete. The Pelican Marx Library occupies an intermediate position between the *MESW* and the complete edition. It brings together the most important of Marx's larger works, the three volumes of *Capital* and the *Grundrisse*, as well as three volumes of political writings and a volume of early writings.

Chronology of Works
by Marx and Engels

Date[1]	Author[2]	Title	English edition[3]
1843	M	*Critique of Hegel's Doctrine of the State*	P *EW*
1843	M	*On the Jewish Question*	P *EW*
1843–4	M	*A Contribution to the Critique of Hegel's Philosophy of Right. Introduction*	P *EW*
1844	M	*Excerpts from James Mill's* Elements of Political Economy	P *EW*
1844	E	*Outlines of a Critique of Political Economy*	P. Engels
1844	M	*Economic and Philosophical Manuscripts*	P *EW*
1844	M	*Critical Notes on the Article 'The King of Prussia and Social Reform. By a Prussian'*	P *EW*
1844	M & E	*The Holy Family, or a Critique of Critical Critique*	*MECW* 4

1. Date of composition, except for *Capital,* where the date of first publication is given.

2. M = Marx, E = Engels.

3. The following abbreviations are used:

P. Engels: Engels, *Selected Writings*, Harmondsworth, 1967.

L W: Lawrence and Wishart.

MECW: Karl Marx and Frederick Engels, *Collected Works,* Lawrence and Wishart, 1975.

MESW: Karl Marx and Frederick Engels *Selected Works in Three Volumes,* Progress Publishers, 1969.

P: Pelican Marx Library.

P *EW*: *Early Writings* (Pelican Marx Library).

P *FI*: *The First International and After* (Pelican Marx Library).

P *R1848*: *The Revolutions of 1848* (Pelican Marx Library).

P *SE*: *Surveys from Exile* (Pelican Marx Library).

Date	Author	Title	English edition
1844–5	E	*Condition of the Working Class in England*	Blackwell 1958
1845	M	*Theses on Feuerbach*	P *EW*
1845–6	M & E	*The German Ideology*	*MECW 5*
1846–7	M	*The Poverty of Philosophy*	*MECW 6*
1847	M & E	*Speeches on Poland*	P *R1848*
1847	M	*Wage Labour and Capital*	*MESW I*
1847–8	M & E	*Manifesto of the Communist Party*	P *R1848*
1848	M & E	*Speeches on Poland*	P *R1848*
1848	M & E	*Demands of the Communist Party in Germany*	P *R1848*
1848–9	M & E	*Articles in the* Neue Rheinische Zeitung	P *R1848* (selection)
1850 (March)	M & E	*Address of the Central Committee to the Communist League*	P *R1848*
1850 (June)	M & E	*Address of the Central Committee to the Communist League*	P *R1848*
1850	M & E	*Reviews from the* Neue Rheinische Zeitung Revue	P *R1848*
1850	M	*The Class Struggles in France: 1848 to 1850*	P *SE*
1850	E	*The Peasant War in Germany*	L W 1956
1851–2	E	*Revolution and Counter-Revolution in Germany*	*MESW I*
1852	M	*The Eighteenth Brumaire of Louis Bonaparte*	P *SE*
1852	M	*Revelations of the Cologne Communist Trial*	L W 1970
1856	M	*Speech at the Anniversary of the* People's Paper	P *SE*
1857–8	M	*Grundrisse*	P
1859	M	*A Contribution to the Critique of Political Economy*	L W 1971
1852–61	M & E	*Articles in the* New York Daily Tribune	P *SE* (selections)
1861	M	*Articles in* Die Presse *on the Civil War in the United States*	P *SE* (selections)
1861–3	M	*Theories of Surplus Value*, Vol. 1 Vol. 2 Vol. 3	L W 1969 L W 1970 L W 1972
1863	M	*Proclamation on Poland*	P *SE*
1864	M	*Inaugural Address of the International Working Men's Association*	P *FI*

Date	Author	Title	English edition
1864	M	*Provisional Rules of the International Working Men's Association*	P *FI*
1865	E	*The Prussian Military Question and the German Workers' Party*	P *FI* (extract)
1865	M	*Wages, Price, and Profit*	*MESW II*
1866	E	*What Have the Working Classes to Do with Poland?*	P *FI*
1867	M	*Capital,* Vol. 1	P
1867	M	*Instructions for Delegates to the Geneva Congress*	P *FI*
1868	M	*Report to the Brussels Congress*	P *FI*
1869	M	*Report to the Basel Congress*	P *FI*
1870	M	*The General Council to the Federal Council of French Switzerland* (a circular letter)	P *FI*
1870	M	*First Address of the General Council on the Franco-Prussian War*	P *FI*
1870	M	*Second Address of the General Council on the Franco-Prussian War*	P *FI*
1871	M	First draft of *The Civil War in France*	P *FI*
1871	M & E	*On the Paris Commune*	L W 1971
1871	M	*The Civil War in France*	P *FI*
1871	M & E	*Resolution of the London Conference on Working-Class Political Action*	P *FI*
1872	M & E	*The Alleged Splits in the International*	P *FI*
1872	M	*Report to the Hague Congress*	P *FI*
1872–3	E	*The Housing Question*	*MESW II*
1874	M	*Political Indifferentism*	P *FI*
1874	E	*On Authority*	*MESW II*
1874–5	M	*Conspectus of Bakunin's Book* Statism and Anarchy	P *FI* (extract)
1875	M & E	*For Poland*	P *FI*
1875	M	*Critique of the Gotha Programme*	P *FI*
1876–8	E	*Anti-Dühring*	Progress, 1972
1879	M & E	*Circular Letter to Bebel, Liebknecht, Bracke, et al.*	P *FI*
1880	E	*Socialism: Utopian and Scientific*	*MESW III*
1880	M	*Introduction to the Programme of the French Workers' Party*	P *FI*
1873–83	E	*Dialectics of Nature*	Progress, 1972
1884	E	*The Origin of the Family, Private Property, and the State*	*MESW III*

Date	Author	Title	English edition
1885	M	*Capital*, Vol 2	P
1886	E	*Ludwig Feuerbach and the End of Classical German Philosophy*	*MESW III*
1894	M	*Capital*, Vol. 3	P

READ MORE IN PENGUIN

In every corner of the world, on every subject under the sun, Penguin represents quality and variety – the very best in publishing today.

For complete information about books available from Penguin – including Puffins, Penguin Classics and Arkana – and how to order them, write to us at the appropriate address below. Please note that for copyright reasons the selection of books varies from country to country.

In the United Kingdom: Please write to *Dept. EP, Penguin Books Ltd, Bath Road, Harmondsworth, West Drayton, Middlesex UB7 ODA*

In the United States: Please write to *Consumer Sales, Penguin USA, P.O. Box 999, Dept. 17109, Bergenfield, New Jersey 07621-0120.* VISA and MasterCard holders call 1-800-253-6476 to order Penguin titles

In Canada: Please write to *Penguin Books Canada Ltd, 10 Alcorn Avenue, Suite 300, Toronto, Ontario M4V 3B2*

In Australia: Please write to *Penguin Books Australia Ltd, P.O. Box 257, Ringwood, Victoria 3134*

In New Zealand: Please write to *Penguin Books (NZ) Ltd, Private Bag 102902, North Shore Mail Centre, Auckland 10*

In India: Please write to *Penguin Books India Pvt Ltd, 706 Eros Apartments, 56 Nehru Place, New Delhi 110 019*

In the Netherlands: Please write to *Penguin Books Netherlands bv, Postbus 3507, NL-1001 AH Amsterdam*

In Germany: Please write to *Penguin Books Deutschland GmbH, Metzlerstrasse 26, 60594 Frankfurt am Main*

In Spain: Please write to *Penguin Books S. A., Bravo Murillo 19, 1° B, 28015 Madrid*

In Italy: Please write to *Penguin Italia s.r.l., Via Felice Casati 20, I–20124 Milano*

In France: Please write to *Penguin France S. A., 17 rue Lejeune, F–31000 Toulouse*

In Japan: Please write to *Penguin Books Japan, Ishikiribashi Building, 2–5–4, Suido, Bunkyo-ku, Tokyo 112*

In South Africa: Please write to *Longman Penguin Southern Africa (Pty) Ltd, Private Bag X08, Bertsham 2013*

BY THE SAME AUTHOR

CAPITAL

Volume 1
Translated by Ben Fowkes, with an Introduction by Ernest Mandel

In Volume 1 (1867) years of research resulted in a marvellously lucid exposition that builds up from the basic unit of the commodity to a detailed consideration of the labour theory of value, the role of money, the modern factory system and the ways in which capital extorts surplus-value from wage-labour.

Volume 3
Translated by David Fernbach, with an Introduction by Ernest Mandel

Although Marx never lived to complete Volume 3 of *Das Kapital*, its trenchant conclusions aroused controversy even before publication. It is in this third volume that he sets out his central, epoch-making thesis that 'the basic laws of motion of the capitalist mode of production lead to explosive crises and its ultimate collapse'. Here we find not only a sustained economic and social description of capitalism as a system and the bourgeoisie as a class but also a full statement of why declining rates of profit and periodic crises of overproduction spell the inevitable end of capitalism and the likely birth of a far better society.